The Marlborough–
Godolphin
Correspondence

Sidney Lord Godolphin.
Lord High Treasurer of England.

SIDNEY, FIRST EARL OF GODOLPHIN

After Kneller. *Circa* 1705

The Marlborough–Godolphin Correspondence

EDITED BY

HENRY L. SNYDER

VOLUME 2

OXFORD

AT THE CLARENDON PRESS

1975

Oxford University Press, Ely House, London W. 1

GLASGOW NEW YORK TORONTO MELBOURNE WELLINGTON
CAPE TOWN IBADAN NAIROBI DAR ES SALAAM LUSAKA ADDIS ABABA
DELHI BOMBAY CALCUTTA MADRAS KARACHI LAHORE DACCA
KUALA LUMPUR SINGAPORE HONG KONG TOKYO

© *Oxford University Press 1975*

ISBN 0 19 822381 1

*Printed in Great Britain
at the University Press, Oxford
by Vivian Ridler
Printer to the University*

600. GODOLPHIN *to* MARLBOROUGH   [*17 June 1706*]

Source: Blenheim MSS. A1-36.

Windsor 17 June 1706

I have received this morning the favour of yours of the 14th[1] by express from Sir Stafford Fairborn by which I find you had written the day before by the post.[2] But that letter not being come, is a very good proof that the correspondence is quicker by this way than by any other.[3]

The Queen is pleased to leave to you the management of the exchange of the 3 French officers you mention, and has ordered a pass to bee sent to *Peralta* as you propose. I can't but think Don Quiros is in the right, and I hope this man will show it by the service he will doe to King Charles the 3d.

As to what you write concerning the Elector of Bavaria you will see my opinion in a former letter that he has but one means left to recommend himself, and I think still if he will bring over Mons, Charleroy and Namur into the King of Spayn's hands, it will bee very right for his Catholick Majesty, the Queen and the States to joyn in endeavoring to gett him restored to his country and not upon any other terms. But if you had those places, it would bee a great security against any diversion the French might attempt in Brabant while you are employed with the army in Flanders.

Sir Stafford Fairborn's letters give us hopes Ostend may not take up so much time as you seem to apprehend, but I doubt he is not a very good judg of that matter, no more than perhaps I am of what may bee proper for you to doe afterwards. But I can't help thinking *Ypres* is the place you ought to desire most of any, because if once you had it you are master of going to Dunkirk, or of leaving it very insignificant, by land; and if you had *Ypres*, that brings you so near France that there is only St. Omer between, soe that whatever motion you made the French would find themselves at liberty to make any diversion on the Brabant side.

Wee have no letters from Lisbon, nor any news from Spayn, but what you have sooner by the way of France. Since the French think fitt to persist in the siege of Turin, 'tis impossible they can send an army to Spayn, till that bee over. I wish our friends in Spayn may not lose this opportunity.

601. MARLBOROUGH *to* GODOLPHIN   [*17/28 June 1706*]

Source: Blenheim MSS. A1-14.
Printed: Coxe, ii. 70 (inc.).

Rousselaer June 28th 1706

What you propose in yours of the 7th[4] of a small frigets bringing the letters to Antwerp, would meet with a great many difficultys in the passage of the

---

[1] The preceding letter.   [2] Letter 597.
[3] See p. 575 about new arrangements for the post.   [4] 5th, letter 589.

Schel, but when you would send any perticular thing with expedition it must be by Ostend. I have write my opinion concerning Brigadier Stanhope by the last post to Mr. Secretary Hedges, for any step of that kind would make all our officers with justice uneasy, unless thay had the same step.[1] [As] for Mr. Harvey and Lord Moon, I think thay aught to be ashamed, and if you aske Mr. Secretary Hedges for a letter which Lord Gallaway write concerning him and his redgiment, that will give just occasion for the sending him to his command. If I were in Lord Moon['s] cercomstances, no law suet should be an excuse for my staying from my command; but it being for his whole estat, it might look heard to punish him for itt. You know I have no partiallity for his Lordship.[2] I think you have done very well in quieting 78 [Ormonde], for this is not a proper time to let him quit; though you may depend upon itt that he is so poor a man, that the hands he is in will never let him serve the Queen as he aught to do; so that in my humble opinion you aught to lose no time in taking measures with her Majesty who should succed him, and be sure to make such a choice, as that 118 [Wharton] may be ashamed to show his anger. For though he has some very extreordinary parts, yett he [Wharton] has such quallitys that it would be scandelous to put such a trust in him.[3] As you have had wishes that the troupes of the descent might be imployed with the King of Spain, you will see by the enclosed letter of the Pensioner,[4] that thay in Holland wish them with the Duke of Savoye. I would give you the same answer I have done to the Pensioner,[5] which is that if thay should be commanded to Spain or Savoye, there would happen so many unforseen accedents, that in all probabillity thay would be of no use anywhere this campagne. Besides, I think the descent must unavoidably give so much trouble to France, that thay will be under very great difficultys. The methode the King of France has taken to make good his word to the Elector of Bavaria, of putting him at the head of an army of 80,000 men, are, the 18 battalions and 14 squadrons which came with the Mareshal de Marsin; the detachement that is now marching from Alsace, of 30 battalions and 40 squadrons; and 14 battalions which the Comte de Gassy[6] commanded in the lyns, which were not at the battaile. These, joined with the troupes that were at the battaile, would make above 100,000 men. But as of necessity thay must put garisons into

---

[1] 13/24 June, Murray, ii. 629, asking the promotion only to be effective for the duration of his stay in Spain. Stanhope was promoted to major-general 1 May 1707, without the reservation Marlborough suggested.

[2] The lawsuit involved the Duke of Hamilton in a contest over an estate which led ultimately to duel with Mohun and their deaths in 1712. Boyer, *Quadriennium Annae Postremum*, iv. 306–7.

[3] Pembroke was made lord-lieutenant in 1707 in place of Ormonde, in addition to his office of Lord President, much to Wharton's chagrin.

[4] 13/24 June, 't Hoff, pp. 237–8.   [5] 17/28 June, 't Hoff, pp. 239–40.

[6] Jean, count of Gassion (died 1713), joined French cavalry 1667; *maréchal de camp* 1692; lieutenant-general 1696; fought in Flanders throughout both wars; as senior lieutenant-general he commanded the French left at Ramillies.

several towns, I flatter myself that thay will find it very difficult to form such an army as will be able to hinder me from making the siege of Menin, as soon as that of Ostend is over. Menin is one of their strongest towns, but there is a necessity of attacking that in the first place, for that will let us into their *pays conqui*.[1] I do hope the descent will oblige them to make a detachment from this country, or force them to raise the siege of Turin. I received last night an expresse from Vienna, with the enclosed letter in Latin from the Emperor, and the powers from the King of Spain in Spanish.[2] That of the King of Spain was a blank signed by him and left in the Emperor's hand. As I have not been able to have the Spanish translated, I do not know exactly the powers. I shall keep it here a secrit til I know from you what her Majesty's pleasure is, as also I shal take measures with my friends in Holland to know how thay will like it, for I must take care that thay take no jealousy. Whatever the Queen's resolution may be, I beg no notice may be taken til the Emperor's minester shal aply to her Majesty. I beg you to asure the Queen, that I have in this matter, nor never shal have in any other, any desire of my own, but with all the submission in the world, be pleased with what she shall think is for her intirest.[3]

602. MARLBOROUGH *to the* DUCHESS   [*17/28 June 1706*]

Source: Blenheim MSS. G1-4.
Printed: *Private Correspondence*, i. 265 (inc.), as 1709.

[Roeselare]

. . .[4] then can be the thought of any other child.[5] Let me be happy with you, and no doubt the children we have, will give us just reason to be contented. I do protest that if I were to aske a blessing of God, it should . . . I received yesterday by expresse from the Emperor a letter in Lattin, and a power from the King of Spain in Spanish, which I send to Lord Treasurer. He will let you know what thay are. I do keep it a secrit here, and so I hope it will be in England til I have communicated with the States, for I would not medle with itt unless it be as well liked in Holland as I beleive itt will be in England; for no honour, or advantage would be of much pleasure to me, unless I did at the same time good to the publick by itt. You will lett 91 [Godolphin] know that I desire to have the opinion of 117

---

[1] The provinces taken from the Spanish Netherlands and incorporated into France by the Treaty of Aachen 1668: Artois, Thionville, etc.
[2] The Emperor's letter of 7/18 June and Charles III's commission are in Blenheim MSS. A1-38. They are printed in *Het dagboek van Gisbert Cuyper*, ed. A. J. Veenendaal (The Hague, 1950), pp. 38–41, the former in Latin, the latter in a translation into Dutch.
[3] This was the offer to Marlborough of the governorship (Representance) of the Spanish Nether-lands. See Geikie, pp. 13–37.
[4] Most of the first folio has been cut off.
[5] See pp. 199, 229, which appear to register the last hopes they had of having another son.

[Sunderland] and his friends, on the powers offered me, for I should be very sorry to make a wrong step in this matter. Besides I must be very carefull of not giving jealousy to 19 [the Dutch] with whome at this time I am extreamly well.

603. GODOLPHIN *to* MARLBOROUGH   [*18 June 1706*]

Source: Blenheim MSS. A1-36.

St James, June 18, 1706

By the return of Sir Stafford Fairborn's express, I acknowledged yesterday the favour of yours of the 25th[1] since which I have now received yours of the 24th[2] by the post with a letter enclosed from the Pensioner to you relating to the affairs of Portugall. Being in great ignorance at present of what they are doing in that country and in hourly expectation of letters, my opinion is, that till wee hear from thence, no resolution can properly bee taken. But the Pensioner's thought of sending somebody from Holland, betwixt this and autumn, seems to mee very good, if it were only that hee may bee an eye witness of Mr. Schonenberg's[3] proceedings, whose envy against Mr. Methuen was the chief occasion of Monsieur Fagells[4] playing the fool all last summer, and indeed of almost all the inconveniences which have hapned either before or since. But the advantage of this proposall will depend entirely upon the choise of a proper person to bee sent both from Holland and from hence also. I shall therefore desire Mr. Secretary Harley to write this night to Monsieur Buys to have his thoughts upon some fitt person to bee sent in case our next letters from Portugall lett us see the occasion of it continues.

The envoy of Savoy[5] gives us an account that Prince Eugene's letters to his master give little hopes of being able to gett into Pie[d]mont time enough for the relief of Turin, and therfore presses for positive orders to the fleet, to bee sent thither with some land men, upon which orders are repeated this day again to my Lord Peterborow, not to send less than 3 battalions. The Duke of Savoy has also desired that my Lord Peterborow may goe with them. That part is left to the King of Spain, who I suppose will not bee uneasy to part with him, and to his Lordship who naturally will bee willing enough to goe, if he dos not suspect it will make the King of Spain and his court easy.

I have directed Mr. Taylour to write very particularly to Mr. Bridges about setting the rate for paying out the money to the army. I hope neither he nor anybody else will take it into their heads to impose upon people in this

---

[1] Letter 599.   [2] Letter 597.
[3] The Dutch minister at Lisbon until 1717.
[4] Commander of the Dutch troops in Spain and Portugal.
[5] Count Briançon.

thing for wee know here to a farthing the difference in the value of the severall species of the money, and so does every common soldier in the army.[1]

Mr. Secretary Harley has notice that the governour, and most of the garrison of St. Omer[2] are Spanyards. If that bee soe, it will bee a great encoragement for your attacking of Ypres before anything else, since [it] opens St. Omer, and St. Omer opens France to you.

604. GODOLPHIN *to* MARLBOROUGH [*18 June 1706*]

Source: Blenheim MSS. A1-36.
Addressed: To his Grace the Duke of Marlborough.

Tuesday night 18 June

To my Grace the Duke of Marlborough

I write these 2 lines, since my letter in Lady Marlborough's packett,[3] only to tell you our Lisbon letters are come, and that I would have sent you the coppyes of them but that Mr. Secretary Hedges tells mee he desires to doe it.

I shall only say therfore, that I think the Pensioner's proposall of sending a person thither is very right, and I wish they would lose no time in dispatching him hither to us.

605. GODOLPHIN *to* MARLBOROUGH [*20 June 1706*]

Source: Blenheim MSS. A1-36.

June 20th 1706

The letters from Lisbon arriving after my letter of the last post was sealed,[4] I sent you a scrip of paper[5] only to tell you, Mr. Secretary Hedges would send you a coppy of what came to him, from Mr. Methuen. But finding in my packett, the coppyes of 2 letters from my Lord Gallway of the 10th and the 11th,[6] I venture to trouble you with them.

Upon the whole matter I am not yett quite out of hopes, that when they have the news of your battell, which had not then reachd them, they may still think it their interest to march onn to Madrid.[7] However wee

---

[1] See p. 609 and n. 4.
[2] Saint-Omer, a fortified town on the Aa, 37 kilometres south-east of Dunkirk.
[3] The preceding letter.   [4] Letter 603.
[5] The preceding letter.   [6] Untraced.
[7] Galway had proposed to the Portuguese a march on Madrid and after some debate his proposal was accepted. The Allied army advanced eastwards on 20/31 Mar. to Alcántara which they took on 3/14 Apr. and reached Almaraz on the road to Madrid on 23 Apr./4 May. Here a decision was taken by a council of war to retreat and attack Badajoz (which they had attempted in 1705) or Ciudad Rodrigo until the fate of Barcelona was known and the disposition of the French army under Berwick could be discovered. The Allies turned north to attack Ciudad Rodrigo, and after its fall on 15/26 May headed east once more towards Madrid, arriving in Salamanca on 27 May/7 June. Galway reached Madrid after little opposition on 16/27 June. Francis, pp. 313-16.

ought not to neglect sending, in my opinion, both from England and Holland, as the Pensioner proposes in his letter to you.[1]

I also trouble you with the informations which Mr. Hill has given mee of the difference of the value of the coyns in Holland and Flanders, and also with a coppy of the letter which Mr. Taylour has written to Mr. Bridges by my direction, that you may the better judg how these orders are complyd with.[2]

Mr. Henry Villiers[3] has comitted so great a misdemeanor in his government of Tinmouth, that I believe he must bee removed, and therfore you will please to lett mee know whom you recomend to the Queen for his successour.[4]

This packett will bee so big, that I will add no more to your trouble. At least not till tomorrow.

606. MARLBOROUGH *to* GODOLPHIN   [*20 June/1 July 1706*]

Source: Blenheim MSS. A1-14.
Printed: Coxe, ii. 56–7 (inc.).

Rousselaer Jully 1, 1706

I have had a letter by the last post from 49 [George Churchill], in which he asures me that he would behave himself in everything as you should like. I do not say this that I am perswadcd that his heart is just as I could wish, but I veryly beleive he would take pains not to offend, and that there must be somebody else that dose mischief besides himself.[5] Your letter of the 9th[6] that came by Ostend was with me three days sooner then that of the 7th,[7] which was write the post before. The siege of Ostend goes on very slow, but this day Monsieur Auverkerk asures me that it will be over in six days. I may be deceeved, but I think 365 [Heinsius] is as to the peace as

---

[1] See p. 586.   [2] *C.T.B.*, xx. iii. 683–4.

[3] Henry Villiers (died 1707), brother of the Earl of Jersey; his sister Barbara (died 18 Aug. 1708) a good friend of the Duchess's, was married to Godolphin's cousin, Viscount Fitzharding. For Villiers's misdemeanour see p. 618. He was given a pension to support his family, below, p. 757.

[4] Marlborough replied that he wanted it for an officer and he asked the Queen to wait until he found someone suitable (p. 603). The ministers also decided that no action should be taken until something could be done for Villiers's family. The Queen's decision to give him a pension in Apr. 1707 freed the place (p. 757). Godolphin then suggested Sutton, whom Marlborough recommended for New York, so that he could be in England as he intended to stand for Parliament (p. 775). The Duke of Newcastle intervened, pressing Sutton (his deputy-governor of Hull) not to accept so that Tinmouth could be given to George Whichcot, an M.P. whose patron he was (p. 784). Marlborough protested that it should only be given to an officer (p. 796), to which the Queen agreed (p. 822), and asked that it be held until the end of the 1707 campaign (p. 832). Then Somerset asked for the governorship for his son, Hertford, and Marlborough promised him the place would not be filled until he returned to England in the autumn (p. 907). The place was finally awarded on 20 Feb. to Major-General Thomas Meredyth, who was a protégé of Somerset's (p. 396 n. 3). The home garrisons were largely made up of soldiers who had grown old in the Service to whom the appointments served in lieu of a pension. Marlborough was anxious to retain these places for this purpose, both for humanitarian reasons and morale factors. See Cardonnel to St. John, 15/26 Sept. 1707, Murray, iii. 568.

[5] See p. 583.   [6] Letter 591.   [7] Letter 589.

wee could wish. However, I think he cannot withstand harkening to good proposalls, though thay should be offered after the subsitys are given. [As for] 116 [Somers], which you beleive a proper man for to be one of the ambassadors, he is certainly very capable, but I should think he would object his not being master enough of the French language. I have a notion for this commission of treaty, which I fear everybody will differ with me. As the Queen will, I hope, whenever this treaty shall begine, declare openly what she shall think just and reasonable, I would not tye myself up to one party, but have one of etch in the commission, that thay might be witness of the Queen's intentions for the publick good.

Monsieur Hop[1] is come to me this day from Bruxelles, and I have comunicated to him the Emperor's letter, and the powers from the King of Spain. He made me great complyments, but I find by him that he thinkes this may give uneasiness in Holland by thinking that the count of Vienna has a mind to put the power of this country into the Queen's hand in order that they [the Dutch] may have nothing to do with it.[2] If I should find the same thing by the Pensioner, and that nothing could cure this jealoussy, but my desiring to be excused from accepting this commission, I hope the Queen will alow of itt, for the advantage and honour I might have by this commission is very insignificant, in comparison of the fatal consequences that might bee if it should cause a jealoussy between the two nations. I have just now received yours of the 13 and 14th[3] but can't answer them til the next post.

I am so uneasy at the slow proceedings at Ostend, that I intend to go thether on Saturday,[4] and return the next day. The inclosed copie[5] is what I have received this afternoon. You will see by it what the King of Spain intends, and that there are no shipes gone on the Italien cost. Some men are bound to make everything thay have to do with uneasy, for now that everything was setled, Lord Mardant's redgiment must go.[6]

607. MARLBOROUGH *to the* DUCHESS   [*20 June/1 July 1706*]

Source: Blenheim MSS. E3.
Printed: *Private Correspondence*, i. 54–5 (inc.), as Bruxelles.

Rousselaer Jully 1, 1706

Since my last I have had the pleasure of yours of the 11th, as also one from 49 [George Churchill], in which he dose asure me that he is desirous of

---

[1] In 1706 Hop was made provisional deputy for the government of Brabant and Flanders and 1709 for the government of Lille and French Flanders. See his correspondence for this year in Vreede.

[2] That is, though it was a great compliment to Marlborough, the fact remained that the Queen had disavowed any claims in the Spanish Netherlands and that the acceptance of this offer could create a misunderstanding between England and the United Provinces. See Geikie, p. 18, and Cuyper, *Dagboek*, pp. 41–2.

[3] Letters 595–6, 598.   [4] 22 June/3 July.
[5] Untraced.   [6] On the descent: see p. 583.

doing everything that might please you and 91 [Godolphin]. I am afraid there is somebody else that makes 82 [Prince George] and Mrs. Morley [the Queen] uneasy. I do from my soul wish her all the happyness in the world, and it is certaine that God has blessed her raine much above what has been for a long time; but we have such a villanous race of vipors amongest us, that whielst she is admired by all people abroad, thay are studying how to make her and those that serve her uneasy. I really am not concerned for myself. I could dispise them and live with much more pleasure retiered, if I were sure that 83 [the Queen] and 91 [Godolphin] would not want my service. It is very mortefying to see that nothing can amend 392 [Lady Monthermer]. I beg of you to do me the justice and yourself the ease to beleive that whatever thay say can have no credit with me, when you asure me of the contrary. I can and do agreive as much as any parent can when a child is unkind. We must hope the best, and be always carefull not to resent their car[ri]age to such a degree as to make the town judge of who is in the right. I am sure 73 [Rochester] nor nobody living can more sincerly attribut the good success to Providence then I do, for I think the enemys taking the resolution to venture a battaile, which was so much against their intirest,[1] could be by no other hand. I have this minut received yours of the 14th, but must answer it by the next post. I am with all my heart and soull yours.

608. GODOLPHIN *to* MARLBOROUGH   [*21 June 1706*]

Source: Blenheim MSS. A1-36.

21 June 1706

I sent you yesterday, by the way of Sir Stafford Fairborn, the coppyes of some letters from my Lord Gallway to Mr. Methuen as also such informations as I have had of the difference of the value of the money betwixt Holland and Flanders. I hope you will receive that packett[2] some days before this letter.

I am willing to flatter myself from those letters from my Lord Gallway, that the Portugheses will yett goe to Madrid. And I find by letters I have seen from thence of the 9th that they begin to bee in earnest very apprehensive of it at that court. However I would not have this opinion of mine bee made use of to divert the sending a person from Holland to Portugall, as the Pensioner proposed. For the sooner that is done I think it will bee the better, and the charge of it is not to bee putt in the ballance with the advantage which the common cause may receive from setting things upon a better foot in that country.

---

[1] Villeroi had been encouraged by Louis XIV to engage in battle to restore confidence in the French army among the inhabitants of the Spanish Netherlands. By their interest Marlborough meant they were safer staying behind their lines and holding their lines, whereas they risked and lost their occupation of Flanders and Brabant by giving battle. Vault, vi. 16, 19, 32.

[2] Letter 605.

I hope wee shall now have the transports from Holland with the first wind, for every day that our expedition is now delayed doth both prejudice the undertaking and increase the charge of it. For now they have brought a proposition to have bread furnished them from hence. This is what I never did so much as dream of, nor can I think it reasonable, in the present case.

Wee hear nothing from Sir Stafford Fairborn, since the batteryes at Ostend have begun to fire, which makes mee a little uneasy for fear that siege should hang longer, than may bee convenient for your other views.

In my letter yesterday I told you Mr. Villiers the governour of Tinmouth has committed a misdemeanour which I think is like to deprive him of his office. I repeat it, that, in case that letter is not yett come to your hands, you may consider of some proper person to recomend to the Queen for that government.

609. GODOLPHIN *to* MARLBOROUGH [*22 June 1706*]

Source: Blenheim MSS. A1-36.

St. James' 22th June 1706

The letters of Tuesday last[1] from The Hague are not yett come to hand. I wrote to you by the post last night, and often of late by the way of Sir Stafford Fairborn. This goes by my Lord Lifford upon a ship that is ordered to joyn that squadron before Ostend. His Lordship is desirous to serve in your army as a voluntier, intending to convince you by that, he was desirous to serve anywhere against France, but that he could not submitt to serve under the Marquis de Guiscard. He has returned, with some difficulty, the commission of Major Generall, which had been given him upon that occasion.

I have had a letter from Blansac to desire his leave might bee prolonged, to which I have answered that it could not bee granted, because the French had refused to exchange Monsieur de *Vaubonne*.[2] When I told this answer to my Lord Lifford, he said Monsieur de Vanbonne had taken party with France, but I was resolved not to believe that unless I heard it from you. The Venetian embassador[3] continues to bee full of his assurances. The republick desires nothing so much as to enter into measures with the Queen, but that they cannot declare against France while the French army lies actually upon their country. He says their Generall Heinan has 16,000 men.

I believe he would have subsidyes or else have assurances that Mantua should bee joyned to the territoryes of the republick. I have not much to say against the latter, nor I don't see that the Emperour or anybody else ought to bee much concerned for preserving that Duke in his territoryes. Could not you sound the Pensioner upon this, and bee pleased to lett mee have your own thoughts of it, as soon as conveniently you can.

[1] 18/29 June.   [2] See p. 588.   [3] Cornaro.

The Queen comes to town next week to the thanksgiving at St. Pauls. I hope one week more after that will finish the Treaty of Union with Scotland.

610. GODOLPHIN *to* MARLBOROUGH   [*24 June 1706*]

Source: Blenheim MSS. A1-36.
Printed: Coxe, ii. 55 (inc.).

Windsor Monday 24 June 1706

The letters of last Tuesday[1] from The Hague are not yett come, but I hope wee shall have them before I make up this.

In pursuance of the instances made in Holland by the minister of Savoy,[2] orders were sent by the States, as also from the Queen here, for sending some regiments by sea to the relief of that prince. But the orders for a squadron to goe to Naples, were sent only from the Queen and not from the States. Now their having positive orders in one case and not in the other, may possibly create a difficulty among the Dutch commanders upon the latter of these poynts. But I don't know how it is capable of ever being prevented. For if upon the arrivall of any informations here, upon which orders are necessary to bee sent to the fleet, if wee should stay till these orders were sent to Holland, and approved there, before they were dispatched, it would lose so much time that they would always come too late to have any good effect.

The Queen complains of the Duke of Northumberland,[3] that upon the Prince's giving leave to Mr. Hawley[4] to sell his *cornett's* place, (I think it was in that regiment), hee has filled it with a little boy[5] whom he presented to kiss her hand. I mention this only to lett you see, that though leave to sell bee sometimes necessary for the good of the Service, yett if it bee not strictly kept to that poynt only, it grows soon to bee made use of to serve every turn.

Tuesday 25th

Since I had written this far, I have the favour of yours of the 28th[6] with the severall papers enclosed. I doe not return you the Spanish paper,[7] not having had time to gett it translated for you, as I intend to doe. But I have been able to read it in English to the Queen who likes the thing very

[1] 18/29 June.   [2] Briançon.

[3] George Fitzroy, Duke of Northumberland (1665–1716), youngest son of Charles II by Barbara Villiers; colonel, Royal Regiment of Horse Guards.

[4] Henry Hawley, cornet, Horse Guards, 1704; captain, Essex's Regiment of Dragoons, 27 May 1706.

[5] Edward Bird, cornet 27 May; replaced by Edward Reading 18 July.

[6] Letter 601.

[7] The powers from Charles III making Marlborough his 'representant' in the Spanish Netherlands.

well and leaves it to you to doe, as you shall judg best for her service and the good of the common cause. I have not communicated this to anybody yett, but 116 [Somers] and to 117 [Sunderland] who are both much pleased with it as what they think is like to keep everything in those countryes upon a right foot, at least, during the operations of this summer. They seemed to think there was no reason for 19 [the Dutch] not to like it as well as wee doe, and both concluded with 91 [Godolphin] that it was one of the rightest thoughts that ever came from 318's [the Emperor] Counsell. 83 [the Queen] has not yett had any notice of it from 349 [Count Gallas].

As to what the Pensioner writes I agree with you intirely, that 'tis too late to take any other measures in that affair of the descent.[1] But I agree with him also, that if the next letters from Lisbon doe not tell us the Portugheses are advancing to Madrid, it will be extreamly proper to send two persons from England and Holland to take new measures and make new agreements with those people.

I am indeed apprehensive the Duke of Savoy may want timely assistance, but it is too late to send anything to him now from this part of the world. I wish the orders sent long since to the fleet may come to bee of any use to him.

Wee hear my Lord Peterborow is gone with the fleet to Alicante and Valentia where he will have 4,000 foot of regular troops. The King of Spayn was to joyn him with the horse on the way towards Madrid.

Thus far their disposition seems to bee right, and unless the Portugheses bee gon home agayn,[2] I doe not see what there is to oppose their march. In the meantime their letters are full of notions very different from views of this kind. They talk of the necessity of getting some port for the fleet to winter in those seas, as if they had no thought of getting possession of the throne, which whenever they obtain, security follows necessarily in the same moment.

As to your own notions, you will see by a former letter of mine[3] that I thought *Ypres* to bee as proper for you as Menin, but you can judg that best. Only if you did not think it too impertinent, I would ask you, if *Alost* bee not a little too farr from your camp for the Prussian and Hanover troops to stay, and whether they may not bee liable to bee insulted there by a sudden conjunction of the Elector with the detachments from Alsace, before you can bee able to reinforce them?

I am sorry to find Ostend hangs so long for many reasons. Our expedition hangs upon it. That is one of the chief of them.

What you say of Harvey and Lord Mohun is certainly entirely right.

The deanery of Rochester is void. The Queen's own thought upon it was, that this might bee proper to give Mr. Hare, and make his step the easyer to

[1] Heinsius wanted to send the troops for the descent to the Duke of Savoy.
[2] See p. 604 n. 4.
[3] Letter 594.

the bishoprick of Oxford. I spoke of it to the Archbishop. He seemed to like it, but had some doubt, that it must not bee a Cambridg man.

Mr. Godolphin had another doubt whether he could bee a dean before he had taken his doctor's degree. Upon the whole, there will bee time enough to consult Mr. Hare himself if you think fitt. This deanery is one of the smallest and not valuable on any other account so much as upon that I have mentioned.[1]

The Queen is come to town to give God thanks next Thursday[2] for your victory. I assure you I shall doe it from every vein within mee, having scarce anything else to support either my heart or my head. The animosity and inveteracy one has to struggle with is unimaginable, not to mention the difficulty of obtaining things to bee done that are reasonable, or of satisfying people with reason, when they are done.

611. MARLBOROUGH *to* GODOLPHIN [*25 June/6 July 1706*]

Source: Blenheim MSS. A1–14.
Printed: Coxe, ii. 58 (inc.).

Harlebeck[3] Jully 6, 1706

I came so late last night to the army from Ostend, and was obliged to march so early this morning, that I must beg pardon that I can't answere yours of the 13 and 14[4] by this post. I sent you by the last post[5] a letter from the Pensioner, and I now inclose the answer I thought was for her Majesty's Service I should make to itt.[6] The inclosed letter of the 3d from him,[7] as also Slingelandt's[8] of the same date, conferms me, that if I should accept of the honour the Emperor and the King of Spain dose me, it would creat a great jealousy, which might prejudice the common cause, so that I hope her Majesty will aprove of what I have done. And I beg you to be so just and kind to me as to asure the Queen that though the apointments of this government are threscore thousand pounds a yeare, I shall with pleasure excuse myself, since I am convinced it is for her Service, unless the States should make itt their request, which thay are very far from doing; for thay have told me that thay think it not reasonable that the King of Spain should have possession of the Low Countrys, til thay had asurances of what Barier

---

[1] See p. 605. Dr. Henry Ullock's death had been expected for some time and Hare had indicated his interest in the place. He heard to his chagrin that it was intended for Samuel Pratt. See his letter to his wife, 9 May, B.M., Add. MS. 28057, fols. 309–11, where he discusses this. Pratt was appointed 8 Aug.

[2] 27 June.

[3] Harelbeke, 19 kilometres south-east of Roeselare, on the road from Ghent to Lille.

[4] Letters 595–6, 598.   [5] Letter 606.

[6] Marlborough errs here, for he refers to Heinsius's letter of 19/30 June and his reply of 22 June/3 July ('t Hoff, pp. 241–3). See the end of this letter where he realizes the omission.

[7] 't Hoff, pp. 243–4.   [8] Untraced.

thay should have for their security. I hope this complysance of mine will give me so much credit, as to be able to hinder them from hurting themselves. For it is certain if thay follow their own inclinations, thay will make such demands upon this country as will very much disatisfie the House of Austria, and be thought unreasonable by all the Allyes, of which the French would be sure to make their advantage. I send you a copie of a letter that was sent me last night from Bruxelles. I do veryly beleive it a trew copie of a letter from Madrid.[1]

The French say thay will do great things when thay have the Duke of Vandome, who is expected in four days. I hope we shall be masters of Ostend by the end of this week, so that in a few days after, the English troupes [for the descent] will be embarked. And I have write to The Hague, that their troupes may be also sheped their.

I now send you the Pensioner's letter of the 30th of the last month, which should have come in my last letter.[2]

612. GODOLPHIN *to* MARLBOROUGH   [*26 June 1706*]

Source: Blenheim MSS. A1-36.

26 June 1706

Though I troubled you with a very long letter by yesterday's post,[3] I began to write again today, beleiving I shall have an opportunity of sending this to Sir Stafford Fairborn, before the next post. And I had a mind besides to add some farther reflections upon the subject of your new government and the consequences of it.

1st I look upon it, in its own nature, to bee a temporary provision, and soe intended.[4] But if it should prove otherwise, and things should soe turn as to make it reasonable to continue beyond the end of this present campagne, in that case, I should think and hope, it should not nor will not hinder your coming into England before the meeting of our Parliament, which in all probability will bee extreamly essentiall to the Queen's affaires, and is an advantage that wee have been deprived of for five years successively by your having been so remote. But you will now bee always within reach of coming over at a week's warning.

2dly in case another Governour is to bee named after the campagne shall bee over and you come into England, would not you think it for your own

---

[1] An anonymous letter dated 7/18 June, Madrid: it reports that 'the news of Ramillies and the entry of the Portuguese into Castile has made Philip V take a resolution of leaving Madrid. Many men of quality are also leaving and they believe all is up as his cause is hopeless.' Blenheim MSS. A2-16.

[2] See above.   [3] Letter 610.

[4] Here Godolphin is more percipient than Marlborough, for this was Charles III's view. See Geikie, p. 16.

ease and satisfaction that it should bee Prince Eugene? And if the warr is to continue another year that must needs bee of the greatest advantage to the Allyes.

613. MARLBOROUGH _to_ GODOLPHIN   [27 June/8 July 1706]

Source: Blenheim MSS. A1-14.

Harlebeck Jully 8th 1706

I received yesterday, almost at the same time, yours of the 20th[1] by Ostend, and that of the 21[2] by the way of Holland. After the behavior of the Portugess, I should not expect much good by the two letters of Lord Gallaway's of the 10th and 11th of the last month. But by the letters wee have from all parts, we have reason to beleive thay are marched forward, and that King Charles was at Madrid on the 20th, the Duke of Anjoue and his Dutchess having left that place on the 18th, and as it is asured, are gone to Pampalona. I have given orders for the embarking of two English redgiments which are now at Ostend, the French marching out of the place this day.[3] I having upon your letter[4] promised Lord Mordant his redgiment should be the thord, [it] gives me some uneasiness, for at my return from Ostend, I found his Lordshipe gone from the army to his lady who is at Gand. Being informed at the same time of the uneasiness his redgiment lay under being ordered to gon on shipboard, I sent an express to desire his Lordship would come to me, but as yett have no answer. For should his redgiment march, the greatest part will disert, so that the Service will be disapointed. The pretence the soldiers take is that I had apointed another redgiment, and that it is not their turn to go. But the truth is, thay do not care to go with their Collonel, who has never been with them since he has had the redgiment.[5] I will take care that this or some other shall be there before the Dutch can be ready to shipe, for it will be for the Service thay should saill together. I was in hopes to have sent Lieutenant General Inglosby with these troupes, but he continues so ill at Gand, that I know not when he will be able to serve, so that there will be a necessity of sending with Lord Rivers, Lieutenant General Earle. For though he may be wanted at the Board of Ordenance, yet that is a much less inconveniency then letting this descent go without a Lieutenant Generall, and I see no other you can make use of. I could give you many reason why you must oblige Earle to go. As to the bread, it must be some man's business to help them when thay are landed, for thay go in a season that thay can't faile of finding corn. If there be time for it, there can be no great expence in

[1] Letter 605.   [2] Letter 608.
[3] Ostend capitulated 23 June/4 July after a severe bombardment.   [4] Letter 595.
[5] A memorial dated 26 June/7 July from the officers of Mordaunt's regiment, protesting the orders, is in Blenheim MSS. F1-20 (3).

sending some meal with them, since the soldiers are to allow for it out of their pay. I am extreame glad of the derections you have ordered Mr. Taylor to give Mr. Bridges, for I do not understand that matter, but shall be always ready in giving such orders as you may think reasonable. Turin being now invested on both sides of the Poo, I am afraid no troupes that can be landed at Onelia[1] can be of service in that siege. But my hopes are, that if the news of Spain be trew, the King of France will be obliged to raise the siege. If Mr. Villiars has given just occasion, I hope her Majesty will make use of the opertunity, for he is a very worthless man; and as I do not doubt but her Majesty would give it to some officer of the army, I shall let you know who may deserve her Majesty's feavour. The King of Prussia has desired me by Collonel Grumkoe,[2] who came yesterday to the army, that I would let it be known only to her Majesty, that he would, with her leave, recall his ambassador, so that she might do the same to Lord Raby, and that he was desirous he might not go back to Berlin. At the same time he has asured me that if the Queen will send an envoye in whome I have confidence, he will live so with him, that he shall be acquainted with everything that passes in his court, he being resolved of doing everything that may please her Majesty. At the same time, he says he has no objection to Lord Raby but his being so well with the Grand Chamberlain's wife, that it gives him a redicule all over the Empire. I do hope this King is ashamed of what he has done, and that [it] may make him be more carefull yearafter. It is of consequence that her Majesty should have power with him, so that I beg you will think well before you apoint anybody, for everybody is not fitt for such a court.

The inclosed is to acquaint the Queen with the reduction of Ostend, and in itt I have obayed your commands as to Lord Sunderland.[3] The inclosed are the letters you desired and that I forgot to send.[4]

[1] Oneglia, a small seaport on the Italian Riviera at the mouth of the Impero, 115 kilometres west of Genoa.

[2] Friedrich Wilhelm von Grumbkow (1678–1739), Prussian minister and general; personal representative of the King of Prussia to Marlborough at the army; undertook several diplomatic missions for the King during the war. Grumbkow worked so closely with Marlborough that he often appeared to be acting at his behest rather than his master's (Geikie, p. 168). He kept Marlborough well informed on the state of the court and the factions at Berlin. After the accession of Frederick William I in 1713 he rose to the directorship of the General War Commissariat and later the General Directory, the finance ministry, in which position he was chief minister.

[3] Marlborough's letter to the Queen is missing. Godolphin sent a draft urging her to take Sunderland into the ministry, which Marlborough incorporated (p. 563). The Queen replied to this on 9 July, H.M.C., *Marlborough MSS.*, 43b (inc.).

[4] Untraced.

614. MARLBOROUGH *to the* DUCHESS   [*27 June /8 July 1706*]

Source: Blenheim MSS. E3.
Printed: *Private Correspondence*, i. 55–7.

Harlebeck Jully 8th 1706

You will have seen by my last letter[1] that yours of the 17th had given me a great deal of uneasyness; but as that gave me trouble, so yours of the 20 and 21 has given me great satisfaction, for the quiet of my life depends upon your dear self and children. What you say in yours of the 20th is so reasonable, that it is impossible but your children must act accordinly, and you may be sure I shall be carefull never to write anything but what may make them sensible of your kindness and the obligations thay have to you.

I have no acquaintance with Doctor Binkes,[2] but I have always heard him reconed amongest the violent men, so that I am not surprised at this proceeding. As wee are now masters of Ostend, I do by this post write the letter to 83 [the Queen] which 91 [Godolphin] desired.[3] I wish with all my heart he meet with less uneasinesses, but in this world it is impossible to live and not have them. Our letters from all parts gives us good reason to beleive that King Charles was at Madrid on the 20th of the last month, and that the Duke of Anjoue and his Dutchess left that place on the 18th, and were gone to Pampelona.[4] If this be trew, the French in reason will be obliged to raise the siege of Turin. By the account you give [the dowager] Lady Sunderland is in a very daingerous condition. I wish she may leave the world with that tenderness I think she owes her son.[5] By your saying nothing to me of your going to Woodstock, I find your heart is not soe much sett on that place as I could wish. Vanbrook writs me that I shall not see him in the army, beleiving that I shal aprove better of his going into Oxfordshire.[6]

[1] 25 June/6 July. Untraced.
[2] William Binckes (died 1712), inflammatory Tory clergyman; Prebend of Lincoln 1683; Dean of Litchfield 1703; prolocutor, lower house, convocation of Canterbury, 1705; his sermon before the lower house on 30 Jan. 1702 was voted scandalous and offensive by the Lords in May; on 1 Mar. 1706 he convened the house after hearing the Queen's order to adjourn, for which he was prosecuted and made submission to the Archbishop. The Duchess also sent an account of this High Church clergyman to the Queen, and probably charged her with favouring his inflammatory doctrines. The Queen disowned knowing Binckes or approving of his principles (fragment in Blenheim MSS. G1-7), but there is reason to believe she was in sympathy with his views. Four years later Harley noted 'in her heart she stil thinks with Kimberly and Bincks' (jotted on a paper of 9 Jan. 1710, B.M., Portland Loan, 29/28).
[3] See the preceding letter.
[4] Charles III never reached Madrid. The Queen left Madrid on 9/20 June followed by Philip V on the 11/22nd. Galway took possession of Madrid on 16/27 June and Charles III was proclaimed there on 21 June/2 July. Owing to the failure of the King and Peterborough to come at once to Madrid Galway left the town on 30 June/11 July to pursue the French army and was not joined by the King until 26 July/6 Aug. at the camp at Gudalajara. Meantime the French re-entered Madrid on 23 July/4 Aug. and the Habsburg attempt to rule Spain was doomed.
[5] She did not die until 16 Apr. 1715.
[6] Vanbrugh had accompanied Halifax on his complimentary mission to present the Regency and Naturalizations Acts to the Electress and the Garter to the Electoral Prince.

615. GODOLPHIN *to* MARLBOROUGH [*28 June 1706*]

Source: Blenheim MSS. A1-36.

June 28th

The paper inclosed[1] was given mee by the Archbishop of Canterbury, and is in his own hand. I have communicated it to 117 [Sunderland] and asked him if that *breach of method*, as it is termed in the paper, were such a difficulty as could not bee overcome upon this occasion. He said, he thought it might bee overcome but at the same time he seemed to think it was not advisable to overcome it in this case, because it would certainly sett the minds of the university so much against *Mr. Hare*,[2] that it would make him a very improper instrument, to incline those people to such a temper, as you would wish to bring them to. And therfore his opinion upon the whole matter, was that you might bee pleased to make what other provision you thought fitt for Mr. Hare, and turn your thoughts to some other person upon whom you can entirely depend, and that shall not bee lyable to this objection. And if you are of the same opinion, I shall bee sure to putt the Queen in mind of Mr. Hare upon the first vacancy of a prebend of [St.] Paul's or Windsor. And somebody else must bee thought of when the Bishop of Oxford[3] shall bee removed, but at present the dreamer [Talbot] is in perfect health.

When I began this letter I thought of sending it by Sir Stafford Fairborn. But now the post day is come, I shall reserve that for another occasion which I expect in a day or two.

616. MARLBOROUGH *to* GODOLPHIN

[*29 June/10 July 1706*]

Source: Blenheim MSS. A1-14.
Printed: Coxe, ii. 61-2, 111-12, as 14 July.

Harlebeck Jully 10th 1706

You will see by three or four letters[4] that I have lately write to you, the care I have taken not to give any occasion of jealousy in Holland, and that I was in hopes that my declining the honour the King of Spain had done me, would give me so much power with the States, as that I might be able to hinder them from doing themselves and the common cause hurt. But such is

---

[1] A letter from Tenison to Godolphin, 26 June, which reads: 'Dr. Ullock, late Dean of Rochester is certainly dead. The deanry may be disposed of by her Majestie when she pleases. As to the Bishopric of Oxford, whenever it comes to be voyd, it cannot, without breach of method, be disposed of to a Cambridgeman. The cours has been to send a Cambridgeman to Ely, and an Oxfordman to Oxford.'

[2] Francis Hare, chaplain-general of the army.

[3] William Talbot (1659?-1730), Tory clergyman; Dean of Worcester 1691; Bishop of Oxford 1699; Bishop of Durham 1721.

[4] Letters 601, 606, 611.

their temper that when thay have misfortunes, thay are desirous of peace upon any terms; and when wee are blessed by God with success, thay are for turning it to their own advantage, without any consideration how it may be liked by their friends and allyes. You will see by the inclosed copie of a letter I have this day write to the Pensioner,[1] that if thay can't be braught to chang their resolution of the 19th of the last month,[2] thay will creat so great a jealousy in this country, that thay shall be under the absolute government of the Dutch, that it will turn very much to the advantage of the French; besides, that the King of Spain will have just reason to complain. Monsieur Hopp tels me the States have derected Monsieur Vriberg to acquaint her Majesty and her ministers with their reasons and proceedings. In my poor opinion her Majesty can't give to[o] kind an answer, but she must be carefull that the King of Spain and the House of Austria have not reason give them to be angry. Now the States have aplyed to her Majesty, you know I can't act with safety but by her Majesty's directions by one of the Secretarys of State. I must beg of her Majesty, for her own Service and the publick good, that she will be pleased to allow of my declining the honour of the King of Spain's commission. Otherways, the party in Holland that are for peace, rather upon ill termes then good, would make a very ill use of itt, though in my opinion the States might have avoyded many inconveniencys and iregularitys that must now happen, if thay had approved of my acting. For I should have done nothing but what must have turned to their safety, and at the same time, thay might have treated with the King of Spain concerning their barier. But by this step of theirs, thay will very quickly be obliged to declare, not only to the Queen, but to everybody else, that thay will keep this country in their own power til thay have their *surity* as thay call it, by having such a Barier as thay shall think reasonable. I dread the consequences of this matter, for I can't write so freely to the States on this subject as I should otherways, if I were not personaly conserned. You may be sure the French have to[o] many partisans in Holland not to be informed of this proceeding, so that thay will be sure to make their advantage of itt. Now that Ostend is over I was in hopes we might have lost no time in attacking of Menin, but Monsieur Gilder-Malsen sends me word that thay have not the necessary preperations ready. But as soon as thay come to Gand, he will lett mee know itt. I am afraid wee shall find at last that some of our friends are of

---

[1] 't Hoff, pp. 245–6, in French. English translation, Coxe, ii. 59–60. This was obviously meant to be shown round. Marlborough's English letter of the same day ('t Hoff, p. 247), expresses his injured feelings in much more passionate terms.

[2] Blenheim MSS. F1-20. The States General arrogated to themselves (and England) the right to govern the Spanish Netherlands in the name of Charles III and appropriate its revenues until a peace treaty was signed guaranteeing them a Barrier. This was a series of fortresses in the Spanish Netherlands which they would garrison to protect their country from a French invasion. The Dutch resolved to establish a Council of State at Brussels to govern the Provinces as in the time of Charles II until a peace treaty was concluded. See Veenendaal, p. 37; Geikie, pp. 24–5.

the opinion that wee have already done to[o] much, for notwithstanding what I said when I was at Ostend, that 2 redgiments would be enough to leave in that place, thay have left six. But I have write to The Hague, and if thay do not give orders that some of them be sent to the army, thay do not intend to have much more done this yeare. This will apear strang to you, but we have to[o] many of these refined pollitiques, that it is hie time we had a good peace. But at the same time I say this to you, much the greatest part of the people in Holland are very honest, and wish well to the common cause. But those that are of the contrary faction, are more active and dilligent. Everything goes so well in Spain that if wee have success with the descent, France must submit to a reasonable peace. The wind has continued so long westerly, that I am afraid severall of my letters are at the Briel, which makes me desire Sir Staford Fairborn to send this. The Dutch have ordered their transports to Ostend, so that you will have their troupes and the English together.

On 11 July Marlborough moved the army from Harelbeke, from which point he had been covering the siege of Ostend, to the south-east, where he camped on the Scheldt with one flank at Helchin.

---

617. MARLBOROUGH *to* GODOLPHIN [*1/12 July 1706*]

Source: Blemheim MSS. A1-14.
Printed: Coxe, i. 61 (inc.).

Helchin Jully 12th 1706

I find by yours of the 25 of the last month[1] you had not had the good news of Spain. We think here that if King Charles makes no long stay at Madrid, but marches with his army into Navarr, the Duke of Anjoue will be obliged to retire into France, for til the siege of Turin be over thay can send no troupes to him. By my last letter,[2] which I sent by the way of Ostend, you will see the measures that 19 [Holland] is desirous to take concerning the management of this country, which would certainly sett this whole country against them, so that I hope you will find some way of not letting them play the fool. You know that I am always very ready of speaking very freely to them, when I think it for their services, but in this matter I am not at liberty, fearing thay might mistake me, and think it might proceed from

[1] Letter 610.   [2] Letter 616.

self intirest. I am sure in this matter I have with pleasure sacrefised my own intirest in order to make them reasonable, which I hope will be aproved on by my friends; for should I have acted otherways, the party that is for peace would have made a very ill use of itt. For the feavourers of the French faction endeavours all thay can to persuaid the people in Holland that the King of Spain will be governed by the Queen, and that this success will all turn to the advantage of England, so that thay must not relye upon anybody, but secure their frontier now that thay have it in their power. This is so plausable in Holland that I am afraid the honest people, though thay see the daingerous consequences this must have, thay dare not speake against it, and I can asure you these great towns had rather be under any nation then the Dutch. I hope in few days we may hear good news from Prince Eugene, for the news from Lille is that there has been action, and if the French had had the advantage, thay would not faile of publishing itt. The Comte Maffie[1] came to the army the day before yesterday. His business is to lett me see the daingers Turin is in. I am afraid the orders that has been given must come to[o] laite, for the French pretend to have it by the 20th of this month. Besides, if Prince Eugene can't force his passage, I do not see any service that five or six battallions could do, for it is most certain thay could not gett into Turin. I send you the Duke of Savoye's[2] and Prince Eugene's letters,[3] that you may read them at your leasure, and put them to such other letters as you have of mine. The reason of the Hanover and Prussien troupes staying so long at Alost is for the security of Bruxelles, and the covering of the 18 hundred workmen that are making redoutes for the better blocking of Dendermont; for that place can't be taken but by famine.

618. MARLBOROUGH *to* GODOLPHIN   [*1/12 July 1706*]

Source: Cardonnel's letterbooks, Blenheim Palace.
Printed: Murray, ii. 692.

Camp at Helchin, 12th July 1706

I have read the copy of the letter Mr. Taylor writes by your Lordship's directions to Mr. Brydges relating to the payment of the army,[4] and am expecting soon to hear from him on that subject from Amsterdam. In the meantime I must beg leave to acquaint your Lordship that, upon my coming into this country, orders were given for the pistoles to be issued to the troops at 9. 15. and the shilling at $6\frac{1}{2}$, and so proportionably all other specie, being the same rate they have always gone at with us, for we have had no other coin in former campaigns from the time we came out of the Dutch garrisons till we returned, unless while we were in Germany; and my

1 Minister of the Duke of Savoy.   2 21 May/1 June, Blenheim MSS. A1-39.
3 6/17 June, Blenheim MSS. A1-39.   4 See p. 594.

greatest care has been that the soldiers might have their full subsistence, according to the English establishment, without any diminution. This rate Mr. Hill could have told you is the current standard of the country, and the same the army was paid at during the last war, whereas what is now proposed is the raised price of the French, which is thought here an oppression. It has been long complained of, and will in all probability be redressed as soon as any government is settled; and if we should pay the army at this rate, I am apprehensive it might have ill consequences; but I should be very glad if anything could be saved to the public at the rate we now pay them, of which Mr. Brydges will be best able to inform your Lordship.[1]

618A. JAMES BRYDGES *to* WILLIAM CADOGAN

[*18 October 1706*]

Source: Printed in G. Davies, 'The seamy side of Marlborough's War', *H.L.Q.*, xv (1951), 34-6.

October 18, 1706

I have forbore writing to you this long, because my Lord Treasurer having an intention that Sir Henry Furnese[2] and myself should attend him at the Treasury in order to settle the affaire of the remittances for the future, whether to Antwerp or Amsterdam I was willing to stay till that matter was determined, that I might at the same time send you an account of it. This having been done this day, I can now acquaint you with the resolution my Lord hath taken, and of which I intend to give Mr. Stratford[3] notice next post. Sir Henry hath upon this occasion shown a malice, that I could not have imagined anyone could have been capable of, much less one who loves his interest and persues it by all such sorts of methods, as he doth, when he cannot but be sensible he endangers that at the same time. At first he reported that yourselfe, Mr. Cardonnel and I had agreed together to pay the army in a different manner to what they ought to be, and that wee had kept up immence riskes.[4] The person who acquainted me with it, told it me under an obligation of not making use of his name, for being concerned in the Treasury it might for ought he knows cost him the loss of his place,[5] but however I taxed Sir Henry with it before the Treasury chamber. He denied it, and thereupon I told him that though I was not a[t] liberty to name the

---

[1] The basis for Godolphin's questioning the rate of exchange is revealed in the following letter by Brydges to Cadogan.

[2] See pp. 630-1.   [3] Francis Stratford, a Hamburg merchant.

[4] Brydges had in fact developed a complex operation for mulcting the colonels of the army and foreign princes who received troop subsidies, taking a percentage of every sum he transmitted. The host agents at every court concerned and Cardonnel and Cadogan were both involved in this scheme. His scheme is best explained in J. G. Sperling, 'Godolphin and the Organization of Public Credit, 1702–10', unpublished Ph.D. thesis, Cambridge, 1955, pp. 151 ff.

[5] One of Brydges's 'contacts'.

person of whom I had it, yet if he did say any such thing, he was a lying rascall, and had he owned it I would have can[n]ed him as long as I could have stood over him; and let those gentlemen present, who heard what I said and heard him say it too, judge of his character who durst not own what he had said, and could bear the language he received. This ended our dispute there, but upon our being called in to my Lord [Treasurer] he did explain to my Lord that over and above the loss by exchange between Antwerp and Amsterdam and the other charges attending it, there was an advantage of 2 or 2-1/4 per cent which he was pleased to say then, he supposed the bankers imposed upon the army and make a profitt of for themselves. I assured my Lord that the army was perfectly well satisfied, that the general officers had desired me to make use of Mr. Stratford and that he had served them to their liking; that the advantage though nothing near soe much as what Sir Henry made it to be, was a gratification they themselves thought reasonable to allow him for his risque and trouble, and that the method this matter had been putt in, was agreed to by the army in generall and not unknown to my Lord Duke,[1] who had never been pleased to contradict it (which knowing Sir Henry's temper and not knowing what use he might make of it, if I should have said approved of by his Grace), was as much as proper I thought for me to say. But my Lord Treasurer laid his finger upon that part—viz.: the 2-1/4 per cent profitt—and said if it was a matter agreed by the army to take the shilling at 6-1/2 why should not that 2-1/4 per cent be saved to the publique. But he could not beleeve it could be agreed to by the army upon any other consideration, than that they thought all things considered, they could not receive their pay upon better terms, whereas 'tis certain he said if Mr. Sweet[2] was at Antwerp he might negotiate all that himselfe without any other banker and thereby save and accompt for to the army that 2-1/4 per cent which now they allow to others, and that therefore t'was his opinion that Mr. Sweet should goe and settle there and ordered me to send him such directions. At least in case he could not goe there himselfe (by reason that the greater part of the remittances must still be made at Amsterdam), that some-body else should be sent there to negotiate that part that was sent directly to Antwerp and who should take care to accompt to the army for that advantage that was made; soe that this has putt an end to the design of carrying the payment on upon the foot it was this summer. The reason why Sir Henry hath carried himselfe with soe much virulence in this matter is, as I have heard, because he was not admitted into the partnership as he expected, if the army had marched into Italy, to have been and concluded that wee had however carried on the design he proposed I remember to us at the meeting at his house.

---

[1] There is no concrete evidence to link Marlborough with this corrupt scheme, although it is hard to believe he could be unaware of it.

[2] Benjamin Sweet, deputy-paymaster at Amsterdam.

619. GODOLPHIN *to* MARLBOROUGH   [*2 July 1706*]
Source: Blenheim MSS. A1-36.

July 2d 1706

Wanting now 3 mails from Holland and having nothing lately from Sir Stafford Fairborn, by reason of the long westerly winds wee have had, I shall trouble you only with my concern that the same winds keep back our transports from Holland and consequently delay our intended expedition longer than is convenient, in many respects. This delay gives time for some of our comittee[1] to think it might bee reasonable to have a 2d view, in case the expedition as it is now projected, should meet with difficultys and disappoinments, which wee did not expect. I am against this, because if one puts any doubts into their heads, I think it is the ready way to hinder the expedition from succeeding. However, in case you can foresee that the landing of those troops anywhere upon the coast near you, could bee of use for promoting any operations you may have in view for the army, I could then comply so farr with this notion, as to consent, the fleet and the troops might have orders, upon any disappointment to come to the islands of Jersey and Guernsey and there expect farther orders from England. But farther than this I cannot possibly [bring] my mind to comply unless you are of another opinion yourself, or that you think the States will bee of another opinion, in either of which cases, I am ready to submitt mine.

I inclose to you the letters of the 25th of June from Lisbon,[2] and of the 15th from Lord Gallway,[3] by which wee are once more encouraged to think wee shall yett have Madrid immediatly. If wee are disappointed agayn, I hope all Spayn will soon follow the example, and declare for King Charles. But it seems very plain by Mr. Methuen's letter that the Portugheses are frighted with the thoughts of a French army, and that they both believe and wish the warr may continue in Spayn, even though Madrid shall have declared for King Charles the 3d. But in this I hope they will find themselves mistaken. Our next letters from Lisbon which wee may expect every day with these winds will clear this whole matter.

But if Spayn bee actually declared, I think it will not bee necessary to keep soe great a fleet in the Mediterranean, and wee may make a detachment of part of them to hinder the galeones from coming into France.[4]

I have no more trouble to give you till I can have the satisfaction of hearing from you.

[1] The Lords of the Committee of the Privy Council, the Cabinet meeting without the Queen.
[2] From Methuen, B.M., Add. MS. 28057, fols. 268–71. Methuen advised that careful plans would be needed to establish Charles III in Madrid (whom he presumed was now there) because strong French reinforcements were on their way and the people of Castile and Aragon preferred Philip V. Charles III needed a strong commander-in-chief and Methuen stated it should not be Noyelles.
[3] Untraced.
[4] The Spanish treasure fleet.

620. GODOLPHIN *to* MARLBOROUGH   [*4 July 1706*]

Source: Blenheim MSS. A1-36.

July 4th 1706

I have received the favour of yours of the 10th[1] by Captain Stanhope, and I must not disown to you, that it both surprised and troubled mee very much. It is amazing that after so much done for their advantage, and even for their safety the States can have been capable of such a behaviour. Those of the French faction must have seen their advantage upon this occassion to fill them with jealousy, of your having, and consequently of England's having too much power, and if this bee at the bottom, wee shall soon see that argument made use of in other occassions as well as this; but your prudence and good temper, will yett gett the better I hope, of all this folly and perversness. The first steps you have made towards it in your letter [to Heinsius] of which you sent mee a coppy, cannot in my opinion bee mended; but I wish very much that Mr. Stepney were at The Hague to second your letters to the Pensioner upon all occasions that may arise, by his instances to the States. You can best judg whether the affairs of Hungary would not suffer by his immediate recall. Otherwise, I think no time should bee lost in bringing him to The Hague.

I am very glad to find you have lost so little time before Ostend. I was much afraid that siege might have lingred so as to disappoint, at least retard too much, your other designs, as also our expedition [the descent] which now I hope may proceed in time, and that the east wind which blowes now, will soon bring us the transports expected from your side. And if the news from Spain prove so good, as that they will not need these troops there, I shall bee a great deal less uneasy than I was about the event of this expedition of Lord Rivers.

116 [Somers] and 117 [Sunderland] were not less struck with your letter than myself, but they flatter themselves that when they come to see the resolution of the States taken the 19th they shall find it was before they knew of the King of Spayn's intentions for you, but I doubt they are mistaken, and I doe not see the least room to bee of that opinion, and I should bee very glad if I did.

The news of the surrender of Ostend[2] has been received here with more joy and satisfaction than you will easily imagine people could have for a thing at which there was so little reason to doubt. I hope wee shall have tomorrow the 4 posts now due from Holland, and after that I shall add to this letter though it bee too long already.

---

[1] Letter 616.   [2] On 23 June/4 July.

621. MARLBOROUGH *to* GODOLPHIN [4/15 *July 1706*]

Source: Blenheim MSS. A1-14.
Printed: Coxe, i. 71 (inc.).

Helchin Jully 15th 1706

Since my last I have received none from England. The embarkation at
Ostend stays for nothing but the Dutch transportes, which this easterly wind
will bring. As the Dutch sends only a brigadier, thay were desirous to have
sent to the Queen, that she might give orders that he might be admitted to
all councelles of warr, as being at the head of their troupes. For the saving of
time I have asured them, that he would be admitted into all councelles.
I hope her Majesty will be pleased to aprove it, and give her orders. But I
hope Lord Rivers will make use of councells of warr but upon extraordinary
occasion. I am very impatient of hearing from Prince Eugene, we having
variety of raportes concerning the action in Italie, which thay say at Tournay
has been so much to our advantage, that thay have quitted the siege of Turin.
A few days will let us know the truth. Monsieur de Gilder Masen came here
last night from Gand, and I find we must not expect all our canon til the end
of this month. But on the 22 I think to invest Menin, and imploye the first
six or seven days in covering some of the quarters, for we can't spare above
32 battallions for the siege. There will remain with me 72, which I hope will
be a sufficient strengh to opose whatever thay can bring, though the Elector
says he has promised 110 battalions. Thay have certainly more horse then
wee, but if thay had greater numbers, I neither think it their interest nor
their inclinations to venture a battaile, for our men are in heart, and theirs
are cowed. If the Duke of Vandome should be obliged to stay in Italie, we are
told that we are then to have the Prince of Conty.[1]

622. GODOLPHIN *to* MARLBOROUGH [5 *July 1706*]

Source: Blenheim MSS. A1-36.

Fryday 5 of July 1706

I was in hopes before this time to have had 4 posts from you, but they are
not yett come.

I forgett to tell you in my long letter[2] which I send with this, that the
subject of it, in answer to yours of the 10th[3] is an entire secrett to everybody
here, except 116 [Somers] and 117 [Sunderland], and will remayn soe, unless
these posts which wee hourly expect from Holland, give occasion to make it
bee publickly spoken of, either by the orders they may bring to Comte
Gallas, or to Mr. Vreberghen.

---

[1] François-Louis de Bourbon, prince of Conti (1664–1709). He did not serve in this war.
[2] Letter 620.   [3] Letter 616.

One immediate good effect of the taking of Ostend, is that the Bank have lent this morning 70,000£ upon the last tallyes struck on the Malt Act, only upon a minute entred to make it good to them in case of deficiency. I am apt to believe the joy for having Ostend is the greater in hopes Dunkirk will fall on the sam fortune, sooner or later, but being fully satisfyed, that besides all the endeavours used by France, to strengthen it, both Menin and Ypres are necessary, in order to come at it. I am come to wish only that in this year you may bee able to carry onn your operations so as that Dunkirk bee streightned by your winter quarters on the Flanders side, which will create an earnest desire and expectation here of attacking of both by land and sea, at the opening of the next campagne.

These are all the views I can have, as to that matter, and the chief end of my troubling you with them, is to lett you see that if the way to Dunkirk bee not open in this year, it will still bee the greatest satisfaction imaginable to all England, if they can but have a prospect of having it in the beginning of the next.

I shall not trouble you with any notions concerning Spayn, or Italy till the arrivall of the 4 posts furnishes more occasion for them.

623. GODOLPHIN *to* MARLBOROUGH   [*5 July 1706*]

Source: Blenheim MSS. A1-36.

Fryday night at 11 July 5

Having just now received your letters of the 1st, the 6th, the 8th and the 12th of July,[1] I would not deferr acknowledging by this post, though I have written a great deal to you before. But not having time to read the papers enclosed in them, I shall not trouble you with my remarks upon them, till the next opportunity of writing which possibly I may have by the way of Ostend, in a day or two.

Besides the good news you send us from Madrid, I have a letter of the 13th from my Lord Halifax from The Hague,[2] with so many particulars of the advantage Prince Eugene has had upon the French that I am resolved not to entertain the least doubt of it.[3]

He writes mee also that he found them full of difficultys at The Hague about the Treaty of Succession, but was in hopes to overcome them. I think

[1] Letters 606, 611, 614, 617.   [2] Untraced.

[3] A French army under La Feuillade had besieged Turin since 3/14 May while a second army under Vendôme covered the siege and defended French territorial gains against an Imperialist relief effort from Austria by holding the Adige, which lay north of the Po, from Garda to the Adriatic. Vendôme's forces were deployed along a 100-kilometre front, which limited his effort to repel a surprise attack at any one point. Eugene arrived with his army at the head of the Adige, between Garda and Verona, where Vendôme expected his assault. Instead Eugene sent troops down river, crossing over near Rovigo on 4-6 July, n.s., and thus turning the French lines. Braubach, ii. 155-6.

his being there was very lucky, not only for this affair of the treaty, but to hinder them from swallowing too farr their own notions about the government of Flanders which has submitted to King Charles the 3d and not to the States. And therfore I don't know what better answer the Queen can give to Mr. Vryberghen's memoriall when it comes, than to say that as King Charles is now in possession of the throne of Spayn, she hopes he will soon find a governour to take possession likewise of his dominions in the Low Countrys and that she shall bee always ready to concurr with the States in such measures as shall bee thought most proper for preserving him in the possession of those he has and for the recovery of the rest.

Somthing to this sence, according as his memoriall shall bee worded, ought to bee the substance of the answer made to it.

Wee may now expect every day the confirmation of King Charles's being at Madrid, by another packet boat from Lisbon. In the meantime, the advances of the Portugall army has putt an end, I suppose, to the Pentionary's thought of sending a minister into that country.

I find by Mr. Stepney's letters of this post, that the great successes of the Allyes in Brabant and Spayn make the court of Vienna return to their naturall aversness to an accomodation with the Hungarians. If soe, I wish, you would allow of Mr. Stepney's coming to The Hague where I doubt he will soon bee wanted.

Lady Marlborough receiving your letters so late at night can't answer them till the next post.

624. GODOLPHIN *to* MARLBOROUGH   [7 *July 1706*]

Source: Blenheim MSS. A1-36.

Windsor 7 July 1706

The last letters wee have had from you were of the 12th[1] from *Helchin*, and the wind has been so fair to have heard from you by the way of Ostend, that I begin to fear wee shall not have the confirmation of Prince Eugene's advantage over the French which wee were putt in hopes of by the last post.

Comte Gallas has been with the Queen this day, to present her a letter from the Emperour and the King of Spain, about the offer of the government of Flanders. Her Majesty was pleased to make some compliments to the Emperour and the King of Spayn, upon the offer, and sayd, that this being a matter of very great consequence she would leave it to you, to doe in it as you should judg most proper for the good of the common cause.

Monsieur Vryberghen has been here also with Mr. Secretary Harley and with mee upon the same subject, and to find out what answer the Queen would make to the Comte de Gallas, and mighty apprehensive least wee

[1] Letter 617.

should make any step here towards accepting the offer. Hee was very well pleased when I told him, the Queen would leave all that belonged to that matter, wholly to you to doe as you should judg best for the common cause. I pressd him then to give a memoriall acquainting her Majesty with the resolution of the States of the 19th,[1] that being a matter (I mean the security of their Barriere) in which the Queen was as much though not so immediately concerned as themselves, adding that I thought he would not easily perswade, that the Barriere in possession of King Charles the 3d was not as much security to them as if it were in their own, but upon his giving in a memoriall all that might bee adjusted between the Queen and them. He sayd he had no directions for that, but he would give an account of what I had said to him.

I design to send this letter to you by the way of Ostend, reserving what I have further to say till tomorrow by the post from London.

625. MARLBOROUGH *to* GODOLPHIN   [8/19 *July* 1706]

Source: Blenheim MSS. A1-14.
Printed: Coxe, ii. 63 (inc.).

Helchin Jully 19th 1706

Notwithstanding the wind has been faire, wee have no letters from England, I supose for want of packet boates.

The English are embarked at Ostend, and I hope to hear this day or tomorrow that the Dutch are so also, the wind having been favourable these three days to bring the transportes from the Texel[2] to Ostend.

I think I have convinced the States General that their resolution of the 19th of the last month,[3] in which thay reserved to themselves the signing all the powers and consequently governing this country in their names, was excluding her Majesty and England from being able to perform to these people what I had promised in her Majesty's name, which if thay had persisted must have produced a very ill effect; for the great towns depends much more upon the Queen's protection, then that of the States.

I shall by the next post send a copie of the commission, and powers, and instructions I shal be obliged to sign for the setelling the Councell of State that must govern this country til the King of Spain can give his directions.[4] I am obliged to do this for the publick good before I am

---

[1] See p. 606.
[2] Texel, an island opposite The Helder at the tip of the Province of North Holland, between the North Sea and the Zuider Zee.
[3] See p. 606.
[4] The unilateral resolution of the States of 8/19 June had been shown to Marlborough in Dutch. Marlborough did not see a French translation until 27 June/8 July, on which occasion he realized that the Dutch had virtually ignored England in declaring what form the government should take

authorised by her Majesty, so that I beg you will move the Queen, that I may have powers sent me, as her ambassador and generall, to act in conjunction with the States Generall what shall be thought proper for the publick good. For my security I beg the date of the power may be some few days after you had the news of my being att Bruxelles. You will be pleased to communicat and take the advice of Mr. Secretary Harley in this matter.

As I have had severall messages from 328 [Elector of Bavaria] to let me see the desire he has of quiting the intirest of 20 [France], I think it would be for her Majesty's Service that I might as soon as possible be authorised to act in conjunction with the States General in that matter, by giving promises, or signing such a treaty as may be for the publick good. There can be no inconvenience in sending such a power, and [it] may be of advantage. But this last must be keep a secrit, so that 20 [France] may not know itt. The French have so many sluces upon the river Lys, now that wee should make use of itt for our canon, we find in severall places that there is not one foot of watter, when of necessity we must have five.[1] So that I have ordered Generall Salish,[2] who is to command the siege, if we can gett watter to make itt, instide of investing Menin, to post himself between Lille and that town, and then destroye all the sluces between those two towns, and if practicable as far as Armentiers.[3] The French are doing the same thing on the Skeel [Scheldt], knowing that we can't make sieges but by the assistance of those two rivers. Instide of the good news we ware expecting from Italie, I am afraid we shall here of Prince Eugene's metting with great difficultys, so that Turin must save itself, or the French will sooner or latter be masters of itt. I had last night letters from The Hague, by which I see the Dutch will insist upon having an article in the treaty for the Succession concerning their Barier, which no doubt is a security to England, as well as to them. However, there must be very great care taken in the wording itt, so that the House of Austria may not be offended; for whatever is thought reasonable in this matter should be transacted with King Charles, and not with the French. But I am afraid some of the Dutch are of another opinion. I shall be more perticularly informed of this by Lord Hallifax, who will be here in three or

in the Spanish Netherlands until a peace was concluded. He refused to sign it and by working with the Dutch persuaded them to replace the resolution with a new statement in which the government was established by the co-operation of the Maritime powers, not just the United Provinces, and English interests were considered. (Geikie, pp. 26–9.) This was the 'Acte d'Éstablishment' in L. P. Gachard, *Collection de documents inédits concernant l'histoire de la Belgique* (Brussels, 1833), iii. 237–41. There are copies of the declaration concerning the Spanish Netherlands and instructions for the Council of State for the government of the Spanish Netherlands, both of 10/21 July, in B.M., Add. MS. 5131, fols. 105–6, 115–16.

[1] The draft required by the boats used to transport the artillery. The French, by diverting the water, rendered the river useless for deep-drafted boats.

[2] Ernst Willem von Salisch (died 1711), Dutch lieutenant-general of infantry.

[3] Armentières, a French town on the border of the Spanish Netherlands, 25 kilometres up the Lys from Menin.

four days, his last letter saying that he should leave The Hague on Sunday last.[1] You will by this post receive a letter from Mr. Bridges concerning the exchange.[2] I do not understand that matter, and do beleive there may be something wrong in itt. All that I beg is that the skillings may be payd to the English as the Dutch pays their troups, and what is over and above may be saved to the publick.

626. GODOLPHIN *to* MARLBOROUGH [9 *July 1706*]

Source: Blenheim MSS. A1-36.

July 9th 1706

Before I received yesterday the favour of yours of the 15th,[3] I had a written a letter to you from Windsor[4] under Mr. Burchett's cover to Sir Stafford Fairborn, giving you an account of what had passed in Comte Gallas's audience of the Queen, upon delivering the Emperor's letter to her Majesty concerning the government of Flanders, and also of the discourse between Monsieur Vryberghen and mee, upon the same subject. And not doubting but you will have that letter before this, I will not give you the trouble of repeating it here.

I am sorry to find by yours of the 15th that the transports from Holland are not yett come and I doubt wee shall still stay a good while for them, though it's more than time that expedition were sett forth. I have sent to Lieutenant Generall Erle, who was in Dorsetshire to prepare himself according to your commands.

I am sorry also to find that during the siege of Ostend your great canon is not yett all come to you, which will oblige you to lose some days. But that is recompenced to us by your opinion that all the endeavors of the French and all the changes they can make of their generalls will not prevayl with their troops to stand you, upon any great occasion.

I wish your expectations from Italy may not bee disappointed. By all the letters of the last post both from France and Holland, which are come to my sight, I see but little ground to believe there has yett been any action there. It's true all the French letters agree the siege of Turin goes onn but slowly.

Mr. Villiers's case stands thus: upon a prosecution of the Commissioners of the Customes, he has a verdict found against [him] to have defrauded to the value of 530£ sterling. But the judgment upon this verdict, will not bee

---

[1] 7/18 July.

[2] Cardonnel informed Brydges on 9/20: 'I have read your letter to Lord Treasurer to my Lord Duke, and am forwarding it by this post to his Lordship. His Grace in what hee writes referrs to it, and only adds that it would be very hard while the Dutch troops receive the shillings at 6–½ stiver the English should be obliged to take them at 7 stivers which indeed is the real and main objection, and which can never be overcome.' Stowe MSS. 58, i. 5, Huntington Library. See pp. 609-10.

[3] Letter 621. [4] Letter 624.

entered till next term, and consequently the Queen cannot bee regularly informed of it till then, so that you have time enough to think of a proper person to succeed him.[1]

Wee have no letters from Lisbon since my last.

627. GODOLPHIN *to* MARLBOROUGH [*9 July 1706*]

Source: Blenheim MSS. A1-36.

9th of July, at night

The Duke of Somersett has been extreamly pressing with the Queen to give my Lord Walden[2] leave to sell his place of Comissary Generall of the Musters, upon the Duke of Norfolk's making him his Deputy Earl Marshall. The Queen agrees that to keep that place, with the Earl Marshall's staff is wholly improper, but being upon all occasions very averse to selling, she has not yett consented to it, but has give leave that I should acquaint you with it, and ask your opinion.

My Lord Walden says he is offerd 2600£ for it by one Mr. Shepheard, a kinsman of Mr. Shepheard[3] of the citty.

I have advised him to take a pension from the Queen of 500£ per annum and lett her Majesty dispose of the place, but he won't hear of this.

Whatever you have a mind should bee don in it, one way or other, I believe the Queen will doe it. This letter is upon this particular matter only, and not disigned to give you any other trouble.[4]

628. GODOLPHIN *to* MARLBOROUGH [*11 July 1706*]

Source: Blenheim MSS. A1-36.

Windsor July 11th 1706

I troubled you so much by the last post, that you might well expect to bee spared for some time, but I am at leisure here, and you are like to pay for it.

Since my last of the 9th,[5] wee have no foreign letters from you, nor from Lisbon. I am much in pain for the transports being so long retarded in Holland. It gives the enemy so much time to prepare themselves everywhere, and if our news bee true, 15 or 16 battaillons are marched from the Low

---

[1] See p. 594.

[2] Henry Howard, sixteenth Earl of Suffolk (1670–1718), styled Lord Walden 1701–6; M.P. 1695–8, 1705–6; commissary-general of the Musters 1697–1707; deputy-earl-marshal 1706–18; created Earl of Binden 1706; succeeded as Earl of Suffolk 1709.

[3] Samuel Shepheard, Whig M.P. for Cambridge 1708–22.

[4] The post went to David Crawford whose commission is dated 31 Mar. 1707. See Somerset's letter to Marlborough of 9 July (Blenheim MSS. A1-46), in which he supported Walden's request. Marlborough approved of it (p. 624).

[5] Letters 626–7.

Countrys for the defence of the coast.[1] This however will have one good effect, since it eases you of so many enemys.

I wish you good success with the siege of Menin, and wish much in my own thoughts you may have time afterwards for Ypres. For while the operations of the army continue near the sea, wee might bee able to strengthen it, from hence upon any occasion at the beginning or the end of the year, and help you to make a siege, when the French would not otherwise expect it from the force left in that part of the country. As for our expedition [the descent], I am myself a good deal apprehensive of it upon severall accounts besides the long delay of it, which after soe much fine weather as wee have had, makes it not reasonable to expect wee shall have much more of it.

Lieutenant Generall Erle[2] was in Dorsetshire when I received your letter,[3] but I have had an answer from him, that though he would have been glad of a little more warning to have prepared himself, he will bee ready to goe in 48 hours.

By all the accounts from Madrid I believe that place upon the approach of Lord Gallway, had declared for King Charles the 3d. But I don't find any certainty as yett of his having been there himself in person. If he takes the resolution of marching, as you seem to wish, towards Navarr, to bee sure, he will not part with any of our troops for the relief of the Duke of Savoy. But what I rather wish in the first place, is the immediate reducing of Cadiz which would enable us to keep a fleet there in the winter, and secure all that has been already done. The uncertainty of events in those parts by reason of the great distance, is extreamly inconvenient and subjects all the resolutions of the Allyes to bee taken, either so soon, that wee can't bee certainly informed of matter of fact, or so late, that no time is left for a remedy.

I shall bee sure to speak to Lord Rivers that the brigadier who commands the Dutch regiments of the descent, shall bee called to all councills of warr.

By the last post I enclosed a letter to you from Mrs. Morley [the Queen],[4] which I suppose was in answer to yours,[5] but she has not yett taken the least notice of it to mee though she has had a very fair occasion to have done so. I believe Lady Marlborough has written to you to know what your thoughts may bee of Mr. How's[6] going to Berlin. What putt it first into my head,

---

[1] Vauban, commander of the French garrisons on the Channel coast, received orders on 25 June/ 6 July to send three battalions of foot to Montreuil at the alarm of the English fleet. Vault, vi. 79.
[2] Lieutenant-general of the Ordnance, he went on the descent as second-in-command to Rivers.
[3] Letter 613.
[4] 9 July, H.M.C., *Marlborough MSS.*, 43b (inc.). The Queen in her letter leaves it up to Marlborough how to reply to Charles III's offer of the governorship of the Spanish Netherlands. She regrets she cannot take Sunderland into her service at this time, as Marlborough had requested (above, p. 603 n. 3).   [5] 27 June/8 July. Untraced. See p. 603.
[6] Emanuel Scrope Howe (died 1709), diplomat; M.P. 1701–8; Groom of the Bedchamber to William III; envoy extraordinary at Hanover 1705–9; lieutenant-general 1709; married Ruperta, natural daughter of Prince Rupert. *D.N.B.* In spite of his wife's indiscreet remarks, Howe was not removed, and remained there until his death.

was, I will own, the observing they were very very uneasy at Hannover, and yett possibly their knowledg of the young princesse there[1] may help to make them easyer at Berlin, than any novice will bee that wee shall send from hence. But if you can suggest anybody that you think will bee more proper, that thought shall vanish.

I hear but little effect yett of the money sent to Geneve.[2] Nothing stirs in Dauphine or the Vivarets, nor indeed doe I much wonder at it considering the behaviour of Prince Lewis of Baden. The Queen has ordered Mr. Stepney to represent to the Emperour the great prejudice that is occasioned to the common [cause] by his insignificancy, and particularly at this time when the great detachments made from the French army upon the Rhyne, leave [us] at liberty to undertake anything there that could bee most to our advantage.[3]

Though I shall bee tomorrow at London I shall hardly give you any more trouble by this post, not expecting to have any foreign letters before it goes.

629. MARLBOROUGH *to* GODOLPHIN   [11/22 July 1706]

Source: Blenheim MSS. A1-14.

Helchin Jully 22th 1706

Lord Lifford has given me yours,[4] and you may be sure I shall make his being here as easy as may be, for I am intierly of your opinion that he has been imposed upon by Miermont. As to Monsieur Vaubon, the French pretend he is a subject of the King's, but the truth is he was born at Avinion. At last I have obtained three months leave for him to go to Vienna, so that with her Majesty's leave I would give a prolongations of 3 months to the officers that are in France, which will be a pleasure to them, and I think noe disservice to her Majesty.[5] We meet with infinet difficultys, the French being masters of the two rivers of the Schell and the Lyse, by their *eselusses*, that thay have at Tournay and Conde[6] for the Schell, and at Menin for the Lyse. Thay have severall other *eselusses* upon these two rivers, but thay not being covered by their fortifyed towns, we are masters of destroying them. We have this morning two English mailes of the 28th of the last month, and the 2d of this.[7] I should be much of your opinion as to Prince Eugene,

---

[1] Sophia Dorothea (1685-1757), daughter of the Elector of Hanover, married 28 Nov. 1706 Frederick William, son and heir of Frederick I, King of Prussia.

[2] To support a rebellion in France. See p. 576.

[3] His illness, the ill condition of his troops, and his lack of reinforcements incapacitated him in this campaign.

[4] Letter 609.

[5] Louis XIV granted Vaubonne leave to visit his home at Orange because he was so impressed by Marlborough's humane treatment of prisoners. See p. 588 and *Mémoires de Saint-Simon*, ed. A. de Bois Lisle (Paris, 1923-30), xiii. 439-40.

[6] Condé, 22 kilometres upstream from Tournai, in France.

[7] With letters 612, 615.

but the Dutch will have none till thay are asured of the Barier thay are so desirous off. I find by yours that the letters I have write to you concerning this matter were not come to you. [As for] the paper you sent concerning Doctor Hare, I am sorry to see there will be a difficulty; for if he can't be made use of, I have so litle acquaintance amongest the cleargy, that I have none to recomend. But since the dreamer[1] is in good health, her Majesty will have time to think of somebody, if it should stile be thought improper for Doctor Hare. But if the objection of the Archbishope's is ever to be dispenced with, it aught to be in this case, it being generally known the estime I have of him, [it] would make him in that imployment more capable of serving the Queen. He has been in 2 battailes, which may be some reason for this distinction.

I hope Lord Rivers, and those that goes with the descent have no doubt of succeeding, for I have always been and am stile of opinion, that all generals that takes his measure before action for a retreat, will be sure to have occasion of making use of itt. As for this campagne, I do not see that their landing near us can be of any use, for our hinderances proceeds from the difficulty of the country, and the want of artillery, and other necessarys for sieges. It is most certaine the French have no thoughts of having a fleet this yeare, so that if the time could be known when the gallions are to return, the intercepting of them would be a great service. But I always see so many accedents happen to almost everything that is projected for the sea, that I have litle hopes of success. But what is right aught to be attempted. The papers I promised you in my last letter,[2] concerning the Councelle of States, are not yet come from Bruxelles. We have a report that Lord Cutts is dead. I hope her Majesty will not be hasty in ingaging herself for his imployement.[3] Menin will be invested tomorrow, but as I am afraid we shall not be able to make use of [the] Lyse, that siege is like to last longer then is to be wished. However, we should have more difficulty with any other town.

I received yesterday the enclosed from the Comte of Noyelles.[4] I send it you that you may see his opinion of the conduct of 127 [Peterborough]. God knows, but I am sure I do not how you will be able to cure this madness. But I am satisfied by all the letters that I have seen which coms from thence, that any treaty or other matter that is to be transacted between him and 315 [King Charles] must miscary.[5]

[1] William Talbot, Bishop of Oxford.   [2] Letter 625.
[3] Cutts died 26 Jan. 1707. He was colonel of the Coldstream Guards; commander-in-chief and a Lord Justice of Ireland; colonel, Regiment of Foot (I); governor of Isle of Wight. See Cutts to Harley, 30 July, H.M.C., *Portland MSS.*, iv. 320, in which he contradicts the report of his death.
[4] There is an undated, unsigned letter in French in Blenheim MSS. A1-14 enclosed with this letter which must be that of Noyelles.
[5] For Peterborough's relations with King Charles see Churchill, ii. 155-63.

630. GODOLPHIN *to* MARLBOROUGH　　　[*15 July 1706*]

Source: Blenheim MSS. A1-36.
Printed: Coxe, ii. 112 (inc.).

Windsor July 15, 1706

Yesterday morning at this place, I received the favour of yours of the 19th[1] by which I was a little surprised to find you complain of the contrary winds having kept back the letters from England, wee having of late made the same complaint here and I doubt wee can not bee both in the right. But the letters from The Hague of the 20th tell us, the Dutch transports are still in the Texel for want of a wind. This is a great prejudice in many respects, among others, one is that it gives more opportunity for people to bee unreasonable. [The] Marquis de Guiscard seems uneasy upon Erle's being declared to goe, and says you always talked to him as if he were to bee the second person in this expedition. But I find he would acquiese in this, if he might command as a Lieutenant Generall in the Queen's troops after Erle. Now there does not seem to mee anything solid in this, for the comission he has will make him however, the next in command to Erle. Lord Rivers has not his health very well at this time, but he seems willing and hearty, which with mee goes a great way to supply many defects. I am sorry to find by yours that you are like to meet with so many obstructions and delays in the sieges you designed.

I have spoken to the Queen about the *severall* powers desired in yours, and given her Majesty's commands upon it to Mr. Secretary Harley, who has promised mee to dispatch them to you with all speed.[2]

I hope the treaty at The Hague about the Succession, as it is now setled by my Lord Halifax cannot fail to succeed, since the Queen will make no difficulty of warranting a Barriere for the States, if they will not bee unreasonable in the manner of asking it.

The talk of any action at the Adige is vanished here. But our letters from Berne persist still that Prince Eugene is passed over that river, and that he has 35,000 men without the Hessians which had not yett joyned him.[3]

And the French letters say Turin holds out very well.

Wee have nothing from Lisbon, *but* by the way of Genoa. Wee hear King Charles was the 17th of June at Barcelona. His long stay there, as things might have fallen out was enough to spoyl that whole affair, but as things are, I hope it will have no ill consequence.

---

[1] Letter 625.
[2] Powers to settle the government of the Spanish Netherlands with the Dutch, and to negotiate with the Elector of Bavaria.
[3] Eugene passed the Adige, 4–6 July, n.s. See p. 614, n. 3.

631. MARLBOROUGH *to* GODOLPHIN   [*15/26 July 1706*]

Source: Blenheim MSS. A1-14.

Helchin Jully 26, 1706

I have received all your letters of the 9th,[1] as also that of the 7[2] by Ostend. The former news we had of Prince Eugene were not trew, but by the inclosed[3] you will see what he has done, and in a litle time I hope to hear he has had farther success, for it is from him only that Turin can be saved.

I am very aprehensive that when the treaty for the Succession is sent to the provinces, that the new party will creat as many difficultys as thay possibly can.

Mr. Secretary Harley has acquainted mee with the answere he has given Monsieur Vriberg,[4] and as it is left to mee, I shall be sure to be carefull of doing nothing but what I shall think for her Majesty's Service. The powers from the King of Spain can no longer be keep a secrit, for I have had compliments from the King of Prussia and several others; so that when you have acquainted the Secretarys, I think Mr. Secretary Harley should be instructed in the [w]hole proceedings, so that he might acquaint the Cabinett Councell with what you shall think proper; otherways I am afraid thay might have reason to be angry when thay hear it from hence, and that nothing has been said to them. I did in a former letter let you know that I thought itt for her Majesty's Service that Lord Walden might have leave to sell, provided there be care taken in the new pattent that the powers this lord had, which were not for the Service, might be left in the Queen.[5]

The Dutch transportes came yesterday morning to Ostend, so that if the wind be faire thay may saile for Portchmouth tomorrow. I am very glad Earle goes with the desent, and if Shrimpton[6] is not imediatly to return to Giberalter, I should think it would be for the Service to send him also with Lord Rivers, and to let him return, when it might be proper for him to go to his government. I am told that Sir George Rook did publiquely refuse to sign the Kentish address. If it be trew it is very unbecoming a Privy Councelor. You will here inclosed have a letter I this afternoon received from the King of Spain.[7] I also send you the Queen's letter.[8]

---

   [1] Letters 626-7.   [2] Letter 624.

   [3] Eugene to Marlborough, 29 June/10 July, in Murray, iii. 28-9.

   [4] In his letter to Marlborough on 9 July Harley enclosed a copy of his answer to Vryberghen, quoted in Geikie, p. 22, n. 4. There is a copy in B.M. loan 29/45 Q/4 together with Vryberghen's acknowledgement.

   [5] See p. 619. If Marlborough did write about this his letter is missing.

   [6] Major General John Shrimpton, governor of Gibraltar. He accompanied Rivers on the descent and was taken prisoner at Almanza.

   [7] 6/17 June, Blenheim MSS. A1-38.

   [8] 9 July. See p. 620 n. 4. This last sentence has been scratched over to make it illegible.

632. GODOLPHIN *to* MARLBOROUGH   [*16 July 1706*]

Source: Blenheim MSS. A1-36.

July 16th at night

I beg leave only to add to my long letter from Windsor,[1] that wee have just now received our Lisbon letters which confirm all the Spanish news by the way of France. I shall not have trouble you with the particulars, since Mr. Secretary Hedges sends you the extracts and coppys of the letters that are come. I don't find King Charles has yett been at Madrid, and till wee hear of him thence, wee can't so well judg what will bee the immediat effects of it through the whole kingdome.

Sir Stafford Fairborn is gone to Spithead, but the Dutch ships are not yett come.

I had by a letter from Mr. Bridges[2] that he has [misunderstood], perhaps wilfully, my intentions about the money. I never meant to deprive the army of the advantage of the exchange, but I would bee glad all the officers and soldiers should share that advantage proportionably, and not that it should bee swallowed by any particular officers, much less by any of the paymasters or their deputyes, but that a regular account bee made by them, both of the advantage itself, and also of the fair and impartiall distribution of it both to officers and soldiers.

Mr. Brydges says in his letter to Mr. Taylour[3] that you don't seem to approve of my directions. But I rather think 'tis he that has mistaken them, and that makes mee give you the trouble to repeat them as I have done in this letter. And I flatter myself if those directions were publickly known to the army, they would not find so much fault with them as I doe at present with those who have taken so much pains to misrepresent them to the officers and soldiers.

633. GODOLPHIN *to* MARLBOROUGH   [*18 July 1706*]

Source: Blenheim MSS. A1-36.
Printed: Coxe, ii. 95-6 (inc.).

Windsor 18 July 1706

Yesterday Mr. Montague,[4] a nephew of my Lord Halifax, and one of my Lord Gallway's ayde de camps, arrived here with letters from his Lordship dated from the camp of Madrid of the $\frac{16}{27}$th of June.[5] But this gentleman

---

[1] Letter 230.
[2] 3/14 July, Stowe MSS. 57, I. 115-16, Huntington Library.
[3] 4/15 July, ibid. 116. Extract with reply, 16 July, *C.T.B.*, xx. iii. 707-8. See above, pp. 594, 608-10
[4] Lieutenant-Colonel Edward Montagu, taken at Brihuega 1710.
[5] B.M., Add. MS. 28057, fols. 258-63.

did not leave him till the 29th. I will not trouble you with particulars because I send you the letters which he brought, desiring they may bee sent to mee agayn at your own conveniency.

The same packett brought mee a letter from my Lord Peterborow[1] of a very old date from Barcelona. It is full of extraordinary flights and artificiall forms but one may see by it that there is room for everything that has been thought and said of his conduct there. And at the same time, by that and by other letters of more credit, nothing ever was so weak, so shamefull, and soe unaccountable in every point, as the conduct of the Prince de Lichtenstein and the rest of the King of Spayn's German followers. If Mr. Crow[2] calls upon you in his return as I hope he will, I shan't need to trouble you with any more of it now, but it looks as if the King of Spayn would never have come to Madrid, if my Lord Gallway had not sent to him from thence, though there was no enemy in the field to hinder them.[3]

In short, as wee have had good luck in what has past, wee shall want it no less in what is to come, except the King of Spayn keeps my Lord Gallway near him at least for some time, as I have most humbly desired him to doe in a letter to himself purely for that purpose.

Wee have two posts due from you but the wind of this day will bring them here tomorrow as I reckon, though not time enough for mee to acknowledg them from hence by this post. It has blown so hard these 2 or 3 days that I am in some pain for the Dutch transport.

634. MARLBOROUGH *to* GODOLPHIN   [*18/29 July 1706*]

Source: Blenheim MSS. A1-14.

Helchin Jully 29th 1706

I have derected Cardonel to send you copies of the severall papers I signed yesterday for the government of this country.[4] I have sent them to Bruxelles, that thay may also be signed by the Dutch deputys. I have not as yet had a copie of their letter, which thay intend to send the Emperor in answere to his.[5] You shall be sure to have it as soon as it coms to my hand. By a letter

---

[1] Perhaps the letter of 1/12 May, in the Osborn Collection, Yale University; autograph copy in B.M., Add. MS. 28055, fols. 154-7.

[2] Mitford Crowe, who had acted in the capacity of English minister to Charles III since 1705, though he carried no credentials.

[3] Charles III gave up the journey to Madrid for lack of money and troops to travel with an entourage appropriate to his royal dignity. With it he lost whatever chance he had of winning the crown of Spain. See Francis, p. 318.

[4] See p. 616.

[5] For the preparation of the letter see Geikie, p. 29. The States' letter, 1/12 Aug., is printed in Vreede, pp. 73-9.

I have received from Mr. Stanhope of the 3 of this month, I find contrary to the King of Spain's first resolution of marching from Valencia to Madrid, he has now resolved to go by Saragose, which must lose him a great deal of time.

I had the favour last night of yours of the 11.[1] You are unkind in making excuses for the leng[t]h of your letters, since I assure you thay are one of the greatest pleasures I have here. It is to be wished the wind had been more favourable, so that we might not have given the French so long time to prepare themselves against the descent. But as yet thay have sent no regular troupes anywhere but to Normandy. In my last letter[2] I told Lady Marlborough my thoughts as to 362 [Howe]. You will find by the letters from Vienna, that there is litle hopes left of an accomodation with the Hungariens, which I am afraid will [make] some in Holland very fond of a peace. There has been some proposals made underhand.[3] If I can have a trew account you shall be sure to have them. In the mean[time] you must say nothing, for that may prevent my farther knowlidge [second sheet of letter torn off.]

635. MARLBOROUGH *to the* DUCHESS   [*18/29 July 1706*]

Source: Blenheim MSS. E3.
Printed: *Private Correspondence*, i. 59–61.

Helchin Jully 29th 1706

I do desire you will make my compliments to the Queen and the Prince for their goodness in remembring Godfrey.[4] For want of rain we are chocked with dust, which I am afraid will make the time of Lord Hallifax['s] stay here seem the more tedious to him. We have no doubt here of King Charles being master of Madrid. However, I am impatient to have the confermation by the way of Lisbon, for the French are so carefull that we receive no letters that way. Our descent begins to give them a good deal of uneasyness, for thay have sent some troupes into Normandy which were designed for this country. The

---

[1] Letter 628.   [2] 15/26 July. Untraced.

[3] Proposals from the French to the Dutch for a peace, made by Gualtherus Hennequin to Heinsius and Buys on 12/23 July. Hennequin was a Dutch merchant who lived at Paris. (Geikie, pp. 58–70; Stork-Penning, pp. 83 ff.) Heinsius sent Marlborough word on 16/27 July which Marlborough received 18/29 July. ('t Hoff, pp. 251–2.) However, Marlborough may also have received the details through Sersander, the agent of the Elector of Bavaria. (Churchill, ii. 151; and above, p. 653.) The inspiration to initiate discussions came from the Count of Bergeyck, Superintendent-General for War and Finance in the Spanish Netherlands. He began conversations with Van der Dussen, Pensionary of Gouda, soon after Ramillies, with the cognizance of Louis XIV and the knowledge of President Rouillé, French representative to the Elector of Bavaria. They took Hennequin into their confidence who transmitted their suggestions to the Dutch. (Torcy, *Memoirs*, i. 116–17.)

[4] Francis Godfrey (died 1712), M.P. 1701–12; Marlborough's nephew, was made Groom of the Bedchamber to Prince George in the place of Henry Graham. Graham, the son of the Tory leader and M.P. Colonel James Graham, was dismissed for voting against the government in the Commons. See the Queen's letter to the Duchess, 5 July, H.M.C., *Marlborough MSS.*, 53b.

Dutch troupes are all embarked, and are to make the best of their way for Portchmouth, where I hope thay will find everything ready, for we are already two months laitter then was at first intended for this expedition. I had last night yours of the 12th, and must agree with you that Mrs. Morley's [the Queen] saying nothing of my letter,[1] must proceed from not likeing the subject matter. I sent by the last post[2] the answere I received,[3] and as she is very sincere and a great many other good quallitys, in which we aught to think ourselves happy, I think 117 [Sunderland] and his friends aught not to take itt unkindly; for as she is every day sensible of the undutyfull and unkind usidge she meets with from the greatest part of 8 [the Tories], [it] will bring her to what I am afraid she is yet uneasy att. I can judge of this matter but by what I hear from you and 91 [Godolphin]. I can't but think you lay a great deal more to 49 [George Churchill] charge then he deserves, for 83 [the Queen] has no good opinion nor never speakes to him.[4] It is most certaine that if the Queen had ill success, as she has been blessed with good, faction is so strong that thay would have made her and those that have the honour to serve her very uneasy. For my own part, when I have nothing to reproch myself, I can't be very uneasy at what mallice can do. But be asured that whenever the angry party [the Tories] can be strong enough, it is not good success shall protect anybody to whome thay have anger.

636. GODOLPHIN *to* MARLBOROUGH   [*19 July 1706*]

Source: Blenheim MSS. A1-36.

Windsor July 19th 1706

Since my letter of yesterday from this place[5] I have the favour of yours of the 22th[6] with the enclosed from Comte Noyelles whose complaints I believe truly are as just, as the matter of them is unjustifiable. But vanity and passion are capable of carrying people who have no principle to doe strange things.

Upon the joyning of our Portugall and Catalonian troops with the King of Spain at Madrid, it has been thought proper for preventing disputes, to settle in whom the superior command of all the Queens troops should bee lodged. The Lords here[7] have been unanimously of opinion that it ought to bee in my Lord Gallway, as having the elder comission from the Queen, and

---

[1] 27 June/8 July. Untraced. See p. 603.   [2] 15/26 July. Untraced.
[3] The Queen's letter of 9 July. See p. 620 n. 4.
[4] The Queen may merely have been circumspect in talking about Churchill with Godolphin. In commenting on Churchill's conduct in the Admiralty to her ecclesiastical adviser, Archbishop Sharp, she said approvingly that he was 'one of the ablest men for that service that could be found'. T. Sharp, *Life of John Sharp, Archbishop of York* (London, 1825), i. 302.
[5] Letter 633.   [6] Letter 629.
[7] Decided by the committee at the Cockpit, 18 July. Harley's minute, B.M. Loan, 29/9.

that the King of Spain's comission to my Lord Peterborow ought not to interfere in this case. I think this is right for the Service, but how it may make him fly out, I can't answer.

I am sorry to find by yours the siege of Menin is like to goe onn so slowly, but I see it is unavoydable. I hope your impatience to make an end of the warr in this year, will not prevail with you to make any unreasonable attempt, nor to push onn anything too fast. For I can't find that taking that place and perhaps one or 2 more, which is the most to bee expected, would putt an end to the warr in this year. Success in Italy perhaps would doe it, or making a lucky use of the powers sent you from Mr. Secretary Harley might possibly have the same effect.[1]

I can't think the Dutch are very reasonable to bee so much in pain about their barriere, as things stand. But it is a plain argument to mee they think of joyning their interest to that of France, whenever a peace comes, and for that very reason, the longer wee can keep it off the better.

Mr. Secretary Hedges will acquaint you what measures are taken about the galeons.[2]

I have received the enclosed from Monsieur de Aligre.[3] The matter of it is news to mee. Pray lett mee know what answer I shall make him.

637. GODOLPHIN *to* MARLBOROUGH [22 July 1706]

Source: Blenheim MSS. A1-36.

St James's July 22d 1706

Lady Marlborough gave mee the enclosed for you this morning at Windsor. I venture it for the first time by the Ostend packett boat,[4] but that will not hinder us from writing regularly by the old way.

The Queen is come to town to receive the Treaty of Union, which has been signed this night by the commissioners on both sides. In case it passes in the Scots Parliament, great preparations are making by the angry party [the Tories] here to oppose it in ours. And now it begins to bee preached up and down that the *church is in danger*, from this union.

---

[1] Marlborough asked for powers made retroactive to settle the government of the Spanish Netherlands and to negotiate with the Elector of Bavaria. The former were sent on 19 July: H.M.C., *Bath MSS.*, i. 86. The latter were not sent until 23 July: below, p. 637. Therefore Godolphin's remark must refer to the former though it sounds like the latter. See also p. 635.

[2] Two galleys from Cartagena, carrying money for the garrison at Oran. Sighted by Leake off Cape Palos, the commander transferred his loyalty (and the money) from Philip V to Charles III. S. Martin-Leake, *Life of Leake* (Navy Records Society, 1918–20), ii. 53-4; Luttrell, vi. 68.

[3] Untraced. There is a correspondence between d'Alegre and the Countess of Rupelmonde at The Hague for May–June 1706 in B.M. loan 29/45D/2.

[4] For the new mail service instituted after the taking of Ostend see above, pp. 575 et seq. Murray ii. 25, 68; Luttrell, vi. 67; *C.T.B.*, xxi. ii. 410.

Ther's no end of their notice and frenzy nor of the folly of the others [the Whigs] in affecting to bring in none but their own creatures and not making the bottom broad enough to bee durable. Betwixt these two extreams one can't fail of passing one's times very agreably.

I am to acknowledg the favour of yours of the 26th and 29th[1] and shall answer them more particularly tomorrow by the Holland post. In the meantime I beg leave just to observe that by yours to Lady Marlborough[2] I perceive you don't think 362 [Howe] competent for the post promised. But all I have to say is that I know nobody here that is better, and I thought that after all that has passed they could not probably bee very easy where they are. But if you have your thoughts upon any other, lett your next bee a little more particular, as to that matter.[3]

Wee hear nothing yett of the Dutch transports from Ostend. However Erle is at Portsmouth embarquing our troops and all the rest of the officers take leave tomorrow. Sir Cloudesly Shovell is now with the fleet upon the coast of Normandy to make a false attacque, that they may draw their force that way.

I am much afraid the slowness of the King of Spayn in advancing to Madrid may prove of very ill consequence.

Nor am I less uneasy at the tampering mentioned in your last.[4] I shall bee sure to say nothing of it, and I don't doubt but you will have a watchfull eye upon that matter.

638. MARLBOROUGH *to* GODOLPHIN

[*22 July/2 August 1706*]

Source: Blenheim MSS. A1-14.

Helchin August 2d 1706

I have had the favour of yours of the 15th[5] from Windsor, and that of the 16[6] from London, in which I find Mr. Bridges dose certainly mistake the orders you have given for the payement of the army. He is not hear, but by his letters I beleive he is lead into the mistake by Sir Henry Fournise's writting that the scelins [shillings] are to go for seven pence, which is impossible, the Dutch paying them to their troupes at six pence half penny.[7] As to the advantage that may be, I think your order is extreame good, it being for the Service that the officer and soldiers should be made sensible of

---

[1] Letters 631, 634.

[2] Untraced. Howe's wife had made his position awkward. See p. 620.

[3] Godolphin had proposed sending Howe from Hanover to Berlin to replace Raby as envoy. For the latter's difficulty see p. 603.

[4] ? Part of the letter (letter 634) was torn off, so this reference cannot be elucidated.

[5] Letter 630.   [6] Letter 632.

[7] For the problem of the exchange and Furnese's role see pp. 608-10.

her Majesty's goodness to them.[1] I am afraid we shall be quickly sensible that King Charles and Lord Pitterborow have been unfortunat in not marching to Madrid, for by it thay have given heart and time to the Duke of Anjoye to take measures that may prove very troublesome. And if thay persist in their resolution of fighting the Portugess, as soon as thay are joyned by Monsieur de Legale,[2] which thay expect should be by the 20th of Jully, by what I have already seen, I do not think the Portuguess will venture a battaile, but resolve to follow their wanted custome of retyering, I am afraid, into their own country, if thay are pressed.[3] This misfortune could not have been if the troupes of Vallancia and Catalonia had marched to join the Portuguess. Thes feares I have proceed from the news we have from France, so that thay may be wrong grounded, which makes me beg that what I write may be keep a secrit, wishing from my soull, that King Charles may meet with no difficulty. Our letters of the 26 of the last month from Paris begins to say that the siege of Turin will be turned into a blockade. The siege of Menin meets with fresh difficultys every day, so that I should be happy if we might be sure of being masters of it by the end of this month. Lord Hallifax goes from hence tomorrow. He has desired me to let you know that the young Prince of Hanover[4] has a mind to be an English duke. I answered that I thought there could be no difficulty in itt, and that it would be very proper for him to speake to you of it at his return. You will be pleased, with my humble duty, to acquaint the Queen with itt. You have forgot to let me know the Queen's pleasure concerning Mr. Pocock, who is now Captain Lieutenant in her own redgiment, and was very much wo[u]nded at the battaile of Bleinheim. My desire is that he might have the company that is vacant in the battallion in Spain, if her Majesty approves of it. I desire Mr. St. Johns may be derected to speak to one of the Secretarys for his commission. The man that Lord Pitterborow recomends to me is Mr. Stanhop's brother, who was an ensigne the last yeare; and it is certainly the right of this gentleman I recomend. Besides, he has the merit of being at Shelenberg, Blenheim, and this last battaile.[5]

---

[1] See p. 568.

[2] François-René, baron de Legal (died 1724), joined the French army 1688; *maréchal de camp* 1702; lieutenant-general 1704; at Blenheim 1704; served in Spain 1705–7; at the siege of Barcelona 1706; returned to Flanders in 1709 where he was made a marquis.

[3] Legal had been sent to Rousillon and from thence into Spain with a contingent of French soldiers after the fall of Barcelona. When Tessé failed to retake Barcelona Legal was ordered to march through Navarre and reinforce Berwick who had retired from Madrid to Xidruque, 100 kilometres north, in the face of the advance of the Portuguese under Galway to Madrid. Legal joined Berwick on 17/28 July, but the latter did not attack Galway. The failure, however, of King Charles to join Galway forced the latter's retirement from Madrid in August.

[4] George Augustus, Electoral Prince of Hanover (1683–1760), succeeded his father in 1727 as George II of Great Britain and Ireland; he was created Duke of Cambridge by the Queen on 9 Nov. 1706.

[5] See p. 580. Pocock was given the company.

639. GODOLPHIN *to* MARLBOROUGH   [*23 July 1706*]

Source: Blenheim MSS. A1-36.

St James's July 23d at night

I writt to you yesterday by the way of Ostend,¹ and just now I receive the enclosed from Lady Marlborough to send to you.

The Treaty of Union has been presented this day to the Queen by the commissioners for each kingdome.

Our troops² are embarking at Portsmouth, and the last officers goe down tomorrow morning. Shrimpton is in the country. Wee have had notice that 30 or 40 sail of ships have been seen off of the Goodwins which wee hope are the Dutch transports from Ostend.

I received yesterday the packett from Mr. Cardinell mentioned in yours³ with the coppyes of the papers you signed for establishing a government in the Low Countryes. They were all comunicated this evening to the Cabinett Counsell, and all that matter is over as you seemed to desire.

I am very much in pain for the contretemps of the King of Spain's staying so long from Madrid. Nobody knows what ill consequences that may produce.

I have left the answer Mrs. Morley [the Queen] made to your letter with Mrs. Freeman [Duchess of Marlborough] who seems very uneasy at it, though I find Mr. Montgomery [Godolphin] did not expect it should bee better than it is.⁴ If I had some directions from you at a proper time to putt her in mind of that letter possibly that may give no rise for some proposalls to smooth the way to it.⁵

I hope as you seem to doe that every post may now bring us some good news from Italy. But I can't bee so sanguine upon our descent.

640. MARLBOROUGH *to* GODOLPHIN

[*25 July/5 August 1706*]

Source: Blenheim MSS. A1-14.
Printed: Coxe, ii. 96-7 (inc.).

Helchin August 5th 1706

I had yesterday yours of the 18th.⁶ I send you back Lord Gallaway's letter. You will have seen by my former letter⁷ the feares I have, that the Duke of Anjoue being joined by Monsieur Legale, may be in a condition to oblige Lord Gallaway and the Portugesse to retier from Madrid, which will make it very difficult for King Charles or Lord Pitterborow to join them. I do

¹ Letter 637.   ² For the descent.   ³ Letter 634.
⁴ The Queen's letter of 9 July, H.M.C., *Marlborough MSS.*, p. 43b.
⁵ See letters 653, 661.   ⁶ Letter 633.   ⁷ Letter 638.

with all my heart wish Lord Gallaway with King Charles, for it is certain since the relief of Barcelona, he has done everything as the French aught to have wished. For had he made use of the time and marched to Madrid, everything must have gone well in that country. The Cabinet Councel are certainly in the right in advising the Queen to give the command to Lord Gallaway, but I am afraid the carector of ambassador is what will be very uneasy to King Charles.[1]

I am taking what care I can to persuaide 328 [Elector of Bavaria] to come into our intirest, but I find 20 [France] has since the battaile been very prodigale in their promises.[2] The Duke of Vandome came last night to Valenchienne,[3] and meets the Elector of Bavaria this day at St. Gillain.[4] All the troupes thay expected from Garmany are also come, so that we shall quickly see how far thay will venture. Monsieur d'Allegree is mistaken as to my Lord Albemarle, his passeport being judged good. The trenches were opened last night before Menin, and in four days thay hope to have the batteries made, and thay promis in 15 days after the canon begins that we shall have the place. I shall willingly give them all this month. The inclosed is what the States will send to the Emperor. It was sent to me, with a desire that I would make such alterations as I should think proper. I think it might have been put in a softer stile, but I would not take upon me to make any alterations. I was desired to send it to England, so that you will be pleased to let Mr. Secretary Harley have itt.[5]

Lord Raby leaves the army in three or four days. I have so far prepared him for his being recalled,[6] by telling him that I was very confident, that as soon as Monsieur Spanheim[7] should be recalled, he would have his orders by the next post. I had the notice given me eight days agoe, that the orders were gone to Spanheim.

641. GODOLPHIN *to* MARLBOROUGH   [*26 July 1706*]

Source: Blenheim MSS. A1-36.

Windsor July 26, 1706

The wind being west, makes mee not hope for the Holland letters due this day till after the going out of the post.

I have nothing to trouble you with but the unfortunate account wee had last night of the embassador Methuen's death who served as well in that

---

[1] Galway was not given the character of ambassador to Charles III, but was accredited to Lisbon in 1708, replacing Paul Methuen.

[2] Marlborough sent Antoine Sersandars an agent of the Elector to him on 23 July/3 Aug. at Mons to try and bring him over.

[3] Valenciennes in France, on the Scheldt, about 40 kilometres upstream from Tournai.

[4] St. Ghislain, seat of a Bernardine abbey, on the Horne, a tributary of the Scheldt, some 30 kilometres west of Valenciennes.

[5] See p. 626 n. 5.   [6] See pp. 571, 603.   [7] Prussian envoy in London.

station, as any man could doe, and all the while under the discouragement of a great deal of groundless censure.[1]

The Queen sends for his son[2] from Savoy, to bee envoye in Portugall, and orders Mr. Chetwind,[3] now at Genoa to goe in his room to the Duke of Savoy, in which court, he seems to bee well looked upon.

The ship that brought this news from Lisbon, was 19 days in coming. Their last accounts from Madrid were that King Charles was proclaimed the 3d but that hee was not arrived there, that the army was marching to Guadalaxara to cover his advance and that the troops of the enemy's army deserted very fast to us. They gave no account, either of Sevill or Cadiz. The King of Spayn's backwardness has, I doubt, been a great hindrance.

As for 362 [Howe], I continue to think of him unless you can suggest a fitter. Here people will bee apt to think of Mr. Hill, or anybody that's wrong.[4]

I beg of you not to forgett writing something to mee upon occasion of what I mentioned in my last[5] relating to 116 [Somers].[6]

I have a letter from Erle which says the troops are all embarked at Portsmouth.

642. GODOLPHIN *to* MARLBOROUGH   [*29 July 1706*]

Source: Blenheim MSS. A1-36.

Windsor July 29, 1706

I have the favour of yours of the 2d of August,[7] and one from my Lord Halifax of the same date[8] which tells more plainly than yours, the true difficultyes of the siege of *Menin*.

It's no new thing to mee that people who can doe nothing themselves, will yett lett nobody else doe anything but themselves.

Your last accounts from Italy make the prospect very hopefull on that side, but in Hungary and upon the Rhyne, the court of Vienna uses us unsufferably.

---

[1] Methuen died 30 June/11 July.

[2] Sir Paul Methuen (1672–1757), envoy to King of Portugal 1697–1705; minister at Turin 1705–6; ambassador to Portugal 1706–8; M.P., Devizes, 1708–10, Brackley, 1713–47. *D.N.B.*

[3] John, second Viscount Chetwynd (died 1767), English envoy to the Duke of Savoy 1706–10; Receiver-General for the Duchy of Lancaster 1702–18.

[4] Godolphin intended to send Howe to Berlin to replace Raby.

[5] Letter 639.

[6] Godolphin errs. He means 117—Sunderland. See p. 641.

[7] Letter 638.

[8] B.M., Add. MS. 28055, fol. 316: 'I was yesterday before Menin, and found them there in a sad way. Wee thought the trenches had been opened the night before, but they will not be there three days yet. The generals are all in quarrells with one another, the Deputies of the States confounded and distrusted among them, and everybody here disatisfied with their delays. It is not to be conceived, without seeing it, how unpracticable these men are without Lord M[arlborough]. He gives them a meeting at Courtray on Wednesday, and then your Lordship may expect to hear they will proceed.'

The more wee exert ourselves for the Emperor and the House of Austria, the less return they make, and not only break off the negotiation with the malecontents, but to strengthen themselves against them they draw their troops from the Rhine, by which they weaken the confoederacy, and furnish an excuse, for the idleness and insignificancy of Prince Lewis of Baden's conduct as if the whole world were under obligations to doe everything for them without any return. In short, I know no way to bee even with them, but that 90 [Marlborough] should make use of the powers lately sent him,[1] for the present ease and advantage of 17 [England] and 19 [Holland], and engage them to make it good, without much concerning themselves, whether it were agreable to 348 [Goess] and his neighbors or not.

I doubt Mr. Methuen's death may prove very unseasonable to our affairs on that side of the world. And the King of Spain's unaccountable delayes occasioned by the folly and weakness of his Germans, joyned to it, may make the entire revolution of that country slow and uncertain, which might have been sure and immediate, if they had followed their advantages, but half so well as some may have done for them. Monsieur Sylvestre[2] has told mee your intentions, in case the French should take the field agayn this year with an army, which indeed I don't expect, but rather retreat from place to place till the winter forces you home, and then depend upon what they can doe with 19 [Holland]. Now in case Mr. Freeman's [Marlborough] powers can bee brought to beare, I should think that might bee a very effectuall way to prevent 19 [Holland] from making any false steps.

I am just going to London, and shall write more from thence, if I find anything worth your notice.

643. MARLBOROUGH *to* GODOLPHIN

[*29 July/9 August 1706*]

Source: Blenheim MSS. A1-14.
Printed: Coxe, ii. 73, 177 (inc.).

Helchin August 9th 1706

I have received yours of the 22[3] by Ostende. It is certainly the quickest passage, but much the daingerous, so that whenever you write that way, it would be well that you send a copie by the way of Holland. I could wish for the rest of this campagne that the Post Office would regularly send all the letters that are for the army by the way of Holland, for should thay devide them and send some tims by Ostende and some tims by Holland, the letters on this side the watter will be neglected at both places, and so we shall receive them very iregularly. What you say of both partys is so trew, that

---

[1] To treat with the Elector of Bavaria for his restoration. See p. 629 n. 1.
[2] Companion to Lord Monthermer, who accompanied Halifax to the Continent.
[3] Letter 637.

I do with all my soull pitty you. Care must be taken against the mallice of the angry party, and notwithstanding their mallicious affectation of crying the church may be ruined by the Union,[1] the Union must be suported. And I hope the reasonable men of the other party will not opose the enlarging of the bottome, so as that it may be able to support itself. My objections to 362 [Howe] was his want of dexterity for so tricking a cort as that of 321 [King of Prussia]. But since you have no better, I think you will do well to send him, for he certainly can never be easy nor do her Majesty any service where he is. Why should you not at the same time offer 363 [Raby] to go to 318 [Emperor], for now would be a proper time to bring 359 [Stepney] to 19 [Holland]. 363 [Raby] has so good an opinion of himself, that if nothing be done for him, he will be very unreasonable. I hope before this comes to you Lord Rivers will be sailled, for the season is very much advanced. It has given a very great allarme in France, but thay have not been able to send regular troupes to any other province but that of Normandy. But in severall places their mellicia [militia] is cloathed like their regular troupes. If Lord Rivers has not been already informed of this, he aught to know itt. The offer that has been made, you will find in the inclosed paper.[2] It has only been in some particular hands, but not communicated to the States. The treaty of Hungary being intierly brooke,[3] I have now noe expectations of Prince Lewis attempting anything on the Rhin, for besides the four redgiments that are already ordered to be sent to Hungary, I do not doubt but more will be sent in the month of September.

I had last night the favour of yours of the 23,[4] and am very glad to find that the commission has so unanimously agreed. I do with all my heart wish the parliaments of both nations may do the same, so that her Majesty may have the glory of finishing this great worke, for which she will not only deserve to be blessed in this, but also in all future aiges.

It is certaine that the King of Spain's not marching with expedition to Madrid may prove very fatal to the quiet of the kingdome, and consequently to the great disadvantage of the common cause. But I have yet some hopes, that the King might, upon Lord Gallaway's letters, not follow his resolution of going to Saragose, but his lordship's of going to Madrid, and so might join the Portuguesse before Monsieur Legale with the French troupes could join the Duke of Barwick. If this should be, and the King keeps Lord Gallaway near him, I should then hope their would be a more reasonable management

[1] The parliamentary Union of Scotland and England.
[2] The peace offers of France conveyed to Heinsius and Buys by Hennequin. See p. 627.
[3] A cessation of arms was settled at the beginning of the year, while negotiations took place between the Emperor and Rákóczi through the mediation of Stepney and Jacob Jan Hamel Bruyninx, the English and Dutch envoys at Vienna. Hostilities broke out again when the negotiations terminated on 13/24 July. Stepney put all the blame on the Emperor for the failure to reach a settlement. For the negotiations see Klopp, xii. 162–89.
[4] Letter 639.

for the futur. Lieutenant General Inglisby continues ill at Gand. I could with all my heart wish him and more generall officers with the des[c]ent. Since Shrimton has no thoughts of going to Gibraltar, I think he might be sent after Lord Rivers.

I have received the powers for treating with 328 [Elector of Bavaria], and am of opinion that he would be of great use if we could make him reasonable. But he is extreamly hartned, by the assurance he has received from 313 [King of France], that he shal spedily have good news from 22 [Spain], and that he shal certainly be master of Turin in this month. I hope 313 [King of France] will be disapointed in both his expectations. The Duke of Vandome having strenghned the garrison of Menin, and ordered severall troupes to march that way, he is to be at Ipres this night, so that I have this day sent 12 battalions to strenghen those of the siege. Our canon begane to fyer this morning. Three or four days we hope will dismount so many of their canon, that we may with security carry on our trenches. Monsieur de Vandome has given orders to all the troupes to be in a readyness to march at 24 hours warning, so that in three or four days he may draw them together. By his languidge we aught to expect another battaile, but I can't think the King of France will venture itt. If he should, I hope and pray that the blessing of God may continue with us.

I have been pressed againe yesterday by Machado[1] to send his demands for the last yeare. This is the fourth time since I have been in the field, but I think itt for the Service to give him no possitive answere til the winter, so that you may see what is reasonable for both campagns together. If Medina[2] should speak to you, you will be pleased that he may have such an answere, as that I may not be troubled til I come to The Hague. In the meantime, if you like it, I can order Cardonell to send the copies of his demand to Mr. Taylor.

644. MARLBOROUGH *to the* DUCHESS

[*29 July/9 August 1706*]

Source: Blenheim MSS. E3.
Printed: Coxe, ii. 135–6 (inc.).

Helchin August 9th 1706

I had the happyness of yours of the 22th by the way of Ostende two days agoe. By the account you give me of the ring Mr. Bridges has sent you, I am confident you will find it is neither a dimont nor a cristol, consequently not of much vallue, but such as your kindness will allow as being my picture.[3] By the same letter I was glad to see you had not forgot poor St. Albans, but

---

[1] Quartermaster-general for the Dutch.   [2] A supplier to Machado.
[3] The Duchess returned it. See below, p. 640, and Green, pp. 112–13.

very sorry to find in yours of the 23 that you had been disapointed of going by sickness. You will allow me on this occasion to say you are very unkind to me, in not doing what I have so earnestly desired; that you would take advice concerning this illness, for you may neglect it so long, that it may not be in the power of the phesitiens to help you.[1] I find both 91 [Godolphin] and 114 [Lady Marlborough] have a mind to remove 362 [Howe], so that I have write accordingly to 91 [Godolphin]. I wish with all my heart we may have good news from Spain, for the letters from Paris are possative that the Duke of Anjoue will venture a battaile. You know that I have often disputes with you concerning 83 [the Queen], and by what I have always observed that when she she thinkes herself in the right, she needs no advice to help her to be very ferm and possative. But I do not doubt but a very litle time will sett this of 117 [Sunderland] very right, for you may see by the letter[2] that thay [the Queen] have a good opinion of them [Sunderland]. I have write as my friends would have mee, for I had much rather be governed then govern, but otherways, I have realy so much estime and kindness for him, and have so much knowlidge of the place you would have for him, that I have my aprihensions, that he will be very uneasy in itt; and that when it is to[o] late you will be of my opinion, that it would have been much happyer, if he had been imployed in any other place of profit and honnour. I have formerly said so much to you on this subject, and to so litle purpose, that I aught not to have troubled you with all this, knowing very well that you rely on other people's judgement in this matter. I do not doubt but thay wish him very well, but in this thay have other considerations then his good, and I have none but that of a kind friend, that would neither have him nor my daughter uneasy. Writting this by kandlelight I am so blind that I can't read it, so that if there be anything in it that should not be, burn itt, and think kindly of me who loves you with all his heart.

645. GODOLPHIN *to* MARLBOROUGH   [*30 July 1706*]

Source: Blenheim MSS. A1-36.

St James July 30th at night

Since my letter was written which I left this morning with Lady Marlborough at Windsor,[3] I have the favour of yours of the 5th,[4] upon which I shall trouble you the less, because mine of this day is a sort of an answer to it, before I had it.

The letters from France by this post are full of their alarms at our preparations for descent. But the wind is so contrary that the Dutch

---

[1] On 16 June Luttrell reported, 'the Dutchesse of Marlborough had lately an apopletick fitt, but [is] well again'. vi. 58.
[2] The Queen's of 9 July. See p. 603 n. 3.   [3] Letter 642.   [4] Letter 640.

transports are not yett to St. Hellens[1] where our troops, all embarked are expecting them.

Here is a Frenchman[2] who says he has had formerly great habitudes with the Prince de Vaudement.[3] He offers his service to goe to him and endeavor to make him embrace the interest of King Charles. I have no great faith in these sort of people, but I find 116 [Somers] is fond of him, so I may perhaps throw away a £100 upon him, and send him with a letter to you.

The letter you sent mee from the States to the Emperour is pretty strong. I think they might doe well to represent as strongly against withdrawing their troops from the Rhyne. The French gazetts are full of the Marshall de Villars's successes.[4] I am glad they have no other to bragg of.

The Hague letters tell us King Charles enterd Madrid the 14th. I doubt it very much, but if it bee true, wee shall have an express with that news in 2 or 3 days.

You may bee sure the Queen will not give a comission for the vacant company in the Guards, but to Mr. Pocock when you recomend, nor confirm any that may have been given by Lord Peterborow. I should have told you this sooner, but that I thought you might have taken it for granted, without my giving you trouble of telling it.[5]

I don't like what you write to Mr. Secretary Harley[6] of the dispositions you find in 17 [England]. I am more afraid and have been so a great while, of that than of anything. But this does not agree with what Monsieur Sylvestre[7] told mee from you.

646. GODOLPHIN *to* MARLBOROUGH [*1 August 1706*]

Source: Blenheim MSS. A1-36.

August 1st 1706

This will bee given you by Monsieur de la Breconniere, to whom I have given a 100£ to carry him to the Prince de Vandemont with whom he says he has a long acquaintance, and hopes he may bee able to perswade him to embrace the interests of King Charles. I have ordered him to goe by Ostend, and receive your commands, and though I think, if he has any credit, hee may

---

[1] A roadstead or rendezvous place for ships entering or leaving Portsmouth, east of the Isle of Wight.

[2] Colonel de La Breconnière. A Franche-Comté adventurer who served equally as a representative of the Allies and an ambassador of France: Stelling-Michaud, p. 346. There is a long memorial from Breconnière in September (to Godolphin?) with an account of his trip to Prince Eugene and the plan he presented in Blenheim MSS. G1-6. See the following letter. For his later activities see p. 1032 n. 2.

[3] A French general in Italy whom Godolphin wanted to bring over to the Allies.

[4] On the Rhine. [5] See pp. 580, 631.

[6] Untraced. None of Marlborough's surviving letters reflects this remark.

[7] See p. 635.

come too late to make use of it, yett I would not neglect a thing that may bee of so great consequence, for the sake of so small an expence.

Wee are in all the concern imaginable here for the contrary winds which still delay our expedition, after our troops are all on board, and in very good heart. But the Dutch transports are still in the Downes.

This have [sic] given mee the occasion of seeing Monsieur Cavalier,[1] who is come post from the Downes, and called upon mee this morning at the treasury, in his way to Windsor from whence he goes to Portsmouth to meet the fleet, when the wind will give them leave to advance.

I intend to goe to Windsor tonight and to write to you from thence by tomorrow's post.

647. MARLBOROUGH *to the* DUCHESS   [1/12 *August 1706*]

Source: Blenheim MSS. E3.
Printed: *Private Correspondence*, i. 61–2.

Helchin August 12th 1706

I have had the hapyness of yours of the 25th, and by itt find the pressent of Mr. Bridges of a much greater vallue then I could have wished itt. I really do not know what to advise you, but I think your letter is very well til you can see him, and I shall take care to send itt to him.[2]

It is very uneasy to have anybody about you that you think is a spye. The best thing you can do is to let Hodges have somebody to watch him, and to endeavour the intercepting of some of his letters; and if you find he is guilty take the first occasion of parting with him, without ever telling him the trew reason. After what you have said to me of Foster and his sister, I shall be sure to have care of him. I always thought them prowed, simple, and Jacobits, but very honest.[3] I find Lord Treasurer thinkes Mr. Methwin a great loose. You know what my opinion has been always of him. I beleive his son by all I have heard of him is an ingenious young man. I did some time after the battaile receive a very obliging letter from 66 [Shrewsbury].[4] I beleive he will be very uneasy at 118 [Wharton] having the place you mentioned, it being a demonstration that he must expect nothing. But I think his pride will make him take care not to have itt seen, but whatever

---

[1] Jean Cavalier (*c.* 1681–1740), leader of the Camisards, French Protestants who rebelled against Louis XIV in 1702. Cavalier came to England after Villars forced the Camisards to disband in 1704. He commanded a French Huguenot regiment on the descent. After his regiment was decimated at Almanza he returned to England and retired to Ireland. See Marcel Pin, *Jean Cavalier* (Nîmes, 1936) and Cavalier's own *Memoirs of the Wars of the Cévennes*, 2nd edition (London, 1727).

[2] See p. 637.

[3] Foster served Marlborough on the Continent, his sister the Duchess in England. Someone had accused them of spying and sending information. It turned out to be of no importance. See the Duchess's letters to Harley in H. M. C., *Bath MSS.*, i. 85, 87, 93.

[4] 22 May, Blenheim MSS. A1-46. See letter 682.

mischief he can do underhand may be expected.[1] I was yesterday at the siege,[2] and am afraid it must last til the 25th of this month, which will be very inconvenient, the Elector having already his army in the field, and next Munday[3] the Duke of Vandome will have all his together. This day two yeares was the battaile of Blenheim. I hope you have not forgote the presenting the Queen with the Collors.[4] The generall officers that were at the battaile dine with me today.

648. MARLBOROUGH *to* GODOLPHIN   [*2/13 August 1706*]

Source: Blenheim MSS. A1-15.

Helchin August 13th 1706

Since my last[5] I have had the favour of yours of the 26[6] from Windsor, by which I see the last letters from Portugale give an account of Ambassadour Methwin's being dead. I think you have done very well for the Queen's Service in sending his son[7] thether, for most people commends him. The French letters will not allow that the King of Spain had joined the Portugale army the 30th of the last month.[8] If this should be trew, it apeares here to us monsterous, that anybody could have power to hinder him from following the desires of Lord Gallaway, for he must have received his expresses time enough to have been there before the end of the last month. We hear nothing of Lord Pitterborough, but we hope your next Portugale letters will let us know where the King and his Lordship are. I did in my last obaye your commands as to sending my opinion concerning 362 [Howe], as I shall now of 360 [Hill]. I think him one of the daingerous men you have in England, and I dare answer for it, you will be sensible of it this winter; so that in my opinion, who ever can think of sending him to 322 [Elector of Hanover], dose not mean the Queen's business should go quietly.[9]

In your last you desire I would say something that might give you occasion of speaking of 116 [Somers]. I beleive you have mistaken the cypher, for I beleive you me[a]nt 117 [Sunderland].[10] If it be so, let me know what you would have me say. I was yesterday at the siege, and by what thay say to me, I find I must have patience til the 25th of this month, which may prove very

---

[1] On 9 Sept. Wharton was made Chief Justice in Eyre of royal forests and parks south of the Trent. He kissed hands for it on 4 Aug. The initiative for the appointment came from Sunderland, who requested the Duchess to propose it to Godolphin. Saturday night [20 July?] in *Private Correspondence*, i. 38–9.

[2] Of Menin.   [3] 5/16 Aug.

[4] The quit rent presented each year to the Sovereign by Marlborough for the royal manor of Woodstock. The flag was presented by their grandson. See p. 647.

[5] Letter 643.   [6] Letter 641.   [7] Paul Methuen.

[8] Charles III did not join Galway at Guadalajara until 26 July/6 Aug.

[9] Howe remained at Hanover until his death in 1709.

[10] Marlborough is correct. See pp. 632, 634.

troublesome, the Elector of Bavaria having his army since the 10th enchamped at La Busiere,[1] between Mons and Charleroy, from whence he may act either in Braband or on the Meuse. At the same time, the Duke of Vandome is drawing his together near Lille, which hinders me from sending the number of troupes that are necessary for the observing the Elector's motions. The Elector's army consistes of the Spaniards, Wallons, Collons, and his own troupes. Thay cal them 20,000 men, but thay can't be so many. The Duke of Vandome['s] army are the French and Swise, their numbers are to be 70 battallions and 140 squadrons. I shall send 30 squadrons and 13 battalions to obsarve the Elector, and keep with myself 40 battallions and 109 squadrons for the covering of the siege. By this account you will see that the Duke of Vandome is much superior to the army that covers the siege. But that gives me no uneasyness, for if he advances towardes me, I have already taken my measures to have 20 squadrons and 25 battallions from the siege, with which by the blessing of God I no ways doubt of beatting him. But my feares procedes from the allarmes the Elector may give on the Meuse or in Braband during the time of this siege; for as soon as this is over, I shal be able to take such measures as will oblige him to retier. In the meantime, we go on in the business I have formerly mention[ed], and I shall not break it til he begins to act offensively, but after that I shall not care to have any farther commerce.[2]

649. GODOLPHIN *to* MARLBOROUGH   [*4 August 1706*]

Source: Blenheim MSS. A1-36.

Windsor 4 August

I have received the favour of yours of the 9th[3] and shall obey your commands in not writing any more by the way of Ostend.

This day the wind seems to incline to change, and I hope our ships may sail. I have spoken to Shrimpton, and he will bee gon in 48 hours to Portsmouth, without insisting upon his commission of Major Generall from the King of Spayn.

Mr. Secretary Harley will take the Queen's commands and acquaint you with them by this post, concerning the alterations of our severall foreign ministers, and will make the offer to Lord Raby mentioned in yours. But I doubt he is whymsicall enough not to like it.[4] However I think 359 [Stepney] should come to 18 [Brussels] the sooner the better.

---

[1] Labuissière on the Sambre, 22 kilometres south-west of Charleroi.
[2] The negotiations with the Elector of Bavaria to bring him over to the Allies. See above, p. 565 et seq.
[3] Letter 643.   [4] For Raby's reaction see p. 647 n. 6.

I think the proposalls you sent mee in the little paper enclosed in your letter extreamly ridiculous in many respects, but in this one especialy. If the Spaniards were uneasy at any partition or separation of their monarchy, does any body think they will like to see Spain itself divided, and a king in possession of one half of it with France at his back?[1]

I have a pretty good opinion of the affaires of Italy, but cannot help being uneasy about those of Spayn till wee hear certainly what is become of King Charles.

As to your matters depending in Flanders, I hope the French doe but talk of fighting agayn, but I hope too you will not depend too much upon that, and upon any ill success in Spayn or Italy, they will venture the sooner.

When Medina comes to mee, I shall bee sure to follow your orders. But I shall bee a week before I see him being to goe tomorrow into Wiltshire for 3 or 4 days to see my horses,[2] which I mention only that you may not bee surprised, if you have no letter from mee by Fryday's post.[3]

650. MARLBOROUGH *to* GODOLPHIN   [*4/15 August 1706*]

Source: Blenheim MSS. A1-14; copy (to Stepney), B.M., Add. MS. 7058, fol. 62.
Printed: Murray, iii. 84.
Note: in hand of clerk; signature only autograph.[4]

Camp at Helchin, the 15th August 1706

Mr. Stepney having writ in his last letters, that seeing the treaty between the Emperor and the Hungarians was at end,[5] without any hopes of its being renewd, he was desirous to make his retreat from Vienna. And finding while I am in the field, and obliged to give my whole attention to the army, we may unavoidably be subject to many mistakes in the administration of this government at Brussells,[6] for want of some person there from the Queen, I would be glad your Lordship would represent this matter, and humbly move her Majesty at the same time that Mr. Stepney might be sent for immediately to be employed in this service, with the like powers as I have, to sign and act in conjunction with the deputys of the States. And in case her Majesty approve of it, I pray no time may be lost in sending for him, that I may be

---

[1] The French proposals to the Dutch for a peace.

[2] Godolphin maintained stables at Tilshead where he raised racing horses. He also owned another set of stables, still preserved at Newmarket. '[It was said by the new ministers] he had a house in Wiltshire, which by the way is a stable of horses.' Duchess to Lady Cowper, 31 Aug. 1710, Cowper Letterbooks, ii. 8, Panshanger MSS., Hertfordshire Record Office.

[3] 9 Aug.

[4] This letter was written for Stepney's benefit and a copy was sent to him. Marlborough to Stepney, 7/18 Aug., Murray, iii. 91.

[5] The cessation of arms negotiated at the beginning of the year.

[6] The Anglo-Dutch condominium.

able to concert and take measures with him before the end of the campagne. Here he will be at hand, too, to supply Mr. Stanhop's place, if her Majesty should find any opportunity of providing for him in the meanwhile.[1]

651. MARLBOROUGH *to* GODOLPHIN   [5/16 August 1706]

Source: Blenheim MSS. A1-14.
Printed: Coxe, ii. 97 (inc.).

Helchin August 16, 1706

Wee have been obliged to stay so long in this camp, that we begine to want both watter and forage. The Duke of Vandome will have tomorrow all the troupes together that the King of France has in this country, and we are told by a lieutenant that was taken two days ago in a sally, that the governor had assured the garrison, that the Duke of Vandome would oblige us to raise the siege before the 20th of this month. We are taking the best measures we can, having above five leagues to cover, but I am more afraid of what the troupes in Braband may do. For if the French should attempt nothing on this side, we shall not be masters of the town this ten days. I have received yours of the 29 and 30th[2] of the last month. It is most certaine the court of Vienna dose not make the returns thay aught to England and Holland, and have nothing att heart so much as the reducing the Hongroise. But as to what you say of my making use of the powers given me[3] for the good of 17 [England] and 19 [Holland] is by the last made impracticable, which makes me beg by this post that her Majesty would have the goodness of joining Mr. Stepney to me, and that he may reside at Bruxelles. For as I am obliged to be always with the army, his being there would be of use to the publick, and the perticular intirest of England.

I agree with you that the Garmains that are with 315 [King Charles] are good for nothing. But I beleive the anger and aversion he has for 127 [Peterborough] is the greatest cause of his taking the resolution of going to Saragose, which I am afraid will prove fatal; for Mr. Crow[4] told me, that he once said to him, that he would never have anything to do with 127 [Peterborough] that he would not accept of health from him. I supose this expression is better in Spanish then English.

The King of Spain was not to be at Saragose til the 15th of the last month, and by our letters from France, Lord Pitterborow had not joyned Lord Gallaway the 1st of this month, nor have we any account where he is. But I am afraid the troupes are so devided in that country, that the Duke of Anjoue

---

[1] Stanhope, now very ill, returned in October to England where he died on 20 Sept. 1707.
[2] Letters 642, 645.
[3] See pp. 616, 629 n. 1. This refers to the government of the Spanish Netherlands.
[4] English representative to Charles III who had just returned.

may be incoridged to attempt the Portuguesse. Mr. Richardes[1] and Mr. Crow will give you so full an account of what passes in that country, that I have already troubled you to[o] much. However, I must repeat to you, what I have already said to Mr. Richards, that I thought the end of June a very wrong time to send of [with] so long a message, the man that has the sole care of the train of artillerie, for Lord Pitterborow could not expect him back till the month of October.

I have this minut an account of poor Cadogan being taken or killed. I hope it is the first and then I can have him exchanged this winter. But for this campagne I must loose his service, which will be very troublesome, having nobody very proper for the execution of his place.[2]

652. MARLBOROUGH *to the* DUCHESS   [*5/16 August 1706*]

Source: Blenheim MSS. E3.
Printed: *Private Correspondence*, i. 62–3 (inc.); balance in Coxe, i. 73 (inc.).

Helchin August 16, 1706

I have had your dear letter of the 30th, and I can't know exsactly what mony has been advanced to Spence[3] til I com to England, but I think it is 130 odd pounds.

Though Woodstock is extreamly at my heart, I very much approve of the resolution you have taken of not letting 91 [Godolphin] be spoke too, for upon my word I had rather never be in the house then put any difficulty upon him. I have taken care to inform myself concerning what you write of Mr. Durell[4] and Fauster,[5] and I can asure you there has been no mony. He is certainly no good sarvant, but I beleive he is an honest man. An officer is this minut come to me to give an account of the forage we have made this day, and tels me that poor Cadogan is taken prisoner or killed, which gives me a great deal of uneasiness, for he loved me, and I could rely upon him. I am now sending a trumpet to the governor of Tournay to know if he be alive, for the horse that beat him came from that garrison. I have ordered the trumpet to return this night, for I shall not be at quiet til I know his fate.

I have opened my letter to tell you that Cadogan is a prisoner at Tournay and not wo[u]nded.

---

[1] John Richards, an Irish Roman Catholic; brother of Michael Richards (q.v.), served with Venetians and Poles before entering service of Portugal in 1703 as a colonel in the Portuguese army and later brigadier-general.

[2] The quartermaster-general, taken while on a foraging expedition. Marlborough asked for his exchange for the Chevalier de Croissy, brother of de Torcy. Vendôme responded by immediately granting Cadogan his parole and asked in return for Lieutenant-General Pallavicini, a Savoyard general in the service of Louis XIV taken at Ramillies (p. 648). Marlborough in turn arranged the return of de Croissy, but this he found was already fixed. Below, pp. 648–9; Murray, iii. 87, 90–1, 106, 124.

[3] Unidentified.   [4] Adjutant-general of the Forces.

[5] Foster, a servant of Marlborough's. See p. 640.

653. GODOLPHIN *to* MARLBOROUGH   [*7 August 1706*]

Source: Blenheim MSS. A1-36.

Tillsett[1] August 7th 1706

I receive the favour of yours of the 13th[2] at this place, from whence I ought not to give you much trouble with my reflecxions. However I can't help saying that I had no thought of employing 360 [Hill]. But I was not without thought that others might propose him, which made mee mention 362 [Howe], as what was most probable to cutt it short, and is in other respects, not improper. For 362 [Howe] will have no whimsys of his own, but bee sure to follow your directions in what every whimsys may arise at that court,[3] where they abound.

You are in the right, to think I mistook the cypher in putting 116 [Somers] for 117 [Sunderland]. I did so, not taking the pains to look upon it, but concluding it was governed by their rank. I wish however you would have rectifyed it before I had owned the mistake, because that will now lose 10 or 12 days time, in the use I would have made of your letter,[4] for a rise to take up that matter with Mrs. Morley [the Queen] to its best advantage. I hope therfore you will doe mee the favour to doe it by the first opportunity.

I think you are much in the right to break off the comerce with that person,[5] in case they take advantage of your present situation, so as to act offensively. But then, if you have not already done it, I think the sooner you lett him know that, the better.

Though I am here in a very fine country with very fine weather, yett I can't help having the spleen, when I think of their childish behaviour in Spain.

I design to leave this place by the end of the week, and hope my next will bee from Windsor.

654. MARLBOROUGH *to* GODOLPHIN   [*8/19 August 1706*]

Source: Blenheim MSS. A1-14.

Helchin August 19, 1706

The inclosed[6] is an account of what has passed in Spain til the 5 of this month, by which you will see, if it be trew, that the Duke of Anjoue is againe master of Madrid. If he should continu so, and the Dutch in their manage-ment here disoblige, as thay do dayly, we shal find greater difficultys in this country then we have heitherto imagined. By my letters from Vienna, I find thay are very much disatisfied with the proceedings of the States Generall, and the States General as much with them. I would beg for the good of England and the Queen's Service, that you would enter as litle as possible into the disputes. For when thay are both unreasonable, it must be the Queen's friendshipe that must interpose, to hinder the French from having

---

[1] Tilshead, site of Godolphin's stables.   [2] Letter 648.   [3] Prussia.
[4] See p. 639. Marlborough wrote as Godolphin requested on 19/30 Aug. (letter 661).
[5] The Elector of Bavaria.   [6] Untraced.

an advantage by itt.[1] Le Bresonier that you mention in yours of the 2d,[2] which I received this morning, is not yett come. I am very confident the mony you give him for his voyage is so much lost. What you have said to the Comte de Gallas[3] is certainly very right, but the court of Vienna is so very wrong in the whole business of Hungary, that it is impossible to sett them right. But in my poor opinion, the Dutch are as much in the wrong in their proceeding concerning the bishopric of Munster, so that I hope the Queen will find some excuses for not entering into that disput to[o] hastely.[4] I hope you will aprove of my proposall, in my last,[5] for the bring[ing] Mr. Stepney with all expedition to the Bruxelles. I know of nobody to go in his place. If you have nobody better, I thinke you might endeavour to perswaid Lord Raby, he having his equipage all ready made.[6] Mr. Secretary Harley in his last letter seems to refer him to me. I desire I may not be thought to be the occasion of his recalling. As Cadagone is absolutely necessary for my ease, so I am indeavoring his exchang. As we made ourselves masters last night of the counterscarp of Menin, we must see in four or five days if Monsieur de Vandome will attempt the relief of the place. The Elector of Bavaria and al his troupes are joined the French. I have very litle intirest with Mr. Johnson,[7] but since you desire it, in a post or two I will write to him.

I hope Willigo will perform the ceremony of the 2 of August[8] many yeares after I am dead.

---

[1] The issues in dispute were the negotiations between the Emperor and the Hungarian insurgents; the poor showing of the Imperial army on the Rhine; and rival candidates for the bishopric of Münster. Marlborough to Harley, 8/19 Aug., Murray, iii. 91–2.

[2] Untraced. See pp. 638–40.

[3] Johann Wenzel, Count Gallas (1669–1719), Imperial ambassador in London, 1705–11.

[4] Münster was the leading German principality in the Circle of Westphalia and important to the Allies as a supplier of troops. The reigning bishop-ruler died on 25 Apr./6 May and there were two candidates to succeed him. The Dutch Republic opposed Karl Joseph, Bishop of Osnabrück, brother of the Duke of Lorraine, and the Imperial candidate, who was supported by England (pp. 650, 685) on the recommendation of Marlborough. To Harley, 30 May/10 June, Murray, ii. 578. They worked instead for the Bishop of Paderborn, put forward by the Archbishop-Elector of Cologne. Urged by the Dutch the English switched their support in November to the Bishop of Paderborn who was elected at the end of 1706, after an earlier election was voided by the Pope and a new election held at Rome. See Marlborough to Hedges, 12/23 Nov., ibid. iii. 230–1. Lamberty, iv. 187–214. M. Braubach, 'Politisch-militarische Verträge zwischen den Fürstbischöfen von Münster und den Generalstaaten der Vereinigde Niederlanden im XVIII. Jahrhundert,' *Westfälisch Zeitschrift*, xci (1936), 154–7.   [5] Letter 651.

[6] On 15/26 Aug. Marlborough wrote Harley: 'As to his [Raby] going to Vienna, he insists on the same allowances Lord Sunderland had [in 1705] and that of being declared [a member] of the [Privy] Council, which last can hardly be refused to any ambassador that can desire it . . . Mr. Stepney has now eight pounds a day, and I am afraid you will find nobody of quality will go cheaper, his equipage being already made, and this commission is likely to last no longer than the war.' H. M. C., *Bath MSS.*, i. 94.

[7] James Johnston (1655–1737), Secretary of State in Scotland 1692–6; Lord Clerk Register 1704–5; a leader of the Squadrone party in Scotland who resided for the most part in England. *D.N.B.* Marlborough wrote to him on 29 Aug./9 Sept. asking him to urge Roxburghe and the other Squadrone members to support the Union in the Scottish Parliament. Murray, iii. 125–6.

[8] The presentation of the *fleur de lis* to the Queen, on the anniversary of Blenheim as quit rent for the royal manor of Woodstock.

655. MARLBOROUGH *to the* DUCHESS   [*8/19 August 1706*]

Source: Blenheim MSS. E3.
Printed: *Private Correspondence*, i. 63-4.

Helchin August 19, 1706

I had this morning yours of the 2d. I wish with all my heart that happy time
were come that we might be at quiet at Woodstock, but I begine to fear that
we must have a litle patience, for our affaires are so managed in Spain that
though we have much the superiority of the French, yett thay have ordered
it so that thay are againe masters of Madrid; at least our letters from France
tels us so. You know that it is always agreable news to me to hear of your
being easy with Mrs. Morley (the Queen). I wish upon all accounts itt may
continue. I grow very weary of this camp, for having been near six weakes in
it, we begine to want forage and watter, for we have had litle or no raine this
two months. I am very sorry our des[c]ent can't have a favourable wind, for their
is already a great deal of time lost. You wish that 82 [Prince George] had an
able and honest man about him. That is much easier wished then found,
for a great many men are capable of everything til thay are tryed, and then
good for nothing. The Duke de Vandome has sent me back Cadogan upon
his parole, and I am now indeavoring an exchange. We are now masters of the
counterscarp of Menin, so that in seven or eight days, if we are not disturbed,
we shall have the place.

656. MARLBOROUGH *to* GODOLPHIN   [*12/23 August 1706*]

Source: Blenheim MSS. A1-14.
Printed: Coxe, ii. 74, 113 (inc.).

Helchin August 23d 1706

Yesterday morning the enemy at Menin planted a white flage on their
breach, and as I was there I emediatly ordered an exchange of [h]ostiges. We
have this morning possession of on[e] of their gates, and on Wensday,[1] being
St. Lewis' day, thay are to march out with the usuall markes of honour.[2] We
must have 8 or 10 days for the leaveling our lins, and the putting the place in
a posture of defence. In the meantime, I am taking measures for the siege of
Dendermont. If the weather continues drye wee shall take it, but if it should
rain we can't continue before it. The Duke of Vandome continues to talke
more then I beleive he intends to performe. However, he strenghens himself
every day, with all the troupes he can possibly gett.

I have had yours of the 1st[3] by Monsieur Bresconier. His expedition can
be of no service.[4] However, at his desire I have writ two wordes by him to

---

[1] 14/25 Aug.   [2] The capitulation is printed in Lamberty, iv. 91-5.
[3] Letter 646.   [4] To bring Vaudémont over to the Allies. See p. 639.

Prince Eugene. As the winds have been at the east these three days, I hope you will quickly hear of Lord Rivers being landed. I send you inclosed a letter I have received from the Pensioner, and my answer.[1] I do not doubt but Mr. Secretary Harley or yourself will hear from Monsieur Buys, as the French are makeing aplications, I beleive, at Vienna, as well as at The Hague. You must be carefull what answere you make; for be asured, thay will not continue this warr much longer, and I am afraid in a very litle time we shall find that the Court of Vienna and 19 [Holland] are more desirous of quarelling with etch other then with 20 [France]. You will see by the inclosed letter from Prince Eugene,[2] that the Chevallier de Croissi is exchanged, so that you will move her Majesty that he may be sent into France. I must hear from the Duke of Savoye before I write to the other two.[3]

657. MARLBOROUGH *to the* DUCHESS   [*12/23 August 1706*]

Source: Blenheim MSS. E3.

Helchin August 23d 1706

I am extreame glad to find by yours of the 4 that you are in a corse of stele,[4] for I am very confident it is what will do you great good. Your willingness of quitting this world is unkind, for I should think the pains of death is nothing in consideration of the uneasiness on[e] has in taking the resolution of quitting forever what one loves and estimes in this world. You will know by this post that we are masters of Menin which I did not expect, nor had thay reason to do yett this six days. As to the battailes you mention, I beleive there will be one in Spain, but I do not think the Duke of Vandôme will venture itt here. We shall now very quickly see what Lord Rivers will be able to do. If it obliges the French to send troupes, thay must go from hence, for thay have drawn almost all thay had in Garmany hether. I thank you for the particular you have sent me of the building;[5] it is more particular then any I have had. I shall keep it in my pocket and read it more then once, which is all the satisfaction I can have in itt at this distance. We have excessive hotte and drye weather, which I am afraid will do hurt to the garden at Woodstock, which gives me more uneasiness then the great dust we have here. By this time you aught to have Lord Hallifax, who has promised to go with you into Oxfordshire. I beleive you will find his having been abroad will not make him lesse fond of England, nor of the Queen's government. What you write mee of 66 [Shrewsbury], a great part of itt proceeds from what has been lately given to 118 [Wharton], for I beleive he reconed

---

[1] 't Hoff, pp. 258–9, discussing the French peace offer.   [2] Untraced.

[3] French officers, prisoners of war, desiring to be exchanged. See above, p. 588.

[4] Iron used medicinally; chalybeate medicine, *O.E.D.* For a report of the Duchess's illness, see p. 638.

[5] Blenheim Palace.

that as his own, so that you may be sure [he] is not very well pleased with 90 [Marlborough] nor 91 [Godolphin]. However, I can't disaprove of the disposale of that place if it gives satisfaction to 118 [Wharton], for though he is capable of executing anything, yet there are many places that I can't wish in his hands.[1]

658. GODOLPHIN *to* MARLBOROUGH [*13 August 1706*]

Source: Blenheim MSS. A1–36.
Printed: Murray, iii. 125.

St James's 13 August 1706

Since my letter of yesterday from Windsor[2] I have received Mr. Stanhope's packett by Mr. Richards,[3] and at the same time, letters from the King of Spayn,[4] and from my Lord Peterborow,[5] by which one may see very plainly their misunderstandings have occasioned all this delay which has already proved so unfortunate, and may yett bee more soe. Upon the whole I am afraid that warr may draw into length, and consequently, unless succeed beyond expectation, wee shall have difficulty enough next winter to justifie that extraordinary expence.

127 [Peterborough] has written a volume to Mr. Secretary Hedges.[6] 'Tis a sort of a remonstrance against the King of Spayn and his ministers in the 1st place, and 2dly a complaint against all the orders and directions sent from hence, and as if he had not authority enough given him either at sea, or land. In a word he is both useless and grieving there, and is preparing to bee as troublesom here, whenever he is called home. Monsieur Vrybergh has given another memoriall very pressing that the Queen would please to recall her recommendation in favour of the Bishop of Osnaberg,[7] and another to desire that England and Holland may concert measures for sending a strong squadron to the West Indies. I suppose Mr. Secretary Harley will trouble you more particularly upon these 2 poynts,[8] and therfore I will say no more upon them, not being without suspence in my own mind till I see whether the French will attempt the relief of Menin, which by what I have heard since yesterday, I now think they will not, and that the Duke of Vendosme's chief aim is to place himself as, when that siege is over, to hinder the further progress of your army. However I shall be uneasy till I hear from you after the place is taken.

[1] See p. 641 n. 1.   [2] Untraced.   [3] See p. 645.
[4] 28 June/9 July, B.M., Add. MS. 28057, fols. 292–3.
[5] 2/13 July, B.M., Add. MS. 28057, fols. 296–7.   [6] Untraced.
[7] For the Münster controversy see p. 647 n. 4.
[8] Harley sent Marlborough copies of the memorials and the Queen's replies in his letter of 13 Aug. (Longleat, *Portland MSS.*, v, fols. 79–80, Harley's letter only). Concerning the second memorial he noted: 'I suppose that of the West Indies arose upon their hearing that the Queen had already ordered a squadron for that service.' The Dutch did not want to be deprived of any opportunity to share the spoils.

659. GODOLPHIN *to* MARLBOROUGH   [*15 August 1706*]

Source: Blenheim MSS. A1-36.
Printed: Coxe, ii. 97-8 (inc.).

Windsor 15 August 1706

Having had yesterday a long conversation with 116 [Somers] and 117 [Sunderland], where among other things much was said of the importance of passing the Union in the Parliament of Scotland, which is to meet the 19th of September, they seemed to think nothing ought to bee neglected in order to that end. And having been informed that Mr. Freeman [Marlborough] has at this time more power than ordinary with 485 [Argyle] they seemed desirous that Mr. Montgomery [Godolphin] might propose to him that he would use all his influence to perswade him return to 26 [Scotland] by letting him know the season of the year, was now so far spent, as to allow of it, that his expence in the jorney should bee born and that 486 [Queensberry] having been last year assisting to him there was now an opportunity of returning that compliment to the satisfaction and good of Mrs. Morley [the Queen]. Those were the chief arguments they suggested, and seemed to lay a great deal of weight upon them. In the meantime 486 [Queensberry] continues here full of unreasonable demands, which seem as much so to them, as they doe to 91 [Godolphin].[1]

Our fleet sayled last Sunday[2] with a fair wind which continued 3 days, but it is now contrary, and so extreamly strong that I am very much in pain for the transport ships. And the long delay of this expedition [the descent] may prove as unfortunate as that of the King of Spayn, in not advancing to Madrid. I have always been of your mind, that they should not have an alternative in their instructions, upon their going to sea. Yett I think the case may bee so farr altered now, that, if by their long delay they should find the difficulty of succeeding increase upon them, or that the affairs of Spayn should turn so as to need their assistance, I think it might bee of good use to know whether the States will like that their troops employed upon this expedition may accompany the Queen's to any attempt upon the coast or ports of Spayn on this side or even as farr as Cadiz itself.

I chidd Mr. Vryberghen soundly yesterday, for repeating his memoriall to the Queen about the Bishop of Munster.[3] He seems to mee as violent in the new party, as any man on the other side of the water.

Mr. Secretary Hedges tells mee, he is causing 127's [Peterborough] long letter to bee coppyed that he may send it to you. It is a sort of a two edged

---

[1] Argyle as High Commissioner and Queensberry as Privy Seal and the key government manager had pushed through the Scottish Parliament, the authorization to treat for a union the previous year. Argyle had left Scotland in the spring to join the army and Queensberry had been reinstated in his former post of High Commissioner, but Argyle's strong support was properly looked upon as essential and he returned to Scotland at this critical juncture. Trevelyan, ii. 257-62, 276.

[2] 11 Aug.   [3] See the preceding letter.

sword, first a remonstrance against 315 [King Charles] in terms as un-mannerly as unjust, and 2dly it is prepared to fall upon any body here that shall bee in his displeasure.

I shall not bee quite out of pain for the event of Menin till I have another letter from you. Though my opinion is the French will pretend to no more then to take such a camp as they hope may hinder your further progress, after that siege is over.

Monsieur Spanheim has taken leave with a good deal of uneasyness to himself, to all his family, and to everybody here. I fancy his master had no other motive for recalling him but to make way for the Queen to doe the same, which being now done, and Mr. Spanheim being very easy to the Queen and by his acquaintance and familiarity here more capable of doing service to his master in this Court, than anybody else, methinks it might bee no hard matter for you to find some means by some of the King of Prussia's officers to insinuate to his Majesty that Monsieur Spanheim's continuance in this Court for some time longer would bee very agreable to the Queen.[1]

660. MARLBOROUGH *to* GODOLPHIN   [15/26 August 1706]

Source: Blenheim MSS. A1-14.
Printed: Coxe, ii. 75-6 (inc.).

August 26, 1706

I have not had the happyness of any of yours since my last, and am very impatient to hear of the descent, so that I beg you will constantly let me have all the particulars you receive of that matter. I saw the garrison of Menin march out yesterday. Thay were near 4,500 men. The fear thay had of being made prisoners of warr made them give up the place five or six days sooner then in decensy thay aught to have done.

My brother will be tomorrow before Dendermont, and I hope the canon may fyer by Monday.[2] And if we have no rain, five or six days may make us masters of that place, which has always been thought unattackable. And in treuth, we should not have thought of it, but the extreordinary drouth makes us venture itt.[3] If we succeed at Dendermont, and can in time have more amunition from Holland, we shall then make the siege of Aith,[4] which will be a security to our winter quarters. Notwithstanding the Duke of Vandome's army, if wee could have been sure of having the necessarys for the siege of Ipers [Ypres], I beleive we should have undertaken it, for that place is very difficult to be relieved when the postes are once taken. But we can't expect the stores that are sent for in less then three weekes, so that we

---

[1] Spanheim remained until his death in 1710.
[2] 19/30 Aug.
[3] See p. 558 n. 3.
[4] Ath, a fortified town in southern Flanders, near the head of the Dender, at the junction of the two main branches.

should have consumed all the forage before we could have been able to have begune the attack. I give you the trouble of all this, that you may see that I should have prefered Ipres before Aeth. But the Dutch like Dendermont and Aeth much the best, so that I hope thay will not let us want amunition for them. By the letters we received yesterday from Italie, I find Comte Maffie feares Turin will be taken, which will give, in his opinion, new life to the French. The French say nothing of Spain, since those I sent you of the 5th of this month, so that I hope you will have received some good news by the way of Lisbon. The inclosed is a copie of a letter from Wratislaw.[1] I have sent the origenal to the Pensioner for his thoughts,[2] and should be glad to have yours by the next post. I have desired Mr. Secretary Harley to acquaint you with what I have write him concerning Lord Raby, so that I shall trouble you with repetition.[3]

661. MARLBOROUGH *to* GODOLPHIN   [*19/30 August 1706*]

Source: Blenheim MSS. A1-14.
Printed: Coxe, ii. 76; Churchill, ii. 144 (inc.).

Helchin August 30th 1706

Since my last[4] I have had the favour of three of yours, of the 7th,[5] 12,[6] and 13th.[7] 328 [Elector of Bavaria] has convinced me that he is willing to do every thing, being sensible that he is neglected and cheated, but 313 [King of France] has taken so just measures that he has nothing in his power, but that of being a tool to them. He would insinuat to mee the same proposition of peace as that which I sent you over some postes ago, that was sent me from The Hague.[8] The same man [Sensanders] that is imployed by 328 [Elector of Bavaria] has promised that I shall know what answere is given by 19 [Holland]. The enclosed is what I have received from 365 [Heinsius].[9] You will by itt judge the temper thay are in, in 19 [Holland], since 365 [Heinsius] is so reserved a man, that he always endeavors to make the best of every thing. I am asured that it is very publickly said at 21 [The Hague], that 20 [France] is reduced to what it aught to be, and that if it should be carryed further, it would serve only to make England greater then it aught to be. In short, I am afraid our best allyes are very fond of a peace, and that thay would ingage 17 [England] to quarell with 318 [the Emperor], for to have a

---

[1] 31 July/11 Aug., untraced; reply, 21 Aug./1 Sept., Murray, iii. 113-14. An offer to send a representative to Marlborough to regulate matters for the next year. Marlborough accepted.

[2] 't Hoff, p. 262; reply, 17/28 Aug., ibid., p. 263.

[3] See p. 647 n. 6.   [4] The preceding letter.   [5] Letter 653.

[6] Untraced.   [7] Letter 658.   [8] See pp. 636, 645 n. 1.

[9] 17/28 Aug., 't Hoff, p. 263, about Prince Lewis and the unwillingness of the other German princes to have their troops to serve under him. The Emperor has been equally remiss and Marlborough should accept the Emperor's offer to confer with his representative about the next campaign.

pretext to come att 5 [peace]. If 366 [Buys] has write concerning 5 [peace], I should be glad to have a copie of the letter, and answer.[1] I agree with you that the business of 22 [Spain] is like to prove very troublesome, and that great part of it is owing to the unaccountable conduct of 127 [Peterborough], and I am afraid all the extravagances in the world may be expected from him. By the enclosed letter from Prince Eugene, I am in pain for Turin. Du Mee[2] the engenier sends me word that he finds much more watter at Dendermont then he expected. I intend to go there in 3 or four days, and then I shal be able to send you the certainty of what we may expect.

I did in a former letter beg her Majesty's favour for Lord Sunderland, and I should be obliged to you in making it easy, as well as putting the Queen in mind of bring[ing] him into her Service. I am very well assured of his zeal, and that he will behave himself as he aught to do.[3] The Duke of Vandôme pretends he shall not have all his troupes together til the tenth of the next month. I am of opinion he will not then venture anything.

662. MARLBOROUGH *to the* DUCHESS   [*19/30 August 1706*]

Source: Blenheim MSS. E3.
Printed: *Private Correspondence*, i. 64–5.

Helchin August 30th 1706

I am to thank you for three of your dear letters, of the 8th, 9, and 13th. I did in my letter of yesterday[4] by Mr. Bridges answere what you write concerning 117 [Sunderland] and 125 [Hedges]. It will not be with you so soon as this, but I thought it a saffer way. What 91 [Godolphin] write to me concerning 360 [Hill],[5] was that he aprehended somebody else would recomend him to be imployed in the place of 363 [Raby], and therfore he was desirous that 362 [Howe] might be named. I agree intierly with your opinion that 360 [Hill] must never be employed unless on[e] is contented to be cheated, for he has both inclinations and capacity to do itt. I find by your letter that you mistake the reason of my not being fond of having 117 [Sunderland] Secretary. However, I have by this post write as 91 [Godolphin] desired,[6] for when I have given my opinion, and my friends are of another mind, I had much rather be governed then govern, by which youmor [humour] I have in the corse of my life found a great deal of ease. I have already lett you know that Cadogan is at liberty. [In] the letter in which you mention him, there are so very kind expressions to me, of which I am so sensible, that I would venture ten thousand lives to make a gratful return. In short my dear soull, if I could begine my life againe, I would endeavour every

---

[1] For Buys's letter, 16/27 Aug., see p. 660.
[2] Lucas du Mée in the service of the Dutch.
[3] Marlborough put this statement in at the request of Godolphin. See p. 632.
[4] Untraced.   [5] p. 646.   [6] See the preceding.

hour of itt to oblige you. But as we can't recal what is passed, forgett my imperfections, and as God has been pleased to blesse me, I do not doubt but he will reward mee with giving me some yeares to end my days with you. And if that may bee with quietness and kindness, I shall bee much happyer then I have ever yett been.

663. MARLBOROUGH *to* GODOLPHIN
[*21 August/1 September 1706*]

Printed: Coxe, ii. 76 (inc.).
Source: Blenheim MSS. A1-14.

[Helchin] September 1st 1706

I have had this morning the favour of yours of the 15th[1] of the last month. I am forced to write this day, though the post is not till tomorrow night, being to go early tomorrow morning to Dendermonde, where our ingeniers, by the raising of the watter, finds more difficulty then thay expected. I hope by my nexte to lett you know that thay have overcome the difficultys, for that place would be very troublesome, it being in the midest of our winter quarters. 485 [Argyll] is with the troupes that are stile at Menin, so that I can't speak to him til my return, which I think will be Saturday.[2] You may assure 116 [Somers] and 117 [Sunderland] that I shall do my best to persuaid him, but I beleive it is in nobody's power to be answerable for his going to 26 [Scotland]; for he is so very fikle, that should he go with a resolution from hence to go thether, it is great odds, but his mind would change on the road. You judge very right as to 350 [Vrijberghen], for he is intierly of the new party, which are now more eager for a peace then ever; and I am afraid thay will very spedily have a new pretext for itt, which is, and I have it from good hands, that the King of Sweeden is resolved to march into Saxony, which you know must have an ill consequence. Mr. Secretary has sent me 127 [Peterborough] long letter. By that and what I have heard, ther is no ill but what may be expected from him. I am told that he has managed the publick mony so very extravagantly, that it will be wholly impossible for him to passe his accounts, and that he did not give the King of Spain one shilling all the last winter. When this comes to be known, I beleive he will find it a very difficult matter to justefie himself in the opinion of the nation. I shall write by the next post to Berlin, and hope to prevaile with them for the stay of Monsieur Spanheim. I shall be very impatient for your next letters, for if you should by that time hear nothing of Lord Rivers, I should then hope he were happyly landed.

[1] Letter 659.   [2] 24 Aug./4 Sept.

664. GODOLPHIN *to* MARLBOROUGH   [*23 August 1706*]

Source: Blenheim MSS. A1-36.

Windsor Fryday 23d of August 1706

This day there are 3 posts due from Holland. I am much afraid they will not bring us good news when they come, because the weather is so fair, that if they had any good to send us, it would make a shift to find the way over though the wind has not been favorable.

Since my last letter to you from this place,[1] my Lord Halifax has been here and upon presenting to the Queen the letters he brought from Hannover, he acquainted her Majesty with the desire of that court to have an English title for the Electoral Prince. She was not very easy at the first proposall of it in your letter,[2] apprehending it might bee made a farther handle for the invitation.[3] But I have endeavored to lett her see, that it must rather have a quite contrary effect, and furnish her servants with a strong argument against it. So she has promised to give directions in it imediatly.

I wish I could tell you that Mr. Montgomery [Godolphin] had succeeded as well in the matter I mentioned to you in my last.[4] But there still continues a reluctancy in that matter which is extreamly unaccountable after all that has been done, and I might add, all that has been sayd upon that occasion. But I dare not troble you with enlarging upon this subject,[5] for fear of infecting you, with some part of my spleen.

Letters are come from Sir Cloudesly Shovell without any objection considerable to the new directions sent him to Torbay.[6]

665. MARLBOROUGH *to* GODOLPHIN

[*23 August/3 September 1706*]

Source: Blenheim MSS. A1-14.

from before Dendermond September 3, 1706

I write to you on the 1st[7] from the army, beleiving I should not have an opertunity of writting from hence. I have found everything here backwarder

---

[1] 20 Aug. Untraced. See p. 658.   [2] Letter 638.

[3] For the Electress Sophia or a member of her family to reside in England.

[4] 20 Aug., untraced.

[5] The problem of persuading the Queen to bring Sunderland into the Cabinet in place of Hedges. In his letter of the 20th Godolphin told Marlborough that he had offered his resignation to the Queen (in writing?) because she would not follow his advice. This can be deduced from her reply on 23 Aug. to Godolphin, offering to take Sunderland into the Cabinet with a pension until a post became vacant. B.M., Add. MS. 56105L. Godolphin replied the next day in terms of resigned submission. Coxe. ii. 138. The Queen wrote to him again in the same vein on 30 Aug. Ibid. 136-8.

[6] The fleet with the troops for the descent was forced to put into Torbay because of adverse winds on 15 Aug., having left Portsmouth on 10 Aug. On the advice of the general officers (p. 658), new instructions were sent to the commander, Earl Rivers, to proceed instead to Seville. See Rivers's correspondence with Godolphin, Hedges, and Harley in H. M. C., *Bath MSS.*, i. 89 et seq.

[7] Letter 663.

then I expected. However, I hope the great drough will inable us to overcome all the difficultys. I shall stay two days longer then I first intended. I have read the long letter of 127 [Peterborough] a second time, and I think you should not neglect this opertunity of making 51 [Hedges] give such an answere, as may in its due time be produced to 13 [Parliament]; for though the letter of 127 [Peterborough] is very extravagant, and such a one as 90 [Marlborough] would be ashamed to produce, yett you may depend of itt, that at the time 127 [Peterborough] write it, he intended it for 13 [Parliament]. It is a misfortune to have to do with so ill a man, but he having showen his inclinations, makes it the easier to take such measures as may expose him. Mr. Crow and Mr. Richardes,[1] which are the two men he refers to, if thay be well handled by Mr. Secretary Harley and Sir Charles Hedges, I should think by what thay have said to me, thay would say enough to shoe that he has been the occasion of the greatest part of the ill measures taken in that country. The first is an admirer of 315 [King Charles], and the last told me that he beleived that the resolution taken by 315 [King Charles] to go to Arragon was occasioned by a letter write to him from 127 [Peterborough], in which he acquainted him that he wanted everything, so that he could not promis that the troupes could be in a condition to advance towards Madrid. I think somthing should be said to Richardes that might give him occasion of saying it to the two Secretarys, for what passed between us was in privat.

666. MARLBOROUGH *to* GODOLPHIN

[*27 August/7 September 1706*]

Source: Blenheim MSS. A1-14.
Printed: Coxe, ii. 77.

Audnar September 7th 1706

The express that carryed the good news to the States of our being masters of Dendermond,[2] was dispatched in such hast, that I could not write to you. I beleive the King of France will be a good deal surprised when he shall hear that the garrison has been obliged to surrender themselves prisoners of warr. For upon his being told that preparations were making for the siege of Dendermonde, he said thay must have an army of ducks to take itt. The truth is, God has blessed us with a very extreordinary season. I do not give myself the honour of troubling the Queen with a letter, so that you will give my duty to her and the Prince, and acquaint them with this good success, which makes it the more remarkable is that this place was never before taken, though once formerly besieged by the French, and the King himself with the army.[3] I hope in seven or eight days, we shall have in this town all the canon

---

[1] John Richards.   [2] 25 Aug./5 Sept., Murray, iii. 118.
[3] In 1667. See p. 558 n. 3.

and amunition that is necessary for the siege of Ath. I should think if you have not already, you should now acquaint the Dutch envoye that her Majesty has derected Mr. Stepney to come to the army, so that he may act with their deputys at Bruxelles in what may be for the publick good, she having commanded me to return to England as soon as the campagne shall be at an end. As Mr. Stepney is to be joyned to me in that commission, so he will have order to follow the derections I shall leave with him. You must also lett him see that this was absolutely necessary, in my absance, so that there might be no opertunity lost for the setling of the Barier with King Charles the 3d. I am the more tedious on this subject, being very sure that the Dutch will not like his coming.

I dine this day at the army.

667. MARLBOROUGH *to* GODOLPHIN

[*29 August/9 September 1706*]

Source: Blenheim MSS. A1-14.
Printed: Coxe, ii. 76-7, 141 (inc.).

Villaine[1] September 9th 1706

I have this morning had the favour of your two letters of the 20[2] and 23d[3] of the last month. I am very sorry to see that the thoughts of the descent is layde aside, for I can't but beleive that if the generall officers could have had a good opinion of the undertaking, but that thay must have succeded. But since thay are of another opinion, it would have been not at al advisable to have given them orders contrary to their opinions. I wish with all my heart thay may succed in what you have now derected. I must on this occasion obsarve to you that the Queen will have three comanders in chief in one kingdome, which can't be good for the Service.[4] In yours of the 20th you say it would be an ease to you to retier from business, the waite of which you can not bare if you are not allowed some assistance. I hope 83 [the Queen] will do everything for your ease but that of parting with you, in which, should you have a serious thought, you could not justefie to God nor man; for without flattery, as England is devided, there is nobody could execut your place with success.

In yours of the 23d you were afraid that if there were any good news from this country, it would have found the way over, whereas you had three packets due. When thay come to you, you wil find everything you could expect from hence. That of Dendermonde, of making them prisoners of warr, was more then was reasonable, but that I saw them in a consternation. That place could never have been taken but by the hand of God, which gave

---

[1] Velaines, 10 kilometres south-east of Helchin and an equal distance north-east of Tournai.
[2] Untraced.   [3] Letter 664.   [4] Peterborough, Rivers, and Galway in Spain.

us seven weekes without any rain. The rains begane the next day after wee had possession, and continued til this evening. We are expecting the news of a battaile between Prince Eugene and the Duke of Orleance.[1]

I have not offered the Duke of Argile the expences he should be at in his jorny,[2] but have promised him that as soon as comes to London, he and Brigadier Web, which is over [our] eldest brigadier in this country, should have comissions for major generals, which I beg her Majesty will aprove of, and that the comission may be ready for him at his first coming, so that he may not have an excuse for staying.[3] He has behaved himself all this campagne with great willingness and corage, so that if the Queen will be pleased to tel him, that she takes it very kindly, his going to Scotland at this time, and that she is very glad of his coming home safe after so much danger, this will please him, and you must not let him stay. If you aprove of the enclosed letter,[4] you will be pleased to seal it and send it to him.

668. MARLBOROUGH *to the* DUCHESS
[*29 August/9 September 1706*]

Source: Blenheim MSS. E4.
Printed: Coxe, ii. 140–1 (inc.).

. . .[5] he has had opertunitys by his . . . this summer to know thet I employe all my time in doing what I think is for the publick good and honour of the nation. I beleive 362 [Howe] near friend[6] is very sincere, but I do not laye much waite on their intelligence. In the first place, there is good reason to hope that 83 [the Queen] will live longer then you or I, and when 322 [the Elector of Hanover] must come upon the stage, his temper is such that he will employe such as he thinkes will be of . . .

What you write me concerning 83 [the Queen] and 91 [Godolphin] gives me a great deal of trouble, for should the consequences be what you say, that there is no relying upon 8 [the Tories], and that 14 [the Whigs] will be out of humor, it must end in confusion, which will have the consequence of 19 [Holland] making 5 [peace] with 20 [France]. I am afraid this is what will gratefie to[o] many of 8 [the Tories] party, but I can see no advantage that can come to 14 [the Whigs] by the ruin of 91 [Godolphin], so that I hope thay are to[o] wise a people to expose themselves and the libertys of Europe, because some things are not done with a good grace.[7] I would not have you

---

[1] Philippe II, duc d'Orléans (1674–1723); Regent of France 1715–22; son of Philippe I, brother of Louis XIV; commander of the French troops in Spain 1707–9.
[2] See p. 651.
[3] Their commissions with several others were backdated to 1 June.
[4] Untraced. Cf. letter 671.
[5] This letter has been mutilated and the dots indicate missing portions.
[6] His wife who visited England at this time.   [7] The appointment of Sunderland.

mistake me, for as farr as it is in my power, for the sake of my country and the intirest of 83 [the Queen], for whome had I a thousand lives I would venture them all, I would have everything that is reasonable done to satisfie 14 [the Whigs], of which I think 91 [Godolphin] is the best judge. . . . If it were not for my duty to 83 [the Queen], and my friendshipe to 91 [Godolphin], I should beg that somebody else might execute my office. Not that I take anything ill, but that the weight is to[o] great for me, for I dayly find a decay in my memorie. Whatever may be told you of my lookes, you will find the greatest part of my hair gray, but I think I am somthing fatter.

669. GODOLPHIN *to* MARLBOROUGH   [*30 August 1706*]

Source: Blenheim MSS. A1-36.

St Albans 30 August 1706

I came thither yesterday from my Lord Wharton's place,[1] and this morning have had the satisfaction to receive the favour of your letters of the 1st and 3d[2] of September in both which you seem to bee full of expectations of mischief from 127 [Peterborough]. But I hope all care will bee taken to prevent it, and I think besides he has so managed those affairs that it will not bee in his power to doe half that hurt here, as where he has been.

I am glad you mention nothing in your letters of Spayn, because it is a sign they have nothing from thence to bragg of in France.

By the last post[3] I sent you a coppy of the letter I had from 366 [Buys] concerning 5 [peace],[4] and by the next I will send you a coppy of the answer I design to send him by that post.[5] I have shown both his letter and the answer to it to 115 [Halifax], 116 [Somers] and 117 [Sunderland] who have all told mee they think the answer is right.

The contrary winds will not yett suffer our fleet to proceed. By our last letters from Sir John Leak he was with his squadron before Alicant in hopes of specialy reducing that place, and by those from the King of Spayn of the 24th of July, he was to march that day to joyn my Lord Gallway, which agrees in time with the French accounts of their junction.

I have a letter from Mr. Stanyan[6] which gives a hopefull prospect for Turin. I wish it may bee other ways confirmed.

Not having seen Mrs. Morley [the Queen] since my last, I can add nothing to what I said of her in that letter. But I cannot conclude my letter from

---

[1] Wimbledon, Bucks.   [2] Letters 663, 665.
[3] 27 Aug. Lost in the post. See pp. 668, 677.
[4] 16/27 Aug. Draft in Rijksarchief, AANW 1865 BXIV A, fols. 53-4. Summary in Geikie, p. 62, n. 2. The main point was that Charles III was to have Spain; Philip V would receive Naples and Sicily.
[5] See letter 672.
[6] Abraham Stanyan (1669?-1732), English envoy to the Swiss cantons, 1705-9.

hence without telling you that if you were here, you could not avoyd taking delight in the work of your own hands, for this garden is really a charming thing.

670. GODOLPHIN *to the* DUCHESS   [*1 September 1706*]

Source: Blenheim MSS. E20.
Printed: *Private Correspondence*, i. 83–5.

Windsor Sunday night

According to your commands I gave your letter last [night] to Mrs. Morley [the Queen], and as she was going to putt it in her pockett, I told her that you had made mee promise to beg of her to read it before I went out of the room. She did so, and then sayd she believed you had mistaken some words at the latter end of the former letter, which she seemed to think had a different sense from that which I had then given her from you. But because you desired I might see it, she would look for it and give it mee, which she did, and desired mee to return it to her today. I come now from giving it back into her hands, and I think I have convinced her that her complaint was grounded upon her having misapprehended the sence of your letter, by not reading it right; that is to say by reading the word *notion* for the word *nation*.

To explain this the more clearly to you, I send you a coppy of the conclusion of your first letter to her, taken as far back as I thought was enough to show the plain sence and meaning of your letter. At the same time I must own that in your originall letter that word *notion* was not soe distinctly written, but that one might as naturally read it *nation*, if the sence of 2 or 3 lines together before, did not fully explain your meaning.[1]

As to the mayn poynt, she has only told mee that she had written a letter to mee, as she said she would, to explain her difficultys, but she must write it out faire before she could give it mee.[2] I shall wait upon her again tomorrow before I come to London, in hopes to have it. The Duke of Shrewsbury has written to Mr. Secretary Hedges, to ask leave for Monsieur de Croissy who is newly exchanged to carry some horses into France with him. I mention this only as a mark of my being entirely out of his favour, or else he would have written to mee sooner than to an absolute stranger, as the other is to him; but I am apt to think, I have not very long to bee the mark of everybody's displeasure.

[1] This dispute was over a misreading of a letter the Duchess had written to the Queen about appointing Sunderland to Hedges's place as Secretary of State (n.d., Coxe, ii. 151–2). The Queen mistook the word 'notion' for 'nation' at the close and taking great offence refused to answer. The Duchess wrote again on 30 Aug. (Coxe, ii. 152–3) and this is the letter which Godolphin delivered. The Queen finally replied to the Duchess on 6 Sept. (Coxe, ii. 154–5).

[2] 30 Aug., Coxe, ii. 136–8.

671. MARLBOROUGH *to* GODOLPHIN   [*1/12 September 1706*]

Source: B.M., Add. MS. 54225, n. f.
Notice: Leeds Sale Catalogue, No. 647.

Villaine September 12th 1706

Though the Duke of Argile has promised me to make hast for England, I believe mine tomorrow will be with you sooner then this. I have told my Lord Argile that you will tel him, on which Secretary[1] he must call for his commission of major generall. He has really behaved himselve extreamly well this campagne, so that I beg both you, and the Queen will make him your compliments. I have given him Stringer's[2] Redgement, and am indeavoring with the province of Holland to get his for my Lord Tillebarden,[3] which I hope may be an ease to the Queen, for he has nothing from his father.

I am ever yours

Marlborough

672. GODOLPHIN *to* MARLBOROUGH   [*2 September 1706*]

Source: Blenheim MSS. A1-36.
Printed: Coxe, ii. 98, 113-14.

Windsor September 2d 1706

I have no letter of yours to acknowledg since my last to you from St. Albans,[4] and the wind is so high and blustring that I scarce hope to have any before the post goes out tomorrow.

I now send you a coppy of the answer to 366 [Buys] from Mr. Secretary Harley and myself.[5] I hope it will have your approbation, and I am pretty sure, it is what the generality of people that one can speak with here, will think very reasonable for us to insist upon. If the very first point bee agreed to, that before any formall stepp bee made towards 5 [peace] both 17 [England] and 19 [Holland] shall engage to warrant whatsoever shall bee concluded upon that occasion, I shall not have much doubt but the rest will follow to our satisfaction.

I beg leave only to add, that I don't see how this first poynt can bee refused with any tolerable honesty or sincerity, and indeed, unless 19 [Holland] bee absolutely resolved to throw off the masque, declare themselves open friends to 20 [France], and not under any obligations to keep farther measures with 83 [the Queen]. This I take to bee no easy task, and therfore I

---

[1] Of State.

[2] Thomas Stringer (died 1706), M.P. 1698-1706; served since 1690; colonel, newly raised regiment of foot, 1702; died in the Low Countries shortly before this date.

[3] A Scottish regiment in Dutch pay which Argyle had commanded since 1702. Tullibardine was made the colonel, 16/27 Nov. 1706.

[4] Letter 669.   [5] Letter 672A.

am humbly of opinion, that to speak plain to them now, is the best way to divert them from attempting it. For the more complaisance is shown them, and the more wee give way to them, it is both their nature and their practice to bee the more assuming.

I trouble you also with a long letter from the King of Spayn.[1] In my answer to it, I have not been able to forbear complaining of his inexcusable delays in not advancing sooner towards Madrid, though I can agree with you that 127's [Peterborough] humour may have given a handle to his ministers to prevail with him against his own interest, from a hope they had of squeezing the people of Arragon as they had before done those at Catalonia. But they have missd their aim in it, as I find by Collonel Stanhop's letter[2] which I also send you. And in a word 127's [Peterborough] extravagance alone could not have hurt us if those Germans had not outdone him both in folly, and everything that is worse.

I write to my Lord Gallway by this post to lett him know how Lord River's expedition is now turned, that he may turn his thoughts the better how to contribute, as farr as it may bee in his power, towards the success of it.

If there bee any occasion, I shall trouble with more, tomorrow from London.

672A. GODOLPHIN *to* BUYS   [*3 September 1706*]

Source: Rijksarchief, AANW 1865 B XIV A, fols. 108–15.

St. James's September 3d 1706

Having comunicated your letter and the plan contained in it to Mr. Secretary Harley and very deliberately considered the same with him, I think myself obliged, in complyance with your desires, to send you our thoughts, both as to the time of treating of a peace with France in generall, and also as to the particulars offered by France, in the plan which you have been pleased to comunicate to us.

Before I mention anything upon the scheme of your letter, I must putt you in mind, that the chief security for preserving those conditions the Allyes shall obtain from France, is the preserving of the Allyance, especially between England and the States, for a just and mutuall warrant of mayntaining the particulars of such a treaty, and the sooner this were sett on foot, it would bee so much the better, and not an improbable way to procure more reasonable terms from France.

---

[1] 13/24 July, in B.M. 28057, fols. 307–8, explaining the disputes over the command of his army, how Peterborough had given way to Galway because of the jealousy of das Minas. The King commended Peterborough highly as well as Stanhope, and indicated his readiness to negotiate a treaty to advance the (commercial) interests of England (cf. p. 673).

[2] 13/24, 16/27 July, Mahon, appendix, pp. xxvi–xxviii.

And now to return to your letter, I shall give you plainly what wee both think thereupon, and will begin with the time.

Wee think the approaching winter may bee a proper time to treat with France but wee beg leave to represent to you, that to make any step towards a treaty in forme, till this campagne bee fully ended, must probably bee much to the disadvantage of the Allyes, for though you are intirely in the right, when you say that all events are in the hands of the divine providence, yett humanely speaking, with regard to the posture of our forces in all parts of Europe, where the warr is now going onn, there is no reason to imagine the affairs of the Allyes shall bee in a worse condition, than they are at present, but in a much better.

In Italie, though the season bee much advanced, our troops are not yett all come to act. Wee are but just entring (as it were) upon the successes which wee hope and expect as the fruit of a very great expence which the Allyes have made and England particularly, in furnishing Prince Eugene with an army to act offensivly, and with all the stores and equipage of warr that were necessary to make his endeavours successfull. And to come to a poynt upon this head, though the French should take Turin, wee shall still have a superiority in Italy, reckoning the troops of Hesse, and those with the Duke of Savoy, but if they are forced to raise the siege, thay lose their reputation in that part of the world, and run the hazard of losing their army also, as they did at Barcelona.

In Spayn, if for arguments sake, wee allow the affairs of that kingdome to bee in a ballancing condition, is it not reasonable to suppose that the fleet and forces now on their way thither, must necessarily turn the scale on the side of the Allyes?

As to the posture of affairs nearer home, it will bee very unnecessary to trouble you with any reasonings concerning them, but upon the whole, it seems to bee very plain, that France will find itself under a necessity of making better offers at the end of the campagne, than they doe now. And as to what is sayd that if their offers are not accepted immediatly they will not stand to them, this is yett a farther confirmation that they will still make better offers.

Besides, that whatever offers they make, they will not stand to them if any advantage happen to them even while a treaty is depending upon the foot of their own offers. All this seems to conclude that a treaty in form, ought not to bee begunn till the campagne bee over.

As to the particulars of the plan, upon the article which relates to the restoring of the Duke of Savoy, and the Elector of Bavaria to their severall countrys, you will give us leave to observe, that the Allyes being in a condition to expect and insist upon such a peace as shall not only give them present quiett but future security, it will bee necessary to keep the Allies in the same union and friendship after the peace, as during the warr.

In order to this end, it seems reasonable they should concern themselves so much for the Duke of Savoy whose firmness to the common cause and sufferings for it, have been very great as to stipulate on his behalf that he should not only bee restored to his own country, but have the full effect of his treaty with the Emperor, which brought him into the Allyance, and which has been ratifyed and confirmed by the Queen and the States Generall.

This is but justice and acting as our treatys oblige us. I will add this further consideration, that the increasing the Duke of Savoy's power and obliging him to keep hereafter firm to the intirest of the Allies, will bee a most effectuall method to ballance the power of France.

As to the restitution of the Electour of Bavaria, it must be remembred that Bavaria, and the upper Palatinat, are upon a different foot, and the Allies will certainly be concerned to have a due regard to the preserving of the Electour Palatin upon that country.

As to the article which relates to the Rhyn and to Alsace, without giving you the trouble to enlarge upon those particulars, it seems reasonable, in generall, that the Emperour and the Circles should have their satisfaction and security in the adjustment of them.

In like manner, the acknowledging the King of Prussia, and the Electour of Hannover in what has been promised by any treatys to any of the Allys, will without doubt bee sufficiently taken care of.

As to the article of Spayn, which you say is the mayn point. Wee must beg leave to repeat what wee have often sayd to you, when wee had the honour to see you here, that no good Englishman nor servant to the Queen, can advise the dismembring of the Spanish monarchy. And as to the difficulty upon France to make a peace, without somthing of this nature, for preserving the name of a king to the Duke of Anjou, he will always bee treated (its probable) in France as King of Spayn, and there is not so much difference betwixt a titular king of all Spayn and the Indies, and a reall king of Naples and Sicily only, as that it is likely the peace should break upon that poynt, when France seems to have so much need of it.

But what is of very great consequence, and deserves to bee well weighed, is, that should a son of France bee master of Naples and Sicily or one of them it would bee so great an addition of strength to the navall power of France, who have Marseilles and Thoulon so near, that not only the trade of the subjects of England and the States to the Levant, would bee precarious, but the Duke of Savoy and all Italie would therby bee under a necessity of taking their measures from France.

As to England, the Queen's title and the Protestant Succession in the House of Hannover being fully provided for, and the whole kingdome having by particular adresses, expressed their resentment of the affront in acknowledging and declaring the pretended Prince of Wales to bee King of England, and the Parliament having addressed to have satisfaction in that poynt, and a clause having been accordingly inserted in the Grand Alliance, it will not look very well if wee should bee treating with France while the pretended Prince of Wales is permitted to continue there.

In the next place, England must certainly insist, upon a treaty of commerce and in that treaty expect to bee relieved from the hardships and oppressions under which their trade with France has layn a long time, as also from severall incroachments and usurpations on the dominions of England in Newfoundland and Hudson's Bay, and elswhere in the Indies; but the former of these is of so great consequence to us, that it will bee strongly insisted upon. And since England has born so great a share in the expences of this warr, and may justly claim so great a part in the successes of it, the Queen not pretending to any conquest or increase of dominion for herself, wee humbly conceive her Majesty may bee very well intituled to insist for the future security and advantage of her subjects, that Dunquerk may bee razed and the harbour forever destroyed, and in this, wee cannot doubt of your concurrence, since that place is equally pernicious to the trade both of Holland and England.

As to the States Generall, wee fully agree they should have a treaty of commerce to their own satisfaction and procure an addition to the dominions of King Charles the 3d in the Low Countrys for a Barriere to the full extent of what they shall judg necessary for their future security.

Lastly as for Portugall, wee are humbly of opinion it will bee for the honour and interest of the Allies, that the King of Portugall as well as the Duke of Savoy should have the full effect of his treaty.

[P.S.] I ask pardon for my ill writing not being willing to trust another hand.

673. MARLBOROUGH *to* GODOLPHIN   [2/13 September 1706]

Source: Blenheim MSS. A1-14.

Villaine September 13th 1706

Wee leave this camp tomorrow. Monsieur Auverkerk marches with 40 battalions and 30 squadrons for the siege of Ath, and I shal cover it with the rest of the army. Wee have all the reason imaginable by the silence of the French to expect good news from Italie. The marchants of Lille and Tournay say that the siege of Turin is raised. The news from Spain by the way of France is not so favourable, for thay think thay shall be able to oblige King Charles to take his winter quarters in Arragon, Vallance, and Catalona, by which thay may make that warr very chargable to England. For it is certaine you will have very litle assistance from the Dutch, who are at this time more desirous of quarelling with the Emperor for the bishoprick of Monster, then for carying on the warr against France. I send you part of the *Paris Gazet*[1] that you may see what thay say of Lord Pitterborough. It is certaine for the good of the Service, there aught to be orders given before the opening of the next camp[ain], that there may be no disputes as to the command. I had a letter two days ago from Prince Lewis,[2] by which I see the Emperor has at last given possitive orders for the Garman army to passe the Rhin, which will be excuted by Velt Marshal Dungen, for Prince Lewis will stay at the watters.

674. MARLBOROUGH *to the* DUCHESS   [*2/13 September 1706*]

Source: Blenheim MSS. E3.
Printed: *Private Correspondence*, i. 52–3 (inc.), as part of letter of 10 June.

Velaine September 13th 1706

I have not had the happyness of any of yours since my last. I hope in my next to lett you know that we have invested Ath, which place is very necessary for the covering our winter quarters in Braband. Our not being able to prosecute the designe of the descent, I beleive vexes me more then anybody else, for I was always more persuaded then any other body, that the descent would have given more trouble to the King of France then anything we could undertake; but since there is an end of that project, we must take our measures for the carrying on of the warr for the next campagne, if we will bring the French to such a peace, as that we may injoye quiet for the rest of our days. By the silence of the French we have reason to beleive that Turin is releived, which will be a great blow to them. The affaires of Spain are so managed that we fear it will turn to such a warr as is now in Polland,[3] which must be very chargable to England, for Holland will chican so as to b[e]ar as litle part as is possible of itt. I do not write to 117 [Sunderland]. You will let him know my thoughts as to these points, which aught to be considered before the opening of the Parliament. I am to have a sett of coach horses from the Elector of Hanover. Thay are to meet me at The Hague, and I would bring them over or keep them here as you shall think best, so that you will let me have your opinion. I am told of a sute of hangings that is at Antwerp that may be baught for eightien hundred pounds, and that thay are worth much more. Would you have mee bye them? Thay have neither silver nor gold in them, nor were ever used. Thay were bespoke by the late King.[4]

---

[1] Untraced.   [2] 27 Aug./7 Sept., Blenheim MSS. A1–42; copy, A2–16.
[3] See the following letter.
[4] Marlborough received the information from Halifax who wrote to him from The Hague, on 11 Aug.: 'At Antwerp and saw . . . a mighty fine set of tapestry hangings which are said to be bespoke by the King at 36gs an ell. Nothing can be nobler, and [they] may be had very cheap for few people can use them. I send your Grace the measures, which perhaps you will transmit to Woodstock. Enclosed is a list of the pieces, ten in all' (Blenheim MSS. A1–46). Marlborough did not buy them.

675. MARLBOROUGH *to* GODOLPHIN   [*5/16 September 1706*]

Source: Blenheim MSS. A1-14.
Printed: Coxe, ii. 141-2 (inc.).

Gramets September 16, 1706

I have had the favour of yours of the 30[1] from St. Albans, and am very much
concerned that those of the 27 are lost, since you tel me you had in that
given me an account of a conversation you had with Mrs. Morley [the
Queen]. 114 [Lady Marlborough] letter of the 28 which mentions that
conversasion has very much allarmed 90 [Marlborough]; for without
flatterie, he is possetivly of the opinion that should 91 [Godolphin] quit the
service of 83 [the Queen], he would not only disturb the affaires of 17
[England], but also ruin the libertys of Europ; so that I beg you to conjure
91 [Godolphin] not to have a thought of quitting til we have obtained a good
peace, and then I hope 83 [the Queen] interest may be so well setled, that
she may allow of 91 [Godolphin] and 90 [Marlborough] living quietly.
But as the affaires of Europe, and that of 83 [the Queen] in perticular, are at
this time, I think both 91 [Godolphin] and 90 [Marlborough] are both in
consience and honour bound to undergo all the daingers and trouble that is
possible, to bring this warr to a happy end, which I think must be after the
next campagne, if we can agree to carry it on with vigor.

Wee have not as yett any perticulars of what has passed at Turin, but we
may be assured by the French silence, that thay are not pleased.

I am afraid this march of the King of Sweden will strenghen the party in
19 [Holland] that are already but to[o] forward for 5 [peace]. I beg you will
not be to[o] hasty in joyning with 19 [Holland] if thay should presse you to the
making any harsh declaration on this march, for though this King is very
much in the wrong, we must consider his humor, and do al that is possible
to keep him from making an allyance with France, which his ministers are
but to[o] much inclined too.[2]

I shall be very uneasy til I hear from you that everything is easy between
Mrs. Morley [the Queen] and yourself, for without that, I shall have no
heart to act in anything, being sure that all things must go to distruction.

---

[1] Letter 669.

[2] Charles XII of Sweden had deposed Augustus, Elector of Saxony, as King of Poland and had
forced the Polish nobility to recognize his candidate Stanislaus instead. The Czar supported Augustus, and when Augustus marched to join forces with him Charles XII invaded Saxony (at the
beginning of September) to force Augustus to submit.

676. MARLBOROUGH *to the* DUCHESS   [*5/16 September 1706*]

Source: Blenheim MSS. E4.
Printed: *Private Correspondence*, i. 69–70.

[Grandmetz]

...[1] confide. .... [I hope] they will let us finish this siege of Ath very quietly, for this army and that of the siege are not above four milles from etch other, so that if there were occasion we could joine. It were to be wished the faire weather had continued a little longer; for as we are to draw the canon for the siege about ...

and I do asure you there is nothing I so much long for in this world, as the blessing of living quietly with you at Woodstock, and that 91 [Godolphin] might be with us. But as to what you say of his quitting, it is wholly impossible, unless it be resolved that everything must go ill abroad as well as at home; for without flatterie his reputation is so great in all courts as well as at home, that such a step would go a great way with Holland in particular, to make their peace with France, which at this time must be fatal to the libertys of Europe. But if we can agree upon carrying on the warr this next yeare with vigor, I no ways doubt but we should have such peace, as that we might end the rest of our days in quietness, and the Queen be justly and gratfully acknowlidged by all the Allyes, as the protectress of their libertys. ....

laufe at him. We have as yet no perticulars of what has passed at Turin,[2] but we may be very sure it has been to our advantage, or the French would before now have acquainted us. I do no ways doubt of my having his Grace of Buckinghamshire's wishes, but I should hope his wealth should make him not wish this army beaten.

677. GODOLPHIN *to* MARLBOROUGH   [*6 September 1706*]

Source: Blenheim MSS. A1-36.

Windsor 6 September 1706

In my letter of the last post from London,[3] I sent you the coppy of what was agreed to bee written to Mr. Buys, and also a letter I had newly received from the King of Spayn, which latter I beg of you to return mee by the 1st opportunity. I ought to have desired this of you by the last post, but I had so many oppressions upon mee that I forgott itt.

Wee have now three posts due from you, and wee wish for them with the more impatience, because wee want some good news from abroad, to keep upp our spiritts. For wee have nothing to entertain you with from hence, but what

---

[1] The letter is mutilated. The dots indicate the portions cut away.
[2] Turin was relieved by Prince Eugene on 27 Aug./7 Sept.
[3] 3 Sept. Untraced. Buys's letter was sent with letter 672.

is intirely disagreable, and the contrary winds wee have had for 6 weeks together, disappoint, or at best, delay all our measures [the descent], which is very distracting.

I wish wee may soon hear anything good from abroad to ballance those complaints but I confess to you, I expect little good from any of 19's [Holland] proceedings, and I have more hopes from Italy and even from Spayn itself than from them. I wish with all my heart I may prove mistaken in this notion.

I can't avoyd to send you the enclosed[1] which I received in a letter to myself, from Mr. d'Aligre. I see by my letter he is extreamly pressing for leave to goe into France, and I believe I need not observe to you, that of al the prisoners that are in England, hee is the last who ought to have it granted because of his particular influence upon 5 [peace].[2]

When one can write nothing more pleasing than I doe, the sooner one releases you the better.

678. GODOLPHIN *to the* DUCHESS   [*7 September 1706*]

Source: Blenheim MSS. E20.

Windsor Saturday 7th at noon

If there bee no opportunity of sending this letter to London today, I wil send one to you on purpose with it tomorrow, though I can tell you nothing but what is disagreable.

By the account I have from 91 [Godolphin], hee letts mee see that upon his continuing as he had done before to press the affaire of 117 [Sunderland], and to make use of all the arguments with which he could enforce what he sayd, he found however it had no sort of effect but to disturb and grieve 83 [the Queen], who after having again repeated the arguments used in Mrs. Morley's [the Queen] letter,[3] and percieving that they made very little impression upon 91 [Godolphin], burst into a passion of weeping, and sayd it was plain 83 [the Queen] was to bee miserable as long as they lived, whatever they did. This 91 [Godolphin] owned to mee was grievously uneasy to him. Yett not saying anything to depart from his poynt, 83 [the Queen] beged not to bee pressed farther upon it till she heard from Mr. Freeman [Marlborough], in answer to a letter she had written to him,[4] upon her being first spoken to of this affair by 91 [Godolphin]. To this 91 [Godolphin] says he seemed to submit, not knowing indeed how to bee otherwise, hoping that answer might

---

[1] Untraced.
[2] He had carried a peace offer from France to Marlborough late in 1705.
[3] 30 Aug., Coxe, ii. 136–8.
[4] 26 Aug. It was lost in the packet-boat sailing 27 Aug., which was taken by the French. Marlborough replied, nevertheless, on 26 Sept./7 Oct. See pp. 688, 694–5.

putt an end to all this uneasyness when it comes; which if it bee a right one, perhaps it will doe; but if not, will only increase all the present difficultys.

After some pause, 91 [Godolphin] says 83 [the Queen] complained of a letter she had received from Mrs. Freeman [the Duchess],[1] which she said with a great deal of stiffness and reservedness in her looks, was *very extraordinary* in her opinion, but she said she was not composed enough to mention the particulars at that time.

What she sayd of having written to Mr. Freeman [Marlborough], is probably the occasion of her having made so many putt offs and delays to 91 [Godolphin]. But what vexes mee most from all this account of 91's [Godolphin] is, that lett Mr. Freeman's [Marlborough] answer bee what it will, this thing cannot end without very great uneasynesses one way or other to all that 91 [Godolphin] and Mrs. Freeman [the Duchess] are and ought to bee most concerned for.

679. MARLBOROUGH *to* GODOLPHIN   [7/18 September 1706]

Source: Blenheim MSS. A1-14.

Gramets September 18th 1706

A trompet of the Duke of Wertembergh which left the French army last night, assures me that the Duke of Vandôme had received the news of the Duke of Orleans being beaten, and that he was wounded, and the Mareshal de Marcin killed, [and] that thay had lost all their canon and bagage. I have the same news this morning from Tournay, so that I make no doubt but the siege before Turin is raised.[2] As for the particulars, we must have patience til we hear from the Duke of Savoye and Prince Eugene, which I fear can't be sooner then towardes the end of this month. I do from my soull wish her Majesty joye of this great success; and if Holland dose not playe the fool, it will be the Queen's and their power to have what peace thay please.

I have write to The Hague to beg that thay would give orders for the sending us more amunition, so that we might be in a condition of attempting something else, if the Duke of Vandome should be obliged to make any detachements from this country. The right of his army will be this night at St. Amand, and the left towardes Tournay, with the rivers of Scharpe and Shelde before him, which shoes plainly he dose not relye upon his numbers. His order of battaile consistes in 158 squadrons and 100 battallions, which are more then we have for the siege and the army that covers itt. but I am very confident he will venture nothing, and also as sure, with the blessing of

---

[1] 6 Sept., printed in *Conduct*, pp. 165–70.

[2] On 27 Aug./7 Sept. Prince Eugene had engaged the French army before Turin and beaten it decisively. Marcin was killed and the French, led nominally by Orléans, retreated into France. The siege of Turin was over.

God, should thay venture wee should beat them, for our army is in great heart, and theirs the contrary. I hope by the end of this month we may be masters of Ath. The march of the King of Sweeden into Saxony, I think should oblige the Queen and Holland to do all that is possible for the keeping the 10,000 Prussiens in this country, and not suffering them to go back. I have write to The Hague about itt, and should be glad by the first to know her Majesty's pleasure, for there is no keeping them in this country but by allowing them some mony, of which the Dutch must pay one half. I wish I could send you any good news from Spain, which was once in our power of being intier masters, had we had the least good management.

By the inclosed copie of Prince Lewis' letter to me,[1] you will see what is intend[ed] on the Rhin.

680. MARLBOROUGH *to the* DUCHESS   [*7/18 September 1706*]

Source: Blenheim MSS. E3.

I have been very uneasy at the great difficultys you tel me 91 [Godolphin] meets with. That joyned with the very unreasonable opinion some have in 19 [Holland] that 20 [France] will be braught to Loo, gives me the spleen. But my hopes is in God, that he will order everything so that we shall at last have an honorable and lasting peace. . . .[2]

I send these letters to The Hague in hopes thay may come time enough to go with the packet boat, that you may have the good news I received last night from the French army of the Duke of Orleans being beaten, by which Turin is saved.

681. MARLBOROUGH *to* GODOLPHIN   [*9/20 September 1706*]

Source: Blenheim MSS. A1-14.

Gramets September 20, 1706

At my return this day from the camp before Ath, I had the favour of yours of the 2d[3] from Windsor, and that of the 3d[4] from London. Your answere to 366 [Buys] letter is certainly very right, and if they had no veu but their trew intirest, thay would think so; but I am afraid you will find thay will make a reply to itt, for the success with which it had pleased God to blesse the armes of the Allyes with this campagne, has made them very jealous of the great power, as thay terme it, that 17 [England] has in the greatest parts of the courts in Cristendome. It is certaine that 19 [Holland] carryes everything with so hie a hand, that thay are not beloved anywhere. I am very much of

---

[1] 26 Aug./7 Sept., Churchill, ii. 190. Now very ill, he had been ordered to turn over his command to his second, Field-Marshal Thungen.

[2] Part of the letter has been cut away.   [3] Letter 672.   [4] Untraced.

your opinion, that before any step be made towardes 5 [peace], we aught to have a treaty with Holland for the guaranty of any treaty of peace we may hereafter make with France, and that there be rome left for the Allyes to come into itt. I think this so much for the intirest of all the Allyes, that if I have her Majesty's commands, I hope it might meet with no oposition at my coming to The Hague. I did in my last acquaint you with the good news we had from Piemont. There is no doubt of its truth, but as yet I have no letters from the Duke of Savoye nor Prince Eugene. However, I have ordered next Sunday[1] to be a thanksgiving day in the army, not doubting of having their letters before that time. I am aprehensive of our hearing some ill news from the Prince of Hesse.[2] Your origenal letters from the King of Spain, I shal keep til I have the honour of being with you, unless you command otherways. As the frute of the Spanish warr, for the good of England, must be a treaty of trade, I hope her Majesty will think it her intirest to comply with what that King so earnestly desiers in his letter.[3] By the winds we have had here, I am afraid Lord Rivers is not yett sailled, so that I can't omit putting you in mind, that Mr. Earle, as Lieutenant General of Ordenance, will be at a great distance from his duty if he goes into Spain. For when I proposed him for the descent, it was stil in my thoughts that her Majesty might have him back in a fortnight's time, when her Service requiered itt. I desire you will beg her Majesty to aprove of what I have been obliged to do; the Dutch having made a promotion of general officers, to preserve the rank of the English, I have provisionally declared the eldest brigadier, Web, major general, and the two eldest collonels, Sir Richard Temple and Lord Dilremple,[4] brigadiers. The comissions of the Duke of Argile and Web must be dated the same day. If her Majesty aproves this promosion, you will be pleased to acquaint Mr. Secretary Harley, that the comissions may be signed baring date from the day of battaile.[5] Mr. Stanhope being very ill has desired me to beg her Majesty's permission that he may have leave to go with the next yackts for England, beleiving that aire will do him good.[6] The trenches were opened last night at Ath, and I hope in a fortnight's time we may be masters of itt, and I shall endeavour to end this campagne so as that I may have the honour of being with the Queen about the end of October, or early in November.

[1] 15/26 Sept.
[2] When Eugene left Verona to cross the Adige as a preliminary to his march to relieve Turin, he left a detachment under the Prince of Hesse to watch the French forces near Lake Garda. Having taken Goito, Hesse laid siege to Castiglione where he was attacked by Count Medavi on 29 Aug/ 9 Sept. and forced to retire having lost half his army.
[3] For Charles III's request see p. 663 n. 1.
[4] John Dalrymple, second Earl of Stair (1673–1747), styled Lord Dalrymple 1695–1707; lieutenant-colonel, Scots Guards, aide-de-camp to Marlborough 1703; colonel, regiment in Dutch service, 1705; colonel, Cameronians, major-general, 1706; succeeded to earldom 1707; envoy to Augustus, King of Poland, 1709; Order of the Thistle 1710; general 1712. *D.N.B.*
[5] They were all dated 1 June. See p. 659.   [6] He died in England on 20 Sept. 1707.

682. MARLBOROUGH *to the* DUCHESS   [*9/20 September 1706*]

Source: Blenheim MSS. E3.

Gramets September 20th 1706

I have had the pleasure of yours of the 1st from St. Albans and that of the 3rd from London. What you say in your first concerning 127 [Peterborough] and his faire lady is certainly very just, for there is no villany that may not be expected from them. I have always obsarved since I have been in the world, that the next misfortune to that of having friendshipe with such people, is that of having any disput with them, so that care should be taken to have as little as is possible to doe with them.

As to what 115 [Halifax] has said to you concerning the title, is what would be very agreable by its being particular. I know not who is proper to mention what I am going to say, which is, the Queen having settled for her life the 5,000 a yeare for the suport of the honour, thay should do it in the act for the suport of the honour, as far as thay carry itt; this is what aught to oblige you and mee. I am sure for myself it will, for next to your dear self, my dear children are my concern, besides the distinguishing honour it will forever be to you and mee, to have such an act passe in our favours.[1]

I did in my last give you an account of the good news we had from Italie. There is no doubt of its truth, but as yet I have had no account from the Duke of Savoye nor Prince Eugene, so that I can send no particulars. I wish I could let you know that 19 [Holland] were as ferme and honest in the matter of 5 [peace] as 17 [England] is, but it is the contrary, for the success that it has pleased God to give, has made them jealous of 17 [England], and consequently, think that 20 [France] may be brought to Loo.

I received by the last post a letter from 66 [Shrewsbury],[2] which I will send you by the next. You will see in it that he has no thoughts of coming to London this next winter, which conferms his being disatisfied. I do from my soull wish myself with you att Woodstooke, but these are vain thoughts; but by the end of October or beginning of November, I flatter myself of being with you at London. The trenches are opened last night at Ath, and I hope in a fortnight we shall have that place. And if I can govern, thay shall be prisoners of warr.

[1] Marlborough's title was inheritable only by direct male heirs. An Act of Parliament was passed this session (6 Anne, c. 6) to confer the title together with the Manor of Woodstock, Blenheim Palace, and the pension of £5,000 a year on the Post Office (6 Anne, c. 7) to his heirs female.

[2] 30 Aug., Blenheim MSS., A1-46; reply, 26 Sept./7 Oct., Murray, iii. 164. Shrewsbury writes him that the progress made on Blenheim Palace 'will give you the curiosity of making it at least one visit this winter, which opportunity I shall take with great pleasure of waiting upon you, since I fear I shall not do it at London.' See pp. 640-1.

If Lord Hallifax bee with you, make him my compliments, and thank him for the *Ten Champions.*[1]

683. GODOLPHIN *to* MARLBOROUGH   [*10 September 1706*]

Source: Blenheim MSS. A1-36.
Printed: Coxe, ii. 143 (inc.).

Windsor, September 10, 1706

There being now 4 posts wanting from Holland, you will not expect one should trouble you very long from this place from whence one can tell you nothing that is agreable. The uneasyness betwixt 83 [the Queen] and Mr. Montgomery [Godolphin], about the affair of 117 [Sunderland] continues as it was.[2] Nor doe I see how it can bee mended, unless 90 [Marlborough] were here to doe it either by his credit with 83 [the Queen] or by his authority and influence with 117 [Sunderland] and 115 [Halifax] and their friends. Not that I think them so much to blame, because they doe really not see the difficultyes as they are and one cannot goe about to show them those difficultyes without too much exposing of 83 [the Queen].[3] Now though I really think 90 [Marlborough] might bee able to ease all this, yett negotiation, not being Mr. Montgomery's [Godolphin] talent, I doubt it may bee past care before 90 [Marlborough] comes, and there is no room to hope for the least assistance from Mrs. Freeman [the Duchess] in this matter.

Yesterday's *Gazette* will give you an account of the reports wee have in our letters from Lisbon of the 7th instant new stile. If there bee any truth in those reports I hope you will before this time have the satisfaction of having them confirmed by the way of France.

The same blustering winds which keep your letters from us, continue to keep the fleet still in Torbay, which is no small mortification.

The Queen has promised the government of the Barbadoes to Mr. Crow.

---

[1] ? Probably a tract by Arthur Maynwaring, 'Remarks on a late Romance', entitled 'The Memorial of the Church of England; or, The History of Ten Champions'. It was written against the Tories and inspired by Dr. Drake's *Memorial of the Church of England*. Though a few copies were printed it was apparently never published. It is to be found in J. Oldmixon's *Life and Works of Maynwaring* (London, 1715), pp. 25-39.

[2] The Queen was supported, if not prompted, in her opposition to Sunderland by Harley. The sense of Harley's memorandums of 21 and 25 Sept. (in B.M., Portland Loan, 29/10, 29/9) are repeated in the Queen's letters. See also his letters to Newcastle (H. M. C., *Portland MSS.*, ii. 196), Marlborough (ibid. iv. 101), and Poulett (B.M., Portland Loan, 29/153/7).

[3] Godolphin met with Sunderland and Halifax and offered them all that the Queen was prepared to give at this time: a place in the Cabinet without office and a pension. The two lords discussed it with their chief, Somers, and decided it was not enough. Sunderland must be given the secretaryship or else they would withdraw their support from the government. Sunderland conveyed this ultimatum to the Duchess on the 17th who transmitted it on to Marlborough and Godolphin. Coxe, ii. 139-40.

684. GODOLPHIN *to the* DUCHESS   [*10 September 1706*]

Source: Blenheim MSS. E20.

[Tuesday] St. James's September 10, at 7

Being just come to town from Windsor, I find I am to return you a great many thanks for the favour of your letter last Sunday. I am sorry you did not meet with any sight to please you at Woodstock, but I am too much inclined too bee of your mind in all that relates to that matter, that I am not surprised with the account you give of it, but shall continue to hope it will always mend, and every day will please you better there. But I doubt you must not flatter yourself with the hopes of enjoying much quiett there, for by that time the races are well over. Upon Monday the 16th the *Vice*[1] and Mr. Maynwaring[2] design to make you a visitt, and Monday the 23rd is the day Lady Harryett and I have fixed for our waiting upon you.

The Queen goes to Newmarkett the first of October, and designs to come to London the 26th of September, and to stay here till that time, and Lady Harryett being to wait the week the Queen goes, you will see by this account that wee shall not pretend to stay with you above 3 or 4 days, because she must bee the 27th at London. But I can't help having it in my head, that the fright of all these visitts may drive you away sooner than you intended, either to the Lodge or to St. Albans, though I can tell you neither of them will bee able to protect you from our visitt, though I believe she is not so fond of St. Albans as I am, but would rather goe to a new place, which I think is one of her chief reasons for going to Newmarket. Not having yett seen any mortall, nor being like to see any tonight, I shall trouble you no farther than just to tell you I will bee sure to write tomorrow night by the Oxford post. The Queen comes to Kensington tomorrow and stops till Fryday. Mr. Godolphin will bee at Oxford with his uncle tomorrow night, and I hope he will take care to send you a piece of a fall stagg which I have given him for you.

685. MARLBOROUGH *to* GODOLPHIN   [*12/23 September 1706*]

Source: Blenheim MSS. A1-14.
Printed: Coxe, ii. 116-17 (inc.).

Gramets September 23d 1706

I have forborn writting til this evening in hopes of having the English letters, or an expresse from Italie, but neither are come. The Garmains have passed the Rhin, but it is so late in the yeare, that we must not expect much

---

[1] Peregrine Bertie, Vice-Chamberlain of the Household.

[2] Arthur Maynwaring (1668-1712), politician, writer; member of the Kit-Kat Club; M.P., Preston, 1706-10; Commissioner of the Customs 1701-5; Auditor of the Exchequer 1705-12; political confidant and secretary of the Duchess; directed Whig press in defence of the Godolphin ministry 1710-12. *D.N.B.*

from them. The 27 of the last month was the post by which you sent me the copie of 366 [Buys] letter. We hear that packet boat was carryed into Callis. I hope they had time to fling the packet overboard, for I should be sorry to have his letter go to Versailles, though I am afraid thay are there but to[o] well informed of the inclinations of 19 [Holland]; for what has passed in 28 [Italy] I am afraid will make them neglect what is fit to be done for the suport of 4 [the war], being not only fond, but as thay think shure, of injoying 5 [peace] before the next summer, which thought can only end in hurting themselves and friends. For as our affaires are in 22 [Spain], how is it possible to imagine that 313 [King of France] can resolve to send for 314 [Duke of Anjou] back? So that there is an absolute necessity of supporting 4 [the war] some time longer, which is what you will find them very averse too. Thay are so angry with 318 [the Emperor] about the election at Munster, that thay very freely say that if 20 [France] were in a worse condition thay might expect from 318 [the Emperor] to be used by him as he dose his own subjects. This joined with the jealoussy thay begine to have of 17 [England] may give such advantage to 20 [France], that he may in few yeares recover so much strengh as to be able to punish them for their folly. Your saying nothing of Woodstock makes me fear you will not have time to go for two days whilest Lady Marlborough is there. I see by the publick news that the Earle of Manchister is to go to Venice.[1] If any good can be had by that embassy, it were to be wished he were now there, and that his equipage might follow him. Our canon and morters will tomorrow begine to fyer at Ath.

686. MARLBOROUGH *to the* DUCHESS [12/23 September 23 1706]

Source: Blenheim MSS. E3.

Gramets September 23d 1706

Wee have had these last three or four days very wete weather, but I hope you may have had itt better at Woodstooke, for I would have you charmed with that place. The inclosed is the letter[2] I promised you in my last. You will see by it he dose not intend to be at London the next winter, but otherways it dose not looke as if he were out of humor. I received yesterday a letter from the Prince of Hesse, in which he acquaints me of his misfortun of being beaten.[3] This would have been a great misfortune if we had not had the good success in Piemont; but as it is I hope it will be of very little consequence, more then the recruting of those troupes, which I have already write into Holland that orders may be given for itt. Hetherto the enemy lets

---

[1] Manchester was sent to Venice to persuade the Venetians to enter the Grand Alliance, or, at the least, to provide troops. His correspondence for this embassy is in Cole. His embassy lasted until Oct. 1708.   [2] From Shrewsbury. See letter 682.
[3] 31 Aug./11 Sept., Murray, iii. 154, reporting his defeat at Castiglione.

us go on very quietly with the siege of Ath. My Lord and Lady Albamerle have both been very ill of a feaver, but are this day something better. I have not yet heard of Cardonel, who went three days ago very ill to Gand. If he should dye it would give me very great trouble, for all the business I have with the foraine courts goes thorow his hands. I am ever hart and soull yours.

687. GODOLPHIN *to* MARLBOROUGH [*13 September 1706*]

Source: Blenheim MSS. A1-36.

September 13th 1706

I am quite tired out with complaining for want of the satisfaction of hearing from you. Wee have now 5 posts due from Holland, for which wee are the more impatient, because the rumours wee have by the way of Calais, are so much to our advantage, that wee almost long to have the particulars. I can't help thinking wee might have heard in all this time, by the way of Ostend, as well as Calais, if not that correspondence had received any encouragement. And by the way, our merchants will soon bee very clamorous, if they must bee obliged to send all their letters to Holland, when Ostend, is in the hands of our friends.

Wee have no letters neither from the sea since my last, nor from the fleet, but that it is still in Torbay, and there it must bee till the wind changes. God knows whether it will not then bee too late for them to pursue any expedition at all. In the meantime, this delay gives occasion to all our Allyes to presse that those troops may goe to the assistance of their severall masters. The envoyè of Portugall presses to have them sent thither, and yesterday the Comte de Briançon told mee he had reason to believe by his letters from Monsieur del Burgh, that the States would bee willing, all the French regiments in their service should bee sent to Oneglia and hoped the Queen will bee as willing to doe the same. But I suppose till wee can have some certainty in what state things are abroad no resolution can properly bee taken in anything of this sort.

Our uneasyness at home continues, and I am afrayd, it is more like to increase than to bee eased.

688. GODOLPHIN *to the* DUCHESS [*14 September 1706*]

Source: Blenheim MSS. E20.
Printed: *Private Correspondence*, i. 66-7.

Windsor Saturday 14, 1706

Though I don't design to send this letter till Monday by Mr. Maynwaring, yett I can't stay so long from beginning to thank you for the favour of yours by my servant, who braught it mee but this morning from Oxford.

You are much better natured in effect than you sometimes appear to bee, and though you chide mee for being touched with the condition in which I saw 83 [the Queen],[1] you would have been so too, if you had seen the same sight I did. But what troubles mee most in all this affair is that one can't yett find any way of making Mrs. Morley [the Queen] sensible of 83's [the Queen] mistakes, for I am very sure she thinks 83 [the Queen] intirely in the right.

The forreign letters being still kept back, I have employed last night and this morning in writing a very long letter to 83 [the Queen], of which I will keep a coppy to show you, when I have the happyness to see you, before which time I reckon I shall have some answer to it; and till I find the contrary, I cannot help flattering myself that it will have a good effect.[2] By the account yours gives of the race, t'was the greatest complement that my Lord Kingston could make you, to order matters soe as that there should bee no running. Wee were disappointed of running our horse at Oxford, where wee had a great design upon the plate, but the articles excluded us.

Mr. Secretary Harley sends mee just now a printed *Gazett* from Paris, in which they own our Italian news to bee all true, as wee at first heard it; that is to say the French army beaten, the Duke of Orleans wounded, the Mareshal de Marcin killed, Turin releived. The same *Gazette* says the French have had an advantage against the troops of Hesse in the Mantouans, but I hope that is not of half so much consequence. Ther's no confirmation of the report wee had of good news from Spayn.

Mr. Secretary Harley writes to mee, that it was reported at Calais, there had been differences betwixt the Elector of Bavaria and the Duke of Vendosme, and that the Duke of Marlborough was gone to The Hague to prevail with the States, that they might make yett another siege, *Dendermond* and *Ath* being taken. This comes only by report from Calais, but I don't think it unlikely.

689. MARLBOROUGH *to* GODOLPHIN   [15/26 *September 1706*]

Source: Blenheim MSS. A1-14.
Printed: Coxe, ii. 117 (inc.).

Gramets September 26, 1706

The Baron Hondorff,[3] who gives you this, is sent by his master the Duke of Savoye, and Prince Eugene, to give her Majesty a relation of the glorius action at Turin. Thinking this opertunity safer then my letters that go through Holland, you shall have my thoughts concerning 19 [Holland].

[1] See p. 670.
[2] 13 Sept. The copy is in B.M., Add. MS. 56105L. See above, p. 656 n. 5. In it Godolphin answers point by point her reasons for refusing to replace Hedges with Sunderland. See the Queen's reply of 21 Sept. in Coxe, ii. 146-8.
[3] Prussian officer, aide-de-camp to the Duke of Savoy.

Thay are possitivly resolved to have 5 [peace], being angry with 318 [Emperor] and jealous of 17 [England]. Thay can't agree amongst themselves concerning their Barier, but the most reasonable are extravagant, so that if that matter be not setled before we come to a formal treaty of peace, the French will certainly make great advantage of itt. Thay are very possative that 314 [Duke of Anjou] must have something given him. In short, thay think by suporting of that thay make their court to 20 [France] at the expence of 17 [England]. I am afraid the management of 4 [the war] and in 22 [Spain] will afford them some reasons so that the only cure I can see is if it be possible to persuaid them to the suporting the warr one yeare longer. You know I have great indulgence for what the States Generall may wish, but thay are so very unreasonable in this disput of Munster, that I hope the Queen will not be persuaded by Monsieur Vriberg to enter into that quarel. The inclosed is a copie of a letter I received last night from the King of Prussia.[1] I have promised to give him an answere as soon as I have her Majesty's pleasure. I also send you a letter I have received from the *Grand Chamberlane*[2] concerning Monsieur Spanheim. This minut the Comte Maffie acquaints mee with the substance of the Duke of Savoye's letter to the Comte de Brienson by this bearer, concerning the government of Millan. I do not acquaint you with the particulars for no doubt he will show you his letter. I think it is what the publick aught to wish for. After the account you will have from the Comte de Brianson if you are of my opinion, I should then think the best way you could take were to write your mind on that subject freely as a friend to the Comte de Wratislaw and send me your letter, and at the same time I will presse to the same effect, for should thay put a governor there that did not in some degree depend upon the Duke of Savoye, the common cause must suffer.[3] I having gote a passport from the duke of Vandome for this gentleman. He goes by Ostend, so that I hope he will be with you before mine, which I shall write by tomorrow's post. If the Duke of Savoye makes good what he assures me of going into France at the beginning of the next campagne he will very well deserve to have the troupes the Queen and Holland pays left with him, for we can nowhere imploye them so well.[4]

---

[1] 6/17 Sept., B.M. 28057, fols. 318–19, informing the Queen of assurances from the King of Sweden not to harm the Protestant interest or compromise the Allies in the war. Frederick I announced his proposal for an alliance between Prussia, Hanover, and Sweden to further the Protestant interest in Europe (see p. 704) and invited the Queen's support for it.

[2] Count Wartenberg. Untraced.

[3] Milan was a part of the Spanish empire but at the same time a fief of the Empire. Much coveted by the Austrians, Leopold I had made his son, Charles, promise to surrender it to Austria upon his possession of the Spanish crown. The Emperor in turn promised part of the lands of the duchy of Milan to the Duke of Savoy as his price for joining the Grand Alliance.

[4] The inception of the Toulon expedition.

690. MARLBOROUGH *to the* DUCHESS [*15/26 September 1706*]

Source: Blenheim MSS. E3.
Printed: Coxe, i. 84–5 (inc.).
Addressed: For the Dutchesse of Marlborough.

September 26, 1706

I have now received the confermation of the success in Italie from the Duke of Savoye and Prince Eugene, and it is impossible for me to express the joye it has given me, for I do not only estime but I really love that prince. This glorious action must bring France so low, that if our friends can be persuaded to carry the warr on one yeare longer with vigor, we could not faile with the blessing of God to have such a peace, as would give us quiet in our days; but 19 [Holland] are at this time unaccountable. The packet boat that braught the letters of the 27 of the last month old stile is lost, so that if you can recolect what you write by that post you should let me know it. I think you were then at St. Albans. I am now in a corse for three days of your rubarb and lickerish, not that I am sick, but for prevention. I would not lose this opertunity of writting, but my dear soull shall hear from me againe by tomorrow's post.

691. MARLBOROUGH *to* GODOLPHIN [*16/27 September 1706*]

Source: Blenheim MSS. A1-14.
Printed: Coxe, ii. 78–9 (inc.).

Gramets September 27th 1706

I write to you last night by the Duke of Savoy's aide camp, who is gone by the way of Ostend.[1] If he can find a passage there he will be with you before this. Wee have nothing new in this country. The enemy continu in their camp, as you see I do in mine. I believe thay have no thought of disturbing the siege of Ath, so that if I march before the siege is ended, it will be for the conveniency of forage. This last success at Turin has so dishartened their army in this country, that if the Dutch can furnish amunition enough for the siege of Mons, I shall endeavour to perswade them to undertake itt. For I am persuaded if the weather continues faire, we should have it much cheaper this yeare then the next yeare, when thay will have had time to recrut their army. But the backwardness I have found in some, even for this siege of Ath, makes me fear that thay will creat so many difficultys, that we shall be obliged to do nothing more after this siege is over, so that I desire you will not speak of this of Mons til you hear more from me. If we shal do nothing after the siege of Ath, but the putting of Courtray in such a condition as that we may leave eight battalions in it this winter, you may then depend

[1] Letter 689.

upon my being at The Hague by the end of the next month. Considering the humour those people are in att this time, I believe there will be a necessity for the Queen's Service that I stay at least ten days, unless you shall order it otherways. I have heard nothing from Monsieur de Buys since he has received your answer, but I should think this good success in Italie aught to make him aprove of your reasoning. But by that I hear from others you may expect a reply.

I have unsealed my letter to put in the inclosed, which I have received this minute. One part of it concerns my Lord Hallifax, and I should be glad to have his and your thoughts what I am to do in itt.[1]

692. GODOLPHIN *to* MARLBOROUGH   [*17 September 1706*]

Source: Blenheim MSS. A1-36.
Printed: Coxe, ii. 85 (inc.).

Windsor September 17, 1706

I have at the last, the satisfaction of receiving 6 letters from you at one time, of the 6, 9, 13, 16, 18 and 20th[2] with the particulars at the same time of the great victory at Turin, the consequences of which will, I hope, answer all our expectations.

I shall not bee able to answer you by this post, so particularly to all your letters as I ought to doe, because I have not yett had the honour to read them to the Queen. I hoped to have done it this morning, but the weather being fair she was desirous not to lose it, and has comanded mee to wait upon her again in the evening, after which it will bee too late to write by this post. But I had yesterday opportunity of speaking to her, Mr. Secretary Harley being present, of the generall officers as you desired, and also, that she would bee pleased to give the Duke of Argyle some words of encouragement when he presents himself to her Majesty. I have not heard of his arrivall though the wind bee now fair which makes mee hope wee shall soon have the letters of last Fryday[3] from The Hague which are not yett come.

I shall bee impatient to hear the next stepps of the Duke of Savoy and Prince Eugene. I am apprehensive the orders of the latter may divert him to the Milanois, but I hope the Duke of Savoy will rather incline to push the French from Pignerol, where as I am informed they cannot protect themselves against a superior army. You will best judg what can bee properly said to them upon this subject, from their Allyes on this side, and whatever is said by yourself, will have more weight with them than from anybody else.

I agree intirely with you that the more successes wee have the more crossness wee are to expect from 19 [Holland]. And therfore I should

---

[1] From Heinsius, 14/25 Sept., 't Hoff, pp. 269–70, referring to the negotiations for the Treaty of the Succession and a Barrier. Halifax had not written to Heinsius as he had promised.

[2] Letters 666, 667, 673, 675, 679, 681.   [3] 13/24 Sept.

think it might not bee amiss, if you made some stepps towards the *pre-liminary treaty* even before your going to The Hague, by letter to the Pensioner. For the sooner that is done, and the rest of the Allyes brought into it, the stronger wee shall bee upon that occasion.

I write to the Pensioner, as you desire, about Mr. Stepney's coming to Brussells, and I take that occasion also to acquaint him with the orders which the Queen has given to the fleet, and to my Lord Rivers, who I hope, will sail this day from Torbay.[1] Monsieur Vryberghen has been very pressing with mee to know the place for which they were designed, but I excused it by saying the Pensioner should bee acquainted with it.

I am very sorry to repeat to you that 83's [the Queen] aversness to the affair of 117 [Sunderland] continues, and her uneasyness with Mr. Montgomery [Godolphin] upon that account, makes him almost distracted, for he sees no possibility of supporting himself, or anything else, in this winter, which is like to bee the nicest and the most criticall of any wee have yett seen, upon many accounts with which I will not trouble you now. He sayes he could die every minute of his life for Mrs. Morley's [the Queen] service, but he can neither encourage nor expect impossibilityes. To make brick without straw, is an Egyptian labour.

693. GODOLPHIN *to the* DUCHESS   [*17 September 1706*]

Source: Blenheim MSS. E20.
Printed: Coxe, ii. 158-9.

. . .[2] to die the next moment, he knows not what to say more than that he has . . .[3]

But what I can't avoyd troubling you upon, is that Mrs. Morley [the Queen] sent for me this morning, and complained much of Mrs. Freeman's [Lady Marlborough] letter, and particularly of the last 2 or 3 lines, upon that part which related to 110 [Cowper].[4] She appealed to mee, upon which I said, I could not but remember she had some difficultys, and I believed she liked this man better than she expected to doe, and from thence I went onn to tell her that I knew very well all Mrs. Freman's [Lady Marlborough] complaints proceeded from having lost Mrs. Morley's [the Queen] kindness unjustly, and her telling her truths which other people would not, to which she sayd, as she has don 40 times, how could she show her any more kindness than she did, when she would never come near her? I sayd she had tryed that severall times and complained it was always the same thing.

[1] 17 Sept., Rijksarchief, Heinsius inventory, 1091, printed in Vreede, pp. 144-5.
[2] The letter is mutilated. The dots indicate the portions cut away.
[3] Compare this line with the close of the preceding letter.
[4] On this subject see the Queen's letter to the Duchess, 17 July, in Brown, p. 211.

Upon that she sayd, Mrs. Freeman [Lady Marlborough] would grow warm somtimes, and then she herself could not help being warmer than she ought to bee, but that she was always ready to bee easy with Mrs. Freeman [Lady Marlborough]. I sayd I hoped then she would bee soe, for that I would die with all my soul, to have them two as they used to bee. Then she said she would send mee a letter for you, and so she did last night, intending I should have sent it by the post,[1] but I thought it was better to keep it for you may see by her letter to Lord Marlborough, which he sent me,[2] that she leans still towards expedients, though I have told her, that to satisfy her, I had tried how far that would go, and the thing was not capable of any expedient, and that I was convinced by what had been said to me by Lord Somers and Lord Halifax,[3] that it was infinitely more for her advantage not to think of any such thing as an expedient. But she told me the other day, she believed I thought it strange that she said nothing upon my shewing her Lord Marlborough's letter;[4] but it was, that though she was very uneasy to see what he writ, she could not, for her life, be convinced but her expedient was better; and when he comes over she will certainly talk so to him; but if he holds firm to what he has written and said, as I do not doubt he will, I dare say she will do the thing.

694. GODOLPHIN *to* MARLBOROUGH   [*18 September 1706*]

Source: Blenheim MSS. A1-36.
Printed: Coxe, ii. 85-6, 114-16 (inc.).

Windsor September 18, 1706

I had time but just to thank you by yesterday's post[5] for 6 letters which I received at once from you. The news they brought at last, was good enough to make amends for our long expectation.

I hope before this comes to your hands, you will have taken Ath, and turned your thoughts, not to any new expeditions, but to end the campagne as soon as the French will give you leave to doe it. I don't think their misfortune at Turin will prevail with them to make any detachments from Monsieur de Vendosme's army, as long as you are in the field. But rather, I am not out of pain, but they may yett venture something to reduce the blow at Turin, on this side when they think the season so farr advanced, as that you could not bee able to prosecute any advantage you might have upon them. And this seems the more reasonable, because it would bee a great help to their negotiations, with 19 [the Dutch] this winter, upon which I believe, *they place their* greatest hopes.

---

[1] 15 Sept. Blenheim MSS. G1-7 (copy), a conciliatory letter.
[2] Untraced.
[3] See Sunderland to the Duchess, 17 Sept., in Coxe, ii. 139-40. See above, p. 675 n. 3.
[4] Letter 661?   [5] Letter 692.

Upon this head, I can't help saying, that though some of the leading men, *of 19 [Holland] I mean,* may bee blind or worse, yett surely the generallity cannot bee imposed upon so farr, as to bee blown up with a jealousy of 83's [the Queen] power, when all that power, bee it great or little, has been, and is still, chiefly exerted for their safety, without the least view or desire or any entent of conquest or dominion for 17 [England], and when it is plain that in 2 or 3 years time 20 [France] with the comfort and assistance of 5 [peace] will bee just where she was before, if the nicest care bee not taken to putt it out of her power, now there is an opportunity in our hands.

But wheras you say in one of your letters wee may now bee sure of a solid and lasting peace *if 19 [Holland] does not play* the fool, that position is certainly right, if wee can agree to carry onn the warr *with vigour* as you call it another year. But the difficulty is in that *agreement,* for I very much doubt whether 19 [Holland] will make so much as a show of doing it. And for 17 [England] though the generallity is intirely for doing it, yett the plain un-willingness in 83 [the Queen] to doe anything for those [the Whigs] who have shown themselves most forward and zealous in promoting all our present advantages, is a discouragement not to bee overcome, at least not by Mr. Montgomery [Godolphin] alone. And there is not one besides in any ministeriall office of the government, that must not bee spoken to ten times over before anything can bee executed, even after it is ordered, as I said before with all the slowness and difficulty imaginable.[1] When I have given you the trouble of telling you this assure yourself that if you saw Mr. Montgomery [Godolphin] he would tell you, it is very short of the dis-agreablenes he finds upon this subject.

The Queen has not yett heard anything from Holland concerning the King of Sweden's march. Perhaps it is because Mr. Vrybergh has not yett been able to digest 6 posts at once. But whenever he applyes your directions will be observed in that matter. And as to the Prussian troops, her Majesty leaves it to you to take the necessary measures for their continuing in the Low Countryes.

The Queen having complyed with her promise to the Bishop of Osnabrug in his pretensions to Munster, and that matter which is really very essential to Holland being now over, I don't see that her Majesty can take any farther part in it, than to doe all that is in her power to compose the difference upon that occasion between the Emperour and the States.[2]

The necessary orders being already given for a squadron of 40 ships to

---

[1] On 30 July, Godolphin wrote in a similar vein to Harley: 'The Admiralty are not so lively and vigilant as they ought to be: I see it every day upon twenty occasions, but yet I don't see how at present it is to be mended.' H. M. C., *Bath MSS.,* i. 83.

[2] For the contest over the election of a new Bishop of Munster see p. 647 n. 4. A confrontation developed between the Dutch and the Emperor when a commissioner appointed by the latter to oversee matters relating to the principality's troops' subsidies during the interregnum threatened to withdraw the Munster troops from the service of the United Provinces. Noorden, ii. 522–4.

winter at Lisbon or at Cadiz, if wee can gett it, might it not bee advisable when you write back to Prince Eugene, to concert with him how to gett the assistance of some troops to joyn with our fleet upon the coast of Provence about the middle of Aprill, by which time the wintering of our fleet in those seas would give them an opportunity of being there? And probably before the enemy could bee in a readiness to make any considerable opposition either by sea or land.

I hope my Lord Rivers did not sail yesterday morning for wee have had here ever since a terrible storm of rain and wind at *northeast* which yett continues. However the letters of Friday[1] last from The Hague are not come to us.

I am sorry the letters from hence of the 27th of August are lost because mine was full upon the subject I mentioned [Sunderland], and Mrs. Morley [the Queen] tells mee she had written to you some time since upon the same subject. And not having had an answer from you by the 6 posts at once, she is afraid her letter was in that boat which miscarryed.

Till wee can hear somthing certainly and directly from Spain, I forbear troubling you concerning my Lord Peterborow and Lord Gallway.

19th

Since I had written the former part of this letter I have the favour of yours of the 23d[2] by which as also by letters I have seen from Paris to the Venetian embassadour here, I perceive 19 [Holland] is running very fast towards 5 [peace] and therefore I think nothing must bee left unattempted of any kind to lett them see that 83 [the Queen] will not bee compelled in that matter. On the other side I am of opinion it would bee right to humour them the more in all reasonable things and particularly, in the affair of Munster. I can't help repeating, that now the election is near by a fair majority I think the Emperour pushes that matter too farr. And since he has not don, nor can't doe anything considerable but as he is helped by England and Holland, it seems to bee an unreasonable assuming, and I doubt Mr. Freeman [Marlborough] will not doe himself a good office with 19 [Holland] by leaving too much to the Imperiall court in this matter.

My Paris intelligencer says Monsieur Rouille,[3] and the Elector of Bavaria carry onn the affairs of 5 [peace] with great vigour and success.

These things make the preliminary treaty still the more pressing to bee begun and dispatched with all speed.

Nor is it less necessary on the other hand to press the Duke of Savoy and Prince Eugene to follow the remainder of the French army which retired to Pegneroll and from thence perhaps into Dauphinè. For if those troops

---

[1] 13 Sept.   [2] Letter 685.

[3] Pierre Rouillé, Seigneur de Marbeuf et Saint-Seine (1657–1712), diplomat; President of the Parliament of Paris; representative of Louis XIV with the Elector of Bavaria 1704–7; French peace negotiator at The Hague 1709. See p. 627.

should bee at liberty to bee employed elsewhere, wee shall soon feel the weight of them upon us in Spayn. I have spoken very earnestly to the Comte de Briançon upon this subject and perhaps a word from you to Comte Maffei and a letter to Prince Eugene and also to the Duke of Savoy himself may bee very usefull. Or otherwise, the consequence of this great victory, to which England has so much contributed, will only serve to make the warr of Spayn, so much more difficult and expensive to us. And considering how ready the Queen has been to doe everything that could bee desired for the support of the Duke of Savoy, she may reasonably expect so much regard from him, as this come to. And besides this, I have gon so farr as to lett the Comte de Briançon hope that whenever 5 [peace] comes to bee adjusted wee would use our best endeavours to keep 20 [France] on this side of the Alpes. I trouble you the more particularly upon this head, both for the great importance of it to England and for that it comes to bear imediately.

As long as my letter is, I have promised my Lord William Hay[1] to write to you, about his brother's regiment.[2] I have also a letter from his father[3] who seems much concerned about it. But when I have named it to you I have don all that can bee expected from mee. You know best, how it ought to bee disposed of.

I have some hopes of gooing to Woodstock the 24th.

Since I began to write this letter the Baron de Handorf is arrived, and I have your letter by him,[4] as well as that of the 27th.[5]

The former part of this letter is as full an answer as I can give to what you write by the Baron de Handorf concerning the disposition of 19 [Holland]. Only I will add, that while they are in that disposition wee ought to bee the more cautious, not to give them any handle too the least jealousy of 17 [England] either about the business of Munster or the subject of the King of Prussia's letter[6] which if not very carefully handled may furnish a new occasion of jealousy. You will receive the Queen's pleasure upon this, from Mr. Secreatry Harley,[7] as also the coppy of my letter to Monsieur Buys[8] in his hand, not being willing to trust it to any other.

When I have heard what the Comte de Briançon has to propose about the government of Milan, you shall have an account of it, and such a letter as you direct for Comte Wratislaw, though with thought of that kind must have ten times more weight from you.

[1] Lord William Hay (died 1723), third son of Marquis of Tweeddale, captain, Second Grenadier Company, Scots Foot Guards; brevet Colonel of Foot 1705; brigadier-general 1710.

[2] Brigadier-general Lord John Hay, died of fever at Courtrai 25 Aug./5 Sept. The Earl of Stair succeeded him as colonel.

[3] The Marquis of Tweeddale.   [4] Letter 689.

[5] Letter 691.   [6] See p. 680 n. 1.

[7] 17 Sept., Longleat, Portland MSS., v, fols. 99–100. The Queen left it up to Marlborough whether she should intervene in the Munster affair. Presumably acting on his advice she switched her support to the Bishop of Paderborn. Marlborough to Hedges, 12/23 Nov., Murray, iii. 230–1.

[8] 23 Sept., Coxe, iii. 118–21. For Godolphin's summary of its contents see below, p. 691.

695. GODOLPHIN *to the* DUCHESS   [*18 September 1706*]

Source: Blenheim MSS. E20.

[Wednesday] Windsor September 18th

Since my last yesterday,[1] I am to thank you for the favour of your letters by the return of my messenger to you, and the particulars you sent mee of Lord Marlborough's letters to you, which are obliging to mee but not of any use, I think, to bee shown to Mrs. Morley [the Queen]. One of his to mee[2] has somthing in it fitter for that purpose, which I did read last night to 83 [the Queen], who upon that was pleased to say I should have an answer in writing to my long letter,[3] by which I begin to doubt again, it is not like to bee so good a one as I hoped it might have been, because I really think it contained a very full as well as a particular answer to the 3 objections in that letter of 83's [the Queen][4] which you saw. She told mee last night she had not had any answer from Mr. Freeman [Marlborough] to the letter she had written, which made her fear her letter was lost in the packett boat of the 27th of August, which is thought to be lost.[5]

The reason why I have never asked to see 114's [Lady Marlborough] extraordinary letters,[6] is because that since this hurly burly I have never had one easy conversation, but all coldness and constraint; and besides, that I have since that written a letter much more *extraordinary* (as it perhaps is thought) upon the same subject, to which I can yett have no answer at all, though the letter has been given ever since Sunday.[7]

Mr. Bridges the Paymaster is come over in the last packett boat.[8] He tells mee 19 [Holland] is violently sett upon 5 [peace], and in great concern for poor 20 [France], but he says too they are not gon so farr as to say they will doe anything without consent of 17 [England].

I am the less surprised at what you write of Mrs. Howe's discourse and behaviour,[9] because I find Mrs. Ramsey[10] is exactly in the same tone here;

---

[1] Untraced.   [2] Letter 675.   [3] 13 Sept. See p. 679 n. 2.   [4] 23 Aug. See p. 664 n. 5.
[5] It was. See Marlborough's reply on the subject of Sunderland, pp. 694–5
[6] See p. 671.   [7] 15 Sept.
[8] Brydges had gone over to the Continent to improve his arrangements for transmitting funds to the army in Flanders, with a particular care to establishing his system for skimming off a percentage for his own profit and that of his confederates. See letter 618A and p. 609 n. 4.
[9] About the Hanover family and the invitation. She fed the Duchess with gossip about the family and the Tories' efforts to influence them. For example, she had written to her on 1/12 Mar. 1706: 'This court [Hanover] has been all along very uneassie about the Bill of Naturiallisation . . . Upon the first report that a man of quallety was to bring it thay were very uneassie and indevoured all thay could to perswade Mr. Howe to write into England to prevent anybody being sent. . . . The last letters has brought them a confirmation that one [Halifax] is to bring the Bills and the Garter at the same time for the Prince Electorall, which thay say will look like paying them with tryfells insteed of calling them over. Your Grace may see by this what power the Torry partie have to infusse notions here. I can't help saying I am surprised to hear all this owned, that I am desiered to doe it to lett your Grace know that it would be most agreeable to the Elector to have the Bill preseanted without any ceremonie and the Garter sent by a hereald' (Blenheim MSS. E44).
[10] Identified as the widow of Lt.-gen. Ramsey, a Dutchwoman (her family name was Buckson)

and nobody, as I have heard, used to give herself greater liberty last winter.

Your 3 a clock visiter's letters are as insipid as his visitts. Tis curious to observe, but I find it by him, that old age betrays one's nature as much as wine.[1]

Lady Haryett thinks it will bee more convenient for her not to goe from hence till Tuesday,[2] so till Tuesday night wee are not to have the happyness of seeing you.

696. MARLBOROUGH *to* GODOLPHIN [*19/30 September 1706*]

Source: Blenheim MSS. A1-14.
Printed: Coxe, ii. 79 (inc.).

Gramets September 30th 1706

The Duke of Savoye has been very pressing by the Comte de Maffie, that I would give him assurances that the 28,000 men paid by her Majesty and the States, should remain in Italie this winter and the next campagne. I have assured him that I will write to The Hague, and do not doubt but thay will consent to their staying this winter. But at the same time, I desired his master would lose no time in sending a project for the effecting what we have formerly desired concerning Toulon, and that would most certainly oblige us to take the resolution of leaving the troupes for another yeare. If you aprove of this, you must make the Comte de Brienson sensible, that all other projects must give way to this of Toulon.

This misfortune of the Prince of Hesse[3] will be an adition to your expence, as well as the stay of the Prussiens, if we can prevaile with them to continue in this country, which I think is for the advantage of the common cause.

The letters of the 15th from Vienna tels me, the Emperor designs the sending the Comte de Senzindorff to me for the taking the necessarie measures for the next campagne. But I believe the trew reason of his jorny, if he dose come, is to informe himself of what is passing at The Hague concerning a generall peace. The Comte de Wratislaw writes me by the last post, that he beleives the Emperor will send him to the King of Sweden. At the same time, he assures me that he will be carefull of neither saying nor doing anything that may give offense to that King, their court being resolved to gaine him by faire means, if possible, being no ways in a condition of acting otherways. Wee have att this time to[o] much rain. However, I continue of

whom Ramsey had married while serving with the Scots Guards in the Netherlands. After Ramsey's death, on 2 Sept. 1705, she was awarded £6,000 by the Scottish Parliament 'for his arrears and services'. Luttrell, v. 595.

¹ Henry Guy?   ² 24 Sept.   ³ His defeat at Castiglione.

the opinion we aught to make the siege of Mons, if we can have a sufficient quantity of stores; for the taking of that town would make us masters of the province of *Haynaut*,[1] which would be a very great advantage to us for the opening of the next campagne, which we must make if we will bring France to such a peace as will give us quiet year after. I expect Mr. Cardonel in two or three days from Gand, and then I shall derect him to send Mr. St. Johns an account of what must be demanded for the remount of the English horse, and as near as I can what will be requisset for the forainers, which will not come to so much as the last yeare, though we had no battaile; for I thank God as yett we have very little of the disease we had last yeare and the yeare before amongest our horses. We have a good many of our general officers sick, amongest them my Lord Albermarle, as also his lady. Thay leave the army tomorrow, in hopes the good aire of Mallines may do them good. My Lord Orkeny is gone sick to Gand, and I beleive when he recovers, will go from thence to England. But I have derected Major Generall Rose to return to the army as soon as he gets strength. Inglesby is also sick but will not quit the siege. I intend to leave him to command at Gand this winter. The greatest part of the English will be in that town. We have now three postes due from England.

697. MARLBOROUGH *to the* DUCHESS [*19/30 September 1706*]

Source: Blenheim MSS. E3.
Printed: *Private Correspondence*, i. 67–8 (inc.).

Gramets September 30th 1706

You m[a]y easily beleive that my impatience is great since we have three postes due from England. The good news from Italie must put you, as well as it has us here, in good humor. The wete weather makes the siege of Ath goes on the slower. However, we hope to have it by the midle of the next weeke. I think I did in a former letter desire of you to know of Lord Sunderland what he would have done with the sett of horses the Elector of Hanover gives him. I have notice that thay will be at The Hague about the midle of the next month. Mine are to go for England or not as you derect, so that he should give his derections, what he would have done with them.[2] My Lady Albermarle has desired me to make her compliments to you. She goes tomorrow from the army very sick, as dose also her lord. I found on a paper in my standish[3] that I am indepted to Lady Fitzharden twelf guines. If it be trew I beg you will make my excuse and my compliments, and lett her be

---

[1] Hainault, one of the nine provinces of the Spanish Netherlands. Named after the river Haine it lies on the French border, between the provinces of Flanders and Namur. Mons is its capital.
[2] See p. 667, where he forgot to mention Sunderland's. They were a gift on the occasion of Sunderland's visit to Hanover with Marlborough in Dec. 1705.
[3] Travelling-desk.

paid. My next will be dated in October, which is the month in which I am used to leave the campagne, so that I begine to please myself with the thoughts that it will not be long before I may have the happyness of being with you, which is extreamly wished for by him that is intierly yours.

698. GODOLPHIN *to* MARLBOROUGH   [*23 September 1706*]

Source: Blenheim MSS. A1-36.
Printed: Coxe, ii. 117–18 as 24 Sept. (inc.).

Windsor 23d September 1706

I have received the favour of yours of the 23d[1] with the enclosed from the Pensioner to you about 5 [peace], in which he is pleased to lay weight upon 2 arguments which seem to mee to have so little [weight] that I can't help saying something upon them to you, because my answer[2] to Mr. Buys's second letter[3] of which I send you a coppy is not so strong upon those particulars as it might have been.

His 2 arguments are:

1st, that I take no notice in my letter[4] of the low condition of their finances.

2dly that France may not bee so well disposed to a peace, at another time, as now. I took no notice in my letter of the state of their finances, because I thought it unnecessary, the answer to it, being so very obvious.

For all arguments of that kind must bee taken comparatively, and though the land and trade both of England and Holland have excessive burthens upon them, yett the credit continues good, both with us and with them. And wee can either of us borrow money at 4 and 5 percent wheras the finances of France are so much more exhausted that they are forced to give 20 and 25 per cent, for every penny of money they send out of the kingdom, unless they send it in specie, by which means they have now neither money nor credit. And the result of this 1st argument, is only, that it absolutely destroys the second, since it is plain the condition of France is in all respects, so low, that the greatest support they have, at present, comes from the *greediness*, if I may use that word, of Holland to encourage and entertain all proposalls of peace. Whereas if the Allyes would agree not to receive or hearken to any proposalls of peace till the state of warr for the next year was settled, I durst venture my little fortune upon it, that France would agree to every point mentioned in my former letter to Monsieur Buys.

---

[1] Letter 685.   [2] In Coxe, ii. 118–21.

[3] 17/28 Sept., draft in Rijksarchief, AANW 1865 BXIV A. Discussed in Geikie, pp. 64–6. Buys wanted to take active measures to seek a peace and considered the time propitious as France showed interest and conditions in the Dutch Republic made some solution imperative. He wanted to begin by drawing up a set of preliminaries in co-operation with England. He also wished to conclude a treaty for a Barrier.

[4] Letter 672A.

As to the project brought over by my Lord Halifax, he will send you his thoughts by this post,[1] as he did by the last to Monsieur Heinsius. Mine you will see in the coppy of my answer to Mr. Buys which goes herewith.

I am the more troublesome to you by this post because after this day you are not like to hear anything very materiall from mee or very regularly, being to goe tomorrow morning to Woodstock from whence you may expect an account of my observations in that place, and from thence to Newmarkett for a fortnight, [or] at least 10 days.

I have told your brother George to have the convoy ready for you, by the end of October.

I hear such fame of this year's champayn, that I hope you will try to bring a little.

699. MARLBOROUGH *to* GODOLPHIN   [*23 September/*
                                                  4 October 1706]

Source: Blenheim MSS. A1-14.
Printed: Coxe, ii. 121 (inc.).

Gramets October, 4 1706

Being to dine at Ath this day, and fearing to return late, I begine my letter, though I have litle to say more then that the governor of Ath surprised us in surrendring his town and garrison prisoners of war, four or five days sooner then we expected. We have five postes due from England, which makes me very impatient of your letters. I hope we may have some of them before this letter goes. The weather is so very bad, that we find difficulty in removing our canon from the batteries, which will be one argument amongst others for our not attempting [the siege] of Mons. But as yett that designe is not laid aside. You will see by the inclosed the offer of the King of Prussia.[2] I have by this post sent the same papers to The Hague, and my opinion that thay aught to have their quarters between the Meuse and the Rhine, since it will save us half the expence. Every post gives me an account of the great desire some in Holland have to end the war before the next campagne. The knowlidge France has of this is no doubt the reason of their having made no new offers since their misfortune in Italie. If Holland can be persuaded to

---

[1] Untraced. On the project of a treaty for the Succession and a Barrier. Halifax's views are set forth in his letter to Heinsius, 8 Oct., in Vreede, pp. 165–70 and to Marlborough, 4 Oct., Blenheim MSS. A1-46. He was concerned that the Dutch moderate their demands and also be more specific in deciding the places they thought essential to constitute a safe Barrier.

[2] Blenheim MSS. A2-16. The conditions for leaving his troops in the Netherlands during the winter. The King demanded the *agio* (that is, an allowance for conversion of money into the local currency, bread, and forage) for his troops to be paid for by the Maritime Powers if his troops were quartered west of the Meuse, that half of these items be paid if they were quartered between the Meuse and the Rhine. See Marlborough to Heinsius, 21 Sept./2 Oct., 24 Sept./5 Oct., 't Hoff, pp. 272, 274; Marlborough to King of Prussia, 5/16 Oct., Murray, iii. 175.

go on with the warr this next yeare, we have reason to expect an honorable, safe, and lasting peace; so that I beg of you that 365 [Heinsius] and 366 [Buys] against my coming to The Hague, may be prepared by letters from yourself and Mr. Secretary Harley, to take with me the necessary measures for the carrying on of the warr the next campagne. I desire you will, with my most humble duty to the Queen and Prince, congratulat the taking of Ath. And if the weather would have permitted the attempting of Mons, the taking of that place would have ended the campagne to my own heart's desire. But God be praised for what has been done. I shall not care to stay longer at The Hague than is absolutely necessary for the Service, being sure thay will be very troublesome concerning the peace. Their notions of that matter in my opinion are very wrong, so that with the Queen's leave I must speake plainly to them, for thay argue as if thay alone were the only people concerned in this warr, and consequently the peace. I have heard nothing from the Duke of Savoye, nor Prince Eugene since the 11 of the last month, but I do not doubt everything goes well there. But from Spain we have nothing good by the way of France, for thay would have us beleive that the intention of King Charles is to take his winter quarters in Arragon, Vallance, and Catalonia, leaving in quiet possession the rest of Spain to the Duke of Anjoue.

If the Service will permit it, I should be glad the convoye might be on this side by the end of this month your stile for I shall be ready to come to you in the first weeke in November.

700. MARLBOROUGH *to the* DUCHESS

[*23 September/4 October 1706*]

Source: Blenheim MSS. E3.

Gramets October 4, 1706

I can now send you the good news of our being masters of the town of Ath, and the five redgiments in it are prisoners of warr, so that the Duke of Vandôme has had the mortefication of three towns being taken since he came to the army, and two of them made prisoners of warr. I hope yet before I seal this letter to have some of your dear letters, we having five postes due. The ill weather, and the goutish humour making me very often sick in my stomack, will make the remaining part of the campagne very tedious. I hope you will take care that the convoye may be for me in Holland by end of October, for I would not willingly stay at The Hague one day longer then may be absolutely necessary; for besides the impatiency I shall have of being with you, I shall be glad to be from a place where I am sure I shall be pressed to what I think at this time not good for the common cause. I mean a peace, for France is not yet braught to what thay aught to be before we can have a safe peace.

I hope we may have something of Spain by the way of Portugale, for France will let us have nothing good from thence. There being no English letters, and the post staying for mine, I must seall this, with assuring of the truth of my heart and soull being intierly yours.

701. GODOLPHIN *to* MARLBOROUGH   [*25 September 1706*]

Source: Blenheim MSS. A1-36.
Addressed: To his Grace the Duke of Marlborough.

Woodstock September 25, 1706

Before I left Windsor, I writt to you soe fully for 2 or 3 posts together that I shall have nothing left to say from hence, but of what belongs to this place.

The garden is already very fine and in perfect shape, the turf all laid, and the first coat of the gravell, the greens high and thriving, and the hedges pretty well grown.

The building is so advanced, as that one may see perfectly how it will bee when it is done. The side where you intend to live is the most forward part. My Lady Marlborough is extremely prying into it and has really not only found a great many errours, but very well mended such of them, as could not stay for your own decision. I am apt to think she has made Mr. Vornbrugge [Vanbrugh] a little [annoyed] but you will find both ease and convenience from it.

Lady Haryett and Willigo have walked all about the garden this evening. I hope when wee doe soe agayn, wee shall have the happyness of your company.

702. MARLBOROUGH *to* GODOLPHIN
[*26 September/7 October 1706*]

Source: Blenheim MSS. A1-14.
Printed: Coxe, ii. 144 (inc.).

[Grandmetz] October 7, 1706

I have by this post sent yours of the 17th to 83 [the Queen].[1] I send inclosed Mr. Harley's letter,[2] by which you will see the letter the Queen write mee was lost. However, I have write my mind very freely, as you will see by the following wordes, which I hope will have a good effect for your ease and the publick good.

As I am persuaded that the safety of your government, and the quiet of your life, depends very much upon the resolution you shall take at this time,

---

[1] Letter 692.   [2] 17 Sept., Longleat, Blenheim MSS. A1-14.

I think myself bound in gratitude, duty and conscience, to let you know my mind freely. And that you may not suspect me of being partial, I take leave to asure you, in the presence of God, that I am not for your putting yourself into the hands of either party. But the behaviour of Lord Rochester and all the hote heads of that party are so extreavagant, that there is no doubt to be made of their exposing you and the libertys of England to the rage of France, rather then not be revenged as thay cal itt. This being the case, there is a necessity as well as justice of your following your inclinations in suporting Lord Treasurer, or al must go to confusion. As the humour is at present, he can't be supported but by the Wiggs, for the other seekes his distruction, which in effect is yours. Now pray consider if he can, by placing some few about you, gaine such a confidence, as shall make your business and himself safe, will not this be the sure way of making him so strong, that he may hinder your being forced into a party? I beg you will beleive I have no other motife to say what I do, but my zeal for your person, and freindshipe for a man whome I know to be honest and zealously faithful to you.

703. MARLBOROUGH *to the* DUCHESS
[*26 September/7October 1706*]

Source: Blenheim MSS. E3.
Printed: Coxe, ii. 145–6.

Gramets October 7th 1706

I am to return you my thankes for five of yours all from Woodstock. I could wish with all my heart everything were more to your mind, for I find when you write most of them you had very much the spleen, and in one I had my share, for I see I lye under the same misfortun I have ever done, of not behaving myself as I aught to 83 [the Queen]. I hope Mr. Ha[w]cksmore will be able to mend those faults you find in the house, but the great fault I find is that I shal never live to see it finished, for I had flattered myself that if the war should happly have ended this next yeare, that I might the next after have lived in itt, for I am resolved on being neither minister nor cortier, not doubting the Queen will allow of itt; but these are idle dreames, for whielst the warr lastes I must serve and will do itt with all my heart; and if at last I am rewarded with your love and estime, I shall end my days happly, and without it nothing can make me easy. I am taking measures to leave the army about three weeks hence, so that I shall have the happyness of being above one month sooner with you then I have been for these last three yeares.

704. GODOLPHIN *to* MARLBOROUGH   [*28 September 1706*]

Source: Blenheim MSS. A1-36.
Addressed: To his Grace the Duke of Marlborough.

St. Albans 28th September 1706

My last was from Woodstock[1] where I left Lady Marlborough in good health last night, and came hither today in my way to Newmarkett, from whence I shall send you, by a messenger on purpose, a great packett from Lady Marlborough which she has taken more pains to write in her own hand, than any clerk of Mr. Cordonell's would doe for 100£.[2]

Mr. Godolphin and I came hither this evening, time enough, to walk once round your garden, which is a charming place and has no fault, unless it bee too shady which will soon mend itself at this time of year.

I received while I was at Woodstock the enclosed letter from Shrimpton and I beg leave to trouble you with it that I may know what answer to send when 'tis possible, but at present I hope he is out of reach of any answer at all.

When I have seen the Queen att Newmarkett, I doubt I shall have occasion to trouble you with a longer letter.

705. MARLBOROUGH *to* GODOLPHIN

[*28 September/9 October 1706*]

Source: Blenheim MSS. A1-14.
Printed: Coxe, ii. 121-2 (inc.).

Gramets October 9, 1706

Since my last I have had the favour of five of yours. I must begine with telling you that the great abundance of rains we have had for these last eight days has obliged us to lay aside the thoughts of attacking Mons, so that we shall do no more this campagne but the putting the town of Courtray in a condition of having a garrison this winter. I am very far from being of your opinion that the French will venture anything on this side, for thay knew of their lose at Turin before we begone the siege of Ath, so that if thay could have had any temptation to venture a battaile, it aught to have been when we of necessity must have been devided. But I beleive thay have sett up their rest in the hopes thay have that their negociations with 19 [Holland] may succed, so that there will be a necessity of 83 [the Queen] giving me leave to opose it in her name, unless thay should offer much better conditions then I have yett heard off. I have write concerning the preliminary treaty you

[1] Letter 701.
[2] The packet apparently contained copies of all the letters that had passed between the Queen and Godolphin and the Duchess on the subject of Sunderland. See p. 708.

mentioned,[1] but I think it would forward itt very much if Mr. Secretary Harley would let me have the heads of such a one as you desire. The business of Munster is like to be a very troublesome business. The Queen can certainly medle with it noe otherways then by doing good offices. I shall be sure to give an account of the Queen's resolution to Prince Eugene of 40 shipes being left in Portugale, or nearer if there be a convenient place, but the proper person to take measures for the designe you have so long wished for must be the Duke of Savoye.[2] 366 [Buys] takes no notice to me of the answer you made to his letter.[3] If he makes you a replie, I should be glad to have it, for that may be of use to me at The Hague. I had a letter last night from the Pensioner.[4] He complains that the treaty for the garanty for the Succession standes stil for his want of hearing from Lord Hallifax. If you have any difficulty in England concerning that treaty I should know itt. If not, it should be pressed, so that I might signe itt before I leave that country.

One of my trumpets is this evening come from the French army. Thay told him there had been an action in Spain, and that thay had had the advantage. But an Ierish Lieutenant told him that he beleived the French had the worst, for since the news came thay had been out of humour. I am afraid it has been no great action, for the last letters from France say possativly that King Charles was marching towardes Vallencia.

706. GODOLPHIN *to* MARLBOROUGH   [*30 September 1706*]

Source: Blenheim MSS. A1-36.
Printed: Coxe, ii. 98.

Newmarkett 30 September 1706

You will receive from mee by this post a letter dated from St. Albans,[5] and I should not have troubled you from hence, but to tell you that Collonel Hamilton[6] has brought mee a letter from Lord Peterborow of the 4th September old stile in which the only matter of fact he tells is that he had left the army and court upon a counsell of warr held at Guadalaxara pretending he had orders from the Queen to goe to Italy. The whole councill agreed to it by which one may conclude, they were as well content to bee rid of him as he to goe.

Collonel Hamilton tells mee thay had the news at Alicant before he left it, of the victory at Turin. I don't find he can give any other account of my Lord's jorney to the Duke of Savoy than to gett some dismounted German troopers, and to carry them back to Spain and mount them. This seems so

---

[1] p. 686. Marlborough to Heinsius, 26 Sept./7 Oct., 't Hoff, pp. 274-5.
[2] The attacking of Toulon.   [3] See p. 691.
[4] 23 Sept./4 Oct., 't Hoff, pp. 273-4.   [5] Letter 704.
[6] Hans Hamilton (died 1721); wounded at Schellenberg; colonel, Regiment of Foot, 1705; quartermaster-general of forces with Peterborough.

slight an occasion to a Generall, that I can't help thinking it might bee worth your pains to engage Comte Maffei to lett you know what he says to the Duke of Savoy, for my opinion is, that it fully deserve[s] your curiosity.

707. MARLBOROUGH *to* GODOLPHIN
[*30 September/11 October 1706*]

Source: Blenheim MSS. A1-14.
Printed: Coxe, ii. 122–3, 142 (inc.), the latter as October 12.

Gramets October 11th 1706

Since my last we have no letters from England, nor any news from France. I expect the Comte de Sensindorff about a fortnight hence, and then I shall be able to lett you know what the Emperor's intentions are for the operations of the next campagne on the Rhine; for if thay can be braught to act offinsivly that will very much help the Allies in all other parts.

It has always, and is stil my opinion that Monsieur Slingelandt is the best inclined for the carrying on of the warr of any of The Hague. This opinion makes me send you the inclosed letter,[1] that you may see how the humor runs in that place. This letter should be seen by none, besides the Queen and Prince, but such as you would advise with to know how I aught to carry myself when I come to The Hague. The Comte de Maffie has shown me a letter he has from Paris, in which he is assured that the French are resolved to make no new offers til I am gone for England, and then thay will offer whatever thay think will be agreable to 19 [Holland]. When I have been at Bruxelles some few days with Mr. Stepney, I think it will be for her Majesty's service that I take Mr. Stepney with me to The Hague, to try if possible to cure their jealoussies, and then send him back to Bruxelles. Having write thus far I have received yours of the 23 of the last month,[2] and a copie from Mr. Secretary Harley of yours to Monsieur Buys, which is so reasonable and just that it will be impossible for him to give an answere, so that the effect of your letter will be, that thay will be angry. For by all that I can larn, thay are resolved to have a peace. But in my opinion, when thay shal endeavour to put it in practice, thay will find it very difficult, for I do not think their people will be pleased with any propositions that are not liked by the Queen. This has given me some trouble, but nothing in comparison of what I now fiel by a letter I have received this morning from 114 [Lady Marlborough], concerning the temper and resolutions of 14 [the Whigs], by which I see all things is like to go to confusion.[3] Yours of the same date mentions nothing of it, which makes me fear you have taken your resolution, which if it be to retier, I must lay the consequence before you, which is that certainly the

---

[1] 25 Sept./6 Oct., untraced; reply, 29 Sept./10 Oct., Murray, iii. 165–6.
[2] Letter 698.   [3] See p. 675 n. 3.

Dutch will make their peace, which will be of fattal consequence, especially considering the advantages we now have, for in all probabilly one yeare's war more would give ease to all Christendome for many yeares. I have write my mind with freedome to 83 [the Queen],[1] so that having done my duty, let what will happen, I shall be the more easy in my mind. Allow me to give you the assurance, that I know you to be a sincer honest man. May God so blesse me, as I shal be carefull that whatever man is your enemy shall never be my friend. As soon as you receive this, I conjure you to let me have your thoughts freely, for til then I shall be very uneasy.

708. MARLBOROUGH *to the* DUCHESS

[*30 September/11 October 1706*]

Source: Blenheim MSS. E3.
Printed: Coxe, ii. 145 (inc).

Gramets October 11, 1706

When I write my last I was as I ever shall be very much yours, but very full of the spleen, and I think with to[o] much reason, For when I am, without flattering myself, imploying my whole time to the best of my understanding for the publick good, and as I do asure you in the presence of God, neglect no opertunity of letting 83 [the Queen] see what I take to be her trew intirest, I do not say this to flatter any party, for I never will do itt, lett the consequence be what it will, for as partys thay are both in the wrong. But it is most certain that 73 [Rochester] and his adherants are not to be trusted, so that 83 [the Queen] has no choice but that of employing those that will carry on the warr and support 91 [Godolphin], for if any other methode be taken I know we shall go to confusion. Now this being the case, I leave you to judge whether I am dealt kindly with. I do not say this to any other end but to have your justice and kindness, for in that will consist my futor happyness. As I am sure I would venture a thousand lives if I had them to procure ease and happyness to the Queen, yet no number of men could persuade me to act as a minister in what is not my opinion; so that I shal never faile of speaking my mind very freely. And as my opinion is that the tackers, and all the adherents of 73 [Rochester] are not for the carrying on of the war, and consequently not in the trew intirest of the Queen and king-dome, you may depend I shall never joine with any but such as I think do serve Her and the kingdome with al their hearts. If the warr continues for one yeare longer with success, I hope it will not be in anybody's power to make the Queen's business uneasy, and then I shall be glad to live as quiet as possible, and not envye the governing men, who would then I beleive think better of 90 [Marlborough] and 91 [Godolphin] then thay now do. I will own frankly to you that the jealoussy that some of your friends have that

90 [Marlborough] and 91 [Godolphin] do not act sincerly, were it not for my gratitude to 83 [the Queen] and concern for 91 [Godolphin], I would now retier, and never serve more; for I have had the good luck to deserve better from all Englishmen then to be suspected of not being in the trew intirest which I am in, and ever will be without being of a faction. As this principal shal governe me for the litle remainder of my life, I must not think of being popular, but shall have the satisfaction of going to my grave with the opinion of having acted as became an honest man. And if I have your estime and love, I shall think myself intierly happy.

Having write thus far I have received your two letters of the 20 and 21 of the last month, which serves to conferme me in my opinion; and since the resolution is taken to vex or ruin 91 [Godolphin] and 90 [Marlborough] because 83 [the Queen] has not complyed with what has been desired for 117 [Sunderland], I shal from henceforward despise all mankind, and think there is no such thing as vertu, for I that know with what zeal 91 [Godolphin] has pressed 83 [the Queen] in that matter. I do pitty him but shall love him as long as I live, and be a friend to none whomesoever can be his enemy. As to myself, I have write my mind very freely to 83 [the Queen] on this occasion, so that whatever misfortunes may happen, I shal have a quiet mind having done what I have thought my duty. And as for the resolution of making me uneasy, I beleive thay will not have much pleasure in that, for as I have not sett my heart upon having justice or any favour done me, I shal not be disapointed, nor will I be ill used by any man. I do not wonder at the reason given by 115 [Halifax] for not coming to 114 [Lady Marlborough], but I think it by no means a good one for 117 [Sunderland] to give.

The horses shal be keep on this side as you desire, but Lord Sunderland should let me have his commands as to his sett.

709. MARLBOROUGH *to* GODOLPHIN   [3/14 October 1706]

Source: Blenheim MSS. A1-14.
Printed: Coxe, ii. 79–80, 123 (inc.).

Cambron October 14th 1706

After having had very bad weather, we have now the finest that is possible. I hope you have the same at Newmarkett.

I send you one shete of the *Paris Gazet*, that you may see what thay say of the affaires of Spain. I hope you will have better news from that country by the way of Portugale. Monsieur de Vandome tels his officers, that he has it in his power of strenghning his army to 140 battallions and 180 squadrons, and that if my Lord Marlborough gives him an opertunity, he will make him a visset before the campagne ends. I beleive he has neither will nor power to do itt, which we shall see very quickly, for we are now camped in so open a country, that if he marches to us, we cannot refuse fighting. What I most aprehend, is that he will have it in his power to give us trouble about Courtray. You will have seen by my last how uneasy I was at some news I have heard from England. I shall continue so til I have your thoughts on that matter, for my trouble proceeds from my friendshipe to you, and my duty to the Queen. For the consequences of what may happen to the rest of Europe, mankind must and will strugle for what is for their own safety. And for myself, I shall be much happyer in a retiered life, when I have 83 [the Queen] and 91 [Godolphin] leave for itt.

I hear Lord Hatton[1] is dead. If it be so, I beg of the Queen, she will be pleased to remember her promis for my brother Charles;[2] and then my Lord Essex may be declared.[3] I shal give myself the honour to write to her by this post about itt. The Dutch makes difficultys about the quarters and expence of the Prussian troupes. I am afraid thay have peace so much in their thoughts, that thay will let these troupes march back to their own country, which may prove al maner of ways of ill consequence. We are asured that the Duke de la Feuliade is going with 15 battalions by sea for the Millanais, by which you may see that the King of France will support that warr, if possible. By my letters from The Hague, I see thay are preparing a great deal of business for me, as to their disputes with the Emperor, their Barier and the peace. But I hope the Queen wil allow me to speak my mind freely, and then come for England; for in my opinion, thay will be so extravegant on their Barier, that it will hinder the treaty for the Succession.

710. MARLBOROUGH *to the* DUCHESS   [*3/14 October 1706*]

Source: Blenheim MSS. E3.
Printed: *Private Correspondence*, i. 70-1 (inc.).

Cambron October 14th 1706

Wee are now in the finest camp I ever saw, with the finest weather, which is very agreable after having had three weeks of the worst could be seen. If my mind were easy, I could in this place have health; but how can that be, when one thinks of the confusion your letters tels me must unavoydably be in England. I see no remidy but patience, for if it were not God's pleasure to punish us for our sins this way, he would never suffer wise men to be so unreasonable; for it is certainly the part of madd men to hurt onsself in order to be revenged of others, especially when they are our best friends. I shal say no more on this subject, having resigned myself to the Almighty's pleasure, and I hope it will do me good for the remaining part of my life, for

---

[1] Christopher, first Viscount Hatton (1632–1706), governor of Guernsey, died shortly before 24 Sept.

[2] To be governor of Guernsey, to which he was appointed in November.

[3] Constable of the Tower, a post for which he had been put forward by the Duchess, vacant since Sept. 1705. For the cause of the delay, see p. 454.

I am sure I will end it without having any further ambition, which makes men slaves.

Since you have no mind to the coach horses as soon as I come to The Hague, I shall send them to Bruxelles to the rest of my horses, which are to be there this winter.¹ If we are to beleive the *Gazett* of Paris, our affaires do not go so well in Spain as I could wish, for thay say that King Charles is gone with his army to Vallencia, and that their King is gone to Madrid; but I hope you have better news by the way of Portugale. We have here no further thoughts of attempting anything more this campagne, but the putting Courtray in a condition to have a garrison this winter, so that if the French attempte nothing which I beleive thay will not, our campagne will end in litle more then a fortnight. I intend to go to Bruxelles about ten days hence, for two or three days, and then return to the army in order to send them to their severall quarters, so that the first weeke in the next month this stile I shall be at The Hague.

711. MARLBOROUGH *to* GODOLPHIN [7/18 October 1706]

Source: Blenheim MSS. A1-14.
Printed: Coxe, ii. 99, 125 (inc.).

Cambron October 18th 1706

The enclosed French letter² is what I received by the last post from the Duke of Lorrain's minester at The Hague.³ He is a very honest man. I send itt that you may see what he writes concerning the peace. He must not be known to have write me such a letter. You may obsarve that the French are trying in all courts but that of England, for the having a negociation for peace, by which thay hope to slaken the preperations for the next campagne, whielst thay are making their utmust effortes. I am very much afraid the court of Hanover will not succed in their negociation with the King of Sweeden,⁴ as thay flatter themselves; for that King has given commissions

---

¹ The horses sent him by the Elector of Hanover. See p. 667.

² 2/13 Oct., B.M., Add. MS. 28057, fols. 322-3, informing him the Bishop of Osnabrück was content to leave the settlement of the Münster dispute to the Pope. The cantons of Switzerland (Berne excepting) offered their services as mediators; Helvetius had returned to The Hague with new propositions for a peace.

³ Charles Baron Parisot, envoy at The Hague 1705-7.

⁴ The Dutch were concerned that the march of Charles XII into Saxony might force the Kings of Denmark and Prussia and the Landgrave of Hesse to withdraw their troops in the pay of the Maritime Powers and send them to the assistance of Augustus of Saxony, with whom these princes were bound by treaty. Heinsius to Marlborough, 26 Aug./6 Sept., 't Hoff, p. 265. Hoping that 'the ill effects of this march might be prevented by a friendly treaty with the King of Sweden', Marlborough wrote the Elector of Hanover for his advice on how the Maritime Powers might act to curb hostilities in the Empire. Marlborough to Heinsius, 31 Aug./11 Sept., 4/15 Sept., ibid., pp. 266-7, to the Elector, 31 Aug./11 Sept., Murray, iii. 129. Responding to this hint the Elector sent one of his ministers, Bodo von Oberg, to Charles XII to see what could be done to ameliorate the situation. The Elector to Marlborough, 10/21 Sept., Murray, iii. 130.

for six redgiments of dragons, and I think takes the necessary measures for the having in the spring at least fivty thousand men, which must disturb all the projects we can make, though he should not declare for France; for such an army must retier into Polland, or find a pretext to advance further into Garmany, for in that country thay can't stay. You will, at your leasure, read Mr. Johnson's answere to my letter.[1] As far as I can judge by itt he has no opinion of the Union, nor will medle so as to be of any use. I do with all my heart wish good success to the Union, and that you may have as litle to do with those men as is possible.

As soon as I hear the Queen has apointed the meetting of the Parliament I shall send the members over. You know thay never finish their mony matters in Holland til the Parliament has made their first votes. I beleive this will find you at Newmarket, where I hope you will gett so much health as will enable you to undergo the labours and trouble of the winter campagne, on the success of which all depends. I have received a letter from my Lord North, in which he desires to succed my brother in the employement of the Tower. It is very trew that I did formerly promis to serve him whenever this should happen, but he had not then behaved himself so as he did last winter.[2] But that which will make this easy is, if the Queen will be pleased to declare her engagement of Constable to Lord Essex, and that she will not as yett put anybody into my brother's place.[3] I beg you will acquaint Her Majesty with this, for if Lord North has not already, you may be sure he will as soon as he receives my letter, come both to the Queen and yourself. His nature is very pressing. I had last night three of yours of the 25, 28, and 30[4] of the last month, but hear nothing of the expresse you mention.[5] But I hear enough from England to be uneasy to the last degree. I am obliged to Sir Charles Hedges for sending mee copies of all that is come from Portugale and Lord Pitterborow, but the bulk is soe great, that I am almost sure that I shall not have time to read them til I am on my way to The Hague. But I have given them to Mr. Cardonel, that he may see if there be anything required from me, so that the Queen's Service may not suffer by my not reading them. I am obliged to you for the account you give me of Woodstock. But if wee must go to confusion, I can be very well contented with my poor garden of St. Albans, which you mentioned so kindly in yours from thence, that it gave me pleasure.

[1] Marlborough wrote urging him and his friends to support the Union (above, p. 647). Johnston's reply referred to here is untraced, but he wrote Marlborough again on 29 Oct., reporting 'since I had the honour to write to your Grace my friends have declared themselves for the Union'. Blenheim MSS. A2-2. See Johnston's letters in *The Correspondence of George Baillie of Jerviswood*, ed. by the Earl of Minto (Bannatyne Club, 1842).

[2] In the House of Lords where he acted with the Tory opposition.

[3] As Lieutenant of the Tower. The post was given to Cadogan, 30 Dec.

[4] Letters 701, 704, 706.

[5] 'A great packet from Lady Marlborough' (p. 696).

The Elector of Hanover has very much recomended to me[1] that the King of Prussia may not know that he is against that treaty which his Majesty preposes to have made with the King of Sweed[en], he being obliged by this marage of his daughter to keep measures with that court.

I send by this post a copie of my letter to the King of Prussia[2] to Mr. Secretary Harley, so that if I should have omitted any part of her Majesty's commands, that I may have his further instructions.

712. MARLBOROUGH *to the* DUCHESS [*7/18 October 1706*]

Source: Blenheim MSS. E3.
Printed: Coxe, i. 155–6 (inc.).

Cambron October 18th 1706

I send you inclosed Mr. Vanbroke's letter,[3] which is write since you were at Woodstock. I send it for your own satisfaction, and beg you will not let anybody know that I have sent itt. I hope you will order it so that after I have been some days at London we may go to the Lodge, and be quiet, for I am quite weary of the world; and since I am afraid there is a necessity of my serving in this country as long as this warr lastes, let me have a litle more quiet in England then I have been used to have, and then I shall be the better able to go through what I must indure in this country; for upon the success we have had this yeare, our friends grow less governable then when thay were afraid of the French. I am sorry to tel you that the peece of hanging you sent by Lady Portland[4] is not as yet to be found, there house-keeper saying it was sent to Lord Albemarle, but at my arrival at The Hague I hope to find it. But for fear of the worst you will send another litle peace by Captain Sanders, for the bargain that is made for the new hangings is that thay are to be of the same fines with those of the Electoris,[5] so that if there be one peece finer then the others, I desire that may be sent; and if you can, to let me know which peece it was that was sent by Lady Portland,[6] so that if it should be lost, that I may have another made. As I have no further prospect of doing any more service to the publick this campagne,

---

[1] 27 Sept./8 Oct., Macpherson, ii. 67. The King of Sweden sought to draw Prussia and Hanover into an alliance recognizing Stanislaus as King of Poland and guaranteeing the Treaty of Altranstädt by which Augustus gave up that throne. Prussia signed a treaty in Aug. 1707 but Hanover did not accede to it, because of pressure from the Maritime Powers, according to one authority (Hatton, pp. 221–2). The Elector's remarks here may be to justify himself to England so as not to jeopardize their support for his candidacy to succeed Prince Lewis as commander of the Imperial army on the Rhine.

[2] 7/18 Oct., Murray, iii. 178–9, regarding his proposal of the triple alliance with Sweden and Hanover.

[3] Untraced. [4] See p. 524 n. 3.

[5] See p. 409. The new hangings were the Alexander set. See p. 750 n. 4.

[6] Lady Portland was to leave it with Stanhope for Marlborough to compare with those made at Brussels at the end of the campaign. Marlborough to Portland, 19/30 Aug., Murray, iii. 111–12.

but that of putting Courtray in a condition, every day is very tedious, and for the two or three days I shall be att Bruxelles I shall be tore to peices, their being twenty pretenders to every place that must be given; for I have not been able to prevaile with the deputys to declare them before my arrivall, which would have given me ease.

Having write thus far I have had the happyness of your kind letters of the 23, 26 and 29 of the last month from Woodstock. The expresse you mention, which also 91 [Godolphin] write me word from St. Albans he would send, yet I hear nothing of itt, though I have received another letter of his from Newmarkett. I have already more then once write my mind very freely, so that my consience is at ease, though my mind is very farr from itt; for I did flatter myself that my zeal and sincerity for 83 [the Queen] was so well known to her, that my representations would have had more waite then I find thay have. But nothing can ever hinder me from being ready to lay downe my life when she can think it is for her Service, for I serve with an intier affection as well as the utmust duty; for you, and I, and all ours would be the most ungratefull people that ever lived if we did not venture all for her good. By this do not mistake me, for I am very sensible that if 91 [Godolphin] be obliged to retier I cannot serve in the ministry. But when these projectors have put all in confusion, I shall then readily not only venture my life, but all that I have to show my gratitude. When the expresse comes by which I shall see all that has passed, I shall once more write as becomes me, and will yet hope it may have its effect. If not, God's will be done.

713. GODOLPHIN *to* MARLBOROUGH [*9 October 1706*]

Source: Blenheim MSS. A1-36.
Printed: Coxe, ii. 365–6 (inc.), but as 1707.

Newmarkett 9 of October 1706

I have but just time to acknowledg yours of the 11th[1] for fear my letter should not come time enough to overtake the mail at Harwich. There came 2 mails from Holland together, but I have not yett received any letter from you of the 14th to myself, though I have seen yours of that date to the Secretary.

I did not want the letter you enclosed from Slingelandt to know their humour in 19 [Holland] for 5 [peace]. I have letters almost every post from 366 [Buys]. I send you the last[2] because I have not time to coppy it. Pray keep it, and when you see him, if you ask him, I beleive he will show you

[1] Letter 707.
[2] 4/15 Oct., in Vreede, pp. 158–61. Buys asked that Marlborough be authorized to prepare preliminaries in conjunction with the Dutch for a peace with France, to include the major conditions of the Allies.

my answer[1] which is in short to repeat, that if they will proceed to settle their state of warr,[2] they may have such terms as will satisfy and secure all their Allyes wheras any other method will create jealouses and distractions among the Allyes and oblige all sides to continue their expenses.

I need not therfore trouble you with anything more to guide you in your behaviour when you come to The Hague especially since Mr. Secretary Harley's letter to you, upon that poynt, is so plain, and so full. I think it was dated the $\frac{4}{15}$.[3]

In a word, after the advantages with which God has blessed the army of the Allyes England will not bee satisfied, nor themselves lose, with less terms than those mentioned in my letter to 366 [Buys].

I cannot say enough to you, nor have I time, for your expression, of kindness to myself. I am apt to think that matter may remayn, as it is till your coming over, which I wish may bee with the soonest, but not much longer.

713A. GODOLPHIN *to* BUYS   [*9 October 1706*]

Source: Rijksarchief, AANW 1865 B XIV A, fols. 157–8.

Newmarkett 9th of October 1706

I have the honour of yours of the 15th by which you seem to think I have not explained myself sufficiently, why the treaty for guaranty of a future peace could not bee in the same instrument with that of our Protestant Succession, and your Barriere.

It is very obvious that wee cannot expect the Duke of Savoy should enter into a guaranty of a Protestant Succession in England, and yett on the other hand, the Duke of Savoy is an ally of too much weight not to bee one of the guarands of a future peace.

As to the authoritys and powers you desire may bee sent to the Duke of Marlborough in what relates to the peace, his Grace is sufficiently impowered and instructed in that matter, and Mr. Stepney has also full powers and instructions for the preliminary treaty.

In short, the Queen desires a solid lasting peace as much as you can doe in Holland but she would not shew such a desire of it, as will bee the only means to deprive us of those advantages with which God has blessed the arms of the Allyes and reduced France to such a condition that whenever you will settle your state of warr for the next campagne, you may bee very

---

[1] The following letter.

[2] The annual report submitted each year by the Council of State to the States General, in which the events of the year were reviewed and budget estimates were presented for the following year. Once approved by the States General the estimates were sent to the individual Provinces for their concurrence as they bore the expense. The statement forwarded 19/30 Oct. 1706 is in Boyer, *Annals*, v, appendix, pp. 146–55.

[3] Longleat, Portland MSS., v, fols. 108–9.

secure, that before it begins France will bee very glad of a peace upon those terms which wee have added to your letter;[1] and without which I beg leave to repeat, your finances will bee eased but for a very short time, but if you show a vigorous resolution of carrying onn the warr another year no impartiall man can doubt, but that it will quickly procure you such terms, as may make the peace lasting and secure for all your Allyes.

714. GODOLPHIN *to* MARLBOROUGH   [*10 October 1706*]

Source: Blenheim MSS. A1-36.
Printed: Coxe, ii. 123-4 (inc.).

Newmarkett 10th of October 1706

Since my last[2] I have also received your letter of the 14th.[3] To that of the 11th I made some answer by the last post, and sent you at the same time, the last letter I had from 366 [Buys] as also the substance of my answer, which was very short.

I believe, as you seem to doe, that notwithstanding the violent passion for 5 [peace] which appears in 19 [Holland] they will have a good deal of difficulty to compass their inclinations against the opinion of 17 [England], especially if they will force us to make it publick upon what terms 83 [the Queen] is willing to approve of 5 [peace]; since I can't but think those will not appear unreasonable, neither to the rest of the Allyes nor to their own people.

The chief poynt, in my opinion, is that Holland, should upon your arrivall at The Hague, proceed to settle their state of warr, for the next year; and though 20 [France] should then make new offers, after you were come too England, they could not fail of communicating them here, before any resolution were taken. Upon the whole matter therfore, it seems best upon all accounts, that you should come over as soon as you can, since you are wanted here as much as there and what you are wanted for here, can't bee supplyed by another, as the business on that side, may, for ought I know, upon any extraordinary occasion which shall happen to occurr, when you are here.

I think it will bee right to give them what ease you can, in bringing Mr. Stepney with you to The Hague, before he enters upon business at Brusselles. I understand by Mr. Secretary Harley, that both you and hee are furnished with all the necessary powers for either of you, in any of the matters to bee transacted there at this time.

I am apprehensive Comte Zinzendorsf's coming to The Hague will rather increase than appease the differences betwixt the Emperour and the States.

The Queen is easy in what you propose[4] for your brother, and my Lord Essex. The rest will remain till you come over.

---

[1] By Halifax's letter to Heinsius of 8 Oct., in Vreede, pp. 165-70.
[2] Letter 713.   [3] Letter 709.
[4] That Churchill be made governor of Guernsey and Essex Constable of the Tower. See pp. 171-2.

715. MARLBOROUGH *to* GODOLPHIN   [*10/21 October 1706*]

Source: Blenheim MSS. A1-14.
Printed: Coxe, ii. 125 (inc.).
Endorsed by Godolphin: This has been readd to Mrs. Morley [the Queen].

Cambron October 21th 1706

I forgote to send by the last post the enclosed letter from the Pensioner.[1] You will see by it the necessity there is of sending me such instructions as I may communicat to him, and Monsieur Buys, who pened the clause for the Barier, so that you must be the more careful in the objections you make to the wording of that clause. By all I hear from The Hague, we must not expect one step to be made to the Succession but as the Barier goes with itt. Thay are so flattered from France, that whatever is easy to themselves, thay think both just and reasonable. But when I come to The Hague I shall use my endeavours to let the honest men see that the project of France is to make them fall out with their best friends, which is the only methode thay have left for the disturbing of the confederacy.

The enclosed is the freshest I have seen of what is doing in Spain. I wish the troupes with Lord Rivers were there, for the affaires of the Allyes, not going well in that country, will be an argument to the Dutch for peace, but in my opinion, aught to be made use of for the carrying on of the warr; for if wee cannot preserve that Monarkie intier the peace will not be of long durance. I have had the favour of yours of the 3 from Newmarket,[2] with the inclosed letters, but it is now so late that it is impossible to say anything on them by this post.

Mr. Stepney is with me.

716. MARLBOROUGH *to* GODOLPHIN   [*10/21 October 1706*]

Source: Blenheim MSS. A1-14.
Addressed: To Yourself.
Endorsed by Godolphin: not read to Mrs. Morley [the Queen].

October 21, 1706

The expresse you have sent came this afternoon.[3] I must own to you that I have been so very much mortefied, at seeing the litle effect my letters of late has had on 83 [the Queen], that I was resolved to write no more, but at my arrivall to have spoke my mind with al submission and duty, very freely, after which I should have given no more trouble. But as it is, if you will send me anything that will do good, I shall with pleasure write itt. For as I

---

[1] 5/16 Oct., 't Hoff, pp. 277–8, in which Heinsius hopes Marlborough will come to The Hague with full powers and instructions to negotiate the treaties for the Succession and the Barrier, which the English ministry seem to have left to Marlborough to conclude.

[2] Untraced.   [3] See p. 696 n. 2.

am resolved to be quiet if 83 [the Queen] persistes in the opinion she is now in, so nothing shall hinder me from venturing my life to give her ease, when these people has braught her business into confusion, as I am afraid it will be even this winter; so I beg of you to take no resolution that shall hinder you from serving her, when her necessitys will require itt.

717. GODOLPHIN *to* MARLBOROUGH   [*13 October 1706*]

Source: Blenheim MSS. A1-36.
Printed: Coxe, ii. 124–5 (inc.).

St James's October 13th 1706

At my arrivall here last night, from Newmarkett, I found the favour of yours of the 18th with the papers enclosed.[1]

I think as you doe, Mr. Johnstone, nor his friends, will not bee of much use to the Union. Wee shall hear now very soon how that matter is like to goe, for upon the 10th their business was to begin. But hapning to begin so late, makes it not possible for the English Parliment to meet so soon this year as it used to doe, and I believe it can hardly sitt, to doe business before the 15th or 20th of November, so that instead of sending over the officers,[2] as you propose, I hope you will take care to bring over yourself, as much before that time as you can. I think it were easy enough to make ourselves very strong in this sessions of Parliament, but the misfortune is, that 83 [the Queen] is very uneasy in consenting to those things, which having been once swallowed, are therfore become necessary to make us soe.

The necessity of the Parliament meeting to take here, may, I fear, furnish a handle to the States to putt off the fixing of their state of warr for next year, which, if they doe, it will bee the greatest encoragmont imaginable to the partisans of France; and they have no ground to take any pretext for delay, from thence, since 'tis necessity and not choyce, which retards the sitting of our Parliament.

As to the letter you sent mee from The Hague concerning 5 [peace][3] I can easily believe that and more. The inclinations of 19 [Holland] are so violent and so plain, that I am of opinion, nothing will bee able to prevent their taking effect, but our being as plain with them upon the same subject, and threatning them to publish and expose to the whole world, the terms which they sollicite for, and the terms to which wee are willing to consent, if they think fitt to insist upon them in conjunction with those Allyes without whose assistance they could not have been able to support themselves.

I hope their own people would think this reasonable. I am very sure the generality of the people in England would not bee satisfyed with less.

---

[1] Letter 711.   [2] Who were Members of Parliament.
[3] From the Duke of Lorraine's envoy.

I am sorry you have not had time to read 127 [Peterborough] long papers, because you will find by them, that he is preparing materialls of all sorts, to perplex and embroyl all the publick affairs this winter, and to that end, he has lodged coppyes of these papers in the hands of his agents here, to bee distributed to such peoples as he thinks will bee glad to lay hold of things of that nature, and I think, one may bee sure 74 [Nottingham] will bee fully possessed of that whole affair.

Now there is a way to prevent any ill effects of all this. If you can by the means of Comte Maffie, or by writing to 317 [Duke of Savoy] gett into our hands the originall letter or an authentick coppy of it, which 127 [Peterborough] wrote some time since to 317 [Duke of Savoy], offering him no less than to putt him into the place of 315 [King Charles the 3d] and I am not sure, but he may yett have the same views; if therfore 317 [Duke of Savoy] can bee prevailed with to part with this letter rather then suffer 19's [England] affairs to bee soe embroyled as to weaken the support which he may otherwise expect from 19 [England]; which once 127 [Peterborough] knows this letter is in hands that can produce it upon occasion it will keep him in awe, so as to make all that matter easy. And I know no other method of hindering it from being very troublesome, and losing, at least, a great deal of time, if it has no worse effect.

These motives rightly explained to 317 [Duke of Savoy] might I should hope, prevail with him, to give that ease to 83's [the Queen] affairs.

115 [Halifax] has shown mee a long letter which he has had from 365 [Heinsius] very intent upon the settling of the Barriere. He says hee sent you a coppy of it.[1] I have desired him to send you also, a coppy of his answer,[2] and I hope he will doe it by this post, since I think it may bee of use to you, when you come to discourse with them upon this affair at The Hague. I am of opinion they will think it reasonable to specifie the particular towns which they propose to have for their Barriere, and are pretty well cured of the folly of affecting the sovereignty for themselves, which however they had to a great degree swallowed from the offers made them by France, last winter, before you had conquered the country.

---

[1] Heinsius's letter of 27 Sept./8 Oct. was copied by Addison and sent by Halifax to Marlborough on 4/15 Oct. Both are in Blenheim MSS. A1-46. See Geikie, pp. 54-5. Heinsius wrote that the mere existence of the Spanish Netherlands as a buffer state constituted no Barrier or safeguard for the Dutch and that his country must maintain troops in such places as they considered necessary, to make it an effective Barrier, which was essential for the preservation of the United Provinces. As only part of the Spanish Netherlands was in the hands of the Allies they wanted *carte blanche* to name the places to be occupied at the conclusion of the war. Halifax warned Marlborough that the Dutch must not be given a free hand in selecting the fortresses for their Barrier and that the places could be selected from the whole country, whether presently in the hands of the Allies or not.

[2] 8/19 Oct., in Vreede, pp. 165-70. Copy enclosed by Halifax to Marlborough in his letter of the same date, Blenheim MSS. A1-46. Halifax accepted the right of the Dutch to a Barrier under their direct control, but protested their demand to have a free hand in occupying whatever part of the Spanish Netherlands they chose.

I am afrayd, wee shall have another difficulty, though of the same nature, with the court of Vienna, about the Duchy of Milan. Italy will bee all up in arms, if the Emperour thinks to keep the possession of it in his own right. But that is not all. No one of the Allyes will like it any better than the princes of Italy.

For this reason the Queen being about to dispatch Mr. Crow to the King of Spayn will cause him to bee particularly instructed to desire that his Catholic Majesty would bee pleased to appoint a governour there in his own right, and to lett him see, that the Emperour's pretensions in that particular will not bee born by the rest of the Allyes.

I think your answer to the King of Prussia, upon his proposalls of the alliance with S[weden] is as well turned as is possible, but Mr. Secretary Harley being out of town, that matter has not been layd before the Cabinet Counsell, nor doe I see at present, any use of bringing it there.

Directions will bee sent for the putting all the Queen's forces in Spain or Portugall, under the orders of my Lord Gallway.

I hope to hear when you come to The Hague, that you have putt an end to all their unreasonable jealousys on that side of the water. I wish there were no such thing anywhere, but wee on this side are not without our share of them.

I have not yett seen or heard of my Lord North, but if he does vouchsafe to make any application to mee, I shall endeavour upon your account, to use him more civilly than he deserves.

718. MARLBOROUGH *to* GODOLPHIN [*13/24 October 1706*]

Source: Blenheim MSS. A1-14.
Printed: Coxe, ii. 74, 126–7.
Endorsed by Godolphin: This has been readd to Mrs. Morley [the Queen].

Cambron October 24, 1706

I find by your last letter,[1] that aplications are made by Mr. Mordant and others for my brother's place in the Tower. I beg you will not be ingaged, and that the Queen will gratefie me on this occasion. I would not have this place disposed of as yett, but when I shall think it a proper time. I would then beg the Queen would be pleased to lett Brigadier Cadogan have itt, since it will be a provision for him in time of peace. As I would put my life in his hands, so I will be answerable for his faithfulness and duty to the Queen. I have for the Queen's Service obliged him this warr to expose his life very often, so that in justice I owe him this good office. I send by this

---

[1] Untraced. This letter must have been sent by the post of 4 Oct.

expresse copies of the Elector's letters to me, and the deputys of the army.[1] I am of the opinion that this matter has been consulted by some in Holland, so that the Queen must be the more careful of the derections she shall think fit to give. For should you show a back-wardness to a good peace, thay would make an ill use of itt; and I beleive on[e] of the designs that France has in this proposall is that it may make Holland lesse zealous in their preparations for the next campagne, whielst thay are doing their utmost. Another is to lett the world see that thay have been managing a treaty these last 12 months. If it were possible to have their proposals without entering into a treaty, I should think that were best. For I am very sure thay would not be liked by the confederates; and if thay have not an opertunity given them to make a proposall, thay will endeavour to make every country beleive that thay should have offered what would have been most agreable to them. I beg I may not be employed in this first step. Mr. Stepney will be very proper. The deputys were very desirous of having my opinion, that thay might have sent it to The Hague, but I desired to be excused by telling them that my opinion in this matter must be governed by her Majesty's commands, and that I was sure the States would give no answere til thay had consulted with her. I shall go to Bruxelles on Wendsday next, being the 27th, and begine my jorny to The Hague on the 2d of the next month. By the enclosed letter from the Pensioner,[2] you will see what he desires of mee. Whatever the Queen would have mee do at The Hague, I beg I may have her commands by the next post, for I shall be very uneasy til I come to England; for I have never been so uneasy, as I am at this time, since her Majesty's coming to the crown.

October 25

I thought to have sent this last night but was disapointed, so that you will have no other by this night's post, being to march tomorrow. I have chose this day for the seeing the army under their armes, which is a sort of taking leave, though I do not intend to quit them til the second of the next month at which time I intend to send them to their severall garrisons.

[1] The Elector of Bavaria, 10/21 Oct., Lamberty, iv. 302–3, 304, making a formal offer on behalf of Louis XIV to treat for a peace in joint conferences with a cessation of arms while it was in progress. For this offer and the response of the Allies see Stork–Penning, pp. 120–7; Geikie, pp. 68, 73–4; Legrelle, iv. 410–15; Cuyper, *Dagboek*, pp. 179–219; and below, p. 734.

[2] 9/20 Oct., 't Hoff, p. 279, hoping he will conclude the Treaty for the Succession and the Barrier when he comes to The Hague.

719. MARLBOROUGH *to* GODOLPHIN   [*14/25 October 1706*]

Source: Blenheim MSS. A1-14.
Addressed: To yourself.
Endorsed by Godolphin: not read to Mrs. Morley [the Queen].
Printed: Coxe, ii. 158 (inc.)

October 25

You will see by the enclosed copie what I write to the Queen.[1] and I hope you will not disaprove of my sending a copie of yours write to 83 [the Queen] on the 13th of the last month.[2] If 83 [the Queen] has complyed with your desires, you will be the best judge of what may be proper to be done with my letter, either to deliver it or burn itt. Monsieur Sesandre of Gand is come to me from the Elector to assure me in the King of France's name, that he had never any thoughts of excluding England in the peace, and that he is very desirous of making such a peace as may be durable. This matter is certainly consulted with some in Holland, but if we can prevaile to have no meeting til the French give their proposals in writing, this must vanish. For whielst King Philipp is at Madrid, the French King dares not offer Spain and the Indies for King Charles, since that would be the most certain way to make all Spain declare for King Charles. I do not doubt but those which have advised these letters have promised the King of France that his grandson shall have Naples and Sicily. If we can't avoyd runing into dist[r]action in England, a peace is the only thing for the Queen, but otherways one campagn more would secure us a good peace.

720. GODOLPHIN *to the* DUCHESS   [*16 October 1706*]

Source: Blenheim MSS. E20.

[Wednesday] October 16

I am extreamly thankful to you for the favour of yours of the 14th, which I received this forenoon, but very sorry to find you have been so pestered with madam 118 [Wharton],[3] who I agree with you is very diverting for a little while, to take and leave as one pleases, but terrible indeed to bee tyed to. I find she has been with you long enough for you to know her character very exactly, but I am afraid she has not been yett long enough with you to make you apprehend her returning so as to doe us any good; but I reckon you are relieved, for 118 [Wharton] went home this morning, but talked as if he would bee here again in a week or 10 days.

---

[1] Of this date (Coxe, ii. 156–8), pressing her to follow Godolphin's advice and accept the Whigs into the Ministry.

[2] See p. 679 n. 2.

[3] Lucy (Loftus), Countess of Wharton (1671–1717), married Wharton, as his second wife, 1692.

I am very sorry too what you say of Lord Marlborough's complaints in his letter to you,[1] and I have reason to bee soe, he seeming to bee so sensible of mine. I am not yett out of hopes but that his being here would goe a great way to ease us both in many of them. His convoy has orders to bee on the other side by the last day of this month, after which my Lord Portland, who is come, says he will bee obliged still to stay 8 or 10 days in Holland; but I hope it will not bee so long. His Lordship is gone to his house at Windsor. I have not seen him, but 115 [Halifax] tells mee he is very sanguine, and does not seem to apprehend the influence of the party in 19 [Holland] who are for 5 [peace]. He says they are but few, and dare not own their inclinations. He sayes poor Mr. Stanhope is very weak, and doubts whether he can live to come over.

I will not forget to move the Queen the first Cabinett Counsel day for my Lord Clancarty's[2] leave; and I hope I shall bee able to gett your poor neighbours' son into the circuit pardon, which usually comes out twice a year, and if I don't mistake, one of the times is not farr off. I wish the time for your coming this way were nearer.

721. GODOLPHIN *to* MARLBOROUGH   [*18 October 1706*]

Source: Blenheim MSS. A1-36.
Printed: Coxe, ii. 164-5 (inc.).

October 18, 1706

Since my last I have none of yours, but the wind being northeast, I hope wee shall have the letters tomorrow. I grow very impatient now, to know how soon I may hope to see you here, for I find plainly nothing will bee sett right with 83 [the Queen] as it ought to bee till then.

I am sensible at the same time that your being sometime at The Hague must bee of very great use to settle and fix the minds of those people. But when you have once seen Mr. Stepney and given him your instructions, those matters may bee left to his care; and the consequence of what you are wanted for here is incomparably greater. I have seen Lord Portland today, and I find him not very apprehensive that the generality of 19 [Holland] will bee so fond of 5 [peace] as wee seem to apprehend here. And I hope if the Dutch will specifie particularly the towns in Flanders which they propose for their Barriere and the number of troops necessary for their defence, you may soon conclude that treaty, and the guaranty of the Succession, which will bee of

---

[1] Letter 712.
[2] Donaugh MacCarthy, fourth Earl of Clancarty (1668–1734), Sunderland's Jacobite brother-in-law, who had been released from imprisonment in 1698 on condition of his living permanently abroad. He may have hoped to obtain the return of some of his estates which had been forfeited to the crown (see above, p. 132). He does not appear to have been given permission to return and died abroad. *D.N.B.*

lesse importance to us every day, if they goe onn as well, as they have begun in Scotland. The letters of this day from thence, give great hopes of carrying the Union. Mr. Johnston's friends otherwise called the new party,[1] seem to have joyned with the Court, which gives a great strength.

52 [James Craggs, Sr.][2] told mee this morning and promised mee to write soe to Mr. Freeman [Marlborough] that 76 [Harley, 61 [   ][3] and one or two more of 90's [Marlborough] particular friends were underhand endeavouring to bring all the difficultys they could think of, upon the pnblick business in the next sessions, and spoke of it to mee, as taking it for granted it was what I could not but have heard of before. I am apt to think they may have made stepps towards this which are not justifiable out of an apprehension that others would have all the meritt. But whatever bee their motive, the thing is destructive and pernicious. I have had a long letter[4] this very day from 76 [Harley] full of professions of being guided in these measures, as in all other by 90 [Marlborough] and 91 [Godolphin], but at the same time I doubt so much smoke could not come without some fire.

Sir John Leak is arrived here almost alone. He has left 20 ships at Lisbon. He says our army is in quarters of refreshment in the kingdom of Valentia. He has taken the islands of Ivyca and Majorca[5] where there is so much corn, that it will bee of great use to the army in Valentia. Our fleet[6] has mett with contrary winds and bad weather in the soundings which had dispersed them very much and disabled some of their transports. But the wind coming fair agayn they are gon onn to Lisbon, which was their rendezvous in case of separation. I am afrayd this will give still a farther delay to that expedition.

Mr. de Guiscard is going to 19 [Holland]. He thinks he could bee serviceable there, in letting people see the unseasonableness of 5 [peace] but I believe his chief business is to wait upon you.[7]

[1] Or the Squadrone Volante.

[2] Coxe identifies 52 as the Duchess but this is impossible because she was not in town (see p. 714). More likely it was James Craggs Sr., Marlborough's confidential agent, who sent him regular political reports.

[3] St. John? Harcourt? Brydges? Brydges may well be the one referred to here. About 20 Nov. he wrote Godolphin proposing that he form a third party of middle men based on the Court and close ranks against the Whigs (Stowe MSS., HM57, I. 46, Huntington Library). More likely it was St. John. See his letter to Marlborough in Coxe, ii. 163–4.

[4] 15 Oct., in H. M. C., *Bath MSS.*, i. 109–11.

[5] Ibiza and Majorca, the two largest islands in the Balearic Isles. Leake appeared before the former on 9/20 Sept. which submitted at once. Majorca submitted after a brief shelling on 14/25 Sept.

[6] Under Shovell and Rivers.

[7] Guiscard had left the expeditionary force under Rivers after its destination was changed to Spain.

722. MARLBOROUGH *to* GODOLPHIN   [*18/29 October 1706*]

Source: Blenheim MSS. A1-14.

Bruxelles October 29, 1706

I have been in such a hurry since I came to this town, that I have but just time to tell you that I have had favour of two of yours,[1] and that I beg you will make my excuse to Lord Hallifax, for my not having time by this post to acknowledge the favour of his, and thanking him for the copie of his letter to the Pensioner, which will be of use to me when I come to The Hague, which will be about the end of the next week.[2] For I shal leave this place on Sunday,[3] and separat the army on the 3d of the next [month], and the same day begine my jorny to The Hague; where my inclinations will lead me to make as litle stay as possible, though the Pensioner tels me I must stay to finish the treaty of Succession, and their Barier; which should I stay the whole winter, I am very confident would not be braught to perfection. For thay are of so many minds, and all so very extravegant concerning their Barier, that I despaire of doing any good til thay are more reasonable, which thay will not be til thay see that thay have it not in their power to dispose of the Low Countrys at their will and pleasure, in which the French flatter them. Mr. Stepney has his power for Holland, but not for this country; but I hope he will meet them at The Hague, where I think it is for the Queen's Service he should bee til I come for England, so that I may be the better able to informe him of all that shall pass. If the letter I sent you by the expresse[4] has no effect with 83 [the Queen], I shall conclude that God intends that way to punish us for other faults. For I think what you write in yours of the 13th of September[5] is not to be answered, for in England no minister can, nor aught to govern without help. God preserve her, and you to serve her long.

723. MARLBOROUGH *to the* DUCHESS   [*18/29 October 1706*]

Source: Blenheim MSS. E3.
Printed: *Private Correspondence*, i. 75.
Addressed: For the Dutchesse of Marlborough.

Bruxelles October 29th 1706

Since my coming heither I have had the happyness of two of yours from Woodstock, with so kind expressions, which makes me happy in spit of many things I see in all most everybody, that gives me disquiet. I have but just time to say this to you, for since I have been here, and as long as I stay in this town, I shall not be master of half an hour's time in the four and twenty.

---

[1] Probably letters 713, 714.   [2] See p. 710.   [3] 20/31 Oct.
[4] For the Queen. See letter 719.   [5] To the Queen. See p. 679 n. 2.

I intended to have returned to the army tomorrow, but shall not be able to do it til Sunday, and on Wensday the 3d of the next month, I shall send all the troupes to their winter quarters, and the same day begine my jorny for Holland.

724. GODOLPHIN *to the* DUCHESS [*18 October 1706*]

Source: Blenheim MSS. E20.
Printed: Coxe, ii. 165–6 (inc.).

Fryday night at 11 October 18th

I can't help making hast to thank you tonight for the favour of your letters, both of Wednesday and Thursday, in one packett, though this has been a day of so much hurry of all kinds that 'tis but just now I have been able to sitt down to write to you. I have written a long letter to Lord Marlborough[1] and enclosed yours in it, though it was as thick as 'twas long, which with my handyness at making up a packett, gave mine a particularly gracefull figure.

The uneasyness which Mr. Montgomery [Godolphin] complained of lately to you is too long a story to bee written, and must bee kept till I have the happyness to see you, which I shall hope is not farr off. The Lodg is a very pretty place, and Lord Marlborough I see in his letter[2] desires to find or carry you thither very soon. I return you his letter with my opinion that it should been sent to Mrs. Morley [the Queen], for though it bee no news to her, it may bee of use to see he continues of the same mind, and will bee soe when he comes hither, for which reason as well as others I confess I am extreamly impatient to have him here. I am glad you did not send him word of 117's [Sunderland] apprehensions, since there is not the least ground for them, and they would only have made him uneasy with him. I am sorry hee and his friends continue so uneasy, since wee have no other bottom to stand upon;[3] nothing shall bee omitted by mee to make them easyer, though 83 [the Queen] is very farr yett from being sensible of her circomstances in that particular.

Our letters today from Scotland are full of hopes to carry the Union. 117 [Sunderland] is much pleased with this news, and 115 [Halifax] much more, which shows mee the other would bee soe too, if he had not uneasyness upon t'other account. All Mr. Johnston's friends have behaved themselves well, soe I am now as fond of him, as you are of his letter.[4] I shall bee against your brother Charles Churchill having the government of Gurnesey for his life, but I am afrayd to mention that thing till Lord Marlborough comes over, for

---

[1] Letter 721. [2] Letter 712.
[3] Sunderland and Halifax had met with Godolphin in the first week of October. Afterwards Halifax reported to Somers that he saw 'no reason to change our resolution'. Hardwicke, *State Papers*, p. 471.
[4] See p. 647.

fear he should pretend to keep the lieutenancy of the Tower, unless his comission bee revoked in the same warrant which constitutes Lord Essex Constable. And if it should bee revoked, there would bee another inconvenience, for Lord Essex being absent there would neither bee a Constable nor a Lieutenant of the Tower upon the place.

725. GODOLPHIN *to* MARLBOROUGH   [*21 October 1706*]

Source: Blenheim MSS. A1-36.
Printed: Coxe, ii. 128 (inc.).

October 21, 1706

I can never thank you enough for all your kind letters which I received, particularly those by this messenger,[1] who goes back to you with her Majesty's opinion, and orders, upon the letter you sent by him from the Elector of Bavaria. I shall add nothing to the particulars which you will receive from Mr. Secretary Hedges,[2] but that they have been considered by all our friends here, as the shortness of the time would allow, and upon the whole, wee think them soe reasonable and so fair, as that you will doe yourself but right, in insisting upon them there, and I think you may depend upon being supported in it here. Besides what is mentioned in Mr. Secretary's letter, the conferences proposed, if they should bee admitted, could not fail of giving an immediate ease and support to all France which lies almost gasping at this time under an excessive want both of money and creditt. I shall long therefore very impatiently for the return of this messenger, and to hear that this blow has been avoyded.

There needs not, I think, any other answer to the letter you have sent mee from the Pensioner, than what you will find in my Lord Halifax's letters to him and to yourself concerning our remarks upon the treaty for the Barriere and the Sucession, which is, in one word that it is too generall, and when they please too particularise the places, they propose for their Barriere, and the troops necessary to maintain them, wee shall agree.

As to the preliminary treaty for guaranty of the future peace, which the Pentioner mentions in his letter to you, I think that must for the present, bee only in generall terms except this treaty for the Barriere and Succession should bee first concluded, in which case, it might bee particularly warranted, in the preliminary treaty.

I shall write to you again tomorrow by the post, and hope to hear further from you before that time. I have thought it best to deliver your letter to 83 [the Queen][3] though I scarce think it will at present have any other effect

---

[1] Letters 718, 719.   [2] 21 Oct., in Coxe, ii. 129-30.
[3] In Coxe, ii. 156-8.

than the rest have had. However I begin to hope, that upon your coming over, wee may bee able to sett all right.

One step towards the Union has been carryed in Scotland by a majority of 66 so wee are all very sanguine in that affair.

The Queen likes your thought for Cadogan and will keep that matter as it is till you come.

I have just now received the inclosed from Lady Marlborough for you.

726. MARLBOROUGH *to* GODOLPHIN
[*21 October/1 November 1706*]

Source: Blenheim MSS. A1-14.

Ghilinghen[1] November 1, 1706

I returned hether yesterday, and the weather is so very good that I am afraid I must keep the army together some days longer then I intended, for fear the French should make use of this weather, and by their passing of Mons give allarms to this country of Braband, which might oblige me to return, though I should be gott to The Hague, so that ill weather would be more welcome at this time with you in England. The enclosed is a copie of the King of Prussia's letter,[2] by which you will see the fickell temper of that prince. You will be pleased to lett me know what answere the Queen would have me give. The Comte de Sensindorf is now with me. His businesses is to speak of the Barier, as also to endeavour to quiet the business of Munster, and to take measures concerning the operations on the Rhine this next campagne. He intends to return to Vienna at the same time I shall go for England.

727. MARLBOROUGH *to the* DUCHESS
[*21 October/1 November 1706*]

Source: Blenheim MSS. E3.
Printed: *Private Correspondence*, i. 75–6 (inc.).

Ghilinghen November 1, 1706

The four days I have been att Bruxelles I have been in so perpetual a hurry, that I now think myself quiet by being in the army. The weather is so very fine that I am afraid I shall be obliged to keep the army four or five days longer together then I intended. By my next you shall know the certainty. I hope

---

[1] Ghislenghien, 8 kilometres north-east of Ath.
[2] 9/20 Oct., copy in Blenheim MSS. A1-37. Reply, 11/22 Nov., Murray, iii. 224–5. The King informs Marlborough he will continue Spanheim at London if the Queen will continue Raby at Berlin. Marlborough's remark stems from the fact that Raby was being recalled solely because of the King's objections to him (see p. 555).

you will aprove of the letter I write by the expresse to 83 [the Queen].[1]
I sent 91 [Godolphin] a copie of itt, and if my life had depended upon itt,
I could not have write with more earnestness, so that I hope it may have its
effect, or I shall despaire of being able to do good. I hope you have had at
Woodstock, the same weather we have had for this fortnight, for I never in
my life saw finer. The hangins I had made att Bruxelles are finished, and the
greatest fault I find with them is their having to[o] much silver and gold in
them; however, I hope you will like them.[2] If I had received the measures
of the apartement you and I are to live in I should have bespoke some more,
but now you may see these, and be the better able to tell me what alterations
you will have made in the next, and I beleive you will be of my opinion to
have no silver nor gold.[3]

728. GODOLPHIN *to* MARLBOROUGH   [*22 October 1706*]

Source: Blenheim MSS. A1-36.

October 22th 1706

I writt to you yesterday[4] by the express which Mr. Secretary Hedges dispatched to you with the Queen's instructions concerning 5 [peace] upon
occasion of the letters you sent us from the Elector of Bavaria. I am apt to
think this letter will meet you at The Hague, almost as soon as the other.

How the opinion which her Majesty has expressed in this affair will bee
received by 19 [Holland] I shall not take upon mee to decide, but I may
venture to say that all those here, who have had any knowledg of it, seem to
think it soe reasonable, that 19 [Holland] may bee under some disadvantage,
by endeavouring to decline it.

When you are at The Hague, would it be amiss to settle with the Pensioner
what ought to bee represented joyntly from England and Holland to the
King of Sweden, upon which the princes of the Empire might bee more
easily inclined to leave their troops in the service of the Allyes?

Our letters of this post[5] give us further alarms, as if the King [of] Poland
[Augustus] by the example of the other, were going to bee as troublesome
of his side and that he talks of coming into Bohemia. Some measures ought
to bee concerted for putting a stop to these savages, or nobody know how far
such a plague may spread. I am afrayd, the King of Prussia is not very unapt
to catch the infection.

Monsieur Spanheim has new credentialls of embassadour, conditionally
that my Lord Raby remain at Berlin in the same character. You must bee

---

[1] 14/25 Oct., Coxe, ii. 156-8.   [2] See p. 529.
[3] See p. 750 n. 4. Only the Art of War set of the tapestries Marlborough commissioned is
'heavily worked with gold'. Alan Wace, *The Marlborough Tapestries* (London, 1968), p. 44.
[4] Letter 725.   [5] See Luttrell, vi. 100.

pleased to unriddle this mystery and tell us what is to bee done with people that are so wavering and uncertain.

All Mr. Johnstone's friends of the new party, have joyned with us for the Union. I have seen him just now but he does not seem to like them the better for it.

The Queen has prorogued the English Parliament to the 22th of November which is late enough, considering what consequences turn upon it abroad, and yett I am very apprehensive they will not have finished in Scotland by that time.

Her Majesty told mee today she would send mee a letter for you before I sealed this.

729. GODOLPHIN *to* MARLBOROUGH   [*22 October 1706*]

Source: Blenheim MSS. A1-36.

22th at night

While I am staying for the Queen's letter,[1] I may trouble you so much longer as to lament the condition of our affairs in Spayn, which grow worse and worse every day, and I will doubt will doe soe till the fleet[2] arrives to support them which I hope they will now very soon doe though they have mett with bad weather. 2 of their transports took shelter at Plymouth, 2 more at Kinsale. Wee must hope the rest are gon onn, and if they cannot succeed at Cadiz, at least they may joyn my Lord Gallway, by the way of Alicante. The last post brought us word that my Lord Peterborow was at Genoa, and designed to goe from thence to the Duke of Savoy, without any orders from hence for it, or any business that wee know of. At the same time he is an embassadour in Spain and generall of an army which I doubt was in distress before he left it.

These are things which seem a little unusuall. What is to bee said for them, or what account to bee given of them I am sure I know not. His Lordship sent mee word, I should hear of him from Genoa, but I can't putt it out of my head, that wee shall see him before wee hear from him agayn.

If the Union succeed in Scotland as I hope it will no one thing could happen more likely to putt people in good humour here, and make them easyer in other things.

In case the States should agree to such a concert as was proposed by 17 [England] and sent yesterday by express to 90 [Marlborough] it will make an immediat necessity of sending over some 3d person from 83 [the Queen] to bee joyned with 90 [Marlborough] and Mr. Stepney. Bee pleased to think

---

[1] Missing. It must have been a reply to his of 13/24 Oct. See p. 713.
[2] Under Shovell and Rivers.

who it should bee.[1] This will make it besides much more easy for 90 [Marlborough] and 19 [Holland] to meet.

The Queen told mee yesterday she had consented to give the government of Guernsey for your brother's life, and she seemed very uneasy at it. I could not say anything to make her otherwise for I am persuaded, it will create her a world of importunityes.[2]

730. MARLBOROUGH *to* GODOLPHIN

[*24 October/4 November 1706*]

Source: Blenheim MSS. A1-14.

Ghilingen November 4, 1706

Wee having two postes due from England, I have none of yours to answere. The army being to seperat on the sixth, I hope to goe to The Hague, so as to write to you by the next post from thence. Ever since my coming from Bruxelles I have been so tormented with a cold, that I can hardly see nor hold up my head. I hope to receive the Queen's commands att my arrivall at The Hague, what answer she would have given to the Elector of Bavaria.[3] The Comte de Sensindorf has shown me his instructions, by which I hope his presence at The Hague may be of good use, especially for the affaire of Munster and the Barier. In both of them he is ordered to follow my derections, so that if 19 [Holland] will be reasonable, I hope we may bring it to some conclusion. Pray let Lady Hariot know that my cold is the reason of my not thanking her for her dear letter.

731. MARLBOROUGH *to the* DUCHESS

[*24 October/4 November 1706*]

Source: Blenheim MSS. E3.
Printed: *Private Correspondence*, i. 76-7.

Ghilinghen November 4th 1706

I have keep the army three days longer together then I first intended by reason of the faire weather, but on Saturday the sixth thay shall be sent too their severall quarters, so that I hope to be on Munday the eight at The Hague. In your last you say that 388 [   ] had write something concerning [sic], and of 90 [Marlborough] that had made you uneasy. I can asure you that 90 [Marlborough] knows 388 [   ] so intirely well, that you aught not to be uneasy at anything thay say of him. Besides, he tels me that he has heard nothing from them this summer except a letter of compliment presently after the battaile. I know not whether this will find you at Woodstock or at

---

[1] See pp. 582, 595.   [2] See p. 701.   [3] See p. 718.

London. If at the last, I should be glad you would let me know what effect
my last letter[1] has had on 83 [the Queen], for I wish her so well, that I am in
the greatest impatience imaginable to know her resolution, which I pray
God may be such as may make her happy. And be you my dearest soull
kind, and then nothing can make me unhappy, for I have not a desire of
being richer, nor any farther ambition then that of ending my days quietly
with you, when this warr shall happily be ended. Wee have now two postes
due from England, and I do not expect the happyness of receiving them til I
come to The Hague, from whence my next letters will be dated.

732. MARLBOROUGH *to the* DUCHESS

[*28 October/8 November 1706*]

Source: Blenheim MSS. E3.
Printed: *Private Correspondence*, i. 77–9 (inc.).

[Rotterdam] November 8th, 1706

I have had the happyness of yours of the 19 by the express, but your long
letters write by the former post I believe is gone to the army, which I shall
not have til I come to The Hague, which I hope will be tomorrow, though
the wind is now very contrary. I embarked yesterday at Antwerp with a
faire wind, and was promised I should be this day at The Hague. I deserve
better from you, then to have you make excuses for a long letter, for when
thay are on a subject that sometimes gives me the spleen, yet coming from
you thay are welcome; for beleive this truth, it is only you can make me end
my days happyly. You say Madam 218 [118–Wharton] is gone so well
satisfied with you, that she intendes to write. Ther is no name to those
figures in my sipher.[2] I know the young man you mention for 397 [   ]
daughter. I have heard a good carector of him, but whielst his father lives,
his revenu will be very smal, so that on all accounts I pity him. What you
have been told of 112 [   ] loaves and mutton [sic] I beleive is very trew.
You know I have no great vallu for him, but it is certain that to the best of
his understanding he is very honest to the common cause. In my next from
The Hague, I shall I hope be able to tell you when I intend to leave that place,
for should I stay to finish the treatys begone, this whole winter would not
suffise; but Mr. Stepney being both capable, and honest, I shall put everything into his hands. I am so fond of some pictures I shall bring with
mee, that I could wish you had a place for them til the gallerie at Woodstock
be finished, for it is certain that there are not in England so fine pictures as
some of these, particularly King Charles on horseback done by Vandick. It

<hr>

[1] 13/24 Oct. See p. 713.   [2] The Duchess meant 118 [Wharton].

was the Elector of Bavaria's and given me by the Emperor, and I hope is by this time in Holland.[1]

Hague November 9

Since my arrivall here I have had the happynes of two of yours, as also from Lord Treasurer. I am sorry to find by one of 91 [Godolphin][2] letters that my letter will not have the effect I desire on 83 [the Queen], for I am sure I have write it with all my heart, in hopes it might have sett everything right. I do not beleive that 48 [Charles Churchill] can live long. However, it is an ease to me in having desired it might be for his life, for should I dye I know him so well that he would be turned out, which thought would make mee uneasy, since I can't but have the tenderness of a brother.[3] You may be sure that I have that consideration and love for you, that my behavior shal be as you would have it to Mr. Godfrey,[4] for I do love you with all my heart and soull.

733. GODOLPHIN *to* MARLBOROUGH   [*29 October 1706*]

Source: Blenheim MSS. A1-36.

October 29 1706

I writt to you yesterday, at his request, by Monsieur de Guiscard,[5] but this letter going over in the same packett boat, will bee with you I suppose as soon or sooner than he.

I hope you will have been some days at The Hague, before this comes to you, and that you will bee in a readyness to come over at the full moon, which often at this time of year, brings an easterly wind.

You will bee very much wanted here for severall things which ought necessarily to bee done before the Parliament. And your being here before their sitting down, must needs have a very great influence toward hastening their preparation for next year.

In the meantime wee are under some impatience to know what the States resolve to doe upon the Queen's answer to the proposalls from the Elector of Bavaria.

---

[1] This portrait was hung in Marlborough House and then in the long library and the great drawing room of Blenheim Palace. It was sold to the National Gallery in the 1880s (Green, *Blenheim Palace*, p. 248). Marlborough was presented with another picture by the States of Flanders. See the resolution of the States of 29 Oct./9 Nov. in Blenheim MSS. A2-10. One of Marlborough's agents was a Seigneur de Schilde who sent Marlborough a list of pictures for sale on 1/12 Nov. (Blenheim MSS. F1-20). Included was a portrait of two English ladies judged to be an original Van Dyke. The shipment dispatched to England was a considerable one. On 19 Nov. Lowndes wrote to the Customs Commissioners advising them that several cases of pictures (about nineteen) and hangings, which had arrived in the Thames, were to be opened in Marlborough's lodgings in St. James. *C.T.B.*, xvi. ii. 99. For a history of this painting see Margaret L. Goldsmith, *The Wandering Portrait* (London, 1954).

[2] Letter 725.
[3] See p. 701.
[4] His nephew? See p. 627.
[5] Untraced. See p. 715.

Mr. Secretary Harley's absence, is not convenient when so many things are to bee transacted betwixt us and Holland, as at this criticall time. I hope he will bee here before this day sennight.[1]

I am thinking to propose that my Lord Manchester may have credentialls to the Duke of Savoy, and wait upon his Royal Highness in his way to Venice, for if the Queen continues to pay troops in Italy another year, it will bee absolutely necessary, to come to some agreement concerning the operation of that army betwixt this and that time.

Wee have now given footing in Italy to the Emperour, and restored the Duke of Savoy to his country. Unless they will agree to enter France next spring, with an army it can't bee expected or imagined that the Queen and the States should pay troops in Italie another year; and except this bee adjusted now they will overwhelm us next year in Spayn. The Venetians begin to bee extreamly uneasy and jealous of the Emperor's power in Italy, and not a little distrustfull of the Duke of Savoy.

They would come into any reasonable measures for keeping the Duchy of Milan in the hands of the King of Spayn.

I doubt Comte Wratislaus has had nothing but compliments from the King of Sweden. That matter too will require some care this winter, for I have no faith in King Augustus's numerous army.[2]

Lord Raby seems absolutely resettled in his post at Berlin, so I expect your thoughts about Vienna.

Wee hear much of my Lord Peterborow at Genoa, but nothing from himself.

734. MARLBOROUGH *to* GODOLPHIN

[*29 October/9 November 1706*]

Source: Blenheim MSS. A1-14.
Printed: Coxe, ii. 165 (inc.).

Hague November 9th 1706

I have had the favour of yours of the 15,[3] 18, and 21[4] by the expresse. In one of them I find you have received a letter from 76 [Harley], full of expressions.[5] I beg you will lay hold of the occasion, and when he is with you, that you would acquaint him with the business of 51 [Hedges] and 117 [Sunderland], and give him your reasons for the chang, for he must not be suffered to go on in the project that 52 [Craggs] acquainted you with; and by gaining of him you will govern the others without taking any pains with

---

[1] Harley had taken his annual holiday in the country at Brampton Castle. He returned on 15 Nov. after five weeks' absence.

[2] Augustus's army was composed of Saxon, Polish, and Russian troops.

[3] Untraced.   [4] Letters 721, 725.

[5] 15 Oct., in H.M.C., *Bath MSS.*, i. 109-11.

them. I have not heard from 52 [Craggs], but I beleive the thing is trew. However, if you take this methode, I am very confident when I shal be with you, you will be able to make 76 [Harley] very usefull to yourself and the Queen's business, and by it you will enable me to make the others sensible of their error.

Since my arrivall I have seen the Pensioner and Monsieur Buys, and tomorrow I shal have a confirence with the deputys of the States Generall, so that I hope in two or thre days I shall be able to send back the courier. I find already it will be impossible for mee to signe the treaty for the Succession, whielst I am here, since that of the Barier must be in itt, unless I have time to send there demand for her Majesty's approbation. For thay will certainly ask so many towns as will make itt impossible for mee to do other then to beg the Queen's possitive commands, since the naturall consequence will bee that of curing the jealoussy that these people have unreasonably against England; or the augmenting of itt, which may be of very daingerous consequences. I send you back part of one of your letters,[1] that you may corect the sipher in the business between 317 [Duke of Savoy] and 127 [Peterborough], for that of 115 [Halifax] must be a mistake. In the meantime, I shall speak to Comte Maffie as you desire, and let him know that I beleive that cypher should have been 315 [King Charles]. Pray send me back the enclosed, that I may put it with the rest of the letter.

735. GODOLPHIN *to* MARLBOROUGH   [*1 November 1706*]

Source: Blenheim MSS. A1-36.
Printed: Coxe, ii. 99-100 (inc.).

November 1st 1706

I have stayd till 10 a clock at night before I began to write in hopes every minute of hearing from you, but wee have still 2 posts wanting though the wind has been and is now fair. Since wee can have no letters, I hope you will make use of it to come yourself, and then I shall have very little impatience for letters, my chief care at present being to learn how they take the Queen's answer in Holland.[2]

I take it for granted Mr. Secretary Hedges sends you extracts of the letters wee had yesterday from Spayn, soe I will not trouble you with repeating them. But I find by Collonell Stanhope's letter[3] to my [sic] that Comte de Noyelles is very well with the King of Spain, and of a temper to make them all very uneasy there. His aim seems to bee that the King should act by himself with a separate body, and the Portughese by themselves. At the

---

[1] Letter 717.   [2] To the peace offers. See p. 718.
[3] 13/24 Oct., Mahon, Appendix, pp. xxxix-xl.

same time they allow that all their troops joyned are not sufficient to oppose the enemy, at present.

My poor Lord Gallway continues soe very pressing to retire and come home, that I really think it would bee too great a barbarity to refuse it him. But what amazes mee, is, that he recomends 127 [Peterborough] as the properest person to succeed him in the care of the whole.

They press very much for recruits but seem to think themselves, ther's noe having them in time, unless whole regiments bee sent them from hence or from Ireland. I should hope, the force gon with Lord Rivers might bee a reinforcement sufficient for them but how the command shall bee setled, when my Lord Gallway comes away, is a matter that I hope you will turn your thoughts to, against your coming over.

The mobb is uneasy at the Union in Scotland, and has been very unruly. The majority in the Parliament for it is so great, that they begin to find it cannot bee resisted but by tumult and open force. What effect this may have I doe not know, but I hope they won't prove the strongest. However the Queen will have the precaution of making some regiments move towards the north of England and of Ireland, and if there were a reall occasion, I hope some of those at Ghendth would be as near.

736. GODOLPHIN *to* MARLBOROUGH   [*3 November 1706*]

Source: Blenheim MSS. A1-36.

Sunday 3d November 1706

I had the pleasure of receiving yesterday 3 letters from you, one from Brusselles, one from Ghilinghen, and the last from The Hague.[1]

I shall begin this with asking your pardon for mistaking the cypher which I have rectifyed by changing 115 [Halifax] as it stood before in my letter, into 315 [King Charles] which it ought to have been.[2] The sence I fear has led you to find out the mistake, and I thank you for what you have don upon it, which I doubt may bee but necessary.

Since you think the treaty of the Succession and the *Barriere*, is like to bee tedious, I hope you will not think of staying to finish it, but to take the opportunity of the light nights to come over. And in case the States should enter into the Queen's thoughts concerning 5 [peace], which I hope wee may yett hear, before I seal this, I say in that case, there will probably bee a necessity of sending over somebody from hence, to concert with them in 19 [Holland] the terms to bee insisted upon; or also, that 366 [Buys] should come over with you, to doe it here, which has been already talked of in 19 [Holland] as I hear.

[1] Letters 726, 730, 734.   [2] See p. 710.

If the news of the last post, of the King Augustus's victory proves true,[1] I reckon one of 366's [Buys] strongest arguments for receiving 5 [peace] imediatly, will have lost much of its force. But I find many people here, doubt the truth of that news.

I hear the Duke of Lorraine and his brother[2] have mett at Mayence. I am afrayd it may bee to encourage his pretensions to the bishoprick of Munster, and to assume some of the Pope's favour and assistance. If this should bee true, it is all fomented by France, underhand, because they knew nothing will reasonably make Holland so uneasy. I hope therefore, wee shall not bee caught, in that snare, and now especially since Monsieur Zinzendorf's orders are to bee guided by you. But I have been wishing rather, some use might bee made of that meeting to bring the Duke of Lorraine into nearer measures with the Allyes against next campagne.

By my last letters from my Lord Gallway and from Mr. Stanhope, I find Monsieur de Montandre[3] is coming from the former to give a particular account of what has past last summer, and Monsieur Zinzerling[4] from the King of Spayn, with his desires of further assistance. Wee expect both these gentlemen by the next Lisbon packett boat. In the meantime I shall send you with this the letters I have had from them, that by the time of your arrivall here you may bee more master of their present circumstances, and bee able to judg the better what further measures are necessary to bee taken in relation to Spayn.

You may remember how earnestly Monsieur Buys pressed mee last spring to remitt 12,000£ to Geneva (though they never remitted a farthing themselves). This was done accordingly, but it never had any effect. I hope he will not bee offended, if I now take the liberty to send for that money again. I am very sure, wee have occasions enough for it at home.[5]

What you write in your letter about 76 [Harley] is certainly right in every part of it. But he is not in town now, and I hope you will bee here before him which will not fall out amiss, in this particular, for if wee speak to him togather upon it, t'will have much more force with him than my speaking to him alone would have had.[6]

[1] The battle of Kalisz on 8–19 Oct. in which King Augustus and the Russians retiring from Poland after giving up the crown by the Treaty of Altranstädt, fought and defeated a Swedish–Polish–Lithuanian army under General Mardefelt. Hatton, pp. 214–15.

[2] Karl, Bishop of Osnabrück.

[3] Francis de Rochefoucauld, marquis of Montandre (died 1739), a Huguenot who served under William III; a friend of Galway; joined the Portuguese army in 1704 as a brigadier-general, under the terms of the Methuen Treaty; major-general and colonel of a Regiment of Foot 1706; lieutenant-general 1710; fought well throughout the war in the Iberian peninsula.

[4] Franz Adolf, Freiherr von Zinzerling, formerly an agent of the Elector Palatine, he had accompanied Charles III to Spain as his principal secretary; sent to his Allies by Charles III to obtain more troops; representative of Charles III at The Hague 1709–11.   [5] See p. 576.

[6] Harley had his conference with the Duumvirs on the problem of Sunderland and the Whigs on 20 Nov. He was forced to give way to their determination to bring the Whigs into the ministry. See Snyder, 'Godolphin and Harley', pp. 260–2.

5 November

Wee have no letters from Holland, and I have nothing to add, but that by a ship come in to Bristoll, wee hear our fleet has been seen off of Vigo making sail towards Lisbon.

737. MARLBOROUGH *to* GODOLPHIN   [5/16 November 1706]

Source: Blenheim MSS. A1-14.
Printed: Coxe, ii. 133 (inc.).

Hague November 16, 1706

I had yesterday the favour of yours of the 29th,[1] but as yett have heard nothing of the Marquis of Guiscard, at which I am not much in pain, for I can't see any use of his coming. The packet boat which should have brought the letters of the 25th has been taken by the French, so that if there were any commands of the Queen, thay must be repeated to Mr. Stepney, for I hope to leave this place before any answere can com to this letter. The States of Holland are to assemble tomorrow, and then the answere to the Elector of Bavaria's letters will be resolved, and I do not doubt but thay will be conform to her Majesty's desires. As I have had much opertunity of discorsing the Comte de Maffie, I should think it for the Queen's Service that Lord Manchister should not have his instructions for the Duke of Savoye til I have the happyness of being with you. This country like others is vexed with different opinions, of which the French must make advantage. I shall not now trouble you with particulars, but I hope all will agree, that the warr must be carryed on til the French be more reasonable, for as yett thay talke of nothing but a partition treaty which is not only dishonarable to the Allyes, but also in length of time distruction, which I have fully declared to be her Majesty's opinion. The business of Saxony gives very great uneasiness here, and those of the French faction makes use of itt. For if the King of Sweden will disturb this next campagne the Allyes, it is next to impossible to find any other remidy then by being on the defensive in Flandres, which these people will never endure.

738. MARLBOROUGH *to the* DUCHESS   [5/16 November 1706]

Source: Blenheim MSS. E3.
Printed: *Private Correspondence*, i. 79–80.

Hague November 16, 1706

I have had the happyness of yours of the 26 and 27 from Windsor, but the packet boat which should have braught the letters off the post before was taken by a French privatier, so that I have not received the letter in which you say you have given me your opinion of my letter to 83 [the Queen].[2] But by

[1] Letter 733.   [2] 13/24 Oct. See p. 713.

what you say in your letter of the 27, I see you do not aprove of my expressions concerning 73 [Rochester] and 39 [the Tories].[1] As I write to her with all my heart for the good of her Service, you will easily beleive I did not write anything with a designe to do hurt, but I am sure whatever I said of those lords and their friends was what I toke to be truth. And if that dose hurt with 83 [the Queen] I can't help itt, but I do hope thay are more reasonable, or we shall be very unhappy. The advice you have given to 392 [Lady Monthermer] is so very right, that I hope in God she will be very carefull in obsarving itt; for though I do from my heart beleive that 125 [Duke of Montager] is capable of everything that is ill, yet it is not for her's nor her husband's intirest to see itt; and you may be sure when I come to England I shall joyne with you in persuading her to obsarve what you have advised. If I receive the answers to my last letters by Sunday,[2] I shall embark the next day, and if the wind be faire I may in two days after have the happyness of being with my dear soull.

739. GODOLPHIN *to* MARLBOROUGH   [*8 November 1706*]

Source: Blenheim MSS. A1-36.
Printed: Coxe, ii. 130-2 (inc.).

November 8 at night

The messenger arrived this morning and brought mee the favour of yours of the 12th and 14th,[3] with the papers enclosed, I have also seen your letter to Mr. Secretary Hedges,[4] with the paper of preliminarys,[5] of which he sends you by this post the Queen's approbations, provided wee keep strictly to every one of them.

If anything should yett bee wanting to fix and establish the 9th electorat, might not some care bee taken of that, as well as of the King of Prussia's pretensions?

The last article leaves room for the Queen to lay claim to reparations for incroachments and damages to the English plantations in America. Though it bee not insisted on as a preliminary, yett if a treaty is to follow, I am apt to think England will hope for some reason from the French in that matter.

I observe the form of these preliminary articles which you have sent over

---

[1] Probably in the letter to the Queen of 26 Sept./7 Oct. See pp. 694-5.
[2] 10/21 Nov.   [3] Untraced.
[4] 1/12 Nov., Murray, iii. 214-15.
[5] Rijksarchief, AANW 1865 BXIV A, fols. 163-6. Summarized in Geikie, pp. 71-2. By them France was shorn of the gains made by Louis XIV from the Empire and the Spanish Netherlands; Charles III was to receive the whole of the Spanish monarchy; the Dutch would have a formidable Barrier; England would obtain a favourable treaty of commerce, recognition of the Protestant succession, and the Pretender would be sent out of France; the other Allies would receive the conditions laid down in their treaties with the Maritime Powers.

is a little different from what was proposed by the Queen. Her Majesty's proposall was that wee should concert and agree the preliminary articles of a peace to bee offered to France, whereas the title of this paper runs thus: preliminarys for a treaty of peace, in case France can bee induced to make the offers in the name both of the King of France, and of the Duke of Anjou. I don't know that there is anything essentiall in this observation, but I had a mind to take notice of it to you, that you might judg, whether this difference in the form were only casuall, or whether it were affected.

I find my letter of the 25th of October has been thrown into the sea. You have escaped a great deal of trouble by it for it was very long, and full of complaints of the Emperour's taking possession of the Duchy of Milan in his own name, though obtained by our troops and money. But if these preliminarys take place, that complaint will bee pretty well cured.

Nor if 19 [Holland] hold firm to them, I am of opinion, that first or last they will take place. For besides all the late ill successes of France, they have a ruine increasing every day upon them in the poynt of their money, which they are not feasible of themselves, nor can't bee able to have a right notion of it from anything that has hapned of that kind within the memory of man in that kingdom. I agree with you, that France will not at first receive these proposalls, but I incline to think they will not absolutely reject them, but endeavour to moderate some articles, and graft something upon others, so as to keep on foot a negotiation upon them, and by that means hope to slacken the preparations of the Allys, and gain time to hearten and encourage their friends in 19 [Holland].

It may therfore deserve your consideration whether there should not bee a time prefixed and limited to them, within which they should bee obliged to declare their finall resolution of accepting or refusing them.

By the enclosed letter from Monsieur d'Aligré you will see I had sent you a letter of his some time since, but that packett hapned to bee lost.

His case is so particular, that the Queen gives him leave to come to London, imediately, and I beleive will lett him goe to Paris, by Calais, and not by Holland, provided he will promise not to hold any correspondence by word or writing with any body in Holland upon word and honour during the time of his absence. But I send you his letter chiefly that you may take occasions of showing it to 366 [Buys] and others of his friends at the Hague, to prevent their taking any jealousy at our sending him over directly to France, in this time of negotiations without passing through Holland.

I don't trouble you with one word about the Barriere, because having communicated the whole to 115 [Halifax] and 117 [Sunderland], I send you a letter unsealed from my Lord Halifax,[1] with whose thoughts upon that subject I entirely concurr; and if they can agree their own demands I don't see why any scruples on our part should take up 2 hour's time.

[1] Untraced.

The powers are sent as you desired for Mr. Stepney, so I hope you will have nothing to hinder you from leaving The Hague soon after you have received these letters.

I received the enclosed for you from Lady Marlborough this morning, and I sent her two letters from you, this evening to Windsor.

740. GODOLPHIN *to the* DUCHESS [*9 November 1706*]

Source: Blenheim MSS. E20.

Thursday [Saturday] 9th of November

I waited on my Lady Sandwich this morning. She told mee the occasion of her doubting mee was upon a letter she had received from you,[1] in which you had told her the Queen's intention of not continuing Lord Sandwich in his place, and she could not but think it so extremely hard that a man should bee discharged after so long and dutifull service, for what was not come upon him by any fault of his own; she sayd but by a sickness, a melancholly which amounted to vapours and no more. She could not give it any other name. She hoped second thoughts would bee taken upon it, and the Queen would think it reasonable to give him leave to goe for his health to the Spa waters which were reckoned the most proper remedy for that distemper. Then she said this was the first instance of this kind; nothing was done like it in the case of Lady Charlotte Beverward. I took the liberty to lett her see the case was very diffirent from that. There were other ladyes of the bed-chamber and but one Master of the Horse. Besides that, hers was a distemper which threatened certain death, and his of a nature rather to promise long life attended with almost an impossibility of ever serving, but that I would represent all she had sayd to the Queen.[2] [She answered] that (if service were the thing in question) she hoped my Lord Hinchenbrook[3] might bee accepted of, and though he was not a man, hee soon would bee one, and could ride on horsback now very well, and that the Duke of Richmond had been Master of Horse to King Charles much younger. To all this I did not think it necessary to give any other answer than a smile. She began again with desiring

[1] 31 Oct., Blenheim MSS. G1-16: 'By what I have heard the Queen say, madam, concerning my Lord Sandwich's misfortune, I found her Majesty ded not think it fitt that the Prince should continue him, or remain longer, without a servant in such a post, and therefore I don't know of any use that I can bee of to your Ladyship, unless you think it for your servise, to use my indeavours with the Queen, and Prince to give Lord Sandwich a reasonable allowance for his better support abroad. In this case I will write to the Queen.'

[2] Sandwich was replaced by Bridgewater (as a deputy?) as Master of the Horse to the Prince in June 1705. He was given a pension of £1,000 a year. Luttrell, v. 570.

[3] Edward Richard Montagu (1692-1722), styled Viscount Hinchingbrooke, M.P. 1713-22; army officer from 1712.

I would speak to the Queen not to crush a family that would die for her service, and had spent much more than they had gott in it.

Then she said she designed to wait upon you. She was afraid you had taken a prejudice against her, and she hoped I would in the meantime endeavour to doe her good offices.

I told her I thought the best I could doe was to desire her not to imagine there could bee any such thing, and so I took my leave. Now upon the whole matter it seems to mee the advantage of this thing is the chief consideration, and if that might remain entire, I am apt to think the rest would bee submitted to, though there were a great many false arguments made use of in almost half an hour's discourse, thus this messenger. But when all this is don, you may see by her letter to Lord Marlborough, which he sent mee, that she leans still towards expedients, though I have told her that to satisfy her, I had tryed some turn that would goe, and the thing was not capable of any expedient, and that I was convinced by what had been said to mee by 115 [Halifax] and 116 [Somers], that it was infinitely more for her advantage not to think of any such thing as an expedient. But she told mee to'ther day she believed I thought it strange that she sayd nothing upon my showing her 91's [Godolphin] letter, but it was that though she was very uneasy to see what he writt, she could not for her life bee convinced but her expedient was better, and when he comes over she will certainly talk soe to him; but if hee holds firm to what he has written and sayd, and I doe not doubt he will, I dare say she will doe the thing.

One would think it were high time for mee to leave off troubling you, but I have not yett done. Ther's a new accident that will make mee bee wronged. The Bishop of Winchester is dead.[1] I have had a notice of it from the Archbishop of Canterbury, and the enclosed letter from the Bishop of Salisbury, and the Bishop of Exeter[2] will never forgive mee if anybody has it but himself. I will endeavour to keep the Queen from coming to any resolution upon it till wee have advised with all our friends.

Mr. Godolphin is come to town, which would bee a satisfaction to mee, if he liked my company as well as I doe his; but I could bear that misfortune with patience if it were the only one I had of that kind.

The letter you sent mee last night for Lord Marlborough cannot goe till Tuesday.

[1] Peter Mews (1619–1706), Bishop of Winchester since 1684, died 9 Nov.

[2] Sir Jonathan Trelawny, third Bt. (1650–1721), one of the seven bishops tried by James II; Bishop of Exeter 1689–1707; sided with Anne and the Churchills against William III 1691; confirmed Bishop of Winchester Apr. 1707. *D.N.B.*

741. MARLBOROUGH *to* GODOLPHIN   [*9/20 November 1706*]

Source: Blenheim MSS. A1-14.
Addressed: To my Lord Treasurer, Whitehall.

Hague November 20, 1706

Since my last[1] I have had yours of the 1st[2] and 12th,[3] and am very sorry to find that Lord Gallaway persistes in retiring, since I think it is impossible to gratifie him. For should he leave that Service, everything there must turn to confusion. You will know by this post, that the peace between the Kings of Sweden and Polland is concluded, which gives great satisfaction here.[4] Mr. Secretary will have mine and the States' [answers] to the Elector's letters.[5] I hope her Majesty will aprove of them. Thay have been this morning comunicated to the foraigne ministers, who are very well pleased. I am afraid I shall leave this place before thay will be able to agree amongst themselves on their Barier. If the wind be faire on Tuesday, I intend to leave this place.

742. GODOLPHIN *to* MARLBOROUGH   [*12 November 1706*]

Source: Blenheim MSS. A1-36.
Addressed: To His Grace the Duke of Marlborough.

12 November 1706

I write these 2 lines only to thank you for the favour of yours of the 20th[6] without giving you the trouble to say anything to the particulars of it hoping that before this can come to your hands, you will have a fair wind though it is not so today, but it is so cold that I think tis not unlike to change.

The Bishop of Winchester's death makes a great ferment here betwixt my countryman the Bishop of Exeter, and your friend the Bishop of Sarum. I know of no other expedient but to keep it vacant, at present.[7]

---

[1] Letter 737.   [2] Letter 735.
[3] Untraced. If this is an error for '2nd', the letter does not survive. If it should be Marlborough's reference to the same letter with both old- and new-style dates, this is the only instance in the correspondence.
[4] The Treaty of Altranstädt, signed 13/24 Sept., but not ratified until 9/20 Oct. Lamberty, iv. 273 ff.; Hatton, pp. 214–15.
[5] For the French offers of peace made through the Elector of Bavaria see p. 712. At a meeting of all the foreign envoys at The Hague on 9/20 Nov. Marlborough and the Dutch announced the rejection of the offer by the Maritime Powers and their determination to carry on the war. The letters of Marlborough and the States are in Lamberty, iv. 303–4, 306–7.
[6] Letter 741.   [7] See p. 733.

743. MARLBOROUGH *to* GODOLPHIN   [*12/23 November 1706*]

Source: Blenheim MSS. A1-14.
Addressed: To my Lord Treasurer, Whitehall.

Hague November 23d 1706

Since my last I have had yours of the 5[1] and 8th.[2] I shall not say anything concerning the prelimenarys nor Barier, hoping to be as soon with you as this; for if the weather will permit it, I intend to embark tomorrow, which must also be my excuse for not writing to Lord Hallifax. I have acquainted Mr. Stepney with all that has passed, also the opinion our friends have in England concerning the Barier, which he must manage with great discretion, for these people are extreame hotte on that point. I beleive the Comte de Guiscard perceives his voyage can be of great use, for he has this minute desired to return with mee. Everything goes well here but the Barier, and in that thay are very obstenatt.

744. MARLBOROUGH *to* GODOLPHIN   [*17/28 November 1706*]

Source: Blenheim MSS. A1-14.
Addressed: For the Right Honourable the Lord Godolphin, Lord Treasurer of England.

Margett November 17th 1706

The wind being contrary, I landed att this place last night, and for want of horses was obliged to stay here till four a clock this morning. If my coach should not be in town, I desire the favour of yours metting mee att the Bacon hous at the top of Shuters hill, seven milles from London, for there I intend to dine, and would have the coach be there by one of the clock. If Lady Marlborough be at the Lodge, I will come derectly to your house. It is on Munday[3] the coach is to meet me.

---

[1] Untraced.   [2] Letter 739.   [3] 18 Nov.

1707

Once again Marlborough returned to England to receive an enthusiastic reception for his achievements in the field. His first task was to resolve the political impasse that arose from the Whig demands for Sunderland to be made Secretary of State in the place of Hedges and the Queen's obstinate refusal, backed by Harley, to make the appointment. In spite of Harley's protestations Marlborough seconded Godolphin's advice to give Sunderland the place. The Queen's objection that it was unfair to displace Hedges without adequate compensation was eliminated when Hedges cut the Gordian knot by resigning his office. Sunderland took his place at the Council table the day Parliament met, thus smoothing the way for close co-operation between the ministry and the Whigs in the session that followed. As a consequence the main bills were all passed and signed before the Christmas recess, an unusual display of speed. The meeting of the English legislature had been delayed in part to await the outcome of the deliberations of its Scottish counterpart on the proposed parliamentary union. When the Scots finally gave their approval, after a stormy session, the English Parliament completed its work and the Union took place on 1 May 1707, one of the great accomplishments of the Godolphin ministry.

In the usual planning for the coming campaign special attention was given to a descent upon Toulon in which the Duke of Savoy, joined by Prince Eugene, would make an overland assault on that port complemented by a naval assault by the Maritime Powers. As well as providing the Allies with a Mediterranean base, and an entry into France from the unprotected south, the capture of Toulon would cause Louis XIV to divert troops from Spain and elsewhere to reinforce his meagre forces on the Mediterranean, thereby giving Charles an opportunity to seize the initiative once more and take Madrid. Marlborough's army would play a secondary role in this campaign, serving chiefly to tie up the large French army in Flanders and protect his recent conquests. Even before his departure for the Continent, the disquieting news reached London of the truce between the Imperialists and the French in Italy. It proved to be the portent of a series of reverses in the various theatres of war during the course of the year that made 1707 as disastrous a year for the Allies as 1706 had been a miraculous one.

Marlborough left London on the morning of Friday, 21 March, to take up his command in the Southern Netherlands once again.

745. GODOLPHIN *to* MARLBOROUGH   [*21 March 1707*]

Source: Blenheim MSS. A2-23.
Addressed: To His Grace the Duke of Marlborough at Margat.

Fryday 21th at 3

I send you the enclosed from Mr. Secretary Harley[1] in answer to a letter I writt to him according to your commands, that you may see it is not my fault, if you have not the letters in time, which you expect from him.

The wind seems here to bee pretty fair for you, but I am not without my apprehensions you will find it otherways at Margat.

The Queen talks of going next week to Windsor for 4 or 5 days, in hopes to hasten the Prince's recovery.

My humble service to Lady Marlborough.

746. GODOLPHIN *to* MARLBOROUGH   [*24 March 1707*]

Source: Blenheim MSS. A2-23.

Monday 24th 1706/7

The Fryday's letters from The Hague came in last night. I don't observe anything new in them, but the story of your partisan[2] who seems to have come off but scurvily with his *enlevement*.

Wee have nothing from Spain, nor Portugall, since you went.

In Italie, the places seem to bee all evacuated, and from Holland they write, that Prince Eugene is going to Naples, which is lamentable, if it bee true. I doubt, I shall scarce bee able to resist writing to Comte Wratislau, upon that subject.[3]

The Queen has appointed a publick thanksgiving upon Mayday for the Union, and she goes to the House today to pass the act for Exchequer bills, the Bill of Mutiny and Desertion, and the Recruit Bill.

I am very sorry to see the wind continue so obstinatly against you, but till it comes more to the southward, there is little hope of changing.

All humble duty to Lady Marlborough.

---

[1] Untraced.   [2] Unidentified.
[3] The draft of Godolphin's letter to Wratislaw, 25 Mar., is in B.M., Add. MS. 28057, fols. 334-7. In it he stressed the importance of the Toulon expedition, the need to send troops from Italy to Charles III, and the necessity of dropping the Naples expedition.

747. MARLBOROUGH *to* GODOLPHIN   [24 March 1707]

Source: Blenheim MSS. B2-9.

[Marget] Munday one a Clock

Since my being here I have had the favour of yours of Friday[1] and Sunday.[2] If this wind should continue some few days longer, I am afraid it would almost make it impossible for me to have time for my going to Saxony.

I should have received her Majesty's derections concerning the inclosed letter from the refugies' minesters in Holland.[3] You will be pleased to lett me have them as soon as possible. Mr. Secretary will show you my letters, which I send him by this express, for the prisoners att Nottingham.[4] I hope the Queen will approve of them.

I send you a letter from Gilder-Malsen[2] of a laiter date then Cadogan's,[2] by which you will see that no possitive resolution[5] will be taken til I can gett theither.

I send you Mr. Secretary Harley's letter[6] that you may take notice to him, of what he desires I should say to you from himself. The wind is so very hie that we have no comunication with the men of warr nor the yackts.

748. GODOLPHIN *to* MARLBOROUGH   [25 March 1707]

Source: Blenheim MSS. A2-23.

March 25 1707

Last night as I was going to bed I had the favour of yours of Monday,[7] and have today read to the Queen the severall letters enclosed in it.

I am glad to find Guldermalsen so sanguine, and only wish you could have a wind to carry you to them, in so good time yett, as (if it were possible) not to disappoint your thoughts of Saxony, and this is not only my own thought, but I come now from 116 [Somers], 117 [Sunderland] and 118 [Wharton] who have all desired mee to write this to you. But when all is done, one must submitt to the winds, though there are so many reasons to grieve extreamly at their continuing so obstinate.

The Queen comands mee to tell you she shall bee extreamly glad to bee instrumentall in restoring the refugiés upon a peace with France, and is willing you should press to have it added as a preliminary, if you find any

---

[1] Letter 745.   [2] Untraced.
[3] Untraced. A petition asking 'that they may be considered in a general peace', also the subject of an address by the Huguenots to the Queen. Luttrell, vi. 155 and the following letter.
[4] D'Alègre and Tallard, 24 Mar., Murray, iii. 337-8, about their parole. The latter was refused.
[5] About inviting Charles XII of Sweden to act as a mediator between the Allies and France and other overtures to the king. See the following four letters.
[6] See p. 737.
[7] The preceding letter.

inclination in Holland to joyn with her Majesty in these good intentions, which I fear you will not. However I think it might not bee amiss to sound them a little upon it now, and if it pleases God to give us any good success, they may then perhaps come the more easily into it.

Mr. Secretary Harley has shown mee your letters to the French prisoners, by which I find I must expect to hear from them when any of the others come back and perhaps before. I acquainted the Queen therfore with the subject of these letters, that it might not bee new to her when the matter comes to bear.

I hope this East wind will carry away our convoys to the West Indies and to Ireland, though I find some of the transport and store ships are not yett gott into the Downs and consequently must expect another opportunity.

My Lord Leven, just came to town, designs to wait upon you tomorrow, but I would not write by him, believing this flying packett would bee with you sooner. Lady Harryette and the children are well. I hope you will continue soe.

749. MARLBOROUGH *to* GODOLPHIN [*26 March 1707*]

Source: Blenheim MSS. A1-37.

Margett March 26, 1707

The little liklyhood of the winds changing makes me send the inclosed letter for the King of Sweden.[1] I beg you will add, or deminish in everything you think may please the King. I think there should be something said as to the Queen's desire of his being mediator,[2] but that can't be done but by her Majesty's leave, and with great caution. Though I send you this draught of a letter, I beg you will with my humble duty assure the Queen that if it be possible for me to go myself, I shal do itt, for the Dutch seems to have so little inclinations of doing anything that may please the King, that I very much dread the consequencys. I hope I may have your answer to this early on Friday morning,[3] and that you will alter every word in the letter if you see ocation.

750. GODOLPHIN *to* MARLBOROUGH [*26 March 1707*]

Source: Blenheim MSS. A2-23.

Wednesday night at 11

I have but just this moment received your letter[4] and the enclosed draught of a letter to the King of Sweden. It is so late that I can't see the Queen

[1] Untraced.
[2] Between France and the Allies to end the War of the Spanish Succession. See pp. 744, 760.
[3] 28 Mar.   [4] The preceding letter.

tonight, nor have the opinion of those you desire may see the letter before tomorrow, for I sent just to my Lord Sunderland, to have endeavored it, but he was not home. But I make no question of dispatching your messenger back again so as that he may bee with you by Fryday[1] noon, as you desire. In the meantime I can give you the satisfaction of letting you know by this messenger (who is dispatched with a packett to Mr. Cardonell) that your friends here agree exactly in your thought, for wee talked it over and over last night, that what you have now proposed would bee proper (in case of necessity). But they would not allow mee to write it last night, for fear of discoraging you from your jorney which they still wish may bee pursued, if you find it possible, when you come on the other side of the water. But when that will bee possible, God knows. The wind continues as obstinate as ever.

751. GODOLPHIN *to* MARLBOROUGH [*27 March 1707*]

Source: Blenheim MSS. A2-23.

Thursday at 3

Last night I acquainted you that I had received yours with the enclosed draught of a letter to the King of Sweden.[2] This morning I waited upon the Queen with them, and I have since comunicated them to those lords.

Wee all agree in opinion with you, in the first place, that, if there can possibly bee time for it, you should still make the jorney yourself, as it was designed.

Next, that if you cannot goe, you should by some officer of trust, send the Queen's letters as well as your own, to the King of Sweden. For this I have asked her Majesty's leave (who agrees to it) and I have accordingly altered the draught of your letter, and made some other not very materiall alterations which have also been approved by our friends. I have been forced to trust Mr. Taylour[3] to write the draught anew for fear partly, that you might not distinguish the amendments, and partly, for want of time to write so much myself. I don't see any good reason for your pressing so much to hear the answer by *tomorrow morning*, however I have endeavoured to comply with it. If your reason were, that you might have time to comunicate something of that matter by the post of Fryday night,[1] either to the Pensioner, or to any-body else in Holland, wee are all entirely against the least taking notice of this thing to anybody there till you are yourself on the other side, and you will then bee able to judg what is best to bee done.

Wee also agree it will bee very dangerous to mention anything of the mediation, *in writing*. If you send Mr. Cadogan, or any officer you can entirely trust, he may bee instructed what to say upon that matter by word

---

[1] 28 Mar.   [2] Letter 749.
[3] John Taylor, First Clerk of the Treasury.

of mouth in case he has encouragement, from any of their discourse to mention it at all.

I can't yett see the least hope of the weathers changing. I heartily wish you patience, and a good passage at last.

752. GODOLPHIN *to* MARLBOROUGH [*28 March 1707*]

Source: Blenheim MSS. A2-23.

Fryday 28th of March 1707

Another Dutch post coming in this morning gives mee the opportunity of troubling you again by this flying packett which Mr. Secretary Harley sends to you with his letters.

Those from the north bring nothing ill, but it looks rather by them, as if the matters in dispute, were not quite uncapable of being accomodated. Those from France, talk bigg now (as I did expect they would) upon the negotiations being broke with Holland [and] of their carrying onn the warr with vigour. All the names of their generall officers, you will find in my newsletter which I send you, because Renard[1] says he has not written to Mr. Cardonell by this post.

I doubt the truth of the article of the Duke of Savoy's having seized the French troops, nothing of it being come to Comte Briançon, but by the news he tells from Spayn I am afrayd one may depend my Lord Gallway has left the command of the army to my Lord Rivers. I have seen a letter from Madrid which says, both Lord Gallway and Lord Peterborow, and also the Condè de Empesa[2] were embarked for Lisbon, and I incline to believe that letter is true. But the same cruell winds that hinder you so long, will hinder our hearing by sea, from those parts of the world.

What I writt last night to Lady Marlborough concerning 4 [Halifax] continues to bee uneasy to himself and to his friends I don't trouble her with a letter tonight, because I didn't doe much yesterday, or else I would have given myself the satisfaction of telling her.[3]

The Queen was very easy in giving to my Lord and Lady Sunderland, the house where my Lord Nottingham lived,[4] in the privy garden.

---

[1] Louis Renard, a newsletter writer at Amsterdam. See p. 526 n. 3.
[2] Not further identified.
[3] Halifax wrote to the Duchess herself this day: he complained of being passed over for Townshend in the selection of a plenipotentiary to serve with Marlborough at the peace table. Coxe, ii. 254–5.
[4] See pp. 390–1.

753. GODOLPHIN *to* MARLBOROUGH   [*31 March 1707*]

Source: Blenheim MSS. A2-23.
Addressed: To His Grace the Duke of Marlborough.

Monday at 10

I was very glad to hear when I came last night from Kensington, that Lady
Marlborough was come to town, concluding you were gon, and that the wind
was more fair than here. But this morning she tells mee you are blown back
again, and that she intends to bee with you as soon as she can. I can't help
telling you, how much I am vexed at all this uneasyness and delay you meet
with, though I have little to say besides that is worth your trouble.

The Prince is much better. The Queen goes this morning to Windsor for a
week. When she comes back, wee expect the sessions will end. As long as
this cruell wind continues wee can have no letters from Spain or Portugall.

754. MARLBOROUGH *to* GODOLPHIN   [*31 March 1707*]

Source: Blenheim MSS. A1-37.

Margett March 31, 1707

I have been so unlucky as to be forced back by a northeast wind yesterday,
after having been seven leagues at sea. The wind continues in the same
corner, so that God knows when I shal be able to gett to Holland. I shal not
repeat what I have writ to Mr. Secretary Harley, the inclosed being a copie.[1]

I fear that whatever I shall writt to the King of Sueden, it will not availe
much, if I have not power to instruct the officer I send with the Queen's
intentions of the King of Sueden's being mediator, when her Majesty shall
think the time proper for the treating of a generall peace. As I can rely upon
Brigadier Palms' discretion, though he dose not speake the languidge, with
the help of Mr. Robison he will do very well with the King, and he is so
intierly master of the French [language], that he will need no help with the
minesters. But I shal say nothing to him, til I see the impossibillity of my own
going. I am very desirous of having the Queen's directions as to the instructions I should give him, and particularly to that of the mediator, with
latetude of adding what I shall think for her Majesty's Service. If the wind
should change I beg your answer by the first packet boat.[2]

---

[1] 31 Mar., in Murray, iii. 339. Marlborough wanted Harley to inform Robinson of his projected
journey to the King of Sweden. Robinson himself was to offer Count Piper and Charles XII's other
ministers pensions to bind them to the Allies. For the presents distributed see R. M. Hatton, 'Captain James Jefferyes's Letters to the Secretary of State, Whitehall, from the Swedish army, 1707–
1709', *Historiskt Magasin*, 35 (1953), i. 15-16.

[2] See p. 739.

755. MARLBOROUGH *to the* DUCHESS   [*31 March 1707*]

Source: Blenheim MSS. E3.
Printed: *Private Correspondence*, i. 85.
Addressed: For the Dutchesse of Marlborough.

Margett March 31, 1707

Fearing my letter might not meet you last night on the road, I writt this though I am not out of hopes of having the happyness of seeing you this afternoon. I was so sick at sea that I am not yett recovered, but I beleive this northeast wind will give me time for it. If fretting will give leave to itt my dear soull, I can't be happy when from you, so that with all my heart I wish for a speedy end of this warr. Pray lett Lord Royalton[1] know the derections I gave to Mr. St. Johns concerning his officer.[2] And I did forgett to speake to you as I promised my brother George I would, that when you renued your pattent for the Park, that you would then do his for life.[3] When you see him pray say two kind wordes to him, as being brother to him that loves you with all his heart.

I do not trouble Lord Sunderland since he will see what I send Lord Treasurer.

756. GODOLPHIN *to* MARLBOROUGH   [*1 April 1707*]

Source: Blenheim MSS. A2-23.

Tuesday noon April 1st

I am very sorry to find by yours[4] which I received this morning that you have had the mortification of being forced back by this obstinate wind.

The Queen being at Windsor, it will not bee in my power to send you her pleasure, as to the latitude you desire, in instructing whomsoever you shall send to the King of Sweden, in case of not being able to goe yourself. But my thoughts of that matter (in the meantime) are that there can bee no difficulty (whenever the Allys shall think it a proper time to treat of a peace) in assuring the King of Sweden that his mediation will bee as acceptable to the Queen, and rather more, than any other. But the nicety of it seems to lie in this: that it may bee dangerous to give him a handle to press the peace and the mediation of it, from any discourse of that nature, since wee have reason sufficient to apprehend, he is but too much inclined to both of them

---

[1] Francis Godolphin was styled Viscount Rialton from the time his father was raised to an earl-dom in Dec. 1706.

[2] Unidentified.

[3] Her patent as Ranger of Windsor Great and Little Park, which was renewed in 1709. The war-rant for the new patent stipulated it should contain 'a grant of the said office of Ranger or Keeper of the Little Park at Windsor of the new Lodge there now inhabited by George Churchill'. *C.T.B.* xxii. 209; *Conduct*, p. 291.

[4] Letter 754.

already. And it was for this reason, as I told you, in a former letter,[1] our friends were of opinion, not to mention anything of the mediator, by writing at all, and that the person you send should bee instructed not to begin that discourse, but to use, or not use any latitude given him upon that matter, according to the rise, that shall bee given him, by those principles in their discourses to him.

I am expecting Mr. Secretary Harley every minute. When he comes, I shall give him my opinion that he may write as you propose to Mr. Robinson, by this night's post. Though, by the way, till the wind turns, I doubt the letters will not bee able to gett over, no more than you, and but yesterday I was told, the boats are all on this side.

Since I began this letter the wind is come more to the southward, and I think so much, it will prove a totall change that instead of sending this letter to Margat as I intended when I began to write I have now desired Mr. Secretary Harley to send it to The Hague and his own too, and only send a flying packett to Margat this night, to give notice, in case you should bee kept there that wee thought it best to send our letters to Holland, hoping they would meet you there, and in case wee ghesse right, you won't bee surprised not to have any letters from Lady Marlborough by this packett, because she went at 5 this morning towards Margat.

757. GODOLPHIN *to* MARLBOROUGH   [4 April 1707]

Source: Blenheim MSS. A2-23.

Fryday 4th Aprill 1707

By the last Holland's mail, I sent you an answer[2] to your letter from Margat[3] about the *mediator*. I gave the Queen at Windsor an account of what I had written to you, and by her answer, which I enclose to you,[4] she seems to approve of it. But I omitted to say anything personally of Collonell Palms. There can bee nobody more proper for the occasion, if you can spare him, and I think there is as little doubt, but the Queen will give you latitude, in any particular that you shall think necessary for her Service. But this cannot bee signified to you in form, till her Majesty's return from Windsor.

I can't help lamenting in every letter the cruell obstincy of this wind which I fear must make your passage to Ostend difficult and tedious, if it does not force you back again to Margate, or to the Downs.

The Parliament will rise upon Tuesday the 8th. All the supplyes are compleated and very effectuall. I wish the Queen may as effectually satisfie those [the Whigs] who have contributed to make the sessions so easy, and so much to her Majesty's advantage.

[1] Letter 751.	[2] The preceding letter.
[3] Letter 754.	[4] Untraced.

The Scots are all expected next week. They will bring with them a great many pretensions, and create us a good deal of trouble but the most uneasy of them all [Argyle] is gon to you. I hope you will not find him so there.

Wee have heard nothing since you went, from Spain or Portugall, nor can wee expect it, till the wind changes. By the last letters wee had from thence it looks as if Sir Cloudesly Shovel would bee obliged to return to Lisbon for provisions.[1] But the orders to hasten him from thence shall bee repeated by every packett.

758. MARLBOROUGH *to the* DUCHESS   [5/16 April 1707]

Source: Blenheim MSS. E3.
Printed: *Private Correspondence*, i. 86.
Addressed: For the Dutchesse of Marlborough.

Brille April 5th 1707

After having been four tedious days at sea, I landed this evening at Helvort-sluce. On Thursday[2] morning at eight of the clock I heard the canon fyer when you went from Margett. I did with all my heart and soull wish myself with you. I am now going to bead to trye to sleep, for my head is so gidy that it is all I can do to writt this letter, that you may by the first opertunity know that I am safely landed. By Tuesday's[3] you shall be sure to hear from mee from The Hague. My service to Lord Treasurer.

759. GODOLPHIN *to* MARLBOROUGH   [8 April 1707]

Source Blenheim MSS. A2-23.

Aprill 8th 1707

By the Ostend packett wee have had the satisfaction of hearing you were landed near Flushing. I hope you are before time at The Hague, and that by the letters of this night from thence wee shall hear whether you find the posture of affairs on that side will allow you the time for your jorney to Saxony, or not. In case you find it impracticable to goe yourself, Mr. Secretary Harley has orders from the Queen to send you by this post her approbation of your sending Brigadier Palmes, and of your giving him such instructions as you shall think best for her Majesty's Service.

Wee have letters this day from Lisbon and Valentia. Sir Cloudesly Shovell was come to Lisbon, hoped to revictuall and putt to sea again by the middle of this month, which I hope will bee time enough.

---

[1] Shovell had taken Rivers's expedition to Spain in Oct. 1706 and had remained in the Mediterranean until Mar. 1707 when he returned to Lisbon to refit his fleet. He had instructions to return to the Mediterranean to assist the Duke of Savoy on his expedition to reduce Toulon. Owen, p. 161
[2] 3/14 Apr.   [3] 8/19 Apr.

Lord Gallway had received the Queen's orders, seemed in good heart at the letters he had received from his friends in England, and resolved to stay in the chief comand. But I find he had not yett seen Lord Rivers and till that interview is over I shall not bee easy about the situation of their affairs, the rather, for that I find all their complaints of Comte de Noyelles continue, and they say he has prevailed with the King of Spain to goe away to Catalonia, and that his Majesty gives them but little hopes of going into the field at all this year. Those resolutions seem pretty extraordinary after [all the expense] the Queen has been at only to make his equipage for his own person, besides the sum she sends to his assistance. I reckon wee must dispatch away Zinzerling immediatly to endeavour to rectifie those false steps before it bee too late.

This is all I have to trouble you with upon the forreign affairs, and as to those at home, I shall say no more at present, but that no foot soldier in your army has a more uneasy life then your humble servant.

760. MARLBOROUGH *to* GODOLPHIN [9/20 *April* 1707]

Source: Blenheim MSS. A1-37.
Printed: Coxe, ii. 190-2 (inc.).
Addressed: To my Lord Treasurer, Whitehall.

Hague [April] 9th 1707

After four tedious days I gott to Helvertsluce, and with difficulty have made these people easy as to my journy to Saxony. But as to the acknowlidging Stanislaw, and the garanty of the peace,[1] thay dare not give mee any powers without the consent of the States, and that the form of the States dose requier their sending to the Provinces, which would requier to[o] much time. But the truth is thay are unwilling to come into the acknowlidging and garanty for fear of disobliging the Zaar.[2]

Since my being here I have received letters from Vienna, by which I see thay persist in the expedition for Naples,[3] and at the same time thay complain of the King of Sweden.

I find that the behaviour of the French has given occasion to these people to wish heartily for good success in this campagne. In two conversations I have had with 61 [Buys], he has been very plain in telling me that he should think it a very good peace if we could persuaid the Duke of Anjoue to be contented with Naples and Sicilie. I am afraid there are a great many

---

[1] Of Altranstädt, between Charles XII of Sweden and the Elector of Saxony.
[2] Peter I, the Great (1672-1725), Czar of Russia from 1682.
[3] The Emperor had designs on Naples and its territories, a dependency of the Spanish crown. The Maritime Powers preferred that he employ his troops in reducing Toulon or assisting Charles III in Spain.

more in 110 [Holland] of his mind,¹ but as wee are very sure I think of making this campagne there may be many alterations before winter.

The ambassador of Moscovy² has been with me, and made many expressions of the great estime his master has of her Majesty, and that he should do everything to meritt her freindshipe; and as a mark of itt he had resolved to send his only son³ into England, but that he desired nobody but the Queen might know itt, since he must pass incognitto through severall countrys. The ambassador tels me that he shall bring six peaces of wine which he begs he may have leave to do. He is also very desirous of the honour as he cals it of the Queen's apointing him a house. As it can be off no presedent to any country but their own, and that the expence is so very inconsiderable, I hope her Majesty will do itt, for it is certain you will not be able to gratefie him in any part of his negociation.

I have undertaken this journey to Saxony to comply with the great desire of our friends. But I own to you that the Pensioner and Slingerland has showen me severall intercepted letters, which have been decyphiered, that show very plainly that almost all about the King receive French mony except Comte Piper.⁴ The agreement for 3,390 foot and 1,125 horse is almost concluded with the Saxon minesters.⁵ Mr. Secretary will have a particular account of itt from Mr. Stepney. The 70,000 crowns that are to be given to put them in a condition to march must be speedily paid, for the troupes can't march til one month after the payement.

I have this afternoon received a letter from the King of Spain of the 6 of March⁶ concerning some imployements in the Low Countrys. He also tels me that he is resolved to go to Barcelona for some short time, til his

¹ Stepney's report on Buys is instructive for his position in the United Provinces: ' 'Tis certain Buys [in code] is under mortification. His endeavoring to be too busy and drawing all negociations to himself has brought it upon him. The main direction of a[ffairs] is entirely in other hands and are likely to be so these 2 years, whereby he is cutt out being plenipo[tentiary] at a peace, or having any share in the secret measures of it. His attempting to go to England last winter did him no good, and if it be true that he offred to go to France on the errand which Mr. Henniken undertook, it is less to be wondered why his conduct is and ought to be censured.

'He is violently against Sweden, and argued with his Grace [Marlborough] to the last moment against his journey. He is likewise more tenacious for Ostend then ever. All his Grace could say on the last of these articles has hitherto made no impression here.' To Lewis, 10/21 Apr. 1707 (P.R.O., S.P. 84/230, p. 324).

² Andrej Artamonovič Matvěev, minister at The Hague 1706–7; ambassador to England 1707–8.

³ Alexius Petrovich (1690–1718). When the ambassador had his first audience of the Queen in May he asked for leave for the Czarevitch to come to England: Harley to Marlborough, 20 May, Blenheim MSS. A2-24. He did not make the trip, however, because of the King of Sweden's campaign against Russia. After the Swedes were defeated at Pultava the Czarevitch was sent to Dresden to study for a year.

⁴ Carl, Count Piper (died 1716), principal minister attendant on Charles XII. Hatton, p. 150.

⁵ 4,639 Saxon troops were taken into the pay of the Maritime Powers by this treaty, which was renewed each succeeding year (*C. J.*, xv. 438, xvi. 221). They were sent to the Rhine rather than to the Low Countries, to compensate in part for the loss of the 12,000 Prussian troops withdrawn the previous autumn. Harley to Meadows, 20 June, *H.L.N.S.*, vii. 463.

⁶ Blenheim MSS. A2-29.

presence may be necessary in the army. I have not time to have his letter copied, but by my next you shall have itt. I have left orders that the first letters that comes from England should be sent after mee, there being now six postes due.

761. MARLBOROUGH *to the* DUCHESS   [9/20 April 1707]

Source: Blenheim MSS. E3.

Hague Aprill 9th 1707

I did write to my dearest soull as soon as I was landed, to lett her know of my being safe. Since my arrivall wee have had noe letters from England, so that if I had stayed for a fair wind I must have been now at Margett. I begine my journey for Saxony this afternoon, so that you will not receive my letters for these next three weekes so regularly, as you shall be sure to do afterwardes. I do undertake this journey in hopes the publick may reap some good by itt, otherways I forsee a great deall of trouble to myself in itt.

I have given orders that all your letters after Friday's[1] post shall be keep here, for fear thay should be lost upon the road. The Muscovitt ambassatrice[2] depends very much upon your acquaintance and friendshipe, so that you must make her some compliments when she coms to London. I desire you will lett Lord Sunderland know that he will see by mine to Lord Treasurer and Mr. Secretary [Harley] all that I can write att this time, so that he shall not hear from me til I have seen the King of Sueden, which I hope to do tomorrow senight. Every hour of my life I wish for Woodstock being finished and my being happly there with you.

762. GODOLPHIN *to* MARLBOROUGH   [10 April 1707]

Source: Blenheim MSS. A2-23.

Aprill 10th 1707

I begin this letter a day before the post believing I shall have letters from you tomorrow to answer. In the meantime I send you my letters from Lord Gallway, Stanhope, and Montandre[3] not knowing whether my Lord Sunderland orders the extracts of his to bee sent you as Mr. Secretary Hedges used to doe.

By all these letters the conduct of the King of Spain seems very discouraging and unaccountable. Wee must send away Zinzerling presently to try if a letter from the Queen, and his representations which he promised you can rectifie it, but surely it will appear very odd in the world if he should decline going in person into the field, when all seems to depend upon his personall

---

[1] 11/22 Apr.   [2] The wife of Matveev.   [3] Untraced.

appearance and after wee have been at so much expence to provide for his equipage and attendance. My Lord Gallway seems to think he has this advice from Vienna but I rather think he has it from Comte Noyelles.

Montandre writes to my Lord Sunderlund that their army will bee compleatly 600 horse, and 20,000 foot, besides what the King can joyn to them which hee seems to think will not amount to above 3 or 4 regiments.

Lord Rivers had not yett seen Lord Gallway, and (whatever they write) I believe he is very uneasy, but whether that will prevail with him to return, I cannot yett to determine. There are no letters from himself, but these letters being only duplicates of what were sent by the *Chatham* not yett arrived, possibly, when that ship comes in, she may bring letters from him.

Sir Cloudesly Shovell writes from Lisbon of the 7th March, that he had left five of his cleanest ships at Alicant, was sending Sir George Bing thither with 20 more, and would follow with the rest when refitted which might bee about the middle of Aprill. He had received a letter from the Duke of Savoy, and cypher by which to correspond with him.

Lord Peterborough was at Valentia but did not meddle with the troops since his revocation, gave out he was going to Italy, and designed to make the campagne with the Duke of Savoy.

This is the substance of all our letters. If I am so happy as to hear from you tomorrow, I'le write more.

763. GODOLPHIN *to* MARLBOROUGH   [*11 April 1707*]

Source: Blenheim MSS. A2-23.

Aprill 11th 1707

I writt to you yesterday,[1] and sent my letter in Mr. St. John's packett, with some of my letters from Spain, and an account of the state of their affairs. If the wrong measures of the King of Spain, are suggested to him from Vienna, one can't expect they should bee altered by our representations, but if not, I should hope, a word from you to Comte Wratislaus, might be of great use to sett him righter.

I was in hopes to have heard from you today before this time, the wind having been perfectly fair, but the letters are not yett come, and till then I shall not trouble you with the uncertain rumours wee have of great insurrections in the south parts of France, nor lay any weight upon them.

All the money bills are past, but the Parliament [is] not quite up. It stands at present prorogued to Monday the 14th, upon a wrangle betwixt the Lords and Commons about the bill to prevent frauds in the drawbacks, and to see whether the Commons will bee willing to renew anything of the same

---
[1] The preceding letter.

nature, that may pass in a few days without prejudice to the Union. But I doubt this experiment will have no other effect than to create a good deal of ferment and ill humour, which wee must live in hope will vanish again before next winter.[1]

42 [the Queen] has never said the least word to mee of Oxford, or the professorship, but in all other things she leans that way, as much as she did in that while you were here, so that one has not only the uneasyness of seeing that men will not (on one side) bee satisfyed with things that are reasonable, but on the other side, that if they would, one could not obtain them.[2]

764. MARLBOROUGH *to the* DUCHESS   [*11/22 April 1707*]

Source: Blenheim MSS. E3.
Addressed: For the Dutchesse of Marlborough.

Osnebourg Aprill 11th 1707

The post being to go from hence tomorrow for Holland, though my head eakes very much with the journey, I could not forbear writting to lett you know that I was gott thus farr on my journey, and hope to be att diner a Sunday[3] att Hanover, and if possible with the King of Sueden on Wensday, for I shall leave Hanover a Munday at daybreak. I have not as yett any letter from you nor Lord Treasurer, and I am afraid shall have very few til my return to the Hague. Pray lett me have the measures of the hangings, which I am to bespeak for yours and my apartement.[4] I am ever yours.

[1] Traders, principally English and Dutch working through Scottish firms, sought to take advantage of the customs union by bringing in goods to Scotland under the lower duties, to be shipped south to England after the Union took effect. By the terms of article VIII of the Treaty of Union a drawback was to be paid on all foreign salt used in the curing of fish which were exported in turn. The drawback was claimed by the Scots as soon as the Union became effective, though no duty had been paid on the salt already imported into Scotland. Legislation was brought in to lower the duties on salt and other goods so that the Scots could not undersell English merchants. The Lords refused to pass the bill because of the harm it might do to the Union. The Queen prorogued Parliament for a week and then allowed it to meet again to work out a satisfactory solution. When it did not she finally prorogued it on 24 Apr.

[2] William Jane (1645–1707), Dean of Gloucester and Regius Professor of Divinity at Oxford, died 23 Feb. *D.N.B.* Marlborough proposed a moderate divine, Potter, as his successor. The Queen preferred Dr. George Smalridge (for whom see p. 907 n. 5). This post, together with the vacant bishoprics of Norwich, Exeter, and Chester, became the centre of a major political struggle with the Whigs ranked behind the Duumvirs and Harley behind the Queen. It was not resolved until the following January. See G. V. R. Bennett, 'Robert Harley, the Godolphin Ministry, and the Bishoprics Crisis of 1707', *E.H.R.*, 82 (1967), 726–46.

[3] 13/24 Apr.

[4] This year Marlborough ordered from de Vos the Alexander set for their bedrooms. They were completed the next year and Marlborough brought them home with him when he returned from the Continent early in 1709. See pp. 704, 974, 1284; *C.T.B.*, XXIII. ii. 90. A paper with the measurements is in Blenheim MSS. A2-34. The contract for the tapestries, 10/21 Aug., is in Blenheim MSS. A2-35. In a cover letter of 1/2 Sept. 1707, Cardonell wrote: 'In case the hangings when made are not approved and accepted by his Grace, the sume paid in advance shall be returned.' Green, *Blenheim Palace*, p. 248.

765. GODOLPHIN *to* MARLBOROUGH   [*12 April 1707*]

Source: Blenheim MSS. A2-23.
Addressed: To His Grace, the Duke of Marlborough.

Aprill 12th 1707

This is only to tell you that I had no letter from you, since your arrivall in Holland which I impute to the hurry you were in upon your going to Saxony. I am glad they have given so speedy a concurrence to it at The Hague, and I wish from my soul, the success of your jorney, may answer the pains of it. I believe you will have no letter from mee, by the next post being in hopes of passing 4 or 5 days at Newmarkett.

766. GODOLPHIN *to* MARLBOROUGH   [*15 April 1707*]

Source: Blenheim MSS. A2-23.

Newmarkett April 15 1707

I received at this place the favour of yours of the 9th[1] from The Hague, and am sorry you are engaged to take so long and troublesom a jorney to Saxony, with no better prospect than you seem to have of any good effect from it.

I like as little the account you give of 110 [Holland] in generall, though as to the particular declaration of 61 [Buys] I am not much surprised for he was always of that opinion, and I believe would rather Naples and Sicily should bee in the hands of the Duke of Anjou than in the King of Spain's. And indeed the conduct of that prince would almost make one think hee himself were of the same mind, since our last letters from Valentia speak very doubtfully of his going in person into the campagne, after all Mr. Zinze[r]-ling's sollicitations and all the expence wee are at in England for the payment of his troops and for the equipage of his own person. This would bee such a *contretemps*, that I have left with the Queen a draught of a letter for her to write by Zinzerling in which she tells him very plainly, that unless he thinks proper to second the endeavours of his Allyes to putt an end to the warr of Spain in this campagne, he cannot reasonably expect any succours from them another year. And by what you write of the intentions of the court of Vienna, it seems not less necessary to speak as plain to the Emperour. Since it is certain that if England continues to act, (as it has done all this warr) with no view but for the generall good of the whole Allyance and that each of the particular Allys act, as they have as steadily done, with no view but that of their own particular advantage wee must needs come by the worst of that at last. And after all, is not the Queen in right to speak plain to the Emperour considering all the assistance England has given him both for the saving of his own country and recovering of Italie, and what ill consequence is there

[1] Letter 760.

to bee apprehended from it? Would it make them goe the sooner into an ill peace? I don't think it would have that consequence. (But even in that case) it were better they should make such a step against our consent, than force us to joyn with them in it, by persisting as they doe, in all cases, to take wrong measures and to turn every success which they could not have without us, to our disadvantage, as soon as they have it. If you are of this mind, I hope you will write accordingly to Comte Wratislaus, as well as to Prince Eugene. I have presumed to write myself to the former,[1] not being able to have patience any longer with their behaviour. And when you write to the King of Spain, I hope you will also second what wee say to him by Monsieur Zinzerling. By some private letters which I have seen, there seems reason to think Lord Rivers is upon his return from those parts.

I will remitt the 70 thousand crowns to Mr. Stepney next week for the Saxon troops, and I think it is right to content the States in that matter, because of the augmentation they have made in their own house, but else, I question much whether these Saxon troops will come time enough to bee of any use this summer.

I shall bee uneasy till I hear you are returned in good health from your uneasy jorney.

767. MARLBOROUGH *to* GODOLPHIN   [*16/27 April 1707*]

Source: Blenheim MSS. A1-37.
Printed: Churchill, ii. 225-6.

King of Sueden's Quarters April 16

I gote to this place last night so early as to have one hour's conversation with Comte Pyper, and this morning a litle after ten I waitted on his Majesty. He keep me with him til his hour of dyning which was at twelf, and as I am told sot longer at diner by half an hour, then he used to do. He also took me again into his chamber, wher wee continued for above an hour, and then his ketledroms called him to prayers. Mr. Robison was with mee all the time, so that I must refere you to the account he gives the Secretary,[2] for I am come soe lait into my quarters, that I have not time to send for a copie of his letter, nor to say more to you, then that I am in hopes my journey may do good.

    [1] See p. 737 n. 3.
    [2] 17/28 Apr., P.R.O., S.P. 88/17; printed in A. E. Stamp, 'The meeting of the Duke of Marlborough and Charles XII at Altranstadt, April 1707', *Transactions of the Royal Historical Society*, new series, xii (1896), 113-14.

768. MARLBOROUGH *to the* DUCHESS   [*16/27 April 1707*]

Source: Blenheim MSS. E3.
Printed: *Private Correspondence*, i. 86–7.
Addressed: For the Dutchesse of Marlborough.

The King of Sueden's quarters, April 16

You will by this know that I am gott safe to this place, and I think with greatt dilligence, being here last night time enough to see Comte Piper, and this morning the King. I have been received with very kind expressions, but as I intend to stay but two or three days at most, I shal not have one hour to myself, so that you must not expect an account of my journey till I return to The Hague, where I long to bee since I see I must expect no letters from you til I come there. The King Augustus of Polland has this evening sent a gentleman to make me compliments, and to lett me know that he is come to Lipsick on purpose to speak with mee, so that I go to him tomorrow, which will ocasion my staying one day longer here then I intended.

769. GODOLPHIN *to* MARLBOROUGH   [*22 April 1707*]

Source: Blenheim MSS. A2–23.
Printed: Coxe, ii. 180 (inc.).

St James's 22th April 1707

It was a great satisfaction to hear by yesterday's post that you came well to Hannover, in your way to Saxony. I hope this will meet you soon at The Hague as well returned from thence, to the great ease of all your friends, and I think I might say of all this part of the world. Whether you will find from this jorney that advantage to the publick, and consequently, that satisfaction to yourself which you proposed, you can now judg. For my part, I shall always bee diffident enough of that matter, till it bee fully cleared to mee by yourself.

The disorders in France, and the discounts upon their *billetts de monnoye*[1] increase every day. They are now made current by a publick edict all over the kingdome,[2] which is much the same case with King James's boast money in Ireland.

However their newspapers never fail to tell us they are sending more troops to Spayn, they are fortifying the passes from Italy against the Duke of

---

[1] The bills of exchange by which the French obtained money on the Dutch and other foreign money markets.

[2] The French were short of ready money to support their army and took to issuing mint-bills backed by the Treasury which the King decreed were to be accepted as gold. They were heavily discounted, nevertheless, because of the uncertainty of their redemption, so the French government then resorted to bills of exchange, promissory notes payable in a year's time. Both sorts of bills circulated in the United Provinces and by this means the French raised ready money to pay their armies. See p. 787.

Savoy, and preparing to act both in Flanders and Alsace with great vigour. But yett, I hope and believe your army will bee in the field before them. Whether the lines they have made will bee able to hinder your progress in Flanders, a little time will try, but if it should prove soe, t'will bee worth considering in time, how farr 'tis possible to transport any detachment to the southern parts of France, where the people [the Camisads] are more than ever, prepared to rise, upon the least encouragement, or hopes of protection. This action is only submitted to your thought in case there should ever bee, either occasion, or room to make any use of it.

The close of the best sessions of Parliament that England ever saw, has been unhappily hindred, by a wrangle between the 2 Houses which is not yett ended.[1] It would bee tedious to trouble you with all the particulars, but it is chiefly imputable, as most other ill accidents are, to private animosityes.

Mrs. Morley [the Queen] seems easier in one or two things, than I have formerly found her, which I reckon is entirely owing to 38's [Godolphin] representations.

770. GODOLPHIN *to* MARLBOROUGH [25 *April 1707*]

Source: Blenheim MSS. A2-23.

Aprill 25, 1707

I have little to add to my last, not having any letter from you, nor hoping to have any till your return to The Hague, which I hope will bee before this letter getts thither; and that you will find your absence has not occasioned any prejudice.

My Lord Rivers, and Lord Essex landed at Falmouth the 20th. He has left the command of the army to my Lord Gallway, after some complements passed between them upon that occasion.

I have seen no letters from Erle by this ship, but I hope he has resolved to stay with my Lord Gallway, who seems to bee in pretty good heart, as to everything but the conduct of the King of Spain, and his court, of which they all complain very much and chiefly of Comte de Noyelles. So if the States have any occasion to recall him to their service, I am apt to think, it might come very seasonably for the affairs of Spain, which seem to turn very much, (as well as our on this side) upon the success of our undertakings in Italy. I hope therfore you neglect no opportunity of pressing Comte Wratislaus and Prince Eugene to hasten their entering into France, as much as possibly they can.

Our Parliament is at last, at an end, but without any effect of the late prorogation.[1]

[1] The drawbacks controversy (see p. 750 n. 1) was the cause of the delay in proroguing the Parliament.

The settling of the affairs, and of the revenues of Scotland, as well as the adjusting of the pretensions of all the Scots men new here, are full of difficulty and uneasiness of all kinds.[1] There will bee no room to satisfy the Duke of Argyle's brother[2] here, so the Duke of Queensberry is in hope you will give him a regiment abroad. I have not given him much encouragement [?] to expect it.

Sir Joseph Tredenham[3] is dead.

771. GODOLPHIN *to* MARLBOROUGH [*28 April 1707*]

Source: Blenheim MSS. A2-23.

28th of Aprill 1707

Since my last,[4] wee have no post from Holland, but are in hourly expectation of its coming, the wind being fair.

My Lord Rivers will bee in tomorrow. By the enclosed letters (which I send you from him to mee) you will best see how he left things in Spayn. Upon the whole, though they parted fair, he seems to bee unsatisfyed with my Lord Gallway, but I must confess myself so dull, as not to see any grounds for his being soe.

They have agreed to putt that army and also the train of artillery upon one establishment, which I hope is right, because 'tis the same thing wee have done here.

In Portugall, they seem both disposed and ready to take the field, if our troops from Ireland had joyned, but wee have not yett heard of their being sailed, though I hope they are so, before this time.

I have desired my Lord Sunderland to send you the coppyes of Sir Cloudesley Shovell's dispatches relating to the project concerted with the Duke of Savoy, by which you will [see] he has taken all the rightest measures that can bee putt in practice for the execution of it.[5]

---

[1] For the changes wrought by the Union see P. W. J. Riley, *The English Ministers and Scotland* (London, 1964).

[2] Lord Archibald Campbell, third Duke of Argyle (1682–1761), created Earl of Islay 1705; became Walpole's chief adviser in Scotland, succeeded his brother as third Duke in 1743; appointed second colonel of Maccartney's Regiment of Foot 6 Mar. 1708; Colonel Alnut's (36th) Regiment of Foot 23 Mar. 1709.

[3] One of the comptrollers of the army accounts.   [4] The preceding letter.

[5] Shovell to Marlborough, 29 Apr., Blenheim MSS. A2-24. Shovell's dispatches are all in this bundle. The project was a co-ordinated land-and-sea attack upon Toulon, which had been worked out by the Duumvirs and the two secretaries in December with Maffei and Briançon. See the 'minutes of the project with the Duke of Savoy in relation to Provence, Dauphine, Dec. 27' in Blenheim MSS. D2-6. The project is printed in Owen, pp. 158–61. A good account of the expedition follows, pp. 158–92.

The Toulon expedition was ill-fated from its inception. The Emperor was more interested in reducing Italy and diverted supplies and troops that were needed on the Toulon expedition

And upon the whole matter I should have great hopes our affairs could goe well abroad this year, if the court of Vienna would have the least regard for all they owe to the Queen and the English nation. But their obstinate persisting upon the expedition of Naples, and their averseness to the design of entering France, makes them deserve in my opinion to bee abandoned by all the world. And I must bee so plain as to add that by my consent, they should never bee complyed with in any one thing they desire, as long as this warr lasts, nor find the least consideration from the rest of the Allyes at making the peace, farther than is necessary for their own interests and security.

And I doe not see what advantage wee have by managing soe changeable, and yett so perverse an ally. But the plainer wee speak to them, I think, the less scurvily wee shall bee used.

772. GODOLPHIN *to* MARLBOROUGH   [*28 April 1707*]

Source: Blenheim MSS. A2-23.

28 Aprill 11 at night

I have now the favour of yours of the 16th by[1] which I see with great satisfaction that you hope your labour has not been lost in going to Saxony. The same post letts us know also, that the French in Flanders have not given the least alarm to Holland in your absence. These are two things which please mee the better, because indeed I was not very confident of either of them. The letter you sent mee from the King of Spain[2] is not soe fresh, as those I now enclose to you.

The settling of the government of Scotland and the management of the revenues there is a grievous burthen, and the uneasyness of people's laying weight upon every trifle after one has overcome the greatest difficultys to satisfie them makes mee weary of my life. Though at the same time if it bee God Almighty's will to bless the Queen with success abroad, whoever is uneasy will hurt nobody by it soe much as themselves.

Tomorrow the Queen declares in Counsell that this present Parliament,

---

(p. 772 n. 3). The Duke of Savoy was more interested in making territorial acquisitions along the way which delayed the arrival of the expedition at Toulon. He quarrelled with Prince Eugene who assisted in the command, and the Prince himself was half-hearted in his support for the project. Because of the slow rate of advance of the land forces the French were able to bring reinforcements into Toulon before the expedition arrived on 15/26 July. Finding the French too strong for the Allies, the Duke of Savoy raised the siege on 30 July/10 Aug. after several attacks failed to breach the main defences. The only real advantage derived from the effort was the destruction of the French Mediterranean fleet based at Toulon. By orders from Louis XIV it was scuttled in the harbour before the arrival of the Allied fleet and few of the ships were ever refitted to sail again. Thenceforth England was supreme in the Mediterranean. For an account of the expedition see Owen, pp. 158–92; Braubach, ii. 194–9.

[1] Letter 767.   [2] See p. 747.

shall bee the first Parliament of Great Brittain which it's generally thought will have the construction of a new Parliament. And as Sir Joseph Tredenham is dead, wee shall by this means lose our other Comptroller of the Army, Mr. *Moor*, who will resign his employment.[1]

The Queen being willing to give Harry Villiers a pension to keep his children from starving, the government of Tinmouth will now bee vacant. Though this bee not worth so much as New York, yett perhaps Collonell Sutton would rather have it than that, having a design by the Duke of Newcastle's help to bee chosen at Newark for the next Parliament.[2] But if you have a mind to place anybody else at Tinmouth, pray lett mee know it as soon as you can.[3]

29th of Aprill

I am in hopes to have seen my Lord Rivers before I sent away this letter, he having written to mee from Exeter that he would bee here tonight, but he is not yett come.

The French letters tell us wee may expect every day to hear of a battell in Spain.

773. MARLBOROUGH *to* GODOLPHIN   [*28 April/9 May 1707*]

Source: Blenheim MSS. A1-37.
Printed: Coxe, ii. 197-8 (as 6 May), 198-200 (inc.).

Hague Aprill 29th[4] 1707

I have used so much dilligence in my journey, that I could not till my return give you an account of the success of my negotiations, which I shal now do with all the exactness I am able. You are already informed that at the audiances I had of the King of Sueden, Comte Piper and Mr. Robi[n]son were always present to interprett between us. On Friday the 29 past, which

---

[1] 'The Parliament of Great Britain being interpreted to be a new Parliament (though consisting of the same members with the last) the clause [in the Regency Act] that incapacitates certain persons from sitting in Parliament takes place immediately, upon which account Mr. More, and Mr. Brewer with others in the like circumstance have quitted their employments, and thereupon (Sir Joseph Tredanham being lately dead) there will be a new Commission of Comptrollers consisting of five in a short time appointed' (Brydges to Tyrawly, 6 May, Stowe MSS. 57, I. 103, Huntington Library). 'There was an intentions once of putting the Comptroll[ership] into five Comissioners (and by the by I hope you don't forgett Negus. Crags and St. John promist to write to you about it to desire you to back what they have wrote to my Lord Duke, but the same [Regency] Act (they have since found out) forbid any comission to be encreast above the number it consisted of at that time, so that it must still be continued in the hands of two' (ibid., to Cadogan, 8 May, p. 108). Brydges and his friends tried to get Anthony Hammond appointed to one of the Comptroller vacancies. (Brydges to Godolphin, 11 May, ibid.). For the persons appointed see p. 765 n. 3.

[2] See p. 548.

[3] Major-General Thomas Meredyth was appointed governor in 1708.

[4] For the correct date see letter 775.

was the day I left Alt Rastadt, the Comte came to me accompanied by
Monsieur Cederheilm,[1] the Secretary *de Cabinett*, to recapitulat in the King's
name the essential of all that had passed before, Mr. Robi[n]son being with
me at the same time. He begane by acquainting me with the great estime his
master had for the Queen, and how sensible he was of the obligations he
owed her Majesty for the assurances I had braught him of her Majesty's
friendshipe, which he would endeavor by all possible means to improve by
making such returns as might be most acceptable to her. He was very particular in the King's acknowlidgements for the comunication he had received
by me[2] of the reasons [which] induced her Majesty to come into the present
warr. Which as he allowed to be very just, soe he wished the like glorious
successes might attend her Majesty's armes as hetherto, in order to the restoring a due ballance of power in Europe, and securing and supporting the
Protestant religion, wherein he said his master was intierly of the Queen's
opinion. He added further that the King agreed the Treatys of Westphalia
aught to be the foundation of a futor treaty of peace as to the affaires of
Germany; and that what has been done in derogation thereoff by subsequent
treatys, especially in point of religion aught to be redressed and reduced to
that standard; his master being likewise of opinion we aught to go one step
farther, by explaining the right of reforming, which by the Treaty of Westphalia is reserved to each Germain prince in his own territory, by vertu
whereof any Protestant prince that turns to the Romish religion, has a kind
of right to oblige his Protestant subjects to change theirs. This he would
have explained in such maner and with such limitations as the safety of the
Protestant religion may requier. This point of religion was what the King
seemed most warmly bent upon, and itt was not without difficulty that I
convinced him and Comte Piper of the necessity of defering everything of
this nature til we come to treat of a generall peace, for fear of weakning the
alliance, by creating unseasonable jealousies among such of the Allyes as are
of the Romish religion. Hereupon I toke occasion to acquaint Comte Piper
that as the King and his ministers had a better insight then we could be
supposed to have in the affaires of Germany, if his master would on occasion
freely open himself to the Queen, her Majesty on her part would be ready
at all tims to concure with him in everything that might be judged for the
mutual intirest and benefit of each other; that I should gladly charge myself
with laying before the Queen whatever his master might think fitt to comuni-
cat to her Majesty; and that with all the secresy and faithfulness the matters
could requier. To this Comte Piper assured mee I might depend upon the
Queen's being informed of whatever offers should be made to the King with
reference to the peace, that their Majestys might take just measures together
against wee come to a general treaty. Here you will allow the caution he

---

[1] Josias Cederhielm, Swedish official, member of the Chancery-in-the-field with Charles XII.
[2] A letter from the Queen. See pp. 739–40.

gave me of keeping this under the greatest secresy, since it may otherways seem, in the eyes of al others conserned, a little too partial in a mediator, as well as inconsistant with his neutrallity. I had almost forgot to tell you, that when I was representing to the King the views the Queen had in the present warr, and how desinterested she was, I toke occasion to mention Dunkerk as a place that had formerly belonged to England; that however her Majesty had not thoughts of reclaming itt, but was desirous at the generall peace to insist upon haveing the fortifications demolished, and the port ruined. To which the King said, he should readily give his helping hand, that place having likewise been a great nusance to his trading subjects, whome he now recomended to a more feavorable treatement in England. And I beleive itt might have a very good effect, if when any occasion offers, her Majesty would please to shew her ready inclinations to gratefy the King in this particular. His Majesty was also pleased to express his satisfaction at what had been done at a conference I had the day before with his ministers and the Baron Goertz,[1] in reference to the disputes between the Prince Charles of Denmark and the adminstrator of Holstein, the result whereof you will find in the two inclosed papers;[2] and desired that all the guarantees might speak the same language, so as to give the less occasion to Denmark to make difficultys in what might be judged reasonable. And here Comte Piper told me that this master having a particular confidence in the integrity of Mr. Robi[n]son and of his knowledge of those matters would be glad he might be imployed by the Queen at the conferences to be held on this subject at Hamborough.[3] To which I asured him of her Majesty's ready concurrance as soon as his attendance on the King could be dispensed with, the Comte having acquainted me before that his master would not allow of any foraine ministers following him into the field. However, I find by Mr. Robi[n]son that as a particular mark of their respect for the Queen, thay will connive at his secretary's[4] accompanying them as a vollantier. This I hope her Majesty will approve off, and in that case be pleased to make him some small allowance towardes his equipage and the expence of the campagne, for which I recon 250 or 300 at most may suffise. Comte Piper at my taking leave of him promised to acquaint me for the Queen's information, with whatever offers

[1] George Heinrich von Görtz (1668–1719), chief minister of Holstein-Gottorp, later in Swedish service.

[2] The dispute concerned the bishopric of Lübeck for which Prince Charles and Christian August of Holstein-Gottorp were both claimants (above, p. 517 n. 2). By the mediation of the Maritime Powers the election of the latter was confirmed. Marlborough enclosed a letter to Daniel Pulteney, the English envoy at Copenhagen, and a model of the renunciation to be made by Prince Charles, which he instructed Pulteney to present to the court of Denmark. The letter is in Murray, iii. 359–60. There is a copy of the renunciation, which Marlborough neglected to enclose (see p. 762), in P.R.O., S.P. 87/2, fols. 598–9; another copy in B.M., Portland Loan, 29/45N, fols. 257–8.

[3] Robinson did so and was resident at Hamburg from 11 Oct. 1707 to 1709.

[4] Captain James Jefferyes; accompanied Charles XII on his campaigns until Pultava. For his reports to the Secretary of State see Hatton, 'Captain James Jefferyes Letters'.

might be made his master from the court of France. Whereupon I asured him he might certainly depend on the like returns from us, the King himself having been pleased to give me perticular asurances that he would adhere to no proposals that might be made him in relation to the mediatorship until he heard from me that the Queen thought it seasonable. He also declared his opinion very freely that the French were not yet reduced to such an ebb as would make them reasonable. Finding the Suedish ministers so well inclined I could not but incorage Mr. Robi[n]son to draw for 12,000 crown, this summe being what her Majesty seemed willing to allow them as a continued yearly pension, to comence from this time; though he was not sure Comte Piper would accept of his share, but his lady has promised to use her intirest to prevaile with him.

I shall trouble you but with one observation more, and that is the uneasiness I perceive the King of Sueden under at the conduct of the court of Vienna. He complains of three perticulars on which he expects satisfaction; the first for the affront offered to his minister at that court; the next on the account of two Suedish officers killed at Breslau; and the thord in relation to the Muscovits on the Rhine, who he insistes to have delivered up to him. But as for this last article, I hope an expedient may be found, by returning the Moscovits to King Augustus, and the Suedes ingaging at the same time, that upon the Czar's releasing the like number of Suedes, these shall be set at liberty. I have pressed the ministers at Vienna to endeavor to satisfie the King on these articles, as fearing otherways, when he coms to march through Silesia in his way to Polland, he may make them very uneasy. It is certain the King designed likewise to have insisted on that court's giving satisfaction to the Protestants in Silesia for the usurpations and innovations comitted in that province,[1] had I not had the good fortune to convince him, as I told you before, of the unseasonableness of it at present. This is the substance of all that passed between me and the court of Sueden, which I hope will meet with her Majesty's approbation, it being very much for the publick good and her Majesty's service that we are sure the King has [not], nor will have any ingements with the French, so as to disturb us in the prosecution of the warr. I must not omitt to inform you that just as I was coming out of the King's closett, Stanislaus[2] arrived from his quarters, upon which his Majesty desired Comte Piper to know of mee whether I had any uneasiness or objection against seeing him, and beleiving I had no reason to make any difficulty, the King went himself and braught him into me, with a great deale of satisfaction. And after the usual compliments, King Stanislaus gave me great

---

[1] The King of Sweden was guarantor of the Treaty of Westphalia which established the rights of the Protestant subjects of the Emperor in certain enumerated places in Silesia.

[2] Stanislaus I (1677–1766), King of Poland and Duke of Lorraine. In 1704 Charles XII compelled the Polish Diet to elect Stanislaus, a Polish nobleman, as King in place of Augustus. When Stanislaus fled Poland in 1709 after the battle of Poltava, Augustus reassumed the crown with Russian support.

asurances of his respect and veneration for the Queen, and of the desire he had of her Majesty's estime and friendshipe.

I must now acquaint you that I had an audience of King Augustus at Leipsig the day before I came away, at which besides many repeated asurances of his repects for the Queen, and of his strict adherance to the intirests of the Allyes, he complained to me of the great hardshipes and extorsions he had suffered from the Suedes, and insinuated his desire, that the guarantys at the same time as thay accepted the guaranty of his treaty,[1] would take care he might have some satisfaction for seven millions of crowns he pretends thay have exacted beyond what the treaty allows, to which I gave him my opinion that is was no ways advisable for him to offer at anything at this juncture that might give the least handle to the King of Sueden to delaye his march out of Saxony. You will have heard when the treaty was concluded here by Mr. Stepney for the Saxon troupes,[2] upon the notice I had of it, and the pressing instances the King made me, I was prevailld with to give Lieutenant General Wackerbart,[3] who is to command them, a bill on Mr. Sweet for 40,000 crowns, payable at fifteen days sight, to enable them to hasten their march, which he promised thay should begine before the time apointed by the treaty, so that I must pray your care in ordering timely remittances for this service. The rest of this King['s] troupes I find are a greater burden to him then he is able to bare, his country being very much exhausted, so that at his desire I have pressed the court of Vienna to take three or four thousand horse into their pay, which thay assure me are in a good condition.

The King of Prussia having sent Brigadier Gromekow to me at Alt Rastat with a very pressing letter to call upon him, I went derectly to Sharlottenburg wher I came on Saturday senight,[4] and rested there the next day. I left the court in so good humor that the King declared to me he would give his consent for restoring the Upper Palatinat to the Elector Palatin[5] and likewise for the putting the Duke of Mantua to the ban of the Empire,[6] but desired me not to speak of this last for some litle time.

---

[1] Of Altranstädt made in 1706.   [2] See p. 747.

[3] August Christoph, Count Wackerbarth (1662–1734), envoy extraordinary from the Elector of Saxony to the Emperor 1698–1714; lieutenant-general, commander of the Saxon troops in Flanders; fought at Malplaquet.

[4] 19/30 Apr.

[5] The Upper Palatinate had been conquered by Bavaria during the Thirty Years War, and Bavaria was permitted to retain it by the Treaty of Westphalia. During the War of the Spanish Succession the Emperor promised the Elector Palatine it would be returned to him when a peace was concluded. The refusal of the Emperor to accept the Utrecht settlement and the military defeats he suffered from the French forced him to concede the retention of the Upper Palatinate by Bavaria at Rastaat in 1714.

[6] Ferdinand Charles of Gonzaga-Nevers, Duke of Mantua (1652–1708), the son of a French nobleman, had inherited Mantua through his mother, the sister of the two preceding dukes. As he had no heir, the succession of his territories was contested by several families, of whom the ducal house of Guastalla had the best claim. The Habsburgs also coveted the territories, some of which,

On munday morning¹ early I continued my journey with all the dilligence possible, by Hanover to this place, where I arrived on Sunday² in the afternoon. And having since acquainted the States with so much of my negociations at the court of Sueden as you will find in my letter to Mr. Secretary Harley,³ I designe to be going tomorrow towardes the army.

One of the papers I mentioned about Holstein is not yet come to my hands. I beleive Mr. Secretary will have itt by the next post from Mr. Robi[n]son.

774. MARLBOROUGH *to the* DUCHESS [29 *April*/10 *May* 1707]

Source: Blenheim MSS. E3.
Printed: *Private Correspondence*, i. 87–9.

Hague Aprill 29th 1707

I returned to this place last Sunday,² by which you will see that I have used such dilligence that I was but eightien days on the journey. Now that it is over I am extreame well pleased to have made itt, since I am persuaided itt will be off some use to the publick and a good deall to the Queen. I shall not enter into perticulars having writt at large to Lord Treasurer.⁴ This journey has given me the advantage of seeing four kings, three of which I had never seen.⁵ Thay seem to be all very different in their kindes. If I was obliged to make a choice it should be the youngest, which is the King of Sueden.

I should be glad to know if itt be trew that 255 [Mrs. Burnet] intends to make a journey to Hanover, because thay have already notice of itt; and the carecter given there of her is that she is a greatt friend off 240 [Lady Marlborough], so that thay think she coms about bussiness, which I know is impossible to bee with the knowlidge of 240 [Lady Marlborough]. I wish with all my heart she may not undertake this journey, for itt must do hurt with 42 [the Queen], and can be off noe use to anybody.⁶

I wish all my soull I had been with you att St. Albans, for every day and action of my life convinces mee that I can't be happy, but by being in quiet

including Montferrat, were fiefs of the Empire. In an armistice in Italy concluded between the Emperor and France in Mar. 1707 the rights of the Duke of Mantua, an ally of France, to be restored to his territories were deliberately omitted from the treaty and a governor appointed by the Emperor was put into the city. The ban of the Empire was a further device to prevent the restoration of the Duke to his lands. See the minister of the Duke of Mantua to Sunderland, 1/12 May 1707, in Cole, p. 476; Braubach, ii. 167–8; M. Landau, *Rom, Wien, Neapel* (Leipzig, 1885), pp. 85–92.

¹ 21 Apr./2 May.   ² 27 Apr./8 May.
³ 29 Apr./10 May, Murray, iii. 357–9.
⁴ Letter 773.
⁵ Charles XII, Stanislaus, and Augustus. The fourth was Frederick I of Prussia.
⁶ Mrs. Burnet suffered chronic ill health and was advised to take the waters of 'The Spa'. She left England 29 May and visited Hanover while abroad, arriving there 18 Sept. After visiting the Electress and the court she returned via Rotterdam where Marlborough greeted her and arranged for her passage to England in one of the Queen's yachts at the end of October. See p. 940; T. E. S. Clarke and H. C. Foxcroft, *Life of Gilbert Burnet* (Cambridge, 1907), pp. 428–30.

with you, which I am afraid will not be so soon as I did hope, for I am very apprehensive that the conduct of King Charles [Spain] will lenghen the warr. I have sent Lord Treasurer a letter from Comte Noyelles, I beleive of a fresher datte than his are, by which I think thay are doing everything that is wrong, which is very crewell since a litle success on that side woud make all things sure.

I had write thus far before wee had the disagreable news from France of a battaile in Spain.[1] I hope it is not so bad as thay make itt, but I am afraid our affaires in that kingdome are in a bad condition. I am to thank you for severall of your letters which I had the pleasure of finding here. Your kindness is the only thing that can make me intierly happy. Mrs. Howe is here and tends for England by the first convoye, which makes her going so uncertain, that I shall not write by her. When I left the court of Sueden I was given to understand, that the king intended his pictur should be at The Hague for me before the end of the campagne.[2] The King of Prussia forced a ring upon mee which is said to be worth one thousand pounds.

775. MARLBOROUGH *to* GODOLPHIN   [*29 April/10 May 1707*]

Source: Blenheim MSS. A1-37.
Printed: Murray, iii. 357 (inc.).

Hague 10th May 1707

You will have another long letter from me by this post,[3] relating chiefly to my negociations in Saxony. I had closed itt yesterday before we received the mallencholly news of the defeat of our army in Spain.[4] I send you here all the perticulars we have of itt as yett.[5] You will obsarve thay come from the French, so that we may reasonably hope our loos has not been so considerable as thay make itt, though I am sorry to tel you I find itt has already created a greatt damp upon people's sperits here.

I had yesterday a conference with the deputys of the States, both in relation to this misfortun, and the affaire of Lubeck. I now give an account of itt to Mr. Secretary Harley.[6] I beg you will take care that this last may be keep in the methode I have putt itt, since you will see the King of Sueden has it very much at heart. On my journey I received a letter from Comte Noyelles dated at Barcelona the 24 of March, which being much fresher then

---

[1] The battle of Almanza on 14/25 Apr., where Galway and Minas attacked a superior army under Berwick and were decisively beaten.

[2] There is no record of a portrait of Charles XII being sent to Marlborough.

[3] Letter 773.   [4] See p. 798 n. 2.

[5] A copy of a letter from a Guards captain of Philip V, 15/26 Apr., Blenheim MSS. A2-16; another copy in P.R.O., S.P. 87/2, fols. 596-7.

[6] 29 Apr./10 May, Murray, iii. 357-9. For Lübeck see p. 517 n. 2. Marlborough's letters to Pulteney and Wratislaw (Murray, iii. 359-61), and a 'modelle de renounciation a faire par le Pr Charles de Danemark'. S.P. 87/2, fols. 598-9.

what you sent me from those parts, you will find it here inclosed.¹ I have
promised that Mr. Robi[n]son shall be imployed at Hamborow to make an end
of this business of Lubeck,² and the Treaty of Travandale, which he may do
as soon as the King of Sueden marches out of Garmany. I hope you will
not join Mr. Wich³ nor anybody else, for Mr. Robi[n]son understands the
business extreamly well. My next will be from Bruxelles.

776. MARLBOROUGH *to the* DUCHESS [*1/12 May 1707*]

Source: Blenheim MSS. E3.
Printed: *Private Correspondence*, i. 92–3 (inc.).
Addressed: For the Dutchesse of Marlborough.

Antwerp May 12, 1707

Since my being here I have had time to hear of nothing but the unfortunat
battaile in Spain. I will stil hope it is not so bad as the French report itt. I
have not time to write to anybody, but from Bruxelles by the next post Lord
Treasurer shall have an account of all I know. Pray lett Lord Royalton know
that I have received his, and will write by the next post. In the meantime I
desire he would lett Mr. Topham⁴ know that I would holly relye on him to
make the bargain for the estate in Oxfordshire; for the tytle, that must be
judged of by some loyer. You should let me know where the gentleman⁵ is
that Lady Tyrconel would have made an officer, and what language he
speakes, so that I may know what nation to speake to. God knows when I
shal have time to write to the children, but kise them kindly from mee. I
am ever yours.

777. GODOLPHIN *to* MARLBOROUGH [*2 May 1707*]

Source: Blenheim MSS. A2-23.

2d of May 1707

I troubled you so much by the last⁶ that it will bee but reasonable to make
you amends by this, besides that since my [last] wee have no Holland letters,
nor any more from Spain. By what 10 [Rivers] has told mee by word of
mouth 2 [Gallway] is upon the worst terms that can be with 44 [King Charles].

---

¹ P.R.O., S.P. 87/2, fols. 596–7, giving an account of the battle of Almanza. Reply, 29 Apr./
10 May, Murray, iii. 362.
² See p. 517 n. 2.
³ John Wyche (died 1713), English Resident 1702–9, envoy extraordinary 1709–13, to Hanse
towns, resided at Hamburg; special mission as envoy to Holstein-Gottorp and Mecklenburg-
Schwerin 1709.
⁴ Richard Topham?, Keeper of the Records in the Tower 5 Mar. 1707; M.P., Windsor, 1698–
1710, 1715–22.
⁵ Unidentified.   ⁶ Letter 772.

I am afrayd this is chiefly occasioned by Comte Noyelles, so what will become of all that business, God knows. And though my Lord Peterborow, who used to complain so much against Austrian politicks, and German ministers, seems at last to have reconciled himself to them, I own very freely 'tis hardly possible for mee to bee in charity with those people after all that has been done for them by the Queen in Germany, in Italy and in Spain.

Yesterday was performed here the solemnity of the thanksgiving for the Union. The streets were fuller of people than I have seen them upon any occasion of that kind. The Bishop of Oxford preached a very fine sermon. When 'tis printed,[1] it shall bee sent to you.

I should be glad to have your answer when you have time, to what I hinted in my last[2] about Collonel Sutton.

Sir Joseph Tredenham being dead and Mr. Moor having resigned his place there is no Comptroller at present of the accounts of the army, but I think not to bee long without proposing one or two for that employment.[3]

Mr. Sollicitor [General][4] seems very well pleased to bee made Attorney, and I hope he will bee very serviceable in that station.

Wee are very impatient to hear of your being well returned to The Hague.

778. GODOLPHIN *to* MARLBOROUGH   [*3 May 1707*]

Source: Blenheim MSS. A2-23.
Printed: Coxe, ii. 204 (inc.).

May 3d 1707

I have this day received the favour of 2 letters from you, one of the 29th of Aprill old stile,[5] with a very particular account of the success of your jorney, and another of the 9th [10th] of May,[6] with the melancholly news of our misfortune in Spayn.

I can never thank you enough for the pains you have taken in writing so much, and so exact a relation of all that has passed, and I think the kingdome can scarce thank you enough, for having settled all things where you have

---

[1] William Talbot, *A Sermon Preached Before the Queen, at the Cathedral Church of St. Paul's on May 1, being the day appointed by her Majesty for a general thanksgiving for the happy Union of the two Kingdoms* (1707).

[2] Letter 772.

[3] See p. 757 n. 1. Marlborough suggested Francis Negus for one (p. 769) but Godolphin said there were too many objections to him (p. 863). The Treasurer proposed Howe, the envoy at Hanover (ibid.), but Howe refused the transfer because it would reduce his income (p. 906). Marlborough asked that the posts be left vacant for a time (p. 944), though during the winter of 1707-8 he and Godolphin had agreed that the latter's nephew, Sir Philip Meadows, would be appointed to one of the places (p. 949). Godolphin again objected to Negus when he was proposed by Meadows (p. 954) and the second post was finally given to Thomas Broderick in June 1708. Luttrell, vi. 320.

[4] Sir Simon Harcourt, Solicitor-General 1702-7; Attorney-General Apr. 1707-8.

[5] Letter 773.   [6] Letter 775.

been, so much to your own satisfaction, and to our advantage. But this good news has received a very great allay by the accounts the French letters give us of the battell in Spain.

I doe not think it is quite so bad as they make it, but I doubt it is so bad, as not to be easily recovered without great impressions upon France from the side of Italy. I see by the coppy of your letter to Comte Wratislaus[1] which you have sent to Mr. Secretary Harley that you have neglected nothing that [will encourage][2] the court of Vienna, to doe what they ought, upon this ill occasion. One would think it should not bee possible for them, after this, to continue their design upon Naples, but if they have any men to spare, to think rather, how they might send them to King Charles's assistance, who I fear may want it now as much as he knows little how to use it, when it comes to him. Lord Rivers had good luck, at least, not to bee in this defeat, but what vexes mee most is to think how Lord Peterborow will tryumph. 'Tis cruell upon all accounts, to bee so long in the uncertainty of our present condition in Spain, and consequently unable to send any proper directions in to take just measures from hence before t'will bee too late for them to have effect. I wish however you had sent us your thoughts, whether the regiments designed to bee employed in Portugall, should continue under their first orders, or whether they should bee sent directly to Spain, to support and sustain our broken forces there. The squadron of Sir George Bing[3] now in those seas might help to gett them provisions from Majorca. But if wee take away the troops from Portugall, so long expected by those people, there is danger, on the other hand, of their running into a hasty peace with Spayn and France.

Success in Italy, if it pleases God, may recover this blow, but I beg of you don't you bee so eager to doe it in Flanders, as to undertake anything rashly in that view, but consider that if you find their lines so strong as not to bee undertaken you may, in case the States please to assist in it, have a very good opportunity of sending a detachment to the river of Bourdeaux, as was designed last year.[4]

As misfortunes seldom come alone, wee have had another ill news today

[1] 29 Apr./10 May, Murray, iii. 360–1.

[2] A word or two here is illegible in the original.

[3] George Byng, Viscount Torrington (1663–1733), admiral; rear admiral 1703; knighted 1704; vice-admiral 1705; served in the Mediterranean 1706–7; prevented the Pretender's invasion 1708; Commissioner of the Admiralty 1709–18; continued to hold offices and commands until his death. See *The Byng Papers*, ed. by B. Tunstall (Navy Records Society, 1930–3), 3 vols. *D.N.B.*

[4] Godolphin pressed the idea of a descent throughout the summer, suggesting that 5,000 troops could be raised in England and Ireland if Marlborough could send a similar number from the Low Countries (pp. 768, 773). He suggested Rivers as the only possible commander unless Marlborough could send someone over (p. 778). Then he gave up the idea for a time when Marlborough said that the Dutch would not permit the release of any troops because of the numerical superiority of the French army over the Allied army in the Spanish Netherlands (p. 793). For Godolphin's revival of the proposal at the end of May see p. 876 n. 2.

of our Lisbon fleets being mett with in the Channell by the Dunkirk squadron, and a great many of them lost. They were the ships outward bound.[1] There is also a very great fleet expected home from thence just at this time. God send they may come soon.

Sir John Jennings[2] tells us from the West Indies, that the Spaniards will not so much as land their galeons there, or lett them come to Europe, till they have certain news of a peace, and that King Charles of King Phillip has quiett possession of Spain, so that if Du Quesne's[3] squadron bee gone into those parts it must bee with some farther design against our plantations there.

Mr. Bridges has order to remitt the 40,000 crowns, as you desired, for the march of the Saxon troops, but I have not much hopes of their coming time enough to bee of use to you, in this campagne.

Mr. Secretary Harley will tell you all you have desired for Mr. Robinson and his secretary will bee done. As also that care shall bee taken of the bills which he has drawn for 12,000 crowns.

779. GODOLPHIN *to* MARLBOROUGH [*4 May 1707*]

Source: Blenheim MSS. A2-23.

May 4th

This morning I received the inclosed letter from Monsieur de Guiscard,[4] which I send you, more, that you might see I am not alone in my opinion of Comte de Noyelles's conduct, than for any other thing mentioned in that letter, though I think most of his own letters to you, are proofs sufficient of his hatred and contempt of my Lord Gallway.

Since this news came I have talked with Brigadier Gorges who came over with my Lord Rivers, and has been all along with the army in Spain. He says he thinks it next to impossible that our troops can have been so much beaten as the French brag of, but if they bee, he seems to think they have no place to retire to (with any tolerable safety) but Alicante.

---

[1] A fleet bound for Portugal and the West Indies was attacked by the Dunkirk squadron under Forbin on 2 May. Forbin captured two of the three men-of-war which were assigned to guard the convoy and twenty-one merchant ships, an exploit for which he was made a count. Owen, p. 195.

[2] Sir John Jennings (1664–1743), naval officer at Cadiz and Vigo 1702; at capture of Gibraltar 1704; knighted 1704; rear-admiral 1705; vice-admiral 1708; Admiral of the White 1709; served with the fleet out of Lisbon 1708–10; M.P., 1705–11, 1715–34. *D.N.B.*

[3] Abraham du Quesne (1654–1726), French naval officer, captain since 1685. For his career see A. Jal, *Abraham Duquesne et la marine de son temps* (Paris, 1873), ii. 567–74.

[4] Untraced. Guiscard wrote Marlborough 3 May, at the same time he wrote to Godolphin, with his advice on what should be done in Spain following the disaster at Almanza. In it he condemns the jealousies raised by Noyelles and speaks of a letter he had received from Noyelles highly critical of Galway (Blenheim MSS. A2-25).

May 5

Since I have written this farr wee have received by the Dutch and French letters the sad confirmation of our terrible defeat in Spain, with the death of poor Lord Gallway[1] and the loss of abundance of our officers and soldiers, and with very little room left to doubt the truth of it. The Queen has taken the resolution of sending my Lord Rivers[2] immediatly, by the way of Lisbon to hearten and encourage those people in the 1st place and afterwards to the coast of Spain, to gather up the remnant of our troops and see what can bee done for preserving by the help of our fleet, the province of Catalonia or the town of Barcelona itself, with the person of King Charles.

At the same time she represents to Holland the necessity of joyning our utmost endeavours to recover the affairs of Spain by strengthing that army whensoever the posture of affairs will admitt of it, and also to press the Emperour, to send some part of the detachment designed for Naples, to the assistance of his brother King Charles.

This is what the Queen can think of doing for the present in this calamity but our greatest hope of relief to Spain must come from the Duke of Savoy's expedition,[3] which by the French letters seems to alarm them very much; and will I hope, oblige them to withdraw most of their troops from thence.

If you could spare us as many troops from Holland and Flanders by July or August as would be replaced by the Saxons, wee might yett endeavour to recover this blow, by a descent upon France, as was intended last year.

780. MARLBOROUGH *to* GODOLPHIN   [4/15 May 1707]

Source: Blenheim MSS. A1-37.
Printed: Coxe, ii. 220–2 (inc.).

Bruxelles May 4/15 1707

Since my last[4] I have seen severall relations of the unfortunat battaile given in Spain, and am sorry to tell you the news does no ways mend on our side. The enemy pretend to have taken five English, five Dutch, and three Portuguess redgiments prisoners, with all our canon and bagage, and 120 coullors and standards, which last I think almost impossible. However, we must expect the worst, and begine to take our measures for repearing this great loos. When we come to hear derectly from Spain I fear we shall find our people confine themselves to the preservation of Alligant and of Catalonia. The States received the news of this fatal stroke with less concern

---

[1] This was a false report.

[2] On Saturday the 3rd, Godolphin wrote to Harley: 'I wish wee had somebody of consideration and sence to encourage Portugall, and to goe onn afterwards to the King of Spain, but I know nobody that has capacity and zeal sufficient for such a piece of service' (B.M., Portland Loan, 29/64/4). Rivers was obviously picked on for lack of someone better.

[3] To take Toulon.   [4] Letters 773, 775.

then I expected. However, it is very likely their deputys may have orders to act here with more caution then the exegency of affaires requiers. And I can't but take notice that 'tis obsarved this blow has made so litle impression in the great touns in this country, that the generallity of the people have rather showen a satisfaction at it then otherways, which I don't attribut so much to the inclination they have for the French as to their aversion to the present government, and the disorders it lyes under, to which I do not forsee any proper remedy can be aplyed during the warr. In the meantime it will make us uneasy. Enclosed I send you copies of two intercepted letters from the court of France to Monsieur Bessenvall,[1] their minister with the King of Sweden, which showes plainly their is noe engagements between the two courts. Monsieur Laseraz, a Swiss minister who does my Lord Albemarl's bussiness with relation to the troupes of that country in the States' service, and has good corrispondance at Paris, has promised to send you from The Hague what intelligence he receives that may be worth your knowlidge, that you may compare it with the advices you have from others. You will see by the letter Comte Wratislaw writs to you of the 30th past, wheroff he has sent me a copie,[2] that the court of Vienna persistes in their expedition against Naples. I wish our misfortun in Spain may open their eyes, and dissuade them from it in time.

I think you have made a very good choice of Collonel Sutton for the government of Tinmouth.[3] In case you should add to the commission of the Controlers of the Army, I am desired by severall friends to recomend to you Collonel Negus.[4] I can asure you he is very capable, and I beleive would act very honestly. I do from my heart pitty you, for all the trouble you are forced to undergoe, and should be very glad it were in my power to give you any ease. Upon Saturday[5] the army will be inchamped att Hall,[6] so that by the end of this month I shall be able to guesse at what the French intend. The Dutch think thay are stronger the[n] wee are. If thay continu of that opinion we shal do nothing.

You will see by the enclosed from Lord Raby[7] the great desire he has of

---

[1] Jean Victor Baron of Besenval, French envoy to Charles XII. The letters were sent to Marlborough by Robethon, in his of 29 Apr./10 May, Blenheim MSS. A2-20. Both dated 17/28 Apr., one is from Louis XIV, the other Torcy (Coxe, ii. 205). Besenval was sent to Charles XII to request him to act as a mediator in the War of the Spanish Succession. The French, like the Allies, also had hope of winning his support in the war. See G. Syveton, *Louis XIV et Charles XII. Au camp d'Altranstadt: La Mission du baron de Besenval* (Paris, 1900). A letter from Besenval to Louis XIV describing Marlborough's visit to Charles XII is printed in Coxe, i. 205-10. There are four other intercepted letters from Besenval to Chamillard, June–July, in B.M., Portland Loan, 29/45v, fols. 266–71, and 29/45P/2.

[2] 19/30 Apr., Blenheim MSS. A2-17.   [3] He was not appointed.

[4] Francis Negus, major, Prince George of Denmark's Regiment of Foot, 1694; brevet lieutenant-colonel 1704; Surveyor of the Queen's Stables. He was not appointed. See p. 765 n. 3.

[5] 10/21 May.   [6] Halle (Hal), on the Senne, 15 kilometres south of Brussels.

[7] 22 Apr./3 May, Blenheim MSS. A2-20. Raby states that he had satisfied Marlborough on the Queen's objection, for his estate was worth more than £4,000 a year and all his brothers and sisters

being an Earle. I wish for his own sake his estate were 4,000 pounds a yeare. Pray let me know what I may say to him, for I take it for granted he can't be gratified.

781. MARLBOROUGH *to the* DUCHESS   [4/15 May 1707]

Source: Blenheim MSS. E3.
Printed: *Private Correspondence*, i. 89–91.

Bruxelles May 4/15 1707

I am to thank you for two of yours since my last. The measures of the roomes are so well explained that I beleive itt will be an advantage to the hangings.[1] I am very sorry to tell you that since my arrivall here, I see by all the letters from France that our misfortun in Spain is much more to our disadvantage then was at first reported. I am afraid we may take it for granted that it is as bad as may be. My chiefest hopes is that the army in Italie will enter France, and in that the court of Vienna does us all the mischief thay can, these thoughts joined with the litle satisfaction you have of the inclinations and beheavior of 42 [the Queen], makes me quite weary of being in the world. Since I left you I have taken more pains then I myself thought I could go through. I shal continu to do my best, but it will always be with a desire of retiring, for their is no being in business with any pleasure. For I must own that I hate myself when I consider the letter I writt to 4 [Halifax] by you,[2] in which I said in few wordes as much as if I had comitted a fault to a man that I owed my fortun too, which has had no other effect, but giving him an opertunity of using me ill, by never so much as taking notice of itt, which is all one could do to a servant of on[e]'s own. I can't forbear venting myself but I conjure you to say nothing of itt. I did say somthing of itt to Lord Sunderland in my last letter,[3] so that he might not think mee in the wrong, when he should come to know that I think myself ill used by 4 [Halifax], as I do. I hope I shall have so much care of myself as to let nobody but you two know itt, and I do promis you that from this minutt it shall give mee no more uneasiness. I do not know who you ment by two men that are prefered[4] which gives discontent to 89 [the Whigs], for

were provided for. Marlborough apparently disbelieved this. Refused by the Duumvirs Raby supported Harley in 1710 and was rewarded with the promotion to the peerage he desired, Earl of Strafford.

[1] See p. 750.
[2] In answer to Halifax's letter of 28 Mar. to the Duchess, complaining that he had not been designated as a plenipotentiary to represent England at the peace conference to end the war, whenever it was held. See p. 741 n. 3.
[3] Sent by Craggs. In his reply on 9 May (Blenheim MSS. A2-24) Sunderland said Halifax was now easy with everyone and had thought it better to let the whole matter drop, which was why he did not notice it.
[4] Sir Simon Harcourt, made Attorney-General, and the Earl of Pembroke, made Lord-Lieutenant of Ireland.

38 [Godolphin] has said nothing to me of any alterations. By your letter I know he must be very uneasy, which I am heartily sorry for, for I can't see a probabillity how he can ever be out of business, nor how he can please considering the temper of 239 [the Queen]. When I left England I was in hopes that everything would go well, but as it is I hope I shall have no hand in the making of 81 [peace], so that I may not be in the power of being used ill, as well as contemptable. Upon Saturday the army will be enchamped att Hall, and then I shall leave this place, so that you will hear very regularly from mee, for I have no pleasur so great as writting and hearing from my dearest soull. For in you are all my hopes of happyness.

782. MARLBOROUGH *to* GODOLPHIN   [8/19 May 1707]

Source: Blenheim MSS. A1-37.
Printed: *Private Correspondence*, ii. 228–9.

Bruxelles May 8/19 1707

Since my last wee have had noe letters from England, nor anything more from Spain. But from Dunkerk we have the ill news of two of our men of war being braught into that place with several marchant men.[1] By letters of the 30th of the last month from Turin, I find Lord Pitterborow was gone from thence, and that he had told the Duke of Savoye he would call upon mee in his way to England. His chiefest business was to persuade his Royal Highness to send troupes to Catalonia, so that thay might be able to make a deversion in Roussillion.[2] I do not send you the news we have from Mons, the post-master telling me that he sends itt to Lord Sunderland. I beg you will make my excuses to the Queen and Prince that I did not sooner send the enclosed letters. I am also to make the King of Sueden's excuse that his letter to the Queen is not in his own hand. The reason given me was that the King could not write French; but the truth is that his hand is so bad, that her Majesty could not have read itt.[3] I shall be with the army att Hall upon Saturday,[4] and shall leave Mr. Stepney here for some time, unless you think his presence necessary at The Hague, for the affaires of this country are in such disorder that I fear the consequences.

783. MARLBOROUGH *to the* DUCHESS   [8/19 May 1707]

Source: Blenheim MSS. E3.
Printed: *Private Correspondence*, i. 91–2.

Bruxelles May 8/19 1707

I have so litle time to myself, that I am glad to begine to write to my dear soull this night, though the post does not go til tomorrow night, and by

---

[1] Marlborough had not yet received Godolphin's account of the encounter, for which see p. 767.
[2] That is, to enter France across the Pyrenees.
[3] Charles XII's letters to the Queen and Prince. Untraced.   [4] 10/21 May.

that I may hope for the happyness of hearing from you. 253 [Lady Tyrconnel] left this place some days before I came, I supose being afraid that I might aske questions, for I no ways doubt of their having been in France. Wee have from Dunkerk the ill news of their having brought in there two of our men of warr, which were convoye to our Portugale fleet, of which thay have taken the greatest part. The misfortun in Spain and this last accedent at sea makes the French talk very impertinently; but my great hopes are that the Duke of Savoye will act with vigor. I have but this morning received yours of the 23d of the last month, which should have come by Mrs. Burnett, but was sent me from Sir Philip Meadhurst. I am extreamly obliged to you for the methode you tel me you have lived with 42 [the Queen]. I hope in time you will find the good effects of itt by being able to do good, for otherways all must go to destraction. The man[1] that is recomended by 17 [Newcastle], I have the same opinion of him you have. I hear from Italie that Lord Pitterborow intends to call upon me in his way for England. I am very glad that Saturday is so near, for I am extreme weary of this place, as I shall be everywhere till I have the happyness of being with you.

784. GODOLPHIN *to* MARLBOROUGH   [*9 May 1707*]

Source: Blenheim MSS. A2-23.

May 9th 1707

I have the favour of yours of the 4th/15[2] from Brusselles with the particulars as they are confirmed of our misfortune in Spain.

Wee reckon here, as you seem to doe, that the best wee are to hope for, will bee that the remainder of our army, may with the help of our fleet, bee able to defend Alicante, and Catalogne, and perhaps only the latter; that the distance will not allow (at present) of taking any measures for reinforcing the army in Spain with men from these parts, and therefore, the only means of giving King Charles any relief in this extremity, must bee by making on all sides such diversions against France as may oblige them to call home their forces from Spain.

In order to doe this, I think the court of Vienna must still bee pressed, and in my opinion threatned, if they will not desist from their enterprise of Naples[3] at this time. I can't but take notice that the Prince of

---

[1] George Whichcot, an M.P. for Lincolnshire, 1705–10, whom Newcastle wanted to be governor of Tinmouth. See p. 787.

[2] Letter 780.

[3] On 2/13 March the Emperor made a treaty with the French for the neutralization of Italy (in Lamberty, iv. 391-8). Under its provisions all the French troops in Lombardy, including prisoners of war, were to be permitted to return to France together with most of their arms, ammunition, artillery, and stores. This incensed the Maritime Powers because it freed some 12,000 seasoned French troops to reinforce the French armies in the Low Countries, on the Rhine, and in Spain

Salma's[1] letters to you,[2] and Comte Wratislau's to myself are full of nothing but false reasonings from one end to the other. I shall not make any reply to Comte Wratislaus because I can't write decently, or with patience to him upon that subject. But I hope you will lett the Prince of Salms see in the civillest terms you can, that the Queen will expect a complyance in this matter both as to the deferring the design against Naples to a more seasonable opportunity, and also the acting with all their force and vigour against France imediatly, or else they must not wonder if her Majesty finds herself obliged to take such measures as may best express her just resentments at the proceedings of the Imperiall court. I own to you it is my poor opinion that when this is said wee shall have reason of them, and never till then.

In the next place wee have been employing our thoughts to gett a body of troops together, if possible, by the end of July in order to make such a descent as was intended last year. The 4 regiments [from Ireland] being gon to Portugall just at this time makes this a greater difficulty than it would otherwise have been. But as it is wee shall hope to gett 5,000 men out of the Queen's dominions, and if you can prevail with the States to lett us have as many from their garrisons in Holland as may soon bee replaced again upon the coming of the Saxon troops, this would make together about 10,000 men which wee shall give out are to recruit the army in Spain, and by that means the design will bee less suspected than it was last year.

Mr. Secretary Harley will send you the particulars both of our calculations and of our desires in this particular.[3]

The States need not apprehend they shall have their troops sent to Spain as last year, and not to France, for wee have no view left now, but of pressing France so on all sides as to force them to a good peace.

Your intercepted letters to Bussenval confirm very well the sincerity of all that was said to you in Saxony by the Swedish ministers.

for the 1707 campaign. With northern Italy now under his control the Emperor sent an expedition south to Naples under General Daun, drove out the Spanish garrisons, and took possession of the Kingdom of Naples in the name of Charles III. Habsburg designs on possessing Italy now seemed assured. This expedition was a further irritant to the Maritime Powers because it resulted in the diversion of men and supplies that could have been used to reinforce the Toulon expedition or Charles III in Spain, both of which they considered should have priority. As a consequence the Maritime Powers held this expedition to be the chief cause for the failure of the Duke of Savoy to take Toulon. For the events in Italy see Braubach, ii. 164–93; M. Landau, *Rom, Wien, Neapel*, (Leipzig, 1885), *passim*.

[1] Karl Theodor Otto, Prince of Salms (1648–1710), Imperial field-marshal; appointed governor to Archduke Joseph, 1685; made first minister by Joseph on his accession as Emperor in 1705; resigned in 1709 when it became obvious his advice was not respected by the Emperor or his ministers.

[2] See Salm's letter to Marlborough, 23 Apr./4 May, Blenheim MSS. A2–17, where he shows how 100,000 men are available in Italy, enough to support both the Toulon and Naples expeditions.

[3] 9 May, Blenheim MSS. A2–24, confirming the details above with a paper showing how 4,350 men (the 5,000) are to be taken out of Great Britain and Ireland.

My head is so full of those forreign affairs that I shall not troubl you in this letter with anything relating to England or Scotland, but that your answer to my Lord Raby may bee that the Queen has not upon the Union, made any promotions to the English [peerage], though much importuned to it, as in some instances, you know.

I am also desired by the Scots lords here in behalf of Brigadier Hamilton[1] in the Dutch service to represent to you the uneasyness of his circumstances he having had a character of major generall in Scotland, and is only a brigadier in Holland. I am not insensible this is pretty hard to bee remedyed.

I suppose the French will not agree to exchange any of our men taken prisoners in Spain, but methinks they might bee contented to change the officers for some of those wee have had here so long.

785. GODOLPHIN *to* MARLBOROUGH [*10 May 1707*]

Source: Blenheim MSS. A2-23.

May 10th 1707

Since my letter of last night, I have received from Monsieur Vryberghen a communication of the resolution of the States of May 17th[2] concerning the affairs of Spain and Portugall. I doe not send you his paper, because by the resolution itself, I find a coppy of it was ordered to bee sent to you and shall therfore only observe upon it, that in case, the States are sincere in the concern they express for the misfortune in Spain and would joyn heartily in their endeavours to relieve King Charles in his present exigency, they ought to make the less difficulty of letting us have the 5,000 men wee desire to make up 10,000 men for a descent on this side, while the Duke of Savoy is acting on the other side of France. I can imagine no way so probable as this to help Spain, or to putt the Allyes upon a foot of expecting, and insisting upon, the same peace, as they might have done before this accident in Spain.

I have a farther thought, which may bee a great argument to induce the States to exert themselves for the relief of King Charles in Spain, if anybody durst insinuate it to them; which is that if they should not doe all that is possible for them to preserve the footing which King Charles is yett master of in Spain, in case he should bee forced to abandon it for want of their assistance, the next step for the Allyes to make would naturally bee to bring him to Brusselles and govern that country himself, and oblige the people to maintain as great a force towards his support as they have at any time done

---

[1] George Hamilton was not made a major-general of infantry (Dutch) until 19 Apr. 1709, back-dated to 1 Jan. 1709; commanded Scots Brigade at Malplaquet; joined the service of the Pretender 1715.

[2] B.M., Add. MS. 5127, fol. 63.

for the Elector of Bavaria and the French. I don't know how farr you may think it proper to touch this string, but I submitt my notion to you. Make what use of it you please, or none at all, if you like that best.[1]

The Queen is willing to give Collonell Sutton the government of Tinmouth and I take it for granted he will like it better than what you designed him, at New York.[2]

786. GODOLPHIN *to* MARLBOROUGH   [*11 May 1707*]

Source: Blenheim MSS. A2-23.

May 11th

My Lord Rivers makes so many difficultys upon going back to Spain, as you will best see by his letter which I send you inclosed,[3] that the Queen has resolved to send back Collonell Pepper[4] to the King of Spain by the way of Genoa, with the assurances of the continuance of her endeavours to support him, by diversions aga[i]nst France, and all other means that are possible, and to send a duplicate of her letters by sea directly to Barcelona.

I send you a coppy of the letters that came this day from Lisbon, by which you will see they had not then heard of the battell in Spain, though 11 days after it. You will see also that they stand still in Portugall, only for want of our regiments in Ireland. I hope they are there before this time, but perhaps the news from Spain will have quite damped the good intentions of the Portughese.

I design to send this letter by the Ostend packett boat tomorrow night, if my mind does not alter betwixt this and that time. My reason for doing it is that I think it will bee with you 2 or 3 days sooner, and there is no danger of the letters being taken for they tie them to a piece of lead.

787. MARLBOROUGH *to* GODOLPHIN   [*12/23 May 1707*]

Source: Blenheim MSS. A1-37.

Lembeck[5] May 12/23 1707

I have had the favour of yours of the 2. and 5.,[6] by which I find you are turning your thoughts how to recover the loose we have made in Spain. I

---

[1] See Marlborough's reply, letter 798. There is no indication he used Godolphin's suggestion.
[2] See pp. 548, 757, etc.   [3] Untraced.
[4] John Pepper (died 1725), colonel, Regiment of Dragoons (8th Hussars), 15 Apr. 1707; brigadier-general effective 1 Jan. 1707; major-general 1710; served throughout war in Spain and Portugal. St. John wrote to Harley on 13 May in reference to Pepper: 'When I heard today at the Cockpit that Pepper was the man pitched upon to go express to the King of Spain I imagined you did not know how scandalously he procured this year a commission of brigadier by imposing a false date of his colonel's commission on the Duke of Marlborough. The thing deserved cashiering, and he seems to have a mark of favour conferred upon him.' H. M. C., *Bath MSS.*, i. 172.
[5] Lembeek, 3 kilometres south of Halle on the Senne, where Marlborough made his headquarters until the army moved on the 15/26th.   [6] Letters 777, 779.

hope you will have an express with the particulars of itt from the King of Spain and what his intentions are before you dispatch Lord Rivers, so that you may be the better able to give your orders.[1] I am very much afraid he will be advised to leave a Vise Roy in Catalonia, and come himself to Italie. This seems to agree with all the measures that are taking att Vienna. I saw in a letter from Italie that 30 [Peterborough] was going for Vienna. His fondness for the project of Naples will make him a favoritt there, but I should think if you oblige him to give an account of his behaviour, and perticularly as to the mony matters, when he returns to 108 [England], he will hardly be a favorit in that country. I hope 2 [Galway] is not dead; but whether he be or no, 30 [Peterborough] must not be suffered to lay his faults on him, for that would be to lett him tryumph. You are certainly very much in the right to incorage Portugale at this juncture. The Dutch have resolved to borrow mony for the paying him[2] what thay are in arrear to him. As soon as wee hear from King Charles, I shall then speak to the Dutch as you desire, and lett you know what their thoughts may be as to the sparing of troupes by the end of Jully, about which time I recon we may have the Saxons. The redgiment of Bothmer[3] will be here sooner. I send you a copie of the Prince of Salm's[4] letter with that from the Comte de Prie, which I received this morning. I shall be very uneasy til I hear the Duke of Savoy is in France, for I think the success of this campagn depends upon itt. The caution of 110 [Holland] and the strength of the French army will oblige me to comply with your desires of not venturing. But should 58 [Duke of Savoy] attack 115 [Toulon] I should then hope 49 [Berwick] would be obliged to make a detachement, which might give an opertunity to 39 [Marlborough] to do something. I am very glad of the good news Sir John Jenyngs sends, that the Spaniards will not send any mony home this summer. If that prove trew France can't continu the warr.[5] By a mistake the King of Sueden's two letters were forgott.

---

¹ For a descent.   ² The King of Portugal.

³ A Hanoverian regiment of dragoons, formerly in Imperial service, taken into the Dutch service on 16/27 Sept. 1707 (Wijn, VIII. iii. 509). It was paid for jointly by the United Provinces and England. See below, p. 814, and the convention for the hire of the regiment between the Elector of Hanover and the Maritime Powers in B.M., Add. MS. 5130, fol. 16.

⁴ 30 Apr./11 May, in reply to Marlborough's of 20 Apr./1 May, Murray, iii. 348-9, enclosing an extract from one from Prié to Lichtenstein of 28 Mar./8 Apr., Blenheim MSS. A2-17. Prié writes optimistically about the expeditions to Naples and Toulon (for which see Salms to Marlborough, 23 Apr./4 May, ibid.). Salms is mainly concerned with Sweden. He inveighs against the machinations of Charles XII, and notes the presence of the French ambassador at his court, but promises Imperial efforts to reach an accommodation. Marlborough's reply, 12/23 May, Murray, iii. 377-8.

⁵ The plate fleet this year made port at Brest in February and what silver was on board apparently remained in France. H. Kamen, *War of Succession in Spain 1700-15* (London, 1969), p. 183.

788. MARLBOROUGH *to the* DUCHESS   [*12/23 May 1707*]

Source: Blenheim MSS. E3.
Printed: Coxe, ii. 222 (inc.), as May 25.

Lembeck May 12/23 1707

I have had your two letters of the 2 and 5, and do with all my heart thank you for your kind expressions in that of the 2d. I do veryly beleive that 255 [Mrs. Burnet] is descritt as possible to be having such a husband, but 240 [Lady Marlborough] may be asured that I shall not be uneasy, though their health should give them leave to make the journey.[1] If I were in the place of 38 [Godolphin], I should take itt very unkindly of the Citty, that upon the first ill success thay should forgett all that is passed, and be so ready to drink confusion to 98 [ministers]. If it were not for the concern I have for 42 [the Queen] and 108 [England], I could wish thay had 30 [Peterborough] and such like favoritts 98 [ministers], and that 38 [Godolphin] and 39 [Marlborough] were at quiet. But I am afraid there must be some time before that will be allowed of, for this ill success in Spain has flung everything backwardes, so that the best resolution we can take is to lett the French see that wee are resolved to keep on the warr til we can have a good peace.

As to what you desire to know of the strengh of the French army,[2] I am afraid thay think thay are strong enough to hinder us from doing anything, but I beleive thay have not so good an opinion of their army as to venture a battaile. The good humor you say 7 [Wharton] was in when he left the town is very comendable, and I do wish it may continu, for I think he is capable of doing great hurt. You know my heart is sett upon the house of Woodstock, and you say nothing to mee how it goes on. I beg you will let mee have an account, and beleive me what I am, with heart and soull yours.

789. GODOLPHIN *to* MARLBOROUGH   [*13 May 1707*]

Source: Blenheim MSS. A2-23.

May 13th 1707

My last was of yesterday[3] by Collonell Pepper who resolved to goe over by Ostend. The Queen sends him with her letter to the King of Spain[4] by the way of Genoa. By all accounts that come, I doubt he will find our friends there in a bad condition, but with the assistance of the fleet which brings them money and some recruits, they may perhaps bee able to preserve Catalonia.

---

[1] Mrs. Burnet's journey to the Continent to visit the Spa and Hanover. See p. 726 n. 6.
[2] The French army in Flanders consisted of 124 battalions of foot and 211 squadrons of horse. Vault, v. 24–5, 297–9.
[3] 11 May, letter 786.   [4] Untraced.

I am now to thank you for the favour of yours of the 8/19 from Brusselles,[1] in which you desire mee to make your excuse to the Queen and Prince for not having sent the *enclosed letters*[2] sooner, but you have not enclosed any letters in yours to mee.

I am sorry to find by yours that the King of Spain's affairs goe no better in Flanders than elsewhere. If the court of Vienna continue to act everywhere as much as they can to the prejudice of the rest of the Allyes, I confess it is no great wonder if nothing succeeds. By this post wee hear from Turin and from Berne they persist in sending a great detachment of their best officers and troops to Naples, and that the attempt to enter into Dauphinè is like to bee baffled by it. I can't help repeating in every letter that I think wee can't hurt ourselves more by speaking very plain to them, than they hurt us for want of it; and if that design against France, bee not pushed with all the vigour they are capable of, it would not surprise mee in the least, if the rest of the Allys endeavoured to make the best conditions they could for themselves, without any regard at all to his Imperiall Majesty.

I find by yours the French talk as if they would venture a battell in Flanders. I should think their success in Spain ought to make them decline it, unless they find themselves pressed within their own country. On the other side, they have more strong places behind them to stopp you in case they were beaten, but in case they had an advantage your great towns are all open. This may perhaps bee a temptation to them.

Monsieur Spanheim has letters from France which say the Duchess of Nemours[3] is dead or dying. This makes him very alerte upon the King of Prussia's pretensions to Neufchâtel. I can see no reason why the Queen should not give him all the assistance she can in that affaire but I believe her Majesty would bee glad to have your thought upon this matter as soon as conveniently you can.

I hope the States will encourage our thoughts for a descent upon France. If they doe wee shall make all the efforts that are possible for us to putt it in execution. I believe they have fewer troops upon the coast this year than they had in the last, and their people still more and more uneasy. I can see nobody here but my Lord Rivers to putt at the head of it. Possibly you may think of somebody to send from that side who might bee more proper. The more experience I have of him, the less fond I am of his temper.

Monsieur Vryberghen tells mee he has leave to goe over to Holland and

---

[1] Letter 782.   [2] From the King of Sweden. See letter 787.
[3] Anne-Marie d'Orléans-Longueville, duchess of Nemours (1625–1707). She died on 5/16 June. As heiress of the last duke of Longueville she had inherited the independent earldom of Neuchâtel and Valengin, a Protestant city and principality in Switzerland. The King of Prussia was one of a number of claimants to this territory. Upon considering the claims of the various contestants the state of Neuchâtel awarded the investiture of the state and its sovereignty to Frederick I as heir to the house of Châlon-Orange, from which the title descended. For a full discussion of the Prussian diplomacy to secure Neuchâtel, see E. Bourgeois, *Neuchâtel et la politique prussienne* (Paris, 1887).

thinks of going about a fortnight hence, before the Queen goes to Windsor. Perhaps wee might easily have a man of better intentions in his room, but he will bee better himself than any new man of the same inclinations.

The Duke of Savoy complains very much not only of the detachment for Naples but that they send all their best officers. However I need not trouble you with repeating this because you will have it more particularly from Comte Maffei. In a word all seems to turn upon the success of the Duke of Savoy's expedition, and if the Emperour will continue to thwart that, I really think the whole Alliance seem to resent his proceeding so much as to bee willing to joyn in protesting against it.

Mr. St. Johns has been ordered to lay a list before the Queen, of such officers upon the establishment of Spain, as are absent from their comands, in order I hope, to make some examples, but I won't answer how farr it will bee done, though I think somthing of this kind is necessary, and if it cannot bee compassed after such a misfortune one must never expect it.[1]

Mr. St. Johns tells mee he will send you every week, what shall bee directed by the Lords of the Comittee, in order to our getting together a body of 5,000 men, as soon as is possible.

On 15/26 May Marlborough moved his army south to Soignies, only to discover that Vendôme had, during the preceding three days, moved across his path from Mons to Gosselies near Charleroi, arriving the day Marlborough marched.

---

790. MARLBOROUGH *to* GODOLPHIN   [*15/26 May 1707*]

Source: Blenheim MSS. A1-37.
Printed: Coxe, ii. 223 (small omission).

Soignies May 15/26 1707

Since my last[2] we have had no letters from England, nor no account from King Charles of the particulars of our misfortun in Spain. The superiority the French persuade themselves to have has incoraged them to quite their lines. Their camp is very strong, and I beleive thay will not stay in any, where thay may with reason be attacked; for though thay have more squadrons and battalions then wee, yet I beleive we have as many men; and for

---

[1] The 'list of officers in England who belong to troops in Spain', dated 12 May, B.M., Portland Loan, 29/45/G/2.
[2] Letter 787.

certaine our troupes are better then theirs. We doe hope that there streng[t]h here makes them weak both on the Rhin and in Dophinee, so that wee flatter ourselves thay can't be long before thay will be obliged to make detachments, and then we may act with more advantage. Being obliged to be on horse-back at four a clock tomorrow morning, I shall give you no farther trouble at this time.

791. MARLBOROUGH *to the* DUCHESS   [*15/26 May 1707*]

Source: Blenheim MSS. E3.
Printed: *Private Correspondence*, i. 93–4.

Soignies May $\frac{15}{26}$ 1707

Since I left my dear soull, til now I have never had any time to myself. Though I am forced to be much on horseback, yett I have the satisfaction of being some time every day alone in my chamber, and if I could be blessed with your company att that time, it would make amends for the other uneasy part of my life; for my misfortune here is that unless it be in what concerns the warr, I have nobody to whome I can speake without reserve. The carector you have given me of 221 [Argyll] is but to[o] treu, so that I shall be upon my guard as much as is possible; but my unhappyness is that I am forced to converse with great numbers amongest which there is not one in a hundred of such a temper as I could wish a friend should bee. I have had a very obliging letter from 245 [Lady Peterborough]. I do not send itt unless you desire itt since the hand is so ill that it would hurt your eyes. By it I beleive she is to meet her husband on this side the watter. Cadogan by some neglegence has had his quarters burnt but I do not yett know what his loos is. The church and the greatest part of the villiage was burnt. The fyer burnt the outhouses of my quarters, but my servants had time enough to take out the horses so that I lost nothing. The French being marched out of their lines, we are this day come to this place. Thay are in a very strong camp, and though thay brag much of being much stronger then wee, I beleive thay will stay in no place where thay may be attacked, so that you need not be afraid of a battaile; but as wee have severall great towns to protect thay may give us trouble. I am heart and soull yours.

792. GODOLPHIN *to* MARLBOROUGH   [*16 May 1707*]

Source: Blenheim MSS. A2-23.

May 16th 1707

Since my last[1] I have none of yours, nor doe I expect the forreign letters before this post goes though the wind bee fair, because it has blown this way

[1] Letter 789.

so long, that I fancy all the boats must bee on this side. I am very sorry for it, all your notions now, being like to bee soe criticall as to give as much impatience of hearing regularly from you.

Wee have nothing neither from Spain or Portugall since the battell. This east wind keeps back everything from thence and won't suffer our Lisbon fleet to come in though wee may hear they are in the soundings.

Our affairs at home goe but heavily and unwieldily onn. They did so last year when wee began the year with so much success. Wee have begon this with a misfortune, which does not contribute to putt people in better humour.

Those of Scotland are not yett settled,[1] and as soon as they are those of Ireland will require some time,[2] and create a good deal of trouble, our friend[3] being not very good at easing of difficultys, though he is more dextrous than he appears to bee at keeping them from himself.

I hope wee shall bee able to gett from Ireland one regiment of horse, one of dragoons, 2 of foot, and from Scotland, one regiment of foot is all wee must look for. But unless Holland will help us with the number we desire from them, it will hardly bee worth the charge of assembling the small force[4] which the Queen can draw together of our own.

All this has but a melancholly prospect. My great hope was in the Duke of Savoy's expedition, and you cannot easily imagine how enraged all people are here at the Imperiall court's persisting in their design against Naples, and sending to[o] great a detachment thither, at this time.

I long to know what effect the news from Spain may have for changing this measure, but I have not much hope that it will, but rather harden them in getting the possession of it, while the opportunity is in their hands. I hope a time may yett come to bee even with them.

For 'tis certain, France is so extreamly pressed within, that nothing but very great success without, can make them hold out long. I say this chiefly that you might not think the blow wee have had in Spain requires you should bee in so much hast to repair it as to undertake anything upon disadvantage.

793. GODOLPHIN *to* MARLBOROUGH   [*16 May 1707*]

Source: Blenheim MSS. A2-23.

May 16 1707

Since I had written my letter[5] which you will receive enclosed in the Duchesse of Marlborough's I have had the favour of yours of the $\frac{12}{23}$ from

---

[1] That is the problems attendant on the Union. A good deal of administrative reorganization was involved.

[2] The Irish Parliament was scheduled to meet on 7 July and Godolphin anticipated some opposition to the government's legislative programme. It went off more smoothly than he anticipated (see p. 854).   [3] Pembroke, the new Lord-Lieutenant.

[4] For the descent. See p. 766 n. 4.   [5] Letter 792.

Lembeck[1] with the letters enclosed from the King of Sweden and the coppies of the letters from the Prince of Salms and the Marquis de Prie by which last it looks as if his master were consenting to the detachment for Naples. But the Comte de Briançon speaks quite another language here.

Those letters, and what you have sent to my Lord Sunderland from Robethon[2] make mee mightily in pain least the Duke of Savoy's expedition should bee disappointed upon which I agree with you, the sucess of this campagne seems chiefly to turn. I must own I am very suspicious too that Mr. Robethon's doubts concerning the views of the Imperiall court may not bee without ground. But if this should bee true, it would bee a proceeding unheard of in any former age, and ought to bee followed with the resentment that justly belongs to it.[3]

Wee send away Delavel tomorrow, by sea to the King of Spain, to encourage him to defend Catalonia, and to assure him of all the assistance imaginable, and to lett him see in case he thinks of any other measures he must forever abandon the thought of being King of Spain. But I think as you doe, that he is very likely to take the advice of going to Italy.

Wee can have no express from Spain as the wind is, and if you stay till you have one by land, before you speak to the States to spare us any troops, I doubt it will bee too late afterwards, to gett all things in a readiness, and wee have no need to make any unnecessary expences.[4]

I don't find you have any letters from Prince Eugene this year. I doubt the reason of it is, that he is ashamed of their maniere at Vienna. I hope still, and shall doe so, till I know the contrary, that the Duke of Savoy will goe onn.

794. GODOLPHIN *to* MARLBOROUGH [*17 May 1707*]

Source: Blenheim MSS. A2-23.
Printed: Coxe, ii. 241-2 (inc.).

May 17, 1707

It was but yesterday that I troubled you with two letters.[5] However I have so many thoughts concerning, the obstinate proceedings of the court of Vienna, after all the obligations they have to the Allyes, that I can't help observing to you, that in case by the answer you expect from the Prince of

---

[1] Letter 787.

[2] John de Robethon (died 1722), a Huguenot refugee, served successively as secretary to Baron Schütz, the Earl of Portland, William III, the Duke of Zelle, and George I as Elector of Hanover and subsequently King of Great Britain (J. F. Chance, 'John de Robethon and the Robethon papers', *E.H.R.*, 13 (1898), 55-70). He regularly provided Marlborough with intelligence. His letter of 2/13 May is in Blenheim MSS. A2-20.

[3] Robethon reported, correctly, that the Emperor was concluding a military convention with France that called for the withdrawal of all French troops from Northern Italy. See p. 772 n. 3.

[4] For the descent.   [5] Letters 792-3.

Salms you should find reason to bee confirmed in Monsieur Robethon's suspitions of their being inclined to a neutrality for Italy, which I look upon as a separate peace, I cannot see any good objection why it might not bee worth your considering with the Pensioner whether measures might not bee taken to bee beforehand with them [the Emperor].

I am sensible this matter is very nice, but I mention it only upon supposing you are thoroughly satisfied of their intentions, and then I should think by restoring the Elector of Bavaria to his country, which would bee no small mortification at Vienna, hee might bee induced to prevail with France rather to gratifie England and Holland in the terms of the peace, than the house of Austria.

And upon this supposition, taking it for granted, that they will putt themselves quite out of the warr, and stick to their neutrality in Italy, and apply themselves to reduce Hungary, I must own very freely, I don't see how the rest of the Allyes can carry onn the warr without great disadvantage, nor can I hope, the Dutch would bee long afterwards, before they followed that example. Though at the same time I agree France is in so ill circumstances at home that they must necessarily sink, if the Allyes would but hold together, and this consideration makes the *contretemps* of the Imperiall court, so much the more unfortunate and more grievous to the whole Allyance. When all this is said, if the Duke of Savoy can, or will goe onn, notwithstanding this detachment for Naples, I shall not quite despair but the project may succeed. Yett in all events, I think wee ought at least to bee very watchfull of the steps of these gentlemen, and take every occasion great and little to lett them see wee are very farr from being satisfied with all their late behaviour.

I ought to ask you a great many pardon[s] for persecuting you with such repeated trouble upon this subject. I am sure it gives mee a great deal of trouble myself and I wish there may bee no occasion of my having given it you.

[19 May 1707]

The greatest objection I can find myself against what I have here hinted, is your letting the Pensioner [know] that wee are capable in any case of receding from the preliminaryes settled with Holland, but I make you judg of that as of all the [sic] and if you please, when you have redd my letter yourself, though you should never think of it again, I shall bee very well contented.

'Tis with the same submission that I trouble you with the enclosed reply which I have made to Comte Wratislaus' letter of which hee sent you a coppy. You may seal and send it forward to him, if you think proper and if not you may please burn it.[1]

---

[1] Wratislaw had written Godolphin 20 Apr./1 May (untraced) to ask that the Maritime Powers agree to send the 7,000 Palatine troops in the pay of the Maritime Powers with the Duke of Savoy to Spain for the relief of Charles III, after the Toulon expedition was over. Wratislaw to Charles III,

Our last French letters bragg that they will venture a battell in Flanders. I think it is what wee ought to wish for but at the same time one can't help being in a great deal of pain, till wee know their intentions more certainly, and that you are not like to bee too much exposed.

Monsieur Vryberghen tells mee he is ordered to press for our payment of the arrears to the Landgrave of Hesse whose minister he says refused to ratifie the last convention[1] made with him, till that bee done. I have told him, I was ready to submitt myself to what you would say ought to bee done in that matter, but if he means the arrears due in the late king's time, those were never yett allowed by the Parliament nor I believe never will bee.[2]

I have told Collonell Sutton, that you had thought of the government of Tinmouth for him, because the Duke of Newcastle seemed soe desirous that he should have something at home, but now his Grace presses rather his going to New York, and the reason of it (I believe) is that he has a mind to gett Tinmouth for a whymsicall of his own, one Mr. Whichcote who is knight of the shire for Lincolnshire but never was in the army that I know of. At the same time the deputy governor's place, of his Grace's own government of Hull is vacant.[3]

I finish this letter a day before the post, but the wind being west, I doe not expect to have the satisfaction of hearing from you in the meantime.

The 4 regiments are at last sailed from Ireland to Portugall with a fair wind. May 19, 1707.

Upon discovering that Vendôme had moved to a strong place north of Charleroi as his own army had moved south to Soignies, Marlborough held a council of war. To besiege Mons would leave Brussels and Brabant exposed; to follow the French was to challenge them to battle which the Dutch field deputies were not authorized to permit. Therefore, when the Dutch also vetoed his proposal to stay at Soignies, Marlborough chose to return north to Brussels and to send a party to Mons to demolish the French lines. On 17/28 May the army returned to Lembecq and on the 18/29th it made camp north-east of Brussels at Beaulieu.[4]

21 Apr./2 May, 'Correspondenz des Königs Karl III mit Wratislaw', ed. A. Arneth, *Archiv für Kunde österreichischer Geschichts-Quellen*, 16 (1869), 42. Godolphin's reply (untraced) must have been encouraging (see p. 803) although critical at the same time of the expedition to Naples. Marlborough sent the letter on (p. 800) and after protracted negotiations the troops were sent early in 1708.

  [1] Made 14/25 Mar. 1707, P.R.O., Treaties, 236.

  [2] In the treaty of 9/20 May 1706 the Landgrave insisted on half at once, the other half at the end of the year, and Marlborough promised to try and obtain payment. No money was ever voted.

  [3] Sutton was made deputy-governor of Kingston upon Hull, effective 11 May.

  [4] Richard Molesworth, an aide-de-camp to Marlborough, wrote to James Brydges: 'Though we may seem to make a tour, and not go the shortest way to the enemy, yet I can assure you 'tis the only one that is practicable and passable by an army such as ours.' 30 May, Stowe MSS. 58, I. 183–4, Huntington Library.

795. MARLBOROUGH *to* GODOLPHIN   [*19/30 May 1707*]

Source: Blenheim MSS. A1-37.
Printed: Coxe, ii. 224 (small omission).

Beaulieu May 30th 1707

Since my last the French have not only drawn as many troupes as was possible out of their garrisons in order to make themselves stronger then wee, but thay have also abandoned their lins, so that we had it in our power to attack any of their towns. But as we could not have our canon in less then a fortnight, and that we had not troupes enough to make a siege [of Mons] and cover it, we thought it best to make this march, in order to hinder the further designs of the French, which you will see by the enclosed copie of my letter to the Pensioner.[1] The trew meaning of my letter to the Pensioner is to lett him see that I am not of the opinion to venture a battaile, unless the advantages be on our side. This caution of mine is absolutely necessary, for instead of coming to this camp I would have marched yesterday to Nivelles,[2] but the deputys would not consent to itt, telling me very plainly that thay feared that march might be the consequence of a battaile. So that unless I can convince the Pensioner that I am not for hazarding but when we have an advantage, thay will give such orders to their deputys that I shall not have itt in my power of doing good, if an advantage should offer itthelf. Besides, the news which wee have from the Rhin[3] will make the Dutch, I fear, persist in their opinion of not venturing. I am also aprehensive that Monsieur Vandome knows from the French partizans in Holland, that the States are against venturing a battaile, which incorages him to act as he does; for he can't but know that our army is better then his and that if wee should beat him, that his master must submitt to such terms as the Allies should think reasonable. I take care not to lett the army know that the Dutch are not willing to ventur, since that must have an ill effect. And though it be a very unpleasant thing not to have full power at the head of an army, yett I do please myself, that I shall do some considerable service this campagne; for I do beleive we shall find the Elector [of Bavaria] and Monsieur Vandome grow insolent, by which thay will either attack, or give me occasion of attacking them. I am sorry to tell you that wee have every day instances that the greatest part of this country are much more inclined to 45 [Duke of Anjou] then to 44 [King Charles], which is occasioned by the unreasonable

---

[1] 30 May, 't Hoff, pp. 311–13. 'Their designe was at the same time [we attacked one of their towns] to have made themselves masters of Braband, and then to have given battaile to the army which should have covered the siege.'

[2] Nivelles, a town 20 kilometres north of the French army at Gosselies.

[3] On 11/22 May Villars had crossed the Rhine and turned the lines of Stollhofen, forcing the Imperial army in the Rhine, under its new commander, the Margrave of Bayreuth, to make a hasty, confused retreat. With its main defensive line broken all southern Germany was open to a French invasion.

behavior of 110 [Holland]. The enclosed from Monsieur Rob[e]than[1] you may read at your leasur. I send them that you may know the thoughts of that court.

796. MARLBOROUGH *to the* DUCHESS [*19/30 May 1707*]

Source: Blenheim MSS. E3.
Printed: *Private Correspondence*, i. 94–5.

Beaulieu May 30th 1707

Since my last from Soignies[2] I have been in perpetual motion, for the French have not only drawen out the greatest part of their troupes from their garrisons in hopes of being stronger then wee, but thay have also abandoned their lyns, so that thay left us at liberty to attack what town we pleased. But upon my having certain knowledge of their intentions of ravaging Braband, I have made two very long marches to come to this camp, which has secured this country, and tomorrow I shall march againe in order to be nearer the enemy. Wee have this morning the news of the French having passed the Rhin, which is shamfull for the Garmain army. I have write my mind as to the business of the warr to my Lord Treasurer, so that I shall not trouble you with itt. The letter you mention by Doctor Hair,[3] I have not received nor hear nothing of him. If he be resolved to come in the packett boat of Ostend, he may very well be obliged to take his way by Dunkerk. I have a great many things which vex me, I mean here abroad, but none more than what Mr. Travers writs to Cardonel, that thay must be obliged at Woodstock to turn the workmen off for want of mony to pay them. This gives me a double trouble, for I am sure their must be great want of mony or Lord Treasurer would not let this bee, therfor pray do not take notice that I know anything of it, for I am sure he must have many troubles, and I should be very sorry to add any to them.[4]

---

[1] 9/20 May, Blenheim MSS. A1-37. Robethon relays a report from Besenval that the King of Sweden will not send his troops against the Tsar but will employ them in Saxony and Bohemia. The Emperor looks upon war with Charles XII as inevitable and will withdraw troops from Italy to fight the Swedes. Besenval believes that Charles does not want to fight the Emperor but rather the Tsar. Robethon suggests that the Queen and Marlborough should do all they can to restrain the Emperor.

[2] Letter 791.   [3] Untraced.

[4] No payment is recorded until 17 Nov., when £3,000, as part of a third order for £20,000 was directed by Godolphin to be paid towards Blenheim; *C.T.B.*, xxi. ii. 494.

797. GODOLPHIN *to* MARLBOROUGH [*22 May 1707*]

Source: Blenheim MSS. A2-23.
Printed: *Private Correspondence*, ii. 230-1.

May 22th 1707

I omitted in my last[1] to take notice to you, that if you should deferr speaking to the States to assist us, in making up a body of 10,000 men either for a descent, or for the succour of Spain, or Portugal, as shall bee found most proper, till you have an express from King Charles, I doubt it will bee too late to gett them in readiness by the time wee propose for ours, and the season of the year may bee too farr spent to make use of them, as really it was last year when my Lord Rivers was so long detained by contrary winds.

I am glad to find the States have shown a readiness to hinder the negotiating of the billets de monnoye from Amsterdam to Flanders, without which the French could not pay their army there. But I am told the lucre of that traffick will make them find ways to evade the placard published by the States, and that nothing will hinder it effectually but a stopp of the posts for 3 months. But I have little hopes this will goe down with them.[2]

The Duke of Newcastle is now come to desire Collonell Sutton may bee his deputy governor at Hull, which being nearer his Grace he says Sutton likes better, and that Mr. Whichcote might have Tinmouth. I told him I would acquaint you with what he desired, but that I believed you would think those sort of employments were most proper for such as had served in the army.[3]

From the hint in your last letter that you thought it likely King Charles might have a mind to come to Italy, there is a very particular instruction sent to Sir Cloudesley Shovell, of which Mr. Secretary Harley said hee would give you an account.[4]

At the 1st [Privy] Counsell called since the Union the Queen added to her Counsell the Duke of Queensberry, Duke of Montrose,[5] Earl of

[1] Letter 794.
[2] For the *billets de monnaie* (mint bills) see p. 753 n. 2. On 21 June/2 July the States General issued a 'Placard' or proclamation prohibiting the acceptance of French bills of exchange unless they stated expressly that they would be redeemed in French crowns after the ancient rate of the year 1685 or their full value in gold. Mint bills were totally excluded. Bills of exchange were not to be accepted unless their expiration date was within ninety days of the date of issue. No mint bills or any other form of security was to be accepted in return for money to support the French army, directly or indirectly. A further placard issued 14/25 July forbade the export of coin or bullion for the rest of the year (Lamberty, iv. 603-5). There is a copy of the printed Placard in Blenheim MSS. A2-33.
[3] See p. 594 n. 4, for the appointment and p. 796 for Marlborough's objection to Whichcote.
[4] Shovell was to follow his former instructions to assist the King of Spain and co-operate with the Duke of Savoy on the Toulon expedition, 'without any regard to the designe of the Germans upon Naples'. He was also to 'discorage the King of Spaine's leaving that country'. Harley to Marlborough, 20 May, Blenheim MSS. A2-24.
[5] James Graham, fourth Marquis and first Duke of Montrose (1682-1742); leader of the Squadrone; created duke 1707, for supporting Union; representative peer 1707-10, 1715-34; Privy Councillor 1707; Lord Privy Seal (S.) 1709-13. *D.N.B.*

Mar,[1] Earl of Lowdun, Earl of Seafeild,[2] and at the same time left out [the] Duke of Buckinghamshire, Earl of Northampton,[3] Earl of Thanet,[4] Earl of Nottingham, Earl of Rochester, Earl of Abingdon, Earl of Jersey, Lord Weymouth, Lord Ferrers,[5] Lord Guernsey,[6] Lord Grenville, Lord Gower,[7] Sir Edward Seymour, [and] Sir George Rook.[8]

Some were of opinion, the Counsell must have been new sworn, but that was declined, and this was all that has been done about that matter. The Duke of Queensberry is very pressing to bee of the Cabinet Counsell.[9]

798. MARLBOROUGH *to* GODOLPHIN   [*22 May/2 June 1707*]

Source: Blenheim MSS. A1-37.

Meldert June 2d 1707

I am to thank you for the favour of four[10] of yours which I have received since my last. That by Collonel Peper braugh[t] me 10 [Rivers] letter to you, which I think is a treu pictor of his base temper. I will have no disput with him, but what he says of 39 [Marlborough][11] is certainly a lye. By what we have now from 127 [Spain] we have hope that 2 [Galway] has recovered his health, which is a very happy and good

---

[1] John Erskine, sixth or eleventh Earl of Mar (1675-1732), colonel, Regiment of Foot, 1702; Secretary of State for Scotland 1705-8; for Great Britain 1713-14; Keeper of the Signet(s) 1708-9; representative peer 1707-14; joined the Pretender 1715. *D.N.B.*

[2] James Ogilvy, fourth Earl of Findlater and first Earl of Seafield (1664-1730), Secretary of State in Scotland 1696-1702; joint Secretary 1704-5; Lord Chancellor 1702-4, 1705-7; a principal court agent and supporter of the Union; representative peer 1707-30; Lord Chief Baron of the Exchequer 1707; succeeded his father as Earl of Findlater 1711. *D.N.B.*

[3] George Compton, fourth Earl of Northampton (1664-1727), Privy Councillor 1702; Tory peer; Constable of the Tower 1712-14; signed protest against the Union.

[4] Thomas Tufton, sixth Earl of Thanet (1644-1729), Tory peer, Privy Councillor 1703, 1711-14; lord-lieutenant of Cumberland and Westmorland 1712-14. Harley had tried to draw him, as a friend of Nottingham, to the Court by the offer of a lieutenancy in 1703: Godolphin to Harley, 28 Mar., 8 May, H. M. C., *Portland MSS.*, iv. 59, 62.

[5] Robert Shirley, first Earl Ferrers (1650-1717), Tory peer, Master of the Horse to Catherine of Braganza 1682-5; Steward of her Household 1685-1705; Privy Councillor 1699; created earl 1711.

[6] Heneage Finch, first Earl of Aylesford (1664-1719), Tory peer, son of the first Earl of Nottingham; Solicitor-General 1679-86; defended the seven bishops 1688; M.P. 1679, 1698, 1701-3; created Baron Guernsey 1703; Privy Councillor 1703-7, 1711-19; Chancellor of Duchy of Lancaster 1714-16; created Earl of Aylesford 1714. *D.N.B.*

[7] John Leveson-Gower, fourth Baronet, first Lord Gower (1675-1709), Tory peer; M.P., Newcastle-under-Lyme, 1692-1703; Privy Councillor 1702; Chancellor of the Duchy of Lancaster 1702-6; created baron 1703; Commissioner for the Union 1706.

[8] Those added were Scottish peers who had supported the Union; those left out Tory opponents of the ministry.

[9] He was appointed a Secretary of State on 3 Feb. 1709, by virtue of which office he was given a seat in the Cabinet.

[10] Letters 684-6, 789.   [11] See the following letter.

reason not to make use of 10 [Rivers]. I can asure you that 39 [Marlborough] dose extreamly aprove of your thoughts, and will do his best with 62 [Heinsius] that you may have the number of troupes you propose from 131 [the States];[1] but as yet 110 [Holland] is to[o] much alarmed by the superiority 71 [Vendôme] has at this time. We now fiel the effects of the treaty in 119 [Italy]. I send an account of the [French] troupes, which has cost our deputys[2] at Bruxelles a good sume of mony. I beleive the names of the redgiments are trew, but I can't think thay are so strong.[3] Wee are also asured that thay are able and resolved that the Comte de La Mott[4] shall make the siege of Huy by troupes thay can draw out of their garrisons, and that this army is to cover itt, and that from thence thay will go to Liege. If this should be their designe, thay must think themselves sure on the side of Italie, and in my opinion that aught to determin the States to venture a battaile, which would deside the fate of this warr.[5] I pray God give us success. The army is in a good condition, but I fear 110 [Holland] will not ventur.

By the letters from Paris thay magnefie very much their advantage on the Rhine. It is very trew that Monsieur de Villars tricked them out of their lyns, but by the officer the Duke Regent of Wertemberg[6] has sent me, with the account of this action, I find the Garmains have lost but 4 men and one leuftenant.[7] The inclosed is the translation of his letter which was in hie Dutch.[8] You will give yourself the trouble also of reading Mr. Ierton's letter[9] by which you will see what he desires. If Doctor Chetwood be in town and

---

[1] For the descent.

[2] The deputies at Brussels who represented the Dutch in the Anglo-Dutch condominium which governed the Spanish Netherlands in the name of King Charles. The money was for intelligence.

[3] A copy of the memorandum on troop movements in the French army is in P.R.O., S.P. 87/2, fols. 628–9.

[4] Charles, Count de la Motte-Houdancourt (died 1728), Vendôme's lieutenant in 1707; French officer, lieutenant-general 1702; fell into disgrace in 1709 for surrendering Ghent contrary to the laws of war.

[5] This was Vendôme's plan, but Louis XIV decided against the siege of Huy and therefore Liège too as unworthy of an army as strong as his and ordered him to remain on the defensive. Vault, vii. 33–5.

[6] Friedrich Karl (died 1724), Duke-Regent of Württemberg from 1677 to 1693 during the minority of his nephew, Eberhard Louis (1677–1733).

[7] On the night of 9/20 May Villars crossed the Rhine and arrived the next morning at Kehl, the Imperial fortress guarding the western end of the lines of Stollhofen. Villars attacked Kehl on the 11/22nd and when he penetrated the lines the following day he found the Imperialists had withdrawn, leaving him in possession of the fortifications. When he advanced to Rastatt on the next day the Imperial commander, the Margrave of Bayreuth, again withdrew his troops, which were stationed about Pforzheim nearby, so that the French enjoyed a series of rapid conquests with virtually no losses on either side. The Allied position on the Rhine, however, was badly compromised. Sturgill, *Villars*, pp. 72–3.

[8] i.e. German. 19/30 May, untraced, sent by Baron de Forstner; reply, 27 May/7 June, Murray, iii. 396–7. See also the Duke of Württemberg's letter to the States, 16/27 May, in *Compleat History for 1707*, pp. 203–5.

[9] Henry Ireton (died 1711), M.P. 1698–1700, 1705–11. Letter untraced.

you speak two wordes to him, I hope you will think that better then my writting.[1] I send you also a short letter I writ to the Pensioner by this post.[2]

799. MARLBOROUGH *to the* DUCHESS [*22 May/2 June 1707*]

Source: Blenheim MSS. E3.
Printed: *Private Correspondence*, i. 95–6, as 9 June.

Meldert June 2d 1707

I am to thank you for four of your letters which I have received by severall ways, the day before yesterday two by the post, one by Brigadier Peper, and the other sent me by Mr. Hare. The enclosed letter of 10 [Rivers] to 38 [Godolphin] is a very extraordinary one. I am sure I do not desire to have any disputt with him, but what he says of my naming Lord Arron is not trew, for itt was himself that first spoke to me of that lord.[3] Instead of a hardshipe I thought I had done him service att that time, but the wisest thing is to have to do with as few people as is possible. If you are sure that 256 [Mrs. Masham][4] dose speak of business to 42 [the Queen], I should think you might speak to her with some caution, which might do good, for she certainly is gratfull and will mind what you say. We came to this camp yesterday, and as the enemy being the strongest governs our motions, I know not how long we may stay; but as my blood is a good deal heated, I hope it may be for some days. This uneasy way of living makes me if possible more confermed that I can have no happyness til I am at quiet with you my dearest soull.

800. GODOLPHIN *to* MARLBOROUGH [*23 May 1707*]

Source: Blenheim MSS. A2–23.
Printed: Coxe, ii. 226 (inc.).

May 23d 1707

I have just now received the favour of yours of the 26 and 30th of May,[5] by which I find the French act otherwise than you expected, and the Dutch no

---

[1] Chetwood was made Dean of Gloucester, 27 Mar. 1707. See his letter to Marlborough, 24 June, Blenheim MSS. A2–30, thanking him 'especially for the kind, and generous fashion of doing it'.

[2] 't Hoff, p. 313, stating his desire to act offensively.

[3] Rivers had sold his third troop of Life Guards to Arran on 2 Mar. 1703. His letter must refer to this transaction, perhaps intimating that Marlborough had insisted on the transfer against Rivers's objections.

[4] Abigail Hill (died 1734), first cousin of the Duchess, and also related to Harley; married 1707 Samuel Masham, created 1712, Baron Masham, Groom of the Bedchamber to the Prince. Her mother had been left a widow and the Duchess found places for her children. Abigail was made a Bedchamber woman to Queen Anne during William's reign and during the years from 1703 to 1707 came to occupy the place in the Queen's affections formerly held by the Duchess. She became the medium through which Harley returned to power in 1710 and secured the disgrace of the Godolphin ministry. She succeeded the Duchess as Keeper of the Privy Purse 1711–14. This letter is the first indication in this correspondence of her growing influence with the Queen.

[5] Letters 790, 795.

otherwise than I expected. I wish you may have an opportunity, of as much advantage, as you seem to hope for. In the meantime I am eased at present of a good deal of agitation of mind, for the event of an imediat action, which I did not think so remote, as it now seems to bee. For whether Monsieur de Vendosme has any notice of the States' inclinations or not, I never looked upon him as a man, that would care to bee cooped up within lines having so great an army.[1] I wish the Duke of Savoy may bee so forward, as to oblige them to make a detachment, very soon. But if you should have any opportunity in the meantime, it may bee of ill consequence to balk your own troops, while they are in so good heart. I make no question but you will have everything in their thoughts, and I hope God will direct you for the best and keep you in his protection.

I find by a letter of this post from my Lord Manchester,[2] that the court of Vienna persists in the detachment for Naples. At the same time he says they are in all the uneasyness that is possible, about the King of Sweden.

This being their posture at Vienna, I can't help thinking that they may yett stopp their detachment to Naples, if you please to lett them see plainly that while they continue obstinate against the desires of the whole Allyance, they need not doubt, but the Allyes will bee vary indifferent at any uneasyness which the King of Sweden gives them; and that the only way to make the Allyes concern themselves in the steps of the Swedes, is for his Imperiall Majesty to prosecute the expedition against France, with all the vigour imaginable, and with another air, than has yett been done.

These measures are absolutely necessary to keep the Allyes together and their breaking can never bee of advantage to any but their common enemy.

801. GODOLPHIN *to* MARLBOROUGH [*25 May 1707*]

Source: Blenheim MSS. A2-23.
Printed: *Private Correspondence*, ii. 232–3 (inc.) as 24 June.

May 25, 1707

This morning wee have received the enclosed letters from Lisbon, by which you will see the great alarms of that court upon the news of the unfortunate battell in Spain. Wee must hope the sight of our troops from Ireland, with the encouragements sent from hence and from Holland will putt them in better heart. In order to that, it will bee necessary, the States should make their first resolution effectuall by paying up the arrears due to Portugall, and in the meantime not neglect to encourage *Pacheco*,[3] at The Hague, for our

---

[1] Vendôme was also restricted, by Louis XIV, from taking the offensive and seeking a battle. This explains the stalemate in Flanders. Vault, vii. 25–6.

[2] See Manchester's letters from Vienna, written in April and May, Cole, pp. 440–55.

[3] Francisco de Souza Pacheco, Portuguese envoy at The Hague, 1694–1708.

Portugall envoyè[1] here, tells mee *Pacheco* in his letters to him takes no notice of that resolution of the States, or that they have any such intentions.

Besides the coppy of Mr. Methuen's letter to my Lord Sunderland[2] and 2 letters from Richards to mee which I send you, I have a [sic] seen a letter from Erle to my Lord Rivers,[3] which gives a very melancholly dissatifyed account, of the whole conduct, since his arrivall there. [He] lay's blame particularly upon the Portughese horse which he says cannot be depended upon and seems to doubt very much whether they shall bee able to gett to Tortosa with the remnant of their army. But the other accounts, which I have seen are not soe apprehensive, as to that matter. All the letters agree my Lord Gallway is so wounded, but not dangerously.

Upon the whole matter, if the Emperour will have so little consideration either of his own brother, or of the rest of the Allyes, as neither to recall his detachment for Naples, nor make peace with Hungary, by which means he may bee at liberty to send some assistance to King Charles, I cannot see how it will bee possible to preserve his footing in Spain, till another year, unless the Duke of Savoy succeeds in his attempt, which might indeed give some new life to our affairs on that side of the world. But till I see that undertaking actually begun, I cannot help having my doubts least the ill news from Spain may one way or other cast a damp upon it.

By a letter which I have received from my Lord Peterborow, by the last post, though it has no date, I find he was then at Genoa, and upon the arrivall of Sir John Norris[4] from Sir Cloudesly Shovel, seemed resolved to return again to Turin. In a former letter he said he had taken leave of that court, and was going to Vienna which makes mee fear his return soe suddenly upon that gentleman's arrivall can bee for no good.

The Comte de Briançon has been with mee to complain, the Emperour refuses to give the Duke of Savoy the investiture of the places belonging to him by treaty,[5] according to the express articles of the treaty which he says, is of great consequence to his master. He also complained that the States are much in arrear of their subsidys which is very inconvenient, and at this time expecially, when he has been obliged to such great expence in preparing the necessary magazins for his expedition, of which he showed mee an account amounting to near a hundred thousand pounds.

[1] Don Luis de Cunha.

[2] 8/19 May, Blenheim MSS. C2-14.

[3] 17/28 Apr., H. M. C., *Bath MSS.*, i. 169-70.

[4] Sir John Norris (1660?-1749), admiral; M.P. 1708-49; served in the navy from 1689; Admiral of the Blue 1709; commander-in-chief in the Mediterranean 1710-11. *D.N.B.*

[5] By the Treaty of Turin, signed 28 Oct./8 Nov. 1703, the Emperor agreed to give the Duke of Savoy that part of Montferrat belonging to the Duchy of Mantua, Alessándria and Valenza belonging to the Duchy of Milan, and the Vigevenasco or an equivalent. This was reaffirmed by a decree of 12/23 Feb. 1707. Lamberty, iv. 402-3. For a statement of the Duke of Savoy's claims and the answer of the Emperor see Cole, pp. 449-50. The investiture did not take place until 1708, and then only at the insistence of the Maritime Powers. See Braubach, ii. 186 ff.

May 27th

After I had written this farr, I received the favour of yours of the 22th[1] from Meldert, with the list of the French army, and the coppy of your letter to the Pensioner, all which considered together, leave mee in a good deal of impatience for the next letters from you, since one can't bee but in great agitation either for the event of a battell which is subject to so much hazard, or that the States should continue unwilling to hazard anything, even when it seems necessary for the common interest.

Every post that comes, shows the difference growing still wider betwixt the Imperiall court, and the King of Sweden. I can't help thinking that the best use England and Holland, can make of that, will bee, to speak plainly the same language to the Emperour that unless he will bee more complying with the reasonable desires of his Allyes and consider the common interest, as well as his own, he cannot expect they should have the same concern for his particular mortifications, as when he took joynt measures with them for the benefitt of the common cause.

I am glad to find by the Duke of Wurtembergh's letter that the forcing of the lines of Stolhofen is not like to have any worse consequences, since the court of Vienna would not in 6 months' time send a generall to the Rhyne. One can't help being the less concerned for any uneasyness of this kind to them, provided it does not leave the French at liberty to send any detachment from thence to Flanders of which, however, I think wee cannot bee secure till wee hear of the Duke of Savoy's march which will soon oblige the French to turn their thoughts that way. In the meantime, while their superiority continues in Flanders you may bee sure I shall not press you for a detachment from your army either for Spain, or for a descent.

I shall take care of your commands to Dr. Chetwood, and add no more to this letter but an excuse for its being already, unreasonably long.

[added by the Duchess]

Lord Treasurer has desired me to add to this leter (which he has forgot), that he hopes you will do what you can to recover our prisenors lost in Spain, by the exchange of those that are now by your favor at their ease in France.

I remember in Mr. Montgomery's [Godolphin] last letter[2] he writt somthing to you of the great desire 220 [Queensbury] has to be in 85 [the Cabinet], which I can't but wish may not bee, for I think nobody should go there that is not in all respects what one would desire, unless their is an necessity of it; and I have known severall things of him I do not like, besides that he is so near relation to 31 [Rochester],[3] and I believe he has been sufficiently

---

[1] Letter 798.   [2] Letter 797.

[3] Queensberry's wife was the niece of Rochester's wife (who died in 1687).

gratifyed already for any servise he has ever don. God send good news from you, my dearest life.

Monsieur Vryburgh told me today; hee went to Holland in three or four days for six weeks.

802. MARLBOROUGH *to* GODOLPHIN   [*26 May/6 June 1707*]

Source: Blenheim MSS. A1-37.

Meldert June 6, 1707

Since my last the Comte de Goes has been with me in the name of 46 [Emperor] to desire my opinion as to two points. The first was what measures 108 [England] and 110 [Holland] would take in case 56 [King of Sweden] should come to a ruptur with 46 [Emperor]. The other was that the Zarr had write a letter to 48 [Prince Eugène] to offer him the crown of Polland.[1] As to the first, I was very plain with him, in saying that I thought it was absolutly necessary for the interest of 46 [Emperor] and 137 [the Allies], that whatever 56's [King of Sweden] beheavior should be, there aught to be all the caution imaginable taken that he might not have reason to push his resentment so farr as to declare 80 [war], since that must turn not only to the disadvantage of 137 [the Allies] but also to the distruction of 46 [Emperor] and 44 [King Charles]. And as to the offer to 48 [Prince Eugene] at this time, it would be what would give to great advantage to 43 [King of France]. I send you inclosed the letters[2] from Prince Eugene,[3] the Comte Wratislaw,[4] and Sinzindorf.[5] There must be no notice taken of them to the Emperor's minister, nor no other foraigner. Whatever original letters I send, you will be pleased to keep them.

About the midel of this month, I think of desiring Mr. Stepney to make a jorney to The Hague, in order to persuaid them to consent to the number of

[1] Marlborough wrote to Wratislaw this same day advising against Eugene's accepting the crown (Murray, iii. 389–90). He did not mention the subject in his letter to Eugene (ibid., pp. 391–2), trusting to Wratislaw to see that the offer was refused. Marlborough's ambivalence about the governorship of the Spanish Netherlands, which the Emperor had offered him on behalf of Charles III in 1706, may have made him reluctant to advise the Prince directly. Eugene had been the most obvious choice for the Netherlands' post (he eventually received it) which had only been offered to Marlborough for expediency's sake (Geikie, pp. 373–5). In any event Eugene refused the offer on 18/29 May, before Marlborough's advice could have reached him. Braubach, ii. 203–5.

[2] The letters all dealt with the same subjects: the plight of Charles III in Spain, for whom only the Maritime Powers could provide aid; the reverses of the Imperial army on the Rhine; the threat of the King of Sweden; and the expedition to Naples which all three men justified. Wratislaw's alone touched on the offer of the Polish crown to Eugene. Marlborough pressed for aid to Charles, urged that a new commander be sent to the Rhine, and advised an accommodation with the King of Sweden.

[3] 20 Apr./11 May, Blenheim MSS. A2-18, copy in A2-16; reply, 26 May/6 June in Murray, iii. 391–2.

[4] 10/21 and 12/23 May, in Blenheim MSS. A2-17; reply 26 May/6 June, in Murray, iii. 389/90.

[5] 11/22 May, Blenheim MSS. A2-17, Coxe, ii. 218–20, as 21 May; reply, 26 May/6 June, in Murray, iii. 392–3.

troupes you desire.[1] Should wee speak of itt at this time in which the enemy have the superiority itt would be to have a deniall. But by that time I hope we shall see what the designs of the enemy are, for as yett wee do nothing but eat forage. Wee could make Monsieur de Vandome much more uneasy, if wee had not the plague of covering Bruxelles, and the rest of the great towns.

By a copie of a letter I have received from Sir John Norris, which Lord Gallaway had writt two days after the battaile [of Almanza] to Admeral Bing, I find he was then at the head of 3,000 horse, but could give no account of his foot, by which it is but to[o] probable that the greatest part are lost. I wish you may have a better account from himself. You will have enclosed a copie of the King of Spain's letter[2] to mee by the Earle of Rivers. You will know [by this] what he would have said to mee if I had had the honour to have seen him. I send to Mr. Secretary Harley the Margrave of Bareith's letter[3] to mee. By itt you will see the great disorders the affaires of the Rhin are in. Nothing is so much wanted there as a good generall, which will be another reason of clamor against the court of Vienna, which I have taken the liberty to let them know by this day's post.

Notwithstanding the bigness of this packett, I send you a copie of my letter to the Comte Piper[4] If the Queen writs, she must not threaten, but indeavour to make him sensible what the advantage it will be to France, and consequently a prejudice to her Majesty and the Prodistant religion.

803. MARLBOROUGH *to* GODOLPHIN [*26 May/6 June 1707*]

Source: Blenheim MSS. A1-37.

[Meldert] 6 June 1707

My other letter[5] is what you may show to the 42 [the Queen], and such of our friends as you please. But this I should be glad you would burn and not let it be seen, for I write it onely to have in time your own thoughts. I find by the Comte de Goes, as well as by Wratislaw's letters, that the court of Vienna are resolved to take no other care of the warr in Spain but by putting the whole expence upon 108 [England], and you may depend upon itt that 110

---

[1] For a descent.

[2] There are letters of 23 Apr./4 May and 26 Apr./7 May in Blenheim MSS. A2-29. Both speak of his determination to persevere in spite of Almanza. The latter requests aid to be sent and proposes the return of Rivers to Spain.

[3] Christian Erfurt, Margrave of Bayreuth (1644-1712), Imperial field-marshal, commander of the Imperial army on the Rhine, succeeding Prince Lewis of Baden. 17/28 May, in Blenheim MSS., A2-21; reply, 27 May/7 June, in Murray, iii. 396.

[4] 26 May/6 June, in Murray, iii. 393-4. Marlborough hoped that the good judgement of the King of Sweden would prevent him from entering into hostilities with the Emperor and pledged the goodwill of the Queen to helping him reach an accommodation with the Emperor.

[5] Letter 802.

[Holland] has the same intention, so that you should in my opinion be very car[e]full of not runing to[o] fast into that expence. I think you should loos no time in sending an order to Lord Gallaway to complett as many redgiments as he can and send the rest of the officers home, so that there might be measures taken for the raising of their redgiments. By this you will come to the exact knowlidge of the troupes you have there, and save a great deal of mony. And if you can find men to complett the redgiments that must return, you will then have a body of foot to send where the service may requier it next spring. For God sake consider the unhappy cercomstances wee are in if it be trew that 44 [King Charles] thinkes 2 [Galway] betrayes him. I would pawn my soull there is no reason for itt, but if it be really beleived it has the same consequencys as if it were trew. You may also take your measures that 116 [the States] will ventur nothing til thay see what 58 [Duke of Savoy] and 48 [Prince Eugene] will do. And should thay not persist and succed in the project agreed upon, you would then very quickly find 110 [Holland] do their utmust for 81 [peace]. Upon this whole matter, when you have a safe opertunity, [do me the favor] of letting me know your thoughts, so that I may be the better able to govern myself.[1]

As I think the good or bad success of this warr, will depend upon what we shall do in this army, I do really think it for her Majesty's service that there should be a premotion made amongest the generall officers of this army. You shall have enclosed the names,[2] but whatever the Queen's pleasur is, I desire itt may be keep a secritt, so that I might take the most proper time of declaring itt. This promotion will be no expence to her Majesty nor the government,[3] and I think a great incoragement to the army. Lord Argile has desired me to beg of you that you would assist his brother[4] in being his lieutenant, by giving Lord Forbus[5] the government of Blackness.[6] I beg you will not suffer the Duke of Newcastell or anybody else to bring anybody into Tinmouth or Hull but officers of the army, and that I may know their names before the Queen is pleased to approve of them;[7] for should it be otherways, all the officers that serve in this present warr would have just reason to think that I take no care of them, which would not be for the Queen's Service.

---

[1] See letter 808.   [2] See the list in Dalton, v. 159.

[3] General officers were not paid according to a standard scale but rather by a specific provision made for them each year in the acts of Parliament for the support of the army. As the establishment for the year had been voted the previous winter no adjustment could be made. Scouller, p. 127.

[4] Archibald, Earl of Islay.   [5] William, thirteenth Lord Forbes (c. 1656–1716).

[6] Forbes was lieutenant-colonel and lieutenant of the Scots troop of Life Guards of which Argyle was colonel and captain. Forbes was not replaced until 6 Mar. 1708 when Colin, Lord Cumberland, son of the third Earl of Balcarres, was given the post. Instead of receiving this place Islay was made second colonel in Maccartney's Regiment of Foot on 6 Mar. 1708 and Colonel of Alnutt's Regiment of Foot on 23 Mar. 1709. The governor of Blackness Castle was Henry Rollo of Woodside. The Earl of Dunmore replaced him as captain of the company there in 1709 but not as governor.

[7] Marlborough's request was observed. See p. 594 n. 4.

804. MARLBOROUGH *to the* DUCHESS   [*26 May/6 June 1707*]

Source: Blenheim MSS. E3.
Printed: Coxe, ii. 240.

Meldert June 6, 1707

I find by your last letter that 4 [Halifax] is not well pleased with 10 [Rivers], which I am not surprised att. However, remember when he is disatisfied you will find that 89 [the Whigs] will be of his side, for partiallity will show itself when party is concerned. I have received a letter from 10 [Rivers][1] with an inclosed from 44 [King Charles].[2] As the whole letter concerns 10 [Rivers], I send him a copie of itt by this post, though I no ways doubt his having seen it before it was sealed. God knows what is to be done for the recovery of the great disorders that are now in Spain, for by what 10 [Rivers] says it is to[o] plain that 44 [King Charles] aprehends that 2 [Galway] betrayes him, which can never enter into my head. However, if thay beleive it, it will poyson all the undertakings on that side. Your kind expressions in yours of the 16th has given me infinet pleasure, and it is trew what you say of Woodstock, that it is very much at my heart, especially when wee are in prosperity, for then my whole thoughts are of retiring with you to that place. But if everything dose not go to our own desire, we must not sett our hearts to[o] much upon that place, for I see very plainly that whielst I live, if there be troubles I must have my share of them. This day makes your humble servant fivety-seven. On all accounts I could wish myself younger, but for none so much as that I might have it more in my power to make myself more agreable to you, whome I love with all my soull.

805. GODOLPHIN *to* MARLBOROUGH   [*28 May 1707*]

Source: Blenheim MSS. A2-23.

May 28th 1707

I have troubled you so much of late that I shall not wonder if you are afraid to see the outside of a letter from mee. But the truth of that matter is, that between the concern I have for your safety, and the agitation of my mind, upon that great event which seems so near, I have very little quiett, myself, and can't helpe making you too sensible of it.

By a conversation I had this morning with 10 [Rivers] I find he has sent you the letter he had from Erle which I mentioned in my last.[3] You will see by it, that poor man has been poysoned with the unjust impressions which

---

[1] Untraced; reply, 26 May/6 June, H. M. C., *Bath MSS.* i. 173, in which Marlborough remarks: 'You say nothing to me of your returning to Spain, but as I see by the King's letter it is what he much desires, if it be not uneasy to yourself I should think you might do good service.'
[2] See p. 795 n. 2.   [3] Letter 801.

10 [Rivers] had given him of 2 [Gallway]. I have seen a letter today from a collonell in that army which says my Lord Gallway had but 17,000 men, and the Duke of Berwick as he says 33,000 of which 9,000 at least horse and dragoons.[1] I send you our line of battell, by which you will see 8 or 9 of the best regiments of foot or horse were absent with the King of Spain. How can he ever forgive himself that absence, or these who persuaded him to it?[2]

The enemy being so much superior in horse, I must own I can't see any reason for fighting in so plain a country, but everybody agrees no men ever behaved themselves better than all our foot, nor horse than the Portughese horse. I find 10 [Rivers] has a mind to return to 144 [44 Charles III] if he can see any hopes of getting together a good body of troops from hence or from Italy or both. From hence, 'tis impossible in point of time so as to bee of any use this year, if it please God that wee succeed in Italy, though it may then bee faisible. Yett it will not perhaps bee so necessary because that must needs bee a diversion so very sensible to France, as will afford them but little leisure to trouble other people. By Mr. Chetwynd's last letter I find he had been at Milan and had very fair promises from Prince Eugene. But I confess I want very much to have the comfort of a letter from him to you, upon the subject of that expedition.[3] I reckon their army is in motion about this time, and therefore if you should not come to any action in Flanders till you hear the event of the Duke of Savoy's march, I am not sure but it may bee for the better. God Almighty direct and prosper you.

30th of May

Mr. Secretary Harley will send you by this post, what Monsieur Schults has proposed from his master towards the composing of the differences betwixt the King of Sweden and the Emperour with the draught of the Queen's letter to the former upon that occasion.[4] I believe you will approve these stepps, though I doubt they may come too late, to hinder a breach in that

---

[1] For a discussion of the strength of the Allies in Spain and at Almanza see I. Burton, 'The Supply of Infantry for the War in the Peninsula, 1703–1707', *B.I.H.R.*, 23 (1955), 59–62.

[2] The decision was made at a council of war at Valencia on 4/15 June 1707. The Spanish and Imperial generals advised the King to divide his army and remain on the defensive. Galway, Stanhope, and the rest of the Allied representatives urged a single command for a second attempt on Madrid. Charles III followed the former advice (encouraged by Noyelles who wanted his own command) and proceeded to Catalonia with the Spanish and German troops leaving those in Allied pay under Galway to proceed towards Madrid. The issue was also the subject of innumerable contemporary pamphlets. Charles III himself blamed Galway for giving battle to the French (to Wratislaw, 23 Apr./4 May, 'Correspondenz des Königs Karl III mit Wratislaw', *Archiv für Kunde österreichischer Geschichtsquellen*, 16 (1869), 42–3). Modern authorities find both parties at fault, Charles III for dividing the army, Galway for attacking with an inferior force. The fullest discussion of the battle is in Wijn, VIII. ii. 213–31.

[3] Godolphin was afraid that Eugene would be sent to confront the King of Sweden instead of going on the Toulon expedition (p. 802).

[4] Harley to Marlborough, 30 May, enclosing a copy of the Queen's letter to the King of Sweden of the same date, both in Blenheim MSS. A2–24. The Queen's letter is printed in Brown, p. 224. The Queen followed Marlborough's advice (above, p. 795) and urged Charles XII not to harm the Allied cause, but reach an accommodation with the Emperor for which she promised her assistance.

side, the differences being come to a great height. But wee must satisfie ourselves with doing all that was in our power to prevent the ill consequences which such a breach may occasion, and especially when the whole world must agree, the Emperor's conduct has very little deserved the Queen's good offices in this case.

Wroth of the Duke of Northumberland's regiment has desired mee to putt you in mind of him. He says, severall of less standing, were made brigadiers, and he hopes you won't lett him lose his rank. I have asked Mr. St. Johns and he tells mee his pretensions are just.[1]

I have had a letter from Lieutenant Generall Erle dated a month before the battell by which he seems to think he could not bee usefull in that service, because in the disputes betwixt 2 [Gallway] and 10 [Rivers] he thought the latter in the right. I suppose what has hapned since does not make him more easy, but till wee hear directly from 2 [Gallway] I don't [know] whether it would bee right to send any orders in that matter, unless you desire it.[2]

I have not yett declared any new comptrollers of the accounts of the army. A great many object against Mr. Negus. I doe not know him personally. Mr. Pauncefort who was Deputy Paymaster pretends to it and I believe he understands it very well. Sir David Nairn also thinks he might bee able to doe service in that office. He has taken pains in the Union and expects to bee gratifyed. Thus that affair stands at present.[3]

I believe wee shall not have the Holland letter till tomorrow.

806. MARLBOROUGH *to* GODOLPHIN   [*29 May/9 June 1707*]

Source: Blenheim MSS. A1-37.
Printed: Coxe, ii. 244–5 (inc.).

Meldert June 9th 1707

By yours of the 17[4] I see you are very aprehensive of 46 [Emperor] making 81 [peace]. I think them extreamly to blame in every thought thay have, but such a proceding would be direct madness. I think thay have many projects more at heart then that of 115 [Toulon], but til I am cheated I must relie upon what 48 [Prince Eugene] promises, which is that he will do his best, so that I do not aprehend a neutrality. But I very much fear that 63 [Wratislaw] and the other ministers may persuaide 46 [Emperor] to such a beheavior as may force 56 [King of Sweden] into 80 [war], which I think would be distruction to themselves, as well as to their friends. I have this minut received yours of the 22 and 23,[5] in one letter. But as to the perticular

---

[1] He was promoted effective 1 Jan. See pp. 808, 836.
[2] Erle was given leave to come home in September on Marlborough's advice. See pp. 892, 899.
[3] For the decision on whom to appoint, see p. 765 n. 3.
[4] Letter 794.   [5] Letters 797, 800.

instructions sent to Sir Cloudsley Shovell concerning 44 [King Charles] going to 119 [Italy], Mr. Secretary [Harley] has said nothing to mee. By a letter I have received from Mr. Chetwin[1] I find the intentions of 58 [Duke of Savoy] is to take three places before he can attempt 115 [Toulon], which I am afraid will discover to[o] much to 43 [King of France] the design we have so much att heart. But whatever the consequences may be, it is to[o] late to take other measures, so that thay must be let take their own way. I have said all that is possible for me to do to the court of Vienna, and have this morning sent your letter to Comte Wratislaw. Yesterday the Comte de la Mott joyned the Duke of Vandome's army, so that I think thay have now all that is possible for them to have; and notwithstanding the noyse thay have made of being in the plains of Fleurus,[2] thay have always been in very strong camps. Thay may in their next march if thay please go into the plains of Fleurus; and then if the 101 [deputies] would allow of it, we might have a decisive action. But by what I can larn thay are no ways inclined to itt.

I did in my last[3] beg that the Queen would not lett anybody have governments but such as have served in the army; for if the Duke of Newcastel and others can prevail, we shall have no other governors but Parliament men, which I am sure is not for her Majesty's Service.

I send by this post a copie of a letter I have received from the Elector Pallatin[4] to Mr. Secretary Harley. You will see what he desires of me. But I should think that neither the consent of the Emperor, nor the Elector himself can be obtained in time, so as to remedy the great disorders in which that army is now in. However, I have write to Vienna.

I did intend to have sent you the enclosed from Sir Rowland Gwynne[5] some time ago. I do really beleive he is sorry for what he has [done]. But if were never so much, it is impossible to do for him what he desires.

---

[1] 13/24 May, Blenheim MSS. A2-18; reply, 28 May/8 June, in Murray, iii. 399-400.

[2] Fleurus, 17 kilometres north-east of Charleroi, site of battles in 1622, 1690, and 1794.

[3] Letter 803.

[4] 26 May/6 June, in Murray, iii. 408-9; Marlborough to Harley, 29 May/9 June, Murray, iii. 400-1. The Elector Palatine wanted the Elector of Hanover to assume command of the Imperial army on the Rhine, which he did in July.

[5] 7/18 Apr., Blenheim MSS. A1-37. Gwynn, when English Resident at Hanover in 1705, had written an indiscreet letter to the Earl of Stamford about the Whigs and the invitation to bring over the Electress. In it he indicated that the court at Hanover favoured the plan. The letter was published and caused great embarrassment to the English ministry who were trying to repair the damage caused by the Tory motion in Parliament for the invitation (see p. 510). The House of Lords ordered the printed letter to be burnt as a libel. The Elector disavowed his remarks and ordered Gwynn to leave Hanover before Halifax arrived in 1706. Howe, the English envoy at Hanover, was ill (he died in 1709) and Gwynn wanted to succeed him if he returned to London, but was never forgiven by the Queen for his imprudent behaviour. He also wrote the Elector at this time asking for permission to return from Hamburg, but was refused. See the Elector to Gwynn, 1/12 Apr., in Macpherson, ii. 92.

807. MARLBOROUGH *to the* DUCHESS   [*29 May/9 June 1707*]

Source: Blenheim MSS. E3.
Printed: *Private Correspondence*, i. 96–8.

Meldert June 9th 1707

I have had the happyness of yours dated the 17 and 19, which gives me an account of 31 [Rochester] having been with 38 [Godolphin]. I am intierly of opinion that 31 [Rochester] if he had or ever shall have it in his power, he would with pleasure hang everybody that wee wish well, so that I think there aught to be no difficulty in giving him all the mortefications which with justice may be done. I see also by your letter that you are in aprehension of a battaile. It is most certain that the enemy have more squadrons and battalions then wee, but ours are stronger and better men, so that for the good of the common cause I do veryly think we aught earnestly to wish for a battaile, which I think the enemy showes; for though thay talke much of being in the plains of Fleurus, thay have never yett taken any other but very strong camps, and it is very plain thay have no confidence in their foot. On the other side 110 [Holland] will not ventur til we can find an advantage, so that both thay and wee are expecting what will be done in Italie, and in the meantime if thay give us an advantage we shall attack them, of which I beleive thay will be very carefull. It is certain that 46 [the Emperor] dose not behave himself as a friend, but we can't resent that but by hurting ourselves. I sent Lord Treasurer by the last post[1] a copie of my letter to Comte Piper, for I own that business is much att my heart. I am extreamly obliged to you for the concern you have for mee. I trust in God he will protect mee, as he has been pleased hethertoo. And as I am persuided that by the great disorders and difficultys the King of France has to gett mony, will make me be cautious of venturing but when I shall think wee have an advantage, so that I beg you to be att ease, and I hope God will bless us so as that wee may end our days in quiet. Having write thus far, I have received yours of the 23 and can[not] imagine what 253 [Lady Tyrconnel] [wrote] for I have neither seen her nor write to her.[2] And as to what you say concerning 57 [   ], you are much in the right for I never name him when I can avoide itt. I less understand what is meant by the great countenance given to Charles' son.[3] He has been two yeares a lieutenant collonel and had this winter my Lord Argile put over his head,[4] but I give you to[o] much trouble on this occasion, for I never spoke three wordes to him in my life. I wish everybody were happy, so that I might be quietly with you.

[1] Letter 802.
[2] Lady Tyrconnel had reported rumours that the Emperor was negotiating with Louis XIV. See pp. 809, 821.
[3] Charles Churchill (died 1745), Marlborough's nephew, natural son of his brother, Charles; aide-de-camp to Marlborough at Blenheim; brevet colonel, effective 1 Jan. 1707, in Prince George's Regiment of Foot; colonel, Regiment of Foot, 1709.
[4] As colonel of Prince George's Regiment of Foot.

808. GODOLPHIN *to* MARLBOROUGH   [*1 June 1707*]

Source: Blenheim MSS. A2-23.
Printed: Coxe, ii. 242-4 (inc.).

June 1st 1707

I have the favour of yours of the 6th with all the papers enclosed,[1] as also your private letter to myself,[2] for all which I give you a great many thanks, and begin today to answer these letters, expecting, as the wind is now, to hear from you again tomorrow.

I think your letter to Comte Piper is as right as is possible, and I hope you will approve as well, the Queen's letter to the King of Sweden of which Mr. Secretary Harley sayd he would send you a coppy by the last post.[3]

If these letters come in time, or are in themselves, sufficient to prevail with the King of Sweden, I think wee are very lucky, for in case they doe not, the court of Vienna seems to mee, neither to doe one thing, nor to have one thought that is not directly opposite to the interest of the Allyes. And by all the coppyes of the letters you send mee it is not only plain that they persist with more obstinacy than ever in sending their detachment to Naples, but it seems to mee as plain, that if the King of Sweden bee uneasy to them, they will encorage the chimericall proposall to Prince Eugene, and send for him and all his troops in Italie to support it, leaving the expedition against France to take care of itself. I take these consequences to bee extreamly probable, and that nothing can hinder them unless you will lett them plainly understand that such proceedings as these will oblige the Allyes to break with them, and abandon the house of Austria to the mercy of France.

As to the affairs of Spayn, I doubt [not] they are in a very bad condition. Collonell Wade[4] is come hither from my Lord Gallway. He was in the battell [of Almanza] himself, and I don't find by him, that any of our foot gott off, but that my Lord Gallway may have about 3,000 horse and dragoons with him at Tortosa, and those not good. He complains of their behaviour in the fight. What Mr. Stanhope writes to my Lord Sunderland,[5] I don't trouble you with repeating, because in that letter he says he writes the same to you.[6]

What you say of 2 [Gallway] is certainly right, and considering the unjust impression of 44 [King Charles] in his prejudice, he cannot bee of use there. But who can? Everybody that is there desires to leave the service, and come home, and I know nobody to send but 10 [Rivers] who perhaps won't care to goe neither without troops from hence; and wee neither have them nor if

---

    [1] Letter 802.   [2] Letter 803.   [3] See p. 798 n. 4.
    [4] George Wade (1673-1748), adjutant-general to the forces in Portugal, 1704; colonel, Regiment of Foot, 1705; served throughout war in Spain; at taking of Minorca 1708; commanded brigade of infantry at Almenara, Saragossa, 1710. *D.N.B.*
    [5] 22 Apr./3 May, Blenheim MSS. C2-15.
    [6] The same date, in Mahon, Appendix, pp. 49-50 on Almanza.

wee had them, would it bee of any use to send them, as you will see by the enclosed[1] from Monsieur de Montandre.

This being the case, it will bee of no use to send to my Lord Gallway to break the regiments into fewer as you propose (however Mr. St. Johns shall find him orders for it), since he has neither regiments to break nor officers to send home, unless wee could gett them exchanged, both officers and men being all prisoners that are left alive. I don't see therfore that there is any better expedient for relief of Catalonia, than by the help of the fleet to trans-port some troops from Italy when either the expedition to Naples is at an end, or that to Provence, or both. For the troops may bee as well taken from Naples itself, by sea, as from any other place. Nor have I any great objection to the Queen's paying the troops that shall goe. She will pay the fewer in some other place, and they won't spare so many, (I doubt) for that service, as to make the charge near so great as it has been to send so many troops of our own from hence.

There is nothing thought soe essentiall here as to preserve Catalonia this winter or if it bee any way possible, and it having been fully considered this night at the Cabinett Counsell, Mr. Secretary Harley has orders to write to you[2] by this messenger,[3] to see if you can either by Comte Wratislaus or Zinzendorf, bring this to bee agreed with the court of Vienna which is at this time so unpopular here that our two dukes,[4] last Sunday night, would have been contented I think to have broke with them, and the least unreasonable of the two would bee satisfyed with nothing less than a joynt complaint and representation from England and Holland together, at their unaccountable conduct. But if they will bee easy in sending troops to Spain, that matter will bee sett right again.

I find by the letters from Turin that Lord Peterborow is returned thither again, though he had formally taken his leave of the Duke of Savoy. He has written a very angry letter to my Lord Sunderland,[5] in which he says he is coming very soon to your camp and you seem to bee much more in his favour than anybody else, that I can't but impute it to my Lady's [Peterborough] good offices, for last winter's visitts [by Marlborough] to her.

The same letters from Turin give hopes their expedition is in so great a forwardness there, that but for the doubt they are in of wanting canon-ball,

---

[1] Untraced. Cf. p. 816 n. 2.

[2] 23 May/3 June, Blenheim MSS. A2-24; copy in Longleat, Portland MSS., v. fols. 157-60.

[3] Young, the messenger, had brought dispatches from Turin and was to be sent back there after stopping off to receive instructions from Marlborough. Marlborough was to propose to the Emperor that after the Naples expedition was over and the outcome of the Toulon expedition known, the Emperor send part of his troops to Catalonia. Harley to Marlborough, 3 June, Blenheim MSS. A2-24. See also Harley to Meadows, 3 June, *H.L.N.S.*, vii. 462-3. Marlborough sent word by Count Lescheraine. Murray, iii. 420.

[4] Probably Devonshire and Somerset, though Newcastle also attended the Cabinet meetings of both 25 May and 1 June.

[5] N.d., but endorsed 'received 31 May', Blenheim MSS. C2-16.

they should think themselves almost sure of success. Orders are therfore sent to Sir Cloudesley Shovell, by this express (who is directed to call upon you) not to bee afraid of unfurnishing the fleet if there should bee occasion, for that care shall bee imediatly taken to replace it from hence. Besides that if they take the place, 'tis to bee hoped they may furnish themselves there with all things they can want of that kind. My greatest apprehension in that whole affair, is least Prince Eugene should not begin his attempt towards Dauphinè, so soon as the other towards Provence; wheras in my opinion, it ought either to bee at the same time or rather sooner; and if you are of the same opinion, I wish you would write accordingly to Prince Eugene[1] by this messenger; and if you have time to write to Sir Cloudesly Shovel[2] about giving the canon-ball that shall bee necessary, I believe a letter from you, will have more weight with him than all the orders wee send from hence.

I think the Elector Palatin's desire in his letter which you have sent to Mr. Secretary Harley,[3] ought to be gratifyed without delay, in relation to the Elector of Hannover. And for what relates to the Saxon troops that ought to bee governed by yourself, and by the States, according to the posture affairs shall bee in, when they draw nearer to you.

I am not at all displeased, that the armyes in Brabant continue to doe nothing but look upon one another. Considering all things, perhaps it is not amiss, that matters should remain soe till the effect of the Duke of Savoy's operations, influence one side, or other to change their measures.

I had the enclosed account of the battell at Almanza from Collonell Wade, and Lady Harryett's letter to you from her own fair hand.

I can't avoyd asking you what I am to doe upon the enclosed petition from Sir Charles Hara,[4] though I am ashamed my packett is so large.

Pray doe mee the favour to speak to Mr. Cardonell to pay Renard[5] at Amsterdam a year, and to draw his bill upon Mr. Taylor.

Having written of so many things, I had almost forgotten to tell you that, as to the promotions you propose, the Queen leaves both the thing and the

[1] 31 May/11 June, Murray, iii. 405–6.

[2] 1/12 June, Murray, iii. 407–8 ordering Shovell to go to Italy and buy 'such a quantity of powder as may put you beyond the possibility of want for executing your project in hand; as likewise some balls'. Norris had protested to the Duke of Savoy and Prince Eugène he had instructions to maintain an adequate supply of powder and ball on board the ships for their own armaments, and could not meet all their needs. Owen, pp. 159, 162–3.

[3] See p. 800 n. 4. Besides expressing a desire for the Elector of Hanover to take command of the Imperial army on the Rhine, he requested that the 7,000 Saxon troops in the pay of the Maritime Powers in the Low Countries be sent to the Rhine. Orders were sent on 12/23 June for the troops to march (Marlborough to Wackerbart, 12/23 June, Murray, iii. 436).

[4] Sir Charles O'Hara, first Baron Tyrawley (1640?–1724), lieutenant-general 1704; colonel, Royal Fusiliers, 1705; created an Irish peer 1706; Galway's second in command in Spain; wounded at Almanza. He requested leave to return to England (p. 816) and was gone from Spain by September (Parnell, p. 236 n.). He made another request for £1,000 for his equippage, and this Marlborough advised Godolphin to ignore as he was coming home. His petition to Godolphin is in Blenheim MSS. A2-29. *D.N.B.*

[5] Renard supplied newsletters from Paris.

time of declaring it wholly to yourself, and you may send her Majesty's pleasure in that matter, when and how you please.

The Duke of Newcastle would have Collonell Sutton his lieutenant
governour at Hull provided Whichcote might have Tinmouth. I believe he
did serve in the last warr, but if you don't like him, send word who you
desire should have it.[1]

809. MARLBOROUGH *to* GODOLPHIN [2/13 *June 1707*]

Source: Blenheim MSS. A1-37.
Printed: Coxe, ii. 245-6.

Meldert June 13th 1707

I had yesterday yours of the 27th,[2] with the enclosed letters that you had
received from Alligant and Lisbon. I have also received a copie of a letter
from Thomas Earle to Lord Rivers, by which, and [by] what the King of
Spain says to me in his letter of the 3d of May[3] from Barcelona, I find 2
[Galway] in very bad cercomstances. For my own part, I think him incapable
of being guilty; but if there be no confidence, the consequencys must be
fatal. I send copies of my letters from Prince Eugene[4] and the King of Spain
to Lord Sunderland, it being in his province, as also my answers, so that if
her Majesty would have me write anything more, that I might have her
pleasure.

The Comte Maffie who is now with me presses very much that more
powder might be sent to the fleet, assuring me that there is none to be baught
in Italie. He also desired me in his master's[5] name to lett you know that all
the mony he had or could borrow he has employed for the project. He begs
that the second 50,000 pounds might be sent, so thay that might not faile
for want of mony. And if thay should be so unfortunate as not to succed,
you might then stop it from his subsity. As this is the most likely project to
make this campagn end well, if possible, thay should have no excuse. As to
myself, I am sure you are so kind as to believe that I will be carefull of taking
the first opertunity of doing good as far as in me lyes, but you know I am not
intierly master. However, I will not dispaire of doing service.

By the express from Prince Eugene, I received the enclosed from Lord
Pitterborow,[6] and if he does not chang his mind I am like to be happy in his

---

[1] See p. 594 n. 4. [2] Letter 801.

[3] Churchill, ii. 234-5; reply, 31 May/11 June, in Murray, iii. 403-5.

[4] Milan, 21 May/1 June, 22 May/2 June, Blenheim MSS. A2-18; reply, 31 May/11 June, in
Murray, iii. 405-6. [5] The Duke of Savoy.

[6] 22 May/2 June, Milan, Blenheim MSS. A2-29; copy, A1-37. All efforts to stop the Naples
expedition were in vain, and he doubts that the campaign in Italy will meet expectations. He will
report to Marlborough at his camp and justify his own conduct to him as he hears from England
it is said he was reluctant to return home. Peterborough protests: 'I would rather put in for a
Teller's place of the Exchequer, than the command of armys, the most fatal employment for an
Englishman, particularly in these parts of the world.'

company. Whatever his project may be you shall be sure to know. I supose the Queen's intentions are that he should return for England, and not stay on this side the watter. I shall not pretend to give him much advice, but shall governe myself by what you shall write me, for I beleive I may have your answer before I shall see him.

810. MARLBOROUGH *to the* DUCHESS [2/13 *June* 1707]

Source: Blenheim MSS. E3.
Printed: Coxe, ii. 226–7 (inc.).

Meldert June 13th 1707

Since my last I have had the happyness of yours of the 27 of the last month, by which I find you were stil under the aprehentions of a battaile. My former letters as well as this aught to put you att ease, but for the publick good it were to be wished it might be had, for our affaires go very ill in Garmany as well as in Spain. For my own part, notwithstanding the noyse the French have made, I think thay would less care to ventur a battaile then our friends. For if thay had a real mind to it, it must have been decided before this time. In the army I must do them right that there is all the desire imaginable to ventur their lives for the publick good, but all other sortes of people on this side of the watter are so very wise, that I am afraid at last thay wil bring us to an ill peace. For myself I am old and shal not live to see the misfortunes that must happen to Christendome if the French be suffered to get the better of this warr. By the enclosed[1] which I received but yesterday, though it be of an old date, you will see the country takes notice that the worke[2] dose not go on as thay expected. Say nothing but burn the letter, for when it is half built it may be enough for you and mee, and I do from my heart assure you that I should be much better pleased to live with you in a cotage, than in all the pallaces this world has without you.

811. GODOLPHIN *to* MARLBOROUGH [3 *June* 1707]

Source: Blenheim MSS. A2–23.

Tuesday June 3d 1707

Besides my great packett of yesterday's date[3] having the opportunity of this express,[5] I beg leave to trouble you with the following reflexions.

By what you write of the unwillingness of Holland to venture anything till they see farther into the event of the Duke of Savoy's attempt, it seems to mee as if they reckoned, that in case that attempt succeeds they should yett bee able to perswade France to give us a good peace; and in case of a

---

[1] Untraced. [2] The building of Blenheim Palace.
[3] Letter 808, 1 June. [4] A messenger rather than the post.

disappointment that they should bee able to oblige us to accept of an ill one; and if this conjecture happens to bee right, they will bee as little willing to venture after that event, bee it how it will, as they are now.

Nor indeed doe I see, to speak the truth, that any success in Provence or Dauphine would oblige the French to weaken their army in Flanders since by having beaten us in Spain and frighted away the Germans from the Rhyne they can from either of those armyes who have no enemy to deal with, send their detachments to Dauphine or to Provence.

I have pressed the Comte de Gallas this morning to send to his court the Queen's earnest desire that they would send some of their detachment at Naples, to Barcelona for the relief of King Charles, and to give their answer soe timely, as that it might not bee too late to give orders to the fleet, upon that matter. He has promised to write by this post, and did not discourage the expectation of the Emperour's agreeing to it.

I must own, I could not forbear telling him, that but for myself who had a particular regard to the house of Austria, the Queen's other ministers could scarce bee kept from coming to a publick remonstrance against the proceedings of the Imperiall court.

My Lord Rivers has brought mee your letter to him, and the enclosed coppy in it of the King of Spain's letter to you desiring mee to read them both[1] to the Queen. I think upon the whole, since both my Lord Gallway and Stanhope desire to come home, and that neither of them can bee usefull there, in case Lord Rivers bee desirous to goe without any Jewish conditions I shall bee for complying with him.

812. GODOLPHIN *to* MARLBOROUGH [*4 June 1707*]

Source: Blenheim MSS. A2-23.

Windsor June 4th 1707

Continuing still without any forreign letters, your trouble by this post will bee very short. I have nothing to add to my last,[2] but that when I was at London the other day to take the oaths,[3] I found 28 s [Shrewsbury] visitt was like to bee very insiped, 4 [Halifax] and 7 [Wharton] having both told mee they had missed him, when they went to have seen him, which looks as if there had been but very little care taken of the interview of any side.[4]

---

[1] See p. 795 n. 2.   [2] Letter 811.

[3] As Lord Treasurer of Great Britain. His office was extended to include Scotland on the Union. See his letter to Harley, 19 June, in H. M. C., *Bath MSS.*, i. 175 and n.

[4] The Duumvirs were still interested in bringing Shrewsbury into the Cabinet to forestall the power of the Junto. They tried to obtain Junto support for giving office to the Duke, but the Whigs could not forgive him for deserting them at the end of William's reign. Marlborough himself approached Shrewsbury again after his return from the Continent during the next winter. See Snyder, 'Godolphin and Harley'. For previous efforts see above, p. 461 n. 4.

38 [Godolphin] has not yett seen him neither, and I am told he goes back agayn, in the beginning of next week.

Some of those [Tories] who were employed formerly in the affair of 51 [Electress Sophia][1] are here and are very lazy of late, which gives occasion to think they may bee endeavouring upon the pretext of 95 [the Union] to revive that matter again.[2] My opinion is, that if they know how to sett about it, they may give a good deal of uneasyness at this time to 42 [the Queen], considering the present posture and disposition of people and things. But if wee could bee so lucky as to succeed at Toloun, that would sett most things right on this side.

813. MARLBOROUGH *to* GODOLPHIN   [5/16 *June 1707*]

Source: Blenheim MSS. A1-37.
Printed: Coxe, ii. 246 (small omissions).

Meldert June 16, 1707

I had this morning yours of the 30th[3] of the last month, with the order of battaile, by which it appeares the enemies were very much stronger then Lord Galway, which makes it very strang that by choice thay should go to attack them in a plain. I have sent the Queen's letter to Mr. Robison.[4] I hope it may have a good effect, but I beleive nothing can hinder the King of Sweden from mortefying the Emperor, by staying in some of his hereditary countrys, and I am afraid it will fal upon Selecia. But though he is angry to the last degree, I dare say he will not declare warr, since that can't but turn to the advantage of France. I am so far from thinking Mr. Wroth's desirs are just, that I think he has no sort of reason to pretend.

You are very much in the right to make no answer to Mr. Earle's letter, til you hear from Lord Galway. I know his presence in England is wanted for the Board of Ordenance. However, I think him the properest man you can leave in Spain, for he has never disobliged 44 [King Charles], and I think is of a temper to please him. And I confess, I think there is the same reason that the King of Spain and his general should command in Spain, as there was for the King of Portugale and his general in Portugale. This is my opinion only to you and her Majesty, and if this should be thought reasonable, Thomas Earle will be very proper to be left, for I take it for granted that my Lord Galway neither can nor will stay. If Kerke[5] should be killed as it is reported, I beg you would desire the Queen's feavor for my sister

---

[1] The invitation to bring her to England. See p. 510 n. 3.
[2] Rochester had paid a visit to Godolphin. See p. 801.
[3] Letter 805.   [4] 5/16 June, Murray, iii. 416.
[5] Piercy Kirk (1683–1741), lieutenant-colonel, Patmore's Regiment of Foot, 1707; colonel 1710; wounded at Almanza.

Godfrey.[1] I take this occasion of giving you my opinion that I think the Queen would do well not to dispose of the redgiments of the collonels which may have been killed, til she has a trew account of the beheavior of all the officers.

You will see by the letters I send Mr. Secretary Harley,[2] that the Saxon troupes are desired for the Rhin,[3] and that the Emperor would give the command of the army on the Rhin to the Elector of Hanover.[4] I beleive he will refuse it,[5] so that army will be without any commander for at least one month longer.

814. MARLBOROUGH *to the* DUCHESS   [5/16 *June 1707*]

Source: Blenheim MSS. E3.
Printed: *Private Correspondence*, i. 88–9.

Meldert June 26, 1707

I have this day had the happyness of yours of the 30th of May, and am very sorry that the indiscresion of 254 [Mrs. Godfrey] has given you so much trouble. I do love her very well, but I know her to be very indiscrit. If Mr. Kerke be killed as is reported, I hope 38 [Godolphin] will prevail with the Queen that she may have his employment, which will put her at ease and me at quiet. You make excuses for your letter being long. I beg you to beleive that if I had much more business then I have, I should leave it with pleasur to read your letters, and if I am ever uneasy, it is when I turn the leafe and find no more writting. The feares you have had upon [what] 253 [Lady Tyrconnell] writte to one of her daughters I dare say is not trew,[6] but my feares are from the unaccountable beheavior of 46 [the Emperor], for he may think it his intirest to recal so many troupes as may put an end to that project [Toulon] on which depends the good or bad success of this campagne. We must have patience for one month longer, which will let us see what we are to expect. I had forgot to tel you in my last that Mr. Cardonel was so sick as to be forced to go to Mallins, but I hear this day he is better. I am ever heart and soull yours.

[1] Presumably he wanted Kirk's post for a son of Arabella Godfrey, his sister.
[2] See Murray, iii. 415.
[3] The request of the Elector of Mainz to Marlborough, n.d. and reply 5/16 June, S.P. 87/2, fols. 644–7. The reply is printed in Murray, iii. 414. The Elector's reply in turn, 8/19 June, is in Murray, iii. 438–9. The Saxon troops were those in the pay of the Maritime Powers in the Low Countries.
[4] Zinzendorf to Marlborough, 24 May/4 June, S.P. 87/2, fols. 648–9.
[5] The Elector accepted this month.   [6] See p. 801 n. 2.

815. GODOLPHIN *to* MARLBOROUGH   [*6 June 1707*]

Source: Blenheim MSS. A2-23.

Fryday June 6 1707

Not having any letters from you since my last by the messenger[1] and the wind being so that wee can't hope for them before this post, I have very little to trouble you with, and indeed after so much as I have given you of late, 'tis but reasonable to allow you some respitt.

10 [Rivers] has brought mee your letter to him,[2] and the enclosed from 44 [King Charles] to 39 [Marlborough] by which it seems plain enough 10 [Rivers] is willing to goe to 44 [King Charles] if 42 [the Queen] desires it.[3] But unless the first overtures arise from himself, I am afraid he may insist upon some things which would bee too unreasonable.

The enclosed letter[4] I am sure must bee from *Parks* at the Leward Islands for I have had just the fellow of it in the outside. If it bee as like mine within, I should advise you not to give yourself the trouble of opening it till you are at full leisure.

Here has been a report this last week that Sir Robert Jenkinson[5] was dead. If it had been true, I doubt it would have caused a new ferment in Oxfordshire. But I hear it has been contradicted, and I beleive he is alive.

816. GODOLPHIN *to* MARLBOROUGH   [*8 June 1707*]

Source: Blenheim MSS. A2-23.
Printed: Coxe, ii. 273 (inc.) as July.

Sunday 8th of July [June], 1707

Wee want still the letters from Holland of last Tuesday,[6] and not having any letters neither from Lisbon, since my last, I have nothing to trouble you with, of any forreign matters, and shall therfore begin this letter with telling you, that as to our home affairs, those relating to Scotland will bee all finished, I hope, in this week. But the apprehensions of creating tumults and disorders among that warm people will bee the occasion of leaving a great many things to bee regulated by the 1st Parliament of Great Brittain, which will make the next sessions more tedious than ordinary. But it can't bee avoyded.

---

[1] Letter 811.   [2] 26 May/6 June, H. M. C., *Bath MSS.*, i. 178.
[3] See p. 795.
[4] Untraced. For résumé of his complaints see his letter to the Council of Trade and Plantations, 4 Aug., *C.S.P.*, Col., 1706–8, pp. 518–21. In it he states: 'The Duke [of Marlborough] promised me the government of Virginia at the battle of Blenheim, but for some reasons of state, that was given to my Lord Orkney, and this given to me with a promise the sallery should be the same which is £2,000 stirling the year. I find myself mistaken and at this distance forgot.'
[5] Sir Robert Jenkinson, third Bt. (*c.* 1655–1710), Tory M.P., Oxfordshire, 1689–1710; a Tacker.
[6] 3 June.

Tomorrow morning my Lord President[1] setts out for Ireland, and I am in pretty good hopes, that he will succeed well enough there. But as to 108 [England], I can't answer how things will goe, 42 [the Queen] being pretty obstinate against some persons and for others, which may bee very uneasy to Mrs. Morley [the Queen], and to her friends and servants in the consequence of it.

By the Bishop of Norwich's[2] being made Bishop of Ely,[3] there are now three bishopricks vacant,[4] and I find 38 [Godolphin] has soe little hopes of their being well filled that he seems resolved to use all his endeavors to keep them vacant till he can have Mr. Freeman's [Marlborough] assistance in those spirituall affairs which seem to grow rather worse and worse, ever since I saw you last with 42 [the Queen] and 38 [Godolphin] and another person [Harley] who I doubt, has not much altered his mind in those matters though he won't own anything like that to Mr. Montgomery [Godolphin].

10th of June

After I had written thus far I received the favour of 2 letters from you of the 13th and 16th of June,[5] in one of which is enclosed a coppy of a letter from my Lord Peterborow. You seem to desire my advice that you may answer to his proposalls. I can't imagine first, what he will propose, or indeed that he can propose anything practicable. But I observe he laments the Emperour's persisting in sending the detachment to Naples, when you can't but remember t'was his own proposall last winter to the Duke of Savoy and to Prince Eugene, and perhaps, the expectation hee gave them of the Queen's concurrence in that project, was the ground of their engaging in that unfortunate design.

As to his comming into England I must own myself to have been of a different opinion from my friends in that poynt. I always thought, that when his power was taken from him, and all his comissions recalled, that he would doe less hurt abroad than at home, and so I think still, it will be found. But I don't at all wonder you should like him better anywhere than with you.

I think what you say of Erle's staying and the King of Spain's comanding are both very right, and I believe as soon as our next Lisbon letters arrive the Queen will take the resolution of allowing 2 [Gallway] to return. But if Erle bee to stay there, I doubt it will bee necessary for yourself to write to him upon that subject, for I don't think anybody else has credit enough with him to make him doe it willingly, as one must doe to serve well.

[1] Pembroke.
[2] John Moore (1646–1714), Bishop of Norwich 1691–1707; of Ely 1707–14; a moderate Whig divine, a friend to the Junto.
[3] Simon Patrick (1626–1707), Bishop of Ely, died 31 May. One of the founders of S.P.C.K. *D.N.B.*
[4] Exeter, Chester, and Norwich.   [5] Letters 809, 813.

My Lord Sunderland has done mee the favour to lett mee see the coppys[1] of your letters from the King of Spain and from the Prince Eugene, with your answers which I think indeed are as right and as full, as 'tis possible, and I can't but have very good hopes still of the Duke of Savoy's expedition. I find too by very fresh letters from Mr. Robinson, that he does not apprehend any sudden breach between the King of Sweden and the Emperour.

I believe the Queen will still leave it to you, to dispose of the Saxon troops as you think best, I can't help saying, that till they agree upon a generall for the Rhyne, they are not like to bee of much use there.

Collonell Wade assures mee that Kirk is alive and well.

817. MARLBOROUGH *to* GODOLPHIN   [9/20 *June 1707*]

Source: Blenheim MSS. A1-37.

Meldert June 20th 1707

Since my last I have received an account of the dates of Mr. Wroth's commissions. I did not know that his brevet of collonel was of so old a date. However, I think there aught to be a difference made when officers do not serve. But there are already so many generals that nevere think of serving, that I can hardly bring myself to refuse anybody.[2] I have received the letters from England of the 3. But yours and Mr. Secretary Harley's, which I understand were sent by a messinger at the same time, I hear nothing of them, though I have had the others these two days, so that it is very likely that some accedent is happened to the man. I have this afternoon received the enclosed from the Comte de Maffie.[3] It is an abstract of part of a letter he has received from 58 [Duke of Savoy]. I think by it, [it] is plain the French are not pleased with the march of that detachment.[4] He begs you will keep this a secrit, and asures that whatever shal come to their knowledge, I shal have itt. The Mareshal de Villars dose what he will in Garmany, though thay now own he has not above twenty thousand men. I am in pain for your letter[5] by the messinger, fearing it may fall into the French hands.[6]

---

[1] See p. 805.   [2] See pp. 799, 808.
[3] Untraced. It contained a report that the Pope offered to guarantee the neutrality of Naples and Sicily for the balance of the war, by taking the government into his own hands. See pp. 813, 824.
[4] The Imperial expedition to Naples.   [5] Letters 808, 811.
[6] Marlborough explained his concern about the messenger to Harley this same day: 'The securest and most expeditious way of sending to me is by the common post, Mr. Van der Poel's couriers being provided with passes, which your messengers cannot obtain without difficulty and loss of time; and if they venture to come on without, there is great danger of their letters falling into the enemy's hands.' Murray, iii. 425.

818. MARLBOROUGH *to the* DUCHESS [9/20 June 1707]

Source: Blenheim MSS. E3.
Printed: Coxe, ii. 247-8 (inc.).

Meldert June 20, 1707

I have had the happyness of your kind letter of the first of this month from St. Albans. From my soul I wish I were with you, but every day gives me less prospect of that happyness. Your reasoning for not venturing at this time agrees exactly with that of 110 [Holland]. For my own part I beseech God Almighty to put into the heart of 39 [Marlborough] what is right. I beleive he is very apprehensive of the consequences on both sides, so that by what I can find by him, he is resolved not to let sleep any favourable occasion, but will not undertake unless others be of the same opinion. What you say concerning 241 [Lady Monthermer] and 25 [Monthermer] I wish you could govern them, but as it is, thay must be left to their own good or bad destiny. 8 [Montagu] is certainly very ill natured, but the divel is good when pleased, and I think thay had it in their power, but I am afraid it is not at this time. I have received a letter from 201 [Erle][1] by which, and by everything that comes from that country, I find there is such a contempt and anger against 2 [Galway], that it will be impossible for him to continue with any satisfaction to himself, or advantage to the publick. But if this be not the opinion of your friends, I desire what I say may go for nothing. The being to[o] much in the sun this day has made my headeak, so that I must end with asuring you with the truth of my heart, of being intierly yours.

819. GODOLPHIN *to* MARLBOROUGH [10 June 1707]

Source: Blenheim MSS. A2-23.

Tuesday night 10th

Since I had written my former letter[2] the Cabinett Counsell has mett, and Mr. Secretary Harley will acquaint you with what was agreed there, as to the Saxon troops and the Elector of Hannover's comanding on the Rhyne.[3]

I have it from very good hand[4] that the Pope is to propose to the Emperour, that Naples and Sicily may bee deposited in his hands till the generall peace, and the French and Spanish troops to bee withdrawn in the meantime from those kingdoms, by which means the King of France would have the service of those troops, and those countryes as much in his power, as now. If I thought it possible for the Imperiall court to bee caught with this proposall I should bee very earnest with you to doe your endeavours to

---

[1] 18/29 Apr., in Blenheim MSS. A2-29; reply, 9/20 June, in Murray, iii. 428-9. On the defeat at Almanza.
[2] Letter 816.   [3] See p. 809.   [4] Count Briançon. See p. 819.

hinder it. But I reckon it would disappoint them of their main design,[1] which I take to bee plunder.

Hitherto the affairs abroad have but a melancholly face, and at home I assure you everybody is extreamly uneasy. Wee must live in hope that before winter things will jumble into a better posture.

820. MARLBOROUGH *to* GODOLPHIN   [*12/23 June 1707*]

Source: Blenheim MSS. A1–37.
Printed: Coxe, ii. 249 (inc.).

Meldert June 23d 1707

I received yesterday yours of the 1st and 3d[2] by the messinger. What you write of the court of Vienna is certainly right; but by the abstract I sent you by the last post,[3] as well as by other letters, I am convinced thay have no intelligence with France. Notwithstanding that, I have write very plainly to them already,[4] that if upon any account whatsoever the project concerted for the entry of France should miscarry, thay must expect that all the fatal consequencys would with justice be laid at their dore. However, I shall obaye your commands, in writting, and att the same time propose to them the sending the greatest part of their detachement of Naples, to the relief of King Charles to Catalonia. I hope you have not as yett told the Comte de Gallas, that the Queen would be contented to pay them. If you have not, I beg you will not lett him nor Sir Philip Meadows[5] know any more then that the Queen as a marque of her zeal for the publick good, and her particular concern she has for the person of King Charles, that she would be contented to allow a subsity towardes the support of such troupes as the Emperor should send from that detachement of Naples. I am perticular as to that detachment, so that thay may not pretend to send any of their troupes which are to enter France. For when that expedition is over, I should be in hopes that wee might be able to spare the King from that army the 7,000 Pallatins which are payde by England and Holande. That expence would not fal upon the Queen alone, as I am afraid any other would do. For 110 [Holland] have so much mind to 81 [peace], and so just a pretence to poverty, that it was with great difficulty, I was able to perswade them to come into on[e] half of the expence of the redgiment of Bothmar.[6] That redgiment and the Saxons[7] makes together 5,400 men. The mony that is saved by the redgiments of foot will more then pay the Queen's part.

---

[1] The Imperial expedition to seize Naples.   [2] Letters 808, 811.
[3] Letter 817.
[4] Marlborough sent notes by Count Lescheraine. See p. 803 n. 3.
[5] English envoy at Vienna 1707–9.   [6] See p. 776 n. 3.
[7] See p. 804 n. 3.

I have write to France to desire I might have a list of the officers and soldiers belonging to the Queen, so that you might know what that expence will be, and that some monys might be sent for their suport. I send by this post to Mr. Secretary Harley an offer made me, and my answer for the exchange of those taken in Spain.[1] The trew intention of France is that thay would have their prisoners delivered to their severall armys, so that thay might be of use to them that campagne, and that ours might be of none til the next. In my opinion, the right time for the exchange wil be about the end of October, and since this matter depends upon the Emperor, the Duke of Savoye, Hollande, and England, I can with ease kepe it off til that time, if her Majesty approves of itt.

I have sent to Mr. Secretary already a copie of a letter I formerly write to Sir Cloudesly Shovell concerning the powder and canon-ball,[2] but will writte againe as you direct, though I can't comprehend their can be a want, for 115 [Toulon] is so litle fortefied towardes the land, that it can make very litle resistance. But my feares are, as you will have seen by a former leter,[3] that I fear thay will attack other places before thay go to 115 [Toulon]. But we are in their hands, and we must have patience, for it is to[o] late to alter any of their measures. I have write as pressing as I am capable of doing to the Duke of Savoye and Prince Eugene,[4] to lett them see the absolut necessity of not only attempting, but also succeding in the project of 115 [Toulon]. I have given the messinger a pasport, so that he may go securly, but by the time he took in coming to mee, I fear the letters would have gone faster by the post, which go now very securly.

In a post or two I expect to hear from Comte Piper. I wish he may lett me know the King's intentions. Notwithstanding all that is said of the resentment the King of Sweden has showen against the proceedings of the court of Vienna, I am very confident he will not proceed to a declaration, since he dose know, what a great advantage that would be to France at this junctur.

I am asured that the Elector of Bavaria has desired of the King of France, that Monsieur d'Arco[5] may march into Garmany with all the Bavariens he has left, which consists of four battalions, and seventien squadrons, which may amount to 3,000 men.[6] You will see by my letter to the Elector of Mayance,[7] that I have sent orders to the Saxon troupes, to derect their march to the Rhin.

[1] The letter to Harley is in Murray, iii. 437–40. The enclosures, in S.P. 87/2, fols. 666–73, include letters from the French comissary, Piuch, to Cardonnel, 12 and 15 June, Cardonnel's reply of 13 June, and Marlborough to Chamillart, 14 June, also in Murray, iii. 412. All deal with English prisoners of war.

[2] 1/12 June, in Murray, iii. 407–8.   [3] Letter 806.   [4] 12/23 June, Murray, iii. 431–3.

[5] Jean Baptiste d'Arco (died 1715), of Piedmontese origin, but long in the service of the Elector of Bavaria; his commanding general 1694; General of Cavalry 1697; President of the Bavarian Council of War, and a field-marshal 1702; commanded left wing at Ramillies.

[6] The rumour was not confirmed.   [7] 12/23 June, Murray, iii. 434.

821. MARLBOROUGH to GODOLPHIN   [12/23 June 1707]

Source: Blenheim MSS. A1-37.
Printed: Coxe, ii. 250 (inc.).

Meldert June 23d 1707

Beleiving it might be reasonable for you to show my long letter[1] to some
that may have a much better opinion of 10 [Rivers] then I have, I send you
my opinion as to the command in Spain apart, so that it may be known to
none but yourself and her Majesty. As I have already told you that it is
impracticable for 2 [Galway] to continue in that Service, and as you aprove
of the reasoning in Montandre's letter,[2] the number of the Queen's subjects
in 125 [Portugal] will be to[o] few for the command of 10 [Rivers]; so that
the best for the Service would be to give the command to 201 [Earle] and
leave no other officers with him but what may be sutable to the number of
men. And as the troupes of necessity that go from Italie must be al foragine,
I think the chief command should be left to the King and his generals,[3]
and that 201 [Erle] should have derections to concern himself only with the
Queen's subjects, and be obedient and assisting to whatever the King should
command. At the same time, I think he should be incoraged by having the
commission of General of the Foot. The train of artillerie aught to be very
much lessened, so that you might be the better able to give subsitys for
Garmain troupes that shall go thether. I should think that you might in
confidence tel 10 [Rivers] that it is impossible to send from 108 [England]
such suplies as are necessarie for the suport of 44 [King Charles] but by the
consent and assistance of 88 [Parliament] so that if thay shall in the winter
resolve on such a suplie as shall enable the Queen, that she will then desire
him to take the command. This aught to please, and I think you will not be
troubled with his service. As I think you will give leave to Sir Charles
Hara, and most of the generall officers leave to come home, the best way
would be to give no answer to his memorial.[4] For should you alow of his
desire it would be a very troublesome president. I must againe beg you to
intercede with the Queen not [to] give way to the sollicitations of 17
[Newcastle], but that the governments may be filled with such officers as
have served since her raine.[5]

---

[1] Letter 820.

[2] 30 May/10 June, Blenheim MSS. A2-29. Montandre advised that no matter how many troops
England sent to Portugal the most the Portuguese could be expected to mount was a frontier war
so long as they had the command of the English troops. 'As they will never agree to any other
arrangement for the command there is no hope for an offensive in Portugal.'

[3] On 9/20 Marlborough wrote Heinsius: 'I think it would be for the good of the common cause
that the Comte de Noyelles as the King of Spain's Generall had the chief derection. But you must
be sure not to make use of my name at any time in this matter.' 't Hoff, p. 319. Cf. with letter 823.

[4] See p. 804 n. 4, for his request.

[5] See p. 594 n. 4 for Newcastle's desire to put George Whichcote into the governorship of
Tinmouth.

822. MARLBOROUGH *to the* DUCHESS   [*12/23 June 1707*]

Source: Blenheim MSS. E3.
Printed: Coxe, i. 263 (inc.).
Addressed: For the Dutchesse of Marlborough.

Meldert June 23d 1707

I have had the pleasur of receiving yours of the 3d from St. Albans, and that of the 6 from St. Jeamses, by which I find something is doing by way of promotions in 171 [the Church] that makes 89 [the Whigs] uneasy.[1] I do asure you I am very sorry for itt, but you know I have very litle to say in those matters. You know how often I spoke about Doctor Potter,[2] and I do not hear that it is as yett done, though the consequence is, that if he has not the Professor's place, I will never more meadle with anything that may concern Oxford. You say nothing of the weather but we have here the hottest that I ever felt. I comfort myself that it is very good for the carrying on of the building att Woodstock, for att last there must be our happyness. And I do asure you as I am now perswaded, if wee were once setled there, that there is no greatness could tempt me to quitt that happyness, if I saw you pleased.

823. GODOLPHIN *to* MARLBOROUGH   [*13 June 1707*]

Source: Blenheim MSS. A2-23.

June 13, 1707

My Lord Sunderland brought a memoriall[3] to the Lords of the Committee this morning signed by the Comte de Gallas, Zinzerling and Hofman in the name of the King of Spain, complaining of their master's want of authority in the army and imputting to that most of the misfortunes which has hapned. There are many insinuations besides, very unreasonable.

It prays in the close that the Queen would assist him with more money and more at his own disposall, and with 4,000 foot of her own subjects, with good experienced officers to command them and that she would use her interest with the Emperour to send him some troops from Italy for his more immediat relief. I could perceive by Monsieur Zinzerling's talk to us today, that he would fain have those troops from the Duke of Savoy's army, but wee told him still the troops that went to Naples, or as many of them as could bee spared, were the most proper, and the nearest at hand.

[1] See p. 750 n. 2.
[2] John Potter (1694?–1747), domestic chaplain to Tenison 1704; Regius Professor of Divinity, Oxford, 1707–15; Bishop of Oxford 1714–37; Archbishop of Canterbury 1737–47. *D.N.B.*
[3] The memorial, 6 June, and Sunderland's reply, 26 June, are in *H.L.N.S.*, vii. 441–5.

All the Lords of the Comittee were very forward to add, that the Queen would not bee unwilling to allow some money for the better support of such troops as the Emperour should send.

I had sayd as much before in private discourse to the Comte de Gallas, which he promised mee to write to Vienna by the last post, but they must not bee suffered by any means to take any of the troops with the Duke of Savoy.

The intercepted letters which Secretary Harley sends you from Rouillè,[1] are a very good picture (if wee wanted one) of the humour of the French nation in generall. But for all their braggs, a number of troops such as wee had the last year, to carry upon their coast,[2] would make them very uneasy yett before winter. A lesser number would serve now, but without the help of Providence, I don't know how wee shall gett them.

824. GODOLPHIN *to* MARLBOROUGH [*13 June 1707*]

Source: Blenheim MSS. A2-23.
Printed: Coxe, ii. 248–9 (inc.).

Fryday June 13th 1707

Not having anything from you since my last,[3] nor likely to have before this post, I shall only trouble you with some further reflexions on the affairs of 44 [King Charles].

I find 4 [Halifax] and 5 [Somers] and their friends are pretty indifferent as to 10 [Rivers] and unconcerned whether he is to return or not, but they are very uneasy to think of recalling 2 [Gallway] (though sensible that he must bee useless) for they carry that matter so much further as to think all those misunderstandings are industriously fomented by 110 [Holland] and by particular instructions to all those who depend upon them, in those parts especially Count Noyelles whom they take to bee the principall occasion and contriver of 2's [Gallway] misfortunes; for which reason they seem to think unless he bee called home either before, or at the same time with 2 [Gallway] or else it would look as if he had been in the right in all he had suggested to 44 [King Charles] and all the reflexions which belong to that matter must light upon 2 [Gallway] and 108 [England]. Now I know no remedy so probable to these difficultys, as that, (if any troops goe to Spain from Italy)

---

[1] 11/22 May, 18/29 May, 21 May/1 June, with Harley's letter in Blenheim MSS. A2-24. There are copies of the letters in cipher and deciphered together with letters by Rouillé of a later date in B.M., Portland Loan, 29/450, fols. 285–310 (the cipher is at fol. 278); 29/45L, fols. 127–8 (10/21 Aug.); and 29/45P/2 (also 10/21 Aug.). The letters were addressed to Louis Mathy, French commissioner at Danzig. Marlborough obtained them on the Continent and sent them to Harley who had the key (Marlborough to Harley, 14/25 Aug. 1707, Murray, iii. 528). He sent this one to Harley on 2/13 June remarking: 'The person who intercepts them thinks [this] may be the last for some time, Monsieur Rouillé being ordered to Paris.' Ibid. 411.

[2] For a descent.

[3] Letter 819.

46 [the Emperour] might order some proper person to take the command of the whole, and Comte Noyelles and 2 [Gallway] bee both recalled.

I have just now received the enclosed letters from Lisbon[1] which I send you that you may have all the light wee have, in to the state of their affairs. The letter from Monsieur de Montandre seems to mee very reasonable, and I think it ought to guide us (as farr as wee are able to follow it) when the Comte de Taroca[2] (whom he mentions) shall arrive here.

825. GODOLPHIN *to* MARLBOROUGH   [*15 June 1707*]

Source: Blenheim MSS. A2-23.
Printed: Coxe, ii. 246-7.

Windsor Sunday 15 June

I received yesterday the favour of yours of the 20th[3] with the extract of Comte Maffei's letter from 58 [the Duke of Savoy]. You will have seen by mine of the last post,[4] that I had been acquainted with the same thing by Comte Briançon here.

I don't think ther's much reflexion to bee made upon it, nor that there is any danger of its taking effect, for the reasons mentioned in my last. And as for the proposition itself, I believe tis as likely, to have proceeded originally from the court of Roome, as from that of France. The detachment for Naples, not having been stopped in time, the next best thing for the Allyes seems to bee that it should succeed quickly, and a part of those forces bee at liberty to bee transported by our fleet to Catalonia. The Imperiall ministers with us doe not seem averse to that, but perhaps those at Vienna, may have other views, in which they may think themselves more nearly concerned.

Our letters of last post from The Hague tell us the Comte de Noyelles has written a letter to the States in which he is pleased to take great libertys with my Lord Gallway. Wee think it pretty hard here, at the same time, that hee who has been the visible occasion of our misfortunes in Spain for 2 years successively, should have the confidence to lay the blame at the doors of others who have suffered so much and at soe great an expence. And as most people are forward to think, and to say that nothing can succeed while 2 [Gallway] is with 44 [King Charles], so here wee shall enter into no expence with much satisfaction, as long as wee find 44 [King Charles] continues under the same ill influence against us.

---

[1] From Paul Methuen and Montandre. Untraced. The advice must be similar to that they communicated to Godolphin on 30 May/10 June, Blenheim MSS. A2-29, that Portugal would never mount more than a frontier war (see p. 816 n. 2) and that it would be very difficult to support the war in Spain based on Catalonia from England.

[2] João Gomez da Silva, Count of Tarouca, Portuguese minister, represented the King of Portugal at the Congress of Utrecht.

[3] Letter 817.   [4] Letter 819.

I am extreamly uneasy to find by yours that my letters by the messanger[1] were not come to your hands, having written more fully and plainly by that man, than I used to doe, nott thinking there was much danger of his being taken betwixt Helvoetsluys and Brusselles. He was also charged with dispatches for Turin which I fear may bee much wanted there, and were judged proper to bee sent by a messenger for more safety, and more dispatch, but it seems it has proved otherwise.

Nothing as yett has hitt right for us; nor doe I much like Mr. Robinson's last letter from Leipsick; but whatever uneasyness happens to the court of Vienna they deserve it richly who would not in all this time send a generall to the Rhyne, though they have been pressed to doe it, to my knowledg, ever since last Christmass.

I reckon the Duchess of Nemours's death engages us to assist the King of Prussia, as farr as wee can in his pretensions to the succession of Neufchastel, but I am sorry it comes to bear at this time, for fear it may putt him upon recalling his troops from Italy to take possession. I hope you will endeavour to prevent this consequence of it.

Though wee are in great want of some good news from the Duke of Savoy, I don't see how wee shall come at it, if there were any, the Marshall De Villars being master of all the passes by which those courriers usually come to Holland.

I hope to hear from you again before this post goes, and if I doe I shall trouble you further.

826. MARLBOROUGH *to the* DUCHESS   [*15/26 June 1707*]

Source: Blenheim MSS. E3.
Printed: Coxe, ii. 263, 264 (inc.); and *Private Correspondence*, i. 99-101 (27th only).

Meldert June 26, 1707

Though the post is not to go til tomorrow, and that I hope to have the happyness of hearing from you before that time, yet I would not loos this hour which I have to myself, of asuring you that you are always in my thoughts; and if it were not for the happyness I prepose to myself of having some part of the remainder of my life of living quietly with you, I could not bare with patience the trouble I strugle with at this time. The weather is so very hott and the dust so very great, that I have this hour to myself, the officers not caring to be abroad til the hour of orders oblige them to itt. It is most certain that when I was in Spain[2] in the month of August I was not more sensible of the heat than I am att this minutt. If you have the same weather it must make all sortes of fruit very good, and as this is the 3d yeare

---

[1] Letters 808, 811.   [2] In Tangier, 1668-70. See Churchill, i. 55-6.

of the tres at Woodstock, if possible I should wish that you might or somebody you can relie on tast the fruit of every tree, so that what is not good
might be changed. On this matter you must advise with Mr. Wise, as also
what place may be proper for the ice house, for that should be built this
summer so that it might have time to dry. The hott weather makes me think
of these things, for the most agreable of all the presents I receive is that of
ice. I expect every day to hear of three looking glasses I have baught at
Paris,[1] that has cost me 300 pistols, of their being come to Bruxelles, as I
shall send them to England, or keep them here til the winter as you shall
direct.

[June 27]

I had last night the satisfaction of your very kind letter of 10th, which has
given me infinett pleasur, as your kindness will always do, for beleive it my
dear soull I can have no lasting happyness but with you. You may give good
wordes to Mr. Duncombe,[2] but I have so many officers here with mee, that
will make it impossible for me to do what he desires. You may assure 255
[Mrs. Burnet] that no man living is more desirous of a good peace then
210 [Marlborough].

46 [the Emperor] is in the wrong in almost everything he dose, but
what she writes[3] concerning his having corrispondance with 43 [King of
France] is certainly not so. The people in 110 [Holland] which seemes
to be favorable to 30 [Peterborough] are of all the worst in that country.
I hear by my last letters from Italie that he is gone to Vienna, to sollicit
troupes for 44 [King Charles], but his mind changes so often that there is not
much waite to be laid upon his motions, nor have I answered any of his
letters not knowing where to send them. I am glad to hear that 28 [Shrews-
bury] is easier then the last yeare.[4] I do not think he can ever be of much use,
but it is much better to have mankind pleased then angry, for a great many
that can do no good, have it *always in their power* to vex and do hurt. What
you say concerning the uneasiness between 42 [the Queen] and 38
[Godolphin], if that continues distruction must be the consequence, as the
cercomstances of our affaires are abroad, as well as at home. I am sure to the
best of my understanding, and with the hazard of my life I shall always
endeavor to serve 239 [the Queen]; but if thay incline more to be governed
by the notions of 208 [Harley][5] then those of Mr. Montgomery [Godolphin],
I would sooner loos my life then persuade him to continue on such cercomstances in the service of 42 [the Queen]. This is only to yourself, but you may

---

[1] For their arrival in Brussels see p. 826.
[2] Identified as Anthony Duncombe (died 1708), M.P. 1698–1708, who apparently asked that his
son, John, a captain in Barrymore's Regiment of Foot, be made an aide-de-camp to Marlborough.
[3] See p. 801.   [4] About his desire for a place? See p. 807.
[5] The Duchess has written 'Mr. Harley' above the code.

depend upon itt, that if ever I be advised with, this will be my opinion. All that I know concerning 30 [Peterborough] is, that he would do anything to gett the payement of an arreare off about 3,000 pounds.

827. GODOLPHIN *to* MARLBOROUGH   [*16 June 1707*]

Source: Blenheim MSS. A2-23.
Printed: Coxe, ii. 250-1 (inc.).

Windsor June 16th 1707

Since mine of yesterday, I have the favour of yours of the 23d[1] which gives mee the ease of your having our letters by the messenger. Hereafter I will write only by the post.[2]

It is a great satisfaction to find your thoughts agree soe exactly with ours in all that relates to Germany, Italie, and Spayn.

I never did once imagine that the Emperour had a thought of making separate terms with France, but yett all his behaviour has been so un-accountable, as to putt the rest of the Allyes under the same difficulty, as if he had acted by directions from Versailles. As to Italie I see you press the expedition all you can, and so wee have done from hence. I agree it is too late to give them new measures now, and I can't but hope those they have taken will have a good effect. By what wee hear from France, that court is entirely uneasy at the Duke of Savoy's expedition, but I have not yett seen any letters directly from Turin by either of these 2 last posts which made mee afrayd the Marshal De Villars might have stopped those courriers.

For what relates to Spain, my own opinion agrees exactly with what you write in your private letter to myself,[3] and in that matter there will bee no difficulty with 42 [the Queen], but as I have told you in my former letter, some of our friends here will bee unwilling to bring home 2 [Gallway] while Comte de Noyelles stays with 44 [King Charles]. So the true way of making all this easy would bee for 46 [the Emperor] to send a good generall with the troops from Italy. The very best would bee the Comte de Thaun[4] who went to Naples with the detachment.

I spoke to the Comte de Gallas myself, in the very terms of your letter, not that the Queen would pay such troops as the Emperour should send to Spain, but that her Majesty had that affair so much at heart that she would bee willing to allow some subsidys for the *better maintaining* of those troops. Some other of our Lords would have gone farther, but I will write to Mr. Secretary Harley to instruct Sir Philip Medows according to this.

42 [the Queen] will bee very carefull not to lett 17 [Newcastle] or anybody else make you uneasy about governments. That of Tinmouth waits your

[1] Letter 820-1.   [2] For the danger of using messengers see p. 812 n. 6.   [3] Letter 821.
[4] Philipp Wirich Lorenz, Count Daun (1669-1741), Imperial field-marshal; served at the relief or Turin 1706; commander of the expedition to reduce Naples in 1707.

orders;[1] that of New York will bee made vacant whenever you propose a proper man;[2] that of New England is also like to bee vacant very soon, there being great clamours depending at this time against Collonell Dudley[3] the present Governor.

I have not yett seen the French proposalls about the exchange of our prisoners, but I take for granted you ghess right, as to their intentions, and I make no doubt but that matter will bee left, as it ought, to your regulation.

You have never said a word to mee how long the French (or your own) army can continue in your present camps. I hope you won't bee obliged to move first, but they having the river [Sambre] behind them, may doe it, with less hazard.

17 June

Having now had the perusall of all Mr. Secretary Harley's letters by this post, I find you are of opinion, the Imperiall court will agree to send some troops to King Charles but that wee should not settle that matter till the month of September. I agree it can't bee executed till that time but if it bee not adjusted without loss of time so as to bee relyed on the orders for our fleet to act in it, will not come to them in time.

I am sorry to find the Elector of Hannover declines the command of the army upon the Rhyne.[4] I can't but think he slipps a great opportunity for his own humour and advantage as well as for the good of the common cause.

By my Lord Raby's letters the King of Prussia seems at present in a good disposition, but as soon as he shall have heard of the Duchess of Nemour's death, all his thoughts will bee turned towards getting possession of Neufchatell which may putt him upon measures very inconvenient for us.

Some French letters speak of the arrivall of our fleet before Monaco as also that Prince Eugene was in march with his troops. If this bee true wee may soon expect to hear somthing good.

828. MARLBOROUGH *to* GODOLPHIN   [16/27 *June 1707*]

Source: Blenheim MSS. A1-37.
Printed: Coxe, ii. 265-6 (inc.).

Meldert June 27th 1707

I have since my last had the favour of yours of the 8th[5] and 10th,[6] and am very glad to find you are so near an end of your Scotch business. For what you are obliged to leave to the Brittish Parliament I am not in much

---

[1] For the appointment see p. 594 n. 4.

[2] Marlborough had named Richard Sutton, but he wanted to remain closer to England and stand for Parliament. See p. 757.

[3] Joseph Dudley (1647-1720), native of Massachusetts; lieutenant-governor of the Isle of Wight 1694; captain-general and governor of Massachusetts 1702-15.

[4] The Elector did accept the command. See p. 809.

[5] Letter 816.   [6] Letter 819.

pain, for I think there must happen so many things on this side of the watter, that of consequence I think will make the sessions either easy or uneasy. And as I can't but hope that God will bless the project of entering France, as well as this army with some success this campagne, I will flatter myself that her Majesty will have a very easy sessions. That which gives me the greatest trouble is what you say concerning 42 [the Queen], for if Mrs. Morley's [the Queen] prejudice to some people is so unalterable, and that thay will be disposing of the preferments[1] now vacant to such as will tare to pieces her friends and servants, that must creat distraction.[2] But you know my opinion was, and is yett, that you aught to take with you 199 [Harley] and to lett 42 [the Queen] see with all the freedome and plainess imaginable her trew interest; and when she is sensible of that, there will be no more difficulty. If there should, you will have performed your duty, and God's will be done. For my own part, I see in allmost every country thay act so extreamly against their own intirest, that I fear we have deserved to be punished. I will endeavor to serve to the best of my understanding, and then shall submitt with much resignation to the pleasure of God, whoes mercys and protection I am very sensible off. And as I do freely and cherfully ventur my life in gratetude to the favours I have received from the Queen, so I do hope and beg of you, that you will take a proper time of letting the Queen know my heart and ferm resolution, with her leave, that as soon as this warr is at an end, that I might be master of myself, by which I might have both time and quietness to reconcil myself to God, which aught to be the end of every honest man.

You will have seen by the letter I sent you,[3] the way by which I heard forst of the proposition made by the Pope. I beleive we may be very sure itt will not bee accepted, for their [the Emperor] greatest designe in that expedition [Naples] is to have the plundering of that kingdome. The Elector of Hanover being resolved, as I am assured, not to accept of the command of the army on the Rhin, I think her Majesty should not expose herself by receiving a deniall. I desire you will give my duty, and thank her Majesty for the leave she has been pleased to give me concerning the generall officers. I shall be carefull not to make the decleration til I see it necessary for her Service, for I am sensible when I shall do itt, the Queen will be tormented by some in England which have not served this warr. I am impatient for the Italien letters, there being a report from the French army of the Duke of Savoy's being ill, which if trew, would be a very great *contretems*.

The Langrave of Hesse[4] threat[en]ing that his troupes in Italie shal not act til his last treaty be performed,[5] I am desired by the Pensioner, and Mr. Stepney, to write to you about itt.

[1] In the Church. [2] See p. 811.
[3] From the Duke of Savoy to Maffei, in letter 817. See pp. 812, 813.
[4] Charles (died 1730), Landgrave of Hesse-Kassel from 1663. [5] See p. 784.

829. MARLBOROUGH *to* GODOLPHIN [*19/30 June 1707*]

Source: Blenheim MSS. A1-37.

Meldert June 30th 1707]

Since my last we have had no letters from England, nor have we any alteration in our affaires in this country, so that I shall not give you much trouble by this post, which will give you the more time to read your letter from Lord Pitterborow. You will see it came open to me. I also send you mine.[1] Thay were braught to me by a Spanish lieutenant generall[2] that was in the unfortunate battaile. He is sent by the King of Spain to give an account of itt to the Queen and States. I beleive he will stay with me two or three days, and then I have promised him a letter to you. You will give him good wordes, but I beleive we can no ways more effectually help his master, then by taking measures for the sending the 7,000 Pallatins, after we have seen the success of our project on that side. I have my doubts, but shall not trouble you with them, since a fortnight or three weakes will lett us see certainly, what thay will or will not do. For that side of the country has been so neglected, that it is most certainly in their power to march to 115 [Toulon]. But God only knows what will be done.

In my last I acquainted you that my letters from Hanover assured mee that the Elector would not accept the command of the army. But last night I received an expresse[3] from the Elector Pallatin, to tell me that his envoye had sent him an expresse to assure him that the Elector of Hanover would take upon him the command. Whether he dose or no, I think her Majesty will do well in not writting, since he must before this have taken his resolution.

830. MARLBOROUGH *to the* DUCHESS [*19/30 June 1707*]

Source: Blenheim MSS. E3.
Printed: *Private Correspondence*, i. 101–2.

Meldert June 30th 1707

I have write to Mr. Travers to desire that Doctor Watkins,[4] Fellow of Magdalen Collage in Oxford, might have a buck[5] when he desires it. You know his brother is one of my secretarys[6] and I could not denie him. If

---

[1] N.d. [27 May/7 June], Blenheim MSS. A2-29; reply, Murray, iii. 448–9.

[2] The Count of Fuencalade. See Marlborough to Stanhope, 30 June, Murray, iii. 448. He arrived in London on 30 June/11 July.

[3] 16/27 June, Blenheim MSS. A2-19; reply, 19/30 June in Murray, iii. 446.

[4] Richard Watkins, demy, Magdalen College, 1683–91; fellow 1691–1700; proctor 1699; B.D. 1701; D.D. 1707; Rector of Whichford 1708.

[5] A deer from Woodstock Park.

[6] Henry Watkins (1666–1727), Deputy-Judge-Advocate of the army; he also served in this capacity under Ormonde and was secretary to the plenipotentiaries at Utrecht 1711–12. See Cardonnel's letters to him in the *Morrison Catalogue*, second series, iii. 39–98.

Mr. Travers should be in the country I beg you will give orders for itt. Since my last we have no letters from England, nor no alteration in our affaires here, nor have we any news from Italie, which we are the more impatient for, there being a report of the Duke of Savoye being sick.[1] I have told Mr. Cardonel the consern you had for him. He is returned and pretty well, but I fear he is in a consumption, so that he will not live long. My glasses[2] are come to Bruxelles and I have bespoke the hangings;[3] for one of my greatest pleasures is in doing all that in me lyes, that we may as soon as is possible enjoye that happy time of being quietly together, which I think of with pleasure as often as I have my thoughts free to myself. I have by this post sent a letter to 38 [Godolphin] from 30 [Peterborough]. His letter to 39 [Marlborough] is much the same but something softer. My last letters from Hanover assured me the Elector would not accept of the command on the Rhin, but by an express I had last night from the Elector Pallatin, he assures me the Elector has accepted of that command. I hope it may make things go better in Garmany, though I much fear he will find it very difficult for this campagne.

831. GODOLPHIN *to* MARLBOROUGH   [*20 June 1707*]

Source: Blenheim MSS. A2–23.

Windsor 20 June 1707

Since my last[4] from this place, I have no letters from you to acknowledg, but the wind has been so, that wee may hope for them every hour.

In the meantime I have little to add to my last. Upon the affairs abroad wee subsist upon the hopes of hearing some good news from Italy, which may furnish us with the means of relieving the King of Spayn from thence, and make things easyer at home, of which there is need enough. But the particulars are too many, as well as too long for a letter.

The Dean of St. Paul's[5] being dead the Queen has given the deanery to my brother,[6] and his prebendary to Mr. Hare,[7] which is all I have to trouble you with by this post, unless I would enter into particulars that would bee endless, besides so many other good reasons for not troubling you with them.

---

[1] It was a false rumour. See Braubach, ii. 193–4. Manchester was at Turin for most of June, new style, and makes no mention of any illness. Cole, pp. 455–8.

[2] From Paris. See p. 821.

[3] See pp. 720, 750, 845.

[4] Letter 827.

[5] William Sherlock (1641 ?–1707); Master of the Temple 1685–1704; refused to read James II's declaration for liberty of conscience 1687; wrote many religious tracts. *D.N.B.*

[6] Henry Godolphin, Provost of Eton.

[7] Francis Hare, chaplain-general of the army. For an earlier effort to find a benefice for Hare see p. 605.

832. MARLBOROUGH *to* GODOLPHIN   [*23 June/4 July 1707*]

Source: Blenheim MSS. A1-37.
Printed: Coxe, ii. 266-8 (small omission).

Meldert July 4th 1707

Since my last[1] I have had the favour of yours of the 13th, old stile,[2] with the enclosed letters of Mr. Methuen and Montandre. I agree with you that the alliance with Portugale should be maintained if possible; but by Mr. Methuin['s] letter I fear it will be very difficult. However, there aught to be care taken that the fault should not be on our side. I own to you that I am a good deal of the mind of Montandre, by which I am confermed in the opinion that the warr in Catalonia must be carryed on by troops from Italie, and not by the Queen's subject[s], by which you may save mony, and the Service be better done; and by that the King and his generall will naturally have the command, which is in [it]self very reasonable. I hear the court of Vienna has had a copie of my letter to Comte Piper,[3] and that thay dislike two expressions; the one where I mention the court of Vienna, and the other the Treaty of Italie. If I hear anything from them of it, I shal let them know the truth, that I meant the letter for their service. If thay take itt ill after that, it will not give me much trouble. I have received letters from Turin of the 15 of the last month,[4] by which I see thay will not begine their operations til about the 25. I shall not be att ease til I hear thay are in France, for the fear of the King of Sweden is so great at Vienna, that God knows what orders may go from thence. I send to Mr. Secretary a letter from the Elector of Hanover's minister at The Hague and my answer.[5] You will see by itt, that the Elector desires that Monsieur Bothmar's redgiment of dragons which is payed by the Queen and Holland[6] might go with him into Germany. It was by no means proper for me to give him the answere, but I should think if it serves with him in Garmany, it would be very unreasonable for the Queen and Holande to pay itt. I have write the same thing to the Pensioner,[7] but have desired him not to make use of my name. Besides, if we allow of this we may be sure, either this campagne or the next, he will press to have more of his troops.

I have had letters of the 22th of the last month from Vienna this morning,[8] by which I see thay have resolved to send Comte Wratislaw once more to the King of Sueden, and if possible to give him satisfaction. If thay

---

[1] Letter 829.   [2] Letters 823-4.   [3] See p. 795 n. 4.

[4] From Chetwynd, Blenheim MSS. A2-18.

[5] Bothmar to Marlborough, 17/28 June, copy in S.P. 87/2, fols. 686-7 and reply, 21 June/2 July, in Murray, iii. 451.

[6] For the regiment see p. 776 n. 3.

[7] 22 June/3 July, 't Hoff, pp. 323-4.

[8] From Wratislaw, 11/22 June, Blenheim MSS. A2-17; reply, Murray, iii. 453-4, and Zinzendorf, 11/22 June, Blenheim MSS. A2-17.

had done this sooner, it would have been better, but I am glad he goes. You will see by the enclosed letter what their opinion is as to our operations for the entering of France. That which I am pleased with is, that thay have left Prince Eugene at liberty in that matter, so that in a litle time we shal hear of the success we are to expect from thence.

I have this evening received your two letters from Windsor of the 15 and 16[1] of the last month. As to what you say concerning Neufechastel, I have said so much to the King of the possitive orders her Majesty has given to her Ministers, for their acting in whatever he shall think proper, that I am sure he is satisfied, so that you need apprehend no ill consequences by the death of the Dutchess of Nemeurs. The King of Prussia is so zealous for the entering of France, that he has already desired that some of his troops may take possession of the princepallity of Orang.

Though my letter is already to[o] long, yet I must answere your desire of knowing how long the enemy and wee may continu in our camps. I beleive with some difficulty we might stay in ours til the end of this month, but I have been some time endeavoring to persuaide our 171 [Deputies of the States] that I might take the camp of Genat. When I can prevaile you will hear of my being there. The reason of their backwardness is, that thay aprehend that might engage the two armys to some action, which thay are willing to avoyd til we hear some good news from Italie. You must have Lord Sunderland cypher[2] for 171.

The two inclosed letters I received by the last post. Mr. Tucker's[3] circumstances you know, and the doctor[4] is a good preacher. I did once speake to the Queen for him.

[1] Letters 825, 827.

[2] A reference to another cipher employed by Sunderland in his correspondence with Marlborough? 101 is the correct code for the deputies in this cipher.

[3] John Tucker, served in Secretaries of States' offices from William's reign; undersecretary to Hedges 1702; stayed in northern office under Harley 1704; but soon transferred to southern office as first clerk under Hedges because he could not get along with Harley. Dismissed in 1706 when Sunderland took office. Succeeded Sir Joseph Williamson as Keeper of the State Papers, an adjunct of the Secretaries' office, in 1701. In his letter of 13 June (Blenheim MSS. A1-37), he reminded Marlborough that during the previous winter when he 'lay under the affliction of a long and expensive fitt of sicknesse and the losse of my place in the Secretary's office' Marlborough and Godolphin had promised to provide for him. Tucker requests they do so now. See reply, 23 June/4 July, in Murray, iii. 457.

[4] James Smallwood, chaplain to the First Regiment of Foot Guards of which Marlborough was colonel. He wrote 13 June (Blenheim MSS. A1-37), asking for one 'of those vacancies which will now be made by the promotions to those bishopricks lately vacant', having waited a long time (fifteen years as a regimental chaplain) for preferment. Smallwood was the author of the first Blenheim panegyric. See the article by R. D. Horn, *H.L.Q.*, 24 (1961), 297–310.

833. MARLBOROUGH *to the* DUCHESS   [*23 June/4 July 1707*]

Source: Blenheim MSS. E3.
Printed: Coxe, ii. 266 (inc.); *Private Correspondence*, i. 102–3 (inc.).

Meldert Jully 4th 1707

By yours of the 13 I find 162 [Archbishop of York][1] is gone into the country in great delight, which I am very sorry for, for it is most certaine that whatever pleases him can't be for the service of 42 [the Queen]. If I were ever capable of giving advise, it would be a rashness to do it at this distance, but I beleive nothing can cure this matter, if I guess right, but Mr. Mongomerie's [Godolphin] giving himself the trouble of writting very plainly what he thinkes is wrong, and send it to 42 [the Queen] without offering to quit, or expecting any answere but as in duty bound to leave it to her consideration. I should hope this would do itt, but if it should not the last and only thing must be that 207 [Harcourt][2] speak very freely to 199 [Harley].

What 240 [Lady Marlborough] says concerning 239 [the Queen] giving 82 [money] depends upon what the gold may be for. Play and charity may take up a great deal.[3] If it be not to[o] late I could wish the Queen would take no notice of what Lady Bridgwater[4] has done, though she is certainly in the wrong; but thay are honest people and a young man must not be ruined for a parent's indiscretion.[5] I am obliged to you for your kind expression concerning Woodstock. It is certainly a pleasure to me when I hear the worke goes on, for it is there I must be happy with you. The greatest pleasure I have when I am alone is the thinking of this, and flattering myself that wee may then so live, as neither to anger God or man, if the latter be reasonable; but if thay are otherways I shall not much care if you are pleased, and that I do my duty to God, for ambition and business is what after this warr shall be abandoned by mee.

I have had this evening the happyness of yours of 16 and 17th of the last month. If I had received them one hour sooner itt might have spared part of this letter, but I must now add to that subject that I hope the Queen will be

---

[1] The Duchess has written in 'B of York' over the cipher and Coxe adopted her identification of 162 as Sharp. This is likely as the affair of the Bishops was the key issue at this time and going against the Whigs. 160 and 161 are ciphers used to represent the *Church* and the *Bishops* respectively. Sharp's satisfaction was the result of the Queen's assurance that she would fulfil her promise to elevate Dawes and Blackall, Sharp's candidates, to the vacant bishoprics. See G. V. R. Bennett, 'Robert Harley, the Godolphin Ministry, and the Bishoprics Crisis of 1707', *E.H.R.*, 82 (1967), 736–40.

[2] Coxe identifies 207 as the *Solicitor-General*. He must mean Sir Simon Harcourt, who was advanced to be Attorney-General in April. Harcourt served on several occasions as a political intermediary for the Duumvirs and Harley.

[3] On 11 June the Queen took 2,000 guineas from the Privy Purse. Receipt in Blenheim MSS. E18.

[4] The dowager Countess, mother-in-law of the Marlboroughs' daughter, Elizabeth.

[5] The 'indiscretion' may have involved her younger son, John Egerton, who seems to have been replaced as a page to the Queen at this time.

pleased to promis Mr. Edgerton[1] the first vacant Guidon's place. As to what 6 [Sunderland] says concerning 44 [King Charles], that nobody will please that dose their duty, I am of his mind, and I have also as good an opinion of 2 [Galway] as anybody can have; but that is no argument for 2 [Galway's] stay, for as it is, it will be impossible for those two to serve togeither. But as I am resolved to medle as litle as possible, pray say nothing of this.

834. GODOLPHIN *to* MARLBOROUGH   [*24 June 1707*]

Source: Blenheim MSS. A2-23.
Printed: Coxe, ii. 269-70 (inc.).

Windsor June 24th 1707

I have the favour of yours of the 30th[2] with my Lord Peterborow's letters enclosed to you and to myself. By his former letters I thought hee would have been with you by this time, but I suppose he will keep at a distance till near the Parliament's meeting. You know my opinion always was that he were better anywhere than here, and so it is still.

Monsieur Vryberghen has sent mee a coppy of a letter the States have written to you[3] about pressing the Emperour to accomodate with the Hungarians. I think ther's no doubt but the Queen will readily joyn with them in any instances of that kind which they shall think fitt to make; though I don't know how she can make them more pressing than she did to stop the troops from going to Naples, without effect. However they may bee willing to show more complyance in the affair of Hungary at this time, when the King of Sweden alarms them so much. But the same reason will goe near to make the malecontents impractionbles, and sett them atop of the house.

I am sorry to find you have your doubts in the affair of 115 [Toulon]. I confess I have had mine a good while, and the more because I see them upon all occasions soe pressing for money beforehand. But I know no remedie. They were not to bee refused, and wee must trust them. If wee are deceived, upon that and many other accounts 38 [Godolphin] is like to pass his time but indifferently next winter; especially since 42's [the Queen] proceedings

---

[1] William Egerton? Marlborough had been importuned for several years to find employments for his son-in-law's brothers. On 12/23 May 1703 he promised Bridgewater that if he sent his brother to the army, 'when he is here you may be assured I shal endeavour to make itt as easy to him as I can' (Ellesmere MS. 9989, Huntington Library). Marlborough must have meant William (not John), who obtained a captain's commission in 1704. As he was already provided for he probably refers in this present letter to John. However, there is no record of his having ever obtained an army post. One son served with distinction at Malplaquet. Marlborough to Lady Bridgewater, 26 Sept./7 Oct. 1709, Murray, iv. 619.

[2] Letter 829.

[3] 19/30 June, in Murray, iii. 460 with reply, 25 June/6 July. See Marlborough's letter to Harley, 14/25 July, Murray, iii. 480.

in some things[1] will give 89 [the Whigs] a handle to bee uneasy and to tear everything in pieces if they can't have their own terms, and 208 [Harley] does so hate and fear 5 [Somers], 6 [Sunderland] and 7 [Wharton] that he omitts no occasion of filling 42's [the Queen] head with their projects and designs; and if Mr. Montgomery [Godolphin] should take him with him upon any occasion of that kind, he would either say nothing or argue against what the other says as he did upon some subjects, some months since when Mr. Freeman [Marlborough] himself was present.

Monsieur Schults tells us the Elector of Hannover will accept the command upon the Rhyne, upon some conditions. But unless he does it quickly, t'wont bee of much use this year, though I am perswaded the appearance of the Duke of Savoy's motions will oblige Marshall de Villars to make great detachments from that army, that will operate upon their army in Flanders. I can't take upon mee to say, but I fear they will not bee under any necessity of weakening that army.

Lady Marlborough went to Woodstock very early this morning.

Since I had written this farr I have seen 239 [the Queen] who desired mee to tell you that she would write to you in a post or 2 as soon as her hand was a little stronger.[2] I suppose the occasion of her letter will bee upon 38's [Godolphin] having read to her some expressions in your letter of the 27th,[3] which she calls spleenatick. However, I think this use may bee made of it to say in your answer, what you think proper, upon the state of your affaires.

835. MARLBOROUGH *to* GODOLPHIN [*26 June/7 July 1707*]

Source: Blenheim MSS. A1-37.

Meldert Jully 7th 1707

Yours of the 20th from Windsor[4] I had yesterday, and am sorry to see by that, as well as by most of your other letters, the uneasiness you have in your home affaires. Heithertoo these abroad has given you no ease. Itt is to be hoped the operations on the side of Italie may succed, which must give a good turn. But should that fail, I am afraid it will make us here more cautious, if possible, the consequences of which would be the passing this campagne without doing any service. Having desired Lord Sunderland to show you my letter,[5] I shall not repeat what I have write concerning the letter from the States, which I send by this post to Mr. Secretary Harley,[6] and beg I may not receive her Majesty's commands til you have seen

---

[1] The appointment of new bishops.
[2] The Queen wrote 26 June (untraced). For Marlborough's reply see letter 845A.
[3] Letter 828.
[4] Letter 831.
[5] 26 June/7 July, in Coxe, ii. 268-9.
[6] See p. 839 n. 2.

my letter, for I am very aprehensive itt might be very unseasonable at this
time to do what is desired. I have as yett no answer from Comte Piper,[1]
which I think must proceed from their not having taken possative measures,
nor do I hear as yett of any answer sent to the Queen's.[2] A trompet from
the French army is now in my chamber, who says that thay had news last
night that Prince Eugene has passed the montagns.[3] If thay did not begine
to march before the 25th as my letters from Italy mention, then as to point
of time, this news is hardly possible, but I would willingly beleive it. By my
next you may know the truth. If the Service dose not suffer in leaving the
government of Tinmouth vacant til towardes the end of the campagne,
I should be glad of it, so that a good officer might be fo[u]nd for itt. But if
her Majesty would have it disposed off sooner you will be pleased to lett
me know itt.[4] Mr. St. Johns has write to me about the filling the vacancys in
the redgiments of the army in Spain. I hope neither the Queen nor Lord
Gallway will dispose of no commission til she has that whole matter laid
before her. I am sure a great deal of mony may bee saved upon that establishment if you take time to consider, and leave no more redgiments in Spain
but such as you have soldiers to complet.

836. MARLBOROUGH *to* GODOLPHIN   [*26 June/7 July 1707*]

Source: Blenheim MSS. A1-37.
Addressed: For the Right Honourable the Lord Godolphin, Lord Hie Treasurer of England,
    Whitehall.

Meldert Jully 7th 1707

Lieutenant Generall Hompech and several others haveing desired me to
recomend this bearer, I hope may excuse me for giving you this trouble.
His name is Powell. He was one of the late King's huntsmen and thay say
a very honest fellow. I beleive a very litle place would please him, for he is in
great want.

837. MARLBOROUGH *to the* DUCHESS   [*26 June/7 July 1707*]

Source: Blenheim MSS. E3.
Printed: *Private Correspondence*, i. 103-4 (inc.), with part of letter of 4 July.

Meldert Jully 7th 1707

I have had the pleasure of yours of the 20th from Windsor. My last letter[5]
is an answer to what you say as to Mr. Edgerton, and I am much obliged to
you for the pains you have taken with 254 [Mrs. Godfrey]. I beleive you

---

[1] See pp. 795, 838.   [2] To the King of Sweden. See pp. 798, 802.
[3] A false report. See p. 836.   [4] For the appointment made see p. 594 n. 4.
[5] Letter 833.

guess right as to the difficultys she makes, for her husband is selfish and very unreasonable. I do intend to begine the next weeke to drink the spaa watters for a fortnight. I remember thay did me good two yeares agoe. As wee see by the letters from Paris, that thay groe uneasy at what may be done by the Duke of Savoye and Prince Eugene, wee grow very impatient of hearing how farr thay are advanced. My last letters from Turin said thay should begine their operations on the 25th of the last month, so that by this time wee hope thay may be in France. I pray God we may quickly hear itt, and that thay may succed in the project, which is the best thing that can happen for England. The enemy and we are in our old camps, and I beleive are likely to stay for a fortnight longer, by which time we shall be sure of having an account of what the Duke of Savoye and Prince Eugene can be able to do, which will very much govern our motions here. My heart is with you.

838. GODOLPHIN *to* MARLBOROUGH　　　　[*27 June 1707*]

Source: Blenheim MSS. A2-23.
Printed: Coxe, ii. 271-2 (inc.).

Windsor 27 June 1707

Not having any letters from you since my last,[1] nor from Lisbon, this serves chiefly to cover the enclosed from the Queen.[2]

My next will bee from London, her Majesty going thither for 2 days in the beginning of the week to accompany the Prince who is to qualifie himself, as well as myself for renewing our offices of Admirall and Treasurer of Great Brittain.

This will necessitate some other renewalls as in the Prince's Counsell, and the officers of the Exchecquer, which may occasion brangles and disputes next winter,[3] of which there will bee no need, for I never saw more preparation for uneasiness in my life.

42 [the Queen] has indulged his own inclination in the choyce of some persons to succeed 161 [the Bishops] and which give the greatest offence to 89 [the Whigs] that can bee; and though 89 [the Whigs] was from other things in a disposition to lay more weight upon it, than in truth, the thing in itself ought to bear, yett it must bee allowed, taking all circumstances together, to bee a very great contretemps; and indeed Mr. Montgomery [Godolphin] is particularly sensible of the load it gives him. But at the same time he sees

---

[1] Letter 834.
[2] The Queen's letter (lost) must have been dated the 26th. See p. 831 for its genesis and letter 845A for Marlborough's reply.
[3] Enlarging these offices by the inclusion of Scotland could be looked upon as the creation of new offices, thus disqualifying subordinate officers from sitting in the Commons, under the place clause of the Regency Act. See Godolphin to Harley, 19 June, H.M.C., *Bath MSS.*, i. 175.

plainly that 42 [the Queen] has gone so farr in this matter (even against his warning) as really to bee no more able, than willing to retract this wrong stepp.[1]

One of the measures which I hear is layd down by 89 [the Whigs] is to disturb 182 [George Churchill] as soon as ever they have an opportunity. 182 is sensible of this, and seemed to have thoughts of preventing anything of this nature by not *renewing*[2] upon the occasion I hinted before. He spoke of it to mee, and though I am of opinion it would bee right for himself and everybody else, I entered no farther into it, than to say, that was an affair in which I thought nobody could advise so well as one's self.[3]

I am sorry to have nothing but such disagreeable subjects to entertain you with. Lady Marlborough is at Woodstock, but I hope she will bee here again next week.

The Comte de Briançon told mee yesterday that the governor of Bavaria[4] had stopped the Palatin recruits, going thru that country as having need of them there. This is new matter of complaint, and ought to bee rectifyed imediatly.

I hope the Elector of Hannover has at last accepted the command. Though it bee of the latest for this year, it may have a good effect, if wee expect to see another.

839. MARLBOROUGH *to* GODOLPHIN   [*27 June/8 July 1707*]

Source: Marlborough's letterbooks, Blenheim Palace.
Printed: Murray, iii. 465.

camp at Meldert, 8th July 1707

Having received this morning the enclosed letter[5] from the Landgrave of Hesse Darmstadt by the late Prince's secretary,[6] who is going to England to solicit, on behalf of the Landgrave, some pretensions of his late master's,

---

[1] For the affair of the Bishops see G. V. Bennett, 'Robert Harley, the Godolphin Ministry, and the Bishoprics Crisis of 1707', *E.H.R.*, 82 (1967), 726–46.

[2] His office as a member of the Prince's Council.

[3] For the problem created by Churchill, and the rumours of his impending resignation, see Churchill, ii. 296–9.

[4] Maximilian Karl, Prince Löwenstein (1656–1718), Imperial diplomat, Governor of Bavaria since its conquest in 1704.

[5] 12/23 June, untraced, and reply, 27 June/8 July, Murray, iii. 465.

[6] Peter Skinner. Sometime after this letter was written Marlborough sent a note by Cardonnel which must have been enclosed in one of his own letters to Godolphin. Now separated from that letter which it originally accompanied (it is in Blenheim MSS. A1-14), it reads: 'Since I had writ a letter to you in favour of Peter Skinner, who served the Lord Prince of Hesse as his secretary at Gibralter and in Catalonia, I have heard so ill a character of him, that I desire no regard may be given to my recommendation in his behalf.'

I could not refuse giving him this letter. Your Lordship must be much better apprised of the justice of what he claims than I can pretend to be. All I have told him is that he must produce very good vouchers before he can expect that any notice should be taken of his demands.

840. GODOLPHIN *to* MARLBOROUGH   [*30 June 1707*]

Source: Blenheim MSS. A2-23.
Printed: Coxe, ii. 272-3 (inc.).

Windsor June 30th 1707

There being now 2 posts wanting from you, and no other forreign letters since my last,[1] in which was one inclosed from the Queen and therfore I shall only trouble you now with what relates to 108 [England] that bee[ing] a very disagreable subject.

By all the conversation I have had since my last I have a good deal of reason to bee confirmed in the great uneasyness of 89 [the Whigs] and also of the occasions as well as of the consequences of it. And though I know 38 [Godolphin] will not neglect anything that is possible to prevent the inconveniences that threaten, yett the difficultys hee meets with, are such, and particularly in the unwillingness of 239 [the Queen] to doe anything that is good and necessary for Mrs. Morley [the Queen], that unless he may hope for Mr. Freeman's [Marlborough] assistance even before the winter, there must bee the greatest confusion imaginable in all the affairs of 88 [Parliament].

I hear 28 [Shrewsbury] is at present with 251 [Lady Westmorland][2] and I suppose whatever bee the pretext the true intent of that visit is to make advances to 89 [the Whigs]. I have not seen him yett but am going this day to London from whence I may perhaps trouble you with some farther account of it.

July 1st

Our forreign letters are still wanting, but those from Lisbon very secure. I have seen an officer who came the 1st of June from Barcelona. He says they were not in much fear of Lerida, or Tortosa, because [the French] had no battering guns nearer than Murcia. He says also, that Cavalier had made his escape and was come to Barcelona though he had been much wounded.[3]

---

[1] Letter 838.

[2] Dorothy, Countess dowager of Westmorland (died 1740), Shrewsbury's aunt. See p. 873 n. 2.

[3] Jean Cavalier, the Camisard leader.

I cannot refuse to send you the enclosed letter from my Lord Dunmore[1] in favour of his son.[2] You will judge best whether there is anything fitt to bee done in his favour when an opportunity offers.

841. MARLBOROUGH *to* GODOLPHIN [*30 June/11 July 1707*]

Source: Blenheim MSS. A1-37.
Printed: Coxe, ii. 270 (inc.).

Meldert Jully 11th 1707

I had the favour of yours of the 24[3] of the last month this morning. As to the letter[4] sent you by Monsieur Vriberg, I write my opinion of it by the last,[5] but shal govern myself in whatever her Majesty shal command. But if the enclosed paper[6] be treu, the obstenacy will not be on the side of the Emperor, but that of the malcontents. If the King of Sueden is resolved to continue in Garmany, that must be of so fatal a consequence to the Allyes, that we must find some way of getting him to speak plainer then he has done. I send you inclosed a draught of a letter, which I would be glad to have in my power to send him, when I shall see a proper time, if the Queen approves of itt. I earnestly beg that you will advise and consider very well this letter, and leave out, or add what may be omitted. As nobody but Cardonel, who has put it into French, knows of itt, so I would be desirous that nobody in Hollande should know of itt but the Pensioner, and that if he should desire an addition that I might have the Queen's leave to alow of itt.[7]

Since you think itt will be of no use to take 208 [Harley] with you to 42 [the Queen], you must find some way of speaking plainly to him; for if he continues in doing ill offices upon all occasions to 5 [Somers], 6 [Sunderland], and 7 [Halifax], it will at last have soe much effect upon 239 [the Queen], whoes inclinations are already that way, it must occasion that no measures will be followed. If Mrs. Morley [the Queen] writs to me, I shal be sure to send you a copie of my answer.[8]

If the Duke of Savoye had marched the 25th, we must by this time have something of itt from France, for what the trompett told us from the French army proves false.[9] Mr. St. Johns writes about Wroth's being declared a brigadier.[10] I beg neither he nor anybody else may be declared til the premotion[11] be made here, which I would defer for some litle time.

---

[1] Lord Charles Murray, first Earl of Dunmore (1660–1710), son of first Marquis of Atholl; created Earl of Dunmore 1686; Privy Councillor 1703; Examiner of Public Accounts 1704; supporter of Union; governor and captain of the Company in Blackness Castle 1709.

[2] John, second Earl of Dunmore (1685–1752), styled Viscount Fincastle 1704–10 after the death of his elder brother; captain 1705; colonel, succeeded to earldom 1710; Third Foot Guards 1713. See below for repeated applications on his behalf.

[3] Letter 834. [4] From the States General to Marlborough concerning Hungary.
[5] Letter 835. [6] Untraced. [7] It was not sent. See p. 849.
[8] See letter 845A. [9] See p. 832. [10] See p. 799.
[11] For the promotion of general officers made this year see p. 796.

The French prisoners have all write as if thay were dyeing, but I have refused them, so that I hope the Queen will not give it to Blanzac,[1] nor any of the others, for thay have been long enough, and the others aught to have their turns.

You have so much business that I am afraid you have forgott to setle with Mr. Bridges the allowance out of the poundage which I desired for Mr. St. Johns. I beg the favour of your doing itt.[2]

842. MARLBOROUGH *to the* DUCHESS   [*30 June/11 July 1707*]

Source: Blenheim MSS. E3.
Printed: Coxe, i. 270–1 (inc.).

Meldert Jully 11th 1707

As I beleive I shall stay in this camp the greatest part of this month, and if we can find forage longer, I shall make use of this time in begining to take the watters of Spaa next Wensday;[3] and as I am obliged to be abroad every day, I shall content myself with one botle. I wish you could take them with me, for besides the satisfaction I should have, I am very confident thay are better here then thay can be in England. I cannot expresse to you the joye I have when your letters are kind, as that of the 23 of the last month was. I received it last night, and as I find you intend to return from Woodstock in a weeke, I shall be impatient to hear you aprove of what has been done. Your expression of the ice house, that it can't be of use this three years, is a very mallincolly prospect to mee who am turned on the ill side [of] fivty seven. I am very sorry that you think you have reason to beleive that 199 [Harley] takes all occasion of doing hurt to 108 [England]. If 38 [Godolphin] can't find a remidy, and that before the next winter, I should think his wisest and honestest way should be to tel 42 [the Queen] very plainly which way he thinks 239 [the Queen] business may be carryed on; and if that be not agreable that she would lose no time in knowing of 199 [Harley] what his scheem is, and follow that, so that 38 [Godolphin] might not be answerable for what might happen. If this were said plainly to 42 [the Queen] and 199 [Harley] I am very confident the latter would not dare undertake the business, and then everything might go quietly. Mr. Mongomery [Godolphin] writs me word[4] that upon reading some part of my letter of the 27 of the last month to Mrs. Morley [the Queen], she thought what I said proceded from the spleen.

---

[1] Marquis de Blansac, taken prisoner at Blenheim. For French demands regarding the exchange and parole of prisoners see Harley to Marlborough, 20 June, with enclosures, including a letter from Chamillard to d'Alègre, in Blenheim MSS. A2–24; Marlborough to Harley, 26 June, 7 July, 3/14 July, in Murray, iii. 461–2, 469–70, and to Chamillard, 28 June/9 July, iii. 466.

[2] The Duke won this augmentation of St. John's salary for him to relieve him of his financial distress. See p. 840.

[3] 2/13 July.   [4] See p. 831.

But if I may be beleived my resolution is taken, though at the same time if I could see that my life could do her any good, I would venture it a thousand tims for her Service. But when a peace is made I can't but think it very reasonable for me to dispose of the litle time I may have to live. I am glad that Lady Portland has lett you know the temper of the people in Hollande. It is certainly trew what she writes, but it is as certainly treu, that thay will repent it next winter. Whatever happens my heart is intierly yours.

843. MARLBOROUGH *to* GODOLPHIN   [3/14 *July 1707*]

Source: Blenheim MSS. A1-37.

Meldert Jully 14th 1707

Having been abroad all day, I shall not answer yours of the 27th from Windsor,[1] til Saturday[2] by Brigadier MaChartney. I send you inclosed a copie of my letter from Comte Piper.[3] The answer to the Queen's which came to me at the same time I do not like.[4] I have also sent a copie to Mr. Secretary Harley, so that those that saw my letter to him[5] may see the answer. The Comte Wratislaw has sent me a copie of his long letter to you of the 2d of this month.[6] If thay succed in the designe against 115 [Toulon] all aught to be well; but if it miscarys, where ere the fault is, we must never forgett it, nor ever [h]earafter expect success on that side. Wee have the letters of the 10th from Paris, but thay say nothing of the Duke of Savoy's army, nor do wee hear by any other way of his having begone his march. Tomorrow wee shall have the Garmain and Italien letters. If thay do not give us an account of his being marched, I shal be very uneasy.

[1] Letter 838.   [2] 5/16 July. See letter 845.
[3] 15/26 June, in Murray, iii. 464; reply, 26 June/7 July, ibid. Piper acknowledged Marlborough's (see below) and repeated that the bases for the discontents with the Emperor were greater now that he had permitted Russian troops in Saxony free passage through the Empire back to Poland in violation of the Altranstädt Treaty by which they were to be surrendered to Charles XII. The King of Sweden was obliged to appeal to the Estates of the Empire and would remain in Saxony until he received satisfaction. For the Russian troops see Hatton, p. 222.
[4] The Queen's letter of 30 May encouraged the King of Sweden to reach an accommodation with the Emperor, the Maritime Powers offering to mediate on the issue of the Muscovite troops. Charles XII's reply, 15/25 June, Blenheim MSS. A2-20, dwells on the repeated refusals of the Emperor to grant him satisfaction and is not conciliatory in tone.
[5] 26 May/6 June, in Murray, iii. 393-4. Marlborough had told Piper not to let the King's troubles with Vienna break out into hostilities as that would only aid France and injure the Protestant cause. He promised the good services of the Queen to reach an agreement.
[6] Blenheim MSS. A2-17, enclosed in one of the same date to Marlborough, Coxe, ii. 235-6. It concerns succours for Spain.

844. GODOLPHIN *to* MARLBOROUGH   [*6 July 1707*]

Source: Blenheim MSS. A2-23.

Windsor July 6, 1707

Yesterday I had the satisfaction of receiving 3 letters at once from you, of the 4th, 7th and 11th of July,[1] with the severall papers enclosed in them.

I am glad to find Comte Wratislaus so firm of opinion that the court of Vienna will not send any more cross orders to Prince Eugene, but I doubt his positiveness in that, may proceed from a presumption of better success with the King of Sweden, than he seems likely to have. For the declining to accept the Queen's mediation betwixt him and the Emperour, does not give us a very favorable impression of that prince's intentions; for which reason I have thought it necessary to take the more precaution in giving you my thoughts upon the draught of the letter which you sent mee, from yourself to his Majesty.

I have had opportunity here of advising and considering upon it, with 4 [Halifax] and 6 [Sunderland] and wee have all agreed in opinion, that with the alterations wee have proposed to the *draught*, which you will find in the margin of that paper, it may have a good effect, and not bee liable to any ill construction from anybody. But wee think it a very nice and hazardous thing to give him any handle to offer his mediation without tying him down, first, to the preliminarys agreed betwixt England and Holland, which in case he shall approve, it will bee an engaging him in some measure, on our side, and in case he shall dislike them, it will lett the Allyes see more clearly, what they are to expect from him.

It will therfore bee necessary to send a coppy of those preliminarys with this letter (if you think fitt to write it as now altered) and as to the Queen's leave for making any alteration in the letter that shall bee proposed by the Pensioner, in case it be a very materiall alteration, differing from our sense of these preliminaryes, it may bee, in that case reasonable enough to propose the alteration itself to the Queen's consideration before you send your letter; otherways to take your own time of sending it.

Mr. Secretary Harley will send you her Majesty's resolution, upon the letter you have received from the States.[2] The posture of the King of Sweden in the Empire at this time gives us a handle to turn the representation to the Emperour, (in which they desire the Queen's concurrence) to an

---

[1] Letters 832, 835, 841.

[2] 27 June/8 July, Blenheim MSS. A2-24. In his acknowledgement of Harley's letter Marlborough wrote: 'I have received the favour of yours of the 9th instant, in answer to the States-General's letter to me, proposing the Queen's joining with them in making one effort more to persuade the Emperor to a peace with the Hungarians, wherein her Majesty seems rather inclined to offer them the alternative to press his making peace either with the Swedes or the Hungarians.' As the problem with the Swedes was in the process of accommodation Marlborough thought the Dutch would not feel it appropriate to intervene, for the Hungarians had withdrawn from all relations with the Emperor. Marlborough would make no answer until he received further guidance from The Hague. (14/25 July, Murray, iii. 480.)

alternative, and to lett his Imperiall Majesty see the absolute necessity of making an imediate accomodation either with the King of Sweden, or with the Hungarians.

The letters by these posts, both from France and Italy, make mee pretty sanguine upon the affair of Tholon, and I can't but hope wee shall soon hear of a good progress towards that matter.

The Comte de Gallas also tells mee the court of Vienna agrees to send any part of the Imperiall troops at Naples to the relief of King Charles, as soon as that kingdom shall bee reduced to his obedience.

The government of Tinmouth may easily remain as it is, till your return. And as to what you write in favour of Mr. St. Johns, I thought it had been done, though I could never have consented to it, as it was at first proposed, to bee don privately, because that was both impossible, and in his case, very unreasonable. But he being contented to own it, and to have it above board, that main objection as removed, and your comands must bee the answer, to any other that shall arise.[1]

I think all that you say about the French prisoners is extreamly reasonable but I doubt 161 [the Bishops] will always bee of the same mind they are now,[2] whatever bee the success at Tholon.

My Lord Gallway writes by the way of Genoa, that the extremityes they were in for want of foot, after the great loss at Almansa had obliged him, by the opinion of all the generall officers to fill up their regiments as fast as they could with Spaniards and Catalans, and to keep up the muster rolls as full. Now this is directly contrary to your advice,[3] and the orders sent to him by the Queen in pursuance of it. I hope therfore he will change this as soon as he shall receive those orders though I am afraid it may have gon so farr already, as that wee shall neither save the money, nor yett have the service of any good troops for it.

The envoye of Portugall gave in a memoriall[4] last night to pray the Queen would bee particular, as to the succors she designs to send the King his master against autumn where they expect to bee much pressed there. Her Majesty has ordered a coppy of this memoriall to bee sent to Holland, that she may know the opinion of the States upon it, and how farr they will bee content to joyn in any further succors to bee sent thither.

The wind is so here, that I am in hopes to hear again from you before tomorrow night.

[1] See St. John's letter to Marlborough, 6 July 1708, and the Duchess's comment on his behaviour in *Private Correspondence*, ii. 277. In the same vein the Duchess wrote to Lady Evelyn, on 17 Oct. 1736: 'At this time [1707] and some time after poor Lord Godolphin would not believe anything to the prejudice of Mr. Harley who he had done everything for that he desired, and the Duke of Marlborough was much infatuated by Lord Bullingbrook. Lord Godolphin sometimes would snap me up notwithstanding his good breeding when I said anything against Mr. Harley.' Evelyn MS. 1896, Christ Church.

[2] A reference to the strength of the Tories among the clergy and their opposition to the war?

[3] In letter 835.   [4] 5/16 July, B.M., Portland Loan, 29/45Y, fols. 231–2.

845. MARLBOROUGH *to* GODOLPHIN   [7/18 July 1707]

Source: Blenheim MSS. A1-37.
Printed: Coxe, ii. 274-5 (inc.).

Meldert Jully 18th 1707

Having this safe opertunity by Brigadier Ma'chartney,[1] I shal write with more freedome then I darst do by the post. I am very sorry to tell you, but it is most certainly treu, that if 43 [King of France] would offer the same conditions he did the last winter, thay would be thought by 110 [Holland] sufficient for the begining of a treaty. But 43 [King of France] seems possativly resolved that 45 [Duke of Anjou] must have 112 [Spain] and the Indies. It is as certain that 110 [Holland] will never more this 80 [war] venture anything that may be decissive, being of opinion that 116 [the States] has already enough in their possesion for their security, and that 43 [King of France] will assist them in disposing of this possession as thay shal think best for their security; and you may be asured that every step thay make for the engageing of 42 [the Queen] in joyning with them, to show the world that 46 [Emperor] is in the wrong, is for no other end but to excuse themselves, when thay appear for 81 [peace]. I am extreamly afraid that the real intentions of 58 [Duke of Savoy] is not to employe what is on board the fleet for the reducing of 115 [Toulon] but of that of Monaco, Villafranch, or of any other that may be of ease to his own country; for it is certain thay have lost time, by which thay have given great advantage to the French. If the intention be really to attack 115 [Toulon], it must be the hand of God that hinders 43 [King of France] from making detachements for the security of that country, for our last letters which were of the fourtienth from Garmany assures us that the Mareshal de Villars is so farr from makeing detachements, he is disposing his magazins, so as to be able to act offensively the rest of this campagne. A fortnight's time will let us see this whole matter, so that in prudence I might be silent til then, but having this safe opertunity I could not forbear letting you have my feares. I pray God we may find them groundless, but if thay should be treu, we must expect no more good on that side.

The Queen's letter from the King of Sueden is very discoraging. However, I am persuaded he dose not make thesse wrong steps intending to favour France, so that I can see no inconveniency in my writting when you have corected it, such a sort of letter as I have sent you; for if we can engage him,

[1] George Maccartney (1660?–1730), colonel, Scots Regiment, 1703, which he took to Flanders; brigadier-general 1705; accompanied Rivers to Spain 1706; taken prisoner at Almanza and paroled 1707; major-general 1709; selected to lead expedition to Newfoundland 1708, but his appointment was revoked on the orders of the Queen, when his housekeeper accused him of rape; forced to sell his regiment; served as volunteer at Malplaquet; appointed colonel, Regiment of Foot, lieutenant-general 1710, acting engineer at siege of Douay; dismissed as partisan of Marlborough's 1711; second to Mohun at duel with the Duke of Hamilton and accused of murdering Duke 1712; fled to Holland; acquitted of murder 1716. *D.N.B.*

we may yett have a good peace.[1] As to 50 [Elector of Hanover], I think in the offer that has been made him, he acts more like a marchant, than a generous man, so that I am apt to think we shall gett very litle advantage by itt.[2]

When 182 [George Churchill] spoke to you about his reneuing, I could wish you had encoraged him in his resolution of being quiet, for it would be very disagreable to me to have him receave a mortification, for I can't be unconcerned in that matter.[3] After the contempt of 4 [Halifax] [in] not answering my letter,[4] [which] I meant with all the kindness imaginable, I shal not be surprised at the hard usidge any for whome I am concerned for shall meet with. I can't on this occasion hinder saying so much to you, whoes quiet I wish as much as my own; but I fear neither of us can have any til we are at Woodstock, so that I could wish some practicable scheem could be made by which her Majesty might be well served, and we both out of the ministry.

The enclosed is a copie of my letter to 42 [the Queen],[5] [which] I write by Machartney. If it gives you any ease, I am happy, but I own to you I am very disponding. I am afraid there is to[o] much conversation between 239 [the Queen] and 199 [Harley]. You on the place can best judge what may be proper to be done in itt, but methinkes one or both should be spoke too.

Collonel Britton[6] is here and I intend to keep him till wee hear what success the Duke of Savoye and Prince Eugene may have had. The enclosed from Comte Zinsendorff[7] I had this morning, by which you may see thay would do everything in their power if possible to satisfie the King of Sueden.

This copy by Marlborough, undated, survives in Blenheim MSS. B2-32. The Queen's letter of 26 [June] to which it refers is missing but may be identified by letters 834 and 838. The sense of Marlborough's argument is also expressed in his letter to the Duchess on 30 June/11 July (842).

[1] See pp. 836, 839.
[2] As a condition of accepting the command of the Imperial army on the Rhine, the Elector of Hanover desired 'that the regiment of dragoons [Bothmer's, for which see p. 776 n. 3] lately taken into the Queen's and the States' pay may join him and yet continue to receive the same pay as if they were serving here'. Marlborough opposed the request fearing 'they may in time demand the rest of the Elector's troops here on the same condition'. To Harley, 23 June/4 July, Murray, iii. 454-5.
[3] See p. 834.   [4] See pp. 741, 770.   [5] The following letter.
[6] William Breton (died 1714 or 1715), served in First Regiment of Foot Guards under William III; lieutenant-colonel of Howe's Regiment of Foot 1702; brevet colonel 1704; colonel, Regiment of Foot, which he took to Spain, 1705; at Almanza 1707; brigadier-general 1710; envoy to Prussia 1712-14 (Dalton, iii. 289 and Horn, p. 104). Breton was on his return to England (to raise troops to replace those lost at Almanza?).
[7] Untraced.

845A. MARLBOROUGH *to the* QUEEN   [*7/18 July 1707*]

I have had the honour of your Majesty's of the 26. of the last month, and wish I could with the hazard of my life, ease you of your spleen, and in gratetude for the many goodnesses you have had for mee and mine, I would venture anything to have the honour of being one hour with you; that I might be able to explaine my thoughts of your present posture of affaires, which can't be done by me in writting so fully as I could wish for your Service. I do agree that both partys have it to[o] much in their heads to governe; but without being of a party, I can't but make this observation, that the interest of the Wiggs obliges them to be more governed by you, then that of the Torrys, so that for your own case, and the good of your business, you should think of the properest measures of making them depend, and be governed by yourself, and those you trust for Madame it must end in betraying your quiet, whoever goes about to persuaide that you can be served at this time by the Torrys, considering the mallice of their chiefs, and the beheavior of the greatest part of the cleargy, besides the Nation is of opinion that if thay had the management of your affaires, thay would not carry this warr on with vigor, on which depends your happyness and the safety of our religion.

I would beg as a favour, if anybody near your person is of opinion that the Torrys may be trusted, and at this time made use off, that you would be pleased to order them to put their project in writting, and know if thay will charge themselves with the execution, then you will see their sincerity by excusing themselves, so that for your own sake and the good of England, come quickly to some resolution, for otherways you will put it out of the power of the honestest and best minister any prince ever had, I mean Lord Treasurer. I may say without flatterie that your Majesty has by God's blessing obtained a greater reputation, and power in foraigne courts then any of your predicessors ever had, the continuance is so absolutely necessary both for the good of our religion and your prosperity, I do earnestly beg, you will lose no time in taking such measures with Lord Treasurer as may make the next sessions of Parliament chearfully enable you for the carrying on of this warr, without which all must run to ruin; for the French are already so insolent upon the success thay have had, that thay talk of nothing but continuing the warr.

As I am resolved that nothing shal ever oblige me to keep any measures with either party, but as your Service shal requier itt, you will believe me when I assure you as I do, that I shall never make my court to any of them, nor be governed by any other principal then that of serving you, which I hope will incline you to excuse the liberty I take.

846. MARLBOROUGH *to the* DUCHESS   [*7/18 July 1707*]

Source: Blenheim MSS. E3.
Printed: Coxe, ii. 276 (inc.), as 11–22 July.

Meldert Jully 18th 1707

Since my last[1] I have not had the happyness of any from you, but by
tomorrow I hope to have the pleasure of receiving two of your dear letters
at once. I wish it may prove treu the good news we have of Forbin's[2] being
beaten in the North Seas by our fleet that is there.[3] We have no news from
Italie, and what wee have from Garmany is bad. Brigadier Machartney is
gone for England this afternoon. I have not write to you by him since you
will have this at the same time. Besides, I do not find my watters cures me
of my spleen. I have sent 38 [Godolphin] a copie of my letter to 42 [the
Queen],[4] though I owne to you that I am disponding as to the good it may do.
However, I have done my duty and God's will be done. By my letter you will
see that I have endeavored to [do] 89 [the Whigs] the best office I can,
but I shal think it a very ill return, if thay fall upon 182 [George Churchill].
I do with all my heart wish he would be so wise as to quite his place, but I
hope nobody that I have a concern for will apear against him. After the
usidge I had from 4 [Halifax], I am concerned but for very few. Therfore, if
there should be occasion, pray say as from yourself two wordes to 6
[Sunderland], for it would be very uneasy to me to have reason to take anything
ill of him, and it is impossible for me to be unconcerned in this matter.
I expect no more then what I would do if he had a brother attacked.[5] This
and many other things shoes there is no happyness but in retierment.

847. MARLBOROUGH *to the* DUCHESS   [*10/21 July 1707*]

Source: Blenheim MSS. E3.
Printed: Coxe, 275–6 (inc.).

Melbert Jully 21th 1707

I received yesterday yours of the 28th from Woodstock, as also that of the
30th and 3d from Windsor. My head is so full of things that are displeasing,
that I am at this time a very improper judge of what would be best for the
work at Woodstock, for really I begine to dispaire of having any quietness
there or anywhere else. What 240 [Lady Marlborough] says of Mr. Prior[6]

---

[1] Probably 3/14 July. Untraced.

[2] Claude, Count of Forbin (1663–1733), French admiral, commander of the Dunkirk squadron.

[3] On 30 June/11 July Forbin narrowly missed seizing ships of the Russian fleet because of a
sudden fog off Kildin Island on the Murman Coast. There was no engagement. On 5/16 July he
was more lucky, taking twelve stragglers near Kildin.

[4] The preceding letter.   [5] See pp. 834, 842.

[6] Matthew Prior (1664–1721), poet and diplomat; secretary to English envoys at The Hague
1690–7, and to plenipotentiaries at Ryswick 1697, and of embassy at Paris 1698–9; member of the

has given uneasiness to 39 [Marlborough], but when you shall know the reason why any consideration was had for him, you will rather pitty 210 [Marlborough] then reproch, but as I am sure he is taking his measurs so as to be out of the power of being sensured and troubled. However, he is to my knowledge resolved to be ill used for a litle time longer. I see by yours of the 30th that I am to be mortefied by the prosecusion of 182 [George Churchill]. I have deserved better from 89 [the Whigs], but since they are grown so indifferent as not to care what mortefications the court may receive this winter, I shal not expect favour. My greatest concern is for 42 [the Queen] and 38 [Godolphin], for 108 [England] will take care of itself, and not be ruined because a few men are not pleased. Thay will see their error when it is to[o] late. I should be glad you would lett me know the conversation that has been between 240 [Lady Marlborough] and 239 [the Queen], and if it were before or after the writting of the letter sent me by Mr. Mongomery [Godolphin], which I answered by Ma'charney [Maccartney]. The intier union you mention between 209 [Godolphin], 210 [Marlborough] and 240 [Lady Marlborough] for the good of 42 [the Queen] and 108 [England] (can there be a difficulty in that union?), but I will own to you that my apre-hensions are that somebody or other (I know not who) has gott so much creditt with 42 [the Queen] that thay will be able to persuade her to do more hurt to herself, then those three you mention can do good. Til I hear againe from you, I shal say no more on this subject.

I shal write about the hangings, and I hope there is time enough to make them of the hight you desire.[1] What you have said to Mr. Travers is very right.[2]

848. GODOLPHIN *to* MARLBOROUGH [*11 July 1707*]

Source: Blenheim MSS. A2-23.

Windsor July 11th 1707

This acknowledges the favour of yours of the 14th,[3] and as the winds have been, I am not in despair of the satisfaction of hearing from you again, before this post goes away. You tell mee you have seen a coppy of Comte Wratislau's letter to mee of the 2d. But you say little either to his excuses for what is past, or his proposalls for what's to come; and indeed all things relating to the latter, may reasonably enough bee suspended, till wee see the event at 115

Board of Trade 1700–7; removed 24 Apr. to make way for Whig nominees, whereupon Marl-borough arranged for him to have a pension of £400 a year. (The Duchess says £500. See her remarks on Prior in her letter to Sir David Hamilton, 3 Dec. 1710, Blenheim MSS. G1-8.) Harley returned him to office in 1711 and appointed him to negotiate a peace with France. *D.N.B.*

[1] See pp. 720, 750, 826.
[2] Probably about a deer for Dr. Watkins. See p. 825.   [3] Letter 843.

[Toulon] for according as that turns our measures must bee guided for the future. But in all events there, supposing the expedition to Naples succeeds, I am still of opinion those troops may bee the best spared, of any, for Spain; and I should think 4 or 5,000 foot would bee sufficient to act upon the defensive, which is all that can bee done there, in this year; and after the affair of 115 [Toulon] is over wee shall judg better what measures are proper to bee taken for the next.

Monsieur de Guiscard has sent mee the coppy of his letter to you of the $\frac{19}{8}$ th.[1] I don't think the latter part of it unreasonable, but I much doubt, the States will never consent to what he mentions of a detachment of foot from your army. Otherwise I incline enough to believe, all that side of France is rather weaker than it was last year because of their fears on the side of Provence.[2] Our last advices fill us with expectations of good news from thence. God send they may bee answered to our satisfaction.

The King of Sweden seems to bee relapsed into all the inclinations which he had before you went to him; and the house of Hanover beginning new to bee apprehensive of the ill effects of them, why might not that bee so impressed, as to gett them and the King of Prussia to joyn with Denmark, England and Holland to stopp his farther progress in the Empire!

I own this measure is pretty nice, and ought not to bee attempted while any hope remains of keeping him within bounds. But in case he continues to decline the mediation of the Queen and the States, and throws off the masque, I don't see what other remedy is left, but this, and even this, the longer its deferred, is like to grow more and more difficult every day.

849. GODOLPHIN *to* MARLBOROUGH [*13 July 1707*]

Source: Blenheim MSS. A2-23.
Printed: Coxe, ii. 283-5.

Windsor 13 July 1707

I am to acknowledg the favour of yours of the 18th[3] with Monsieur Zinzendorf's letter and the answer the Queen is to have from Vienna, concerning the transporting to Spain, some of the troops from Naples. I take the substance of that answer to bee that if Naples bee reduced, the

---

[1] There are letters of 1/12 and 18/29 July in Blenheim MSS. A2-25, but not one of this date.

[2] Guiscard revived his plan for a landing on the Gironde near Bordeaux. The ministry had prepared an expedition to carry out the plan in 1707 but changed the destination of the force when it was found necessary to send reinforcements to Spain (see p. 526 n. 2). Godolphin having already proposed a descent to Marlborough for this year (p. 776) picked up his idea enthusiastically (pp. 863, 874). Recommending Rochefort and Saintes on the Charente as the objectives (p. 882) he suggested first Ingoldsby (p. 874) and then Withers as possible commanders (p. 890). He was dissuaded by Marlborough, who sent similar advice from Heinsius (p. 880). The project was given up (p. 903) but Marlborough did support a descent for 1708 (pp. 900, 906) which was in fact implemented (see 1708 letters, *passim*).

[3] Letter 845.

Emperour will not only send, but maintain, them while they are in Spayn, and if not, he will still send them, if the Allyes will maintain them there. I wish either of those ways may bee taken, since it is now neither reasonable, nor hardly possible to send troops to Catalonia from hence; nor is Mr. Methuen of opinion, (as perhaps he may tell you himself in the enclosed),[1] that 'tis like to bee of much use to send any more troops to Portugall itself. He says nothing will prevail with them to enter Spayn again, and the most that can bee expected from those people is a frontier warr. This being the case, all that seems necessary for us is to support them, so as to keep them firm to our allyance, by which means wee shall continue to have the convenience of their ports which wee cannot well bee without, while the warr against Spain subsists, and can bee supported by the Allyes which from Italy I hope it may bee, and cheaper than hitherto from hence.

All this shows the necessity of getting as many troops, as wee can, and as soon as wee can, from that side, for I am so farr from being of opinion with 110 [the States] that 43's [King of France] advantages in this year, ought to incline the Allyes to accept of his proposalls in the last, that to this moment, I think yett, 43 [King of France] is every day more and more pressed, and that if 110 [the States] will stand firm, they will yett find the effects of it before the end of the year. But in case they doe not, or will not see their own interest in this poynt, it is my humble opinion, (with submission to better judgments), that 42 [the Queen] must speak very plainly to them, and lett them see that if ever they make any step towards 43 [King of France] but with the participation and consent of 108 [England], they must expect the last resentment from 42 [the Queen] upon such a proceeding. This is at present, but my own privat opinion, upon what you have written in yours of the 18th, but as soon as I have an opportunity of doing it, I will send you the thoughts of our friends as well as my own, upon this subject, which I take to bee very nice, and of the greatest consequence.

In the meantime give mee leave to add from myself, that in case wee succeed at 115 [Toulon], I believe wee may have reason from 116 [the States], and in case wee shall stand more in need of it, than before, I submitt it therfore to your thoughts whether wee should not endeavour without loss of time, to make farther and stricter alliances with 47 [King of Prussia], 50 [Elector of Hanover] and the rest of 137 [the Allies] for going onn with 80 [war] and not hearing of 81 [peace] but by generall consent. The greatest obstruction I can foresee to this is 56 [King of Sweden] because of his antipathy to 46 [Emperor]. But if those differences were capable of being accomodated, and 56 [King of Sweden] satisfyed, that objection would not bee so strong. And wheras 39 [Marlborough] says, 116 [the States] is satisfyed with the possession of what they have now [with] the assistance of 43

---

[1] 30 May/10 June, Blenheim MSS. A2-29, with copies of letters of the same date to Godolphin and Sunderland.

[King of France] to secure them in that possession, I leave you to judg what 88 [Parliament] will say to that, and how they will bee persuaded either to goe onn with 80 [war] only for the advantage of 110 [Holland], or indeed to *submitt* to those advantages by the means of 81 [peace] without expressing the last resentment at the proceedings of 116 [the States].

I am glad Bretton is with you for severall reasons because he can give you a full account of all that has past in Spayn, and most exactly of all that relates to 30 [Peterborough] and his proceedings, which may bee of use to you, to bee informed of, before he comes to you.

Mr. Freeman's [Marlborough] letter to 42 [the Queen][1] was as right, and as full, as is possible, and was no more than is extreamly necessary and it will bee as necessary to continue in the same style upon all occasions both before and after 39's [Marlborough] return.

850. MARLBOROUGH *to* GODOLPHIN   [14/25 *July 1707*]

Source: Blenheim MSS. A1-37.
Printed: Coxe, ii. 278.

Meldert Jully 25th 1707

I have had the favour of yours of the 6th from Windsor,[2] but have not time to give an answer til the next post. The enclosed letter from Comte Wratis-law,[3] I received this morning. I must own I think it a more reasonable letter then I have seen from that court a great while. I shal not give any answer til I have yours, 4 [Halifax], 5 [Somers], and 6 [Sunderland] thoughts of what may be proper to answere. I hope tomorrow we may have the good news confermed of the Duke of Savoy's being in Provence. You will be [by] this post have an account in print of the reception of the Garmains at Naples.[4] Pray make my excuse to Lord Sunderland, that I can't answer his of the eight[5] by this post. I send Sir John Norris' letter[6] that you may see what he desires concerning the bils of exchange.

¹ Letter 845A.   ² Letter 844.
³ 2/13 July, in Coxe, ii. 278–80. Wratislaw doubts that the Duke of Savoy's army can stay in Provence after the campaign is over because of the danger of losing the army by a French counter-attack. The war in Spain should be treated only as a diversion rather than a principal theatre. Let the Portuguese do what they want with their own troops and allow Charles III enough troops to maintain his position and perhaps advance into Roussillon. If he does remain then he must be reinforced; if not the Allies must go on the defensive in Italy. Wratislaw favours keeping a fleet in the Mediterranean and preparing for a descent on the Atlantic coast of France. He says nothing about Germany or the Low Countries.
⁴ The Imperial army entered Naples on 6/17 July and was greeted with great demonstrations of joy and enthusiasm. The townspeople pulled down a statue of Philip V and mobbed the French-men remaining in the town. A band of Italian partisans helped the army drive out the remaining Bourbon troops in the countryside. See the account in *Compleat History for 1707*, pp. 275–8, which is based on contemporary newsletters and prints.   ⁵ See p. 849.
⁶ 20 June/1 July, Blenheim MSS. A2-18, to pay for the powder and shot Shovell had purchased 'according to the course of exchange for the support of his credit in those parts'. See p. 804 n. 2.

851. MARLBOROUGH *to the* DUCHESS [*14/25 July 1707*]

Source: Blenheim MSS. E3.
Printed: Coxe, i. 338 (inc.), as 27 July.

Meldert Jully 25th 1707

I have had the happyness of yours of the 6th from Windsor. I had write about the hangings, but have had no answer, but shall keep them to the first dementions, since you think that will be best. I should be glad that anything in my letters which you show to 42 [the Queen] might incline them to take such measurs as are wished by 38 [Godolphin]. I am a good deal surprised at what you write concerning 28 [Shrewsbury], for he is well bread, and has certainly a mind to be employed. His pride is capable of making him take wrong measurs, but as far as I can judge, I think his pride should have obliged him to have given a visset, and I can't but think he will yet do itt.[1]

I have had a letter from 6 [Sunderland] by which he lets me see the ill consequences that must happen if 42 [the Queen] can't be prevailled with in the affaires of 171 [the Church]. It is pretty hard to me to give him an honest answer, since it would lay to[o] great a weight upon 239 [the Queen]. If other things go well, that will be done as thay wish, but I am rather disparing then otherways. I have done what I can, and let what will happen I hope to have nothing to reproch myself, and then God's will be done.

Wee have no news from Italie, but what coms by the way of France, so that we are in doubt of the truth, but what we have is good. I have good reason to hope the differences between the Emperor and the King of Sueden will be accomidated. Wee must flatter ourselves with good news from other parts, for here we shal do nothing. I have been obliged to quit the watters, it being impossible to live so regularly as thay requier, so that at last thay did not pass at all, which made my head uneasy. Whielst I have life I am yours.

852. MARLBOROUGH *to* GODOLPHIN [*16/27 July 1707*]

Source: Blenheim MSS. A1-37.
Printed: Coxe, ii. 281-2.

Meldert Jully 27th 1707

Being obliged to be abroad almost the whole day of the last post, I could not answere yours of the 6th[2] as I aught.

You may be assured that I shal not send the letter to 56 [King of Sweden], but as corrected and approved by yourself and friends; but by what I have

---

[1] Shrewsbury had been visiting his aunt, Lady Westmorland, at Whitton, and had not used the opportunity to visit the court at Windsor. See p. 873.
[2] Letter 844.

from thence I am in hopes there will be no occasion of writting.[1] But if there should I beleive we must do it without acquainting 62 [Heinsius], for it is certaine that 110 [Holland] will never consent to have the prelimenarys sent, for I am afraid thay are of opinion thay will never be obtained from 43 [King of France]. However, I am of your opinion that 108 [England] must never depart from them.

You will see by my last letter to 199 [Harley][2] that I shal delay the answere to 116 [the States] letter, for by what is write from Vienna of the beheavior of the Hungariens, I think even 116 [the States] will be of opinion that this is not a proper time for the pressing 46 [Emperor].

You have done very well in sending the memorial of Portugale to Holland, for by it you will gaine time and at last you will be answered with the impossibillity of their helping, and their hopes of the Queen's generossity in helping the King of Portugale. Would it not be a good expedient to gaine more time, as soon as you have the States' answer to the memorial, to send 2 [Galway] to 129 [Portugal], by which you may amuse that court? For whatever expence you make in that country, I looke upon it as mony flung into the sea, for thay have neither officers nor good inclinations, but by this methode you may keep them in hopes til the next spring. I can't but think it extreamly for the Queen's Service, that you continue ferm in the resolution of paying no more redgiments in Catalonia then there may be English soldiers to complet. And whatever Spaniards or other foraigne troups England would be at the expence of, that aught to be by subsity and not regular pay; and theire aught to be care taken that the cloathing which are thereupon the account of privat redgiments, should not be given to other people, for that expence at last will fal upon the Queen.[3]

The copie of Wratislaw's letter, which I sent you by the last post,[4] agrees extreamly with the notion I have for the schem of the next campagne; for should 115 [Toulon] not be taken, the warr must be continued; but if that should succed I should then hope 111 [France] would be forced to give such conditions as 108 [England] should think reasonable. 210 [Marlborough] assures me he is so weary of all this matter, that nothing can make him happy but being in quiet at 122 [Woodstock].

I received last night the enclosed letters from Prince Eugene and Sir Cloudesley Shovell.[5] I am extreame glad to find thay have resolved to attack Toulon in the first place. If thay succed it will be the greatest misfortune [that] could have happened to France. The last two lins in Prince Eugen's letter should not be seen but to few. You must not be to[o] much allarmed at his expression, for it is his way to think everything difficult til he coms to put them in execution, but then he acts with so much vigor,

[1] See p. 836. [2] 14/25 July, in Murray, iii. 480.
[3] See p. 893. [4] Letter 850.
[5] 2/13 and 3 July, in Murray, iii. 483–5.

that he makes amends for all his disponding. Though he writs in this maner to me, I am sure to the officers of the army his discorse is the contrary. I would not stay for the post, but send this by Collonel Britton so that her Majesty might have this good news as soon as possible. With my humble duty, I beg you will assure her of my hearty congratulation and prayers that she may ever be happy.

853. MARLBOROUGH *to the* DUCHESS   [*16/27 July 1707*]

Source: Blenheim MSS. E3.
Addressed: For the Dutchesse of Marlborough.

Meldert Jully 27th 1707

I received last night an expresse from Prince Eugene, with the good news of their haveing entered Provence on the 13th of this month. I send a copie of his letter as also that of Sir Clowdsley Shovell to Lord Treasurer, by which you will see thay are resolved to march derectly to Toulon, and not besige Antibes.[1] If this succeds it will be the greatest blow that we could wish to France. I have received yours of the 9th with Vanbrook's letter to you.[2] If the wals he speakes off do not cost much, what he says of there being a time for them to dry is reasonable, but I leave it intierly to you to order what you think is best, and what pleases you I am sure I shal like.[3] I have write so much this day, that I must refer you to Lord Treasurer's letters.

854. GODOLPHIN *to* MARLBOROUGH   [*17 July 1707*]

Source: Blenheim MSS. A2-23.
Printed: Coxe, ii. 285-6 (inc.).

Windsor July 17, 1707

Since my last wee have no forreign letters. Two posts will bee due tomorrow, but wee can't expect them, as the winds have been here.

In the meantime I continue to hope for good news from Italy, being more perswaded in my mind, than you seem to bee, that they will act in earnest on that side; and indeed if they doe not, 'tis next to impossible for 137 [the Allies] to continue together as they are, this winter. But if the affair of 115 [Toulon] succeed, I should think wee are in a better way than ever to have reason from 43 [King of France]; and therfore, our chief concern at present ought, in my opinion, to bee what measures to take, and how to deal with 110 [Holland] in case the affair of 115 [Toulon] should not turn, as wee wish it. For by the picture which 39 [Marlborough] has lately made of them, (and which I must bee so just to 38 [Godolphin] as to say hee always suspected, and

---

[1] A coastal town 110 kilometres east of Toulon.   [2] Untraced.
[3] This refers to the foundations for the bridge. See p. 851 and Vanbrugh, *Works*, iv. 212-13.

expected), it seems to mee that no time ought to bee lost in 42's [the Queen] endeavouring to make use of the influence of 108 [England] to strengthen and augment 137 [the Allies], to receive as many into the fraternity, as can possibly bee procured, and that the foundation of the whole should bee never to admitt of 110's [Holland] inclinations to 81 [peace], but in generall to declare against 81 [peace], except as in the letter to 56 [King of Sweden] corrected and altered as it was sent back from hence.[1]

Perhaps it may bee thought and said, that this is visionary and impossible. But what will 88 [Parliament] say? [Neither] 88 [Parliament] nor 108 [England] won't lie down and die, because 116 [the States] find their account by 81 [peace]. But [I] rather incline to think, that soe strengthned as I have been wishing, they may gett the better both of 43's [King of France] and 116 [the States] together. And if 116 [the States] bee once convinced, as I think they ought to bee, (and perhaps the sooner the better), that 42 [the Queen] and 108 [England] are capable of coming to this resolution, I cannot help being of opinion, they will think more than once before they give them a just provocation to doe it.

The extream hott weather last week has given mee a great cold in my head and a deafness with it, which makes mee very uneasy to myself, and to every-body else, that I talk with. However I can write still, and no infirmity but the gout in my right hand will hinder mee from persecuting you with my letters.

855. MARLBOROUGH *to* GODOLPHIN   [17/28 July 1707]

Source: Blenheim MSS. A1-37.

Meldert Jully 28th 1707

Since mine of yesterday by Collonel Britton,[2] I have received none of yours, nor no farther news from France; but we hear from Franckfort that the Mareshal de Villars had detached 30 squadrons, and 24 battalions,[3] the truth of which we shal know by tomorrow's letters. But it is very probable, for we are assured that Monsieur de Vandome should have said publickly that the King could detache troupes enough from the Rhine and Roussillion to force the Duke of Savoye into his own country. The best we can wish for, is that thay would neither detache from the Rhin nor their army in this country. I have a great mind to send Brigadier Palmes to the Duke of Savoye and Prince Eugene, so that I may be exactly informed how thay hope to end this campagne, and what their thoughts may be as to the project for the next.[4] I intend he should stay with them til the siege of Toulon is finished, so

---

[1] Marlborough's lettert. See pp. 836, 839.   [2] Letter 852.
[3] On 21 July/1 Aug. Louis XIV ordered Villars to send six battalions of infantry and a regiment of dragoons to Provence (Vault, vii. 242).
[4] Their plans for the balance of this year's campaign and that of 1708 (p. 900).

that if he be with me by the midle of September I shal have time enough to acquaint you with the whole, and have your thoughts before I take any measures with the Emperial Court, or our friends in Holland. The weather is now as extravegantly cold, as we have had itt hott. The enclosed I received some time ago. I send it, that you may see what temper he is in. I think nobody but the Queen should see itt, and then you may burn itt.[1]

856. MARLBOROUGH *to the* DUCHESS   [*17/28 July 1707*]

Source: Blenheim MSS. E3.

Meldert Jully 28th 1707

I was in such a hurry yesterday when I write by Collonel Britton, that I could not answere yours of the 9th so fully as I should have done. As to the house and bridge, whatever you judge best, I shall be well pleased with. But if the stoneworke he proposes dose not excede 2,000 pounds, I should be glad it were done, for that work aught to have one hole yeare to drye before any weight is laid upon it. Besides til this be done it will be impossible to know what the foundation in that bottome will bare.[2] Notwithstanding what I say do what you like best, for by what Vanbrugh says in his letter[3] I am afraid my life will be to[o] short for the seeing the house finished. I would advise you to let him know that you can't with any quiet or satisfaction lye in the house til the two great rooms are finished. I mean the hall and sallon. Thay did make me hope the hall and sallon would be covered this yeare, but by his letter I see it is quit[e] otherways.

Since the Duke of Savoye has taken the resolution of going in the first place to Toulon, and not besieging Antibes, I hope the project in that country will succed. But if thay will stay there this winter thay must ventur a battaile for it, the King of France having detached from the army on the Rhin 30 squadrons and 24 battalions, that with what thay can draw from Roussilion[4] will make them strong enough, as the Duke of Vandome says, to hinder the Duke of Savoye from staying there in the winter. But if this entering of France should incorage their subjects to be mutinous, I believe Monsieur de Vandome will be obliged to send some troupes. Whatever he dose I am afraid we shall do litle on this side, for our friends will not ventur. I know not wether it proceeds from the watters I have taken, but I am so chile and cold, that I have att this time a fier in my chamber. I am with all my heart yours.

[1] Untraced.
[2] The foundation for the bridge is the subject of these remarks. See p. 851.
[3] 15 July, in Blenheim MSS. A2-31; reply, 24 July/4 Aug., Murray, iii. 500-1.
[4] The French province adjoining Spain on the Mediterranean.

857. GODOLPHIN *to* MARLBOROUGH   [*21 July 1707*]

Source: Blenheim MSS. A2-23.

Windsor 21 July 1707

The wind continuing contrary wee have now 3 posts due, so your trouble will bee short at this time, since I have nothing to add to my last letters[1] but that since I sent them, I find that 4 [Halifax], 5 [Somers] and 6 [Sunderland] are entirely of 38's [Godolphin] opinion, as to the measures which 108 [England] ought to take with 110 [Holland],[2] and that the sooner this is explained to them the better. They agree that this ought not to depend upon the event of 115 [Toulon], for a good success there will make the affair[3] less difficult, so disappointment will make it yett more necessary and consequently that wee ought to try it, in all events. There may bee some nicetys to bee observed in the method of doing this, but I forbear troubling you with any of my thoughts as to the method of doing it, till I have yours as to the thing itself.

The Parliament in Ireland has begun very well, and I hope they will give the necessary supplys, and make a short sessions.

The regiments designed to have been taken from thence, are in a readyness, but if wee can have none to joyn them from Holland, wee cannot add enough to them from hence to make them of use for any descent, that should recompence so extraordinary a charge. 'Tis too farr, to send them to Catalonia, and as for Portugall, 'tis plain by our last letters, and by all wee have had from thence since the battell of Almansa, they will never think of acting offensively against Spayn any more.[4] This being the case, to send horse and dragoons thither from Ireland, would bee to no purpose, besides that it is an extraordinary expense not provided for by the Parliament. So indeed is that of the 4 regiments of foot sent thither already,[5] but they arrived there so seasonably for their support, that I hope all well meaning people will approve of that stepp.

I have of late been much out of order in my health, which is another reason for not giving you any farther trouble, at this time.

---

[1] Letters 849, 854.

[2] To ensure the Dutch do not negotiate with France for a peace without 'the participation and consent of England' (p. 847).

[3] To draw the Allies into 'stricter alliances . . . for going onn with war and not hearing of peace but by general consent' (ibid.).

[4] The King of Spain was wholly dependent on the Maritime Powers, especially England, for support, and never more so than after the defeat at Almanza. Stanhope used this advantage to force Charles III to sign a commercial treaty with England (29 June/10 July 1707). It gave the English special trading rights both in Spain and the West Indies. A secret article provided for the establishment of an Anglo-Spanish trading company after the war which improved upon these privileges to the exclusion of the Dutch and the French. Though ratified on 9 Jan. 1708 it never became fully operative because of Charles III's tenuous hold on his kingdom. When it became known to the Dutch it evoked their angry protests. It was to be the inspiration for the concessions made by Spain to England at Utrecht which led to the founding of the South Sea Company. Geikie, pp. 147-8, 154; B. Williams, *Stanhope* (Oxford, 1932), pp. 60-1.

[5] Pearce's, Newton's, Sankey's, and Stanwix's.

858. MARLBOROUGH *to* GODOLPHIN [*21 July/1 August 1707*]

Source: Blenheim MSS. A1-37.
Printed: Coxe, ii. 286–8 (small omission).

Meldert August 1st 1707

I am very impatient of hearing from Comte Wratislaw, for Mr. Robinson's letter of the 19th from Lipsick,[1] speakes very doubtfully of the reception that comte may have. If it be possible 56 [King of Sweden] should use 46 [Emperor] harldly after the advances the latter had made, I agree intierly with 38 [Godolphin] that we must take such vigorous measures as may put a stope to his proceedings, but it must not be sooner then the end of this campagne. But I own to you, that I can't persuade myself, that he will make such a step, as must necessarely give so great an advantage to 43 [King of France], for I am sure he earnestly desires the continuance of 80 [war]. This bearer[2] is a Member of Parliament. He comes from Spain, and seems to be a very modest man, but as much as he cares to speak, he is of the same opinion with all that I have seen, which in short is that neither 2 [Galway] is an officer or zealous. Thay all say that he is also grown very proude and passionat, which you know is very different from the temper he formerly had. I will not pretend to judge how right it may be to lett the friendshipe and opinion of 89 [the Whigs] govern in this matter, but I am very certaine the opinion 44 [King Charles] and all the officers have of him (though unjust) will make it impracticable for him to do anything that is great or good. I have sent Brigadier Palmes to the Duke of Savoye and Prince Eugene, with orders to stay there til thay can judge how the campagne will end on that side, and then to have their thoughts on a project for the next campagne. I have acquainted them with my opinion.[3] I expect him back about the midle of September so that I may have yours and our friends' thoughts before I setle any part of them with the court of Vienna, and the States General.

[1] 9/20 July, Blenheim MSS. A2-20. Wratislaw would be allowed to talk with Piper but it was not decided if he could see the King.

[2] Henry Worsley, M.P., accompanied Rivers to Portugal and Spain in 1706, carrying messages from Lisbon to Barcelona and back. Worsley was selected to go as envoy to Charles III at the beginning of 1708, with Rivers as the troop commander. Then his instructions were cancelled and both posts were given to Stanhope. Alexander Cunningham attributes the change to Marlborough's jealousy of Rivers (*History of Great Britain* [London, 1787], ii. 204–5). More likely it was due to the solicitations of Charles III in favour of Stanhope. See Snyder, 'British Diplomatic Service', p. 61. Worsley to Oxford, 'Saturday morning', B.M., Portland Loan, 29/45Y, fols. 129–30. James to Philip Stanhope, 2 Mar. 1708, in Aubrey Newman, *The Stanhopes of Chevening* (London, 1969), p. 36.

[3] Eugene did not advise taking the offensive in Savoy next year, but rather only a diversionary campaign to tie up French troops. Marlborough suggested that Eugene should not serve with the Duke again, and there was no doubt he would not. He also could not serve under or alongside the Elector of Hanover on the Rhine. The Allies wanted Eugene to serve in Spain but the Emperor would not have him so far away. From the beginning Eugene's own preference was to serve on the Moselle or with Marlborough in the Low Countries and in fact he took up his command at first in the former and then with the latter. See below, *passim*, and Braubach, ii. 209.

I have had the favour of yours of the 13th[1] which is answere to mine of the 18[2] new stile. I am glad for the sake of the Queen and England, that you are of opinion that the warr in Spain aught to be carryed on by subsistys, which may gett foragne troupes, for her Majesty's subjects can never come in time nor indeed be keep in good order in that contry for want of recrutes. If wee suceed at Toulon, as I hope we shal since thay have not made the litle sieges, which must necessarily have lost so much time, as must have given the French and [an] opertunity of having their detachements, which I hope will not be able to joyne the Mareshal de Tessee til the siege of Toulon be happyly over. When that place is in the hands of the Allies, besides the ruin it must be to his navall stores, it will make it very difficult for the King of France to suport the next campagne, which I hope will incorage 110 [Holland] to have no thoughts but of 80 [war].

I allow al your reasonings to be very right concerning 118 [France], 116 [the States], and 88 [Parliament], and that 80 [war] must be continued. But no reasoning or success, can prevaile with 116 [the States] to think anything reasonable, but what tends to their own particular intirest. However, during 80 [war] it would be to[o] daingerous of making any allyances in which 110 [Holland] were not concerned. I have received letters of the 15th from Sir Cloudesley Shovell with copies of the demande signed by the Duke of Savoye and Prince Eugene, and the Admeral's answere.[3] By the demande and answer it lookes as if Shovell had not the copie of the points setled between the ministers of Savoye and the Lords apointed by her Majesty this winter.[4] If he has it not, it should be emediatly sent him, for in that paper it is stipulated that the shipes, and what belongs to them are to be her Majesty's, and the stores of the town for the Duke of Savoye. I think I mentioned this once before,[5] but having had no answere, you will excuse my zeal. I send enclosed a copie of a letter[6] I have received from Don Quiros.[7] You may read it at your leasure. I have this morning received a letter from the Pensioner,[8] who is very much allarmed at the proceedings of 56 [King of Sweden]. Whatever does happen, I am very confident we shall hurt ourselves if we make a noyse

---

[1] Letter 849.   [2] Letter 845.

[3] Blenheim MSS. A2-18. The Duke and Prince demanded to know what support Shovell would give them. Enclosed is a council of war of 3/14 July where the operations were decided. See the letters of Eugene, 2/13 July, and Shovell, 3/14 July, in Murray, iii. 483-4.

[4] For the detailed project settled for the Toulon expedition see Owen, pp. 158-61. Marlborough was correct. The Duke was to furnish powder, ammunition, and mortars for the land forces. The English fleet would furnish cannon and a limited amount of powder.

[5] Marlborough had already written to Shovell, telling him to give all the powder he could spare and to buy more so as not to jeopardize the expedition. See p. 804 n. 2.

[6] 20/31 July, Blenheim MSS. A2-22, on sending troops to aid Charles III in Spain.

[7] Don Bernardo de Quiros (died 1709), administrator-general; he was appointed governor of Limburg by Charles III on 18/29 Mar. as successor to Goess. The Dutch considered his instructions to take an oath of homage to King Charles from his subjects, a challenge to the Condominium, but Marlborough supported Quiros's pretensions.

[8] 19/30 July, 't Hoff, pp. 330-1.

til the end of this campagne. You will have received the considerations of the court of Vienna, as to sending troupes for the suport of the King of Spain. I have received a copie from Comte Senzindorff[1] but shall make no other answere, but that we must see the success of the expedition into Provence, before we can judge what may be faissable for the releife of King Charles. By this I shal gaine time for the return of Brigadier Palmes. I intend to write to the Pensioner that the Dutch may give the same answere.[2]

859. MARLBOROUGH *to* GODOLPHIN [*24 July/4 August 1707*]

Source: Blenheim MSS. A1-37.
Printed: Coxe, ii. 290–1.

Meldert August 4th 1707

By the last post I had not time for the copying of the enclosed from Lore Pitterborow.[3] His motions have been so incertaine that I have write but ono letter in answere to four of his, which I sent to Sir Philip Meadhurst, who write me that it came after the Earle was gone, but that he should send it td Hanover, beleiving it might meet him there. By one expression in his letter, I believe his justefication is meant to be printed.[4] I should think it for his service, as well as the quiet of the Queen's business, that nothing of this kind should be printed. If he gives me occasion I shall put him in mind of the English saying (litle said is soon mended), but I know he will govern himself, and I had much rather it should be so, then your humble servant have anything to do in itt. I do not hear the Elector of Hanover has yett declared any time for his going to the army on the Rhine, so that for this campagne we must not, I am afraid, expect any other thing but the obliging Monsieur de Villars to keep on the other side of the Rhin, so that thay may detache the greatest part of their army for Provence. I hope tomorrow wee may have the good news of the Duke of Savoy's being att Toulon the 23d of the last month.

Having write thus far, I have the favour of yours of the 17th,[5] by which I see you want t[w]o mailes from Holande, in which letters you will find us full of hopes of success of the project of Toulon. But if that of 115 [Toulon] should not succeed, you will find no hearts left in 110 [Holland]. You must see this month of August passe, before you will be well able to judge what measures may be proper to be taken. I am sorry for the uneasiness your cold gives you and do with al my heart wish you might never have any other

---

[1] Enclosed in his letter of 25 June/6 July, Blenheim MSS. A2-17, reinforcing Zinzerling's request for aid to Charles III. See p. 817 n. 3.

[2] 21 July/1 Aug. ('t Hoff says *c.* 2 Aug., pp. 332–3).

[3] 11/22 July; this copy in Blenheim MSS. A1-37; printed in Coxe, ii. 238–9, telling of his visit to the King of Sweden and criticizing Stanhope's actions in Spain.

[4] It was, by Dr. John Freind, his physician: *An Account of the Earl of Peterborough's Conduct in Spain* (London, 1707).

[5] Letter 854.

uneasiness, but what of necessity you must undergoe for the good of the publick. I have been uneasy in my head ever since I left off the watters, but if the siege of Toulon goes prosperously, I shall be cured of all deseases but old age.

860. MARLBOROUGH *to the* DUCHESS   [*24 July/4 August 1707*]

Source: Blenheim MSS. E3.
Printed: Coxe, ii. 291–2 (inc.).

Meldert August 4th, 1707

Since my last wee have had so much rain that I can hardly stur out of my quarter, the durt being up to the horse[s'] bellies, which is very extraordinary in this month. However, I think we must stay here til wee hear what success the Duke of Savoye has att Toulon. By a letter I have received from 30 [Peterborough] he should be at this time att 141 [Hanover], where no doubt he will be a great favoritt to 51 [Electress Sophia]; but I do not think his humor will be agreable to 50 [the Elector]. I send a copie of his letter to Mr. Mongomery [Godolphin]. I did last winter desire the Queen's favour in giving her picture to Comte Wratislaw, which she was pleased to promis, so that I thought it had been at Vienna, but by the last post I received a letter from the Emperor['s] Resident[1] that Sir Godfrey Neiller says he can't begine the pictor til he has a warrant from Lord Chamberlain.[2] Pray give my duty to the Queen, and that I desire she would be pleased to give Lord Kent her orders, for Wratislaw has sett his heart on the honour of her pictor, and Sir Godfrey might order it so that her Majesty need not have the trouble of setting but once. But the next yeare I must beg the favour of the Queen that she will allow Sir Godfrey to come three or four tims to draw hers and the Prince's pictor for Bleinhem. If I am ever to enjoye quietness it must be there, so that I would have nothing in my sight but my friends. Since France gives litle or no account of the Duke of Savoy's march, we think it a signe that all goes well, and that we may by tomorrow's letters hear that he gott to Toulon by the 23d of the last month. At Paris thay must have letters from Toulon of the 30th, and thay speak of nothing fresher then the 20th. If anything had happened for their advantage, thay would have taken care to have let us have had itt. Having write thus farr, I have received yours of the 18th, by which I find there were two Dutch postes due. What 73 [Howe][3] tels you[4] is a mallincolly prospect, but when thoughts are carryed anywhere

---

[1] Johann Hoffman.   [2] The Earl of Kent.
[3] Howe returned to England during the summer and apparently sought employment in England because of his health (see p. 863). Unsuccessful, he returned to Hanover by the end of November and remained until his death in 1709.
[4] On 18 July, the same day on which the Duchess wrote the letter that Marlborough answers here, she wrote in a similar vein to the Queen: 'I wish you could have heard all Mr. and Mrs. Howe

else thay are daingerous, so that of two evels you must chuse the least. I am more concerned at what you say of 42 [the Queen], since that is what may hurt emediatly. But as to 50 [the Elector of Hanover], I hope it is at a great distance, and will own to you that the litle gratetude or sence 108 [England] have of their peculier happyness, makes me less concerned. But I would ventur a good deal to make 139 [239–the Queen] happy, for I am persuaded thay mean very honestly. You have againe in this letter made use of 273 [Walpole]¹ and my cypher goes not so farr.²

861. GODOLPHIN *to* MARLBOROUGH   [25 *July* 1707]

Source: Blenheim MSS. A2-23.
Printed: Coxe, ii. 288–90 (inc.).

Windsor July 25, 1707

I am now to acknowledg the favour of yours of the 21th,³ 25th,⁴ and of the 27th⁵ by Mr. Breton as also of the 28th⁶ by the post. And to begin with what is uppermost with all people here, wee are now in greater expectation than ever of good news from Thoulon, finding plainly that the Duke of Savoy and Prince Eugene will not lose any time, and as plainly by the French letters that they must bee there before the Marshall de Thesse. Besides that they seem to bee superiour to him till his succours arrive from Alsace and Roussillon which may come perhaps in time to oppose farther progress into the country but can never, as I hope, and think come far enough to raise the siege of Thoulon; for which, if more foot should really bee wanted as Sir Cloudesly seems to hint,⁷ I don't see why the fleet might not bring the English and Dutch Garrisons in Girona⁸ and Barcelona in 4 days time; and they might return again before they could bee wanted in either of those places.

told me of the court the Torrys have made to the hous of Hanover of their pretended zeale for the invitation, how well they are with them, and how hardly the friends to this government are thought on for supporting you, and the government from confussion. 'Tis a wonder to think, how that sort of people find a way to poysen all princes, for both the hous of Hanover and Mrs. Morley [the Queen] is equally fond of them, at the same time that they design bringing in the Prince of Wales.' Blenheim MSS. G1-7. Cf. p. 688 n. 9.

¹ Sir Robert Walpole, Earl of Orford (1676–1745). Prime Minister under George I and II; M.P., Castle Rising, 1701–2, King's Lynn, 1702–12, 1713–42; member of the Prince's Council 1705–8; Secretary at War 1708–10; Treasurer of the Navy 1710–11. *D.N.B.*

² The use of *273* in the cipher raises questions. In 1710 it was definitely used to stand for Walpole. In 1708–9 it seems to have been an alternative designation for the Duchess. It is impossible to be certain what was intended here, but as Marlborough could not recognize its meaning by context alone from the Duchess's letter, it could have meant Walpole in this instance. For the letters in which this number is employed see Cipher G in the Appendix.

³ Untraced.   ⁴ Letter 850.   ⁵ Letter 852.   ⁶ Letter 855.

⁷ Shovell's letter of 3 July, Murray, iii. 483–4. The Admiral reported that the Duke of Savoy was hesitant to move on to Toulon 'leaving garrisons behind even in his own country and troops of the enemy's', who could cut his communications and impede his retreat. 'They expect a great number of troops will oppose them, but hope to be at Toulon before they can get together.'

⁸ Gerona, Spanish town held by the Allies 90 kilometres north-east of Barcelona.

The Queen approves your thought of sending Brigadier Palmes to the Duke of Savoy for the reasons you give. And at his return will certainly bee the most proper time to speak plain to 116 [the States] and 62 [Heinsius], for you will please to consider, that sooner or later, there seems to be an absolute necessity of doing somthing of this kind.

108 [England] had entirely swallowed the advantages[1] they hoped for against 43 [King of France] this summer, and since it is now like to pass over without any endeavour or attempt of that kind, 88 [Parliament] will certainly enter into the reasons and causes of this proceeding, and will not probably bee very well satisfyed unless they find there has been some expostulation upon it with 116 [the States] and some better regulations made. And if this should bee wholly neglected, or but too long delayed, it would certainly give the greatest handle imaginable against 80 [war].

I thank you for the coppy of Comte Wratislau's letter which I can't think soe reasonable throughout, as you seem to doe. All that he says of what is past is entirely unreasonable, and particularly his doubts whether 108 [England] would make the right use of sucess at 115 [Toulon] by continuing the warr; and where he talks of their having ventured and exposed their army in Italy only to gratify 108 [England]. Had they ever had Italy or an army, but for the extraordinary efforts and expence of England? And is it now thought too much to doe what is really the most solid advantage to themselves, only because it is particularly gratefull to England? I confess this is a little harsh to my ear.

As to his future views,[2] I approve them very much, and shall endeavour as farr as I can to make them practicable. But I see by the last letters from Sir Philip Medows the Court of Vienna effects still to have the Palatine troops sent to the King of Spain from the Duke of Savoy's army which can't bee don by no means if the enterprise succeeds at Thoulon. For in that case, even by Comte Wratislau's own scheme, the Duke of Savoy's army ought to bee strengthned and augmented so as that he may winter in France. 'Tis true indeed, if wee should bee bottled there and hee obliged to retire, so great an army on that side would not bee necessary, and then the Palatins might goe to Spain. But at present I think wee ought to insist still upon having some of the troops from Naples, as most at hand, and because of the remoteness of the place very difficult to bee made use of this year, any other way than by transporting them to Catalonia by sea.

Comte Wratislaus touches one thing in his letter against which I beg leave to precaution you in time, and that is the thought of sending for Prince Eugene to the Rhine, the latter end of this campagn. Now the affairs of the Rhyne for this year, seem to bee at an end by the troops detached from Villars' army, and I believe the Elector of Hannover would like to have that command

---

[1] The defeat of the French army in the Spanish Netherlands.
[2] Discussed p. 848 n. 3.

another year. Besides I doe really not think him sincere in dropping that expression to you, for if they had Prince Eugene at Vienna, they would not think of sending him to the Rhyne but rather make use of him to bridle 56 [King of Sweden].

Upon the whole, I think it might bee right to answer him that in generall his views are like to bee approved, and that if the Emperour has any doubt England would make use of the success wee hope for at Thoulon, not to continue the warr, his Imperial Majesty has but to make it his request to all the Allyes not to make peace till the monarky of Spain bee restored to the house of Austria, and he will soon see if England will not bee ready to joyn with him in procuring such a declaration from them. And perhaps this would not give a very improper rise for what will bee necessary to bee said to 116 [the States] upon the subject of the former part of this letter.

If Count Zinzendorf comes to you, (as I hope), hee may bee of great use in concerting all these things against the return of Brigadier Palms, which I wish might bee sooner than the middle of September both because before that time the siege of Thoulon must bee over one way or other, and also because after that time, to speak very plainly, it will bee no more than abso-lutely necessary that you should make hast into England to look after our affairs at home.

I agree in all you say concerning Spain, and Portugall, but if they are like to bee pressed in autumn, as the French bragg, wee must bee at some extraordinary expence to keep them firm to our allyance. At present I think wee are upon pretty good terms with them.

Mr. Robinson's last letters give yett but a very doubtfull account of the matters depending between the Emperour and the King of Sweden, not-withstanding all the advances made by the former.

I hear my Lord Peterborow has been with him,[1] and don't doubt but from thence he will goe to Berlin and Hannover before he comes to you, by which time he will bee furnished with sufficient matter for one whole week's conversation.

Since I had finished this letter I have shown it to 42 [the Queen] for her approbation. She commanded mee to remember her very kindly to you, but did not say the least word of her having had a letter from you.[2]

I had almost forgott to observe one thing to you, upon what you write that subsidyes would bee better than a regular pay for the troops to bee sent from Naples to Spayn. This is most certainly true, if any honesty remained in the world. But as the case stands, if that method bee taken, the subsidys will bee sent to Vienna, and the troops, I doubt, will starve in Spayn.

---

[1] For Peterborough's visit to Altranstädt, where he saw Charles XII, see Coxe, ii. 236 ff.

[2] 7/18 July. See letter 845A, in which Marlborough tells her the future safety of her happiness, her religion, and her country depends upon her co-operating with the Whigs. If 'anybody near your person' (an oblique reference to Harley) can do better than Godolphin, have him put 'their project' in writing. She will find they cannot promise to implement it.

862. GODOLPHIN *to* MARLBOROUGH   [*27 July 1707*]

Source: Blenheim MSS. A2-23.

Windsor 27th of July 1707

I have the favour of yours of the 1st of August by Collonell Worseley,[1] with whom I have not yett had time to speak about 2 [Gallway] though I don't doubt but his opinion is, as you say, the same with the rest, since he went over with 10 [Rivers] and is a particular friend and favorite of his. But whether 2 [Gallway] bee changed, as they say, or the same wee have always known him, I agree he cannot bee of use where he is and I wish for any good opportunity of his being removed from thence, though at the same time nobody will bee found that can struggle better with the naturall difficultys of that service. But if wee succeed at Thoulon those difficultys will not bee soe great as they have been, since the French will bee obliged to recall their forces there, for their own defence, the resolution of the Duke of Savoy to march directly to Thoulon being grounded chiefly upon Sir Cloudesley Shovel's promises[2] to keep a squadron of ships and transports there all winter to assist him either with provisions or troops, as there should bee occasion; and I see by Comte Briançon, his master is very willing to enter into this measure upon those assurances, and that the 28,000 men paid by the Allyes may continue there another year.[3] But concluding, in this view, as is but reasonable, that the French will draw still more forces from Spain, and from the Rhyne, the Comte de Briançon is also very earnest that the Elector of Hannover would not only accept the command of the army of the Empire without any farther delay, but hasten personally to the Rhyne himself, because his presence there would make it more difficult for the French to send any farther detachments from that side. I think this is right in itself, and I trouble you with it, the rather because Mr. Schultz has shown mee a coppy of his master's[4] letter to you of the 26th of July[5] in which he seems to delay taking any finall resolution about the command, till the Baron de Goerts whom he sends to Mayence, shall have made him a report of the condition in which he finds that army. I hope therfore you will enter

---

[1] Letter 858.

[2] At the council of war held on 3/14 July the Duke of Savoy had expressed his concern that his communications and retreat would be cut off if he continued his march to Toulon. Shovell, in his letter which Marlborough had sent to Godolphin by Worsley, 'promised, if we take Toulon, I shall be the more able to keep our ships, and if it be not possible to retreat by land, we could carry him [the Duke of Savoy's land forces] back by water, for then I should be able to leave a squadron here to assist in the attack of any places on the sea coasts'. Murray, iii. 484.

[3] The Duke of Savoy was not permitted to keep all the troops. The 7,000 Palatines in the pay of the Maritime Powers in his service had already been suggested for Charles III in Spain once the Toulon expedition was over. See p. 783 n. 1.

[4] The Elector of Hanover.

[5] In Macpherson, ii. 93–4. In it he asks for Bothmer's Regiment of Dragoons and 1,000 cavalry in the pay of the Maritime Powers to be sent to him at the Rhine. See p. 827.

so farr into the Comte de Briançon's reasonings, as to doe what you can, to hasten the Elector's coming to the Rhyne, in person. Whether he does anything there this year, or not is not so materiall, as his appearing but one month or 6 weeks, upon the place.

July 28

I believe you judg very rightly that 56 [King of Sweden] has no intentions or inclinations to gratify 43 [King of France]. However all his actions have the consequence of doing it to some degree, but I am not in dispair of a sort of a polished up agreement betwixt him and 46 [Emperour] for the present, which may help to gain time for farther measures in the winter. At the same time I am apt to think, in that case, the Swedes will take the pretext of the guaranty to continue a body of their troops in Saxe, and expect the event of Thoulon, and the consequences of it, before they declare themselves farther.

Upon the approaches of the Duke of Savoy towards Provence, the French have drawn away all their troops from the coast of Guienne[1] and Poietou,[2] and not daring to trust the people with arms in the absence of their troops, they have wholly disarmed those provinces.

This being the case, I can't see but 5 or 6,000 men are like to make more impression there at this time than double their number could have done in the last year,[3] and I submitt to you whether 110 [Holland] would not lett us have 3 or 4 English and Scots battaillons from thence; especially considering, there is no likelyhood of any action, and that their motives for being against it, will I doubt, bee a very sore poynt next winter, if somthing bee not said to them very soon pursuant to the subject of my 2 last letters.[4]

Mr. St. Johns has promised mee to send you by this post,[5] a state of the force wee have in readyness, by which you will best judg if any such addition can bee made to it, as may render it usefull in the present weakness of France, on this side.

I have not yett appointed any persons to bee comptrollers of the army. There are objections to Mr. Negus, and you have named no other to mee as I remember. What doe you think of Brigadier Howe for one? He is too much a cripple with the gout, ever to serve again in the army and I believe his post abroad is not easy to him.[6]

---

[1] Guyenne, province of France, on the south-west coast, with Bordeaux as its capital.
[2] Poitou, province of France on the Atlantic coast below Brittany, with Poitiers as its capital.
[3] The project of a descent. See p. 846 n. 2.
[4] Letters 857, 861.
[5] 29 July, Blenheim MSS. A2-25. From Ireland Ormonde's Regiment of Horse (418 men), Tunbridge's Dragoons (443) and Wynn's Foot (7,250), totalling 1,586 men. From England 434 Dragoons, the remainder of Carpenter's and Essex's regiments and 2,066 foot, the regiments of Barrymore and Paston. Two further regiments of foot were proposed, but he has no orders. A battalion of 600 marines will be furnished by the fleet.
[6] For the appointment of Meadows and Broderick to these places see p. 765 n. 3.

I forgott to observe to you the answer to Comte Wratislaus[1] was very easy when he tells you wee asked nothing from them at first, for the warr of Spain, but the person of the Archduke [Charles]. It is very true, and if wee had had nothing but his person, he had been at this houre upon the throne of Spain. But the folly and greediness of those they sent with him, hindred him from it though for a month or six weeks together, he had only to stepp into it and take possession.[2]

863. MARLBOROUGH *to* GODOLPHIN [*28 July/8 August 1707*]

Source: Blenheim MSS. A1-37.
Printed: Coxe, ii. 296-7.

Meldert August 8th 1707

I find by yours of the 21[3] that you want four packets from Holand, and as the wind is I fear thay are stil on this side. The news we have this morning from Paris is much better then what we received by the last post. The Duke of Vandôme has detached 12 battalions, and 9 squadrons, but continues stil in his camp. I hope this detachment will incorage 101 [the deputies], so as that I may make the march[4] I have been preposing to them for these last six weeks. If thay alow of it my next will be from another camp. You will by Mr. Walpool[5] have an account of all our affairs in Catalonia. However, I trouble you with a copie of my letter from Thomas Earle.[6] The other two papers, I have not had time to have them copied; thay should not be showen to many. By that from Hanover[7] 42 [the Queen] may see the obligations she has to

---

[1] In his letter of 2/13 July, sent by Marlborough to Godolphin on 14/25 July (p. 848), Wratislaw had written: 'It is pretended in England that the troops which the Emperor may send into Spain, ought to be maintained by us. . . . It ought to be remembered, that when the Archduke [Charles III] was demanded of us, we were reproached in the same manner, for making a difficulty to send him; because nothing was then asked for this war, be this person only.' Coxe, ii. 280.

[2] Godolphin refers to Charles III's failure to respond to Galway's urgent plea to meet him in Madrid in July 1706 (p. 604 n. 4).

[3] Letter 857.

[4] See p. 785. Marlborough had wanted to make a sudden march towards Mons and threaten Vendôme's line of communications, expecting this feint would force him to withdraw and give Marlborough an opportunity of attacking his rear-guard if not drawing him into battle. Marlborough was finally allowed by the Dutch to move on 31 July/11 Aug. See pp. 865-6.

[5] Horatio, first Baron Walpole of Wolterton (1678-1757), diplomat, younger brother of Sir Robert Walpole, M.P. 1702-56; secretary to James Stanhope 1706-7, to Henry Boyle 1708-9; to Viscount Townshend at The Hague 1709-11. *D.N.B.* Walpole had been sent to England with the Treaty of Peace and Commerce with Spain which Stanhope had concluded with Charles III on 29 June/10 July. He had stopped off at Marlborough's camp *en route*.

[6] Untraced.

[7] Robethon to Cardonnel, 22 July/2 Aug., in Coxe, ii. 295-6, describing the scheme of Scott, an Englishman residing in Hanover, to secure an invitation for the Electress Sophia to live in England by the aid of the Tories. Sunderland saw it as a warning to the Queen not to antagonize the Whigs any further as it might drive them to support the invitation, 'not to anger two courts at once' to Marlborough, 5 Aug. (Coxe, ii. 339). Godolphin arranged for Scott's removal from Hanover. See pp. 870 n. 2, and 878 n. 1.

some of her subjects. Though 50 [Elector of Hanover] has behaved himself in this business as I always thought he would,[1] you may depend of itt that Mr. Scot dose nothing but by the derection of 51 [Electress Sophia], and I dare say you will see this matter attempted in the winter. The other is from Businvall, the French minister to Torcy.[2]

By a letter Mr. Cardonel has received from Lord Pitterborow, he should be here this evening, or tomorrow.

I here inclose the resolution of the States[3] given me this day by the deputys of the army. It is an answere to my having pressed them to gett fuller powers. It would do them hurt with the States if thay should know thay had shown me the whole resolution, so that I beg it may be comunicated only to 4 [Halifax], 5 [Somers], and 6 [Sunderland]. You will see by their reasoning of this resolution the humor thay are in. I should be glad to know what your opinions are of the use I aught to make of this resolution.

864. MARLBOROUGH *to the* DUCHESS [*28 July/8 August 1707*]

Source: Blenheim MSS. E3.

Meldert August 8th 1707

By your short letter of the 21th I find you are likely to receive four letters of mine together, and it may be this at the same time, for the wind has been and is stil very contrary. Mr. Cardonell received this evening a letter from Hanover; I have sent it to Lord Treasurer. I desire you would aske for itt. Our news of this day from Paris, joined with the detachement the French army are obliged to make for Provence, makes me hope that all goes well with the Duke of Savoye, though as to particulars we are keep very much in the dark. I hope my next will be from another camp, I having been long weary of this. This night or tomorrow I shall have the happyness of 30 [Peterborough] good company. I shal and must hear all thay will please to say, but you may be sure I shall be very carefull of my own beheavior. I must not now trouble you with a long letter, for you will certainly receive this at the same time with several others of mine.

Frustrated in his plan to attack Vendôme in his camp (p. 864 n. 4), Marlborough won the consent of the Dutch deputies to make a surprise march to the south-west

[1] The Elector had disavowed Scott's negotiations with the Tories. See p. 878 n. 1.

[2] An intercepted letter recounting Peterborough's meeting with Charles XII of Sweden, in Coxe, ii. 237–8. There are other intercepted letters from Besenval to Chamillart of June and July. See p. 769 n. 1.

[3] 27 July/7 Aug., Blenheim MSS. A2-16; another copy, A2-33. The States do not want to risk battle and jeopardize the success of the war while the outcome of the Toulon project is depending.

at night. His aim was to threaten to cut Vendôme off from his base at Mons and his supply lines, and thus force his withdrawal. At 9 o'clock in the morning he sent off his heavy baggage to Brussels (crossing the Dyle at Heverlee). He did so in order to be relieved of this encumbrance and not as a feint, which Churchill suggests (ii. 268). Vendôme did the same, sending his impedimenta to Charleroi.[1] The slow-moving artillery was ordered to pass the Dyle at St. Joris Weert. The troops marched at 4 o'clock in the afternoon, crossing the Dyle on temporary bridges at Florival and continuing on all night, not stopping until 3 o'clock in the afternoon of the 31st/11th. Receiving word of his march, Vendôme broke camp that evening and marched in the same direction, maintaining a safe distance from Marlborough. Vendôme made his camp on 31 July/11 August at Seneffe.

---

865. MARLBOROUGH to GODOLPHIN [30 July/10 August 1707]

Source: Blenheim MSS. A1-37.
Printed: Coxe, ii. 292–3, 301.

Genap August 11th 1707 [Meldert, August 10th]

I had not time by the last post to answere that part of your letters of the 17th and 21.[2] of the last month, in which you say that it is not only your own opinion, but also that of 4 [Halifax], 5 [Somers], and 6 [Sunderland] that there should be no time lost in taking measurs, and at the same time letting 110 [Holland] know the ferm resolution of 42 [the Queen] and 108 [England] never to think of 81 [peace] til thay can bring 43 [King of France] to those preliminarys agreed to last winter. I think this is very rightly judged, but the execution will be very difficult, for as the prelimanarys were never in form braught to 116 [the States], so you may be sure thay will pretend to know nothing of them. By what I hear from Lipsick, I beleive the fate of Toulon will be decided before the negociation of the Comte de Wratislaw[3] will be finished. When I told you that I aproved of the greatest part of 63 [Wratislaw] letter, I did not mean his reasoning upon what was passed, for my humor is to look forward, so that I meant as to the managing of the warr for the next campagne.[4] You may be in the right to wish Prince Eugene to continue where he is, but if [he] himself and the Emperor shall think fitt to have him in Garmany, itt would be very harsh in the Allyes to oppose itt. But I shall be better able to speake on this subject after the return of Palmes, which

---

[1] 'The Ostend mayle that came in since the rest, confirmes the decampment of the armyes in Flanders that of the French having made detachments moved off in the night, and his Grace had sent back his heavy baggage in order to be upon them, but they [the French] had got to the strong campe of Genap [Seneffe].' W. Sloper to Brydges, *c.* 29 July, Stowe MSS. 58, II. 23–4, Huntington Library.

[2] Letters 854, 857.   [3] With the King of Sweden.

[4] See pp. 848, 850, 860–1.

can't be til the midle of September. By the last post[1] I sent you the last resolution of 116 [the States] by which you will see their great caution. I can't forbear giving you my opinion as to what you say of 88 [Parliament] setleing the management of 80 [war] with 116 [the States]. It is a matter I think 31 [Rochester] and all his friends would be extreame glad off, and therfore I think should be avoyeded, for it is certaine that there could be no good end of such an enquiery; and although 39 [Marlborough] can't prevaile with them [the Dutch] to do even what is good for themselves, yett thay will trust him with much more power then thay will ever be braught to do by treaty.

[Genappe, August 11th]

I had write thus farr in our old camp. The march I made last night and this day has had the effect I always assured the deputys it would have. As soon as the Duke of Vandome had the assurances of my being marched, he emediatly gaves orders for dechamping, and accordingly begone to march at twelve a clock last night, knowing very well that if he had staid til I had been in this campe he could not have marched without action. I hope this will convince our friends in 110 [Holland], as it had done our deputys, that if thay had consented to my making this march six weeks ago as I pressed to do, the French would have done then, as thay now have, a shamefull march, by which both armys sees very plainly that thay will not ventur to fight. We have nothing since my last from Provence and I am so very sleepy, not having shut my eyes last night, that I shal give you no further trouble.

866. GODOLPHIN *to* MARLBOROUGH [*31 July 1707*]

Source: Blenheim MSS. A2-23.

St. James's July 31th 1707

While wee are expecting with great impatience, a good event at Tholoun, our thoughts are employed upon all the ways of improving it, either by strengthening the Duke of Savoy's army there, or by giving otherwise so much work to France, as to disable them from coming upon him with a great superiority. In order to the former, might wee not try (now they are out of reach of France) upon what terms the Venetians would lett us have some of their troops? They are the nearest of any wee can think of, and the only temptation to them would bee, that England and Holland would bee answerable, Mantua[2] should not (after a peace) remain in the hands of the Emperour. This will bee a very difficult poynt with the court of Vienna, to whom however it ought first to bee mentioned; and the way of mentioning it to them, in my opinion, ought to bee, by representing to them the necessity of

[1] Letter 863.
[2] Occupied by the Imperialists in February. See p. 761 n. 6.

strengthning the Duke of Savoy's army in France; and the great advantage of it to all the Allys in generall, and particularly to the Emperour, by making it impossible for the French to have an army on the Rhyne, while he continues to give them so great a diversion in the south of France; that there does not appear any means of doing this with effect, but either by the Emperour's own troops, or by his joyning the rest of the Allyes in the necessary measures for procuring troops from the Venetians; and since he will certainly decline the former of these, wee shall bee the stronger in our instances to that court, for their complying with the latter.

In case wee shall not bee able anyway to send troops to the Duke of Savoy, the next way of assisting him, and perhaps the most effectuall of any would bee to give France a diversion and alarm them from this side, as wee did the last year.[1] I need not trouble you with particulars now, having troubled you so much upon this head, in my last,[2] and Mr. St. John's having acquainted mee since, that he had also written to you as I had desired him, upon that subject.

I hope Monsieur Zinzendorf is with you by this time, for in case 110 [Holland] will bee on any terms persuaded to continue 80 [war] it will bee absolutely necessary, to adjust and settle everything beforehand, that is to bee expected from 46 [Emperour] and in a more plain and certain manner has hitherto been done; and that he, or some other should reside at The Hague with more trust, and more powers, or better inclinations than Comte de Goez, seems to have had.[3]

Windsor August 1st 1707

The former part of this letter was written yesterday at London. I have little to add to it from hence, but that I have had a letter from Collonell Stanhope from Barcelona of the 6th of July new style[4] in which he says he had also written to you,[5] for which reason I don't trouble you with his letter to mee. But the sum of it was, that unless Comte Noyelles were recalled, any troops sent thither from Italy without a generall of more figure, would signifie very little. For that unless Comte Noyelles comanded all, he would certainly spoil all.

I am told by 4 [Halifax] that Mr. Stepney is in so ill a condition of health, that he must bee forced to come over here for remedies. If this bee soe, I should think the sooner the better, for he can ill bee spared there whenever you come away.[6]

   [1] By a descent.   [2] Letter 862.

   [3] Goess had been recalled and left The Hague at the beginning of September. Zinzendorf did not remain, perhaps to his regret, for personal difficulties at home made him anxious to get away. Geikie, p. 37 n. 2.

   [4] Chevening MSS., box 37/12.

   [5] 27 June/8 July, Blenheim MSS. A2-29.

   [6] Stepney came over at the beginning of September and died in England on the 15th.

The enclosed paper was brought to mee yesterday, by the gentleman himself, Mr. Barton.[1] He is a good pretty man, and the two Lords[2] that recommend him, are very deserving to bee gratifyed. You will please to lett mee know what should bee done in it.

867. GODOLPHIN *to* MARLBOROUGH   [*4 August 1707*]

Source: Blenheim MSS. A2-23.
Printed: Coxe, ii. 297-8 (inc.).

Windsor 4th of August 1707

I received yesterday the favour of yours of the 4th and 8th of August[3] with the severall papers inclosed.

The coppy of my Lord Peterborow's letter is a perfect picture of himself, and some paragraphs of it are very well explained by the letter intercepted from Busenval,[4] but you having by this time had enough of the originall I shall say no more of it now, but that I hope you have advised him not to bee so troublesom, as his own temper and inclination would naturally lend him to. I think it very probable that he may have entered into all the views of 51 [Electress Sophia] and joyn with those people in that and in other things when he comes hither unless 39's [Marlborough] lessons have power enough to hinder him from it.

You take no notice in any of your letters of the King of Spain's letters[5] to yourself, of which I have had the honour to receive a coppy by Mr. Walpool. What he says there of 5 or 6,000 foot from Italy is certainly necessary, and with the soonest, I wish all our instances may bee able to obtaine them even by allowing subsidys for them, to his brother the Emperour.

What he proposes also of one general to command the whole, seems reasonable in itself, as well, as necessary in the present circumstances. All our endeavours shall bee used with the court of Portugall to make them easy in that poynt, and if the Emperour will send anybody from Italy or Germany, wee shall all acquiese in it. But our people will bee very uneasy to submitt to Comte de Noyelles to whom the King's inclination seems to goe.

For what relates to his future subsidys from England, that must bee left to the Parliament, and therfore, as well as for other reasons he ought to bee a

---

[1] Robert Barton, a lieutenant in Meredyth's Regiment of Foot wanted a company in one of the Almanza regiments, whose men were taken prisoner. The regiments were to be newly raised in England at which time Marlborough recommended he be awarded a company (p. 876).

[2] Halifax was one. See his letter to Marlborough, 25 June, Blenheim MSS. B1-7.

[3] Letters 859, 863.   [4] See p. 865 n. 2.

[5] 31 May/11 July, Blenheim MSS. A2-29; copy in B.M., Add. MS. 28057, fols. 338-9. Charles III wrote about his need for 5,000 men from Italy, which the Maritime Powers alone had the resources to underwrite; the need for an Allied fleet in the Mediterranean the year round; and his need for a commander-in-chief. For the last he suggested Prince Eugene, Rivers, or Noyelles.

little more concerned to satisfye this nation, than hitherto he seems to have been.

I thank you for the letter[1] you sent mee from Hanover, because I hope it will doe some good with 42 [the Queen]. I am sure it ought to doe soe. 199 [Harley] will have orders from 42 [the Queen] to lett 50's [the Elector of Hanover] minister [Schütz] know the person mentioned [Scott] in that letter ought to bee recalled imediatly.[2]

I have comunicated to 4 [Halifax] and to 6 [Sunderland] the resolution of 116 [the States] inclosed in yours of the 8th from Meldert. Their construction of it, is that 39 [Marlborough] will bee more at liberty than he has been, and your letters received today of the 11th from Genap,[3] seem to confirm that construction. Wee agree that this month of August must pass, and the fate of 115 [Toulon] bee over before any just measures can properly bee taken, as to what ought then to bee sayd to 110 [Holland].

The Paris letters of the 8th which wee have this day, bragg much of the good condition of defence Thoulon is in. I hope the next post will revive us again as to that matter. In the meantime, the hast they are in, for making detachments from all parts, is no ill symptome for us.

Monsieur de Plessis Chastillon[4] is arrived here. He has been mighty earnest with mee to write to you, that he may bee exchanged for Brigadier Macartney. You can best judg what is fitt to bee don in that matter.

August 5th

I am much afraid our affairs grow every day worse and worse with 56 [the King of Sweden], not that I really think he is in any engagements with 43 [the King of France], but his own naturall unreasonableness, and his uncertainty, is like to have the same effect, and I doubt 30 [Peterborough] has done all he could, to make mischief there as well, as in other places where he has passed, and unless he bee gon from you before this comes to your hands, a little good advice from you, will have more weight, than from anybody to hinder him from hurting himself and being very troublesome to others.

After resting overnight at Genappe Marlborough moved his army on 1/12 August west to Nivelles, a distance of about 10 kilometres, the right flank resting on

[1] From Robethon, p. 864 n. 7.

[2] Harley worked through Schütz to neutralize Scott's activities and press for his removal from Hanover. See p. 878 n. 1, and Godolphin's letters to Harley, in H. M. C., *Portland MSS.*, iv 421–2; *Bath MSS.*, i. 175–6, 177, 178.

[3] Letter 865.

[4] Louis du Plessis, marquess of Plessis-Châtillon and Nonant (1678–1754), French officer; colonel of a regiment of Provence 1700; captured at Blenheim; brigadier Oct. 1704.

Arquennes. From the heights of the latter the left of the French camp at Seneffe was visible. The Dutch General Count Tilly was given orders to attack the French rearguards if they marched, but Vendôme managed a skilful night withdrawal, stopping temporarily at midday on the 2/13th between Haine-Saint-Paul and Haine-Saint-Pierre. Hesitant to venture against the enemy in the dark, Tilly did not set out until early in the morning. Albergotti, commanding the French rearguard, was able to hold him off while retiring to join the main French army, which now had a sizeable lead. After marching 10 kilometres, Tilly gave up the pursuit at Abbaye-de-l'Olive and returned north to rejoin Marlborough. Vendôme resumed his march at two in the afternoon and did not stop until he reached Saint-Denis, a march of more than 40 kilometres. On 3/14 August the Allied army set off for Soignies at six in the morning but the rain and mud were so terrible that the 20 kilometres march took eleven hours and the last stragglers did not arrive until noon on the 4/15th. Vendôme moved at the same time, finally reaching safety the same day at Cambron, putting the Dender between himself and Marlborough.

---

868. MARLBOROUGH *to* GODOLPHIN   [4/15 August 1707]

Source: Blenheim MSS. A1-37.
Printed: Coxe, ii. 303-4 (small omission).

Soignies August 15th 1707

I was in hopes this might have given you an account of some action, for on Friday[1] we marched to Nivell[es], and camped about half a league from Seneff, where the French army was enchamped. We came to[o] late for the attacking them that evening. As soon as it was dark thay begone to make their retreat, without making the least noyse, not tutching neither drume nor trompett; so that the Comt de Tilly, whome I had detached with 40 squadrons and 5,000 granadiers to attack their rear garde, in case thay should march, knew nothing of their marching til daylight; so that their reargard was gott into the inclosiers before he could join them, so that there was very litle done.[2] Our lose was three officers and some few soldiers. I beleive theirs was also very inconsiderable, but by these four days' march, thay have lost very considerably by desertion,[3] for we gave them no rest, so that thay were two days without any bread. Thay were in one continued march from Friday night from Seniff til Sunday 12 a clock to Cambron, so that thay may now have their bread from Mons. This army is also very much fatigued, so that I shall be obliged to take 3 or 4 days' rest in this camp, and then I shall march towardes Ath. Monsieur Vandôme's avoyding twice to fight within these

---

[1] 1/12 Aug.
[2] The failure of Tilly to fall on the rearguards aroused much controversy. See Taylor, ii. 43-5; Churchill, ii. 268-71; Wijn, II. 203-7; Milner, pp. 201-2.
[3] The estimates ran from 2,000 to 4,000.

four days, I hope will convince our friends as well as enemys, that his orders are not to venture.[1] The consternation that has been amongest their common soldiers aught to assure us of victory if we can ever engage them. But as thay will not venture, thay are now in a country where thay may march from one strong camp to another, and so end the campagne, which I fear thay will do.

I have this morning had the favour of yours of the 27th,[2] by which I see you think this may be a proper time to attempt on the co[a]st of France. The season is very much advanced, but if you have any fixed project setled with the officer that is to command, if you would lett me have itt, you may depend upon having 3 or 4 battalions as you desire.[3] For though 110 [Holland] should not be willing, I would take upon myself for so inconsiderable number of men. But should you not be almost sure of success, I should not think itt advisable for you to run into such an expence as unavoydably this must be. But if you are sure that the people[4] will join with you, and that thay can be suported this winter, it aught not to be neglected. If I could have persuaded, 50 [Elector of Hanover] had been at the army before now. But thay are so very dillitary and act with so much caution, that I am afraid thay will not do much good.

The employement you mention for Mr. How, [seems proper] provided he quits his redgiment. What I have from Saxony makes me fear the King of Sueden. I do not acquaint you with what Mr. Robison writes, beleiving Mr. Secretary Harley has the same, but the enclosed papers[5] you can have from nobody else.

Comte Dona[6] has been some days with me, and his account differs very much[7] from that of the English officers concerning 2 [Galway]. My Lord Pitterborow has been here ever since Tuesday,[8] and I beleive thinkes of staying some days longer. He assures me that he shall be able to convince yourself and Lord Sunderland that many stories has been made of him, in which there are no truth; and that he hopes to justefie himself in every perticular to the Queen's satisfaction; and that his intentions are to be employed by the Queen as she shal judge best; and that if she dose not make use of him, that he may have her leave to serve elsewhere. He has very obliging letters from the King of Spain, and the Duke of Savoye has a kindness for him.

I beg you will put in one bundle all my inclosed papers, for some times there is not time to copie them.

[1] For Louis XIV's orders to Vendôme not to fight see p. 791 n. 1.   [2] Letter 862.
[3] For the descent see p. 846 n. 2.   [4] The French Huguenots.
[5] Untraced. Probably from Besenval. See p. 769 n. 1.
[6] Johan Frederik, Count of Dohna-Ferrassières (died 1712), Dutch general; brigadier 1710; major-general 1704; lieutenant-general 1709; governor of Bergen in Henegouwen; colonel, infantry regiment, Gelderland, from 1695; colonel, Swiss regiment in pay of Holland, 1708; accompanied Galway on his march to Madrid; present at Almanza; killed at Denain 1712.
[7] That is, he gave a favourable account of Galway. Cf. p. 855.
[8] 29 July/9 Aug.

869. MARLBOROUGH *to the* DUCHESS [*4/15 August 1707*]

Source: Blenheim MSS. E3.

Soignies August 15, 1707

Since my last[1] I have not had the happyness of having any of yours, nor have I had very little rest, having been in perpetual motion. If the enemy had not marched one Friday night, we had had a battaile the next day, wee being camped in sight of etch other, but it was to[o] laite to begine that night. If we had faught it would have been on the 13th, which was the day of Blenheim, and I do veryly beleive God would have blessed us with the same success. Wee have keep them for these four last days in perpetuall alarms, so that thay have lost a great many men, but thay are now in a strong camp, where thay may have their canon and bread which thay have wanted three days. I have this minut received yours of the 26 and 27th. By them I now understand what you meant by 276 [   ]. I agree with you in a good deal of your opinion concerning 208 [Harley], but there is no possibilly [sic] in my opinion of acting otherways then making use of him, so that there should not only be pains taken in possesing 42 [the Queen] of a just charecter, but also of convincing 199 [Harley]. You speak of a new methode 38 [Godolphin] has taken with 193 [the Queen]. 240 [Lady Marlborough] should let me know itt, that I might att least do no hurt. I am glad you are pleased with the discretion of 243 [Lady Sunderland], but certainly you are in [the] right not to lett them tel 6 [Sunderland] til there be an absolut necessity. I have by this post received the enclosed from the Duke of Shrewsbury.[2] I desire you will give it to Lord Treasurer, and if it be necessary to lett the Queen see itt, for I am persuaded what he says in his letter is very treu. The methode you have taken to content Vanbrook I beleive is very right, and I am very glad of itt, for I am desirous of having everybody easy.[3]

870. GODOLPHIN *to* MARLBOROUGH [*7 August 1707*]

Source: Blenheim MSS. A2-23.

Windsor 7th of August 1707

As the wind is I can't hope for any letters from you, before this post goes out. In my last I forgott to observe, that as it is very true, if the Emperour and Prince Eugene are desirous he should come to Germany, it must bee so. On the other hand, since the Elector of Hannover takes the command

---

[1] 30 July/10 Aug. Untraced.

[2] 26 July, in *Private Correspondence*, ii. 234-6; reply, 4/15 Aug., Murray, iii. 513. Shrewsbury had been near Windsor but had not visited the Court, thinking 'it best to give no new jealousy to any in places, or in expectation of them'. Marlborough chided him in his reply for not making a call.

[3] She had stopped work on the bridge over the Glynne at Blenheim but had retracted her order on Marlborough's advice. See Vanbrugh to Boulter, 10 July, Vanbrugh, *Works*, iv. 212.

upon the Rhyne, and Starembergh is in Hungary, I am not quite out of hopes there may yett bee no occasion for Prince Eugene's coming to Germany.[1]

I have had two or three very pressing letters from Monsieur de Guiscard to push onn a descent from hence, though but with a small number of men. You will see by my former letters, that I am a good deal of his mind, but he cannot command this expedition himself, and wee have nobody here, that is any way proper, in my opinion. If you could spare Lieutenant Generall Ingoldsby to bee at the head of these men, I believe wee could yett gett them altogether by the middle of next month, at farthest, in case the impressions in Provence, so farr answer our expectations, as to encourage us to venture them.[2]

By all the officers lately come over, and by other ways too, I am very much concerned to hear Mr. Stepney is in so ill a state of health. Methinks he ought to have immediate leave to come over, for some proper remedies, in case his strength will permitt him to make use of it. I beg you to think quickly, how you would have his station supplyed. 'Tis of the last consequence to have somebody there upon whose prudence, as well as zeal for your orders you can intirely rely. I own to you I can't yett think of anybody here to whom I have not an objection of one kind or other. But whoever is resolved upon should (I think) bee sent away imediatly to you, and receive his instructions from you, how to govern himself, both at Brusselles and at The Hague.[3]

As to 56 [King of Sweden], since 116 [the States] will not hear of the guaranty,[4] why should not they bee pressed to enter into stricter measures with the *Czar*, who is one of the greatest bridles wee can have for 56 [King of Sweden], and if those two by the means of 43 [King of France], should agree upon 81 [peace] the consequences of it would be terrible.

---

[1] Eugene was with the Toulon expedition. He joined Marlborough in the Spanish Netherlands in 1708.

[2] For the descent see p. 846 n. 2.

[3] Stepney returned and died on 15 Sept. There were many candidates for his job including Matthew Prior, the Earl of Berkeley, and William Walsh. Raby, Abraham Stanyan, James Vernon, Sr., and James Stanhope were all proposed. The last two were the candidates favoured by Godolphin. Marlborough was ready to accept Stanhope, but as he was not immediately available William Cadogan was appointed temporarily on Marlborough's recommendation to serve during the winter. Stanhope was told he could have the position when he returned from Spain at the end of the year and was expected to go, but the pressing instances of the King of Spain persuaded the ministry that Stanhope should return there instead. Cadogan continued at Brussels until 1711 but the business was often carried on by his secretary, John Lawes, as was the business at The Hague by James Dayrolles, until Townshend was sent there in the spring of 1709. See Snyder, 'British Diplomatic Service', pp. 59–61; James Stanhope to Philip Stanhope, 2 Mar. 1708, in A. Newman, *The Stanhopes of Chevening* (London, 1969), p. 36.

[4] Of the Treaty of Altranstädt (1706), by which King Augustus gave up the throne of Poland in favour of Stanislaus. The Maritime Powers refused to guarantee the treaty although England did recognize Stanislaus as King of Poland: Hatton, p. 227 n.

871. MARLBOROUGH *to* GODOLPHIN   [7/18 August 1707]

Source: Blenheim MSS. A1-37.
Printed: Coxe, ii. 305-6 (inc.).

Soignies August 18th 1707

I have this morning had the favour of yours of 31 and 1st of this month.[1] I think your thought of the Venetiens is very good, but I very much question your bringing itt to bare in any reasonable time. For that of landing in France, I gave you the trouble of my thoughts by the last post.[2] I should have sent you the enclosed copies of the King of Spain's letters some time since but by a mistake thay were forgott.[3] I also send you a copie of what I have received this morning from Comte Wratislaw,[4] it giving more hopes of an accomodation then his last. But I am afraid at last he will find that the Suedes presume so much on the favourable conjuctor, that thay will be very unreasonable. It is not to be expressed the rains we have had, and that continu stil, so that if the safety of the common cause depended upon our marching, neither the enemy nor we could stur out of our camps; for it is with the greatest difficulty, that the generals getts to my quarters for orders. All the comfort we have is that the enemy do at least suffer as much as wee. Sinserlin [Zinzerling] has acquainted me this day with the asurances he has had from her Majesty of her assisting the King [Charles III] his master, and pressing me at the same time that troupes might be emediatly sent. I have endeavored to lett him see that til we have more certainty of the expedition of Provence, nothing could be done. But in the meantime, he aught to press the court of Vienna to have those troupes in Naples ready to be transported, if that should be found for the Service.

I have by this post received a letter from 241 [Lady Monthermer] to acquaint me of 240 [Lady Marlborough] being so unsatisfied with her, that she is forbid coming to her. I do know nothing of the quarrell, but I will take it for granted that 241 [Lady Monthermer] is to blame. However, I beg you will take no notice that I write to you, for 240 [Lady Marlborough] has said nothing to me of itt, but that you would make them friends; for should it be known it would make a disagreable noyse, and be of great prejudice to the young woman. 30 [Peterborough] has said all that is possible to mee, but says nothing of leaving the army. By what he tels me he thinkes he has demonstration to convince you that he has been injured in everything that has been reported to his disadvantage.

My Lord Orkney has desired me to send you the litle paper in favour of

---

[1] Letter 866.   [2] Letter 868.
[3] See p. 869.
[4] 30 July/10 Aug., Blenheim MSS. A2-16; reply, 7/18 Aug., Murray, iii. 522. The firmness of the English and Dutch mediators had had a good effect on the Swedes and Wratislaw was hopeful of an accommodation between Charles XII and the Emperor.

his brother Archbold.[1] You will do in it just as you please, for I am no ways concerned.

What you desire for Captain Barton,[2] may be done by telling Mr. St. Johns, that when those redgements are to be completed, that there might then be care taken that he may have a company. For til the Queen is informed of the state of those redgiments, there aught to be no commissions given, by which a very considerable some of mony may be saved.

872. MARLBOROUGH *to the* DUCHESS [*7/18 August 1707*]

Source: Blenheim MSS. E3.
Printed: Coxe, i. 305 (inc.), as 15 August.

Soignies August 15th 1707

Since my last we have had one continued rain, so that nether the enemy nor we can stur out of our camps. I have at this time my winter cloaths and a fire in my chamber, but what is worse the ill weather hinders me from going abroad, so that 30 [Peterborough] has the opertunitys of very long conversation. What is said on[e] day the next destroyes, so that I have desired them [him] to putt their [his] thoughts in writting. My Lord Pitterborow has showen me severall very obliging letters of the King of Spain to himself, which I can't but wonder att after what he [the King] has write against him. He dose also asure me that he is some thousand pounds the worse for the services, having lost two equipages upon the whole he swares, and I beleive his estate is very much in dept. The English post of the 31 is come, and I have had this minut the satisfaction of reading yours. I believe Mr. Burton[3] is a very honest man, which is the best of securitys, so that you do well in taking that morgage. The estate of Lord Lovlace's,[4] which is to be sold the next term, will not be ours, if you leave it only to the care of Mr. Guidot, for his temper is such that some other will bye itt; but you must not lett him know this, but Lord Chancelor might advise who might be a proper person to be joined with him. I am obliged to you for Lord Royalton's letter,[5] as also the accounts of Woodstock. I wish the hall and sallon could have been covered, but I find that must not be expected. My heart is set on this place, but if I can come to have quiet with you, I shall think myself happy in any place.

 [1] Lord Archibald Hamilton. The paper is untraced. Hamilton was a captain in the navy and Orkney may have requested a promotion for him. He was made a rear-admiral in Jan. 1708. Luttrell, vi. 254.
 [2] See p. 869 n. 1.   [3] Unidentified.
 [4] John, fourth Baron Lovelace of Hurley (died 1709), cornet and major, first troop, Life Guards; colonel, Regiment of Foot, 1706; governor of New York 1708; died there 1709.
 [5] Untraced.

873. MARLBOROUGH *to* GODOLPHIN   [*9/20 August 1707*]

Source: Blenheim MSS. A1-37.
Printed: Coxe, ii. 306.

Soignies August 20th 1707[1]

As I have had the favour of Lord Pitterborow's company ten days, he has not only shown me, but left with me the copies of several letters to resolutions of councels of war, to demonstrat the falsety of several facts malliciously reported of him.

He has given me the enclosed paper[2] of what he hears is reported against him. My having been so constantly abroad makes me ignorant not only as to this paper, but also what other facts may be laid to his charge. But as he is resolved to acquaint you and Lord Sunderland with everything, in order the Queen may have a treu information, I shal say no more, but that as far as I am capable of judging, I veryly think he has acted with great zeal.

874. MARLBOROUGH *to* GODOLPHIN   [*11/22 August 1707*]

Source: Blenheim MSS. A1-37.
Printed: Coxe, ii. 307.

Soignies August 22d 1707

If we had had any tollerable weather we had staid but one night in this camp, but as the rains continu God only knows when we shall be able to get out of it.

Lord Pitterborow left us on Saturday.[3] I have endeavored to lett him see that for his own sake he aught to clear the objections against him, in order to which I have given him a letter for yourself;[4] and he has promised me that he will acquaint you and Lord Sunderland with all he has to say. At the same time I must acquaint you, that by what I am told of the discourse of 30 [Peterborough], that he will not be able to be governed. But I have said so much to Lord Pitterborow that I hope you will have it in your power to make him easy, which may prevent the mischief of 30 [Peterborough], who will most certainly run into the notion of 51 [Electress Sophia], and all other things that may be crose. The opinion of 50 [Elector of Hanover] should be

---

[1] This tongue-in-cheek letter was written at Peterborough's request for him to carry to Godolphin and the Queen. Cf. Marlborough's opinion in the following letter.

[2] In Blenheim MSS. A1-37. It lists five charges that had been made against him followed by his justification. For a similar list see Sunderland's letter to Peterborough, 28 Sept. 1707, and Peterborough's reply, n.d., *H.L.N.S.*, vii. 398, 400–4 et seq. The charges were: not marching to Madrid upon notice from Galway and discouraging Charles III from going; declining to serve under Galway who was senior to him; going to Italy and leaving his duties in Spain without orders; negotiating with the Duke of Savoy without authority from the Queen; drawing bills for some £50,000 which had never been accounted for.

[3] 9/20 Aug.   [4] Letter 873.

made as publick as possible, for I very much fear that this next winter 42 [the Queen] may receive a mortefication on that subject.[1]

I see by yours of the 5th[2] which I received last night that you are of the opinion that the chief command should be left to the King of Spain and his generals. I think the best argument that can be given in Portugale is that her Majesty being resolved to leave only a lieutenant generall in Spain, thay aught to do the same, by which that matter would be setled. But as for the number of troupes that should go from Italie, I can know no certainty til the return of Brigadier Palms.

I beleive it is very treu that 56 [King of Sweden] has no engagement with 43 [King of France], but his unaccountable obstenacy, and the litle knowledge he has of the affaires of Christendome may make him take engagements this winter, expecially if it be treu what is write from Paris, of the Duke of Savoy's having attacked the retrenchement, and was repulsed, with a very considerable loose. The enclosed from the Comte Wratislaw[3] is what I have received since my last, and is the only one which gives me some hopes of an accomodation.

My trompet is this minutt come from the French army, and says thay have no news from Toulon since the nynth, so that the Duke of Savoye's being repulsed is false.

875. MARLBOROUGH *to the* DUCHESS   [*11/22 August 1707*]

Source: Blenheim MSS. E3.
Printed: Coxe, ii. 308 (inc.).

Soignies August 22th 1707

I am obliged to you for your kind concern in yours of the 5th, which I received last night. The litle indisposition I had was occasioned by my being obliged on the march to take burnt wine which stoped my lousness, which made me very often sick in my stomack. But I hope now all is over, I having taken two days together the lickerish and rubarb, so that my stomack is easy.

---

[1] Marlborough was concerned about the machinations of Mr. Scott who had come over to England with the connivance of the Electress Sophia to work with the Tories. She still desired an invitation to come to England though the Elector disavowed Scott's efforts (M. Knoop, *Kurfürstin Sophie von Hannover* [Hildesheim, 1964], pp. 207–8. Marlborough wrote to Harley a confidential note on this same topic, addressed 'for yourself': 'By yours [of the 5th, Blenheim MSS. A2-24] I find you have by direction of the Queen desired that Mr. Scott may be recalled to Hanover. I should think her Majesty might reasonably expect to have him disgraced, otherways he will remain there as an agent to the discontented. Nobody having write to me of this matter but yourself, I desire you will let my opinion be known to none but the Queen and Lord Treasurer, but in zeal to her Majesty's Service, I beg the opertunity may not be neglected, in letting all England know the Elector's opinion [p. 864 n. 7], for I have but too much reason to know, that the invitation is intended to be pressed this winter' (P.R.O., S.P. 87/2, fols. 748–9). By his of 2 Sept., Harley reported 'Mr. Scot it is said is gone' (Blenheim MSS. A2-24).

[2] Letter 867.

[3] 2/13 Aug., copy in Blenheim MSS. A1-37; reply, 14/25 Aug., Murray, iii. 532.

I do asure you I did not mean 89 [the Whigs] when I spoke of ingratetude,[1] but I meant it in generall to 108 [England], and if you will do me justice you must beleive that I have done all the good offices that is possible at this distance. I do not say this to make my court to 89 [the Whigs], but that I am persuaded it was good for my country, and for the Service of 42 [the Queen], for I do really beleive that 84 [the Tories] will do all thay can to mortefie 42 [the Queen]. In this whole matter I have no concern but the zeal I have for 42 [the Queen] and 108 [England], for I am now both att an age and humor that I would not be bound to make my court to either partys, for all that this world could give me. Besides, I am so dishartned that when I shall have done my duty, I shal submit to providence. But as a friend I will fortel you the unavoidable consequence if 89 [the Whigs] mortefie 91 [the Court]; that 38 [Godolphin] will be dishartned, and 199 [Harley] have the power and credit of doing what he pleases. This I know will hurt both 42 [the Queen] and 108 [England], but I see no remedie. I hope our last news from Paris is not treu, which says the Duke of Savoye had attacked the retrenchement before Toulon, and was repulsed.

I open my letter to send you the good news that what was said of the Duke of Savoye is not trew.

876. GODOLPHIN *to* MARLBOROUGH   [*12 August 1707*]

Source: Blenheim MSS. A2-23.

Windsor August 12th 1707

Wee have now 2 posts due, though the wind has seemed favorable 2 or 3 days together. I am afraid the packett boat is taken, which would bee very grievous at this time, when wee are so impatient to hear from you, and to know what passes at Thoulon, which is of so great consequence that our *all* seems to depend upon it.

While wee are under so much suspence in these great matters, I shall have very little to trouble you with, unless it bee to observe, that in case things should turn so abroad, as that there might bee any encouragement to proceed with our small expedition,[2] it would be convenient that Maccartney's exchange might bee perfected, with the soonest, he being an officer who seems to mee [more] capable of conducting such a number of men than anybody else within our reach here.

The last letters from Lisbon, represent the Portugheses in great fear of being pressed hard, in the autumn, and at the same time, in no good condition of defence, and that to send more troops thither, would bee so much

---

[1] Probably in the missing letter of 30 July/10 Aug.
[2] A descent upon France.

thrown away. In the meantime, wee must give them, as good words, as wee can, and endeavour to keep them from being frighted into a peace.

Mr. Methuen is very pressing to come home, and wee have no great plenty of proper person to send there or (indeed) anywhere.[1]

877. MARLBOROUGH *to* GODOLPHIN   [*14/25 August 1707*]

Source: Blenheim MSS. A1-37.
Printed: Coxe, ii. 309-11.

Soignies August 25th 1707

I send you enclosed a copie of the Pensioner's letter with my answere.[2] That of the desent and the oaths to be given this country, as well as the Barier. I should be glad to be derected what I might say farther to those points. It is near six weakes since I have had anything directly from Provence, and what we have by the way of Paris can't be relied upon. If we should not succed at 115 [Toulon] I find by all my letters from 110 [Holland] that thay shall be very much dishartned, so that our friends fear thay shal not be able to make them act with vigor. But 39 [Marlborough] hopes the contrary, if 56 [King of Sweden] gives no disturbance, so that I could wish your thoughts might be employed to see if you can't find some proposition that might be made to him, to bring him more into the interest of the Allyes. Mr. Stepney is in so daingerous a condition that I despair of his life. The Queen will have a loose, and I am afraid it will be very difficult to find a proper person to fille his station in this country.

Having write thus farr, I this minut receive yours of the 8th.[3] What you say of Prince Eugene we can have no just thoughts til the return of Mr. Palmes. I have this morning received letters of the 20, 24, and 29 of the last month from Mr. Chetwind,[4] and others from the army in Provence, and I am very sorry to tel you that I obsarve by all of them, that there is not that friendshipe and relyance between 58 [Duke of Savoy] and 48 [Prince Eugene], as should be wished for the making so great a design succed. I beg this may be known to nobody but yourself and the Queen, hoping God may reconcil them and make them act for the best.

---

[1] Methuen was not recalled until 29 Apr. 1708 when Galway arrived to replace him.
[2] 9/20 Aug., in 't Hoff, pp. 336-7; reply, 14/25 Aug., ibid., pp. 338-9. Heinsius thought it was too late in the season to attempt a descent. Quiros had sent Heinsius an authorization from Charles III for Quiros to administer the oath of Allegiance to his subjects in the Spanish Netherlands (see p. 856). The Pensionary considered it improper as the Maritime Powers had taken the government into their own hands for the duration of the war (see p. 616). He thought it was time their two countries took up the negotiations for a Barrier again (p. 606) and brought that affair to a conclusion.
[3] The 7th, letter 870.
[4] Blenheim MSS. A2-18. That of the 29th is excerpted in Churchill, ii. 253.

By my letter I received this morning of the 17th from Mr. Robi[n]son,[1] he thinkes 56 [King of Sweden] is resolved not to be reconcilled to 46 [Emperor]. I do not send his letter, not doubting but he writes the same thing to Mr. Secretary Harley. The desire you have that 116 [the States] should enter into stricter measures with the Czar, may be right, if the Emperor and King of Sueden should not agree. But by the enclosed I send of Comte Wratislaw of the 17 from Leipsick[2] gives great hopes. I have also a letter from Comte Recteren of the 10th from Vienna,[3] that asures me the Emperor has agreed as to the point of religion, desired in favour of the Selesiens by the King of Sueden. I have received another letter from Thomas Earle;[4] he presses very much to come home [from Spain]. He should either be made easy in that Service, or have leave to return. If you shall see it practicable, and for the service to make a de[s]cent this yeare, I would recommend Withers rather then Ingolsbey; for the first is very brave and dilligent, and will make no other demands then what is absolutly necessary; the other will be desiring a train of artillery and such expences as you will not be able to comply with. But upon the whole, if wee do not succed in Provence, it will not be reasonable to attempt the landing of men this yeare. A very little will clear this matter, for I recon Brigadier Palmes was with the Duke of Savoye about ten days ago, so that I may hear from him in a weeke.

878. MARLBOROUGH *to the* DUCHESS   [*14/25 August 1707*]

Source: Blenheim MSS. E3.
Printed: Coxe, ii. 308 (inc.).

Soignies August 25th 1707

Since yours in which you desire I should look on the seals of your letters, I have done itt for two or three posts, and I am very confident thay have not been tutched. As long as you are carefull to send them to Mr. Secretary Harley, you may be sure thay will come safe. The continuall ill weather wee have had which keeps us in this camp gives mee the spleen, for it is not in this place I would stay. If 30 [Peterborough] should when he coms to England at any time write to you, pray be carefull what answere you make, for sooner or latter it will be in print. If you would have mee bye five peeces for yourself and daughters, pray lett me have the coullors, and number of Dutch elles or English yardes, so that I may bye no more then what is necessaire. Most of your letters being full of feares for this winter, I can't forbear asuring you, that I would not only wish prosperity and quietness to

---

[1] Blenheim MSS. A2-20; reply, 14/25 Aug., in Murray, iii. 532.
[2] Blenheim MSS. A2-17.
[3] Ibid., reply, 21 Aug./1 Sept., Murray, iii. 544.
[4] 15/26 June or 16/27 July, both in Blenheim MSS. A2-29. He pleaded his bad state of health. See also p. 892.

42 [the Queen], but I would take pains and venture any hazard to make her business go well; so that for God sake, if you think I can contribut, lett me know itt;[1] for I can asure you, that if wee have not success at Toulon, there will be this winter a great deal of uneasiness in most of the forain courts. So that should we at the same time have divissions in England, how could the warr be carryed on with vigor this next campagne, which must be done to bring France to reason? I have received yours of the 8th, and I am of the same opinion I was in a former letter,[2] that Lord Lovlace's estate will not be baught by Mr. Guidott unless he has somebody joined with him. I shal inquier into what Mrs. Brinkfield writes, but it is certain he can't be payd but to the time of his death.[3] I thank you for Mr. Bolter's[4] letter, for I am always glad to see an account of the building, for that must be my resting place.

879. GODOLPHIN *to* MARLBOROUGH   [*15 August 1707*]

Source: Blenheim MSS. F1-31.
Printed: Coxe, ii. 311–13 (inc.).

Windsor August 15, 1707

I am to acknowledg the favour of your letters from Soignies of the 15th and of the 18th,[5] with the severall letters and papers enclosed, which I shall bee sure to keep very carefully according to your directions.

By yours of the 15th, the French seem to have very narrowly escaped your hand, and I doubt the very ill weather, and the country in which they now are, will secure them from falling any more this year into the same danger. This I reckon, will putt you in a condition of more easily sparing 3 or 4 regiments for our descent, in case the season of the year and other circumstances will admitt of our putting it in execution.

It is impossible to bee sure that any attempt of this kind shall succeed, but all the assurances from those parts are very encouraging to it. Besides that, wee know all the force of France is at this time moving towards Provence, and their people on this side left both unguarded, and also in many places, disarmed, for fear of revolts. With your assistance, I see wee might bee able to have about 6,000 foot and 1,000 horse and dragoons, which if they were well on the other side, I should think might bee sufficient, with a good man at their head, to make themselves master of Rochefort and

---

[1] Marlborough did write to the Queen by this post but the letter is untraced. See p. 891 n. 1.
[2] Letter 872.
[3] Arrears of pay due to the widow of his aide-de-camp, killed at Blenheim.
[4] William Boulter, joint (with Henry Joynes) comptroller and clerk of the works for Blenheim Palace. Joynes was first appointed in May 1705. Boulter, a creature of the Duchess, according to Vanbrugh (*Works*, iv. 182) was added in June 1705. On his death Tilleman Bobart was appointed, in Sept. 1708.
[5] Letters 868, 871.

Saintes,[1] which opens to them the provinces of Xaintage and Augoumois[2] where the Protestants are the most numerous, and the people said to be the best disposed of any. But all this will turn upon having a proper person at the head, and in great measure also, upon success at Thoulon, which I hope in a good way, though all the French accounts endeavour to fright us very much with their good posture there, and the great preparations they are making to disappoint the Duke of Savoy's design upon that place.

I am glad you have no other objections to the Venetian troops but your doubt of them not coming in time, for they are certainly nearer at hand than any others whatever, except those which the Emperour has in Italy already. And I am very glad to find by Sir Philip Medow's last letter that he is in hopes the Imperiall court will bee easy in letting us have some of the troops from Naples for strengthening the Duke of Savoy's army, which I take to bee equally usefull to us as if they lett us have them for Catalonia.

I doubt 50 [Elector of Hanover] will not bee willing to lett the Saxon troops now upon the Rhyne advance towards Italy, because he is soe pressing to have others from 39 [Marlborough]. But I think 'tis very plain there will bee no farther occasion of them this year where they now are, unless 50 [Elector of Hanover] would show more diligence and vigour than his motions hitherto seem to promise, or indeed then the season of the year seems now to admitt of.

I enclose to you a letter I had lately from 199 [Harley],[3] which I desire you not to lose, that you may see his thoughts concerning 30 [Peterborough]. I must own to you at the same time, that if one could imagine there were the least truth in what 30 [Peterborough] has taken so much pains to profess to 39 [Marlborough], my own opinion would bee not make 30 [Peterborough] desperate, till he had first given clear demonstration it was impossible for him not to bee troublesom. But in this, as in all other things, I can submitt to better judgments, and I incline to think that the opinion of 4 [Halifax], 5 [Somers], and 6 [Sunderland] would in this particular bee the same that 199 [Harley] seems to have.

As to what you write about 241 [Lady Monthermer], I hope you will receive satisfaction from 240 [Lady Marlborough], who always sees what 39 [Marlborough] writes to Mr. Montgomery [Godolphin], and I don't doubt will bee concerned to doe what is best for both, and to prevent any disagreable noyse in that matter.

---

[1] A French town on the Charente, 30 kilometres inland from Rochefort.

[2] Saintonge, and Augumois, coastal districts of France lying between La Rochelle and the mouth of the Charente.

[3] 13 Aug., Blenheim MSS. B2-33; relevant portion in Coxe, ii. 313–14. Harley suggested Peterborough be required to 'give an account in writing of his proceedings' in Spain and on his journey home. If the Cabinet found he had acted 'contrary to his instructions, ought he not to be committed?' Though he could be bailed he would be tried in court 'by a common jury for a misdemeanor' which would keep him busy and out of mischief.

I have written to my Lord Manchester by this post,[1] in my Lord Sunderland's absence, that he would lose no time in proposing to the Venetians to come into the great Allyance, upon promising subsidys for ten or twelve thousand men to joyn the Duke of Savoy, and giving them assurances of taking care of their interests at the general peace, and that no peace shall bee made without their participation.

880. GODOLPHIN *to* MARLBOROUGH   [*16 August 1707*]

Source: Blenheim MSS. A2-23.
Printed: Coxe, ii. 314 (inc.).

Windsor 16 August 1707

Mr. Hare came hither yesterday, and finding he resolves to return to you, by the very next packett boat, I have a mind to mention some particular things to you, by so safe a hand, which I should not care to venture by the post.

I reckon one great occasion to Mrs. Morley's [the Queen] obstinacy, and of the uneasyness she gives herself and others, especially about the clergy, proceeds from an inclination of talking more freely than usually to 156 [256 Mrs. Masham]. And this is layd hold of, and improved by 199 [Harley] upon all such matters, if not upon others, to insinuate his notions (which in those affairs) you know by your own experience, from the conversation wee had together, before you left England, are as wrong as is possible. I am apt also to think, he makes use of the same person to improve all the ill offices to 89 [the Whigs] which both hee, and that person are as naturally inclined to, as 42 [the Queen] is to receive the impressions of them.

Now this must needs doe a great deal of mischief, and I am afraid wee shall find the effects of it in the winter if a timely remedy bee not putt to it which I think cannot bee done but by Mr. Freeman [Marlborough] and 38 [Godolphin] speaking very plainly at the same time to Mrs. Morley [the Queen], both of 199 [Harley] and a great many other things, and settling a rule for preventing (before it is too late) all those uneasynesses for the future. But how this will bee done in time I cannot see, unless your affairs on that side will allow of your being here some time before the meeting of the Parliament, and to satisfie you of how great importance it is, that you should bee here before that time, is the chief reason of my giving you this trouble.

[1] On receiving the letter, Manchester's secretary, Christian Cole, advised the envoy that only the Queen or a Secretary of State had the power to issue him instructions. He advised Manchester to write to Sunderland for a clarification. This incident has been reported by historians as an instance of Godolphin's meddling. At this time, however, there was no Secretary on hand at Windsor to attend the Queen. The Lord Treasurer deputized (by command of the Queen) rather than bypassed the Secretary and kept Sunderland fully informed of his actions. Godolphin to Manchester, 15 Aug., and Cole's comments thereupon, Cole, pp. 473–4; D. B. Horn, *B.D.R.*, pp. 4–5; M. A. Thomson, *The Secretaries of State, 1681–1782* (Oxford, 1932), p. 100; Godolphin to Sunderland, 14, 20–1 Aug., Blenheim MSS. D1-21.

One thing, which I take to bee immediatly necessary to your liberty of coming over early, is, that you should think and fix upon some proper person to succeed Mr. Stepney without delay, so as that he may bee setled in that station, and possessed of the severall parts of his business, before you leave The Hague. And unless this bee done to your full satisfaction, I doubt it will bee too great a difficulty upon all the rest, and you will bee obliged to stay too long there, to have the fruit which I hope for by your being here before the Parliament. When all this is sayd, I have nobody in my thoughts to offer to yours, nor can I judge so well as you can who will bee more or less proper for the severall parts of business which attend this station, and will really require a man of very good application and capacity.[1]

In my letter of yesterday I took notice of what you had written to mee about 241 [Lady Monthermer], who must certainly bee to blame to 240 [the Duchess]; for both you and I have seen a thousand times how kind and indulgent 240 [the Duchess] has always been to 241 [Lady Monthermer], who (I doubt) is apt to presume too much upon her own understanding; and though she has a great deal of sence, yett the want of good counsell and ex-ample makes here ready to fall into errours, which people of less sence and more complyance might very easily avoid.

I have made this letter so long that I will leave the rest to write by the post, which I believe is like to bee with you before Mr. Hare.

881. MARLBOROUGH *to* GODOLPHIN [*18/29 August 1707*]

Source: Blenheim MSS. A1-37.
Printed: Coxe, ii. 341, 311 (inc.).

Soignies August 29th 1707

I have had the favour of yours of the 12th[2] by which I see you want two foragne mailes. I am afraid thay will not bring you good news, neither from Saxony, nor Provence. You will see by the enclosed what the Duke of Savoye's envoye[3] writs me from The Hague, which confermes what I have received by other letters from that army. I also send you the Pensioner's answer to mine of the 25th, which you had a copie off.[4] By Lord Sunderland's letter write to 2 [Galway],[5] I find it is preposed to him to be Ambassador, so that you might be easy in granting the request of Mr. Methuin, for I can't but

---

[1] Cadogan was left in charge. See p. 874 n. 3.　　　　　　　　　　　[2] Letter 876.
[3] The Marquis del Borgo. His letter of 14/25 Aug., Blenheim MSS. A2-30 with an extract of a letter from the Duke of Savoy of 19/30 July. See the following letter for the contents.
[4] See p. 880. Heinsius's answer of 16/27 Aug., in 't Hoff, pp. 339-40. Heinsius was discouraged by the news from Toulon and the poor prospects for a peaceful settlement between the Emperor and the King of Sweden on the condition of the Silesian Protestants. The Pensioner approved in principle the idea for a descent upon France but thought it was too late for one this year.
[5] 24 June, P.R.O., S.P. 104/208, pp. 111-13.

think but 2 [Galway] will be glad of being there or anywhere, rather then where he now is.

I am a good deal concerned att a letter I received by the last post from 240 [Lady Marlborough], in which she tels me that 208 [Harley] has the intier confidence of 239 [the Queen].[1] If she has good reason for this opinion, I can't but think there should be no time lost in speaking plainly to 42 [the Queen], in letting them see what 38 [Godolphin] and 39 [Marlborough] thinkes her intirest. If she be of another opinion, I think 38 [Godolphin] and 39 [Marlborough] should honestly lett her know, that thay shall not be able to carry her business on with success, so that she might have time to take her measures with such as will be able to serve her.

I shall always be ready to sacrefise myself for the prosperity of the Queen, but I will not be thought to have credit, when her business is managed in a way, which in my opinion must be her ruin. I beg you will let me know your thoughts on this matter, and what you think may be proper to be done, for though I am weary of all sorte of business, I know her meaning is so sincerly honest, that I would undergo any trouble or hazard that you think may do good. On the other side, if I can't do good, nothing can make me so happy as a quiet life.

The weather begining to be good I intend to make the canon and bagage march tomorrow, and the army the next day. I beleive the French will march from Cambron, before I passe the Dandre, for it is very plain thay will avoyde the comming to action. I shall take care as soon as I can for the exchang of Machartney, but I beg that none of the prisoners in England may have any incoragement, for the French do not use us well, pretending to govern absolutly in the exchange of prisoners, by making their choice. For att this minut, thay act as if thay were our masters.

882. MARLBOROUGH *to the* DUCHESS   [*18/29 August 1707*]

Source: Blenheim MSS. E3.
Printed: Coxe, i. 310–11.

Soignies August 29th 1707

I have had yours of the 10th and your nott of the 12th with Vanbrook's letter,[2] by which I see the hall and sallon must be left for the next yeare. As our business of this yeare goes I am afraid it will be time enough, especially if the news we have from France be trew, which says that the town made a sally on the Duke of Savoye on the 15, by which we suffered very much.[3]

---

[1] Cf. the preceding letter.   [2] Untraced.
[3] On 18/29 July the Allied forces had taken the heights of Sainte-Catherine, overlooking Toulon. It was retaken by the French on 4/15 Aug. by a fierce assault in which the Allies lost the commander, the Prince of Saxe-Gotha, and 600 men. The Allies gave up the siege within a week.

If you have good reason for what you writte of the kindness and estime 239 [the Queen] has for 256 [Mrs. Masham] and 208 [Harley], my opinion should be that 38 [Godolphin] and 39 [Marlborough] should tell 239 [the Queen] what is good for herself, and if that will not prevaile, to be quiet and let 208 [Harley] and 256 [Mrs. Masham] do what thay please; for I own I am quite tiered, and if 42 [the Queen] can be safe, I shall be glad. I hope 38 [Godolphin] will be of my mind, and then we shall be much happyer then by being in a perpetuall strugle. For if 38 [Godolphin] and 39 [Marlborough] have lost the confidence of 239 [the Queen], it would be the greatest folly in the world in them to act so as that the world may think as thay now do, that it is in their power to do everything, by which wee shall not only be made uneasy, but loose our reputations both at home and abroad. I shal always be ready to sacrefise my life for the quiet and safty of 42 [the Queen], but I will not be imposed upon by anybody that has power with them. For as I have served them with all my heart, and all the sincerity imaginable, I think I deserve the indulgence of being quiet in my old age.

883. GODOLPHIN *to* MARLBOROUGH   [*19 August 1707*]

Source: Blenheim MSS. A2-23.

Windsor August 19, 1707

Wee have now two posts due from you, but no hopes of their comming before this goes away. This keeps us in great suspence as well as in great impatience for the event of Thoulon. Everything seems to turn upon it, and particularly (while that is uncertain) our designed expedition[1] must remain under the same uncertainty. But if at last, the season of the year and other circumstances encourage us to goe onn with it, the troops you can send us to joyn those already here, must bee sent to Ireland, to take in the rest there; by which method, if anything happens to disappoint the design, wee shall avoid the unnecessary trouble and charge of bringing those forces hither.

My Lord Steward[2] dyed yesterday. The Queen seems resolved that his son[3] shall succeed to his employment; and I hope she will lett my Lord Manchester return to his place, of captain of the Yeomen of the Guard, to which there are a thousand pretenders. But he is now in the Queen's service abroad, and has always behaved himself well, so that it would bee a sort of injustice not to restore him, and consequently, all pretenders will more easily submitt to him, than they would to one another.[4]

[1] A descent on France.   [2] William, first Duke of Devonshire.
[3] William, second Duke of Devonshire.
[4] Manchester had previously held the post, 1689–1702. He resigned it upon being declared Secretary of State, 'not thinking it reasonable, nor honourable to keep two such posts'. To Godolphin, 25 July/5 Aug., Cole, p. 466. The Marquis of Hartington, heir to the Duke of Devonshire, had succeeded him. Instead of giving it to Manchester, who did not return to England from his embassy at Venice until the end of 1708, the Queen gave it to Townshend. Godolphin made him the offer in a letter of 6 Nov. 1707. See Sotheby sale catalogue, 11 May 1970, item 132.

Mr. Hare designes to goe over in this packett boat. I have written another letter to you, by him,[1] which I hope will come safe to you, but I believe this will bee sooner with you than he can bee.

On 19/30 August Marlborough sent off his heavy baggage towards Ghislenghien and the next day broke camp and marched his troops to the west. They stopped at noon when they reached the Dender just south of Ath. Marlborough made his headquarters at Attre, across the Dender from the French camp which Vendôme left precipitously that morning when news reached him of the Allied movement. Leaving quantities of provisions and baggage behind as booty for Marlborough's soldiers, the French did not stop until they reached the safety of the Scheldt, close to the fortress of Tournai, a march of 30 kilometres compared to 15 for the Allies.

---

884. MARLBOROUGH *to* GODOLPHIN

[*20/31 August 1707*]

Source: Blenheim MSS. A1-37.
Printed: Coxe, ii. 316-17.

Attre September 1st 1707

You will know by the letters of this day, upon our marching hether, the enemy dechamped in great hast, and I beleive our march tomorrow will oblige them to passe the Skell.[2] The deputys are convinced that if we had made the march to Genap two months ago, when I pressed for itt, the Duke of Vandôme would have been obliged to retier as he now does. I know nothing of the Duke of Savoy's quitting the siege of Thoulon, but what I am told by the Duke of Vandôme's trumpet, who says it was on the 22th.[3] I believe this will naturally put a stop to the descent you intended, and if you have good reason for a descent, as yours of the 15th[4] seems to think, it is most certain [that] early in the yeare when thay have the whole summer before them, is a much properer time.

What 199 [Harley] says in his letter concerning 30 [Peterborough] may be right, but I think as you do that you must do no step in that matter but in conjunction with 4 [Halifax], 5 [Somers], and 6 [Sunderland], and if possible with 7 [Wharton] also, or he will play you tricks. By what I have heard him say I beleive he thinks he can justefie himself in every perticular, but I should think itt is impossible to justefie the aplication of the mony; for whenever you have those accounts, I believe you will find the greatest con-

---

[1] Letter 880.   [2] The Scheldt.
[3] The siege was given up on this date and the Allied army retired into Italy.
[4] Letter 879.

fusion imaginable, so that I think Mr. Bridges should make himself master of that account as soon as possible.

Upon this ill news from Provence, I am already pressed by Monsieur de Quiros[1] that emediat orders might be given for the sending troups to King Charles. Til I know what the Duke of Savoy and Prince Eugene['s] project may be, by Mr. Palmes, who I beleive might leave them as soon as thay marched from Thoulon, I shall not be able to give any answere. In the meantime, I should be glad to know what your thoughts in England are as to that point. The enclosed from Comte Wratislaw[2] I received this morning. You will see it gives much more reason for hopes then Mr. Robinson's letters.

885. GODOLPHIN *to* MARLBOROUGH   [*22 August 1707*]

Source: Blenheim MSS. A2-23.
Printed: Coxe, ii. 314–15 (inc.).

Windsor August 22th 1707

I have the favour of yours of the 22th and 25th[3] and am very sorry you have had so much bad weather. Wee had our share of that, and therfore I hope you have yours of the fine weather wee have here at this time.

I have not yett heard of 30 [Peterborough], though our letters from The Hague tell us he was to come over in the last paquet boat. But whatever he shall say, it cannot bee relyed on. He will bee governed by his animositys or his interest; I can't answer which of them will prevail.

You ask my opinion, about taking the oath of fidelity to King Charles in the Low Countryes and also about settling the Dutch Barriere. I take you to bee a much better judg in both these points. However, I am always free and ready to give you my opinion.

I think then there is no colour of reason for not giving the oath to those people, and for the States to pretend to any part of the soverainty of them,[4] seems to mee the most extravagant thing in the world. I must own at the same time I think this has been too long delayed, and that the right time of doing it had been, when the King of Spain offered you that government. And though you were not willing to assert it upon that occasion, because it

---

[1] 20/31 Aug., draft by Quiros, Rare Book Department, Boston Public Library.

[2] 13/24 Aug., copy in Blenheim MSS. A1-37. He told Marlborough, 'he was resolved to sign the treaty with the Swedish ministers, unless he had orders from Vienna to the contrary by Monday last [18/29 Aug.]'. Marlborough to Harley, 21 Aug./1 Sept., Murray, iii. 542.

[3] Letters 874, 877.

[4] Godolphin misunderstands the Dutch conditions for a Barrier. He made a similar statement to Lord Chancellor Cowper. 'Dutch would have sovereignty of Barrier towns, particularly Ostend (which England can't tolerate). [The King of] Spain insists [the inhabitants of Flanders] should take oath of allegiance to him, which Dutch oppose and Duke of Marlborough can't shew, he can do more in Flanders' (in Snyder, 'Formulation', p. 160). The Dutch did not claim *sovereignty*, only the right to *garrison* troops in the Barrier towns.

might have an air as if you contested with the States for yourself, yett your easyness upon that account has been a reall prejudice to the King of Spain, and an encouragement to 116 [the States] to encroach upon his just rights.[1]

However, if this matter of tendering the oath of fidelity gives a new occasion of resuming (at this time) the discourse of their Barriere, it is certainly best to putt itt off; for towards the end of the campagne they will take a handle from the least dissatisfaction about their Barriere to run head-long into all the offers that will not fail to bee made them from 43 [King of France]; especially, if wee might yett hope for good news from 119 [Italy]. But I must own with much concern, the 2 last posts have abated the reasonable expectations which I thought wee had of that matter.

Whithers is certainly in all respects, the best man in the world (if you can spare him) for the descent. But that matter as well as most others must depend entirely upon our fate at 115 [Toulon].

I am very glad Sir Philip Medows finds the court of Vienna so ready to strengthen the Duke of Savoy's army in Provence. I am also in hopes of getting troops from the Venetians.

886. GODOLPHIN *to* MARLBOROUGH   [*25 August 1707*]

Source: Blenheim MSS. A2-23.
Printed: Coxe, ii. 342-3 (inc.).

Windsor August 25 1707

I have the favour of yours of the 29th[2] with the papers enclosed. I keep them all by mee and if at any time you want any of the papers you send mee, I can readily find them.

Though I have written fully to you by Mr. Hare[3] about 42 [the Queen], and though I am not very willing at any time to say much upon that subject by the post, yett desiring in yours of the 29th to know my thoughts upon what 240 [the Duchess] had written to 39 [Marlborough], I am under a necessity of endeavoring to make you comprehend as well that both Mr. Montgomery [Godolphin] and Mrs. Freeman [the Duchess] have thought it best to read to Mrs. Morley [the Queen] 39's [Marlborough] last letter to 209 [Godolphin];[4] all except one word, which was the name of a person[5] not fitt to bee mentioned. They did very well foresee this would certainly have the consequence of making yett more uneasiness in Mrs. Morley [the Queen] toward Mrs. Freeman [the Duchess] but did hope it might bee of so much use another way as to over ballance that.

Whether their thoughts will prove right in the latter of these, I cannot tell. But in the former, I am very sure they have not been mistaken, and I believe

---

[1] See pp. 573 et seq. and 856, n. 7.   [2] Letter 881.   [3] Letter 880.
[4] That is, letter 881.   [5] 208 [Harley].

39 [Marlborough] will soon bee of the same mind in that matter, by a letter which I am told he will have from 42 [the Queen]¹ as soon as this. And I can't but think it is of so much consequence that 42 [the Queen] should not bee countenanced and encouraged in complaints of 240 [the Duchess] that when you have an opportunity of talking with 39 [Marlborough] of these matters, you would advise him to take great care of his answer in that particular. I will only add, that when you write yourself anything [to] 38 [Godolphin] which you would not have 42 [the Queen] know, it ought to bee in a letter apart.

I am so much distracted with my doubts and apprehensions concerning 115 [Toulon] that I can't say anything to the purpose about that matter or the consequences of it; but as the wind is I believe wee shall have another post tomorrow.

In the meantime I am convinced by all the accounts I have seen from Leipsick that if the accomodation bee not perfected betwixt the Emperour and the King of Sweden it is absolutely Comte Wratislau's fault. But I hope he will not have made so fatall an errour, as that would prove to bee. And therfore if I may suppose that agreement made, the readyest stepp (in my opinion) towards improving the consequences of it, by entering into stricter measures with 56 [King of Sweden], would bee for you to congratulate with him upon that occasion; and to tell him this proceeding will bee so agreable to the Queen, as that she cannot fail of being desirous of comming into stricter friendships and measures with him; and that you shall look upon it as a great mark of his confidence, if he will bee pleased to charge you with his proposalls to her Majesty for that end.

I find by the Pensioner's letter, he is very much for a descent, if it can bee made in time, but as I told you in my last, all that depends upon the Duke of Savoy's success, and while wee are heartless on that side, everything goes onn heavily on this.

Wee want to hear from 2 [Gallway] upon my Lord Sunderland's proposall,² but I am farr from thinking the embassy will please him. If I were in his place, I'me sure I should not take it. I believe he is very fond of coming home and presses now again for leave in every letter. When his answer to Lord Sunderland comes that matter ought to bee determined.

I have not seen Lord Peterborow, nor he has not yett waited upon the Queen. In my Lord Sunderland's absence, he made his application to Mr.

¹ 25 Aug., in Coxe, ii. 343–4, and Brown, pp. 230–1 (misdated as early September), in reply to one from Marlborough, 14/25 Aug., untraced. In answer to charges that she followed advice from Harley rather than Godolphin, the Queen protested she did follow Godolphin's advice and that Harley had never spoken to her about the two bishops she had nominated over the objections of the Whigs.

² Sunderland wrote to Galway 24 June (P.R.O., S.P. 104/208, pp. 111–13) pressing him to take the post of ambassador to the King of Portugal in place of Paul Methuen who was anxious to return home. Galway accepted and left Spain for Lisbon in Feb. 1708 to take up his new post. Marlborough made the suggestion to Godolphin independently (p. 850) but after Sunderland had written.

Secretary Harley who is rather worse disposed towards him (if possible) than his colleague. Severall letters and answers have passed between them which all tend (I think) more to increase the misunderstandings, than to lessen them. He has sent mee your letter with his answer to some objections, he states in it. I must own I think his answers even to those objections stated by himself are frivolous enough. I believe I shall see him tomorrow or next day at Quainton plate,[1] where I am told he intends to bee.

Finding by your last you designed to move in a day or 2 towards Ath, I have been thinking Holland would like well enough of your besieging of Tournay, if the season permitts and that you have strength enough for it. They would bee glad to extend their contributions and t'would bee no great charge to bring their great canon by the Scheldt. But this I believe is determined one way or other before you can have this letter.[2]

On 22 August/2 September Marlborough sent his artillery and heavy baggage off to cross the Dender at Lessines. The army followed the next day and stopped at Nederbrakel. On 24 August/4 September the army reached the Scheldt at Ename. The impedimenta crossed that afternoon and the army on the 25th/5th, joining up at Petegem. Meantime Vendôme continued in his camp at Antoing.

---

887. MARLBOROUGH to GODOLPHIN

[25 August/5 September 1707]

Source: Blenheim MSS. A1-37.
Printed: Coxe, ii. 317 (inc.).

Petteghem September 5th 1707

Since my last[3] we have made three marchs in order to passe the Schell, which wee have done this morning. We shal stay in this camp tomorrow, and the next day march to Helchin, by which we shall oblige the enemy to eat upon their own country, which I am afraid is all the hurt we are like to do them, for I am very confident thay will be carefull not to give occasion for action.

I have had two letters from Mr. Earle [in Spain], both being possitive that if he has not leave to return he must dye.[4] If the Queen will alow of his

¹ On 26 Aug. Harley wrote to Marlborough, 'my Lord Treasurer...is gone to Quinton Hall in Buckinghamshire' (Blenheim MSS. A2-24). This was the site of an annual horse race, the 'Quainton plate'.
² Tournai was not attempted this year.   ³ Letter 884.
⁴ 20/31 July, Blenheim MSS. A2-29.

coming home, I should be glad to know itt, that I might write to him. He says the 2,500 English horse and dragons are not above 500, and those in a bad condition. The mony that might be saved this yeare in that army might help you in the next yeare, but by what I hear Lord Galway employes the mony in paying Catalons, which certainly aught not to be approved off; for if that should be once setled, you will be obliged to that expence during the warr.[1] As soon as Brigadier Palmes returnes, I do intend to send him to give you an account of what the Duke of Savoye and Prince Eugene has said to him. I can't gett any account from France of the number of the common soldiers taken in Spain. I beleive the reason is that thay have by ill usidge made the greatest part of them take service, which thay aprehend, with reason, we should take ill.

I have had a second letter from the Pensioner concerning the Bearier,[2] fearing if there should be nothing done in that affaire it might be of ill consequence. Pray lett me know, if Monsieur Vriberg presses this matter, and what answer he has, so that I may know how to govern myself. I send the enclosed[3] that you may also see what Lieutenant General Earle writs to Cadogan. The letters of the 13th are just come, but I am so tiered that I can only thank you for yours.

'Yesterday the army marched from Petteghem to this camp, from whence we covered the siege of Menin last year. The French, who pretended to take the camp of Pont d'Espierre upon the first notice of our passing the Scheldt on Tuesday [6 September], likewise passed that river the same evening near Tournay, and continued their march to Pont-a-Tresin, where they are now encamped with their right, and with their left at Lille, having the river Mark before them.'[4]

---

888. MARLBOROUGH *to* GODOLPHIN
[*28 August/8 September 1707*]

Source: Blenheim MSS. A1-37.
Printed: Coxe, ii. 324–5 (inc.).

Helchin September 8th 1707

Your two letters of the 16 and 19 by the post and Mr. Hare,[5] I have received. By both I see you had not received the ill news from Thoulon. What you write concerning 239 [the Queen], 199 [Harley], and 256 [Mrs. Masham] is of that consequence, that I think no time should be lost in putting a stop to that management, or else to lett them have it intierly in their own hands. I did mention this to you in a former letter,[6] but have had no answer. I do not

---

[1] See p. 850.   [2] 20/31 Aug., 't Hoff, pp. 340–1.   [3] Untraced.
[4] Marlborough to Harley, 28 Aug./8 Sept., Murray, iii. 550.
[5] Letters 880, 883.   [6] Letter 881.

see anything to the contrary, but that the campagne in this country might be finished by the end of October, and I beleive eight days wil be sufficient for my stay at The Hague. But I beleive the Elector of Hanover will be desirous to have a meetting for the setling the operations of the next campagne, but as yett I have heard nothing from himself; but his General [Bülow] here has told me that he beleived it would be desired.

The dainger Mr. Stepney is in gives me a good deal of trouble, for I am afraid it will be very difficult to find a proper person to fill his place, for itt must be one that is capable of the business of Flandres as well as that of Holande. But whielst there is any hopes of his life, I beg nobody may be spoke to. If I knew anybody proper for this station I would take the liberty of naming, but as I know none, I hope you will think of somebody that has dexterity and no pride. For if the Queen be not very well served in this country, she will quickly fiel the ill effects, for not only the people in this country but the Dutch also must be pleased, which is a pretty hard task.

The weather is so very fine, that I have beged of Lady Marlborough to make a vissett to Woodstock, and if your business will permit of it I should be glad you would see it, though but for one day. If I could flye I would be there, but my fate is to row in this gally. If I can ever be so hapy as to be free, I shal then endeavor to end my days in quiet, which is much more longed for then I can expresse.

I wish for the service of the Queen, that she may have no thoughts of disposing of the blew ribons, til she may find the giving of them be a satisfaction to herself, or of some use to her business.[1] Besides, I think if we should ever have a treaty with the King of Sueden, that might be a proper time for him to desire itt, and her Majesty to give itt. My letters from Leipsick by some accedent are miscaried, but by what I hear from others, you aught to have an account from Mr. Robinson, that the treaty was signed on the 30th of the last month.[2]

I open my letter to send you the enclosed,[3] which I have received this minutt. Prince Eugen's letter[4] should not be seen by anybody but the Queen.

---

[1] The Duchess had written that Kent wanted the Garter. See p. 895.

[2] See below, p. 896 n. 2.

[3] From Robinson, 20/31 Aug., Blenheim MSS. A2-20, and Wratislaw, 20/31 Aug., Blenheim MSS. A2-17; reply, 4/15 Sept., Murray, iii. 561-2. They informed him the treaty would be signed the next day and described its terms. In his Wratislaw enclosed a letter from Prince Eugene of 24 July/4 Aug. (in Coxe, ii. 325-6).

[4] Eugene complained of the Duke of Savoy and said this was the most difficult operation in which he had ever been involved. Cf. Eugene's letter to Marlborough, 9/20 Aug., in Coxe, ii. 321-2.

889. MARLBOROUGH *to the* DUCHESS

[*28 August/8 September 1707*]

Source: Blenheim MSS. E3.
Printed: Coxe, ii. 324 (inc.).

Helchin September 8th 1707

By the last post I was so tiered, and received yours so late, that I had neither time nor force to answere itt. I am sorry for what you write concerning 181 [182, George Churchill]; it is certain he is a very indiscrit 84 [Tory], and has so litle judgement that he is capable of any indiscretion; but I am very sure he would not say or do anything that he thought might prejudice the Queen or her Government. I am very glad to find by yours that the Queen has it in her thoughts of giving the white staff to the now Duke of Devonshire, for I think him a very honest man, and that he will prove a very usefull man. I find by Lord Treasurer[1] he hopes the Queen will restore Lord Manchister to that of the Gardes. Besides his being now in the Service, and I think ever since the late King's death, he has always behaved himself well. I am very sure he is much better then any of those named in your letter. As to what you write of 40 [Kent] pressing for the blew ribon, it would be scandelous to give it him, since he has no one quallity that deserves itt.[2] What you write me of Cox[3] I have heard but never saw any proff. He is certainly a cunning man, and it may be a knave, but he lets nobody cheat you but himself, so that I am afraid you will not find a better. I have by the last post received a letter from Mr. Travers.[4] I inclose it that you may see that what Mr. Bolter promised [balance missing].

890. GODOLPHIN *to* MARLBOROUGH   [*29 August 1707*]

Source: Blenheim MSS. A2-23.

St. James's 29 August 1707

I am here expecting every hour the Holland letters, which are not yett come though the wind seems to have been fair.

In the meantime I am to thank you for the favour of yours of the 1st of September.[5] The unwelcome news of the raising of the seige of Tholon, will not allow time at present, to complain of the occasions of it. Wee have little enough left to prevent the ill consequences of it.

'Tis obvious that the French will lose no time in sending back the detach-

---

[1] Letter 883.
[2] Cf. Marlborough's remark in the preceding letter which was prompted by the Duchess's letter.
[3] Coggs, the goldsmith, and her banker?
[4] 19 Aug., Blenheim MSS. A2-31, describing the progress of the works at Blenheim.
[5] Letter 884.

ments from all sides which they had ordered to march to Provence, and that fear being now over, their first thought will bee to overrun Catalonia, and oppress King Charles there this winter.

'Tis (I think) as plain that ther's no possibility of breaking this blow but by troops from Italy, either out of those already in the pay of the Allyes, or rather (if that can bee obtained) out of the Emperour's own troops, which are more proper in this case, and for which in my opinion wee might encourage the court of Vienna, to expect subsidyes from the Allyes to begin from the first of January next, provided they bee sent thither imediatly. This last clause is indispensable, since otherwise they can neither come in time to save Catalonia, nor can our fleet stay in those seas to transport them, now the enterprise at Tholon has failed.

To the same effect with this letter to you, Mr. Secretary Harley will write by this post to Sir Philip Medows. But I cannot ground much confidence in his instances at Vienna, unless they bee supported by yours also to your friends in that court, which is the chief intent of my giving you so much trouble upon this head.

I have desired Mr. Secretary to send you a coppy of my Lord Gallway's last letter to mee,[1] which will show you his thoughts relating to Spain. But his schemes being grounded upon success at Tholon, seem to bee of no great use since our unfortunate disappointment there.

Only in case the agreement should hold with the King of Sweden,[2] and the Elector of Hanover being settled in the command upon the Rhyne, why might not the Emperour consent to send Prince Eugene with his troops to command all the forces in Spain? Nothing could so much contribute to give new life and reputation to that affair, nor consequently, bee more essentiall to the interest of the whole common cause in generall, nor particularly to that of the house of Austria.

This ought not to hinder, but it will rather mightily encourage, our endeavours to strengthen the army in Italy by all the ways wee can imagine of hiring troops for that end from the Venetians, from King Augustus, or any other princes of Germany.

And in case the King of Sweden agrees with the Emperour, I don't see how he will bee able to support so great an army, as he has now. I can't easily think he will part with them; and therfore might it not bee proper some way or other to sound that court about receiving subsidyes from the Allyes for a part of them?

These notions in a hurry are my first thoughts upon the melancholly news from Tholon. I can easily believe Mr. Palmes will bring you better, yett

---

[1] Untraced.

[2] With the Emperor, concluded at Altranstädt, 21 Aug./1 Sept., in Dumont, VIII. i. 221-3. By its terms the Emperor agreed to restore the Silesian Protestants to the rights they were granted at Westphalia in 1648; granted Charles XII permission to march his army across Silesia; accepted the Holstein-Gottorp candidate for the bishopric of Lübec.

these if allowed immediatly will bee of more effect than better, that are longer delayed.

As to 30 [Peterborough] he has not yett seen 42 [the Queen] nor 38 [Godolphin]. He is ordered to give an account of his proceedings in writing, which I suppose he will comply with.[1] His whole behaviour here seems very unaccountable. If wee can unite with 89 [the Whigs] and bee upon good terms with 88 [Parliament] which I take to bee a consequence of the former, wee shall gett the better both abroad and at home. But wee shall want Mr. Freeman's [Marlborough] help in the last, as much as in the first.

891. GODOLPHIN *to* MARLBOROUGH   [*1 September 1707*]

Source: Blenheim MSS. A2-23.

Windsor September 1st 1707

I have the favour of yours of the 5th new style[2] by which you seem to think the enemy will take care to avoyd any action, and consequently your campagne is as good as finished. And since that is the case, I would wish it were really finished that you might bee the sooner at liberty to return; which I think can hardly bee too soon, with respect to our affairs at home. Though at the same time, I think it would not only bee right, but necessary, to adjust a new scheme for carrying onn the warr next year with the States, and the ministers of the Allyes, while you are at The Hague, in your way hither.

In order therfore to doe this effectually I offer to your thoughts whether you would not send imediatly to Vienna that either Comte Wratislaus or Comte Zinzendorf may meet you at The Hague by the end of the campagne. By what the Emperour will agree to doe, wee must take our measures for all that relates to Italy and Spain in the next year, and these measures ought to bee all concerted in one place. It loses more time than wee have to spare, to send forward and backward, between London, The Hague and Vienna. When I have said this I beg your patience to lett mee lay before you, what I wish might bee the scheme for next year, upon which you may judg, first how farr it is right, and 2dly how farr it is practicable.[3]

By the letters from Leipsick of last post, I take it for granted, the agreement is made between the Emperour and the King of Sweden that the Queen and the States are to bee the guarantees of this treaty;[4] and Mr. Dayrolles' last letters say, the envoyè of Denmark[5] is soe enraged at this, that he has publickly said his court cannot bear it, and must take new measures. I hope

---

[1] The correspondence of the Secretaries of State with Peterborough is in *H.L.N.S.*, vii. 394-409.

[2] Letter 887.

[3] Godolphin's plans were developed in conversations with Lord Cowper at Windsor on 1 and 8 Sept. See Cowper's notes of these meetings in Snyder, 'Formulation', pp. 144-60.

[4] Neither England nor the United Provinces became guarantors of the Treaty of Altranstädt of 1707, nor, more important, that of 1706, although England at least did recognize Stanislaus as King of Poland early in 1708, one of the conditions of the latter treaty. Hatton, p. 227 n.

[5] Johann Heinrich von Stöcken, the elder (died 1709), Danish envoy at The Hague, 1699-1709.

this will not hinder the States from confirming the guaranty, which is soe necessary, but that they will think of some proper methods not to lose Denmark, which will agree enough with their own inclinations.

By this step of the King of Sweden's I would fain flatter myself that the Emperour would not want the service of Prince Eugene in Germany, but that he might bee perswaded to send him with a good body of troops from Milan and Naples to the succour of his brother King Charles in Spain. This would bee so popular in England, that I have no doubt but the Parliament will bee very ready to allow subsidyes for the support of those troops from the first of January next; especially, if they bee sent so timely, as that wee may hope to defend Catalonia this winter.

In the next place I could wish that the 28,000 men might continue to bee payed by the Allyes, and to act under the orders and directions of the Duke of Savoy next year, which will oblige France to keep a great army on that side to prevent his impressions, and consequently make them less strong in Spain, upon the Rhyne, and in Flanders.

As to this last, I wish that wee may provide for as strong an army there as usuall, that is to say for the 40,000 men and for the 10,000 men; but I am very much of opinion that the experience of this year is enough to convince all the world (and especially our own people) that wee ought not to make use of them. For since it is plain that the greatest and the best armys can bee of no use in that country, till both sides agree to fight; what an opportunity have wee lost by not having 10,000 men less there this year and of carrying them to the coast of France where there were no troops within 500 miles of them; and consequently, they might have done what they pleased, on that side. I say all this to show, that an army in Flanders strong enough to cover the great towns and to hinder the French to make any siege, or to putt Holland into a pannick fear, is more for the advantage of the common cause, than to have so great an army there (as disables us to have troops for a descent) upon a view of acting offensively, which is always in the power of the enemy to avoid.

As to Portugall, I reckon wee must send some regiments thither, even before next year, to keep them in our allyance and encourage them to defend their frontiers but without the least hope or expectation of their acting offensively.

I had written the greatest part of this letter when I received the favour of yours of the 8th from Helchin[1] with the enclosed from Comte Wratislaus and Mr. Robinson. I shall observe your caution about Prince Eugene's letter to him.

Mr. Robinson's letter to you is enough to give one new alarms about the treaty, but I hope the next post will bring news that all is concluded with Comte Wratislaus. As he readily acknowledges the great obligations the

[1] Letter 888.

Emperour has to the Queen and the States, for sheltering him as they have don from this King of Sweden, so I wish he would as readily consider what returns the court of Vienna makes for these, and all their other obligations.

The separate treaty in Italy[1] and the sending of those troops to Naples[2] was infallibly the cause of disappointing us at Thoulon. I don't say this to make them a useless reproach for what is passed, but rather to putt you in mind of arguments to make use of, for pressing them to exert themselves the more, to give speedy relief to King Charles in Catalonia, since there is not time for it to come but from them; and if it bee possible, that they would send Prince Eugene thither.

I don't see that your going to the Elector of Hanover, is either reasonable in itself, or like to bee usefull at this time. How can you concert operations with him for next year before you know what troops you can depend upon? He may appoint some person of trust[3] to meet you at The Hague with Comte Wratislaus or Zinzendorf, as I propose in the first part of this letter. And (besides) this jorney would keep you soe long out of England where there are matters of much more consequence, which cannot end well without you. When I redd to the Queen, what you write about the blew ribbands, she sayd she understood that the King of Sweden had never shown the least inclination to have one.

She gives leave to Mr. Erle to come home.

892. MARLBOROUGH *to* GODOLPHIN [*1/12 September 1707*]

Source: Blenheim MSS. A1-37.
Printed: Coxe, ii. 326-8 (inc.).

Helchin September 12th 1707

I find by yours of the 22th,[4] which I received last Friday,[5] that you had not then received the ill news from Thoulon. By the letter I have received from Mr. Secretary Harley,[6] as well as by what you say of 30 [Peterborough],[7] [I find] that he had not been with the Queen, nor anybody in her Service, which I wonder att, for he told me he would in the first place waite upon you and Lord Sunderland. He is very capable of poshing his animossitys so far as to hurt himself, and give a good deal of trouble to others, which were to be wished might have been avoyded, especially this winter. What you

---

[1] Between the Emperor and France for the neutrality of Lombardy, 2/13 Mar. 1707. See p. 772 n. 3.
[2] See p. 848 n. 4.
[3] Marlborough met the Elector of Hanover and Wratislaw at Frankfurt in October.
[4] Letter 885.   [5] 29 Aug./9 Sept.
[6] 26 Aug., Blenheim MSS. A2-24. 'The Erle of Peterborow has been in London since Wednesday. He continues to avoid waiting upon the Queen, because he is left out of the Council, upon the reforme when the Northerne Lords were brought in [in May].' See pp. 787-8.
[7] See p. 896.

say of the oaths of fidelity is very reasonable, but by 62 [Heinsius] letters thay are of another opinion, so that I beleive thay will not alow the oaths to be given.[1] God knows what is best to be done in that matter. But I am afraid the business of the Barier, which is next to impossible to be setled, will occassion very great uneasiness between 108 [England] and 110 [Holland]. I can very easily keep it off til my return to The Hague, but then I must be instructed. Don Quiros and Monsieur Sinzerlin have been with me. I have write by Sinzerlin to the Elector Pallatin[2] to know to what number of his troupes, payd by England and Holande, he wil consent should go for Spain. As soon as I have an answere you shall have itt. I beleive Holande will consent those troupes should be sent to Catalonia, and the truth is, we have no others that can go. By what we hear from France, thay are sending back the Duke of Barwick with the troupes that came from Spain, and 4,000 men more, and, as thay say, orders for the attacking of Geron [Gerona].

Now that the agreement is signed between the Emperor, and King of Sueden, I beg you will be carefull of making any step with the Moscovitt ambassor that may give offense to the Suedes, for should thay return into the Empir during the war, it would oblige us to make an ill peace with France. You will see by the copie of the letter I sent you by the last[3] of 48 [Prince Eugene], that he and 58 [Duke of Savoy] can't serve any more in the same army, and 50 [Elector of Hanover] being in possession of the command in the Empire, I see no place wher he can serve but in 112 [Spain], in which place I am afraid we can't succeed. I long for the coming of Palmes, that I might know what the Duke of Savoye at Prince Eugene intends for the remainder of this campagne, and their thoughts for the next. It is now very plain that the French having no troupes in Italie enables them to be strong in all other places, so that we must think of strenghning the army on the Rhin and in this country, or the next yeare we shall be beaten in one, if not both places. God knows how we shall be able to do this, but if we can't we shal run great hazardes. Notwithstanding the Catalon redgiments which Lord Galway has raised, which I hope your orders will put an end too, I could wish for the Queen's Service and the good of the common cause, that you would do all that is in your power for the raising those redgiments of foot which were taken at Almanzor, by which you may have in the spring a body of foot to employe in a desent, if practicable. I should I think the raising of these redgiments very difficult, but that I am persuaded that the greater part of the officers are at liberty, or vacant. When you shall resolve to take this methode, I shall then presse the States to do the same thing.

I inclose the copie of a letter from Comte Noyelles,[4] which I received but

---

[1] The Dutch refused to permit the oaths to be taken, and Quiros did not press it (Veenendaal, pp. 131–2).
[2] 30 Aug./10 Sept., Murray, iii. 552–3.   [3] Letter 888.
[4] 18/29 June, in Blenheim MSS. A1-37. Noyelles reviews recent military operations in Spain. He stresses the need to have a fleet wintering in the Mediterranean and suggests the port of Alicante.

yesterday, though it is of an old date. You also will see what Monsieur Zinzerling['s] business is to The Hague.[1] That of the Palatins thay will consent to, but I beleive thay will give no possative answere to any of the other articles.

Sir Rowland Guin has write twice to me to desire I would write to you, in favour of his petition he sent to her Majesty imploring her pardon. If you have received such a petion pray lett me know what answere I might make. I have sent the Marquis of [du Plessis-Chàttilon and] Nonan[t's] letter to Mr. Secretary Harley.[2] If what he says be trew, it would be a cruelty to refuse him 4 months' leave.

893. MARLBOROUGH *to the* DUCHESS   [*1/12 September 1707*]

Source: Blenheim MSS. E3.

Helchin September 12th 1707

On Friday last[3] I had yours of the 22th of the last month, by which I see you agree with me that if 89 [the Whigs] persistes in the resolution of mortefying 91 [the court], the whole is likely to fall upon 38 [Godolphin], which may hurt 42 [the Queen] and 199 [Harley], but can do no good to 89 [the Whigs]. This confermes me in the opinion of what I have formerly write, that I would have 38 [Godolphin] not only speak plainly to 42 [the Queen], but also to 89 [the Whigs], and if that has no effect upon 42 [the Queen], and that 89 [the Whigs] will continue sullen, I would then as a friend have him retier. I do not mention 39 [Marlborough] because I know his fixt resolution of medleing with no business when 38 [Godolphin] is out.

Though 6 [Sunderland] agrees with the opinion of 199 [Harley],[4] I am afraid it is for different reasons; and though 30 [Peterborough] is much to blame, he may give more disturbance then were to be wished, especially this winter, which made me take a good deall of pains with him. I shall say no more, knowing long before this coms to you, the resolution concerning him must be taken. I had a letter from Lord Portland two days before he was to embarke,[5] but he said nothing of his Lady nor the stuffs,[6] so that I desire you will lett me have your commands. I am not att all surprised att any unreasonable or unjust thing done by 8 [Montague], but I am very well pleased that

It could provide grain from Majorca and the Barbary coast for Barcelona. Charles III will need a continuation of his subsidy next year from England.

[1] Zinzerling had come to England in the spring and then had gone to the Continent to obtain aid for Charles III. He presented a similar memorial in England before going to the Continent.

[2] 29 Aug., P.R.O., S.P. 87/2, fols. 763–4. The Duke of Montague and the Countess of Peterborough also interceded with Marlborough for him. See Murray, iii. 554, 560–1.

[3] 29 Aug./9 Sept.   [4] See p. 883 n. 3.

[5] 19/30 Aug., The Hague, Blenheim MSS. A2-25.

[6] Dress fabrics for the Duchess and her daughters. See p. 881.

25 [Lord Monthermer] is of a contrary temper.[1] The letter you sent of 241 [Lady Monthermer] makes me hope in time she will behave herself to 270 [Lady Marlborough] as she aught. I do asure you that nothing goes so near mee, as when I see you are made uneasy by your children. May you and yours be ever happy, and that you may live long to enjoy the blessing of your grandchildren, is and shall be my constant prayer; for I do love and estime you with all my heart, and if I can enjoye a few yeares in quiet with you, I shall think myself recompenced for many troubles.

The particular you have sent of Lord Lovlaise's estate seems to be very unreasonable, but thay will not be able to sell it til thay bring it to a reasonable price.[2]

Pray lett me have your thoughts what you think will be best for the service and quiet of 38 [Godolphin], for whatever it be I think it aught to be put in practice before the meeting of the Parliament.

894. GODOLPHIN *to* MARLBOROUGH   [*2 September 1707*]

Source: Blenheim MSS. A2-23.
Addressed: To his Grace the Duke of Marlborough.

Windsor September 2d 1707

In my long letter[3] which you will receive with this, I have troubled you the more particularly with my notions about a scheme for carrying on the warr next year, both because I am persuaded, they are generally speaking, the notions of those here, who wish nothing so much as a good end of the warr; and also because I know that nothing will lend more to make them zealous and hearty in obtaining the necessary supplyes for it, than being satisfied that there is a desirable and a probable scheme adjusted and settled betwixt us and our Allyes.

I am apt to fear that the greatest difficulty of putting any such scheme in practice, as I have mentioned in my other letter, will bee with 110 [Holland]. And (in that case) to bring them *that length*, as the Scots express it, I should think they might bee encoraged to expect any reasonable assistance from us, as to their *Barriere*, except what relates to Ostend. But that must never bee yielded.[4] Monsieur Vryberghen has never yett said one word to mee of that matter. 'Tis true he has not had much health since his arrivall.

---

[1] Cf. p. 885.
[2] For Marlborough's interest in buying Lovelace's estate, see p. 882.
[3] Letter 891.
[4] The negotiations for a Dutch Barrier in the Spanish Netherlands, begun in 1706 had ended at the close of that year without resolution (see p. 520 n. 1). They were not taken up in earnest again until 1709. Throughout the discussions the English were adamant that Ostend should not be included. As the main port of entry for English goods into the Low Countries, they could not permit it to be in Dutch hands.

All thoughts of our descent for this year are laid aside, the transports for the horse and dragoons discharged, but some of the foot must (I think) bee sent to Portugall.[1]

895. MARLBOROUGH *to* GODOLPHIN [*4/15 September 1707*]

Source: Blenheim MSS. A1-37.
Printed: Coxe, ii. 328-9.

Helchin September 15th 1707

Since my last I have had the favour of your two letters of the 25 and 29th.[2] I think your thoughts for the affaires of Spain, and the retrieving of our misfortune at Thoulon by strenghning the army in Italie by the Venetians, if possible, is very right. But I am afraid you will find those people more backward. You will see by the inclosed[3] that the King of France promises the Elector, that he shall have, the next campagne, an army strong enough for the regaining of Braband. I am not concerned for what may happen here the next campagne, in comparison of the aprehensions I have for the Queen's business this winter in England. If that goes well, I hope we may be able to strugle with the French in this country. I am sorry to see you are of opinion that 2 [Galway] will not care to go for Portugale, for there he might do service, and where he is I think itt impossible. I think it might be for the Queen's Service, and the publick good, to endeavour to persuade the States to make an augmentation, for the carrying on the warr with more vigor, or we shal never come to a good peace. Whatever you say to Vriberg, must at the same time be said at The Hague. The French intending this day to forage Templeuve,[4] I marched thether with 20,000 foot and 5,000 horse. Upon their having notice, thay did not suffer their foragers nor escort to leave their camp, but suffered me to forage the whole country, though I was three leagues from my own camp, and not a league from theirs. But thay will ventur nothing this yeare.

You will see a letter I have sent Lady Marlborough,[5] which I received by the last post from Lord Pitterborow. By that you will see that he intends to be in good temper. But I confess I can[not] understand the meaning of his not waiting upon the Queen, and that there is no notice taken of itt. In my poor opinion you should resolve to be pleased or to be very angry.

[1] For plans made for a descent this year see p. 846 n. 2. Five squadrons of foot, totalling 912 men, were sent to Portugal in the spring of 1708.
[2] Letters 886, 890. The latter bears the date of 27 Aug.
[3] Untraced.
[4] A village lying midway on the road between Roubaix and Tournai.
[5] Letter 896.

896. MARLBOROUGH *to* GODOLPHIN   [*4/15 September 1707*]

Source: Blenheim MSS. A1-37.
Printed: Coxe, ii. 346.

[Helchin] September 15th 1707

I inclose a copie of my letter to the Queen,¹ and I leave it to your discretion to deliver it or burn itt. And I think I am obliged, let the consequence be never so fatal, to the friendship and love I have for you, to tel you my opinion very freely, that if 89 [the Whigs] will continue in that unreasonable humour of being angry with 38 [Godolphin], whenever 42 [the Queen] dose not do what thay like, [it will cause everyone's ruin, including their own]; for the truth is, thay are jealous that 38 [Godolphin] and 39 [Marlborough] have inclination to try once more 84 [the Tories]. You and I know how false this is. However, if 42 [the Queen] will be governed by 199 [Harley], thay will have just reason given them to be angry; and if 38 [Godolphin] and 39 [Marlborough] continues in business, al England will beleive what is done was by their advice, which will give power to 89 [the Whigs] to mortefie whom thay please. So that I think you must speak very freely to 89 [the Whigs] and 239 [the Queen], and if thay will not aprove of your measures have nothing to do with either; and if we were well out of this warr, we should then be happy.

897. MARLBOROUGH *to the* DUCHESS   [*4/15 September 1707*]

Source: Blenheim MSS. E3.
nted: Coxe, ii. 346-7 (inc.).

Helchin September 15th 1707

I have received yours of the 25 and 26 of the last month, and by the enclosed letter you sent of 42 [the Queen]² I am afraid that nothing can go well this winter. I am confermed in this thought by what 243 [Lady Sunderland] writs as from her Lord.³ I will make no reflections, but I own to you that I think the expressions are very hard, when I consider what pains 38 [Godolphin] and 39 [Marlborough] takes. I have sent a letter to 38 [Godolphin] for 42 [the Queen] and a copie of my letter, and have left it to his discretion of burning or delivring itt. For my own part, I am out of hart, and wonder att the corage of 38 [Godolphin]; for were I used, as I do not doubt but I shall, as he is by 89 [the Whigs], which threatens to abandon him, whenever 239 [the Queen] displeases, I would not continu in business for all this world could give me, and I beleive they would be the first that would have reason to repent. I do not send you a copie of my letter, being sure 38 [Godolphin]

¹ 4/15 Sept., in Coxe, ii. 344-6. Marlborough urges her to accept Godolphin's advice, and co-operate with the Whigs. He offers to go to England secretly for a day or two if necessary to consult with her.
² 25 Aug. See p. 891 and n. 1.   ³ Untraced.

will shoe it you. I did desire your opinion as to 38 [Godolphin] quitting but you have never made me any answere; for as I would serve 42 [the Queen] with the hazard of my life, so my friendship to him obliges mee to wish that he would venture nothing, since everybody pretends to be angry. Yours of the 29th is com this morning. It is most certain that I had the happyness of very long audiences from 30 [Peterborough], but it was generally after my business was done, and I must own to you he was very diverting. The inclosed[1] is what I received from him by this post. I shall give no answere to itt till I hear something more from England, for he should either have been with the Queen or the Queen should be angry. I send you back 243 [Lady Sunderland's] letter that you may read it once more, for I think it is plain, thay beleive that 38 [Godolphin] and 39 [Marlborough] have a mind to bring in 84 [the Tories], which is very obliging. I have always obsarved the seals of your letters, and I dare say thay have never been opened. I was in hopes to have meet with some of the French army this day, thay being to have foraged the same place I have done this day, but one the notice thay had thay did not come.

898. GODOLPHIN *to* MARLBOROUGH   [5 September 1707]

Source: Blenheim MSS. A2-23.

St. James's September 5, 1707

I have nothing to add from hence to what I troubled you with yesterday[2] from Windsor, but that wee have letters from Lisbon of the 26th [in] which they are under a good deal of apprehension from the enemy on that side, and [have] no good preparations made for their defence. The Marquis de Fronteira,[3] who had the best reputation among them, had layd down the command of the army, which is given to the Condé d'Alvor,[4] who has neither reputation nor experience. However I think since the descent is now layd aside, I doubt wee must send 2 or 3 regiments of foot more, to encourage them to continue in our allyance, since wee cannot now bee without the port of Lisbon. If wee had succeeded at Tholoun wee should not have been forced to make so much court to them.

Erle having the Queen's leave to come home, and my Lord Gallway and Stanhope being both very earnest for the same favour, I believe it will very soon bee granted them, in which case the command of her Majesty's subjects there will naturally fall upon Hara, unless you think it may bee better to send any other person from hence to take that command.

---

[1] 26 Aug., Blenheim MSS. A2-29; reply, 4/15 Sept., Murray, iii. 560.
[2] 4 Sept. Untraced.
[3] Portuguese general, made commander of the Portuguese army in 1707. He continued in the command the rest of the war.
[4] Portuguese Councillor of State, formerly viceroy of Goa.

I have not yett appointed any comptrollers of the army. Mr. How's ill health makes him desirous to serve at home rather than abroad, but at the same time [he] does not seem very willing to part with anything of his present income.

899. MARLBOROUGH *to* GODOLPHIN [8/19 September 1707]

Source: Blenheim MSS. A1-37.
Printed: Coxe, ii. 329-30 (inc.).

Helchin September 19th

The inclosed is a copie of a letter I have received all in cypher from 63 [Wratislaw].[1] I am afraid his carectors are very just. However, his project, in my opinion, is very daingerous att this time; but I have not nor shall I give any answer til I hear from you. I agree intierly that the more troupes we can keep in Italie, the greater numbers the French will be obliged to keep on that frontier and in their own country. But as for the troupes of the Langrave, I beleive he will not be persuaded, nor do I beleive his country is able to recrutt them; and [except] for the Pallatins, we have no other troupes we can send to the King of Spain. As to your desire of Prince Eugene's going for Spain I think he can serve nowhere else, for I dare say he will not serve under the Elector of Hanover nor can he serve with the Duke of Savoye. I shal inclin you to think as Sir Edward Seamour said in the House of Commons that he never knew admeral or generall that had ships or troupes enough. I am of the opinion that the warr will be desided in this country by a battaile early in the next campagne, for thay see that no success in any other part of the world can gett them peace; so that I am persuaded thay will have a very great strength here at the opening of the field. However, I shall endeavour to govern myself agreable to what you think will please in England. If you have any perticular place in which you think great service might be done by a desent, that aught to be known to none but England and Holande, and I think might very easily be acomidated with the service of this country. For a desent can't be put in practice til the begining of Jully, and before that time I dare say we shall have decided the business here. For if we have not a battaile by that time we may shipe the troupes at Ostend, and will not give so much notice to France, as if thay were shipped from England. I expect Brigadier Palmes in [a] few days. I am of the opinion to send him over as soon as he comes, so that you may know their thoughts, and mine also. It is very trew the King of Sueden has never shown inclinations for the bleu ribon,[2] but when he shal enter into stricter friendship with the Queen, I hope he

[1] 23 Aug./3 Sept., Coxe, ii, 330-3; reply, 21 Sept./2 Oct., Murray, iii. 606-8.
[2] See p. 899.

will have a mind, as also the King of Denmark. The inclosed from Lord Galway[1] came to me under a flying seal. The derections the Queen has sent him concerning the troupes is certainly much righter then his notions.

900. MARLBOROUGH *to the* DUCHESS   [*8/19 September 1707*]

Source: Blenheim MSS. E3.
Printed: Coxe, i. 347-8 (inc.).
Addressed: For the Dutchesse of Marlborough.

Helchin September 19th 1707

I have received yours of the 30th and 2d. I have received no letter from 267 [the Queen?] since that you sent me, and you may be sure I shall never mention 256 [Mrs. Masham] neither in letter nor discorse, and I am so weary of all this sort of management that I think it is the greatest folly in the world to think any strugling can do good, when both sides have a mind to be angry. When I say this I know I must go on in the command I have here as long as the warr last[s], but I would have nothing to do anywhere else, for really what I hear from England gives me great disturbance, and sometims vexes me so that I am not the same man. If 240 [Lady Marlborough], 38 [Godolphin] and 39 [Marlborough] were out of business, I should be more capable of doing my duty here. I have a letter from the Duke of Summersett[2] in which he tels me the right he has to the government of Tinmouth, and att the same time askes it for his son.[3] I have made him a sivil answer,[4] and that I shall not be engaged til my return, which was what he desired. I find by some of your letters that you think I may have credit with 42 [the Queen], but I do assur you I have not, and I will give you one instance; that Smaldridge[5] has been able to hinder the disposing of the Professers.[6] I see this but that must not alter my doing the best service I can. I would be estimed but I am not ambitious of having power.

[1] 3/14 Aug., Blenheim MSS. A2-29. Galway wanted to build a superior force in Spain and was concerned that satisfactory arrangements had not been concluded for exchanging prisoners. He needed those men taken at Almanza to fill his regiments. The delay, as Marlborough explained to St. John, was because 'the French are so obstinate, that to this day I can get no account of the numbers of our private men, nor so much as learn where they are, but his lordship might easily know that they were immediately marched away for France' (8/19 Sept., Murray, iii. 570).

[2] 26 Aug., Blenheim MSS. A2-25.

[3] Algernon Seymour, seventh Duke of Somerset (1684-1750), styled Earl of Hertford until 1748.

[4] 7/18 Sept., Murray, iii. 567-8, and n.

[5] George Smalridge (1663-1719), tutor of Christ Church; M.A., Oxford, 1689; D.D. 1701; deputy to Regius Professor of Divinity 1700-7; his influence is evidenced by his later appointments as chaplain to the Queen 1710; Dean of Carlisle 1711-13; Dean of Christ Church 1713; Bishop of Bristol 1714-19. *D.N.B.*

[6] Regius professorship of Divinity at Oxford, vacant since the death of Dr. Jane in February. Smalridge had been acting as Jane's deputy since 1700 and the Queen promised him the post. Marlborough proposed Dr. John Potter and the Whigs supported his candidature. Potter was finally awarded the professorship in Jan. 1708. For the struggle to obtain Potter's appointment see G. V. Bennett, 'Robert Harley, the Godolphin Ministry and the Bishoprics Crisis of 1707', *E.H.R.*, 82 (1967), 736, 746.

901. GODOLPHIN *to* MARLBOROUGH   [*9 September 1707*]

Source: Blenheim MSS. A2-23.
Printed: Coxe, ii. 333-5 (inc.).

Windsor September 9, 1707

In all my late letters you have had so fully my thoughts about carrying onn the warr next year, that it is almost superfluous to say any more upon that subject, if every letter I receive from you did not furnish some new occasion which makes itt impossible for mee to avoyd repetitions.

By yours of the 12th and 15th[1] I find you expect still the return of Brigadier Palmes with an account of those Princes'[2] thoughts both as to the ending of this campagne, and the beginning of the next, before you can come finally to determine your own resolutions. I am much afrayd, the miscarriage at Tholoun, is owing to the little good understanding betwixt those two princes, or rather, in truth betwixt the Imperiall court and the Duke of Savoy; for which reason, I think little or nothing can bee hoped from them in this year, nor, I doubt, in the next neither, unless measures are taken this winter, to remove and cure the jealousys between the Emperour and the Duke of Savoy. This makes mee repeat once more to you the necessity of Comte Wratislau's meeting you at The Hague at the end of the campagne,[3] that both this thing which is extreamly essentiall, and also Prince Eugene's going into Spayn, may bee there concerted and settled. The latter of these will bee a very popular thing in England and very much contribute to obtain the necessary subsidyes in the Parliament.

I am the more particular upon what relates to Spain and Italy, because those places [being] most remote, the necessary measures for carrying onn the warr there ought to bee adjusted in the first place, because else there will want time to putt them in execution. Spain can't bee supported this winter without Prince Eugene, and some troops from Italy; and Italy can't bee made usefull next year to the common cause, but by putting the Duke of Savoy at the head of an army to act offensively against France, and by giving him the view and assurances of it imediatly.

When these things are well provided for France will bee less able to have any great superiority either upon the Rhyne or in Flanders, and those parts being not so remote the consideration of them is not so pressing.

As to the Rhyne, besides the troops of the Empire, of which that army usually consists, why might not the Elector of Hannover, who is now at the head of it, find means to sound the King of Sweden whether he would not bee willing to lett a body of his troops come into the pay of the Allyes and serve under his Electoral Highness if his present expedition does not detain him all winter. And if he keeps his agreement with the Emperour, as I hope

---

[1] Letters 892, 895.   [2] Eugene and the Duke of Savoy.
[3] Wratislaw met Marlborough at Frankfurt and they travelled together to The Hague. See pp. 935 et seq.

he will, he may want some such expedient for the support of a part of his great army. In case things turn soe, as that this notion comes to bee thought practicable the proposall can't come so plausibly any other way as from 50 [Elector of Hanover].

As to Flanders, I am sorry to find you think there will bee a necessity of augmenting that army. I doubt it will prove no small difficulty here to keep it upon the foot it now stands, considering how little fruit 116 [the States] has suffered it to yield us this summer; nor how 110 [Holland] are like to bee perswaded to any augmentation on their part, can I see much ground to hope. What you say of their averseness to lett King Charles's own subjects take the oath of fidelity to their sovereign, and of their renewing at this time their instances about settling their Barriere, seem to mee as if they sought rather for a handle to be cross, than really to joyn heartily with us in prosecuting the warr. If they had (as they have not) any just pretension to the soveranity of any part of Flanders hereafter upon a peace, the taking of [an oath] of fidelity to King Charles in the meantime, till such stipulation bee made, does not interfere with that pretension. And as to their Barriere, I continue of opinion that England never will nor can admitt that Ostend should bee in their possession, but in the possession of King Charles. That being granted, I think wee might agree with them in the other desires they make as to their Barriere, provided they will agree with us in an augmentation of their forces, and a vigourous prosecution of the warr in the next year. But for all these things poor Mr. Stepney will bee extremly much wanted. His condition is thought desperate by most people here, and if it were possible for him to recover, it would bee impossible for him to assist in those things which come to bear imediatly, and will continue all this winter to require a man in that station of the best sence and integrity. If you can spare Cadogan till spring I believe he is the most sufficient for this service. But you are the best judg of the whole as well as of this particular.

I doubt the season is too farr spent for you to think of any siege, otherwise Ypres or Niewport would open a way to Dunkirk next year, and consequently give a pleasing prospect to our people.

By our letters from Lisbon of the 3d I find they will expect more regiments from us for the defence of their frontier, or take a handle for the want of them to make up with France and Spain. I think therfore wee must send them 2 or 3 regiments more by the 1st convoy.

Till I speak with Mr. St. Johns I cannot give you an answer as to the raising the regiments taken at Almanza. His grandfather is dying,[1] which obliges him to bee near him.

By the next post 42 [the Queen] tells mee she will give mee an answer to your letter.[2]

---

[1] Sir Walter St. John, third Baronet (*c.* 1622–1708), M.P. intermittently 1656–95; died 9 July 1708.   [2] 4/15 Sept. See p. 904.

902. MARLBOROUGH *to* GODOLPHIN [*11/22 September 1707*]

Source: Blenheim MSS. A1-37.
Printed: Coxe, ii. 335-6 (inc.).

Helchin September 22th 1707

The winds have been so contrary, that I beleive this may come at the same time with that I write by Mr. Hill.[1] Since that I have received the enclosed letters[2] concerning the march of the Pallatins for Catalonia. I have sent copies of them also to the Pensioner,[3] desiring him to loose no time in returning an answere, and that I should take upon mee in the Queen's name so that the troupes might be emediatly sent. But I fear 116 [the States] will not willingly promis what is desired by the Elector.[4]

You will find enclosed a copie of my letter to Comte Piper.[5] If you think I aught to write anything more particularly you will let me have your thoughts. I have heard nothing from the Elector of Hanover since his being with the army, but I think he will not be able to do much this yeare. I wish he may take good measures for the next. I have write by this post to Mr. St. Johns,[6] to desire there might be an order given to the redgiments of foot guardes to fill up their companys, there being none of their battalion left that were in Spain but what are prisoners, and of those we shall have but very few. You will allow me once more to send you another letter I have received from Sir Rowland Guyn.[7] I should give him some answere.

I have not yett Brigadier Palms, but expect him dayly. I hope he will bring Prince Eugene's consent to serve in Spain, since you say it is what is desired in England. If there be need of it I shall be sure to press him. Besides, as the commands are now settled, he can serve nowhere but in Spain or Hungary. The King of Sweden will certainly not come into the Grand Alliance since that would put him out of all hopes of his mediatorshipe, which we must continu to flatter him with. [As] for the troupes of King Augustus, it is just that thay should be entertained by the Emperor and Empire, but I fear thay are not able to comply with the expence. However, thay ought to be pressed by England and Holland. It were to be wished that we could please the Portuguese without sending any more troupes, since

---

[1] Letter 899.

[2] Elector Palatine and Zinzerling, both 4/15 Sept., in Murray, iii. 573-4, giving permission for them to go.

[3] 9/20 Sept., 't Hoff, pp. 346-7.

[4] The Elector laid down a number of conditions about pay, transport, etc., which were all quite reasonable. The one special point he did insist on was that he would possess the sole right to the commissary, the agency for managing the pay, stores, and provisions for the troops. This was the point on which Marlborough thought there might be some dispute.

[5] 7/18 Sept., in Murray, iii. 568-9. A complimentary letter on the peaceful settlement of the disputes between King Charles and the Emperor.

[6] Murray, iii. 578.

[7] Untraced. Gwynn repeatedly wrote for leave to return to England. Earlier this year he asked to succeed Howe at Hanover. See p. 800.

thay must be useless. If Mr. Stepney should dye pray lett me have your thoughts, who you think may be for the Queen's Service to succed him, for if it be practicable he should meet me at The Hague.

I had the favour of yours of the 4[1] and 5[2] last night. I send you a copie of what I write this day to the King of Prussia,[3] but I despair of having any of his troupes in Prussia, as I propose. However, it is but a letter lost. If he should not comply, I desire you will say nothing to Spanhem, for I must do it personally with the King.

If her Majesty continues in the intention of Lieutenant General Inglosby's commanding the troupes in Ireland, and that Lord Pembroke has leave to come this winter for England, it might be proper to take care that he might be one of the justices, in which there can be no difficulty if Lord Pembroke has notice.

903. GODOLPHIN *to* MARLBOROUGH   [*12 September 1707*]

Source: Blenheim MSS. A2-23.
Printed: Coxe, ii. 348-9.

Windsor 12 September 1707

My last[4] acknowledged the favour of yours of the 12th and 15th[5] from Helchin, and there is now but one post due this day, and wee shall not have that before these letters goe.

I believe you will have an answer by this post from 42 [the Queen], but whether it will bee inclosed in this I cannot tell.[6] By a long conversation between Mrs. Morley [the Queen] and Mr. Montgomery [Godolphin],[7] of which I have had some account, I find they both agree that for 39 [Marlborough] and 108 [England] to see one another before the naturall time, might be liable to many great inconveniences; and those in the nature of them so uncertain, that no humane precaution is sufficient to prevent the ill consequences that may happen from those uncertaintys. Besides that, to say the plain truth, in case one should run that venture, one cannot at this time depend upon the fruit of it, with any certainty, 38 [Godolphin] having lately spoken very fully upon all those subjects of which Mr. Freeman's [Marlborough] head and heart seem to bee so full. And though there has yett appeared but very little encoragement to think the arguments used upon that occasion are

---

[1] Untraced. [2] Letter 898. [3] Murray, iii. 578-9.
[4] Letter 901. [5] Letters 892, 895.
[6] The Queen's letter of 12 Sept., untraced. She sent it by the Duchess. See pp. 915, 924-5.
[7] On 10 Sept. Godolphin followed up the meeting with a letter to the Queen on 11 Sept., urging her to satisfy the Whigs. Blenheim MSS., B2-32, abbreviated in H. M. C., *Marlborough MSS.*, 41b. She replied on 12 Sept. in a strong letter that she was not 'to be hectored or frighted into a compliance' by the Whigs. The present whereabouts of the letter are unknown. An extract is printed in Brown, pp. 231-2.

like to prevail, yett one may conclude in this case as the scriptures doe, in the very words of our Saviour;

> *If they hear not Moses and the prophets neither will they bee perswaded, though one rose from the dead.*

Mr. Hare can explain this sentence to you, if there bee need of it.

I have troubled you so much in my 3 or 4 last letters upon the subject of our affairs abroad, that I shall not repeat anything but that it seems indispensible to have a congress of the ministers of all the Allys at your return to The Hague, for a thorough concert of all that is to bee done next year. The time will not allow you to give yourself the trouble of going to 50 [Elector of Hanover] or anybody else. The sooner this concert can bee made the better; for wee shall never bee able to gett our Parliament to enter upon the particulars of the warr next year till wee are able to comunicate some scheme for it from abroad which will bee encouraging and agreeable to them. I am very sensible that in other years, the encouragement to our Allyes abroad, has often proceeded from their votes in the first week of the Parliament. But our misfortunes and disappointments in this year, will make that very difficult, at present, even though wee could obtain those things to be done, which are necessary to putt them in good humour.

904. GODOLPHIN *to* MARLBOROUGH   [*14 September 1707*]

Source: Blenheim MSS. A2-23.

Windsor 14th September 1707

I gave you so much trouble by the last post[1] that I shall not add much to it by this, there being no appearance of receiving any more letters from Holland before it goes.

Mr. Robinson's letters of the 3d give us the certainty of the treaty's[2] being signed the 1st, after his last letter to you was sent away. So (I think) no time ought now to bee lost in improving that step, by endeavoring to gett the King of Sweden into the Allyance; or at least, by getting the remainder of King Augustus's troops into the pay and service of the Allyes. This latter (I should hope) need not require much time. The former perhaps must wait upon the event of his march and bee guided very much according as that shall happen to succeed.

By the letter you sent mee from Prince Eugene,[3] it is very plain, that from the time they came with the army before Thoulon, there were great difficultys in that enterprise. But I think it is as plain that if they had hastened their march, as they might easily have done, and arrived but eight and forty

---

[1] Letter 901.
[2] Of Altranstädt, between the Emperor and the King of Sweden. See p. 896, n. 2.
[3] See p. 894.

hours sooner before the place, they must have been masters of it in 8 days' time.

I think, as I hinted in my last, that wee have nothing now to doe, but to overlook what is past, and only to lett the Imperiall court see they ought to make us amends for that unhappy treaty,[1] made in Italy without consent or so much as knowledg of the Allyes, which indeed has been the true, and originall cause of this disappointment; notwithstanding which great provocation, the Queen and the States have (as I reckon) saved the Empire a 2d time, by influencing the King of Sweden to finish and sign this treaty. Comte Wratislaus himself has given it you under his hand, that it could not have been compassed but by their assistance.

I am the more tedious and troublesome to you, upon this head, in hopes that by sending one of those ministers to The Hague, mentioned in my last, they will give you an opportunity of letting them see, that for so much support and assistance as the Allyes (and especially the Queen) has given to the house of Austria, some better returns will bee expected here (and really you will find it soe) than they have hitherto thought fitt to make.

905. GODOLPHIN *to* MARLBOROUGH   [*15 September 1707*]

Source: Blenheim MSS. A2-23.

Windsor September 15, 1707

I had been informed that the East India Company were buying up great quantitys of silver in Holland to export to the East Indies; and concluding that would bee very prejudiciall to the great remittances wee are obliged to make for the support of the warr, and that it would occasion a security of many both in Holland and England, I sent for the United Company to the Treasury chambers to speak to them of it. By the enclosed minutes you will see what passed upon that occasion;[2] and I have been since informed, that the discourse had very little effect upon them; and that they continue their negotiations in Holland for buying up silver, with design to bring it over in the yachts and convoy which are to bee sent for you.

I thought it necessary to acquaint you with this. You can judg as well as anybody of the consequences and mischief of it. And you will also judg better than anybody can whether a stopp can bee putt to this madness on that side, without doing it in such a manner as may make a heart burning between the merchants of both nations, of which there is no need at all at any time, and more especially at this time.

[1] Of Milan.
[2] 5 Sept., *C.T.B.*, xxi. ii. 44–5. The Company protested they could not carry on their trade without exporting £500,000 in silver. Godolphin replied 'he cannot hinder them, but thought it, however, necessary to give 'em this caution'.

906. MARLBOROUGH *to* GODOLPHIN   [*15/26 September 1707*]

Source unknown.
Printed: Leeds Sale Catalogue, no. 648 (summary).

Helchin 26 September 1707

'Relating to the augmentation of the troops; the success of the French in the last campagne beyond their expectations; the necessity of opposing their endeavours at the opening of the next campagne; sending the Pallatine troops to King Charles, and other important matters. A most interesting letter, the names of some persons who are alluded to being in cypher. In concluding, his Grace desires that this letter be burnt.'[1]

907. GODOLPHIN *to* MARLBOROUGH   [*16 September 1707*]

Source: Blenheim MSS. A2-23.

Windsor 16 September 1707

I am to acknowledg the favour of yours of the 19th by Mr. Hill,[2] with the paper of 63 [Wratislaw] enclosed in it. I take his characters to bee just and the paper written with a good deal of witt and spirit; but I hope ther is no occasion (at present) for putting it in execution, since wee seem to bee secure this winter from the storm wee feared on that side.[3] And before wee propose any measures to prevent the like for the future, I think it ought to bee tryd (as I have formerly hinted) whether by the means of 50 [Elector of Hanover], wee may hope for some of 56's [King of Sweden] troops to serve with him, next year. As to the other parts of your letter, I think as you doe that it will bee difficult to gett the 28,000 men compleated for Italy next year. But I think also, wee must still pretend to doe as much as wee can in that matter both for the encouragement of our friends on that side, and that the French may not think themselves secure, but bee obliged to keep a good body of troops in those parts, which will make any operations less difficult on our side. And I agree your army in Flanders may bee made as strong as you please in the beginning of the spring, with a view still of employing them upon the fleet,[4] in case nothing can bee done there with effect, for the advantage of the common cause. And I like it the better, because it will very well disguise any intention of that kind till near the time of putting it in execution.

But I think our more immediat views at present lead us to doe all that is possible to support King Charles in Catalonia and to encourage Portugal.

---

[1] This is the summary given in the Leeds sale catalogue.   [2] Letter 899.
[3] The ministry had been afraid a war might break out in the Empire between Charles XII of Sweden and the Emperor over the situation of the Protestants in Silesia. This was avoided by the settlement made at Altranstädt.
[4] i.e. a descent.

To the former of these nothing will contribute so much as the presence of Prince Eugene, with some of the Emperour's troops added to the Palatins. And I hope therfore you will write to him and to the court of Vienna, in the most presing manner imaginable, that being certainly more imediatly necessary than any other thing whatsoever. And as for Portugal the Queen is sending 2 or 3 regiments more thither, all extraordinary, though at the same time wee can't gett so much as an answer from Holland, whether they will or will not concurr in anything of that nature.

I think the place wee ought to attempt next year by a descent (if on the south of France) is *Rochfort*, but that wee ought to doe and say everything to give the French a jealousy that wee intend to renew our attempts at Thoulon next year. In case your army can act so in the beginning of the year, as to come at the besieging of Dunkirk, wee could easily furnish ships and men and ammunition and provision to assist you in that attempt, without much disturbance to any other measures.

I find Monsieur Vryberghen very averse to our proposing to the States any augmentation of troops for next year. He says whatever is to bee done, of that kind, must arise from the measures that shall bee concerted at The Hague, and in this particular I agree with him.

908. MARLBOROUGH *to* GODOLPHIN [*18/29 September 1707*]

Source: Blenheim MSS. A1-37.
Printed: Coxe, ii. 349–50 (inc.).

Helchin September 29th 1707

I have had the favour of yours of the 12th.[1] I have also received the letter you mentioned from 42 [the Queen].[2] I am sure 240 [Lady Marlborough] must have acquainted you with itt. 38 [Godolphin] being on the place must judge infinetly better then 39 [Marlborough]. But he bids mee tell you, that by what he has from 108 [England] he thinkes everything must go ill. And therfore, he continues of the opinion, that unless 239 [the Queen] will be pleased to be guided by 272 [Godolphin], or that 4 [Halifax], 5 [Somers], and 6 [Sunderland] makes it their business to persuade 38 [Godolphin] to have patience for some time longer, if neither of these two things happens, I hope that 38 [Godolphin] will take such measures that it may apear very plainly to 108 [England], that he dose not approve of the measures now taken. The wordes in your letter I think I understand so that I shall not speak to Doctor Hare, but since one from the dead can't gain belieffe, pray be carefull of the living, for I am convinced that 42 [the Queen] will not be guided, til thay see that the advice thay now follow has braught their affaires into confusion.

[1] Letter 903.   [2] 12 Sept., untraced.

Nothing shall disharten me from endeavoring to do all the good I can here abroad. Our prospect is by no means good, but I think in the begining of the next weeke to go for two days to 121 [The Hague], in order to hearten and take measures with them, so that I might not be obliged to stay long at The Hague when the campagne is done, though I am persuaded my being in 108 [England] this winter will be of very litle use to the publick. But I shall have the satisfaction of being with 272 [Godolphin] and 240 [Lady Marlborough] notwithstanding.

I shall by this post or the next write my opinion to Mr. St. Johns, what aught to be laid before the Parliament concerning the troupes. For if I take time for my doing what is necessary on this side the watter, thay will have meet above a fortnight before I can be at London. And if we must be so unhappy that this sessions at their first meeting should not act with vigor, it must add to our misfortunes abroad.

Brigadier Palms is taken with a violent fitt of the goutt in the Vestervalt,[1] so that I know not when I shall see him, but I have desired him to writt to mee to 121 [The Hague]. Mr. Lomley[2] goes for England tomorrow. I shall send you by him the copies of some letters from the Duke of Savoye.

909. MARLBOROUGH *to* GODOLPHIN [*18/29 September 1707*]

Source: Blenheim MSS. A1-37.
Printed: Coxe, ii. 350-1 (inc.).

Helchin September 29th 1707

I take this oppertunity of sending by Lieutenant General Lumley a copie of the Duke of Savoy's letter to the Count Maffie, as also two other letters he has sent mee.[3] Upon the whole I am afraid we must not expect much more good from that side of the world. However, I think wee should do all that is in our powers to oblige the Duke of Savoye.

The uneasiness of 89 [the Whigs] and the obstinacy of 42 [the Queen] must unavoydable give an opertunity to 84 [the Tories] of showing their mallice. I am a good deal concerned for the mischief this must do, both at home and abroad, but I am satisfied it will be impossible for 38 [Godolphin] and 39 [Marlborough] to influence 42 [the Queen] to anything that is right, til she has tried this scheem of 199 [Harley] and his friends. What it is God knows, but that there is one I am sure. If there be anything in the world can hinder her from runing this hazard, it must be her knowing you will quitt. For myself, I would not for anything this world could give mee, act otherways

---

[1] Westerwald, a forest region east of Bonn and Coblenz.
[2] Henry Lumley (1660-1722), brother of Richard, first Earl of Scarborough; major-general 1696; M.P., Sussex, 1701, 1702; lieutenant-general, governor of Jersey 1703; fought at all Marlborough's great battles; General of Horse 1711.
[3] Untraced.

then to show that I am not in the skeem,[1] so that I have no concern left, but the wishing you may do what is right. If you stay in your place, though you are noways consenting, yet all that shall be amise you must be answerable for. And on the other side, I am very sensible that if you do quit, the business both at home and abroad must very much suffer. For whatever 42 [the Queen] and these new skeemers may think, 137 [the Allies] will expect nothing from 108 [England] when thay shall see that 38 [Godolphin] and 39 [Marlborough] have lost their creditt, after having served with so great success. I hope your answer to this will lett me know your possative resolution, so that I might govern myself; for whielst you are in I shall send my opinion.

910. MARLBOROUGH *to the* DUCHESS [*18/29 September 1707*]

Source: Blenheim MSS. E3.
Printed: Coxe, ii. 349.
Addressed: For the Dutchesse of Marlborough.

Helchin September 29th, 1707

Though I have write a long letter this day by the post,[2] I would not lose this safe opertunity by Mr. Lumley. I am so extreamly concerned for the quiet and safety of 38 [Godolphin], that I can't be at ease til I know what resolution he has taken. If he stays in his place and dose not intierly govern 239 [the Queen], he will be duped by 199 [Harley]; and if he dose what is certainly best for himself, quitt, he will do great hurt both to the business at home and abroad. However, there is nothing else left to make 239 [the Queen] sensible of the dainger she is runing into, and if that will not do, we must leave itt to providence. I do with all my heart pitty 42 [the Queen], being very sure she dose not know the fatal step she is going to make.

911. GODOLPHIN *to* MARLBOROUGH   [*19 September 1707*]

Source: Blenheim MSS. A2-23.

Windsor September 1707

I have all this day expected the Holland letters, but they are not yett come, so I shall give you but little trouble by this post.

I enclose to you a coppy of Mr. Vrybergh's memoriall[1] left yesterday with Mr. Secretary Harley. I like very well that they leave it to you and the deputyes to send the necessary orders to the Palatin troops, because I reckon 'tis high time they were in Spain. But I can't well imagine what is meant by the latter part of the memoriall, where they desire to bee informed what measures the Queen has taken with the Emperour, what orders she has given to the admirall, [and] what care she has taken to provide corn for the voyage. All this makes mee incline to suspect thay have a mind either to create difficultys and delays in the succours for Spain, or to take exceptions at our forwardness, neither of which is very desirable at this time.

The Queen's part has only been to press the Emperour and the rest of the Allyes with all the earnestness imaginable to send some imediate succors to Spain; and to send generall orders to her admirall and to all her ministers everywhere, to contribute whatever was in their power to that end; and I could wish (if it were to any purpose) that they had done so too.

Poor Mr. Stepney being now dead[1] I am perswaded you will lose no time in determining your thoughts as to his successor in Holland and Flanders. Some think of Mr. Robinson, who has asked leave to come home. But can he bee allowed, at present, to bee anywhere but as near the King of Sweden, as his irregular motions will suffer him to bee. My Lord Sunderland's first thoughts are for Mr. Stanyan who has a good understanding, and I believe very capable of improving. The Duke of Somersett is zealous for Mr. Stanhope, in Spain, and I don't know any greater objection to him than that he is in Spain, and this affair can hardly wait for his return. Upon the whole, the sooner you lett the Queen know your mind the better, for this ought to bee done before you leave that side of the water, and that ought to bee soon.

912. GODOLPHIN *to* MARLBOROUGH   [*22 September 1707*]

Source: Blenheim MSS. A2-23.

Windsor September 22th 1707

I am now to thank you for the favour of yours of the 22th and 26th[2] with the severall papers enclosed in them.

The affair relating to the Palatin troops being left wholly to you, will (I hope) bee dispatched as soon as is possible (though hardly as soon as is necessary), the enemy as wee hear being already before Lerida. But wee have the satisfaction of knowing no instances have been neglected from hence, of sending timely succors to King Charles in Spain. Sir Philip Medows pressed the court of Vienna two months agoe to send some troops from Naples, while it was possible for the fleet to stay in those seas to transport them. Now, 2 months after, they desire the fleet may stay in those seas and assist them to take Sicily, which would furnish both ports and provision. That is time enough, if wee send it; but ther's no endeavoring it after this season of the year, and the distance, besides, is too great for it to bee of much use to us.

---

[1] He died 15 Sept.   [2] Letters 902, 906.

The enterprise upon Tholoun might have succeeded (as it was) if they had been hearty and diligent in it; but it could not have failed but for the treaty made in Italy, and the detachment to Naples. I mention this now only to show, how much more complaisance the court of Vienna owes us, than they seem willing to pay upon any occasion. Their late deliverance from the King of Sweden makes them turn their thoughts readily, too, to avoid falling again into the same danger, but not to make any return to us who have freed them from it.

Your letter to the King of Prussia is very right. I shall not take any notice of it to Spanheim, but leave that matter wholly to his Prussian Majesty and yourself.

But I can't help being of opinion that your letter to Comte Piper, might and ought to bee fuller at this time. For since the King of Sweden owned to you before the beginning of this campagne that France was not yett low enough for a peace, the successes thay have had since might reasonably incline him to lend some troops to bring them lower, before they will consent to our preliminarys, the only reasonable foundation for a treaty, and consequently of a mediation, which he has so much in his head. You ought, I confess, to know his views better than I. But I incline to think they may bee very much changed since you saw him.

The letter you sent mee from Prince Eugene putts mee in mind to continue pressing you not only that he might serve in Spain next year, but that he might goe, or (at least) bee declared to goe immediatly. For nothing will engage our people to support that warr, after the loss wee have sustained there, so much as the knowledg of his being there, or being declared to serve there. But the first of those 2 is much the best, and if Sir Cloudesley Shovell leaves a convoy behind him to bring the Queen of Spain[1] to Barcelona, that might afford him a good opportunity of going thither.

As to what you write about continuing the warr in Flanders next year with a greater force than in this, I hope and believe most people here will allow you to bee the best judg of what is fitt to bee done in that matter; though (at present) I must bee so sincere as to say this notion is under some prejudices here. And therfore I am very glad to find by the letters from The Hague, though not from yourself, that the campagne is ending, and that you may soon bee at The Hague. I beg of you to hasten that as much as is possible, that you may bee here at least a week or 10 days before the Parliament sitts down. And in this view the Queen has last night directed the yachts and the convoy too bee sent over for you immediatly. There is time sufficient for this in all poynts, except your concerting with the Allyes the operations of the warr for next year, before you leave The Hague. But I beg you to reflect, whether this concert may not bee made with more advantage after you have been a

---

[1] Princess Elizabeth Christine of Wolfenbüttel (1691–1750). Betrothed to King Charles III by proxy, she was brought to Spain by Leake in July 1708, and married to Charles on 21 July/1 Aug.

fortnight in England, by which time the Parliament will have passed all their votes and taken their resolutions for carrying onn the warr. After this I propose (indeed) that you should take the trouble of returning to The Hague, to finish the matters to bee concerted with all the Allyes. And this I think you will probably doe with better success, when you shall bee able upon your own knowledg to hearten and encourage them with the resolutions taken in England. This scheme I have had opportunity to communicate to 4 [Halifax] and to 6 [Sunderland] who both mightily approve it, and think it next to impossible that anything should goe right, either at home or abroad, by any other method.

I ought to say in my own justification that I was indeed against your leaving the army in the field and coming over in a manner incognito, because one could not see through the ill consequences that might have hapned upon it.[1] But the campagne, once at an end (which I hope you will hasten as much as is possible), all the rest that I have mentioned is naturall as well as necessary.

Since then I must beg leave to flatter myself with the hopes of seeing you here about the 10th or 12th of our October, the time of the Queen's returning from Newmarkett. I shall not need to trouble you with 38's [Godolphin] thoughts of retirement, farther than that I find they are the same with yours and that he desires to bee absolutely guided by Mr. Freeman [Marlborough].

913. MARLBOROUGH *to* GODOLPHIN

[*22 September/3 October 1707*]

Source: Blenheim MSS. A1-37.
Printed: Coxe, ii. 352-3.

Helchin October 3d 1707

I shall go tomorrow towardes The Hague, where I intend to stay but two days at most, being resolved to return to this camp. I have thought as well as I can how to leave the business of this country at my return for England, and I think it must be Cadogen. So that if the Queen pleases, I shall acquaint the States Generall, and the Councell of State of this country, that in the absence of Mr. Stepney, he is charged with the care of her Majesty's business.[2] My journy this time to The Hague will not only enable me to take measures for the operations on the Rhin for the next campagne but also make my stay much shorter at the end of the campagne. You will have known by the last letters from France, that the King has given orders as thay write for an augmentation of 30 redgements of foot, and 20 of horse. This aded to the superiority thay had the last campagne in Garmany, Flanders, and Spain, as also the advantage thay probabilly will have of having some of their troupes from Spain, must give a very mallincolly prospect for the next yeare's service,

---

¹ See p. 904, n. 1.   ² See p. 874, n. 3.

if we are not willing and able to make a considerable agmentation.[1] I shall endeavor to make them sensible of this att The Hague, though I am sensible their expence is already so great, that though thay should have the will, I fear thay have not the power. You shall be sure to know by the next post from The Hague, in what humour I find them. And if there should be a necessity of my going to Franckford, I shall so order itt as not to delay my coming for England. For if I do go, I will return to this army before thay seperatt, so that I desire the yackts may be in Holand by the end of October, old stile.

914. MARLBOROUGH *to* GODOLPHIN
[*22 September/3 October 1707*]

Source: Marlborough's letterbooks, Blenheim Palace.
Printed: Murray, iii. 611–12.

Camp at Helchin, 3rd October 1707

I have formerly written to your Lordship in behalf of Mr. [Josiah] Sandby, one of our chaplains, who has been my brother's [Charles] secretary for some years past, and particularly ever since we have been masters of Brussels, where he has been so useful that I should be very glad some means were found for his encouragement. I therefore give him this, to introduce him to your Lordship, and pray you will please to recommend him to her Majesty or my Lord Chancellor for such dignity as may become vacant, either in the church of Worcester or elsewhere, suitable to his merit and character. His ambition does not look higher than a prebend, which I hope you will not think too great a reward for his services.[2]

915. GODOLPHIN *to* MARLBOROUGH   [*23 September 1707*]

Source: Blenheim MSS. A2-23.

Windsor September 23d 1707

Since my letter of yesterday[3] which you will receive at the same time with this, I have had the favour of yours of the 29th[4] and am glad to find by it, that you were going to The Hague, in hopes these letters will find you there,

---

[1] There was no general augmentation made of the Allied army in the Spanish Netherlands in 1708. The forces for the descent under General Erle were sent to Ostend in the late summer and that resulted in an addition of 4,500 men, but that was the only addition of importance made and it came late in the campaign.

[2] He was instituted a prebend of Worcester 18 June 1708.

[3] Letter 912.

[4] Letter 908.

and give you an opportunity, of settling with them, and afterwards of following the measures proposed to you in my letter of yesterday; since if 39
[Marlborough] and 108 [England] doe not meet by the time mentioned there,
all the concerts abroad will signifie very little; and if they doe, 38 [Godolphin]
does not wholly despair, but that things may bee brought to some consis-
tency both here and there. It's true this will cause an additionall trouble to
Mr. Freeman [Marlborough] at an ill season of the year, but I hope it will
save him a great deal of what he must otherwise have, when a good one
returns.

This preliminary being (in my opinion) a foundation indispensable, I
cannot therfore say anything but in pursuance of it, hoping that you will [want
it] from yourself, and, all your thoughts accordingly and settle only at
present with 62 [Heinsius] that whatever remains unfinished of the necessary
concerts with 50 [Elector of Hanover], and 63 [Wratislaw] or with 137 [the
Allies] in generall, may bee prepared and adjusted against the middle of
November; by which time, I believe, it will bee necessary Mr. Freeman
[Marlborough] should promise to wait upon 121 [The Hague] in order to see
the finall dispatch of that matter. And this way, I would fain flatter myself,
he may bee furnished with proper materialls, but by any other method, I beg
leave to repeat, it is aiming at impossibilityes.

This day sennight the Queen designs to goe to Newmarkett. While wee
are there I shall hope for your answer to this, for which I shall bee very
impatient, that accordingly wee may take our measures here.

I am sorry for Brigadier Palmes's illness.

Wee can't yett think of anybody proper for Mr. Stepney's post abroad. A
great many appear very desirous of it. I take Stanhope to bee really the
fittest, but hee is too farr off. I doubt therfore you will bee under a necessity
of leaving Cadogan, at present, to take care of all that business, and when
you are here another may bee agreed on.

By what you write Mr. Lumley may probably bee come over with this
packett, but he is not yett come hither.

916. GODOLPHIN *to* MARLBOROUGH   [*26 September 1707*]

Source: Blenheim MSS. A2-23.

St. James's September 26, 1707

Since my last I have no letter from you, the wind being contrary, which I
hope will have brought you my last[1] before you left The Hague, that you may
the better concert with them there your coming over here before the Parlia-

ment, which indeed is extreamly necessary; though I own, I think it will oblige you to cross the seas again before Christmas.

Mr. St. Johns has been with mee today to tell mee he is preparing the estimates for the Parliament according to your commands.[1] Some of the regiments have officers enough to bee going onn with their levyes, but others have none at all.

I don't yett hear any news of Mr. Lumley, and am very sorry Brigadier Palms has been so long detained. Here are a hundred storyes made about the occasion of our disappointment at Tholoun, and a great many private letters from the fleet which lay the fault openly upon 48 [Prince Eugene].

I won't take upon mee to determine where it lies, but I am too sensible it is not to bee repaired without all the industry and endeavours imaginable.

Unless I hear from you between this and Monday night,[2] my next will bee from Newmarkett. I received the enclosed from Lady Marlborough this morning by the post.

917. MARLBOROUGH *to* GODOLPHIN
[*26 September/7 October 1707*]

Source: Blenheim MSS. A1-37.
Printed: Coxe, ii. 353-4.

Hague October 7th 1707

Since my coming here[3] I have had two conferences with the deputys of the States. Thay are very desirous I should meet the Elector of Hanover, for the taking measures with him for the next yeare's campagne, and att the same time to press that the Emperor and Empire, might take the 6,000 Saxon horse into their service. I shall so order it that my going to Mayance shall not delay my return to England, for I intend to return to the army before thay seperatt. I leave this place this evening and hope to be with the army on Sunday night,[4] and stay with them til the Saturday following, where I shall leave them incamped where thay shall continu til my return, which I intend shall be by the 28 or 29th of this month. In two days after my return I intend to send them to their garrisons, after which I am afraid it will be necessary for me to be att Bruxelles for some few days. By what I have now done, I hope my stay at The Hague need not be above six days. I

---

[1] The Secretary of War was responsible for preparing the establishment for the coming year and an estimate of the total cost before the House of Commons. He gathered the information by consulting the commanders in the field for their recommendations then drawing up a consolidated estimate of what was required. Once the Commons approved it then they concerned themselves with the problem of raising taxes to support it.

[2] 29 Sept.

[3] On 24 Sept./5 Oct.

[4] 28 Sept./9 Oct.

am the more particular that you may know when to expect me in England, which I think may be about the 7th of November.

Having this safe opertunity by Collonel Pendergrass,[1] I must acquaint you that I see very plainly that 110 [Holland] will not only not ogment their troupes, but will act the next yeare as thay have done this last, which is so disheartning that I do wish with all my heart, if it were possible for 39 [Marlborough] to be excused from being att the head of their troupes. I am very impatient of hearing the certainty of what 38 [Godolphin] will do, for that shall govern mee. I shall say no more on this subject, since you will see my mind by the enclosed copie of what I write to 42 [the Queen].[2]

Brigadier Palmes came to me yesterday. He hopes to be in a condition to pass with the next packett boat. He will give you an account of all that the Duke of Savoye and Prince Eugene has said to him.

918. MARLBOROUGH *to the* DUCHESS

[*26 September/7 October 1707*]

Source: Blenheim MSS. E3.
Printed: Coxe, ii. 354–5.
Addressed: For the Dutchesse of Marlborough.

Hague October 7th, 1707

I thank you for yours of the 16, as also the copies[3] you sent me. God's will must be done. I have thought as well as I can, and have prepared myself for the worst.

I return tomorrow for the army, and as it is thought necessary for me to go to Mayance or Frankford, I shall begine that journy about ten days hence, and return againe to the army before thay go to their winter quarters, so that this journy will not delay my coming for England as I intended in the first weeke in November. I have had so litle time to myself here that I shall not

---

[1] Sir Thomas Prendergast (died 1709); created Bt. 1699; lieutenant-colonel, Orrery's Regiment of Foot; colonel, same regiment, 1707; killed at Malplaquet.

[2] 26 Sept./7 Oct., *Morrison Catalogue*, first series, i. 148, plate 120 (facsimile). Asking her to alter her resolution, of following advice contrary to that Godolphin has given her, or she 'will not only disturb the quiet of your own life, but also ruin the Prodistant Religion, and all the libertys of Europ[e]'. The resignation of Godolphin must be the consequence if she does not change (that is, agree to accept the Whigs).

[3] Probably the Duchess's letter to the Queen of 14 Sept. (Blenheim MSS. G1-7), with which she enclosed Marlborough's letter of 8/19 Sept. (letter 900), and complained how the Queen ignored the advice of the Duumvirs; the other enclosure would have been the Queen's reply of 16 Sept. (Brown, p. 229).

trouble with a longer letter, but refer you to what I write to 38 [Godolphin].
He will lett you see what I have write to 239 [the Queen] in answer to two
letters[1] I have received from them.

919. MARLBOROUGH *to* GODOLPHIN

[*27 September/8 October 1707*]

Source: Blenheim MSS. A1-37.
Printed: Coxe, ii. 356–7.

Antwerp October 8th 1707

I received this afternoon yours of the 23d,[2] by which I see you are desirous
I should come for England. Your two letters of the 12th and 16th,[3] as well as
42 [the Queen],[4] telling me that your opinions were that it would make to[o]
much noyse, made me take the measures I have now done at The Hague, to
meet the Elector of Hanover, and one from the Emperor at Mayance the 20th
of this month. And accordingly, I have write letters to all the courts of
Garmany, so that it will be impossible for me to putt the journey off. But
since the Queen is desirous I should come, I will order itt so as to be with you
by the first of November if the wind gives leave. I am afraid my presence
will be but of very little use, but if 42 [the Queen] and 38 [Godolphin] be of
another opinion, 88 [Parliament] aught then to be put off for a fortnight.
And if the intelligence I have from 108 [England] be trew, their meeting are
noways to be wished, til 42 [the Queen] is pleased to take a ferm resolution
of what she will do. For if 89 [the Whigs] will not suport, and 84 [the Tories]
will be mallicious, what must be the consequence but ruin. But if anybody
has a good scheem[5] which is like to succed, the sooner they meet is the better.
I find my thoughts are very different from those of 42 [the Queen]. My
comfort is that a litle time will convince her, that I am much more concerned
for her quiet and good then I am for my own life. Whielst I am thought to
have a share in her ministry, I must tel my mind freely when I see distruction
at hand. When I have nothing to do I shall not displease, and shall always be
ready to help whenever I shall think my service can be of use.

920. GODOLPHIN *to* MARLBOROUGH   [*28 September 1707*]

Source: Blenheim MSS. A2-23.

St James's 28 September 1707

I have received since my last the favour of your letter by Lieutenant Generall
Lumley,[6] with the enclosed letters from the Duke of Savoy, which are very

---

[1] Untraced.
[2] Letter 915.   [3] Letters 903, 907.   [4] Of 12 and 16 Sept. Untraced.
[5] See p. 861, n. 2.   [6] Letter 909.

materiall and very particular. I agree intirely with 39 [Marlborough] that 58 [Duke of Savoy] ought to bee satisfied as farr as it is in our power. But I reckon, that, like most other things, must bee done chiefly by 39 [Marlborough] and by his personale influence with 63 [Wratislaw] and 46 [Emperor] where the greatest difficulty of satisfying 58 [Duke of Savoy] is like to lie. The sooner therfore he setts about it the better in my opinion. And as in those letters it is said of 48 [Prince Eugene] that he is *destinè ailleurs* for next year, the sooner that too is made publick, the better effect it will certainly have.

I am sorry to find by Lieutenant Generall Lumley that he thinks you are not like to meet with a very good disposition in 116 [the States] since that is the foundation of the whole; and except that bee right, no good can bee expected, whatever pains are taken.

I am now also to acknowledg the favour of yours of the 3d of October[1] by the post and am glad to find by it, that you have agreed that Cadogan shall *for the present* supply poor Mr. Stepney's place abroad. I believe you can't spare him to attend that business very long, soe I look upon it but as a temporary provision. And I am the more willing to doe so, because I have discoursed with a man for that post, who I find is willing to bee commanded, and I believe you may think him, as I doe, very capable of doing service in that station, since nobody has better inclinations, and he wants neither temper, discretion, capacity or integrity. He wants indeed a little more youth and health. Not to keep you longer in doubt, whether I mean the Earl of Berkeley[2] (who tells mee he has written to you upon this subject),[3] I mean Mr. Vernon the father who was Secretary of State.

But this matter must now remayn as it is, at least till you come over, which I hope still will bee very soon, according to what I have written to you for 3 or 4 posts successively, and particularly in my last[4] which I wish may have come to your hands at The Hague. Because I reckon that will make it the easyer for you to settle all your affaires on that side pursuant to the desires of those letters. And as to 38's [Godolphin] affairs here, and his resolutions, they will (as I have already told you)[5] bee entirely in the disposall of Mr. Freeman [Marlborough].

[1] Letter 913.
[2] Charles, second Earl of Berkeley (1649–1710), envoy to the States General 1689–95; Custos Rotolorum and Lord-Lieutenant of Gloucestershire and Surrey from William's reign until his death.
[3] 26 Sept., Blenheim MSS. A2-25.
[4] Letter 916.   [5] Letter 912.

The news of the last post from the Rhyne[1] pleases here, but it won't bee of any great use, unless it hinders the French from winter quarters on our side of that river.

921. GODOLPHIN *to* MARLBOROUGH   [*29 September 1707*]

Source: Blenheim MSS. A2-23.

St Albans September 29, 1707

I came hither this morning to see Lady Marlborough and take up my Lord Rialton in my way to Newmarkett. And finding my lady sends to London tomorrow, I have a mind to add to what I told you in my letter yesterday[2] of Mr. Vernon, that in case you relish that proposall and are inclined to see him at The Hague before you come over, you may have time at eight and forty hours warning, whenever you please. But when I have said this I hope it will not occasion the least delay in your coming over, for all turns upon it. I hope therfore you will separate the army imediatly, and then nobody will wonder at your coming. I shall press the going over of your convoy, as fast as is possible. Sir John Jennings who commands it is a very good man, and has promised mee to hasten all he can.

I can tell you nothing from hence but what you know already, that this garden is extreamly agreable.

922. MARLBOROUGH *to* GODOLPHIN

[*29 September/10 October 1707*]

Source: Blenheim MSS. A1-37.

Helchin October 10th 1707

Not being very well, and having troubled you with so many letters this week, you will I am sure excuse the shortness of this. The weather has been so very weat that I can't make the march I intended to Ath, but must pass the Schell within two leagues of Gant, so that the army may be able to have their bread by the conveniency of the *Grand Chossy*.[3] If her Majesty approves of Cadogen's being employed this winter att Brussels, you will be pleased to speake that the Secretary may signefie the Queen's pleasur to him, and then there will be time of finding a proper personne against the spring. I shall march tomorrow from hence, the bagage and canon being marched this day.

[1] The Elector of Hanover sent a detachment under Count Mercy to attack French troops under Lieutenant-General de Vivans who were encamped near Offenburg. They awaited reinforcements in order to attack and seize Homburg. The French were caught completely by surprise on 13/24 Sept., when the Imperialists killed some 800 men, put the rest to flight or took them prisoners, and captured their baggage and money.

[2] Letter 920.

[3] The *Grande Chaussée*, a stone-paved road connecting Soignies with Brussels.

923. MARLBOROUGH *to the* DUCHESS

[*29 September/10 October 1707*]

Source: Blenheim MSS. E3.
Printed: Coxe, i. 357 (inc.).
Addressed: For the Dutchesse of Marlborough.

Helchin October 10th 1707

I having had oppertunitys of writting four letters[1] to you this weeke, and my head eaking and none of yours to answer, will be an excuse for this short letter. I leave this camp tomorrow, and shall certainly have the spleen to see the poor soldiers march in durt up to the knees, for we have had a very great deal of rain. I shall write to you once more before I leave the army, after which my letters will come iregularly til my return from Garmany. I hope to make the jorney in fortien days. I shall take the best care I can of your five pieces,[2] for Will Lovegrove[3] is sick att Gant. I hope you have your provission of wines, since you desire none.

924. GODOLPHIN *to* MARLBOROUGH   [*2 October 1707*]

Source: Blenheim MSS. A2-23.

Newmarkett October 2d 1707

I have received at this place the letters from The Hague of the 6th new style but none from you; which troubles mee very much, because I was in hopes not only to have heard from you from The Hague, but to have heard you had received there the English letters of the 23d September old style.[4] But Sir Thomas Frankland's son who is here, tells mee, he has seen a letter which says you were gon from The Hague, that you had not time to write from thence, but that you designed to write from Antwerp by the way of Ostend. So that wee must have patience for those letters to know what you resolve as to the time of your coming over, which continues to bee entirely necessary in all respects. What I can doe towards it here, is only to tease Mr. Burchett as I doe every day, to hasten your convoy. He told mee yesterday that he hoped it was gone, but I can't help fearing it is not.

By the French news of this post the Duke of Savoy seems to press *Suse* very vigorously,[5] and I don't find they bragg much of any great progress at Lerida, so that if our Palatin troops arrive there, one might hope that country might bee preserved this winter. But the accounts from Naples look

---

1 Only letter 918 survives.
2 Of cloth. See p. 881.
3 William Lovegrove, Marlborough's steward, who attended him in the field.
4 Letter 915.
5 After giving up the siege of Toulon, Prince Eugene and the Duke of Savoy assembled their iorces at Scalenghe and on 7/18 Sept. Eugene took one body of troops to besiege Suza which lay west of Turin in the Alps. It capitulated on 23 Sept./4 Oct.

as if wee were not to hope for any Imperialists from Italy which grieves mee the more because I doubt Prince Eugene's going turns upon that, and upon his going (in my opinion) the whole turns.

I believe wee shall bee here about a week longer. My Lord Sunderland came last night to my Lord Orford's,[1] but I have not yett seen him, nor his foreign' letters of this post; so perhaps he may write more particularly to you.[2]

On 29 September/10 October Marlborough sent off the garrisons for Menin and Courtrai and started the artillery and heavy baggage towards Ghent. The next day he moved the army to Petegem and on 1/12 October to a camp near Asper. The 2nd/13th the army crossed the Scheldt at Gavere and encamped at Wetteren.

---

925. MARLBOROUGH *to* GODOLPHIN [2/13 October 1707]

Source: Blenheim MSS. A1-37.
Printed: Coxe, ii. 358–9 (inc.).

Westrem[3] October 13th 1707

If you have so ill weather as we have here, Newmarkett must be very disagreable. I was not very well when we begone our march on Tuesday,[4] and these three ill days has made me more uneasy. However, I am resolved to begine my journey next Saturday, that I may return to The Hague, so as I may be in England by the first of November. You know that Mr. Craggs keeps company with 84 [the Tories], which makes me send you his enclosed letter,[5] which I desire may be shewen to 42 [the Queen]. For if 89 [the Whigs] will not opose these measures,[6] I beg that 88 [Parliament] may be putt off for some litle time; but you and 42 [the Queen] can judge much better then 39 [Marlborough]. But his zeal is such that he can't forbear sending his opinion, for if 84 [the Tories] succeds it will not be in anybody's power to do service. I also inclose a letter Mr. Cardonel received this last post from the Earl of Pitterborow.[5] I have also received one from him,[7] but it being nothing

---

[1] Edward Russell, Earl of Orford (1653–1727), admiral; lieutenant 1671; joined the service of William of Orange after the execution of his cousin, William, Lord Russell; carried invitation to him to invade England, 1688; Treasurer of the Navy and Admiral of the Blue 1689; defeated French fleet at La Hogue 1692, which made him a Whig hero; First Lord of the Admiralty 1694–9, 1709–10, 1714–17; one of the Whig Junto. *D.N.B.* His house at Chippenham, Cambs., was probably the seat for a Junto conference. Another had been held at Althorp in August.

[2] See Sunderland's letter of 8 Oct., in Coxe, ii. 355–6, telling him that the Duumvirs had not heeded warnings about Harley and that all would go to ruin if the changes demanded by the Whigs were not made.   [3] Westrem, a village 5 kilometres south of Wetteren.

[4] 30 Sept./11 Oct.   [5] Untraced.

[6] A proposal to invite over the Electress Sophia. No such motion was made during the 1707–8 session of Parliament, but the prospect of such an action was a constant threat to the ministry.

[7] 15/26 Sept., Blenheim MSS. A2-29; reply, 2/13 Oct., in Murray, iii. 619.

but compliments I do not send itt. When I was last at 121 [The Hague] I found everybody so disponding, that should 88 [Parliament] not begine with their usual vigor, it must give great advantage to 111 [France], especially should thay show any inclinations for 81 [peace]. And should thay succed in their invitation, 110 [Holland] would think themselves undone, for thay put their trust intierly on the sincerity of 42 [the Queen]; for the news of the invitation was gote to 121 [The Hague] so that I know that 62 [Heinsius] thinkes it will disturb al business, which will incorage in their country the partizans [of] 111 [France]. I beleive Mr. Secretary Harley is gone into the country, for by this post of the 26th I have received nothing from either office. Til his return my Lord Sunderland should let me have her Majesty's commands. You will be pleased to send your letters as formerly, and I shall give directions to Van der Pool[1] to send them after me; but I am afraid nether yours nor mine will come very regularly till my return.

I intend tomorrow to make use of the Queen's leave, in making the enclosed promotions.[2]

926. MARLBOROUGH *to the* DUCHESS   [2/13 October 1707]

Source: Blenheim MSS. E3.
Printed: Coxe, ii. 357–8.

Westrem October 13th 1707

I have had yours from Woodstock of the 25th. I wish you may find the building advanced as you are told, but by what is write to me I beleive you will not. I have been a good deal out of order these four or five days. However, I intend to begine my journey on Saturday,[3] so that I may be in England, since it is desired, by the first of November. I pray God I may be able to do any good when I shall be there. I have no heart nor sperits left, and would give a good deal to avoyd this troublesome journey. Wee have had, and have stil very ill weather, which will make the roads intollerable. I am very much afraid I shall not have the pleasur of receiving many of your letters til my return. However, I will take the best care I can to have them follow mee, so that I beg you will be regular in writting, and I will take all opertunitys of doing the same. I have often had the spleen, but never with so much reason as now, I finding almost everybody dishartned, I mean on this side the watter; and if wee have att the same time uneasinesses in 108 [England], how is [it] possible to strugle? England I am afraid dose not know their happyness, I mean in comparison with other countrys, but if thay oblige the Queen to a peace, as the circomstances of affairs are now abroad, thay will be sensible in a very litle time of their error. For my own part it will give me ease and the pleasur of being with you, which is what I most earnestly desire.

---

[1] Director of the post at Brielle.
[2] The promotion of general officers he requested in the spring. See p. 796.   [3] 4/15 Oct.

927. GODOLPHIN *to* MARLBOROUGH [*7 October 1707*]

Source: Blenheim MSS. A2-23.
Printed: Coxe, ii. 363-5.

Newmarkett 7 October 1707

I am to acknowledg from this place the favour of yours of the 8th from Antwerp,[1] by an officer (whom I don't know), with the enclosed to the Queen,[2] which I delivered to her last night; also that of the 10th from Helchin,[3] and of the 13th from Westrem[4] with the letters and papers inclosed. I am extream sorry to find by them, that you complain of want of health, at the same time you are to take a great jorney in this ill weather, which is the same with us as with you, and makes the Queen very apprehensive of a fitt of the gout coming upon her here. I saw her very uneasy last night, but they send mee word this morning she is a little better; and if she is able, she designs to goe to London the 10th.

I am very much troubled to find our letters of the 23d of September[5] did not reach you before you left The Hague, and had settled with them, your jorney to the Rhine. For it is most certain that must have had a better effect, after you could have been able to have encouraged them from hence; and it is as certain that your coming over in time would have contributed to that encoragement more than anything else can doe. It is very true both 42's [the Queen] and 38's [Godolphin] letters were against your coming for a day or soe only, while the armyes were in the field.[6] For that could not but have made a great noyse and exposed all things to great hazard, with not allowing time enough for your coming to have been of any effect. But when the armys were, or might have been separated, when you had opportunity of giving at The Hague the reasons for you coming over, that must needs have been of the greatest use here; and if it had succeeded, would have enabled you, to have adjusted everything on that side much more to the advantage of the common cause. But ther's an end of that now, and it remains only to bee considered whether 88 [Parliament] can bee deferred a fortnight without doing more hurt than good. I confess I think it putts us under a great deal of difficulty and (I doubt) 88 [Parliament] can't be putt off without discoraging of our friends, retarding all our preparations, and encouraging the opposing party, already grown insolent from our ill success abroad in this year.

On the other side, nothing is fixed here to make 88 [Parliament] succeed, nor can 38 [Godolphin] doe anything so shamefull as to abandon 42 [the Queen], but upon a joynt measure with Mr. Freeman [Marlborough], who now cannot bee here till after that thing comes to beare; and the resolution must bee taken one way or other. Upon the whole matter, I can come to no

---

[1] Letter 919.	[2] Letter 917.	[3] Letter 922.
[4] Letter 925.	[5] Letter 915.	[6] See p. 904, n. 1.

other conclusion but that it will still bee best for you to hasten hither as soon as you can. Accidents may happen to delay the proceedings of 88 [Parliament] so that nothing very materiall may bee decided finally before you come.[1]

In severall of 39's [Marlborough] letters to Mrs. Morley [the Queen] I find he often repeats, *that the rashness of some people's schemes may prove fatall.* But there is really no such thing as a scheme or anything like it from anybody else; nor has 42 [the Queen] as yett any thought of taking a scheme, but from Mr. Freeman [Marlborough] and Mr. Montgomery [Godolphin]. The misfortune is that 42 [the Queen] happens to bee intangled in a promise that is extreamly inconvenient, and upon which so much weight is layd, and such inference made, that to affect this promise would bee destruction; at the same time 42 [the Queen] is uneasy with everybody that but endeavours to shew the consequences which attend it.[2]

As to any forreign affairs, though there are 2 posts come, I have not seen any of the letters, and consequently I shall spare you till next post.

10 at night

This afternoon the Queen told mee she hoped to write to you herself by this post, but just now she sends mee the enclosed[3] which I send you, because it is less trouble to mee than to write the substance of it by candlelight.

928. GODOLPHIN *to* MARLBOROUGH   [*10 October 1707*]

Source: Blenheim MSS. A2-23.

Newmarkett 10th October 1707

I acknowledged the favour of yours of the 13th from Westrem[4] by the last post,[5] since which I have none from you, nor much expect any while you are in your jorney. In my last I told you so fully how much better it had been to have deferred all you design to doe there, till after the Parliament had mett here, that I shall not now trouble you with repeating or complaining; and all now left to bee done, if the Parliament must bee put off, is, that you make what hast you can to us. If by the means of 50 [Elector of Hanover] anything can bee done, to bring 56 [King of Sweden] into stricter measures with us, that will bee a good effect of the pains you have taken, and some recompence for the disappointments it will give us here. But I must own to you I am not in much apprehensions of the French efforts upon the Rhyne next year.

If the court of Vienna could have been perswaded in 6 months time but only to have named a generall for that command, none of those mischiefs

---

[1] Parliament was fixed to meet 23 Oct. On that day the Queen ordered the Commons to choose their Speaker and prorogued Parliament until the 30th, when she prorogued it again until 6 Nov. She made her speech on the 7th but the Commons did not start on business until Monday the 10th. Marlborough arrived on the 7th.

[2] The appointments of Blackall and Dawes to the bishoprics of Exeter and Chester.

[3] Untraced.   [4] Letter 925.   [5] Letter 927.

had hapned for the want of it, which wee have felt in this year. And now I imagine the very same good counsells will take care of nothing else this next year, and leave King Charles to shift for himself in Spain. In case that bee their intention I think wee should lett them know very early, they are not to expect one single ship from us for their assistance at Naples, till King Charles bee at ease in Catalonia; for it is very plain that court is not much burthened with generosity, and the more is done for them the less gratefull they are. It is certain to a demonstration that the whole misfortunes of the past summer are justly imputable, to their delay of naming a generall upon the Rhine, and to their treaty of Italy without the consent or knowledg of the Allys; and their wilfull obstinacy of making the detachment to Naples. Is it fitt then that those men should direct the measures for another year?

The Queen has been a little out of order here, but she is well again, and goes to London the 13th.

929. GODOLPHIN *to* MARLBOROUGH   [*10 October 1707*]

Source: Blenheim MSS. A2-23.
Addressed: To his Grace the Duke of Marlborough.

Newmarkett Fryday night 10th October

I am comanded by the Queen to add these two lines to my letter of this morning only to tell you, that she designed to have written to you herself tonight, but that she is not so well, but that it is uneasy to her. She hopes you will excuse her, and that she shall see you very soon here; and indeed soe doe I too.

930. MARLBOROUGH *to* GODOLPHIN   [*12/23 October 1707*]

Source: Blenheim MSS. A1-37.

Frankford October 23d 1707

I had yesterday the favour of yours of the 28 and 29th of the last month.[1] It was impossible for me to avoyde this journey. I find everything in confusion which makes the Elector wish with all his heart that he had not undertaken this troublesome employement. Wratislaw will not be here til tomorrow, so that Wenesday, the 26 will be the soonest I can leave this place. I am re-solved not to return to the army, but go the nearest way to The Hague, by which I shall gett 5 or 6 days, so that if the convoye be ready and the wind feavorable, I hope to be with you before November. I have received a letter from the Earle of Berkley,[2] but I think Mr. Vernon would do the Queen better service in that post. But I wish nothing may be done in this business, til I have an opertunity of acquainting her Majesty and you of the temper of

[1] Letters 920, 921.   [2] See p. 926

116 [the States]. Besides, for this winter I beleive Cadogan will do better then anybody. I have received the enclosed from Doctor d'Avenant,[1] and I beleive when I return to The Hague it will be thought necessary that the Queen and States should send to Ratisbon, to press their takeing into the Emperor's service the 6,000 Saxon horse. My next will be from The Hague.

931. MARLBOROUGH *to the* DUCHESS   [*12/23 October 1707*]

Source: Blenheim MSS. E3.

Frankford October 23d 1707

By your two letters from St. Albans, I find you expect me sooner in England then it is possible for me to be, there being an absolute necessity for my coming to this place. I expect Comte Wratislaw tomorrow, and hope on Wensday[2] to begine my journey for The Hague, having resolved not to return to the army, so that I may if the wind be favourable be with you by the end of October. I am not surprised to find 50 [the Elector of Hanover] so very desirous as he seems to be of being quit of this troublesome employement, for the truth is everything here is in more disorder then with us. I am glad you have desided the covering of the teritt. I wish you had done the same for the bowe windoe. As for myself, I could have agreed with you in wishing the house had been lesser so that it might have been sooner finished; but as it will be a monument of the Queen's favour and aprobation of my services to posterity, I can't disaprove of the modell, nor of what you have done in desiring that one half of the house may be made habitable, though I am afraid I shall not enjoye that for some yeares. For if I am to continue in the Service til we gett a good peace, that must take upp [a] great part of my life, and one the other side, if my fate shall be to retier, I shall take more pleasure in the Lodge, then to be with so many workmen, as of necessity must be for the finishing of that house. Att my going through Gand I could not resist the temptation of being [buying] some pictors, which I shall bring with mee.[3]

932. GODOLPHIN *to* MARLBOROUGH   [*14 October 1707*]

Source: Blenheim MSS. A2-23.
Addressed: To his Grace the Duke of Marlborough.

Newmarkett October 14, 1707

I think I should not have troubled you again from hence, but to cover the enclosed which the Queen has just now sent mee for you.[4] She has been out

---

[1] 30 Sept., in Blenheim MSS. A1-37, asking him to intercede with Godolphin to pay the arrears of his son Henry Davenant, English Secretary at Frankfort, 1703-11. Payment was ordered 26 July 1708. *C.T.B.*, XXII. ii. 37.

[2] 15/26 Oct.   [3] See p. 724, n. 1.   [4] Untraced.

of order some days which has kept her here longer than she intended. But I hope she will goe to London in 2 or 3 days.

Palmes was so ill of the gout when hee landed at Harwich that he was obliged to goe to London, so I have not seen him, nor doe I know one word of what he brings. But I see by other letters the uneasyness is very great betwixt the Duke of Savoy and Prince Eugene.

I hope you will bee in England so very soon after you receive this letter that it would bee to no purpose now to give you any farther trouble.

933. MARLBOROUGH *to* GODOLPHIN   [*16/27 October 1707*]

Source: Blenheim MSS. A1-37.
Printed: Coxe, ii. 359-60.

Frankford October 27th 1707

I was resolved to have left this place on Munday last,[1] but the two Electors[2] were so very pressing that I would stay for the arrivall of Comte Wratislaw that I could not refuse. He is not yett come but thay say he will be here this night. I have taken my measures to begine my journey on Saturday, and hope to be att The Hague by the 3d of the next month, so that with a faire wind I may yett have the happyness of being with you by the 1st of November, old stile.

The two Electors are very zealous and desirous that the Emperor and Empire may entertain the 6,000 Saxon horse, which would be a very necessary augmentation for this army. I have promised to press the Comte Wratislaw that the court of Vienna may do there part, which is said aught to be one half of the expence. I beleive I shall have good wordes, but I am afraid it may end there. However, I shall be very plain with him. The Elector of Hanover tels me very possativley, that if the Empire dose not put this army in a much better condition then it is at this time, he will not return to itt the next campagne. I can be very sensible of the uneasiness he is like to meet with, by what I suffer in Flanders. What I am going to say dose not proceed from the spleen, but really from the vexation I have in my mind, which make mee less capable of serving with success as I have done hethertoo; so that if I can't prevaile to have Prince Eugene sent to Catalonia, I should think the next best thing for the Service will be that he commands in chief in the Empire, and that the Elector of Hanover takes upon him the command I have in Flandres. For if things goes as I think thay will both in 108 [England] and 110 [Holland], nothing shall be able to prevaile with mee to loose that reputation I have hazarded for this warr. Til I have had an opertunity of acquainting 42 [the Queen] and having her leave, I shall lett nobody know of this intention of mine but the 62 [Pensioner], who is an honest man, and

[1] 13/24 Oct.   [2] The Electors of Hanover and Mainz.

so much my friend that he will say nothing of itt til he has my leave. I send you the Duke of Savoy's letter and project,¹ as also my answere, so that in what I may have been wanting, the Lords of the Cabinett may advise her Majesty, the States having by an expresse given me power to assure the Langrave of Hesse, that thay will satisfie him for his arrcares if he will consent to leave his troupes one yeare longer in Italie. I shall this afternoon send an expresse to Cassell,² and presse him in the name of her Majesty as well as that of the States Generall, but I fear he has already sent his orders. From The Hague you shall know what effect my letter to the Langrave has had.

934. MARLBOROUGH *to the* DUCHESS   [*16/27 October 1707*]

Source: Blenheim MSS. E3.

Frankford October 27th 1707

When I write my last³ I was in hopes my next would have been from The Hague, but the two Electors have been so pressing with me to stay for the arrivall of the Comte de Wratislaw, that I could not refuse. He is not yett come, but thay assure me he will be here tonight, so that if the wind prove faire when I am in Holand, I hope to have the happyness of being with you by the 1st of November, old stile. I find 50 [the Elector of Hanover] not very fond of serving this next campagne, at which I am not surprised; but I have taken the liberty to tell him that since he is in the gally he must row the best he can. I have write a thought of mine to 38 [Godolphin] by this post, which if I can compose, I hope it may be agreable to you, since it is what will give me great quiet, and give me an opertunity of ending the remainding part of my life to my own heart's desire.

935. GODOLPHIN *to* MARLBOROUGH   [*17 October 1707*]

Source: Blenheim MSS. A2-23.
Addressed: To his Grace the Duke of Marlborough.

St James' Fryday 17 October 1707

I am just now at 7 this evening come back from Newmarkett with the Queen, who is, God bee thanked, in very good health, and has endured the jorney very well. With more than this account I shall not trouble you till next post, before which I shall have seen Brigadier Palmes.

¹ 30 Sept./11 Oct., with a council of war of 28 Sept./9 Oct. and a memorial of 3/14 Oct. signed by Van der Meer, the Dutch commissioner, Chetwynd, Prince Eugene, and Rehbinder, commander of the Palatine troops. (Blenheim MSS. A2-16 (the project is wanting); reply, 16/27 Oct., Murray, iii. 625-6.) The Council considered alternative plans for the Duke of Savoy's operations the next year, either a penetration into Dauphiné or Provence, and set forth his requirements for troops and provisions. For a discussion of the project see Eugene to the Emperor, 9/20 Oct., *Feldzüge*, ser. 1, ix. 198-210.
² In Murray, iii. 628.   ³ Letter 931.

In the meantime I hope you will hinder all you can the recall of the Imperiall troops from Italy. And indeed what need is there of it, now the King of Sweden is so farr off.

I am vexed at this long east wind which keeps back your convoy. Pray make what hast you can.

936. GODOLPHIN *to* MARLBOROUGH   [*21 October 1707*]

Source: Blenheim MSS. A1-36.

Tuesday October 21th 11 at night

Though I have already troubled you with a very long letter by this post,[1] yett the wind being now west, I believe these letters may bee at The Hague very soon. I have a mind to add 2 or 3 lines only to tell you, that the Queen resolves to goe Thursday next the 23d to the Parliament and to direct the Commons to present their speaker to her that day sennight, the 30th of our October, by which time, if the winds bee favorable, wee are in hopes you may bee here.

937. GODOLPHIN *to* MARLBOROUGH   [*24 October 1707*]

Source: Blenheim MSS. A2-23.
Printed: Coxe, ii. 366.

24 October 1707

The wind being westerly I must still continue to write, though I long extreamly to see you here; for till you come, I doubt nothing will goe right, what ever it does then. 38 [Godolphin] labours as much as he can, and trys every way that can bee thought of to prevent 42's [the Queen] spoiling everything. But I am much afrayd t'will bee too late, unless Mr. Freeman [Marlborough] helps to make a solemn treaty, from which there is to bee no departing upon any terms whatsoever, without which it will bee next to impossible for Mr. Montgomery [Godolphin] to continue where he is. And the consequences of that, I need not enlarge upon to you.

Mr. Secretary Harley came to town the night before the Parliament mett. They chose the same Speaker yesterday without any obstruction, and he is to bee presented to [the Queen] the 30th, at which time I am afrayd there will bee a necessity for her to speak, though if it could bee without too much murmuring, I would rather her speech were deferred till you came.[2]

---

[1] Untraced.

[2] At a Cabinet Council on 26 Oct. Harley noted: 'Draught for Queen's speech read by Earl Sunderland and again paragraph by paragraph. Wednesday one a clock Lords to attend the Queen at Kensington when further to be considered.' In his minutes for the Cabinet meeting on the morning of the 29th Harley remarked: 'Draught of Queen's speech mended approved. Houses [of Parliament] to adjorne until November 6.' (B.M., Portland Loan, 29/9.)

938. MARLBOROUGH *to* GODOLPHIN

[*24 October/4 November 1707*]

Source: Blenheim MSS. A1-37.
Printed: Coxe, ii. 366-7.

Hague November 4th 1707

A little after my arrival here last night, I received five packets from England. The convoye is also come, and I am using all the dilligence I can to dispatch what of necessity must be, before I leave this place. Comte Wratislaw and Quiros being here, with powers from the Emperor and the King of Spain, will creat so much business, that should I stay a month, I should not have one day to myself. I have declared to them, as well as to the States, that I shall be obliged to make use of the first faire wind after this next Tuesday,[1] the wind being now very contrary. I may probabilly be with you as soon as this letter, which I beg with my duty you will lett the Queen know is the reason of my not doing myself the honor of answering hers of the 14th.[2]

I send you inclosed my letter to the Langrave of Hesse, his answere,[3] and the States' letter to me[4] on that subject.[5] I also send you the letters I have received by two expresses from Turin. You will be pleased to acquaint her Majesty with the contents, and such as may be proper, with her leave, may be comunicated to the Cabinet Counsell. I shall do my utmost to persuade the Langrave's minister[6] that his masters' troupes may continu one yeare longer in Italie. I do not see by Prince Eugene's letter[7] that he has any thoughts of going for Italie, and by what I find by Comte Wratislaw I am afraid the Court of Vienna are desirous of keeping him in Garmany. The Pensioner has promised me to second my endeavours with the Comte, that the Prince may be sent.[8]

62 [Heinsius] tels me that the King of France has given the necessary orders for an ogmentation of threscore thousand men, which I beleive is not in his power. However, it has a very ill effect here. I have many things to say but shall give you no further trouble at this time, being resolved of being with you as soon as possible.

---

[1] 28 Oct./8 Nov.   [2] Untraced.
[3] 16/27 Oct., Murray, iii, 628; reply, 18/29 Oct., Blenheim MSS. A2-19, insisting the States abide by the convention signed in March, that his troops would return north after the campaign in Italy.
[4] 12/23 Oct., in Blenheim MSS. A2-28.
[5] On leaving his troops in Italy with the Duke of Savoy for another year.
[6] Johann Reinhard von Dalwigk, envoy extraordinary from Hesse-Kassel at The Hague 1702-20.
[7] 8/19 Oct. Turin, in Blenheim MSS. A2-18.   [8] To Spain.

939. MARLBOROUGH *to* GODOLPHIN
[*28 October/8 November 1707*]

Source: Blenheim MSS. B2–9.
Printed: Coxe, ii. 367–8.
Addressed: To my Lord Treasurer, Whitehall.

Hague November 8th 1707

I had ordered my business so as that I might have sailled this day, having sent my servants on board yesterday, and ordered the yackts to Helvertsluce, where thay are now with the men of warr, so that we might go to sea with the first opertunity. But the wind is not only contrary, but also blowes very hard, so that God knows when I shall be able to be with you. But you may be assured that I will not loose one hour when the wind will allow my going to sea.

I have this morning had the favour of yours of the 24th,[1] and am much troubled to see that 42 [the Queen] continues in the making you uneasy. I am afraid you do me to[o] much honour in thinking that my presence is necessary, but you may depend that I shall be governed by you in doing whatever you think may do good. But I must confesse that by what I see, as well abroad as att home, [it] lookes as if it were resolved by destiny that nothing should go well this winter. My last letter[2] I hear is blowen back, and as the wind is it is impossible for this to go, so that I may be as soon with you as this.

940. MARLBOROUGH *to the* DUCHESS
[*28 October/8 November 1707*]

Source: Blenheim MSS. E3.
Printed: Coxe, ii. 368.
Addressed: For the Dutchesse of Marlborough.

Hague November 8th 1707

I was in hopes not to have writt but to have been at sea this night, having sent my servants on board the yackt yesterday, but the wind being as contrary as possible and blowing a storme, I have continued in this place, but shall not send for my servants back, being resolved to make use of the first wind that will alow of my going to sea, having finished what I was to do here, and very desirous of being with you. I am afraid my friends will then see that I am not of much use, but I shall be governed. I am sorry to tell you that the inclinations 110 [Holland] has for 81 [peace] will occasion their hurting themselves and their friend, as much as our unhappy differences in 108 [England].

I am sorry for poor Mr. Chudleigh's condition.[3] If he has not been employed to receive any mony this summer, he has none of mine in his hands. I am to

[1] Letter 937.   [2] Letter 938.
[3] Avener and Clerk Marshall as well as equerry to the Queen. He died 26 Oct. See the Queen to the Duchess [27 Oct.?] in Brown, pp. 209–10.

thank you for yours of the 24th which I received this morning. What you say of 256 [Mrs. Masham] is very odd, and if you think she is a good weather-cock, it is hie time to leave off strugling, for beleive me nothing is wroth rowing against wind and tyde; at least you will think so when you come to my age.[1] I have been to waite upon Mrs. Burnett,[2] and have ordered her a yackt. I am ever yours.

941. MARLBOROUGH *to* GODOLPHIN
[*31 October/11 November 1707*]

Source: Blenheim MSS. A2-39.
Addressed: To my Lord Treasurer, Whitehall.

Hague November 11th 1707

This is the thord post since my being here, and Vanderpool tels me that not only these letters, but also some of mine from Frankford, are keep on this side of the watter by the continuell stormes and contrary winds. If there be not a faire wind by tomorrow morning, of which there is no liklywhood, the tydes will fall so late that the men of warr can't gett to sea til Tuesday,[3] though the wind should be faire; so that I intend on Munday to go to the Brile and go to sea whenever Sir John Jenings will ventur out, for I am impatient of being with you; and any longer stay here will but creat only trouble to myself, for these people here will most certainly take no farther resolutions till thay see what the Queen and Parliament will do. I pray God all may go for the best, for otherways the insolence of the French will be intollerable. I am this afternoon to have a conference with the deputys, and afterwardes with the Pensioner. If anything passes worth your knowledge, you shall be sure to have itt.

942. MARLBOROUGH *to the* DUCHESS
[*31 October/11 November 1707*]

Source: Blenheim MSS. E3.
Printed: Coxe, ii. 368-9 (inc.).
Addressed: For the Dutchesse of Marlborough.

Hague November 11th 1707

I have had yours by Lieutenant General Lumley, but have not taken the fisick, being resolved to go from hence the minutt the wind proves the least favourable. This crose wind vexes me a good deall, for besides the satisfaction I

---

[1] For the complaints of the Duchess about Mrs. Masham see the Duchess to the Queen, 29 Oct., *Private Correspondence*, i. 106-12.
[2] On her return to England from the Spa and Hanover. See p. 762.
[3] 4/15 Nov.

should have in being with you, I find 38 [Godolphin] very desirous of my being with him. I have no opinion of my being able of doing any good, but uncertainty is the worst of all conditions, for death itself is easier, then the fear of itt. If you were treuly sensible of the great desire I have of ending my days quietly with you, I flatter myself your good nature would be contented to bare many inconveniencys, and to lett the rest of the world govern itself after its o[w]n methode. This is the thord I have write since my being here, and the postmaster tels me that not only those, but some of mine from Frankford are stile on this side, so that I shall not make this longer, then by assuring you of my being with all my heart and soull yours.

1708

Marlborough landed at Dover on Thursday, 6 November, at noon, and was in London by the afternoon of the next day. His first task was to resolve the political stalemate that had continued since his departure. The Queen was adamant in her refusal to admit more Whigs to her Cabinet, and without their support the ministry could not expect to survive another session of Parliament. In contrast to the previous year, Marlborough was unable to arrange a satisfactory solution. As a consequence the parliamentary session was a most difficult one, with both Tories and Whigs bent on forcing the Duumvirs to submit or driving them from office. Harley proposed admitting more Tories into the ministry and retaining only those Whigs who would forsake the Junto. Marlborough and Godolphin eventually decided against him, having long agreed that they could only carry on with Whig support. The treasonous activities of one of Harley's clerks, William Greg, weakened his position. Under the spur of the Whig-inspired investigation that followed and his failure to persuade Godolphin and Marlborough to adopt his plan for a remodeling of the ministry, Harley apparently intimated his intention to resign at the end of the session. In reality, he planned a coup, to turn out Godolphin and follow a Tory scheme with himself as the centre of power. When news of the plan to unseat him reached Godolphin, the aggrieved Treasurer broke with the Secretary and together with the Marlboroughs delivered to the Queen a demand for his dismissal. Upon her refusal they retired from Court only to return when Harley voluntarily resigned, having found that he could not command sufficient support in the Parliament to maintain a government without Marlborough's assistance.[1]

Harley's departure from the ministry, together with that of his closest supporters, Henry St. John, the Secretary at War, Sir Simon Harcourt, the Attorney-General, and Sir Thomas Mansell, the Comptroller of the Household, was not the principal topic of coffee-house debates for long. It was followed immediately by the long-expected, attempted Jacobite invasion, led in person by the Pretender. This proved abortive and no landing was carried out, but not before hasty preparations were made, ten battalions were summoned home from the Netherlands, and Admiral Byng, who had been cruising in the Channel, went in pursuit of the Pretender's fleet.

Warned by reports from the Continent that Louis XIV was building a still larger army in Flanders to try and recoup his losses of the past year, Marlborough was anxious to put his own troops early into the field. The Dutch did not feel secure so

---

[1] For a summary of Harley's activities this winter and his plans see Snyder, 'Godolphin and Harley', pp. 262–71. The details of Harley's scheme can only be surmised as the evidence is scanty. Angus McInnes was unable to provide any additional clarification in his *Robert Harley, Puritan Politician* (London, 1970), pp. 97–102.

long as he was absent and the Emperor urged him to confer with Prince Eugene, whom he sent to The Hague for that purpose. Marlborough left England as soon as arrangements had been completed at home for the support of his army.

Marlborough's departure from London came at 3 o'clock on the morning of 29 March. Embarking at Margate he crossed the Channel that night and made his way to The Hague where he arrived 31 March/11 April. He was accompanied by Stanhope who attended The Hague conferences with him before returning to Spain to take up his duties. Godolphin hoped that Marlborough would return to England once the meetings with Heinsius and Eugene were concluded and the plans for the 1708 campaign decided. The General was still needed at home to settle the outstanding differences between the Queen, the Duumvirs, and the Whigs. Very likely Marlborough had already decided to avoid any further unpleasant confrontations in England and had no real intention of returning, though he did not send the Treasurer his apologies and excuses until 6/17 April (letter 947).

---

943. GODOLPHIN *to* MARLBOROUGH   [*30 March 1708*]

Source: Blenheim MSS. A2-38.

March 30, 1708

The wind and weather are both so fair here, that I hope this day has safely landed you in Holland, and if the troops are ready to sail from Tinmouth there is great appearance of their having a favourable passage.

I omitted to ask you before wee parted whether you would yett allow mee to appoynt comptrollers for the accounts of the army.[1] I cannot but look upon that, as a very necessary office.

The gentlemen of the House of Commons[2] who mett last night at Mr. Boyle's agreed that the returns should bee layd before the house today by Mr. Walpole, of what had been done relating to the recruits in pursuance of the late Act of Parliament.[3] But I have not yett seen anybody since, that could tell mee what has passed there upon this subject.

By the forreign letters of this day I hear Prince Eugene has assured Mr. Palmes at Hannover,[4] that the Emperour will have 20,000 men upon the

[1] Sir Philip Meadows and Thomas Broderick were appointed in June. For the background of their appointments see p. 765, n. 3.
[2] The government managers in the Commons, all office-holders.
[3] 6 Anne, c. 45. The address for the account was passed 30 Mar.: *C.J.*, xv. 642. The report, showing 868 men had volunteered for the service for 1708 is printed, ibid. 645-6.
[4] Palmes had been sent to the Continent in February to make arrangements with the Allies for the 1708 campaign, and in particular, for the support of the Duke of Savoy, who was expected to make a thrust into France through Dauphiné. He went over to The Hague in February, visited Hanover in March, Berlin and Vienna in April, and stayed at the latter until August when he went to Savoy. At Vienna he was mainly concerned with obtaining the award of certain territories promised by the Emperor to the Duke of Savoy (p. 989, n. 4) without which the latter would not take

Rhyne with all the necessary equipage for their acting offensively by the middle of May. I shall doubt the truth of this till I hear it from you. But if it bee true, I conclude Prince Eugene will act at the head of them himself; and if it bee not true, that he only says it to encourage the Elector.

Since I had written thus far I have seen Mr. Secretary Boyle, who tells mee he has given you an account of what has passed in the House today,[1] by which you will see that as soon as the fright of the invasion is pretty well over, the enemy[2] begins to pluck up a spiritt agayn. This matter depends upon what the House will doe tomorrow. But I plainly see their design is to turn the blame of not executing the Act upon the administration. And my opinion is they will doe nothing tomorrow that will bee worth delaying to putt an end to the session in expectation of what they may doe farther. The old argument about their election returns, and makes greater impression upon their minds, as the time draws nearer.

Orders are given tonight[3] for Sir George Bing to come to the Downes, leaving 3 ships to cruise upon the coast of Scotland to prevent and intercept their correspondence.[4] The troops are also ordered to return this way by easy marches.

Greg's[5] paper was the most trifling impertinence that ever was seen; and may help for ought I know to make him bee hanged, though the Queen is averse to it.

Recruiting was a perpetual problem with which the government had to contend. It was carried on in two ways. Each regiment sent back teams in the autumn of the

the field. Eugene was on his way to The Hague to meet Marlborough to make plans for the campaign. He stopped *en route* at Dresden, Berlin, and Hanover (where he met Palmes). Braubach, ii. 217–18.

[1] The Commons addressed the Queen to send them an account of what number of men had enlisted or been impressed. The Tories moved for the addition of a clause asking what money had been given to this out of bounty money and what orders had been issued to encourage recruiting. Boyle to Marlborough, 30 Mar., Blenheim MSS. B1-1; Walpole to Marlborough, ibid., B1-2.

[2] The Tory opposition in Parliament.

[3] Burchett to Byng, 30 Mar., inclosing orders for Prince George, *The Byng Papers*, ed. B. Tunstall (Navy Records Society, 1930–2), ii. 121–3.

[4] i.e. the Jacobites in Scotland and the Pretender.

[5] William Greg, a clerk in Harley's office, had been discovered sending copies of official papers to the French, enclosed with prisoners' mail that was being censored in the office of the Secretary of State. A careful investigation was made, first by the Cabinet, then by the House of Lords at the initiative of the Whigs, who hoped to implicate Harley. Greg was found guilty of treason and executed on 28 Apr. On 29 Mar. he was taken from Newgate to Sunderland's office to be examined at his own request and must have delivered in the paper (untraced) referred to here. It probably included an exoneration of Harley, whose innocence Greg consistently defended, even on the scaffold. For the investigation see Trevelyan, ii. 331–3; *H.L.N.S.*, vii. 548–51; *The Report of the House of Lords, being the Trial and Confession of W. Greg* (London, 1708).

year, after the campaign was over, to recruit new troops during the winter for the next campaign. Bounty money was paid to the officer who enlisted the recruit, and levy money to the recruit himself, as an inducement. The Justices of the Peace were empowered by the successive Recruiting Acts to conscript able-bodied men without visible means of support and to release capital offenders from prison who volunteered to enlist. This system of recruitment never met the needs of the army. In the 1707–8 session of Parliament the government tried to introduce a system of compulsory levies to total 16,000 men on the parishes and counties, which would make them responsible for supplying a fixed quota of men. This failed in the Commons as it did on several other occasions during the war when it was proposed. The Act which was finally passed (6 Anne, c. 45) did include an order for the Justices to organize a drive in March to bring in recruits, and raised the bounty to the constables who carried out this duty for the magistrates, and increased the levy money to volunteers. This was the best the government was able to manage.[1]

---

944. GODOLPHIN *to* MARLBOROUGH   [*31 March 1708*]

Source: Blenheim MSS. A2-38.

Wednesday night 31 March

I gave you some account by last night's post of what passed yesterday in the House of Commons relating to the recruits. That matter has ended this day in an address to the Queen to putt out a proclamation for enforcing the former act, and strictly enjoying all Justices of the Peace and officers of the army not to neglect their duty in this matter. You will find the address in the printed *Votes* which I conclude Mr. Cardonell will have sent to him.

Wee had a meeting at the Speaker's[2] this morning, and I found by all the gentlemen of the House of Commons present this was all that was possible to bee done in that matter, without continuing the Parliament as long as it could sitt by law, which would have been attended with endless inconveniences. This being the case, I believe the sessions will end tomorrow. And in that case I shall goe to Newmarkett for 5 or 6 days which makes mee give you this account so long before the post day, because I hope to bee gon before it comes.

The letters of this day from Scotland say that the Earls of Arroll[3] and Marshall[4] have sent worde they will surrender themselves, but the Duke of Atholl declines coming in, upon pretence of want of health.

---

[1] For a discussion of recruiting during the war see Scouller, pp. 102–25.

[2] John Smith.

[3] Charles Hay, thirteenth Earl of Erroll (*c.* 1680–1717), apprehended on suspicion of treason at the time of the Pretender's attempted invasion and imprisoned in Edinburgh Castle.

[4] William Keith, eighth Earl Marischal (*c.* 1664–1712), Privy Councillor, Scotland, 1701; arrested and lodged in Edinburgh Castle because of Jacobite sympathies at time of the Pretender's invasion.

945. GODOLPHIN *to* MARLBOROUGH [*3 April 1708*]

Source: Blenheim MSS. A2-38.

Newmarkett 3d of Aprill 1708

I am very uneasy not to have heard, as yett, of your safe arrivall in Holland, the wind having appeared to us here very fair all Thursday last,[1] to have brought over the forreign letters. It is so this day to carry the troops from Tinmouth, so I hope, you will soon hear of their being safely arrived at Ostend.[2]

I trouble you with the enclosed letter[3] which I have received at this place, from Lieutenant Generall Erle, by which you will see somebody or other makes it their business, to fill other people with as much uneasyness as they can. I shall endeavour to satisfy him as soon as I come to town; for I think very much depends this summer, upon his being in good humour.

You will have heard from London how the sessions ended, so I will not trouble you from hence with anything but my good wishes that you may have all manner of happyness and satisfaction.

946. GODOLPHIN *to* MARLBOROUGH [*5 April 1708*]

Source: Blenheim MSS. A2-38.
Printed: Coxe, ii. 408.

Newmarkett 5 Aprill 1708

I had the satisfaction to receive here last night, the favour of yours of the 31th of March[4] from The Hague, and Prince Eugene having been there before you. I hope your affairs on that side will soon bee dispatched to your mind,[5]

[1] 1 Apr.
[2] These were the ten English battalions sent over from Ostend on the alarm of the Pretender's attempted invasion. Not needed after all, they never landed at Tynemouth as planned but returned to Flanders after lying some days off the coast. Those sent were the 1st Battalion of Guards, the regiments of Orkney, Argyle, Webb, North, Ingoldsby, Tatton, Howe, Godfrey, and the Scotch Fusiliers. See John Deane, *Journal of a Campaign in Flanders of 1708* (London, 1846), pp. 3-4.
[3] Untraced. Erle's field pay as a general had been stopped on his return from Spain. (He still drew his salary as Lieutenant-General of the Ordnance.) His grievance is explained in a letter Godolphin wrote him this same day: 'What was done for the person [Rivers] you name was done, by a sort of bargain with the Duke of Marlborough before he went over, and in consideration, partly, of former mortifications, but you have no reason so much as to imagine there can bee the least competition betwixt you in the opinion of the Queen or in the Duke of Marlborough. I am very sure, there is none of that of [mine].' (Osborn Collection, Yale University Library.) As the ministry intended to employ him again in the field, as commander of the descent, Marlborough recommended his pay be continued from the time he left Spain (pp. 961-2).
[4] Untraced.
[5] At The Hague conference Eugene and Marlborough decided on the strategy to be employed by the Allies this year. A new army of 40,000 men was to be formed on the Moselle for an invasion of France up the river, which Prince Eugene would command, although the two generals prepared alternative plans which were implemented for Eugene to join Marlborough in the Low Countries. The Duke of Savoy was to be provided with 20,000 Imperial troops to make a thrust into French

which is the more necessary, because it is plain those on this side, will not bee soe without your assistance.[1] And yett I am not in despair, but your being one fortnight here, would obtain what is reasonable to bee done, and sett things upon a tolerable foot, which otherwise are like to come to great extremitye's next winter, in the opinion of your humble servant.

947. MARLBOROUGH *to* GODOLPHIN   [6/17 April 1708]

Source: B.M., Add. MS. 28057, fols. 344–7.

Hague April 17th 1708

I have had the favour of yours of the 30th[2] of the last month this morning and am very sorry to see that the recrutes is not like to go well, since it must be very prejudicial to the Service.

I send you enclosed the project[3] for the armys on the Moselle and the Rhine, by which you will see that the Imperial troopes are not near 20,000 men, since in our project we are obliged to take 9,000 Pallatins to make up the number of 20,000[4] we are to join the Hessiens, and Saxons, to the army on the Moselle, as also to add 5,000 men more to make that army 40,000. This project if it be her Majeste's pleasur may be communicated to the Cabinett Councel, for it cannot long be keep a secrit since it must have the aprobation of the Elector Pallatin, and Hanover. I believe the last will very unwillingly consent. I am rather of the opinion that he will opose it all he can, and att last take the resolution of not serving, especially if he knew the resolution taken by Prince Eugene and myself, that if the Prince sees that he cannot act with success on the Moselle, he will then loose no time in making such a march as that he may join me in Flanders, that we may have some days of acting before the King of France can give orders for the strenghning Monsieur Vandome's army. The success of this will very much depend upon the secrit, which will bee very hard to keep.

Dauphiné. The Elector of Hanover would command an army of 45,000 on the Rhine and was expected to parallel the Duke's advance with a drive up the Rhine into Franche-Comté. Marlborough would take the offensive in the Low Countries and provision was made for Eugene to join Marlborough with his army (the real aim of the two generals) and overwhelm the French in the Spanish Netherlands. The Imperial general, Count Starhemberg, would take command in Spain, with James Stanhope in command of the troops in English pay. The plan for a descent on the French coast, which Godolphin had urged the previous year (see pp. 768, 773), was to be implemented under the command of Erle. Spain was regarded as the seat of defensive operations although every encouragement was given to the commanders to take the initiative. Marlborough explained some of his plans to Boyle, 2/13 Apr., Murray, iii. 698–9.

[1] The political crisis in England had not been completely resolved with the resignation of Harley and his associates. The Queen had still not given her consent for Somers and Wharton to be admitted to the Cabinet. Godolphin hoped that Marlborough would be able to persuade her to accept them if he returned. Marlborough did not return and the two Whigs were not given office until the end of the year, after the death of Prince George broke the Queen's resistance.

[2] Letter 943.   [3] 5/16 Apr., in Murray, iii. 709–11.
[4] The 20,000 men were sent to the Duke of Savoy (see p. 1007).

I send you a copie of the paper Mr. Stanhope and I have drawn,[1] of the orders we think are allready given, for the government on those heads. I have given Prince Eugene the same paper signed by mee, that he might send it to the Mareshal Staremberg.[2] I also send you a copie of Prince Eugene's minutes of what we have agreed at the several conferences,[3] so that if her Majesty has no objection that the necessary orders may be given. I have write to Mr. Secretary concerning the 4,000 Garmain foot, and the impossibillity of replacing them, but by the Emperor's own subjects, so that nothing but money can do itt.[4] What every answere you think it most for the Queen's Service, should be given by the next post, for til this matter is resolved those 4,000 men are of no use to the publick.

You will give mee leave to trouble you with a letter I have received from the Earle of Bertley.[5] You will see that he continues in the desire of being employed in this country, but I should hope when Sir Philip Meadhurst [Meadows] is made on[e] of the controlers,[6] the Earle of Bertley might be properer for Vienna then this place. When you know the Queen's pleasur, you will speak to his Lordship for I must refer him to you.[7]

I am extreamly pressed by the States not to return for England, and also by Prince Eugene, for my meetting him att Hanover, in order to persuade the Elector to agree to our project. I am told the States has this day write to the Queen to desire I might not leave this country.[8] Thay are the more allarmed by the hearing nothing of our horse nor foot, and the French pretending to enchamp 30 battalions, and 50 squadrons the 20th of this month. But I believe there real intentions, are, not to come into the field, til we oblige them to it.

By the discourse I have had with 48 [Prince Eugene] I am afraid we must

1 The lists in Murray, iii. 710–11?

2 Count Guido von Starhemberg (1657–1737), the most celebrated Imperial general after Prince Eugene; appointed to command in Spain, 1707, without consultation with the Maritime Powers who had requested Eugene. See A. Arneth, *Das Leben des kaiserlichen Feldmarschall Guido Starhemberg* (Vienna, 1853); Emperor to Anne, 20/31 Dec. 1707, *Morrison Catalogue*, first series, ii. 350.

3 Untraced. Part of these relating to the admission of Russia to the Grand Alliance, were sent to Boyle on 9 May. (See Murray, iv. 8 n.) This portion is in S.P. 87/3, fols. 50–1. Eugene's letter to the Emperor, 6/17 Apr. was full of details about troop dispositions for the armies in the Low Countries and on the Rhine and Moselle as well as details of what the Queen would contribute to sending 4,000 men from Italy to Spain. *Feldzüge*, ser. 2, i. 65–78.

4 To Boyle, 6/17 Apr., Murray, iii. 702–3. Eugene proposed that the Maritime Powers take 4,000 Imperial troops in Italy into their pay and send them to Spain, asking that the Queen provide the levy money to recruit men to replace these troops. Marlborough thought he asked for too much money and recommended that the Queen offer only a portion of the sum requested (to Boyle, 23 Apr./4 May, Murray, iii. 717–18), and the Emperor accepted. Marlborough to Sunderland, 26 June/7 May, to Boyle, 19/30 May, Murray, iv. 7, 43–4. The troops arrived in Spain after the fall of Tortosa to the Bourbons. Parnell, p. 249.

5 Untraced.　　　　　　　6 Comptrollers of the army accounts. See p. 765, n. 3.

7 For Cadogan's appointment as envoy at The Hague and Brussels to succeed Stepney see p. 874, n. 3. For the replacement of Meadows by Palmes as envoy at Vienna, see *B.D.R.*, p. 31.

8 6/17 Apr., B.M., Add. MS. 5130, fol. 205.

not expect much success[1] from 58's [Duke of Savoy] army nor from that of 50 [Elector of Hanover] which makes me very mallincolly, knowing very well the difficulty we shall meet with in this country, and the uneasiness which consequently must be with 88 [Parliament] this next winter.

I have this minnut received the Friday's letters,[2] by which I see there is nothing done for the recruting the redgiments which will be a great prejudice to the Service. God grant that I may be in the wrong, but I do fear everything will grow worse. The enclosed letter of Sir Philip Meadhurst to Mr. Negus[3] I should have shown you before I left England. Notwithstanding the unreasonable bigness of this packet, I must send Vanbrook's.[4] Pardon this and you shall never more have so much trouble att once from your faithfull friend and servant.

948. GODOLPHIN *to* MARLBOROUGH   [*8 April 1708*]

Source: Blenheim MSS. A2-38.
Printed: Coxe, i. 412 (inc.).

Newmarkett 8 of Aprill 1708

I have the favour of yours of the 13th[4] and am very sorry you have so little time to yourself while I am so idle as to bee here. One of my best reasons for it was the hopes I have to meet you at London at my return thither. But I must own, your letter leaves that matter very uncertain, since you seem to think the enemy's forming a small camp near Ypres will oblige you to goe to Flanders. For my part, I can't see much ground to apprehend the French preparations there, or anywhere, since their disappointment in Scotland which seems to have very much disordered all their measures.

I entirely dislike all Prince Eugene's projects[5] even if they could succeed. For considering how the court of Vienna used us as soon as they were

[1] That is, they would not act offensively.
[2] 3 Apr. See Boyle to Marlborough, 2 Apr., Blenheim MSS. B1-1; Walpole to Cardonnel, 2 Apr., Letterbook, Cholmondeley MSS., Ch. (H) 2, Cambridge University Library.
[3] Untraced. It discussed their serving together as joint comptrollers of the army accounts. Godolphin found too much opposition to Negus and appointed Thomas Broderick instead. See p. 765, n. 3.
[4] Untraced.
[5] See p. 949. Eugene had proposed a major offensive on the Moselle with an army of 70,000 men, made up by drawing 30,000 men out of the Allied army in Flanders, and an offensive on the Rhine to include the siege of Strasbourg. He also proposed sending 4,000 Imperial foot from Italy to Spain and 1,000 horse from Flanders to Spain. (Marlborough to Boyle, 2/13 Apr., Murray, iii. 698-9.) Marlborough countered with a proposal that Eugene have an army of 40,000 on the Rhine which could be sent if conditions warranted to join Marlborough's army in the Spanish Netherlands (below, p. 961). Marlborough's plan was adopted. The foot were sent to Spain, but as 9,000 horse were already ordered from Italy to Spain it was decided that sending the additional 1,000 was not warranted (ibid. 6/17 Apr., pp. 702-3).

masters in Italy, it would surely bee very unadvised to putt it into their power to doe the same again, by making them masters again upon the Rhyne and Moselle, and by neglecting the opportunity of our own advantages nearer home, of which our people will bee much more sensible. I wish therfore most earnestly that your notion may prevail with Prince Eugene, but not at the price of those 2 Electors; because that could not fail of being called here a *pretext* not to return into England, our world being not much better natured than when you left it.

I send you the enclosed from my Lord Halifax.[1] My Lord Steward[2] who is here joyns in that request.

The wind is now so fair for your coming over, that I would fain flatter myself I shall meet you Saturday night[3] at London.

949. MARLBOROUGH *to* GODOLPHIN [9/20 April 1708]

Source: B.M., Add. MS. 28057, fols. 348–9.

Hague Aprill 20th 1708

This day Prince Eugene is sett forward for Dusseldopf, and I have promised to mett him this day senight att Hanover, where I beleive we shall pass the two days we intend to stay there very disagreably. For by the discorse I have had with the envoye of Hannover,[4] I am confermed the Elector will not like our project,[5] though it is the most likelyest to give uneasiness to France.

Having this safe opertunity by Courant,[6] I send you inclosed the minutes of Prince Eugene of what passed betwene the Pensioner, that Prince and myself this morning, concerning propositions made by King Augustus to the Emperor.[7] The Emperor having promised that nobody should be acquainted with this matter, you will keep it, as a secrit from everybody but her Majesty, and that you will be pleased to let me have her pleasur, and your thoughts on this subject; for I am engaged no farther then my opinion of what aught to be done, and the Pensioner has been full as cautious as myself.

I must acquaint you and the Queen with the same desire of secressy, of a thing which gives me very mallincolly reflections, which is that Wensday last the Burgemasters of Amsterdame desired I would appoint them an hour, and accordingly thay and their Pensioner[8] came, in which thay endeavoured

---

[1] Untraced, but carrying the request that Lord Irwin be appointed governor of Scarborough Castle *vice* Anthony Duncombe, M.P., Hedon, who died 4 Apr. (p. 954). Irwin was not appointed until 22 June 1709.

[2] The Duke of Devonshire.   [3] 10 Apr.

[4] Hans Kasper von Bothmer.   [5] To form a third army under Eugene on the Moselle.

[6] A messenger.

[7] Untraced. Prince Eugene had visited Augustus at Dresden on 19/30 Mar. The King offered the Emperor a further 3,000 cavalrymen, which he no longer needed (or could support) now that he had withdrawn from the Great Northern War: Braubach, ii. p. 217 and n. 123.

[8] Willem Buys.

to show mee the impossibillity of their being able to continue the warr longer than this campagne. The next point was that of their Barier. I gave them the best arguments I could think off, to make them comprehend that the best way to have a good peace, would be to act so, as that France might have reason to beleive that we had no thoughts but that off carrying on the warr with vigor. Notwithstanding all that passed they pressed me to acquaint you with what they had said, but I possetivly refused to have any other part then that of sending whatever they should give me in writting. I must own to you that by all that I can observe on this side, and the rising of the Parliament without making provision for the recruting the redgiments gives me a very mallincolly prospect not only for this summer but also for the next winter.

950. MARLBOROUGH *to the* DUCHESS   [*9/20 April 1708*]

Source: Blenheim MSS. E4.
Printed: *Private Correspondence*, i. 124–5 (inc.), as 20 and 27 April.

Hague April 20th 1708

Courant being desirous to return for England, I take this opertunity of writting rather then by the post, and at the same time take the liberty of telling you how uneasy I am in my mind, being convinced by your two letters which I have received since my being here, of your resolution of living with that coldness and indifferency for mee, which if it continues must make me the unhappyest man alive.

I know it would be but a trouble to you to have an account of what I do here, but I can't forbear saying so much, by all that I can obsarve we must expect infinett troubles.

I have promised Prince Eugene to meet him this day senight at Hanover, where we are to endeavour to gett his consent to the project, which we are persuaded is that which is most likely to give trouble to France. However, I do not beleive the Elector will consent to what wee shal propose. I know noe remedy but that of submitting to Provedence, and endeavour to be contented when on[e] has nothing to reproch on[e]'s self. I have been troubled very much with the headeak since my being here, but I hope the going into the eare will do mee good. I send the two keys for my closett, not knowing but you might have occasion for some of the writtings.

951. GODOLPHIN *to* MARLBOROUGH   [*11 April 1708*]

Source: Blenheim MSS. A2–38.
Printed: Coxe, i. 412–13 (inc.).

Sunday night Aprill 11

The wind has been so fair all the while I was at Newmarkett that at my return from thence Saturday night I was not out of hopes to have found you here. But instead of that I find very plainly by yours of the 17th[1] that you don't think of comming, which I must own, is a great mortification to mee. For I had much sett my heart upon the hopes of seeing you, and endeavoring once more to have sett Mrs. Morley's [the Queen] affairs upon a right foot; and I really think it would bee very hard for her to have resisted the plain reasons with which our arguments might have been enforced at this time. I say this chiefly because I really believe one of your chief reasons for your not making use of the fair wind that presented, was, your apprehension that your being here would not bee able to doe any good. For you must give mee leave to say that I can't think you will goe to Hanover, or that you think yourself, there is any occasion at present for your going to Flanders.

As to the project you sent over, the Queen leaves it to you to agree to whatever you judg most for the advantage of the common cause. If it ends in Prince Eugene's acting with 20 or 30,000 men in Flanders, that may bring Monsieur de Guiscard's plan[2] to your mind, or enable you to attack Lisle, or Ypres which is better, in case it opens your way to Dunkirk. For my opinion is that France would venture the loss of a battail much sooner than the loss of that place at this time.

In case the Elector of Hanover agrees to the project, all possible means should bee used to hasten him to the Rhyne. In case he does not, but rather declines to serve, 48 [Prince Eugene] should not bee flattered in his notion of besieging of Strasbourg,[3] for the reasons I gave you in my former letter;[4] and [which] are indeed very obvious of themselves, besides that it makes it impracticable to act offensively in Flanders at the same time.

Our French letters say they continue their naval preparations at Brest and Rochefort as well as at Dunkirk. I hope therefore the States will continue their intentions of sending their ships to act in conjunction with the Queen's fleet, for the blocking up Dunkirk, and preserving our superiority in the North Sea, and throughout the Channel.[5]

I believe it will bee necessary for you to make them sensible of this, or else, the [Pretender's] expedition to Scotland being now over, I am afraid they may have a mind to save their ships, and the charge of them. But really, wee shall not bee able to doe anything considerable without them.

My Lord Sunderland will lett you know[6] the Queen leaves it to you, to agree for the 4,000 men to bee sent to Spain, in case you think them

---

[1] Letter 947.

[2] To make a landing near Bordeaux and enlist the aid of the French Protestants in that region. See pp. 553, 874.

[3] Strasbourg was the headquarters of the French army on the Rhine. Eugene did not besiege it but joined Marlborough in the Spanish Netherlands instead.

[4] Letter 948.

[5] The Dutch sent ships to join an English contingent. Together they made up a squadron of twenty ships, which spent the summer watching Dunkirk. Owen, p. 270.

[6] 13 Apr., Blenheim MSS. B1-1.

absolutely necessary. But my notion of that matter is, that it's just so much money given to the Emperour and the men will never bee replaced.

You don't explain it in your letter but the *project* shows us plainly that the States and Prince Eugene have not so much mind to oblige King Augustus, as you seemed to have.

I am very sorry for what 48 [Prince Eugene] tells you of the little to bee expected from 58 [Duke of Savoy]. I confess I had great hopes somthing might have been done with effect on that side, where there seems to bee the least preparation for any resistance.

My Lord Sunderland has the Queen's directions to send instructions to Mr. Stanhope pursuant to the paper you sent mee over.[1]

I am surprised at Sir Philip Medow's letter to Mr. Negus, nor can I imagine from whence he takes his incoragement. For as often as you have spoken to mee about that matter, I have always told you it was impossible for mee at this time to doe it for Mr. Negus.

When I see Mr. Vanbruggh I shall talk with him about what you have written to mee [in] his favour.

Monday 12th

I should have told you that I have not comunicated the project but to the two Secretaryes of State, and to my Lord Chancellor. The rest need not know it till it begins to bee talked of some other way.

A good many people seem to bee uneasy here at your sending for 3 regiments but I hope that will soon bee over, if the diligence of Lieutenant Generall Erle, joyned to the great allowances which I have made at the Treasury for restoring the Almanza regiments, can bee sufficient to have them compleated by midsummer, the time assigned them for that purpose. He goes tomorrow to Northampton to review such of the troops as are upon their return from the borders of Scotland.

The Duke of Devonshire and Lord Halifax repeat their request for your favorable recomendation of my Lord Irwin[2] for the government of Scarborough Castle.

952. MARLBOROUGH *to the* DUCHESS   [*11/22 April 1708*]

Source: Blenheim MSS. E4.
Printed: *Private Correspondence*, i. 126.
Addressed: For the Dutchesse of Marlborough.

Hague April 22th 1708

I did not write to you by the last packet boat, Courant going at the same time with the yackt, but as the wind is this morning changed, the packet boat may gett for England, and the yackt may be forced back, so that I leave this letter to go by Tuesday's post.[1] I leave this place this evening, in order to meet Prince Eugene at Hanover next Friday. I shall stay there not above two days, and then return to this place, til when I shall have no opertunity of writting unless it be att Hanover. The credit of 256 [Mrs. Masham] occasions a good deal of disagreable discorse in this country.

953. GODOLPHIN *to* MARLBOROUGH [*13 April 1708*]

Source: Blenheim MSS. A2-38.
Printed: Coxe, ii. 413 (inc.).

13th of Aprill 1708

Since my former letter, of the 11th and 12th,[2] the letters of the 20th are arrived from Holland, and to my great surprise I have none from you; nor had Lady Marlborough received hers when I saw her this morning. So I conclude some accident must have hapned to her letters and mine. By yours to Mr. Boyle,[3] I am very sorry to find you resolve to goe to Hannover. It will bee looked upon here as a very full conviction, than any place is more agreable than England, and I am afrayd the pains you take in going thither can have no other effect than to increase 50's [Elector of Hanover] jealousy of 48 [Prince Eugene] and render him still fuller of difficulty's and irresolution.

By the French letters of this post it appears that Monsieur de Vendosme does not pretend to begin the campagne sooner than the 20th of May, and that all their measures have been changed, since the news of their disappointment in Scotland. However I am afraid both 50 [Elector of Hanover] and 48 [Prince Eugene] will bee too backward to make any great advantage of the present disorder they are in. Wee are told they have not lost less than 5,000 men in this expedition.[4]

954. GODOLPHIN *to* MARLBOROUGH [*13 April 1708*]

Source: Blenheim MSS. A2-38.

13 Aprill 12 at night

I am just now to acknowledg the favour of yours of the 20th[5] by Courant with the paper of *minutes* enclosed, in which poynt I think your resolutions are extremely right.

I wish I could think the same of your jorney to Hannover, but I have no more hope of your success ther, than I can find by yours you seem to have

---

[1] 13/24 Apr. [2] Letter 951. [3] P.R.O., S.P. 87/3, fols. 16-17.
[4] Untrue. There were only 6,000 men on the expedition and they never disembarked. The English captured only one ship, the *Salisbury* (*Mémoires du Comte du Forbin*, ed. A. Petitot et Monmerque (Paris, 1829), p. 250).
[5] Letter 949.

yourself, and I should bee contented if 50 [Elector of Hanover] would but resolve to doe or not to doe what you propose. But what I most of all apprehend is dilatorynesse and irresolution.

I am very sorry for what you tell mee of your visitt from Amsterdam. It can bee of no use even for what they themselves seem so much to desire, unless they think you want to bee excited to some action that would bee finall, which is impossible to imagine.

I have troubled you with so long a letter by this post already,[1] that at this time of night, 'tis reasonable that both of us should rest.

955. GODOLPHIN *to* MARLBOROUGH [*16 April 1708*]

Source: Blenheim MSS. A2-38.
Printed: Coxe, ii. 413-14 (inc.).

16 Aprill 1708

In my last,[2] I acknowledged yours of the 20th,[3] with the account from Prince Eugene of King Augustus's proposalls to the Emperour, in which matter the Queen does fully agree with your opinions at The Hague.

As to what was sayd to you by those of Amsterdam concerning their Barriere, wee in England shall bee easy I believe, in giving them any satisfaction about that matter, with these two conditions;

    1st, that Ostend remain in the hands of Spayn; and,

    2nd that Dunquerk bee demolished.

I think wee are undone, whenever wee consent to any peace without these 2 articles.

I am now to acknowledg yours of the 22th[4] and I have shown to Lieutenant Generall Erle the commands you gave mee for him. He will take care to embark the 3 regiments you desire, and to send you an account of the condition in which he finds the others, as soon as he has reviewed them, for which purpose he goes to Northampton tomorrow. He thinks of Seymour[5] for his major general and thinks that choyce may perhaps strengthen him with some of the marines; but is pretty apprehensive he shall not bee able to gett 4 or 5,000 men together till the end of June.[6] I wish he may have them even by that time; and I doubt, the ships will not bee ready much sooner, for wee don't yett hear of Sir George Bing's being come to the Downs, or Baker[7] to Ostend.

---

   [1] Letter 951.   [2] Letter 954.   [3] Letter 949.   [4] Untraced.
   [5] William Seymour (died 1728), second son of Sir Edward Seymour, Bt.; lieutenant-colonel, Coldstream Guards, 1692; colonel, Regiment of Foot, 1694; his regiment constituted as Regiment of Marines 1703; brigadier-general 1702; major-general 1704; lieutenant-general 1707; wounded at Landen and Vigo. He served under Erle on the descent.   [6] For a descent.
   [7] John Baker (1661-1716), served in the Mediterranean 1691-1707; rear-admiral 1708; vice-admiral of the Blue and second-in-command in the Mediterranean 1709-13. *D.N.B.* Baker was returning the troops brought over at the time of the Pretender's invasion (p. 947, n. 2).

When all shall bee ready for our proceeding upon this expedition, wee shall not bee able to send ships enough for this service, and block up Dunkirk at the same time, unless the Dutch help us with some of theirs for the latter. I trouble you with repeating this particular in every letter, because I am sure the whole thing must fail, if they don't think it of consequence enough to comply with us in this poynt. By the letters received yesterday from Lisbon, which I send enclosed,[1] you will see they are pretty perverse in Portugall. But at the same time, they doe not seem to bee in much apprehension of what the enemy can doe this spring. I hope the French preparations are not much more forward, on the side of Catalonia, and consequently that Sir John Leak will arrive there in time to relieve all their wants.

I wish your next letter from Hannover may give us a good account of your having had success there. But I must own, 'tis more than I expect.

956. MARLBOROUGH *to* GODOLPHIN   *[16/27 April 1708]*

Source: Blenheim MSS. A2-39.

Hanover April 27th 1708

I would not lett the post go without writting, though I have nothing to say but that I am safely arrived, and that wee have had a conference with the Elector in which we have acquainted him with our thoughts as to the operations for this campagne. We find his Electorall Highness thinkes we have to[o] few troupes to act in three places at once. It is plaine by the letters come this day, from France, that thay are taking measures to have an army on the Moselle, which is to be commanded by the Duke of Berwick.

957. MARLBOROUGH *to the* DUCHESS   *[16/27 April 1708]*

Source: Blenheim MSS. E4.
Printed: *Private Correspondence*, i. 125.
Addressed: For the Dutchesse of Marlborough.

Hanover Aprill the 27th 1708

The English post came in this morning, by which I was in hopes to have heard from you. But I had no letters. I beleive I shall not be able to leave this place til Munday,[2] so that I may yett hear from you, for a Sunday night we may have letters. As I thought I should have returned to England, I omitted telling you that I am advised by everybody to have the portico,[3] so that I have writt to Vanbrook to have itt, and which I hope you will like, for I should be glad we were allways of one mind, which shall always be endeavoured, for I am never so happy as when I think you are kind.

---

[1] Untraced.   [2] 19/30 Apr.
[3] The more elaborate porticoes proposed by Vanbrugh in 1705 (p. 467) were built. Green, *Blenheim Palace*, p. 84.

958. GODOLPHIN *to* MARLBOROUGH [*19 April 1708*]

Source: Blenheim MSS. A2-38.
Printed: Coxe, ii. 420 (inc.).

Aprill 19, 1708

This shall not bee long because I intend to trouble you tomorrow by the post. But Mr. Foster[1] going over with the same pacquett, I could not resist telling you by him, that Mrs. Morley [the Queen] continues so very difficult to doe anything that is good for herself, that it puts us into all the distraction and uneasyness imaginable.

I really believe this humour proceeds more from her husband than from herself, and in him it is very much kept up by your brother George, who seemed to mee as wrong as is possible, when I spoke to him the other day. And finding him, I spoke so freely and so fully to him, of what wee must all expect next winter, and himself in particular, if things were to goe on at this rate, he appeared to bee much less resolute, after I had talked a while to him, and thanked mee for speaking so freely. If he did not doe this out of cunning, I beleive your taking notice to him that Mr. Montgomery [Godolphin] seemed to fear he putt Mr. Morley [the Prince] upon wrong measures, might posssibly have no ill effect. But you are the best judg of this. The vacancy's in the Prince's Counsell, will not (I believe) bee very well filled,[2] and the difficulty's of filling the Attorney Generall's place[3] is as great as that in which you left us, and which still remains as when you left us.[4]

I have been today with the Queen's leave to see the Duke of Hamilton. Mortifications are of use to some tempers. I found him less unreasonable than I expected, but very desirous however to bee sett at liberty, and to bee distinguished from the rest of his countrymen.[5]

959. GODOLPHIN *to* MARLBOROUGH [*20 April 1708*]

Source: Blenheim MSS. A2-38.

April 20th 1708

The Dutch post that came in yesterday brought no letters from you, nor indeed did I expect any till you had been at the court of Hannover. I hope

[1] A servant of the Duke's.

[2] Godolphin tried to get Byng and Jennings to join, both of whom refused, which nearly kept the former and did keep the latter off the Board appointed to succeed Prince George in November. See Godolphin to Byng, 26 June, in *Byng Papers*, ii. 189–90.

[3] Vacant by the resignation of Harcourt. The Duumvirs proposed promoting James Montagu, the Solicitor-General and brother of Halifax. The Queen resisted for many months and this was one of the main points of friction between the Whigs, the ministry, and the Queen this year.

[4] See p. 948, n. 1.

[5] Hamilton and other suspected Jacobites were taken prisoner at the time of the Pretender's attempted invasion and brought to London to be examined. Sunderland arranged for Hamilton's release in May on the condition he would support the Whigs in the parliamentary elections to be held this spring.

this will find you returned from thence, and that for the future wee shall hear as regularly from you, as the winds will allow.

In my letter of last night by Mr. Forester,[1] about a particular matter, I told you I would write agayn today, by the post. What I reckon you will bee most concerned to hear of from hence, is how our preparations advance, for the embarcation you propose.[2] We shall bee able to tell you more certainly what strength wee can depend upon, when Lieutenant Generall Erle returns from Northampton. In the meantime the men of warr and the transports will easily bee gott ready before the regiments can bee in condition. And I have gott my Lord President's consent that wee may have one, if not two regiments from Ireland, rather than that wee should fall short of our number. And I have ventured to give more than reasonable encouragement to the officers of the Almanza regiments provided they bee compleat by the end of June.

They must encamp at the Isle of Wight and it will bee given out they are going to Portugall, and when this service is over, the best use wee can make of them, perhaps would bee to send them there in earnest; especially, if in the meantime my Lord Gallway, who has taken upon him the character of embassadour there, can bee able (by his dexterity) to bring that court into reasonable measures for the future carrying on the warr, in that country.

By our last letters from thence, which are very fresh, they don't seem much alarmed at the enemy's preparations for this present campagne, which though it was not then begun, the season for action in those country's was almost at an end.

I hope the French are not forwarder anywhere else, and if wee may believe our intelligence from Paris and Mons, you will bee in the field before them. But what they seem most of all to neglect, is Dauphinè. So I hope you will always tease Comte Maffei, to press his master to begin early on that side. I am afrayd these easterly winds keep Baker, and the troops still on this side.

960. GODOLPHIN *to* MARLBOROUGH [22 April 1708]

Source: Blenheim MSS. A2-38.
Printed: Coxe, ii. 421-2.

Aprill 22th 1708

Having this safe way of writing to you by Mr. Durell, I am desirous to tell you, that last night the Dukes of Newcastle and of Devonshire were with Mrs. Morley [the Queen] again to press her upon the subject of Lord Sommers.[3] After she had long defended herself upon the old argument of

---

[1] Letter 958.   [2] The descent.

[3] Pembroke held the posts both of Lord President of the Council and Lord-Lieutenant of Ireland. The Whigs wanted to remove him and give the former to Somers and the latter to Wharton. At this point they despaired of winning both posts and concentrated on that for Somers. See Maynwaring to the Duchess [7 Apr. 1708?] in *Private Correspondence*, i. 126-30 and 9 Apr., ibid. 121-3.

_.-_é#

not doing a hardship to Lord Pembroke, they proposed to her to call him for the present to the Cabinet Counsell without any post at all, which being new to her and unexpected, she was much at a loss, what to say. At last, she sayd she thought it was very unusuall, upon which they offerd some instances of its being done. And then she said, she thought the Cabinet Counsell was full enough already, so they took leave in much discontent. And she was also very uneasy, being sensible of the disadvantage she should bee exposed to by this refusall, since her main argument, upon which she had hitherto insisted, was taken away by it.

This morning she sent for Mr. Montgomery [Godolphin] to give him an account of this visitt, and to complain that she saw there was to bee no end of her troubles. He says he told her that the matter was much changed by this proposall, and that he could not but think it entirely for her service to accept of it. That it was a very small condescention if they would bee satisfied with it; that it gayned her poynt absolutely in relation to Lord Pembroke; that it would make all her affairs easy at once; and that if Mr. Freeman [Marlborough] were in town, he was sure it would bee his mind as much as it was Mr. Montgomery's [Godolphin]. She seemed still very uneasy, and very unwilling, but she said she would write to Mr. Freeman [Marlborough][1] about it tonight or tomorrow. I hope therfore you will endeavour to prevail with him to make such an answer to her, as that this thing may bee no longer delayd. For as it stands now, you will give mee leave to say, the refusall is of much worse consequence, and exposes her much more than as it stood before.

If Mr. Freeman [Marlborough] has no mind to enter into particulars, why might not hee answer in generall, that he begs her to comply with Mr. Montgomery's [Godolphin] desires in this affair, who (he is sure) will never propose anything to her, but what shall bee as much for her honour as for her advantage?

I shall write agayn tomorrow by the post if there bee any occasion.

961. MARLBOROUGH *to* GODOLPHIN [*22 April/3 May 1708*]

Source: Blenheim MSS. A2-39.
Printed: Coxe, ii. 415-16 (inc.).

Hague May 5th 1708

At my return here last night, I had the happyness of your three letters of the 3d, 5th, and 8th,[2] by which I am sensible of your kind desires for my return. I am now thoroly convinced if I had avoyded being at Hanover at the same time with Prince Eugene, not only the project made at The Hague had miscaryed, but also these people would have laid the fault at my dore.

---

[1] 22 Apr., Coxe, ii. 422-3 and Brown, p. 246.   [2] Letters 945, 946, 948.

After a very great deal of uneasiness the Elector has consented to the project for three armys, but we have been obliged to leave on the Rhyn two Imperial redgiments more then we designed, so that Prince Eugene wil have 2,000 horse less on the Moselle. And as for the joyning the two armys, we thought it best not to acquaint the Elector with it, so that I expect when that is put in execution he will be very angry. But since the good of the campagne depends upon itt, I know no remidy but patience.

The Burgemasters of 113 [Amsterdam] were above two hours with me this morning, to convince me of the necessity of a sudent 81 [peace]. I need not repeat to you their reasons. The greatest part of them were such as you have heard formerly from 61 [Buys]. That which gave me the greatest surprise was that thay hoped 239 [the Queen] would come into measures with them for the proposing 81 [peace] to 43 [King of France], in case 111 [France] should make none to 110 [Holland] by the month of Jully. This from the most zealous part of 110 [Holland] has very much alarmed mee. The next thing thay desired was that the Queen would be pleased to lose no time in giving her orders for begining a treaty for their Barier, and that thay on their side were willing to take any measure her Majesty should propose for the security of the Union, and the Prodestant Succession. Thay insist on the same Barier thay formerly proposed with what they call an expedient, which is that half the garrison of Ostend might be Spaniards.[1] Thay make difficulty of giving me this in writting, but at last I beleive thay will do itt. In the meantime, I beg you will acquaint the Queen, and that I may know her pleasure. Though thay pressed me very much to acquaint you by this post, at the same time thay were very earnest that you should lett nobody know itt but her Majesty. Not only in this conversation, but that which I had with them before I went to Hanover, I find thay think 84 [the Tories] is in the interest of 54 [the Pretender], and that 91 [the Court] is divided. This opinion may prove very fatal to 42's [the Queen] interest. Everything has so ill a prospect that I should dispair, were itt not for the hopes that God will give me, this campagne, an opertunity of serving the Queen and common cause.

Before I left England I did speak to the Queen, that in this promotion, the Earle of Rivers might have a commission of General of the Horse, he being the only lieutenant general of the last warr. If her Majesty pleases, I think it reasonable that his commission should be dated from the time he was sent for Portugalle.[2] I have read Lieutenant General Earle's letter. As to what he says of his pay, it seems to me very reasonable that he should be continued

---

[1] For the Barrier discussions of 1706, see p. 520. The English had immediately declared that the Dutch could not garrison Ostend, seeing it as a veiled threat to their trade in the Low Countries, for which Ostend was the entrepôt (p. 562). The Dutch, unwilling to give up the anchor town on the string of fortresses they had proposed (for which see Geikie, p. 75) now sought to allay English fears by sharing control of the garrison with the Spanish.

[2] It was backdated to 16 Sept. 1703.

[in] his pay from the time he left Spain, as long as you shall continue to imploye him. By the next post I shall write to Lord Galway and send his letter open, so that you may lett the Queen see my thoughts as to the service of Portugale. If thay are not approved you may burn my letter.

Cadogan has behaved himself so very well this winter at Bruxelles, that Don Quiros has, in the name of the King[1] his master, desired of me that he might be continued for the six months in the summer.[2] I shall do everything, so that the expence will only bee for the six months in the winter. If the Queen approves of this, there must be care taken that whoever be designed for this place, must understand that he has nothing to do with Flanders. I shal leave this place in two or three days, and shal take care that your letters be sent after mee. The ten battalions are safely arrived, but as we hear nothing of the horse I am uneasy, since thay will not be able to take the field at our first enchamping, which may be the liklyest time for action.

You forgott to inclose Lord Hallifax's letters, so that I am ignorant of what he desirs.

I own to you that I expect no good natur from my dear countrymen, but I beg that justice and friendship of you to beleive that I could noways avoid my journy to Hanover, without the hazarding the project wee have made for this campagne. Lord Raby is very desirous he might have leave to come for England for six weeks. I can forsee no inconveniency in his absance from Berlin.[3]

962. MARLBOROUGH *to the* DUCHESS   [*22 April/3 May 1708*]

Source: Blenheim MSS. E4.
Printed: Coxe, ii. 414–15.

Hague May the 3d 1708

At my return last night to this place, I had the pleasure of receiving yours of the 5 and 9th. I am very sorry and do assure you that it was never my intention that any letter of mine should give uneasiness to 240 [Lady Marlborough],[4] but the contrary, for 39 [Marlborough] can have no content if he must live

---

[1] Charles III.

[2] Cadogan was made envoy extraordinary at Brussels on 12 Nov. 1707 until a successor to Stepney could be found. He held the post until 1711 and in so doing acted as England's representative in the condominium which governed the Spanish Netherlands. Marlborough himself was the other English representative in the condominium. He still had pretensions to the governorship of the Spanish Netherlands. This desire coupled with the need to work in close co-operation with the Brussels government, whose assistance in provisions, intelligence, and other matters, was vital to the prosecution of the war in the Low Countries, prompted Marlborough to continue Cadogan as envoy, knowing he would protect the interests of Marlborough (q.v. below, p. 1220, n. 1) and the army.

[3] Raby was given leave and was absent from Berlin from 10 May to 20 Sept.

[4] Untraced. Marlborough must have written to the Duchess on 31 Mar., 2/13, 6/17, and 9/20 Apr., and none of these has survived. The strained relations between them is evident, however, from letter 950, the first surviving from this year.

without the estime and love of 240 [Lady Marlborough]. The letter writt by
116 [the States]¹ proceeded from my possativly refusing of them, and not
from any desire of not returning. I must own to you that 210 [Marlborough]
has never been one day since he left 108 [England] without very dismall
thoughts, for he is very much of your opinion that 42 [the Queen] inclinations
is such as that 89 [the Whigs] must be angry, and consequently 38 [Godol-
phin] and 39 [Marlborough] not only uneasy but also unsafe. All this 39
[Marlborough] could bare, if he could be so happy as to gaine the love and
estime of 270 [Lady Marlborough]; for however unhappy the passion and temper of 39 [Marlborough] may make 270 [Lady Marlborough], when he has
time to recolect, he never has any thought but what is full of kindness for her.

The hopes you have by the good instructions that has been given to 11
[Devonshire] in order to persuade 42 [the Queen] is what I am afraid will
signefie very litle, since the power and inclinations of 256 [Mrs. Masham]
will be opositt. For my own part I shall this campagen do my utmust for the
good of the common cause and the Queen's Service, after which I should
from my soul be glad of being excused from any farther service. I shal leave
this place in two or three days, and shall take care to have your letters follow
me to Bruxelles.

The inclosed paper you sent me,² I should think would do good.

963. GODOLPHIN *to* MARLBOROUGH   [23 April 1708]

Source: Blenheim MSS. A2-38.
Printed: *Private Correspondence*, ii. 239-41.

April 23d 1708

I writt to you yesterday by Mr. Durell³ who goes over (I believe) in the
same packett with this, so 'tis likely you will receive both my letters at the
same time.

I have little to add, in this, but that after I had sent him my own letter
for you, the Queen sent mee a letter for him to carry to you, which I hope
he will deliver to you.⁴

To this moment wee have not heard of the arrivall of the troops, at Ostend,
though they must certainly have been there long before this time. Lieutenant
Generall Erle is not yett returned from reviewing the regiment at Northampton, so I can't yett give you any certain account in what condition they are

---

¹ To the Queen, requesting Marlborough remain on the Continent. See p. 949.
² Untraced. Probably the draft of a letter to the Queen, from the Duchess, either 4 or 8 Apr.
The letters charged the Queen with giving her confidence to Abigail Masham in preference to the
Duchess, and then denying the fact. The existence of these letters (untraced) can be deduced from
letters of Arthur Maynwaring to the Duchess [7], 9 Apr., *Private Correspondence*, i. 126-30, 121-3
and the Queen to the Duchess [10 Apr.], H.M.C., *Marlborough MSS.*, p. 53b.
³ Letter 960.   ⁴ See p. 960, n. 1.

like to bee. He has chosen William Seymour, for his Major Generall who seems to bee well pleased with it and very desirous to serve.[1]

Mr. Boscawen tells mee his friend and countryman my Lord Mohun seems willing to part with his regiment, if you would approve of it, and appoint the person with whom he should treat for it. Since he never will apply himself as he ought to doe, I think upon all accounts, he were better out of the army than in it.[2]

Sir George Bing is come to town, but has not yett had that countenance shown him, which either his past diligence, or the hopes of his future behaviour in this summer's service, might naturally lead him to expect.[3] Those who have most creditt with Mr. Morley [Prince George], doe him all the ill offices imaginable. Mr. Montgomery [Godolphin] has taken some pains to change this temper, and to reconcile them; but I am not certain what will bee the effect of it. This I am certain of, that if those prejudices can not bee cured, the advices they occasion will ruine the Service, and those that give them.

In a word, wee must hope, you will doe miracles abroad, and afterward that those may produce yett greater miracles at home.

964. MARLBOROUGH *to* GODOLPHIN   [25 April/6 May 1708]

Source: Blenheim MSS. A2-39.
Printed: Coxe, ii. 417 (inc.).

[The Hague] May 6th 1708

I am to thank you for yours by Foster,[4] and three others by the post,[5] which came this morning. I find by yours, but more by those of Lady Marlborough, that some of my friends are persuaded it was in my power to have returned. I can assure you if I had not gone to Hanover we had had no project for this campagne. Besides I think my presence would have been but of very litle use. When Prince Eugene comes to Vienna, I beleive he will give me an account of what he has been able to do with King Augustus. But we shall have none of them to replace the 4,000 Garmain foot.[6] However, having received

---

[1] On the descent.

[2] With Marlborough's permission (p. 973), James Dormer purchased the regiment from Mohun for £3,000 and was made colonel on 1 May. Lewis to Harley, 20 May, H.M.C., *Portland MSS.*, iv. 490.

[3] See his letter to Godolphin of 25 Dec. 1707 in *Byng Papers*, i. 248–50, complaining of the lack of promotions for himself and others and attributing it to the influence of George Churchill. The four senior positions in the service were vacant. They were all filled in January, Byng receiving that of Admiral of the Blue. For Godolphin's offer to Byng of a seat on the Prince's Council and Byng's refusal see p. 1405, n. 4 and *Byng Papers*, ii. xvi–xvii.

[4] Letter 958.   [5] Letters 951, 953, 954.

[6] The Emperor offered to send 4,000 Imperial troops in Italy to Spain, where they would be taken into the pay of the Maritime Powers, on the condition that the latter would pay for the recruit of replacements (p. 949, n. 4). Eugene wanted to hire the troops offered the Emperor by King

possitive orders from Lord Sunderland for the agreeing with Prince Eugene, I shall write by Tuesday's post[1] to him, as also to Mr. Chetwin,[2] to take care of their embarkation, if the Emperor should send orders for their going; for when I parted with Prince Eugene, I thought it so extravegant to give such unreasonable leavi mony, that I gave him very litle incoragement. But since it is thought otherways by the Cabinett Councel, I shal do my best.

I send you inclosed my letter to the Earle of Gallaway,[3] by which you will see my thoughts as what I wish might be done for Portugale, in case Lord Galways gives hopes of success. If her Majesty will be at this expence, the eight battalions and some of the dragons should be the body of men that are to allarm the enemy's cost,[4] and when thay are sent for Portugale, Mr. Earle should have orders to return for England, and Lord Tyrolly should be sent for Portugale. I should think it might be fore the Service that at least one of the Scotch regiments of dragoons should be sent for Portugale.

The Pensioner's sickness hinders me from seeing him, but I have pressed Monsieur Fagel, the Grifier,[5] that their shipes might be hastened to you.[6] Yesterday's letters from Paris assures that the Duke of Burgundy is to command in Flanders, and that thay pretend to have a superiority of 30,000 men, which I think is impossible. But if thay send him, thay think themselves strong enough to act offensively, by which we may have action. Those who are angry at the comming over of the three battalions, do not know that thay are part of our 20,000 as also the redgiment of Raby. But I am so sensible of some peoples being glad to find fault, that I am quit[e] weary of serving, for though I give myself no rest, and ruin my constitution, I cannot please without doing impossibillitys. I shall write to my brother Georg as you desire. As I think there is very litle or no allowance to the governour of Scarborow Castel, if it will oblige Lord Irwin, I should think it were for her Majesty's Service to give itt him. I go from hence tomorrow morning, but shal not be at Bruxelles til Thursday, being resolved to go by Gand to give the necessary orders for the English. The recrute horses not being come, will make it very difficult for the English horse to take the field at the same time with the rest of the army. When you have read the enclosed from Monsieur Lafont,[7] I beleive you will think it reasonable that the two Secretarys and yourself to speak with him.

Augustus (p. 951, n. 7) for his own army on the Moselle (Braubach, ii. 220–1), which meant no replacements could be obtained for those sent to Spain. The Emperor had demanded levy money, therefore, from England to raise new regiments for Italy.

[1] 29 Apr./10 May.
[2] The letters are dated 25 Apr./6 May, in Murray, iv. 5–6.
[3] 25 Apr./6 May, Murray, iv. 2–4.   [4] The descent.
[5] François Fagel (1659–1746), *greffier* (clerk) of the States General, one of the 'big four' who were the leaders of the Dutch Republic.
[6] The Dutch ships for the Channel fleet (p. 953).
[7] Untraced.

965. MARLBOROUGH *to the* DUCHESS   [25 April/6 May 1708]

Source: Blenheim MSS. E4.
Printed: *Private Correspondence*, i. 131–3.

Hague May the 6, 1708

Going from hence tomorrow morning, I leave this for the Tuesday's post.[1] I like so well the advice to the electors[2] that I have read it twice. Though it is al very good, yet I think the latter part is that which will do the most good. The pad[3] of Collonel Southwel's[4] I wish may be to your mind, for I think riding will doe you a great deal of good. I wish your happyness with all my heart, and shall be glad to part with anything I have in this world with pleasure, if I might think it gave you ease. My claret is baught to serve the several tables, so I beleive thay will find better for you at Rotterdame, which Will Lovgrove will doe, but I very much fear his finding an opertunity of sending itt. I am of your mind, and not that of Mr. Berty's,[5] for 256 [Mrs. Masham] will not have that preferment[6] since it must prove their ruin; but I am afraid thay will have the power of doing all the mischief that is possible to 42 [the Queen]. There is care taken by letters write from England to persuade these people that 42 [the Queen] has no kindness for 240 [Lady Marlborough], 38 [Godolphin] and 39 [Marlborough]. I take this to be a pollatique of 199 [Harley] for the inducing these people to a peace, which God knows thay are but to[o] much inclined. I am to thank you for three of yours which I received this morning. I should be glad to have your second letter of 42 [the Queen],[7] that I might be the better able to judge of that fatal corrispondance with 199 [Harley], which will prove her ruin. I must own to you that I am of the same mind with your friends, that you can't oblige 239 [the Queen]. However, I vallu your quiet and happyness so much, and being almost

---

[1] 27 Apr./8 May.

[2] A pamphlet by Maynwaring. See Snyder, 'Daniel Defoe, the Duchess of Marlborough, and the *Advice to the Electors of Great Britain*', *H.L.Q.*, 29 (1965), 58–62.

[3] An easy-paced horse. *O.E.D.*

[4] William Southwell, served in Hamilton's Regiment under William III; major in James River's Regiment of Foot, 1702; lieutenant-colonel 1704; colonel 1706; served in Flanders and Spain; at taking of Barcelona; retired 14 June 1708.

[5] Peregrine Bertie, Vice-Chamberlain of the Household.

[6] There were rumours that Mrs. Masham would receive one or more of the Duchess's posts, which included Keeper of the Privy Purse, Groom of the Stole, and First Lady of the Bedchamber. The Duchess had offered to resign her places in February on the occasion Marlborough and Godolphin also offered to resign their posts (p. 943). The resignations had not been accepted. On hearing these new rumours the Duchess wrote to the Queen on 31 Mar. (Blenheim MSS. G1-7) reminding her she had promised her some time ago to give the posts to her daughters if she quitted them or died before the Queen. The Queen replied the same day (ibid., E18) saying she would never remove the Duchess.

[7] The Duchess and the Queen exchanged several further letters, concerned primarily with Mrs. Masham's replacement of the Duchess in the Queen's affections. The existence of the Queen's second letter (untraced) may be inferred from Maynwaring's letter to the Duchess of [7 Apr.], in *Private Correspondence*, i. 126–30.

persuaded that is next to impossible to change the inclinations of 256 [Mrs. Masham], more then by being att a distance with 239 [the Queen], I would not have you constrain yourself in anything.

I find by yours that some friends of mine are angry at my not returning. It is most certaine if I had not gone to Hanover wee should have begun this campagne without any project. God knows how this will succed, which we have agreed on, but this pleasure we have that it gives uneasiness in France. Besides this, I own to you, that if I had come I should not have been able to have done any good with 42 [the Queen]. For til thay suffer by the unreasonable advice of 256 [Mrs. Masham] and 199 [Harley], itt will not be in my power to do her any service. So that unless 240 [Lady Marlborough] will have itt otherways, I know it is the intention of 39 [Marlborough] to use his endeavours of making it necessary his staying abroad this next winter. The account of the behavior of 182 [George Churchill] is unaccountable. I shall be sure to write to him my mind very freely. My Lord Chancelor[1] did tel mee that he had given directions for the putting Mr. Gapp[2] out of the commission of peace. If it should be forgott, I beg he may be spoke to, to do it; for should thay be so ungratfull as not to chuse my brother[3] it will vex mee, so that I beg you will not give the thoughts of it over, but spend no mony, and oblige my brother to go down three or four days before the election. You are unjust in thinking that I am not concerned when you omitt writting, for when thay are kind thay give me more pleasure then all other things in this world can do.

Mr. Cardonel thinkes your letters will be taken more care of by Mr. Tylson,[4] then by Mr. Jonnes,[5] he having given him a particular charge.

966. GODOLPHIN *to* MARLBOROUGH   [*26 April 1708*]

Source: Blenheim MSS. A2-38.

Aprill 26, 1708

Not having yett any letter from you since you went to Hannover, I shall trouble you with very little, by this post, more than that by Doctor Hare, who will goe from hence in a day or two, I may write somthing more particular to you, than I dare venture by the post.

Everybody here is very busy at present about elections, and there hapning to bee a great distemper, almost universall among the horses, it falls out very

---

[1] William, Lord Cowper.

[2] John Gape, opponent of the Marlborough interest at St. Albans.

[3] George Churchill did not stand at St. Albans (see p. 977), but was elected for Portsmouth 6 May.

[4] George Tilson, Under-Secretary of State to Harley and Boyle; Auditor of the Revenue and Excise Duties in Scotland 1707.

[5] A clerk in the office of Secretary Boyle.

inconveniently for some people, who can't find any to carry them into the countrys.

Among others ther's one concerned in elections which (I believe) you little expected. My Lord Orkney has asked the Queen's leave to goe to Scotland to bee elected one of the 16 peers. I was not against his obtaining it, because, if he were refused I was sure he would bee in very ill humour, and very uneasy with you and everybody else. But I fancy he will hardly bee chosen, and especially when he is upon the place.[1]

Erle being not yett come back, I can give you no account of those regiments. But for fear they should fall short, I have prevailed with my Lord President to lett us have Munden's[2] regiment from Ireland.

The Queen agrees to lett my Lord Rivers have a comission of Generall of the Horse.[3]

My Lord Ryalton come[s] back from Newmarkett tomorrow, to goe directly to Oxfordshire. The election for that county is to bee tomorrow sennight.[4]

967. MARLBOROUGH *to* GODOLPHIN [*27 April/8 May 1708*]

Source: Blenheim MSS. A2-39.
Printed: Coxe, ii. 423 (inc.).
Addressed: To my Lord Treasurer, Whitehall.

[Antwerp] May the 8th 1708

I have just now received on the road yours of the 22d by Durel,[5] and 23d by the post.[6] I have but time to assure you that by the next post I shal follow your directions to Mrs. Morley [the Queen], for if 42 [the Queen] be obstinat, I think it is a plain decleration to al the world that 38 [Godolphin] and 39 [Marlborough] have no credit, and that all is governed underhand by 199 [Harley] and 256 [Mrs. Masham]. I did promis my Lady Orkney to use my endeavours that her Lord might for this next Parliament be one of the 16. I intend[ed] to have consulted you at my return, but I must now beg you will speak to the Duke of Quinsborow, and the two Secritarys and Lord Chancelor,[7] as a matter I should take kindly of them.

---

[1] Orkney, unbeknownst to Godolphin and Marlborough (below), was in collusion with the Junto and their Scottish allies, the Squadrone. He and his brother the Duke of Hamilton threw their lot in with the Whigs and both were elected. The Queen was so incensed at Sunderland's conduct in working against the Court nominees, she sought to dismiss him. See p. 1023, n. 3.

[2] Richard Munden, served as captain and lieutenant-colonel of the First (Marlborough's) Regiment of Foot Guards at Blenheim; lieutenant-colonel of Lovelace's newly raised Regiment of Foot in Apr. 1706; succeeded Lovelace as colonel 20 Mar. 1708.

[3] For Marlborough's request for Rivers's promotion see p. 961.

[4] Ryalton had run for Cambridge University in 1705 but had been defeated by the efforts of the Tories, a deliberate rebuff to Godolphin. See p. 432. This year he stood for Oxfordshire and he won, swept in by a Whig landslide.

[5] Letter 960.   [6] Letter 963.

[7] Queensberry, Sunderland, Boyle, and Cowper.

968. MARLBOROUGH *to the* DUCHESS   [*27 April/8 May 1708*]

Source: Blenheim MSS. E2.
Printed: *Private Correspondence*, i. 133.

[Antwerp] May the 8th 1708

I have received this morning on the road yours of the 22th by Durell, and yours of the 23d by the post. I have only time to thank you for them, and if I have any opertunity you shal be sure to hear from me by the next post from Gant, for I shal not come time enough to Bruxelles. You will excuse the shortness of this since by the same post you will receive on[e] much longer.

969. MARLBOROUGH *to* GODOLPHIN   [*28 April/9 May 1708*]

Source: Blenheim MSS. A2-39.
Printed: Coxe, ii. 423.

Gant May 9th 1708

Having been obliged with my own hand to copie my letter to Mrs. Morley[1] [the Queen], I have but just time to tel you that I beg that nobody may see the originall letter of Mrs. Morley [the Queen] but Mrs. Freeman [Lady Marlborough] and that you would keep it for mee.

I have enclosed my letter to Mrs. Morley [the Queen] to Mr. Secretary Boyle,[2] so that if she takes no notice, you may let her know that I had write you word that I had done myself the honour to answere her letter, but I think it would be best not to own the having received a copie. I shall stay here tomorrow and go the next day for Bruxelles.

970. MARLBOROUGH *to the* DUCHESS   [*28 April/9 May 1708*]

Source: Blenheim MSS. E2.
Printed: Coxe, ii. 425.
Addressed: For the Dutchess of Marlborough.

Gant May 9th 1708

I have sent to 38 [Godolphin], 42 [the Queen] originel letter, which I have desired nobody but yourself may see. In it you will see her possative resolution. Mr. Montgomery [Godolphin] will show you that I have write to her. I wish it may do good, but I fear all is undone, for our affaires here abroad

---

[1] 28 Apr./9 May, Coxe, ii. 423–5 in answer to the Queen's of 22 Apr. (for which see p. 960, n. 1). Marlborough told the Queen that the Dutch were anxious for peace; not because they feared the French, but because of 'what passed in England last winter, and from the continued intelligences they have of your Majesty being resolved to change hands and partys'. He pleaded with her to admit Somers to the Cabinet and 'to follow the advice and good Councell of Lord Treasurer'.

[2] This date S.P. 87/3, fols. 44–7. In an autograph postscript (omitted from Cardonnel's copy in Murray, iv. 7–9), Marlborough added: 'I beg with humble duty, the inclosed may [be] given to her Majesty.'

goes every day worse. I stay here tomorrow, and the next day go for Bruxelles, from whence you shall be sure to hear from me.

The writting and copieing of Mrs. Morley's [the Queen] letter has so tiered me that I can say no more.

971. GODOLPHIN *to* MARLBOROUGH   [*29 April 1708*]

Source: Blenheim MSS. A2-38.
Printed: Coxe, ii. 426–7.

April 29, 1708

In my last[1] I told you I would write by Mr. Hare, som things more particular than I could doe by the post.

By yours of the 5th of May,[2] which I have received this day, it is very plain what mischief the divisions of 89 [the Whigs] does even among the people of 110 [Holland]. And yett 42 [the Queen] is still extreamly obstinate, not only in refusing hitherto the proposall about 5 [Somers], of which I sent you an account by Mr. Durell,[3] but in the matter relating to 4's [Halifax] brother[4] is as inflexible to all that can bee said upon that subject, by all these who have access to 239 [the Queen], and are concerned that 89 [the Whigs] should not bee divided. For 'tis most certain nothing is like to bee so ruinous to 42's [the Queen] interests as those divisions, and 'tis as certain 42 [the Queen] might yett easily prevent it by a very little complyance with Mr. Montgomery's [Godolphin] advice in the matter of 5 [Somers]. But this will not bee long in 42's [the Queen] power, and nothing else in the world can keep 89 [the Whigs] from being divided.[5] I hope therfore your answer to the letters that went by Mr. Durell, will bee very full to that point. But I am afrayd wee shall not have it so soon, as I hoped, since by your letters of this day, I find you designed to leave The Hague last Monday and I doubt Durell will not have been able to reach it, before your going to Flanders.

But in all your letters pray remember that nothing is like to have better effect with 42 [the Queen] than to show the ruine that must unavoydably follow from the divisions among 89 [the Whigs], which in my opinion can only bee prevented by the assistance of 5 [Somers].

---

[1] Letter 966.

[2] Actually 22 Apr./3 May. Letter 961.

[3] Letter 960.

[4] Sir James Montagu (1666–1723), barrister, Middle Temple; M.P. 1695–1701, 1705–13; knighted 1705; Solicitor-General 1707; Attorney-General 1708–10; First Baron of the Exchequer 1722. *D.N.B.* The Duumvirs had proposed him to the Queen as Attorney-General.

[5] See the similar analysis of Maynwaring in his letters to the Duchess on 7 and 9 Apr. *Private Correspondence*, i. 126–30, 121–3.

972. GODOLPHIN *to* MARLBOROUGH [*30 April 1708*]

Source: Blenheim MSS. A2-38.
Printed: Coxe, ii. 431, 443-4 (inc.).

Aprill 30, 1708

Last night by Mr. Hare I writt to you upon a particular matter.[1] Whether you will receive that letter so soon as this, is uncertain. I rather think Mr. Hare will not travell so fast as the post.

I am now to acknowledg the favour of yours of the 5, 6, and 8th of May,[2] by which last you referr mee to the next post, for your answer to mine by Mr. Durell. But you take no notice of your having received Mrs. Morley's [the Queen] letters which Mr. Durell also carryed to you. I hope your answer to both,[3] will bee such as may bring that matter to a good end at last, which has hung unreasonably long, considering either what is past, or how much all that is to come depends upon a right decision of that affair. What I have mentioned to you in my letter by Mr. Hare, is much of that same nature, and almost of the same consequence.

I think all you have done with the Elector[4] and Prince Eugene is entirely right, and will (I hope) have a very good effect, if they come timely enough into the field. But the generall backwardness of the Germans is extreamly discouraging. The Duke of Savoy makes heavy complaints by this post, that Generall Visconti[5] has refused to send him 6,000 men for a particular expedition which he had designed.[6] I hope, he letts you know the same things by Count Maffei, for there will bee no remedy of this from Vienna, but by your means; and it would bee [a] great pitty the Duke of Savoy should bee stopped by his friends, for I don't see that our enemys are like to bee, on that side, in any condition of stopping him.

I am very well pleased with their changing their generalls in France,[7] and I think it is no good sign for them. The Elector of Bavaria's going to the Rhyne will make all Flanders uneasy, and jealous that the French design to give them up to 110 [Holland] as I really believe they intend to doe, in case of any check, or considerable disadvantage. And for that reason, they are willing to have him out of the way, though they endeavour to make him like

---

[1] Letter 971.   [2] Letters 961, 964, 967.
[3] From the Queen and Godolphin.   [4] Of Hanover.
[5] Hannibal, Marquis of Visconti (1660–1750), general of cavalry, commander of the Imperial troops in Lombardy. Chancellor of Milan, installed by the Emperor.
[6] An expedition into Dauphiné for which the Emperor was to supply a general (p. 974) as well as troops.
[7] Vendôme remained the actual commander in Flanders while the Elector of Bavaria was sent to the Rhine to make way for the Duke of Burgundy, Louis XIV's grandson, as titular commander. Villars, on bad terms with the Elector, traded places in turn with Berwick and took his post in Dauphiné. Villars's exploits in 1707 had cost the Allies heavily on the Rhine so that Godolphin was pleased to see him removed to a location of less strategic importance, for it was evident the Duke of Savoy would not take the offensive.

it by telling he will bee so much nearer to the opportunity of getting into his own country.

I am of opinion the Duke of Burgundy[1] and the rest of those Princes that accompany him, will bee rather a hindrance, and a perplexity to Monsieur de Vendosome, and not any advantage. But I agree with you that it may very soon bee the occasion of some action, not so much from the superiority the French pretend to have, as from the impetuous temper of that Prince, who is full of ambition and desire to gett a reputation in the world. I should think this consideration ought to make you act with the greater caution in the beginning of the year, till the Germans come into the field, and oblige the enemy to weaken their army. And I hope you will allow mee to putt you in mind of one thing more, which is, that even after the Germans shall bee in the field, the communication from the French armyes to one another, is quicker than it can bee, between Prince Eugene's army and yours. Consequently, you may bee full as 'tis able to bee surprised by any sudden motion of theirs, as they by yours.

What you write about Portugall, and of our annoying the coast of France, is extreamly right, and shall bee followed here, as farr, as wee are able to doe it. But I have always told you wee cannot doe it, without the assistance of the Dutch ships to lie before Dunkirk,[2] and as yett I see no assurance of them.

973. MARLBOROUGH *to* GODOLPHIN [3/14 May 1708]

Source: Blenheim MSS. A2-39.
Printed: Coxe, ii. 443 (inc.).

Bruxelles May 14, 1708

Since my arrival to this place I have had the favour of yours of the 26,[3] which makes me impatient for the arivall of Doctor Hare. The great want of rain will oblige me to put off the assembling the army til the 21. of this month. The French continues to threaten us with the Duke of Burgondy and a vast army. I hope the Duke of Burgundy will come, and for their army I can not see how it is posssible for them to be stronger then thay were the last campagne. I have had a letter from Lord Orkney to excuse his going for Scotland. I beg the other generals may be hastned away. I send you the enclosed[4] that you may be the better able to judge of their tempers att The Hague. As to 58 [Duke of Savoy], it is most certain that the French leave

[1] Louis of France, Duke of Burgundy (1682–1712), eldest son of the Grand Dauphin, in turn eldest son and heir of Louis XIV; after his father's death in 1711, heir presumptive; titular commander of the French army in Flanders in 1708 and at Oudenaarde.
[2] See p. 953, n. 5.   [3] Letter 966.
[4] From Slingelandt, 30 Apr./11 May, Blenheim MSS. B1-15. Slingelandt notes with concern the resolution of Louis XIV to send the Duke of Burgundy to the army. He stresses the importance of Liège as a major objective to be taken and says that it is more important to mount an offensive in the Low Countries than on the Moselle and the Rhine. The last point is underlined.

fewer troupes in Dophinee then was expected. I hope thay may be the dupes in that matter, for I think it impossible that 58 [Duke of Savoy] can rely on any promises of 43 [King of France]. I have had a letter from Lord Mohon.[1] Collonel Dormer[2] which he proposes for his redgiment is a very good officer, so that I believe it must be for the good of the Service, if her Majesty will give her consent. You have done well in getting Collonel Munden, and if you can prevaile to have Collonel Lapelle,[3] you might send Gorge,[4] and another redgiment in their places, which I should think Lord Pembrooke would like.[5]

974. MARLBOROUGH *to the* DUCHESS   [*3/14 May 1708*]

Source: Blenheim MSS. E4.
Printed: Coxe, ii. 425–6.

Bruxelles May 14th 1708

Since my arrivall here I have had yours of the 27th of the last month, and am very sensible of the indiscrit behavior of 182 [George Churchill]. I know not what effect it may have. I have write my mind freely to him.[6] As to what you say of the Garter, I think it should not be given til the Queen is sensible of the sham it would be to let so worthless a creatur as 40 [Kent] so much as expect itt. Not only this but everything I hear puts me very much out of heart, that I expect nothing but confusion. If my letter to 42 [the Queen][7] has no effect, I hope both 38 [Godolphin] and 240 [Lady Marlborough] will be convinced that I have no creditt, and will accordingly take their measures. We are in so great want of rain, that I shall be forced to delay the meetting of the army for four or five days. Besides, the French seems to chang their resolutions every day, so that I beleive their taking the field will depend upon our motions.

I was yesterday to waite upon 253 [Lady Tyrconnel], who I think is grown very old, and her horseness much worse then it was when I saw her last.

---

[1] Untraced.

[2] James Dormer (died 1741), lieutenant and captain in the Foot Guards, commanded by Marlborough 1702; lieutenant-colonel 1704; served at Blenheim and Ramillies; brevet colonel 1707; succeeded Mohun 1 May; sent to Spain 1709; brigadier-general 1711; fought at Saragossa and Brihuega, where he and his regiment were taken prisoner. His career may have been assisted by Mrs. Burnet, for her only sister was married to Dormer's brother Robert, Justice of Common Pleas.

[3] Nicholas Lepell, colonel, Regiment of Foot, 1705; sent to Spain 1708; brigadier-general 1710; became commander of English troops in Spain between capture of Stanhope and arrival of Argyle.

[4] His regiment, purchased from the Earl of Donegal in 1706, had been on the Cadiz expedition 1702; then was sent to the West Indies; was sent to Spain in 1704; at Almanza 1707.

[5] Lepell's and Munden's, among others, were employed on the descent in 1708 and were sent to Spain in 1709.

[6] Untraced.   [7] See p. 969.

I have been to see the hangings for your apartment and mine.[1] As much as are done of them I think are very fine. I shall not send them over til the winter, unless you desire them. I shoul be glad at your leasure you would be providing everything that may be necessary for furnishing those two apartments, that you would direct Vanbrook to finish the breaks between the windoes in the great cabinett with looking glasses, for I am resolved to furnish that roome with the finest picturs I can gett. I shall be impatient for Doctor Hare, since you have write by him.

975. GODOLPHIN *to* MARLBOROUGH [*4 May 1708*]

Source: Blenheim MSS. A2-38.
Printed: Coxe, ii. 427 (inc.).

May 4th 1708

I have received this morning the favour of yours of the 9th from Gandt,[2] with the papers enclosed, in which I shall bee sure to obey your commands very exactly.

Mr. Secretary Boyle being obliged to attend the poll today for the Westminster election,[3] hee sent mee the letter you enclosed to him for 42 [the Queen], to deliver, which I did. But she layd it down upon her table, and would not open it, while I stayed in the room, by which, I am afrayd, it is not like to have any more effect, than some other representations of the same kind have had, from your humble servant, who has endeavoured to lay the consequence of this sort of proceeding so fully before Mrs. Morley [the Queen], that it is astonishing to find how very little, they prevail. The originall letter which you send mee seems to take it for granted, that what has been desired of Mrs. Morley [the Queen], is no less than *destruction*, without giving one reason why it is thought so, and when in truth, the contrary is really that *destruction* and this the only way to avoyd.

A time is coming when (I doubt) this will bee plainly demonstrated, but it will bee too late then to think of a remedy. And when it is known to bee soe, than I expect to bee called upon to try it. I ask your pardon for dwelling so long upon a subject so disagreable. But if you were in my place, I fancy you could scarce forbear venting yourself sometimes to your friends.

My next complaint will bee of a very different nature. Mr. Chetwynd writes that the Duke of Savoy is enraged to the last degree at the proceedings of the court of Vienna. They concert nothing with him, though the campagne ought now to begin. They refuse the 6,000 men he has desired, for an immediat expedition.[4] They have not yett named the generall who shall

---

[1] The Alexander set woven by De Vos. See p. 750, n. 4.
[2] Letter 969.   [3] He was declared elected after a scrutiny on 7 July.
[4] Into Dauphine. The Duke of Savoy in turn refused to take the field until he received the investiture of territories promised him in 1703. This did not take place until July. See p. 989, n. 4.

command them. This way of acting, seems very unaccountable to us, and wee know nothing so likely to make them alter is [it] as your writing plainly upon this subject to Prince Eugene and Comte Wratislaw. 'Tis very discouraging that the Allyes themselves should hinder France from being pressed on the side where it lies most open and exposed.

The French letters give us hope that they are not like to make any great progress this spring, either in Catalonia or Portugall. And if wee may credit the reports from thence, all their generalls are discontented at the late changes made in the commands of their armys.[1] I must own I think them so like to bee fatall to France, that nothing could have prevailed in it but their opinion that 81 [peace] could never take place, till these removes were made, by which means they will have it more easily and certainly in their power to gratifie 110 [Holland] so far as to engage them to assist them effectually in the matter of 81 [peace]. But in case wee are so happy as that they are to receive a blow, this may have an effect very contrary to what they designed by it.

As for 81 [peace] my former letters will have told you fully my opinion of that, and of the Barriere which can never bee any reall security to us, if Ostend bee not in the hands of King Charles, or if Dunkirk continue in the hands of France.

Erle being returned from Northampton will send you himself, the state of the regiments he has reviewed. I hope they will bee in readyness by the end of June. He says the 3 you have sent for, are gon to Harwich to embark, and that the battalion of the Guards, is the worst of the three. However, I wish they were with you, for if there is to bee action I doubt it will bee before they can come.

God send us always good news from you.

976. GODOLPHIN *to* MARLBOROUGH   [6 May 1708]

Source: Blenheim MSS. A2-38.
Printed: Coxe, ii. 427–8 (inc.).

Thursday night May 6

As the wind is now I expect letters from you tomorrow, after which I shall write again by the post. In the meantime I can't resist the safe opportunity by Mr. Withers of telling you that though Mr. Montgomery [Godolphin] has had two conversations with Mrs. Morley [the Queen] of 2 hours a piece, upon the subject of Mr. Freeman's [Marlborough] letter,[2] 42 [the Queen] continues hitherto inflexible on that poynt, and resists all the plainest reasons and arguments that ever were used in any case whatsoever. At the [same time] 42 [the Queen] renounces and disclaims any talk of the least commerce with Mr. Harley, at first or secondhand, and [is] positive that she never speaks with anybody but 41 [Prince George] upon anything of that kind. From whence 41's [Prince George] notions come, is not hard to conjecture.[1] Upon the whole I find Mr. Montgomery's [Godolphin] life is a burthen to him, and like to bee soe more and more every day. After I have sayd all this, I know nothing to bee done but to persisit upon all occasions in the same language, and hope that time and accidents may open people's eyes as the danger comes nearer. But as often as you have any occasion to write, I think you should still continue to represent, that the longer that matter is deferred, the less good effects must necessarily attend it.

I would have had Withers take a fregatt in the Downs, and goe over to Ostend, that he might bee the sooner with you, but he thinks the packett boat both quicker and surer.

977. MARLBOROUGH *to* GODOLPHIN [6/17 *May 1708*]

Source: Blenheim MSS. A2-39.
Printed: Coxe, ii. 446-7 (small omission).

Bruxelles May 17th 1708

I have this morning had the favour of yours of the 30th,[2] and in a day or two expect yours by Dr. Hare.[3] I do intend, if the enemy will give me leave, to follow your advice by gaining of time, so that the Elector and Prince Eugene may have time to act. As yett the French have sent no troupes to the Moselle. You will see by the enclosed[4] what Mr. Stanhope desires, and particularly as to that of the fleet. There aught to be no time lost, for it is most certain that warr can't succeed unless a squadron be left in those seas.

I have write very pressing to Vienna in favour of the Duke of Savoye.[5] Palms writes mee[6] that the Prince of Salms endeavours to mortefie that Duke in eveything, which I fear at last may prove very fatal. It is most certain the French have drawn [a] great part of their troupes from that country. 73 [Howe] says that 50 [Elector of Hanover] apeares very much out of humour, and noways fond of his journey, not begining by eight days so soon as he promised. I pray God bless 39 [Marlborough] with sucess, for I expect none from 50 [Elector of Hanover].

[1] George Churchill.
[2] Letter 972.
[3] Letter 971.
[4] From Milan, 25 Apr./6 May, Chevening, Stanhope MSS., box 66/2; reply, 8/19 May, in Murray, iv. 21-2. He urged that a naval squadron be stationed in the Mediterranean through the winter. Such a command had long been desired but waited the possession of a proper port. This was answered by the taking of Port Mahon.
[5] To Wratislaw, 6/17 May, in Murray, iv. 14-15.
[6] Palmes to Cardonnel, 28 Apr./9 May, ibid. 14.

978. MARLBOROUGH *to the* DUCHESS   [6/17 May 1708]

Source: Blenheim MSS. E4.
Printed: *Private Correspondence*, i. 135–6.

Bruxelles May 17th 1708

I have this morning had the happyness of your two letters of the 30th. The trew reason of my writing for Lord Orkney was that I promised his Lady. I am much obliged to you for your expressions on this occasion, and I do in return assure you, that I would ventur everything to make you happy. What you say concerning 182 [George Churchill] is very reasonable, but there is no avoyding natur. I can say nothing in his deffence. Though I have many mallincolly thoughts, I can't but hope we shall have some time at Blenheim, so that if you have not already write to Lord Manchister, I should be glad you would, that he might chuse some velvets and damasques, and send them home by some of the men of warr this winter.¹ I was yesterday a long while with 253 [Lady Tyrconnel], who complains very much of the non-payment of their rents. By what thay say I am afraid thay are very unjustly delt with. By what you tel me of my brother George not going to [stand at] St. Albans,² I supose his name will not be made use off, so that I shall not know who is for or against mee. I think the best thing I can do in that, as in most things, is to medle as little as possible. Since my last wee have had a good deal of rain, and now very fine weather, so that I intend the army shall begine to camp on Munday next.³ I am glad you think that 256 [Mrs. Masham] dose not medle with business, for I am of the opinion it will be much easier struling with 182 [George Churchill] then with her. I pray God that 39 [Marlborough] may have it in my power to act so this summer that we may have 81 [peace], otherwais I see nothing but confusion. I hope before my next I shall have yours by Doctor Hare.

979. GODOLPHIN *to* MARLBOROUGH   [7 May 1708]

Source: Blenheim MSS. A2-38.

May 7th 1708

Having written to you last night by Lieutenant Generall Withers,⁴ this trouble will bee the shorter.

I had this morning the favour of yours of the 14th⁵ with the enclosed from Monsieur Slingelandt. It is strange to mee they should bee so much to

---

¹ The Duchess must have written soon after receiving this. Manchester replied from Venice, 25 June/6 July, describing the sorts of fabric available: H.M.C., *Manchester MSS.*, p. 100. On receiving his letter the Duchess ordered 3,500 yards of damask, velvet, and satin. 1 Aug., William, seventh Duke of Manchester, *Court and Society from Elizabeth to Anne* (London, 1864), ii. 387–9.
² In the parliamentary election (see p. 967). Churchill stood for Portsmouth instead, for which he was elected.
³ 10/21 May.   ⁴ Letter 976.   ⁵ Letter 973.

seek for the motives of removing the Elector of Bavaria from Flanders, for they seem very plain to mee. And if the French receive a blow, they will soon bee as plain to them. For while he was at the head of that government, 43 [King of France] could not have it so entirely in his power to gratifie 110 [Holland] in the matter of 81 [peace], as now he may doe whenever his affairs press him to doe it.

I have done all I could to hasten away Withers to you. He and Ross, are the only officers here that I wish were with you. I hope your foot that was at Tinmouth will have had time to refresh themselves. The French own that theirs is in lamentable condition, but they say their horse are very fine.

Though it bee true as you observe that 58 [Duke of Savoy] can never trust 43 [King of France], yett I find everybody here very much concerned that the usage of the court [of Vienna] gives him so much discouragement, not to call it provacation.

'Tis certaine the French withdrawing so many troops from Dauphiné gives the Duke of Savoy very fair play, if he can gett the Imperiall troops that have been today promised him.[1]

I don't find wee are like to bee much pressed on the side of Catalonia or Portugall, and the appearances are hitherto promising enough at the beginning of this campagne. But a great deal of good luck against 43 [King of France] in the summer, will hardly bee able to support 42 [the Queen] in soe much wilfulness when winter comes.

980. MARLBOROUGH *to* GODOLPHIN [*10/21 May 1708*]

Source: Blenheim MSS. A2-39.

[Brussels] May 21, 1708

I have had the favour of yours of 29th by Dr. Hare,[2] and am very much troubled at the difficultys you meet with in the carrying on of 42 [the Queen] business. I beleive everybody as well as myself must agree with you, that if the only people that are able to carry on the business of the government be devided, all must go to confusion. I am so much of this opinion, that I indure many mallincolly hours, and our affairs here do not as yett give me much content, the French having made no detachment towardes the Moselle. If I do not hear from 48 [Prince Eugene] by the end of this weeke, I intend to send an express to desire he would lose no time in making the march wee agreed on, for til the junction of those troops, we shal be able, I am afraid, to do nothing. But you may be assured that I am thoroly sensible that the Queen's affaires abroad as well as at home, requiers my venturing this

---

[1] For his expedition into that province.   [2] Letter 971.

campagne, so that no occasion shall be neglected. I am so weary of all business, that [it is] nothing but the concern I have for the quiet and wellfaire of 42 [the Queen] that makes me act with any sort of pleasure, for I meet with nothing but what is disagreable. At this time I am bussy in discovering a treacherous corispondance held by the French with some officers of the cittadell of Antwerp.¹ That which gives mee the greatest trouble in this matter is that a Spanish collonel,² who commands in the cittadel, and on whome I most relyed on, was yesterday taken prisoner. I should not write thus freely, but that it goes by a safe hand, so that you will have no other by this post.

981. MARLBOROUGH *to the* DUCHESS   [*10/21 May 1708*]

Source: Blenheim MSS. E4.
Printed: *Private Correspondence*, i. 136–7.

[Brussels] May 21, 1708

Since my last, Doctor Hare has given mee yours of the 29th. I write this by Collonel Harrison³ rather then by the post, he going in the same packett boat, and promises to be at London as soon as the letters. I am very sensible of the mallincolly prospect we have for the next winter. I am impatient to hear of the success my letter to Mrs Morley [the Queen]⁴ may have had concerning 5 [Somers]. If he be taken in, I shall then hope that 42 [the Queen] will comply in every other reasonable thing; but if thay continue obstinat in that, I am of the opinion with 38 [Godolphin], that anything else will be but of litle use; for if the body of men that must serve be divided, how can it be other then confusion? I begine to camp the troops this day, and by the 24th shall have them all together. But as the French have as yett sent no troops to the Moselle, I must have for some time patience, thay being very strong, in hopes that as soon as Prince Eugene shall begine to act, thay will be obliged to send some of their troops from hence. I write this that you may see the difficultys I meet with; but as our troops are good, and that our present circomstances requiers action, I hope God will bless us with success this campagne, or else the prospect will be as mallincolly here, as that of England. I hope in ten days to hear of Prince Eugen's being in motion, and that I shall be the better able to give an account of our hopes in this country.

¹ The discovery was made by the Dutch and discounted at first by Marlborough. See A. Veenendaal, 'Opening Phase of Marlborough's Campaign of 1708 in the Netherlands', *E.H.R.*, 65 (1950), 39. Cardonnel to Tilson, 10/21 May, and Marlborough to Sunderland, 13/24 May, in Murray, iv. 25, 31.
² Manuel José Laspiur, Marquis of Villala. He had joined the Allies with his regiment in 1706 after the taking of Antwerp.
³ Thomas Harrison, captain and lieutenant-colonel, First Foot Guards, 1705; brevet colonel 1707; adjutant-general in Spain, 1708, where he was going; commanded sixth Foot at Saragossa.
⁴ 28 Apr./9 May. See p. 969, n. 1.

I send the enclosed[1] only for you to read and burn itt. You know I have no good opinion of the auther, so that I shall give no answere to his letter, but I am afraid he is in the right of what he wishes.

982. GODOLPHIN *to* MARLBOROUGH   [*11 May 1708*]

Source: Blenheim MSS. A2-38.
Printed: Coxe, ii. 431 (inc.).

May 11, 1708

Wee have no letters from you, since my last, nor doe I expect any, as the winds have been here, before this post goes out. I hope the generall officers you expect from hence, are with you before this time. The wind has been fair for them.

Everybody here is busy at present about elections, and the talk of them. The generality of them, are as good, I think, as can bee desired, and there is little reason to doubt, but the next Parliament will bee very well inclined to support the warr and (I hope) to doe everything else that is reasonable, if they can have but reasonable incouragement. All seems to turn upon that. Mrs. Morley [the Queen] continues to bee very inflexible. I still think that must alter. My only fear is that it will bee too late.

All our preparations goe onn for the intended expedition,[2] and [it] will bee ready I hope to operate by the 1st of July. The ships could bee ready sooner, but not the troops.

Wee have letters from Catalonia of the 11th of Aprill. Staremberg was not then arrived, but they thought themselves stronger than the enemy. Wee have also letters from Lisbon of the 8th of May, which say Sir John Leak was sailed from thence with the money. Upon his arrivall at Barcelona, I hope all will goe well there. My Lord Gallway writes that in Portugall too, they are superiour to the enemy. I will send you his letter to mee by the next post.

983. GODOLPHIN *to* MARLBOROUGH   [*11 May 1708*]

Source: Blenheim MSS. A2-38.

May 11 at midnight

Since I had sent away my letter of this day[3] in Lady Marlborough's, I have received, just now, yours of the 17th,[4] with the enclosed papers from Mr. Stanhope.

[1] A copy of a letter from Raby to the Elector of Hanover in which he must have requested the Elector's assistance in obtaining the earldom of Strafford for him. The letter must have been sent to Marlborough by Robethon, the Elector's secretary. Raby had made the request without success to the Queen, Godolphin, and Marlborough. His most recent attempt with Marlborough was in a letter of 15/26 May (Blenheim MSS. A2-37) in which he explained he had an estate of £4,000 a year to justify his claim, apparently as an answer to a previous response from the Queen that his income was not large enough to sustain the dignity. His ill-advised approach to the Elector angered the Queen and caused her to refuse his request (p. 1047).
[2] The descent.   [3] Letter 982.   [4] Letter 977.

I commend his concern in sending an express for the more speedy procuring of orders to bee sent to Sir John Leak, about the transporting more forces from Italy. But ther's no need of doing it, his orders being already so express in that matter, that he has stayd a fortnight at Lisbon, only to fitt the transport shipps to carry horse. I agree, that nothing is more essentiall for carrying on the warr in Spain, than to winter a squadron in those seas. But how can it bee done with safety, while the French have Thoulon, betwixt us and the ports of Italy? Besides, the charge, as well as the hazard of carrying all our navall stores for that squadron to soe great a distance, makes it impracticable anywhere nearer than Lisbon, or the ports of Spain itself. For this reason as well as many others, I mightily approve Starembergh's plan of carrying the warr (if wee can act offensively), by the sea coast towards Andalusia. And I am not out of hopes but before the end of the summer Sir John Leak may bring them troops enough to make a superiority.

I am very glad to find you approve of my advice. Indeed it is my opinion that the French design to venture, because though they should bee beaten, they have taken such measures by sending away the Elector of Bavaria with his troops, as to secure themselves of 81 [peace] by the means of 110 [Holland]. But I doubt, if they give you a fair occasion, you will scarce bee able to forbear them till Prince Eugene comes, which I fear will not bee so soon, as you seem to expect him.

I am not all surprised at what you say of 50 [Elector of Hanover] and I wonder you should bee soe. For my part, I have never desired more of him, than to bee upon the place, and only make a show as if he intended to doe something, which perhaps would bee much better than to expose himself to the danger of being beaten.

984. MARLBOROUGH *to* GODOLPHIN [13/24 May 1708]

Source: Blenheim MSS. A2-39.
Printed: Coxe, ii. 431-2, 445-6 (inc.).

[Brussels] May the 24th 1708

I have had the favour of yours by Lieutenant General Withers,[1] as also that by the post of the 7th.[2] I am extreamly sensible of the difficultys you meet with, that were it in my power I should despise any danger to make your life easier, for we must ventur both life and quiet for the Service of 42 [the Queen] or all is undone. I beg you will read the inclosed letter[3] to 239 [the Queen]. She may depend upon the truth of itt, for the auther of the enclosed drew

---

[1] Letter 976.   [2] Letter 979.
[3] From Robethon, 7/18 May, Blenheim MSS. A2-39, Coxe, ii. 432. Peterborough had written the Elector and Electress on 3/14 Apr. of the necessity of having a member of their house reside in England. He also declared his intent of visiting Hanover.

the answere to 245 [Peterborough] by 50 [Elector of Hanover] order.[1] What the answere of 51 [Electress Sophia] was, I do not know.

Tomorrow I shall march towardes Hall where we shall join the English and the rest of the troups which come from Flanders. You know already my intention of gaining time til Prince Eugene can act with his army, which I am afraid cannot be till about the midle of the next month. I have and shall continue to write to Vienna as I am commanded. I inclose a letter of Comte Maffy's[2] which I received last night. By that and some others I have received, I very much fear we must not expect any great things from 58 [Duke of Savoy] this campagne, so that my onely dependance is on the junction of 48 [Prince Eugene] and 39 [Marlborough]; for if thay should not be able to do somthing considerable, our affaires in all parts will be in a bad condition. The discovery we have made of the designe the French had for the seasing the cittadell of Antwerp, will oblige, I beleive, Monsieur Vandome to chang his measures.[3] Next Saturday[4] is apointed for their generall *reveu*. After that we shall have their order of battle, by which we shall know their numbers of battalions and squadrons. You will see by the letter from Hanover,[5] that the Prince Electorall is to serve with his father's troupes in this army. It would have been more naturall for him to have served with his father, but I supose thay have a mind he should make acquaintance with the English officers.

If the Queen and Prince have not already disposed of Collonel Alnot's redgiment,[6] I should think the mony might be saved by not giving the commission til there comes a time for the raising the redgiment, it being one of those which is to pay the prisoners.[7]

985. MARLBOROUGH *to the* DUCHESS   [13/24 May 1708]

Source: Blenheim MSS. E4.
Printed: Coxe, ii. 428–9.

[Brussels] May 24th 1708

I have had the pleasure of your kind letter of the 4th, and it has been a pleasur to mee that you approve of my letter to 42 [the Queen].[8] If it has the effect I wish, it would incorage me to hope that 42 [the Queen] business might

---

[1] A portion of Peterborough's letter of 3/14 Apr. and the Elector's reply of 15/26 May are in Macpherson, ii. 110–11. The Elector replied he would do nothing regarding Great Britain except in concert with the Queen.

[2] 1/12 May, Blenheim MSS. B2-15; reply, 13/24 May, Murray, iv. 32.

[3] See p. 979, n. 1.   [4] 15/26 May.

[5] See the Elector to Marlborough, 16/27 May, Macpherson, ii. 111.

[6] Thomas Alnutt (died 1708), captain, Charlemont's Regiment (later 36th Foot), 1701; succeeded as colonel 1706; sent to Spain 1705; the regiment suffered severe losses at Almanza where Alnutt was taken prisoner. Alnutt died 7 May. See p. 1212.

[7] Instead of bringing all the regiments decimated at Almanza up to strength, some of the money appropriated for them was used to provide for the men taken prisoner. See p. 994, Marlborough to Walpole, 7/18 June, Murray, iv. 67.   [8] See p. 969, n. 1.

go smothly this next winter, without which wee can never gett out of this warr with honour and safety. You are so good as to say you will never write of pollatiques that may be disagreable to me if I desire itt. You know in friendship and love there must be no constraint, so that I am desirous of knowing what your heart thinkes, and must beg of you the justice to beleive that I am very much concerned when you are uneasy.

When I toke leave of Lady Tyrconell, she told me that her jointur in Ireland was in such disorder, that there was an absolut necessity of her going for two or three months for the better setling of itt; and as the climat of Ireland will not permitt her to be there in winter, she should begine her journy about ten days hence; and that she did not intend to go to London, but hoped she might have the pleasur of seeing you att St. Albans. I have offered her all that might be in my power to make her journey to Holland or England easy, as also that if she cared to stay att St. Albans, either at her going or return, you would offer it her with a good heart. You will find her face a good deal changed, but in the discorse I have had with her she seems to be very reasonable and kind. I have this morning received yours by Lieutenant General Withers, as also that of the 7th by the post. The copies of the severall letters you have sent me, I shall not have time to read til tomorrow, that I go to the army, for in this place I have very litle time to myself.

You will see by the two inclosed letters from Mrs. Morley [the Queen],[1] both which were write since she received mine. I desire that nobody may see them but Mr. Mongomerie [Godolphin], for I beleive 38 [Godolphin] and 240 [Lady Marlborough] are of opinion with me, that 239 [the Queen] should not know that their letters are sent to anybody. If I receive any other you shall be sure to have itt, and you will keep them til my return. You may asure 38 [Godolphin], that on all occasions I have to write to 239 [the Queen], I shall follow the directions he has given in his letter by Lieutenant General Withers, though I must own to you that I am thorowly convinced, that until 42 [the Queen] has suffered for the obstinat opinion thay are now in, that neither 38 [Godolphin], 39 [Marlborough] or 240 [Lady Marlborough] will be able to prevaile, though never so reasonable. But when 42 [the Queen] shall be sensible of their having been ill advised, thay will then readyly agree to all that may be advised by 38 [Godolphin], 39 [Marlborough] and 240 [Lady Marlborough]. I pray God it may not be then to[o] late. Whatever happens, if you are kind I will flatter myself with injoying some happy yeares at Bleinheim. I am sorry for the death of Mr. Bolter,[2] and glad you are going thether, so that the finishing of the inside may be to your own mind.

---

[1] 4 May, Blenheim MSS. B2-32, and 6 May, in Coxe, ii. 430–1. In the latter she comments upon his 'being prest in two conferences for the makeing steps towards a peace'. She comments: 'I shall never at any time give my consent to a peace but upon safe and honorable terms.'

[2] Assistant Surveyor of the Ordnance.

986. GODOLPHIN *to* MARLBOROUGH [*14 May 1708*]

Source: Blenheim MSS. A2-38.

May 14, 1708

I troubled you so much by the last post[1] that, having none of your letters to acknowledge since that time, I shall make this very short.

Enclosed I send you my Lord Gallway's letters[2] as I promised you in my last. You will find by it, that they don't apprehend the enemys this campagne, and that if they are to act offensively there next year he proposes more troops may bee sent thither before the end of this; which agrees well enough with our schemes as to that matter, in case he can bring them, in the meantime, to any reasonable conditions, as to the pay or the command of their troops, which he seems very heavily to endeavour.

Though Sir John Leak has carryed £90,000 sterling to Catalonia, he has left behind him in bills at Lisbon £75,000 more, which had been remitted thither from hence for the service of Spayn. I doubt it will bee a long time now before wee can gett it thither.

I am glad Palms has given you so right an account of the difficultys which the Imperiall court finds out, to discourage the Duke of Savoy, and to delay the execution of his treaty.[3] That usage is so prejudiciall to the rest of the Allyes, and soe imperious to the Queen and the States who are the guarands of that treaty, that it is really unpardonable. However, if our last accounts from thence bee true, the French have recalled the troops they had ordered from Dauphinè.

The weather is so fine here, that I make no doubt but the armyes are in the field, which will make us very impatient of constant news from you.

987. GODOLPHIN *to* MARLBOROUGH [*16 May 1708*]

Source: Blenheim MSS. A2-38.

May 16, 1708

By the favour of yours of the 21th[4] which I received yesterday morning, I find your army is drawn together before this time, and the enemy's (as *they say*) much stronger. But I am very much concerned that you seem to think, the affairs abroad, as well at home, are in such a condition, as to require that you should venture (particularly) at this time, more than would bee thought reasonable at another.

In this thow I must beg leave to differ since our letters of last post both from Germany and Italy, speak very hopefully of the Duke of Savoy's

---

[1] Letters 982, 983. [2] Untraced.
[3] The treaty between the Duke of Savoy and the Emperor, 28 Oct./8 Nov. 1703. See p. 989, n. 4.
[4] Letter 980.

intentions to take the field very soon, and to act with all possible vigour. If that bee once done, and 50 [Elector of Hanover] and 48 [Prince Eugene] doe but come to their stations, I hope you will soon find the French will not bee able to preserve any superiority against you. And therfore I am of opinion, if they doe not make it their business to come to some action with your army before June, you may depend they will avoyd it as carefully this year, as they did in the last. And I confess, I doe not see how 'tis possible for them to make head against 48 [Prince Eugene] and 58 [Duke of Savoy] (not to name 50 [Elector of Hanover]) without making very considerable detachments from Flanders. These considerations make mee think, that the affairs abroad doe lesse require venturing in the beginning of this year, than ever they have done. And for those at home, they stand upon another foot, and must run into great confusion in the winter, unless there bee a change at home, lett the success abroad bee what it pleases God to give us.

I have taken occasion to read your last letter (which was very moving) to 42 [the Queen] without leaving out one syllable. But whether it was for want of time, or for hardness of heart, I could not perceive that it made such an impression as might reasonably have been epected from it.

Lord President has consented to lett us have Munden and Lepell's regiment too,[1] to bee replaced by two of the Almanza regiments. I wish wee may bee able to gett them hither in time.

I have thoughts of going Tuesday[2] to Newmarkett for 4 or 5 days. If I receive no letter from you while I am there, I shall not trouble you at all by the post of Fryday the 21th.

988. GODOLPHIN *to* MARLBOROUGH [*17 May 1708*]

Source: Blenheim MSS. A2-38.
Printed: Coxe, ii. 432–3 (inc.).

May 17, 1708

I have just now received the favour of yours of the 24th,[3] much to my surprise, the wind having been here for some days not only contrary, to our thinking, but very strong.

I give you many thanks for Comte Maffei's letter which you sent mee inclosed. The latter part relating to 110's [Holland] confidence in 39 [Marlborough] is very satisfying to mee, because nothing is (in my opinion) of so much consequence, as to have that continue, whether this campagne bee successfull or not. And as to the former part of his letter, where he speaks of 58's [Duke of Savoy] inability to doe anything considerable, being so ill seconded by the court of Vienna, I look upon that to bee more playing

---

[1] For the descent.   [2] 18 May.   [3] Letter 984.

the part of a faithfull servant and a good minister, than anything else; and am in great hopes by the letters from Vienna of the 9th, that the Duke of Savoy will soon bee enabled to act both with vigour and with satisfaction.

I have had an opportunity to read yours of the 24th to 42 [the Queen] with the letter from Hannover. She was not much surprised at it and seems prepared to expect a great deal of trouble upon that matter in the winter, but can't bee prevailed with upon that or any other account to doe what can only in my opinion prevent it.

4 [Halifax] tells mee he has heard there is a letter in this town.[1] I believe it must bee from Scott,[2] which pretends to say that when Mr. Freeman [Marlborough] was lately at 50's [Elector of Hanover] house, 39 [Marlborough] should have told 50 [Elector of Hanover] that there would bee a necessity something of that kind[3] should bee done next winter, because of the extream perversness and imbecillity of 42 [the Queen]. As ridiculous and preposterous as this story seems yett I intend to acquaint Mrs. Morley [the Queen] with it, because I think it not unlikely to bee an invention of 199 [Harley] who perhaps intends to make his uses of it.

All our French newsletters of this last post are full of braggs of what the Duke of Burgundy will doe, that he will attack you, and afterwards makes no doubt of reconquering all Flanders and Brabant.

The only use I would make of this, is to confirm you in what seems already to bee your resolution that is to say, not to lett them attack you where they can make use of the superiority of their horse. And if nothing passes till Prince Eugene comes in to the field, they will bee very calm afterwards.

All our accounts from Hamburgh makes their affairs[4] look so black, that I wonder you are silent upon them. But I suppose you have enough of your own.

---

[1] The story was sent by Lewis to Harley on 22 May: 'All the letters from Hanover say positively the Electoral Prince is to make the campaign under the Duke of Marlborough though our prints do not mention it, and I think it may be observed that our news writers are more cautious what they say in relation to that family, than to any other subject. I am further told that the Duke will next winter bring him or his grandmother over hither, in such a manner that they shall have the obligation neither to Whigs or Tories, but entirely to himself and Lord Treasurer; whether they will think fit to communicate it to the Queen I cannot tell.' H.M.C., *Portland MSS.*, iv. 490.

[2] For Scott, an English resident at Hanover in league with the Tories, see p. 864, n. 7.

[3] An invitation to bring over a member of the house of Hanover.

[4] Krumholtz, a Lutheran minister in Hamburg, had stirred up the populace of this Imperial city against the burghers, and the city was torn by factions. The other members of the Circle of Lower Saxony, Sweden, Prussia, Hanover, and Wolfenbüttel, surrounded the city with their troops and forced their entrance to restore peace. The King of Denmark, who made claim to the city, looked upon the armed intervention as a direct challenge to his own rights. In a memorial delivered to the Queen on 15 May he threatened to withdraw his troops from the Allied army in the Low Countries for use in safeguarding his interests. She urged him to desist from recalling his troops on 25 May and he complied. An Imperial commission settled the disputes in Hamburg. The English envoy to the King of Sweden, John Robinson, who was at Hamburg to mediate between Denmark and Sweden, added his efforts to avoid further strife. *Compleat History for 1708*, pp. 194–205.

Marlborough left Brussels on 15/26 May, taking with him the troops encamped in the vicinity, and assembled his army at Bellingen, 19 kilometres south-west of Brussels, for the opening of the campaign.

---

989. MARLBOROUGH *to* GODOLPHIN   [*17/28 May 1708*]

Source: Blenheim MSS. A2-39.
Printed: Coxe, ii. 448–9.

[Bellingen] May 28th 1708

Having this opertunity by Collonel Huniwood[1] I may ventur to write freer then by the post. The motions the French have made makes me begine to be of your opinion, that thay are in the mind at this time to ventur, and by their having sent no troupes to the Moselle thay are certainly a good deal stronger then wee are. If wee should come to action in this part of the country it must be desided in a great degree by the foot, which is what we aught to wish for. But what I fear is, if thay have a sufficient strengh, that thay may post themselves so as to attack Ath, and take it before Prince Eugene can join, but this I beg you will say nothing of to anybody. I hope thay will not ventur it, but as thay are now camped, it is in their power. I believe you judge very right of the reason of sending the Elector[2] away, for 43 [King of France] dose know that on[e] way or other, 110 [Holland] will have 81 [peace], which must make 42 [the Queen] business more difficult in 108 [England]. Besides, I have some reason to believe that severals will be of the opinion of 30 [Peterborough] for the invitation,[3] which must be very mortefying. I am very glad to find by yours of the 11th[4] that you have hopes that Mrs. Morley [the Queen], though late, will do what 38 [Godolphin] desires. Nothing else can make us happy in serving her well. For though 39 [Marlborough] should have success, that might give safety abroad, but would not hinder disagreable things att home. You may see that I have very mallincolly thoughts. But be assured that I shall use my utmost endeavours that this campagne may be glorious to the Queen and nation.

---

[1] Philip Honeywood (died 1752), captain, Huntingdon's Regiment, 1702; brevet major 1703; served in Spain under Galway; colonel, Townshend's Regiment of Foot, 1709; brigadier-general 1710; deprived of regiment in 1710 for Whiggish views. At this time he was carrying dispatches from Spain to England.
[2] Of Bavaria. See p. 981.   [3] See p. 981, n. 3.
[4] Letter 982.

990. MARLBOROUGH *to* GODOLPHIN   [*17/28 May 1708*]

Source: Marlborough's letterbooks, Blenheim Palace.
Printed: Murray, iv. 35-6.

Camp at Bellinghen, 28th May 1708

This will be presented to your Lordship by the Comte de Bergomi,[1] whom I met lately at Hanover in his way to England with the character of envoy from the Duke of Modena[2] to her Majesty. I was desired, as well by that court as by Prince Eugene in the name of the Empress Dowager,[3] to recommend him to his Royal Highness [Prince George] and your Lordship. I have accordingly given him a letter to the Prince, and pray this may introduce him to your Lordship. I should not have so readily complied with the request, though made to me by persons of so great power, if I could foresee any inconveniency in his going to England merely on a compliment.

991. GODOLPHIN *to* MARLBOROUGH   [*20 May 1708*]

Source: Blenheim MSS. A2-38.
Addressed: To his Grace the Duke of Marlborough.

Newmarkett 20 May 1708

If I had been at London, instead of being here for 2 or 3 days, in great quiett and little company, I should have had no letter from you to thank you for by this post, nor consequently anything to add to the long letters I have troubled you with from thence of late, there being no change at my coming out of town, of the temper, which I complain of so much, and which will, without extraordinary accidents, create all the difficultys imaginable next winter. But still I think ther's remedy for all things but death, iff 39 [Marlborough] can bee here in time to concert, and take, the necessary measures.[4]

15/26 May, the day Marlborough moved to Bellingen, the French came to Soignies, 'about three leagues from us, but the continued rains we have had since have made it impracticable for them to move from thence. They give out that they are resolved to venture a battle. Tomorrow I shall make a motion forwards [to Saintes] to show them we will not decline it.'[5]

[1] Giovanni Francesco, Count Bergomi, representative of Modena at the Ryswick Peace Conference. He visited Vienna, Berlin, and Hanover before arriving in England to press for Modena's right to participate in the peace conferences. After remaining in England a year he removed to The Hague where he was accredited until 1714 and from thence to the peace conference at Baden.

[2] Rinaldo d'Este, Duke of Modena (1655-1737), whose wife was the sister of the Empress Wilhelmine, consort of Joseph I.

[3] Eleonora Magdalena Theresia of the Palatine (1655-1720), widow of Leopold I.

[4] Cf. p. 955.   [5] Marlborough to Boyle, 17/28 May, Murray, iv. 35.

992. MARLBOROUGH *to* GODOLPHIN   [20/31 May 1708]

Source: Blenheim MSS. A2-39.
Printed: Coxe, ii. 449 (inc.).

[Saintes] May the 31, 1708

I have this morning had the favour of yours of the 14th[1] with Lord Gallaway's letters, by which I have the pleasur to see that we may fear nothing on that side.

I have forgott in my former letters to tell you that the ten English battalions that were embarked this last expedition, were part of those which were embarked in the late King's time, and thay were then allowed their subsistance whielst on shipeboard, so that I have thought it for the Queen's honour and Service to promis them the like, which I hope will be aproved of.[2] Comte Senzindorf writes me by the last post,[3] that Palms has so well succeded in his negotiations, that the Duke of Savoy will have reason to be satisfied, and that the Elector Pallatin's affaires are setled to his mind,[4] and that the Emperor consents to the sending the 4,000 foot for Catalonia, which by this time I hope Sir John Lake is taking care of their embarkation.[5] I am sorry to see in some of your former letters the difficulty there is in leaving a squadron in the winter in the Mediteranien, for I am very much persuaded that til a squadron stays the whole winter, you will not succed in Spain.[6] I received the inclosed by the last Italian packett from Mr. Stanhope.[7] I was in hopes he had been att Barcelona, for I beleive his presence is necessary.

---

[1] Letter 986.

[2] The ten battalions were those sent over from Ostend on the alarm of the Pretender's attempted invasion (see p. 947, n. 2). They had been sent to the United Provinces in the spring of 1701 by William III under treaties by which the Maritime Powers had pledged aid for mutual security (see p. 6, n. 2).

[3] 5/16 May, untraced; reply, 19/30 May, Murray, iv. 39–40.

[4] The Duke of Savoy refused to take the field until he received the investitures of the territories in Italy promised him by the Emperor. The Elector demanded the Emperor grant him the investiture of the Upper Palatinate, taken by Bavaria in the Thirty Years' War. The Emperor conceded both in June, Marlborough to Wratislaw, 21 June/2 July, Murray, iv. 91–2. See Palmes to Cardonnel, 28 Apr./9 May, Murray, iv. 14.

[5] Leake brought the troops from Italy to Spain. See S. Martin-Leake, *Life of Sir John Leake*, (Navy Records Society, 1920), ii. 194–215.

[6] See pp. 976, 981.

[7] From Turin, 1/12 May, Blenheim MSS. A2-39. Stanhope says not much can be expected from the Duke of Savoy except the taking of Exilles, Fenestrelle, and Cesana (which were taken). The main deterrent is the Emperor, and if permission can be obtained to have the German troops winter in Italy a penetration into France next campaign is feasible; for it is 'certain that no project which will not lead us to winter on the other side of the mountains can be significant'.

993. MARLBOROUGH *to the* DUCHESS [*20/31 May 1708*]

Source: Blenheim MSS. E4.
Printed: *Private Correspondence*, i. 140–1.

[Saintes] May 31, 1708

Wee have so much rain and cold weather, that I am writting by a fier. I hope you have better in England. We comfort ourselves in beleiving the French suffer more then wee, thay being camped in lower ground then wee are. I had a letter yesterday from your sister Terconnel, in which she tels me she leaves Bruxelles in two or three days, and that her stay in Holand will be no longer then by going by the first safe opertunity, so that you will hear very quickly from her. I desire you would know of 6 [Sunderland], as from me, if Duke Hamilton pretends to be chosen, and by what party, for I am sometims told such extravagances as are very hard to beleive.[1] I have this morning had the happyness of yours of the 14th, and att the same time the inclosed from Mrs. Morley [the Queen],[2] which I send, it being an answere to my letter; but I beg that she nor nobody but Mr. Montgomery [Godolphin] may know that I send itt. You will be pleased to give the same caution to him. I have not time to say more, but that I am with all my heart *yours*.

994. GODOLPHIN *to the* DUCHESS [*22 May 1708*]

Source: Blenheim MSS. E20.
Addressed: To her Grace the Duchesse of Marlborough att Windsor.
Endorsed by the Duchess; Nothing in this letter but to shew the continual discouragment from Mrs. Morley [the Queen] to carry on her own service, 1708.

Newmarkett 22 May

I thought to have come to London tonight, but having yesterday a very discouraging letter from Mrs. Morley [the Queen],[3] and knowing one should not have the satisfaction of seeing Mrs. Freeman [Lady Marlborough] there till Monday at soonest, I have not been able to resist my own inclination in staying here till Monday morning.

My Lady Hervey[4] did not come back as she said she would, but was here last night, and goes home again today. She says she shall not come to London this sommer. I beleive you will have the Dutch post before I have the favour to see you.

---

[1] See p. 968, n. 1.
[2] Untraced. 14 May? The Queen probably wrote him about his proxy for use in the Scots peers election. See the Queen to Marlborough, 18 June, Brown, pp. 249–50, in which she makes reference to such a letter.
[3] 20 May. Present whereabouts unknown. The Queen objected to making James Montagu Attorney-General. She proposed instead Sir Thomas Parker and Robert Eyres as Solicitor General (in place of Montagu who currently held the post). Leeds sale catalogue, no. 54.
[4] Elizabeth (1676–1741), daughter of Sir Thomas Felton, Bt.; married, 1695, John Hervey, created Baron Hervey 1703. She was a close friend of the Duchess.

995. MARLBOROUGH *to* GODOLPHIN   [*24 May/4 June 1708*]

Source: Blenheim MSS. A2-39.
Printed: Coxe, ii. 449-50.

Terbanck[1] June 4th 1708

I have this morning received the favour of yours of the 16[2] by Captain Coot,[3] and that of the 17th by the post,[4] by which I see you have had the pleasur of Newmarket. You will see by my letter to Mr. Sectretary[5] that the French having marched al Friday night and Saturday,[6] with the intention as I was assured to continu their march for Louvain, I thought it for the Service not to camp at Bruxelles, but continu the march to this place, where the head of the army arrived yesterday, between aleaven and twelf a clock in the morning. If the French would have ventured thay might have been here at the same time, but thay finding I continued my march, I beleive occasioned their staying at Braine L'aleu, where thay now are enchamped, which makes me think, notwithstanding their braging, that thay will not ventur a batle. You have one expression in your letter of the 17th which is very malincolly, that success can't secure quietness next winter. By the last letters from Vienna you might see that the business of the upper Pallatinat was setled to the Elector's content, upon which he sent orders for his troupes to march. But two days after, an express arrived at Dusseldorp from Vienna, upon which he has sent possative orders to his troupes not to march. I do not know what the difficultys are, but I fear we shall not have the use of those troupes a good while, which may in a great degree break our measures, thay being 10,000. You may by this see the great advantage the King of France has over the Allyes. Since we depend upon the humours of several Princes, and he has nothing but his own will and pleasur. The Elector[7] should have been on the Rhin by the 20th of the last month, but my letters from Hanover says that he did not intend to leave that place til the 30, notwithstanding that thay knew that the Elector of Bavaria would be at Strasbourg the 21. I know not what to make of this but I am afraid wee must expect no good from thence this summer. I would not willingly blame Prince Eugene, but his arrival at the Mosele will be ten days after his promis. I beleive his stay at Vienna is occasioned by the difficultys of the Pallatinat.[8] I am so tiered and am to be upp so early tomorrow, that I can't read my letter, so that you will excuse any errors.

  [1] Terbank, a village lying just outside Louvain on the south-west.
  [2] Letter 987.
  [3] Identified as Thomas Coote, captain and rank as lieutenant-colonel, First Foot Guards, 1709; or (less probably) as Richard Coote, captain, Schonburg's Regiment of Horse, 1703; succeeded brother as third Earl of Bellamont 14 June 1708.
  [4] Letter 988.   [5] Boyle, Murray, iv. 48-9.
  [6] 21 May/1 June-22 May/2 June.   [7] Of Hanover.
  [8] The investiture of the Upper Palatinate demanded by the Elector Palatine from the Emperor. See p. 989, n. 4.

996. MARLBOROUGH *to the* DUCHESS   [*24 May/4 June 1708*]

Source: Blenheim MSS. E4.
Printed: *Private Correspondence*, i. 141–2.

Terbank June 4th 1708

Since my last I have had the happyness of yours by Captain Coot, as also another by the same post, and you may be sure henceforward, whenever I writt by an officer, you shall not faile of having a letter by the post; for doing what you like and your thinking kindly of mee, is what will make me most happy. Your desire of my following Lord Treasurer's advice is very kind, and you may be sure as long as I think you so, I shall be very desirous of living. I do not say this to flatter you, nor am I at an age of making fond expressions, but upon my word, when you are out of humor, and are disatisfied with me, I had rather dye then live; so on the contrary, when you are kind, I covett of all things a quiet life with you. What we hear from France and the languages of the princes in their army, I think are very different with their motions, for their last march makes me begine to think that their intentions are not to ventur a batle. Whatever happens, my dearest soull may be assured that I shal be carefull in doing as far as the Service will permitt what she desires. You know my mind in a former letter as to the invitation, and what you advise as to the alarming 42 [the Queen] by letting them know itt. Mr. Mongomery [Godolphin] may informe you, that he gave me an account by this post,[1] that he had read a letter of 39 [Marlborough] to 42 [the Queen] on that subject, and that he did not obsarve that thay were much concerned. I am intierly of your opinion that this last mark of favour to 220 [Queensberry] might have been spared, but beleive it must be thought by 86 [the House of Lords] that 239 [the Queen] has the power of doing it, so that in prudence 89 [the Whigs] should not attempt what can't be aproved.[2] I know not what caracter you have had of 52 [the Electoral Prince], but in my opinion he is far from being the worst; but in a few months I shall be able to give you a better account of him.

---

[1] Letter 988.

[2] Queensberry was made a peer of Great Britain, Duke of Dover, like Argyle, who was made Earl of Greenwich. Both claimed the right to sit in the Lords by virtue of their patents. Godolphin feared the Whigs might oppose their admission into the House. There were protests but both took their seats, though Queensberry was disqualified by the House from voting for Scottish representative peers. In 1711, when Hamilton received a similar honour, the Lords ruled that he was ineligible to sit in the Lords as of right as he already possessed a Scottish peerage. This ban remained until 1771. See p. 1028. For the representative peers of Scotland see William Robertson, *Proceedings Relating to the Peerage of Scotland* (Edinburgh, 1790) and Sir James Ferguson, *The Sixteen Peers of Scotland* (Oxford, 1960).

997. GODOLPHIN *to* MARLBOROUGH [25 May 1708]

Source: Blenheim MSS. A2-38.

St James May 25th 1708

I am to acknowledg the favour of yours of the 28th and the 31th of May.[1] In the former you seem to think, as I did, that the French hadd intentions to venture a battell, but as matter[s] now stand, I believe they don't intend to provoke it, but rather to observe your motions. I should not bee sorry if matters continued in this posture till Prince Eugene's comming, though 'tis plain that is not like to bee so soon, as you were promised. When he comes, it looks to mee, as if the French would bee very much embarrassed; especially if 50 [Elector of Hanover] makes good his post, for 58's [Duke of Savoy] affairs seem now again in a hopefull encouraging way. And I don't find there is anything to [be] feared on the side [of] Catalonia, and less yett in Portugall, as you will see by the letters which Mr. Boyle has orders to send you by this post, of the $\frac{15}{4}$ and the $\frac{23d}{12}$ from Lisbon.[2]

Lord Gallway's scheme[3] layd down in these letters seems reasonable and good, but I question whether 110 [Holland] will doe what is necessary in order to make it usefull. I believe the Queen, with what is already there, may have about 9,000 foot in that country about the middle of October; and Sir John Leak being to return with the fleet to Lisbon about that time of the year might have orders meet him at Gibralter, to bee asisting to their design if it goes on. But I doubt the arrears of subsidy from Holland, will not bee easily obtained. You see he inclines to have the French half pay officers sent to him. I have no objection to that, but on the contrary I think it a good riddance of as many as will goe. But I beleive a great many will excuse themselves.

By what you write of deserters which come to you, of the prisoners taken at Almanza, the French seem to have been in the right[4] very much not to suffer, *Arnold*,[5] whom you sent for that purpose, to see the English prisoners

---

1 Letter 989, 992.

2 From Galway to Sunderland. Boyle sent the originals which were to be returned to Sunderland. Blenheim MSS. C2-11.

3 Galway outlined a plan to invade Andalusia and make a siege of Cadiz, 'which of all other expeditions is of the greatest consequence to Britain'. The Portuguese would oppose it as it would lessen the importance of Lisbon to the Allies and therefore they must not be told. It is of no use to subsidize any more Portuguese troops as they will never leave their frontiers. Galway suggests instead raising an army of 12,000 foreign troops, adding to them the best of the Portuguese troops by taking them into English pay and placing the whole under an Allied general to take the offensive.

4 When Marlborough first conveyed the French refusal to England (6/17 Apr., Murray, i. 702–3), Sunderland admitted in his reply that it depended 'a good deal upon the truth of what they alledge, in relation to the like demands of their's being refused here; which I find nobody here remembers, [but] in generall, they cannot in everything of this nature, be treated in too high a manner'. 13 Apr., Blenheim MSS. B1-1.

5 John Arnott, captain in Portmore's Regiment of Foot; taken prisoner at Almanza 1707; charged by the Queen with care of English prisoners in France 1708; Marlborough to Chamillard, 19/30 Jan. 1708; Murray, iii. 669.

in France. For I am perswaded, there are few or none left there, though bills are drawn very regularly from time to time for their subsistance.

The Queen thinks it very reasonable to allow the subsistance to your 10 battalions during the time of their being a shipboard.

Our French newsletter which comes to my Lord Sunderland[1] seems to think the design upon Scotland is not at an end, and talks of 8 or 10 battalions at Brest. I think it is only to value himselfe, and his correspondence, but the matter of fact seems to mee impossible; nor can I imagine that while the French have their hands so full on all sides, that they will keep 8 or 10 battalions at Brest ready to embark upon an uncertain expedition, being certain at the same time, to meet stronger fleets in their way, if not stronger armyes.

I wish, as you doe that Mr. Stanhope were in Catalonia, rather [than] in Italy. What mony soever can bee taken up there, 'tis plain by his own letter, that Mr. Chetwynd can doe it as well, or better than hee.

The Queen has the gout, but talks of going next week to Windsor. I cannot yett find the least alteration in Mrs. Morley's [the Queen] temper.

998. GODOLPHIN *to* MARLBOROUGH [*26 May 1708*]

Source: Blenheim MSS. A2-38.
Printed: Coxe, ii. 433 (inc.).

May 26th 1708

Having a little more time to write now than I had by last night's post,[2] I am desirous to observe farther to you, upon the letters from my Lord Gallway sent you yesterday by Mr. Secretary Boyle, that, wheras he talks much of augmenting the subsidys to the Court of Portugall, upon his new scheme, it will not bee possible to augment the subsidys to Portugall in this year. But supposing he can obtain, that the Portughese troops in Catalonia shall bee payd for the future by the Queen, deducting the amount of that pay, from the subsidys to Portugall, and that the troops which her Majesty designs to send thither in September, added to those already there, shall bee a sufficient inducment to them to act offensively another year as my Lord Gallway proposes; and in that case, I have written to him that the Parliament may perhaps bee prevailed with to grant a farther subsidy to Portugall, but nothing more to bee expected in this year.

---

[1] The newsletters may have been sent by Daniel de Martine or Martines, an apparently clandestine agent or correspondent at Paris of Prussia, 1701-8, Hanover, 1706/7–23/4 and Hesse-Cassel, 1699–1726. Robethon may have arranged for Marlborough to receive copies (J. F. Chance, 'John de Robethon and the Robethon papers', *E.H.R.*, 13 (1898), 57 ff.). They have been almost totally ignored, but undeservedly so. See Churchill, ii. 549, n. 1. They are in Blenheim MSS. D1-15/18, and cover the period Sunderland was in office.
[2] Letter 997.

As to what Mr. Stanhope presses so much, and you also mention in yours of the 31th[1] concerning the wintering of a squadron in the Mediterranean, I must own to you, I doe not see how it can bee practicable, with any tolerable hopes of safety, while the French are masters of Thoulon. And consequently the whole strength which they have in that place, lies in the way of hindering us from sending all the necessary stores and provisions for such a squadron; besides that the squadron itself could not bee secure from their insults in any port of Italy.

This makes one regrett afresh the not taking Thoulon last year when it was so much in our power, and I am afrayd no successe which 58 [Duke of Savoy] could have in this, would lead him that way again; or any thing wee could doe for him, bee a temptation sufficient to doe us that peice of service, though it should bee in his power. And if this bee the case, as I doubt it is, the next best thing, is, as far as it is in our power, to pursue my Lord Gallway's scheme so effectually as to make ourselves masters of Cadiz, either this winter or next spring. Besides all other advantages of that conquest, this would fully answer all the ends of wintering a squadron in the ports of Italy for the service of Spayn.[2] And I know nothing besides, that could doe it, but that which I mentioned before, *of Thoulon*. I submitt to you, whether any success on that side will ever encourage you to name it to Comte Maffei. By what I can collect from some talk which I have had today with Collonell Honywood,[3] it looks to mee as if your armyes in Flanders would both continue in the camps where they now are, till Prince Eugene's motions oblige the French to take effectuall measures to oppose him, which I doe not find they have yett done, but I am sorry to see in Palmes's letter of the 19th that that Prince was still at Vienna, and no day sett at that time, for his leaving it.

My Lord Raby is just arrived here.[4] He has not yett opened any pretensions, but I take it for granted he will bee importunate to bee made Earl of Strafford, before his return to the court of Berlin.

I have had a letter from my Lord Conningsby[5] whose judgment and experience in all the affairs of 88 [Parliament] I value very much. He tells mee he has had sore eyes which makes it uneasy to him to write, but that in a

---

[1] Letter 992.

[2] The Prince's Council was consulted. On 23 June Burchett wrote Sunderland their advice, who passed it on to Marlborough on the 25th. 'You will see the opinion of the Prince's Councill in relation to the wintering of a squadron in the Mediterranean, and indeed I believe they are in the right, that it can be with no safety, but at Port Mahone' (Blenheim MSS. B1-1 with enclosure).

[3] He had just come from Spain carrying dispatches.

[4] Home on leave from Berlin. See p. 962.

[5] Thomas, Earl Coningsby (1656?–1729), M.P., Leominster, 1679–1710, 1715; Vice-Treasurer of Ireland 1693-4, 1698–1710; created Irish baron 1692; baron in British peerage 1715; earl 1719; government manager in the Commons and principal adviser to Godolphin on Ireland. See 'Lord Coningsby's Account of the State of Political Parties during the Reign of Queen Anne', *Archaeologia*, 38 (1860), i. 3–18. *D.N.B.*

little time he will send mee his thoughts[1] very fully as to the measures which ought to bee taken about 88 [Parliament]. And he adds that a little more delay will goe near to make everything that is good impossible to bee effected. 38 [Godolphin] seems to bee intirely of the same mind but finds 42 [the Queen] so perverse and soe obstinate *without* the least foundation, that nothing in the world is (in my opinion) so unaccountable, nor more dreadfull in the consequences of it. I can only say in this case, as I have heard my Lord Crofts[2] say a great while agoe in things of this kind; *Well Sirs, God's above.*

May 28th

I have had hopes all this day to have heard from you before the going out of the post. But now I am in dispaire of it, and shall only add that Lillingston, whose regiment is in the Leeward Islands, having positively refused to goe to it, severall have made application to buy it of him; among others one Fielding,[3] a relative of my Lord Denbigh's,[4] and brother to the querry.[5] But the Prince seems inclined rather to give the regiment to the lieutenant collonell[6] who is, as he is informed, upon the place, rather than lett Lillingston sell. I have really no objection to that, because in itself, I think it is right. But then that method should bee followed in other cases as well as in this, and without partiality which I much wish. But I doubt, I shall not live to see it.

999. MARLBOROUGH *to* GODOLPHIN   [*27 May/7 June 1708*]

Source: Blenheim MSS. A2-39.
Printed: Coxe, ii. 451 (small omission).

Terbanck June 7th 1708

I have the favour yesterday of yours of the 20th[7] from Newmarkett, where I should have been glad to have been with you, for besides the pleasur of your company, I should have injoyed quietness, which is what I long extreamly after, but God knows when I shall have itt. You will know by this post that the Elector of Bavaria has been obliged to make a detachment for the Mosele,[8]

---

[1] For his later letter see p. 1030, n. 4.
[2] William, Baron Crofts of Saxham (1611 ?–77).
[3] William Fielding, M.P., Castle Rising, lieutenant of the Yeoman of the Guards, which he resigned in June.
[4] Basil Fielding, fourth Earl of Denbigh (1668–1717), Master of the Horse to Prince George 1694–7; lord-lieutenant of Leicester 1703–6, 1711–14; Teller of the Exchequer 1713–15.
[5] George Fielding, equerry to Queen Anne.
[6] James Jones, who was granted the regiment effective 2 June. See Marlborough to Walpole, 7/18 June, Murray, iv. 67 and below, p. 1023, n. 4.
[7] Letter 991.
[8] Receiving word that the Imperialists had moved towards Kreuznach and that the Hessians had crossed the Rhine at Rheinfels, the Elector determined to reinforce his troops on the Moselle, which he saw as the Allied objective. Vault, viii. 311 et seq.

which will give an opertunity to the Elector of Hanover to pass the Rhin. You will have seen by my last that we are like to lose the 10,000 Pallatins, at le[a]st for some time. I have writt to Prince Eugene that I think time is so pretious that he aught not to stay for the Pallatins. The enclosed[1] was sent me by Don Quiros, who assures me that I may depend upon the truth of itt. Not knowing whether Mr. Stanop's letter may be come to you, I send mine,[2] which I received this day. The enemy continues in their camp at Braine Laleu, and I shall not march til thay do, or that I hear from Prince Eugene; so that I have begone this day to pass in reveu the right wing of horse of the first line, and tomorrow shall see half the foot of the same line, and so continue every day til I have seen the whole army. I shall by the next post do myself the honour of sending the Prince [George] an order of battel of the enemy's as well [as] our army. If you have curiosity, the Prince may let you have a copie of them.[3]

1000. MARLBOROUGH *to the* DUCHESS   [*27 May/7 June 1708*]

Source: Blenheim MSS. E4.

[Terbank] June 7th 1708

I had yesterday the favour of yours of the 20th from Woodstock, and am extreamly pleased at your being so well satisfied with the place. I assure you I do with all my heart return your compliment, that whatever you order I shall like. It is treu that I do intend picturs for that room of the bow windo, but am sorry to hear that your apartement and mine is not to be finished this sumer, since it was agreed to be done in the estimat. Considering the expence of this house, there can be no disput but the first flower [floor] must be all right wenscott. I hope you will have had time to have seen my Lady Dash-wood,[4] for if I can be so happy as to live at Bleinheim with you, I should be desirous of living well with our neighbours. Amongst the Parliament men chosen Mr. Guidot is marked for a Wigg; but if there be not pains taken with him, by what I have heard, I fear he will be found otherwais. When you see him, you may speak as your not doubting of his being for the carrying on of the warr, til a safe peace can be had, by which you will see his inclinations.

---

[1] Untraced.

[2] The letter enclosed here was dated either 28 Apr./9 May, Chevening MSS. 66/2, or 5/16 May, Blenheim MSS. B1–9. In the latter Stanhope reports on his efforts to raise money for Charles III and gives notice of the death of Noyelles on 10/21 Apr. See reply, 31 May/11 June, Murray, iv. 59–60.

[3] For the French order of battle see Vault, viii. 377–80.

[4] Penelope (Chamberlayne) (died 1735), wife of Sir Robert Dashwood, first Bt. (1662–1734), whose seat was at Kirtlington Park, not far from Woodstock. A Tory, he was M.P. for Banbury, 1689–98, and for Oxford, 1699–1700.

1001. GODOLPHIN *to* MARLBOROUGH   [*30 May 1708*]

Source: Blenheim MSS. A2-38.

May 30, 1708

I give you this trouble before the post day at the request of Mr. Molesworth,[1] who does earnestly desire my recomendation to you. I suppose he must mean by that, to serve near your person, as farr as the duty of the post you have given him will admitt. I think he is extreamly zealous and affectionate in your service. He has been long sick in his northern jorney, and the dreggs of it, remain yett in his face. But I hope he may bee quite recovered before he getts to your camp. Since my last, I have the favour of yours of the 4th of June from Terbank,[2] which I acknowledg now, expecting I shall have another to thank you for before Tuesday's[3] post.

I am sorry to find by yours that you seem to have counted so much upon 50 [Elector of Hanover] and 48's [Prince Eugene] being upon their stations so exactly according to the time named and agreed on. Wee here are not much surprised at such sort of failours. But I confess I can't help being much troubled to find the letters of this last post from Vienna so directly contrary to the former, both in what relates to the Elector Palatin, and to the Duke of Savoy. This will enrage people here to a degree that will make it impossible to keep any measures with that court, unless these difficultys are eased as suddenly as they have been raised.

Since my last[4] in which I mentioned some thoughts about Thoulon, I have had a letter from Mr. Chetwynd, in which he says 58 [Duke of Savoy] has had sure advices that that matter is easyer than it was last year. I intend therfore to speak of it to Comte de Brianncon in such a manner as may lett him see 58 [Duke of Savoy] may expect everything from 42 [the Queen] and 108 [England], both in present and when 81 [peace] appears, in case he shall see room to make any sucessfull attempt in that matter. But otherwise I am much afrayd all Stanhope and Chetwynd seem to wish he should doe this year that soe he might bee ready to enter France in the next, will only bee looked upon by our Parliament as a shoing horn to draw more extraordinary subsidys from them, another year.

Wee have news today that upon the 20th 6 or 7 French men of warr came to the port of Gallway in Ireland with design to have taken our East India ships, which have layn there some time. But the men in the fort behaved so well, that they sunk one of the French men of warr, and forced another to run ashoar. However the East India ships in the road have been so frighted that they ran themselves also upon the strands by which means I suppose

---

[1] Richard, later third Viscount Molesworth, aide-de-camp to Marlborough. His father was envoy to Denmark 1689–92. The nature of this journey is not disclosed.

[2] Letter 995.   [3] 1 June.   [4] Letter 998.

all their goods will bee saved, but the hulls of the ships, I think must bee lost.[1]

My Lord Dursley[2] sailed the 20th from Spithead with 17 clean ships, he may have a hitt to meat the French in their return.[3]

1002. GODOLPHIN *to* MARLBOROUGH   [*31 May 1708*]

Source: Blenheim MSS. A2-38.
Printed: P.C., ii. 242-3 (inc.).

May 31, 1708

My last was of yesterday by Mr. Molesworth.[4] I have received this morning as I expected the favour of yours of the 7th,[5] with the enclosed paper from Don Quiros of news from severall parts of Spain, which I believe is all true, since wee have it confirmed from France and Italy, with other particulars not mentioned in your paper; but more considerable as that Sir John Leak has mett with a convoy of provisions designed for the support of the Duke of Orleans's army. He has 80 sail of them and dispersed the rest which were about 40 more. Besides the relief which this will bring to our friends in Catalonia, it may chance to putt the French army into great distress. For it is sayd, they depended chiefly upon this convoy for their summer's subsistance.[6]

I hope therfore upon the whole, that wee have a fair prospect of hearing constant good news from that side of the world.

Not only by your letter, but by all the other advices of this post, the French seem very much to apprehend their affairs upon the Moselle. And it is plain by the detachments they make from thence they will leave the Rhyne very weak, and consequently putt all into 50's [Elector of Hanover] power to doe something considerable for the common good, if he bee well guided. I offer it therfore to your thoughts, whether you would not propose to him (if you think fitt) what might bee done in that side, with most effect. You know best how farr the intelligences in Frenche Comtè subsist, and whether this bee not as favorable an opportunity as could bee expected to make advantage

---

[1] See Luttrell, vi. 310.

[2] James Berkeley, third Earl of Berkeley (1680–1736), styled Viscount Dursley 1699–1710; M.P., Gloucester, 1701–2; captain, Royal Navy, 1701; served in Mediterranean 1704–7; created Baron Berkeley 1705; raised to flag rank 1708; succeeded as Earl of Berkeley 1710; First Lord of the Admiralty 1717–27. *D.N.B.*

[3] Godolphin may have been misinformed about the condition of Dursley's ships, because Entick (p. 669) reports that Dursley met three French ships on 26 May 'but his ships being most of them foul, and the French clean, they stood away for their own coast and escaped'.

[4] Letter 1001.   [5] Letter 999.

[6] The convoy was intercepted 11/22 May. It was bound for Peniscola, for the Duke of Orleans who was besieging Tortosa. Catalonia was on the verge of famine so the taking of the grain fleet was providential for the Allies. *Life of Leake*, ii. 209–12.

of them;[1] expecially now about the time when 58 [Duke of Savoy] will probably bee taking the field, which would bee a great encouragement to him. And by what Mr. Chetwynd writes by this post, he appears so out-ragious of the proceedings of the court of Vienna, that he will very much want to bee encouraged. And if he has not speedy satisfaction from them I doubt wee shall find the last ill consequences of it. I wish therfore that Palmes would lose no more time in getting to him; for though he may have been usefull at Vienna, he would bee more usefull there, upon this account chiefly, as well as upon others.

You have done certainly very right in pressing 48 [Prince Eugene] to hasten, even without the 10,000 Palatins, for time is more than all the rest. But this delay in the court of Vienna is more unpardonable than all the mischief they have done before it. And if wee ever come to have such a share in 81 [peace] as is but justly due to 42 [the Queen] I know one that won't forgett it, though everybody else should bee inclined to have that com-plaisance.

June 1st

The Comte de Briancon tells mee he had a letter from his master in which he bids him tell mee the affair of Thoulon is easyer than it was last year. You will easily imagine I was not backward in saying everything that I thought proper to encourage him to have it always in his view, if ever it were in his power to make that attempt with success; and particularly that it would turn more to 58's [Duke of Savoy] honour and advantage to doe it now, than it would have done last year when he had the assistance of 48 [Prince Eugene]; but now that it would bee all owing to himself alone. This conversation ended with great appearance of satisfaction in both sides.

But I am now going to give you an account of one this morning betwixt Mr. Montgomery [Godolphin] and Mrs. Morley [the Queen], which ended with the greatest dissatisfaction possible to both. They have had of late many great contests, as I am told, upon the subject of 4 [Halifax's] brother, but without any ground gained on either side. This day it held longer than ever. The particulars as they have been repeated to mee, are both too tedious and unnecessary to trouble you with them. In short, the obstinacy was unaccountable, and the battell might have lasted till [evening], if after the clock had struck 3 41 [Prince George] had not thought fitt to come in and look as if he thought it were dinner time.

I hope your next will acquaint us with Prince Eugene's arrivall, which will bee very welcome news to mee.

---

[1] A two-pronged movement was planned into south-east France, the Elector of Hanover ad-vancing into Franche-Comté, the Duke of Savoy into Dauphiné. It failed because the Hanoverian advance never materialized. See p. 1035, n. 2.

1003. MARLBOROUGH *to* GODOLPHIN

[*31 May/11 June 1708*]

Source: Blenheim MSS. A2-39.
Printed: Coxe, ii. 452-3.

Terbanck June 11th 1708

Since my last I have none of yours to answere, and I have been bussy every day in reveuing the troupes. The greatest part are in extreame good order. I shall continue in this camp, unless the enemy march, til I hear from Prince Eugene that he is in motion, for as yett I have no account of his being gone from Vienna. The news we have from Spain is more favourable then we could reasonably exspect, and I find by Lord Galway's letters that we have nothing to fear on the Portugale side. Wee do flatter ourselves that the detachement the Elector of Bavaria has been obliged to make may give an oppertunity to the Elector of Hanover of doing something on the Rhin. The continuall complaints of 58 [Duke of Savoy] is, I am afraid, a forerunner for our not expecting much on that side. The disapointement of the Pallatin troupes, and 48 [Prince Eugene] not being able to put in execution by at least a fortnight what was agreed betwine him and 39 [Marlborough] gives great disadvantage. However, 39 [Marlborough] has taken his measures that nothing may be wanting at the arrivall of 48 [Prince Eugene], he being persuaded that our greatest hopes must be in what we shall be able to do in the first four or five days, for their foot will be able to joyne them as soon if not sooner then ours. But if 48 [Prince Eugene] uses that dilligence he has promised, he may with his horse joyne me some days before thay can, by steling a march, which time we must make use off. I have this afternoon received yours of the 25,[1] but have not time to do more then thank you til the next post.

1004. MARLBOROUGH *to the* DUCHESS

[*31 May/11 June 1708*]

Source: Blenheim MSS. E4.
Printed: Coxe, ii. 451-2.

[Terbank] June 11th 1708

Whenever I have any leasur, and my mind a litle at ease, I make use of that time to writt to my dear soull. The post dose not go til tomorrow, but as I am that morning to see the left wing of horse, I make use of this time to tell you, that I am in my health, I thank God, as well as one of my age, and that has not his mind very much at ease, can be; for what I concerted with 48 [Prince Eugene] will not be executed by 15 days so soon as was resolved, which will be an advantage to the Duke of Vandome, by giving him time; but the slowness of Garmains are such that wee must always be disapointed. Our news from Spain is as favourable as we could expect, and by Lord Galway's letters we have nothing to fear on the side of Portugale. The Elector of Bavaria having been obliged to make a considerable detachement from his army for the Moselle will, we hope, enable the Elector of Hanover to do something on the Rhin. By this time we flatter ourselves that the Duke of Savoye is taking the field. The greatest difficulty he will meet with is the mountains he must pass before he can gett into France. As for us in this country, we have a very good army, but the French think themselves more numirous. However, I hope with the blessing of God that this campagne will not pass without some good success on our side. You will easily beleive me when I tell you, that I do from my heart wish that the favourable account I now give you of the postur of our armys, may meet with no disapointment, and that this campagne may be so successfull, that I may have the happyness of being in quiet with you this next summer, and for the remaining part of my life. I have this afternoon the favour of yours of the 23d and 25th, but am returned so late to my quarters that I must answere them by the next post.

1005. GODOLPHIN *to* MARLBOROUGH   [*3 June 1708*]

Source: Blenheim MSS. A2-38.

June 3, 1708

Since my last of the 1st[1] wee have no forreign letters, nor can wee hope for them, as the wind is, till after the post of tomorrow night. In the meantime Mr. Meredith going away tomorrow morning, I cannot refuse him a letter to you, though I have very little to add to my last. Everything here continues very disagreable, at present, and the prospect from it next winter very melancholly. But providence I hope will take care of us, as long as wee doe not omitt to use all proper means.

Lieutenant Generall Erle is out of town and will bee soe yett a week longer. However all our preparations goe on,[2] and will bee ready (I believe) by the end of the month. I send you 3 papers herewith, that you may see what he proposes for his establishment, and the comparison betwixt this, and that of Lord Rivers.[3] I [think] the chief argument for allowing of this, must bee, that it will last but a little while, and is of such a nature as to pay for its expence.[4]

---

[1] Letter 1002.   [2] For the descent.

[3] Rivers's expedition to Spain in 1706, which was originally intended for a descent on a plan similar to that formulated for Erle's. See p. 541, n. 2.

[4] The descent was a short-term venture, only expected to last a few months and force the French to divert troops from the main theatres of war.

The face of our affairs in Spain changes very much for the better. God send us good success there and everywhere.

58 [Duke of Savoy] would never revive the affair of Thoulon to us, as he has done, both by Mr. Chetwynd, and by Comte Briancon, but that he has either a mind to value himself, by doing it in earnest, or else he is making terms with 43 [King of France] and has a mind to amuse us with that expectation.

1006. MARLBOROUGH *to* GODOLPHIN   [3/14 June 1708]

Source: Blenheim MSS. A2-39.
Printed: Coxe, ii. 453-4.

Terbanck June 14th 1708

By the letters of Lord Gallway, as well as what you write me in yours of the 25 and 26th,[1] I can't but obsarve that his project that he now makes dose no ways agree with the project he sent by Mr. Stanhope. That would have been expensive, but this is likely to be much more. There can be no doubt but Cailles [Cadiz] would be of great use, but I beg you to consider how impossible it will be to have success unless it be done by surprise, and how impossible that will be when the much greatest part of the troupes are to march by land, and that you are to decieve the Portuguesse, as well as French and Spaniards. But if it be practicable, itt must be this yeare and not the next, for when you shall the next winter put your troupes into such quarters as may be proper for that expedition, you may be assured that thay will take such precaution, as will put that place out of dainger. You know that by the treaty, England and Holland are obliged to give every yeare to the King of Portugale upwards of 4,000 barels of powder, which is more then is expended by France and all the Allyes in their armys, so that I beg you will be cautious of giving any incoragement of having an English train established in Portugale. For if the attempt of Cailles goes on, the canon and everything for that expedition must be furnished by the fleet. As for the refugie officers, I think he setts a much greater vallu on them then thay deserve. If he can make any use of them, I should thank thay would be better there then in Ireland.

I am very sorry you have so much ocasion to put you in mind of Lord Croft's saying, but as *God is above*, so I trust in him or else our prospect is very dreadfull.

The enclosed copie is what came to me by expresse from Comte Recteren.[2] You will see by itt, how uncertain all measures taken with the Germains are, for the army on the Moselle was to be formed at farthest by the 27th of May, and by this letter we must not expect it til the begining of Jully. Patience is a vertue

[1] Letters 997, 998.
[2] The Dutch envoy at Frankfurt 27 May/7 June, Blenheim MSS. B1-15; reply, 31 May/11 June, Murray, iv. 61. See also the exchange between Marlborough and Eugene in Coxe, ii. 454-6.

absolutly necessary when one is obliged to keep measures with such people. I beg you will informe her Majesty and the Prince that thay may not think me neglegent, and if the Queen approves of it, I think Comte Rectern's letter might be read to the Cabinet Councell, so that thay might see the reason for my staying in this camp. What you mention [of] 115 [Toulon] is not now to be thought on. I own to you that I fear we must not expect this campagne much from 58 [Duke of Savoy], but the best thing we can do is to make him beleive that we flatter ourselves with great success on his side, and that we relie intierly on him, not doubting but he will take the best measures.

1007. MARLBOROUGH *to the* DUCHESS   [3/14 *June 1708* ?]¹

Source: Blenheim MSS. E3.
Addressed: To the Dutchesse of Marlborough.

[beginning missing]

. . . likly, since it is very probable that I shall dye long before the Queen, and then Sandridge, the 5,000 pounds a yeare given by Parlaiment, and what I shall leave in my will, will be added to your present fortune.

I hope to be able to take such measures as that I nede not be obliged allways to live under a roufe [with] Mrs. Massum, much less make my court to her as was hinted the other day, nor do I think I shall ever live in the house [you] have a mind to build. But since you have told me your mind very freely on that subject, I will lett you know mine, which is, that if you will setle the house on mee for my life, and after that on yourself and to whome else you please forever, I shall be ready to give towardes the building and furnish of itt, seven thousand pounds, provided that if you do not think fitt to setle it on the tytel as it is in the Act of Parliament, then the house shall be a security for the payment of the seven thousand pounds after your death, and not before. And in like maner, if you shall think to setle this house on the tytel, then thay shall be obliged to pay to your order the mony which you shall have laid out on the house and furnitur over and above the seven thousand pounds.²

¹ The Duke makes reference to the cost estimates for Marlborough House in his letter of 20 June/1 July (letter 1023). One can infer from that letter that the terms for financing its construction had already been worked out between them, placing this fragment at some earlier date in the year. All Marlborough's letters to the Duchess up to 3/14 June survive except for the first few he wrote immediately after his departure for the Continent. One presumes that he wrote her on 31 Mar., 2/13 and 6/17 Apr., as he customarily wrote her on post days, at the same time he wrote the Treasurer. If we assume that the arrangements for the house were worked out in their correspondence between June and September (see letter 1121) and that the Duchess's query regarding the lease (reply, letter 1023) followed the settlement of the financial details, then this date, rather than the other June dates (7/18, 10/21, 17/28) for which no dated letter to the Duchess survives seems the most probable.

² This letter refers to plans for Marlborough House in St. James's Park. Construction was begun the next year and the Duchess moved there in 1711.

1008. GODOLPHIN *to* MARLBOROUGH   [*4 June 1708*]

Source: Blenheim MSS. A2-38.

June the 4th 1708

I sent Mr. Meredith a letter for you last night,[1] but he going over but with this packett, this letter will bee with you sooner than that, for he seems not to bee in a condition of making hast.

I am much pressed by my Lady Oglethorpe[2] to desire you would obtain leave for Monsieur le Marquis de Levy,[3] to goe into France for three months. It seems a relation of his has marryed her daughter,[4] and the young woman hopes to bee better used for the future by her husband's relations, in case she can obtain this favour. I have already mentioned it once,[5] and if it appears that you have no objection to it, I beleive t'will bee done.

Flotard[6] makes use of your name to mee for some favour which he says you promised him. I know you have never written to mee about it of late, nor indeed am I thoroughly convinced that the man has dealt fairly in all that matter with which he was trusted.

I should not trouble you with these things which signifie little but that I have troubled you so much of late, upon other subjects which are more materiall, and I was unwilling, though I had written yesterday by Mr. Meredith, that the post should bring you no letter from mee.

[1] Letter 1005.

[2] Lady Eleanor Oglethorpe (died 1732), widow of Sir James Oglethorpe (1650–1702), brigadier-general 1688; deprived of his places after the accession of William III. *D.N.B.*

[3] Charles-Eugène, marquis of Lévis (died 1734), French officer; brigadier 1702; *maréchal de camp* 1704; lieutenant-general 1708; taken prisoner from the *Salisbury*, a ship in the Pretender's expedition captured by Byng.

[4] One daughter married the marquis of Maziera in Picardy, another the marquis of Bellegarde.

[5] Untraced.

[6] David Flotard, a Huguenot living in London, was sent by Miremont to the Cévennes in June 1703 to promise aid to Cavalier in the Queen's name: J. Cavalier, *Mémoires sur la guerre des Cevennes*, ed. by F. Puax (Paris, 1918), pp. 154–5, 298. After returning and giving the English ministry a report of the conditions he found there, Flotard was sent back to Geneva to help manage assistance provided for the Camisards: Stelling-Michaud, pp. 165–6, 185; Flotard's correspondence with Hill in *Correspondence of Richard Hill* (London, 1845), pp. 165, 185. Returning again to England he was made a brevet captain of Dragoons, to go with Rivers's expedition in 1706. When the destination of the expedition was changed, he apparently left it with many other of the French refugees: Rivers to Hedges, 11 Sept. 1706, H.M.C., *Bath MSS.*, i. 98. He was at The Hague in the spring of 1709 and while there pressed the States for a pension for his services. From there he wrote to Godolphin and Marlborough warning them of the treachery of Guiscard: Flotard to Marlborough, 22 Mar./2 Apr., enclosing a letter from d'Étienne de la Fous about Guiscard, Blenheim MSS. B1-16; to Godolphin, same date, Blenheim MSS. G1-6; another copy, B.M., Portland Loan, 29/45 I/22. Marlborough wrote to the Queen in 1709 about a pension and he was given £60 a year. By 1713 he was complaining to Oxford it was two years in arrears. See Marlborough to Boyle, 5/16 June, 20 June/1 July, Murray, iv. 506–7, 523; Flotard to Oxford, 14/25 Aug. 1711, B.M., Portland Loan, 29/45R, fols. 308–9; 15 Sept. 1713, ibid. 29/45T, fols. 100–1 (recounting his services and discussing his pension).

1009. MARLBOROUGH *to* GODOLPHIN [7/18 *June 1708*]

Source: Blenheim MSS. A2-39.
Printed: Coxe, ii. 456-7.

Terbanck June 18th 1708

Since my last[1] I have had the favour of yours of the 31 and 1st[2] of this month. I am not surprised at the conversation you have had with 58 [Duke of Savoy] minister,[3] though I am very confident he has no thoughts of that expedition for this campagne, but he knows very well how fond every honest Englishman is of that project.[4]

The opinion of 39 [Marlborough] as he tels me is, that 58 [Duke of Savoy] knowing to[o] well that he shall be able to do nothing considerable this campagne, the Allyes may grow weary of leaving so many troupes with him the next yeare, unless he can by some plausable offer engage 108 [England].

By what I have received this morning from 48 [Prince Eugene], the difficulty of the Pallatin troupes continues, and he is not certain when the 4,000 Imperial horse can be at their rendevous. In the meantime, you will see by the enclosed paper[5] the dilligence and care taken by the Elector of Bavaria. It is most certain that the few troupes which the French leave on the Rhin gives a great occasion to the Elector of Hanover, and I should think a good opertunity for that of Franch Comty. I shall follow your advice in letting 50 [Elector of Hanover] know what 39 [Marlborough] thoughts are, but I must own frankly to you, that I take the humour of 50 [Elector of Hanover] to be such, that the sure way of not being disapointed, is to expect nothing from thence.

I send you the letter I have received this morning from Monsieur Buys, with the answere I have made to itt.[6] You will see by it that thay are not changed in their opinion, so that it will be necessary for you to think well of what answere I shall give, for it will be communicated to the four Burgemasters. I am afraid that 113 [Amsterdam] is very much determined for 81 [peace], and if that should be once known by 116 [the States], it might be of a very daingerous consequence this winter. When 61 [Buys] and his companion spoke of this matter to me, thay assured me that thay had acquainted nobody but myself, being sensible of the consequence. Your letter by Molsworth[7] is not yett come to me.

[1] Letter 1006.   [2] Letter 1002.
[3] Count Briançon.   [4] To seize Toulon.
[5] Untraced.
[6] 5/16 June, Blenheim MSS. B1-5; reply, 7/18 June (with copy of Buys's), ibid., B1-15; Buys and Burgermaster Hooft had reported on their conversations with Marlborough about peace at The Hague in April (see p. 951). They hoped he now had a reply to give them from England on the points raised.
[7] Letter 1001.

1010. GODOLPHIN *to* MARLBOROUGH   [*8 June 1708*]

Source: Blenheim MSS. A2-38.

June 8th 1708

I am to acknowledg the favour of yours of the 11th,[1] by which I see you are very uneasy at the long delay of 48 [Prince Eugene]. I did always doubt, it was impossible for him to come so soon as he had promised you, considering how many things he had to doe, and what difficultys he must expect to meet with in some of them. But I hope they are all over by this time, for Sir Philip Medows writes from Vienna, that the Palatine troops march, and that the Duke of Savoy has the entire disposition of the 20,000 men, and Generall Thaun [Daun] to command them. So I hope wee shall soon hear some good effect of it. Comte Briancon gives great assurances, and I have written very earnestly to Mr. Chetwynd, to see that no opportunity bee lost of pressing the warr on that side and in case there bee any opportunity of resuming the affair of 115 [Toulon], that all possible assistance and encouragement bee given for it.

There is no doubt, but the French have left themselves weak upon the upper Rhyne, and that 50 [Elector of Hanover] may if he pleases make advantage of it. But I submitt to you, whether you will not think it proper to give him some hint which way he may act most usefully, and whether this might not bee a proper opportunity of executing the design so long since projected in the Frenche Comtè. When 48 [Prince Eugene] and 39 [Marlborough] meet, as I hope they have done before this time, they will best judg what is proper to bee done in this matter. Upon the whole matter, if our last accounts from Vienna are true, both 48 [Prince Eugene], 50 [Elector of Hanover], and 58 [Duke of Savoy] are all by this day in a condition to act. And if you expect any diversion from our expedition,[2] that will also bee all in readyness by the end of this month; and their first attempt being designed upon the coast of Normandy, it may probably oblige the enemy to draw some troops from the garrisons in Flanders which are nearer to it.

As slow as the Germans are in most things, I doubt they have been too quick in sending the Queen of Spain; and I am very apprehension [apprehensive], that their attention to carry her to Catalonia, may keep the fleet too long from more essentiall operations; and also that her Majesty's presence there will but augment the expence of the court of Spain, and consequently divert too much of that money which ought to bee applyed to the warr.

Mr. Erle is not yett come to town, but I hope he will make amends by his diligence when he comes, for his too long absence.

I received the enclosed letter by the last Dutch post, from *la Martinerie*.[3] In the late King's time wee used to look upon him as half mad. However,

---

[1] Letter 1003.   [2] The descent.   [3] Untraced.

I am apt to think there may bee a good deal of that humour stirring which he mentions in his letter. I don't intend to make any answer to it but as you direct mee.

1011. MARLBOROUGH *to* GODOLPHIN   [*10/21 June 1708*]

Source: Blenheim MSS. A2-39.

[Terbank] June 21, 1708

Since my last[1] I have had the favour of yours by Mr. Molsworth,[2] as also that of the 4th of this month by the post.[3] I sent you so many inclosed copies of letters in my last, that I am glad I have but litle to write by this post, fearing I might tier you.

I can no ways judge of the inconveniencys that may arise upon giving leave to the Marquis de Levy, he being taken at sea. But the behavior of the court of France as to our prisoners, dose no way deserve theirs should meet with any favour, and I beleive my Lady Ogletherp as litle. At the same time I would beg the Queen's favour for Monsieur Jolly[4] for a pass for 4 months. Hee has been always in England since his first comming. I have thought it just to refuse the giving any longer time to those in France, so that thay are ordered back, and I would humbly beg that her Majesty would direct her subjects to return without lose of time according to their parole. I know not what Flotard means by making use of my name. I am sure I must know something better of him then I do, before I should recomend him to you.

1012. GODOLPHIN *to* MARLBOROUGH   [*11 June 1708*]

Source: Blenheim MSS. A2-38.
Printed: Coxe, ii. 433-4 (inc.).

June 11th 1708

Having no letters from you since my last, nor nothing either from Spain or from Portugall, I shall have very little to trouble you with by this post, unless I would give you an account of Mr. Montgomery's [Godolphin] complaints which indeed would bee endless. And if I can judg rightly of him, I think he would rather chose to sink under the burthen of them himself, than to give you the trouble of them, to no purpose, who have so many things of greater consequence to take care of.[5]

---

[1] Letter 1009.   [2] Letter 1001.   [3] Letter 1008.

[4] Joly, lieutenant-colonel of Dragoons, taken prisoner at Blenheim.

[5] Godolphin had just received a long carping letter from Halifax complaining about the failure to appoint his brother James to the vacant Attorney-Generalship and the lack of recognition for his own efforts. 10 June, Blenheim MSS. B1-7.

1008 *Godolphin to Marlborough, 11 June 1708*

I cannot say anything more to you of our intended expedition, than that the troops will bee at the *rendesvous* by midsomer, all except the regiments from Ireland; and Sir George Bing, Sir John Jennings, and Lord Dursley with above 20 men of warr are at sea with intentions of bringing them hither by the latter end of this month.

Mr. Erle does not come to town till the 15th. When I saw him last, he did not seem to bee very sanguine in this affair. But I flatter myself, it may prove quite otherwise, if it bee well conducted.

If 39 [Marlborough] and 48 [Prince Eugene] should happen to bee soe successfull, as to gett into 43's [King of France] country, you will remember, that such a fleet as wee have now at sea, can at a very little warning bee able to carry a great quantity of provisions to any place.

1013. GODOLPHIN *to the* DUCHESS [*11 June 1708?*]

Source: Blenheim MSS. E20.
Endorsed by the Duchess: The difficultys with Mrs. Morley [the Queen] were about Lord Somers.

Treasury, Fryday morning

Before I had the favour of a letter from you, I designed (if I could find time) to wait upon you about the subject of it.[1] I had a letter yesterday from Lord Hallifax to speak with mee, and I conclude it must have been about this matter.[2] I answered him, I would come to him as soon as I went abroad this morning.

Since I had written this farr, he has been [to see me]. What he sayd to mee has pleased mee, and what I have said to him, he seemed to bee well satisfyed with, but I am very much afrayd of difficultys with Mrs. Morley [the Queen].

I don't think I shall have time to see you before you goe out to dinner, but if I cannot, I hope I shall find you at home in the evening, and show you my letter from Lord Marlborough which I received last night, the moment I left you.

1014. GODOLPHIN *to* MARLBOROUGH [*13 June 1708*]

Source: Blenheim MSS. A2-38.
Printed: Coxe, ii. 434-5.

13 June 1708

There will bee 3 posts due from you tomorrow; and Collonell Sutton telling mee he designs to goe over in the packett boat of the 18th I begin to write

---

[1] Halifax's letter of 10 June? See p. 1008, n. 5.
[2] The appointment of his brother and/or Somers.

this letter beforehand, without consequence to those I shall continue to write to you every post; because by so safe a hand I may venture to write more freely than I am willing to doe by the ordinary post.

42 [the Queen] continues so averse to everything Mr. Montgomery [Godolphin] can propose for the support of Mrs. Morley's [the Queen] affairs, that he is soe tired out of his life at present, and has so little prospect of any tolerable ease in the winter, that he has been obliged once or twice to begg of 42 [the Queen] either to follow his notions, or to dismiss him, and not lett him bear the burthen and load of other people's follys. But all this hitherto has been to no purpose, and seems to make no manner of impression.

The case with 41 [Prince George] is little better. He is sometimes uneasy at the apprehensions of what he shall meet with, but unadvisable in what is proper to prevent it; whether from his own temper, or made soe by [1]82 [George Churchill] I cannot judg. But [1]82 [George Churchill] is not, at least seems not to bee, without his own uneasynesses too, in which I always confirm him when wee talk together, and he appears to bee upon those occasions very much of my mind. But, however, he has great animositys and partialitys, and he either cannot, or will not prevail with 41 [Prince George] to doe any good.

This being the case here at present, and not very like to mend before 88's [Parliament] coming to town, I had a mind, by so safe a hand as Collonel Sutton, to prepare you to expect that it will not bee possible for 38 [Godolphin] to continue as he is, till 88's [Parliament] arrivall; unlesse it may consist with Mr. Freeman's [Marlborough] affairs to see 108 [England], and settle measures both with 38 [Godolphin] and 42 [the Queen] before the arrivall of 88 [Parliament], for at least 15 days.[1]

1015. MARLBOROUGH *to* GODOLPHIN   [*14/25 June 1708*]

Source: Blenheim MSS. A2-39.

[Terbank] June 25th 1708

I have had the favour of yours of the 8th,[2] and am very glad to find by it that the expedition under Lieutenant General Earle will be in a readyness by the end of this month, for no doubt that will occasion a deversion that will oblige the enemy to detache some troupes for their co[a]st. By the letters I have received this morning from Coblence, I fear their army will not be in a condition of marching til the begining of the next month. I did in

[1] Marlborough did not return until early in 1709, halfway through the parliamentary session which began 16 Nov. 1708. The Queen finally capitulated in October and the death of the Prince in that month broke down all her resistance for a time.

[2] Letter 1010.

a former letter acquaint you with my thoughts concerning 115 [Toulon]. I wish I may be mistaken, and that 58 [Duke of Savoy] might do that service to the Queen. I think you are very much in the right, in letting Earle have the establishement he proposes, since it will last so litle a time. Otherways thay are the same allowances I have. I should be glad you would lett mee know which are the generall officers that are to go with him, so that I may give you my opinion of such as may be proper to return with him.[1]

I do not trouble you with returning Monsieur la Martinerie's letter, which has more truth than he is acustumed to write. You know his carector is above half-madd, very vain and a lyer, so that if you can avoyde answering his letter that would be best. I write to you by the Duke of Lorrain's Minister in French, having sent him the letter under a flying seal, that he might see what I write to you, thinking it for her Majesty's service to oblige that Prince, especially since the equivelant can hardly be any otherways then at the expence of France.[2] The Electorale Prince of Hanover came to the army last Friday,[3] and has hethertoo dined every day with me. I am told he has a great equipage and intends to keep an open table. He seems to be very sivill, otherways nothing extraordinary.

The inclosed letters from Bercelona[4] I have received but this minutt.

1016. MARLBOROUGH *to the* DUCHESS   [*14/25 June 1708*]

Source: Blenheim MSS. E4.
Printed: *Private Correspondence*, i. 143-4.

[Terbank] June 25th 1708

By the disapontments that Prince Eugene has meet with in getting his army together, and which are not yett over, make me resolve to take the watters of Spaa, this camp being very quiet. But the weather is so very wett and cold that I have not taken them this morning. But as soon as wee have a litle sunshin I shall take them, for by the news I have from the Mosele I am afraid I shall continue ten days longer in this camp. You will know by the publick news that the Prince Electorale of Hanover came to the army on Friday last.[5]

---

[1] To Spain, after the descent. See p. 1021.

[2] Untraced. A similar letter was sent to Sunderland: Murray, iv. 77. The Duke of Lorraine pretended to the Montferrat, which the Emperor had promised to the Duke of Savoy. Lorraine received no equivalent at the Peace of Rastatt.

[3] 11/22 June.

[4] Stanhope's of 23 May/3 June, Chevening, Stanhope MSS., 66/2; reply, 15/26 June, Murray, iv. 83-5. Stanhope enclosed his letters of the same date to Godolphin (untraced) and to Sunderland. See B.M., Add. MS. 28055, fols. 363-4, Mahon, Appendix, lxv, reporting on the state of affairs in Spain.

[5] 11/22 June.

I have had the happyness of yours of the 8th. The declaration made by 42 [The Queen] to 148 [   ] is very surprising. What you write of 11 [Devonshire] I beleive is very trew, for I had a letter from him by which I could see he was disatisfied with 42 [the Queen].[1] He is a very honest man, and has had opertunitys to know the pains 38 [Godolphin] and 39 [Marlborough] have often taken with 42 [the Queen], to no purpose, so that I dare say he will do justice to them upon all occasion, for as much as I can obsarve, he governs himself by reason. I wish I could say so of all our acquaintance. You are so kind as to be in pain at what may happen when 48 [Prince Eugene] coms. Put your trust in God as I do, and be assured that I thinke that I can't be unhappy as long as you are kind.

1017. GODOLPHIN *to* MARLBOROUGH [*15 June 1708*]

Source: Blenheim MSS. A2-38.

June the 15 1708

I am now to acknowledg the favour of yours of the 14, 17, and 21th[2] with the severall letters and papers enclosed in them. It is very disagreable upon the whole to find the Imperialists and Germans so slow in complying with their promises and engagements to you. But one must endeavour to make the best of everything, and hope they will yett make you amends when once they begin to act; for I see plainly nothing but success will bee sufficient to keep up the hearts of 61 [Buys] and his friends. Upon the account you gave mee of the conversation you had with them at The Hague, I sent you my thoughts of that matter.[3] But since I find by this repeated instance of 61 [Buys] (who abounds extreamly in his own sence), that he desires an answer in a little more time, I enclose an answer, as from the Queen, in a paper by itself,[4] which I hope may restrain them (at least some time) from undoing themselves, and everybody else.

I think you reason very rightly upon my Lord Gallway's proposall,[5] and I agree entirely with you, that if anything of that kind bee attempted, it ought to bee in this year much rather than in the next, for many reasons; and among others, a main one is, that wee must send some of those regiments born upon the establishment of Portugall and Spain, at least as farr as Portugall by the middle of September. But I am very much afrayd, that the transporting of the Queen of Portugall[6] will disorder all the operations

---

[1] Devonshire had pressed the Queen to admit Somers to the Cabinet. See p. 959. For Devonshire's reaction to Marlborough's reply to his letter see p. 1036.
[2] Letters 1006, 1009, 1011.   [3] Letter 955.
[4] Letter 1018.   [5] An attempt upon Cadiz.
[6] Marie Anna, Duchess of Austria (1683–1754), a younger daughter of the Emperor Leopold I. She was married by proxy to the King of Portugal on 28 June/9 July. She made her way to England from where she was taken to Lisbon by an English fleet under Leake, arriving there 16/27 Oct.

of our fleets in these seas, as that of the Queen of Spain will doe in the Mediterranean.

58's [Duke of Savoy] minister continues to give assurances here, as well upon the affair of 115 [Toulon] as upon other things. I am apt to think the troubles which seem to bee breaking out in the heart of Italy, (I mean the Pope's territorys)[1] will make him still think it the more necessary for him to mannage us in England.

50 [Elector of Hanover] seems to have a fair field, if he has a heart and a head to make use of it. I am glad you have thought fitt to encourage and incite him.

Here is one *la Breconniere*, a *Suisse*, born near the *Frenche Comtè*, capable of being very usefull in those parts. I design to send him to you by the next packett,[2] that you may send him forward with a letter to 50 [Elector of Hanover].

1018. GODOLPHIN *to* MARLBOROUGH   [*15 June 1708*]

Source: Blenheim MSS. A2-38.

June 15th 1708

I have received the favour of yours of the 18th[3] with the enclosed from Monsieur Buys, which I have comunicated to the Queen, who has comanded mee to make you the following answer.[4] Viz:

That her Majesty is as desirous of a good and lasting peace, as any of her Allys can bee. But it is her Majesty's opinion, that the only way of attaining such a peace is to expect the first overtures of it from France; and not to make them on the part of the Allys, which can have no other effect, than to make the French persist in all the unreasonable offers which they have made of late. Wheras if the Allys hold firm, her Majesty thinks the time of bringing France to reason, is not farr off, since there is a very fair and reasonable prospect of a prosperous campagne, by the blessing of God, upon the army of the Allys.

---

[1] Rinaldo d'Este, Duke of Modena, brother-in-law to the Emperor, had laid claim to Ferrara as a proper part of his domains. It had been taken by Pope Clement VIII in 1597, as a fief of the Holy See, on the grounds that the rule could not pass to the bastard claimant, Cesare d'Este, as heir to the last reigning Prince. This claim together with other disputes between Pope Clement XI and the Emperor, in particular the Pope's refusal to recognize Charles III as King of Spain, led the Emperor to invade the papal domains. Imperial troops occupied Comacchio on 13/24 May, laid siege to Ferrara, and threatened the frontiers of the Papal States on both sides, with the Allied fleet blockading the ports in co-operation. The Pope formed a league of Italian princes to support him and a desultory phase followed which lasted until 4/15 Jan. 1709 when the Pope recognized Charles III as King of Spain. Hans Kramer, *Habsburg und Rom in den Jahren 1708-1709* (Innsbruck, 1936) and Marcus Landau, *Rom, Wien, Neapel* (Leipzig, 1885).

[2] See p. 639, n. 2.   [3] Letter 1009.

[4] See p. 1012.

1019. GODOLPHIN *to* MARLBOROUGH   [*17 June 1708*]

Source: Blenheim MSS. A2–38.

June 17th 1708

I send this by la Breconniere[1] who thinks he can bee very usefull to 50 [Elector of Hanover] in any design upon the Frenche Comté, or even in Dauphinè, if there were occasion.

In case you have time to speak with him, you will best judg by the accounts he gives you, what may bee proper for you to write by him to 50 [Elector of Hanover]. Mr. Spanheim recommends him much, and says he has great acquaintance and correspondence in those parts, and that he may bee entirely trusted. My Lord Sunderland is very fond of sending him to you, and all I can say more upon it is that I wish he may deserve the £150 which I have given him upon this occasion.

1020. MARLBOROUGH *to* GODOLPHIN   [*17/28 June 1708*]

Source: Blenheim MSS. A2–39.
Printed: Coxe, ii. 457–8 (inc.).

[Terbank] June 28th 1708

I had not time by the last post, to do any more, but inclose the letters that came by expresse from Barcelona. What I have from thence are very pressing for a squadron to be left this winter in the Mediteranien. The Dutch are so much convinced that the Service requiers it, that if measures be taken in time thay will make no difficulty for their proportion. By what I hear, if 16 shipes were left, that number would be sufficient. The proposion for England would amount only to ten, so that I hope and beg you will lose no time in pressing the Prince's Councell to give the necessary orders for this squadron; for without it the whole expence made in Spain is to no purpose. Measures must be emediatly taken with Holande, so that thay may be preparing their stores. If thay refuse to joyne with you in this, you may take it as a decleration of their thoughts of 81 [peace] this winter, for thay know we can not suceed in Spain but by having a squadron all the winter there.[2] By letters I received last night from 48 [Prince Eugene],[3] he gives me hopes of his being in a condition of begining his march, either tomorrow or the day following, and that he will the night before his march send a copie of my letter of the 24th to 50 [Elector of Hanover]. The inclosed is a copie of my letter.[4] 48 [Prince Eugene] thinkes 50 [Elector of Hanover] will not approve

---

[1] See p. 1019.   [2] See p. 976.
[3] 14/25 June, Blenheim MSS. A2–36; reply, 16/27 June, Murray, iv. 86.
[4] To Eugene, in Murray, iv. 76. See also Marlborough's letter of 19/30 May, in Murray, iv. 37–8. Both letters were written for the same purpose, to be shown to the Elector of Hanover

of his march, which is the reason of his not acquainting him soner with my letter, so that he might not have itt in his power to hinder the march, which he thinkes otherwais he would do. That which gives me the greatest uneasiness is that I find 48 [Prince Eugene] thinkes that their horse cannot joine 39 [Marlborough] in lesse then 10 days, and that their foot must have 14 or 15 days. If thay cannot make a greater expedition, I fear the horse of 49 [Duke of Berwick] will gett before them, which I have write to the Prince by expresse this morning. According to the answere I shall receive from him I shall give the necessary orders for eight days bread, which I shall take with me, when I leave this camp, my designe being to engage their army if possible, or to oblige them to retier to such a post as that I may have it in my power to make the siege of Charleroy. But if thay take such a camp as will cover Charleroy, I shall then be obliged to stay for foot, before I begine my march for Flanders, since the disapointements 48 [Prince Eugene] has meet with has lost us above a month, and that the enemy know to[o] much of our designe. The best thing we can hope for is that we may be able to oblige them to some action, for it is the opinion of 48 [Prince Eugene], as well as of 210 [Marlborough], that thay must not expect any ease from 50 [Elector of Hanover], which is a misfortune, but such a one as I know not how to remedie. We were in hopes to have heard that the Elector of Hanover's army had passed the Rhin, the French being at this time very weake on that side. The letters from that army dose not come til tomorrow, but our letters from Francford says that thay will not passe that river til Prince Eugene['s] army begins to act. The inclosed is from Mr. Laws,[1] who was secretary to Mr. Stepney, and is a very hopfull young man.

1021. MARLBOROUGH *to the* DUCHESS   [? *17/28 June 1708*]

Source: Blenheim MSS. G1-4.

[Terbank]

[fragment only]

... see plainly that what is proposed by 38 [Godolphin], 39 [Marlborough], and 240 [Lady Marlborough] is the only way for her to govern, with quiet and safety. Should you take any other methode it would serve only to make her [the Queen] more obstinat, and shy of speaking to you even when she changes her mind. As for 38 [Godolphin] and 39 [Marlborough], thay must

and to reconcile him to Prince Eugene's march to join Marlborough in the Low Countries. The second letter is translated by Coxe, ii. 447–8 with some commentary on Marlborough's plans.

[1] John Lawes, secretary to Stepney; in charge of affairs between departure of Stepney and arrival of Cadogan 1707; appointed Secretary at Brussels 1708; remained until 1712, managing affairs in the absence of Cadogan and Orrery (1711–12).

persist in pressing her and I do assure you I shall take all occasion of letting her see her trew intirest.

The French being stronger then we I am using my endeavours to hasten the march of Prince Eugene, which will I hope put us in a condition of acting offensively.

Lett me have the continuance of your estime and love, and I am happy.

1022. GODOLPHIN *to* MARLBOROUGH [*18 June 1708*]

Source: Blenheim MSS. A2-38.
Printed: Coxe, ii. 437 (inc.).

June 18 1708

Since my last of the 14th,[1] acknowledging your letters of 3 posts which wee received together, I have written to you by Collonell Sutton,[2] who goes over with this pacquett; also a letter by la Breconniere[3] who has promised to goe at the same time.

The wind has been northeast these 2 days, so I hope to have a letter from you before the post goes out tonight. In the meantime I begin to trouble you with an account that your commands are obeyed in behalf of Monsieur *Joly*, and the Queen will give her orders for sending back all her own subjects who are here upon their paroles, as you desire.

Yesterday arrived a Lisbon mail; the letters are very old. I intend to send you mine from my Lord Gallway. You will see by it, that he cannot bring those people to any reason. He seems to think and really soe doe I, that they have personally a mind to bee ridd of him. However I think wee must make one tryall more before he bee recalled, and I should think speaking very plain to their envoyé here, and telling him the Queen will not send any more troops thither, unless she can have a separate army under the command of a generall of her own, might gayn this poynt. But they seem pretty easy in Portugall at present knowing their army to bee superiour. Though I must own to you I am afrayd the Marquis de Bay[4] is soe much a better officer, that the last news by the way of France, of the 2 armyes being so very near, gives me a good deal of pain for our friends there; and I could bee very well content this campagne might pass on that side without any fighting. For though the Portugheses should have the advantage, they would not follow it, as they ought to doe; but if they should bee beaten, the others would follow them to Lisbon.

Sir John Leak's taking the provisions for the Duke of Orleans's army was very seasonable, and will hinder him from being able to doe anything before the other troops come from Italy, and then 'tis to bee hoped our army will

---

[1] Letter 1017.
[2] Letter 1014.
[3] Letter 1019.
[4] Alexander, Marquis of Bay (1650–1715), a Spanish lieutenant-general who served throughout the war in Spain. Appointed governor of Estramadura in 1705 he was largely responsible for preventing its conquest by the Allies.

bee superiour. But I am much afraid the Queen of Spain's comming to Barcelona may prove as unseasonable, and make that court think of nothing but divertisements, instead of following their advantage.

I was in hopes when I began this letter that I should have heard from you by this houre; but now I give it over.

The letters wee have today from Scotland are full of the heats and animosity of that country about the election of the peers. I have no mind to trouble you with the particulars, (for they could bee endless). Besides, since you must needs see very often, both the Duke of Argyll, Lord Stairs, and Lieutenant Generall Ross, you cannot easily avoyd hearing what passes there upon this troublesome occasion.[1]

1023. MARLBOROUGH *to the* DUCHESS   [20 June/1 July 1708]

Source: Blenheim MSS. E4.
Printed: *Private Correspondence*, i. 144-5, with the balance in Coxe, ii. 435.

[Terbank] Jully the 1st 1708

Yours of the tenth from St. Albans came when my last letters were sealled, so that I could not then thank you for them. I hope to have another letter from you before tomorrow night's post. I am glad the windoes you have made in the drawing room at St. Albans are so well done as to please you. My heart being sett upon having some litle quiet at Woodstock, if possible, I shall not be fond of doing anything anywhere else but what is of necessity. It is most certaine that Mr. Gapp should not have been left with the power of Justice [of the Peace] in the town. I beleive it proceded from the ignorance of Lord Essex,[2] for I beleive that depends upon him. In my opinion what you write of Vanbrugh is very right, and I should think that any reasonable man would be satisfied, if you could find a proper opertunity of letting him know them; for bysides the reasons you give against a pentions, it is more for his intirest to have patience til something happens which may be lasting.[3]

Your desiring to know which is best, of fivety yeares or three lives, I should think the term of yeares to be much the best, but those things are good or bad according to your own thoughts, so that you are the properist judge.[4] Besides, you know I have no great opinion of this project, for I am very confident that

---

[1] See p. 968.   [2] As Lord-Lieutenant of Herts.
[3] See Maynwaring to the Duchess [15 June], in *Private Correspondence*, i. 153-7. Vanbrugh was in severe financial troubles, his activities as an impresario having saddled him with heavy obligations. He apparently asked the Duchess for a pension in recompense for his labours at Woodstock.
[4] The Duchess's grant of land in St. James's Park passed the Great Seal on 25 Oct. The lease was made for a period of fifty years, at a rent of 5s. per annum. The Duchess also had to pay £2,000 to the survivor of the trustees of the previous lessee. (See p. 219, n. 2.) A new grant was made in 1709 to incorporate additional land required for her house. (*C.T.B.,1708*, XXII. ii. 379-80; *1709*, XXIII. ii. 191-2.)

in time you will be sensible that this building will cost you much more mony then the thing is worth; for you may build a better appartment then you now have, but you will never have so many conveniencys as you have in your lodgings, and you may depend upon itt that it will cost you double the mony of their first estemat.[1] It is not a proper place for a great house, and I am sure when you have built a litle one you will not like itt, so that if you have not sett your heart upon itt, I should advise you would think well of itt; for it is certainly more advisable to bye a house then to build one. Though we are in the month of Jully I am now writting by a fyer, the weather being very weat and cold, which I am very sorry for, since it must be very inconvenient to Prince Eugen's army, who are now on their march. God knows what we shall be able to do when we join. I am sure of nothing so much, as that I earnestly long for the doing something that may putt an end to this warr, so that I might have the happyness of being in quiet with you; for were this warr ended, nothing could persuade me to torment myself with business and absance.

I have received yours which should have been dated the 15th, by which I see the intentions of 89 [the Whigs].[2] I need make no other answere then what I have already assured you, that 39 [Marlborough] will be glad to strenghen them, but never to devide them.

1024. MARLBOROUGH *to* GODOLPHIN   [*21 June/2 July 1708*]

Source: Blenheim MSS. A2-39.
Printed: Coxe, ii. 458 (inc.).

[Terbanc] Jully 2d 1708

Since my last I have had the favour of yours of the 11th and 15th.[3] By the first I see the uneasy circomstances you labor under, and I do assure myself that you do me the justice to beleive that for your sake, as well as for 42 [the Queen], I would chearfully ventur my life to make you two of one mind; for unless that can be, it were quieter and better [for me to] be under grownd. I beg you to beleive that my love and zeal for you two is such that I should not vallu the difficultys I meet with here abroad.

I have by this night's post sent yours of the 15th to 61 [Buys]. What answere he makes you shall be sure to have. I am told that he is so possest with the thoughts of 81 [peace], that he could not forbear saying latly, to an honest man who was not of his opinion, that if we had not good success this campagne, thay must have 81 [peace]. I am told that 74 [Raby] presses to be sworn of the [Privy] Councell.[4] I should think considering his temper,

---

[1] See p. 1307.
[2] They threatened to go into opposition to the Court. See the letter of Maynwaring referred to on the preeeding page and [16 June?] in *Private Correspondence*, i. 150-3.
[3] Letters 1012, 1017, 1018.   [4] He was not made Privy Councillor until 23 June 1711.

that reward would be more seasonable when he has finished his foraigne business, for he is of so craving a natur, that at his return he will be angry if something else be not done for him. I beleive if you write in time to Vienna you may order it so that the Queen of Portugale coming to Holand may be so timed as not to hinder any service the fleet is to do this summer. Besides, a very few shipes might serve, when the Dunkerk squadron can't be at sea. Sir John Lake's orders from the King of Spain is not to stay for the Queen if she bee not ready, but to make all the expedition possible with the troupes, so that I hope thay will come time enough to hinder the taking of Tortose, the French letters saying possativly that the Duke of Orleans will attack itt, and that it was to be invested by the 15th.

You know I have in all tims been inclined to think Sir Rowland Guyne an honest, indiscrit man, which is the occasion of my troubling you with his[1] and Mr. Robison's letter.[2] I do veryly beleive he dose sincerly wish all happyness to the Queen, and that he dose hartely repent him of his indiscretion, so that I hope her Majesty will forgive him. I do not mean that he aught now to be imployed. La Breconnier which you mention I beleive is a French man and not a Suisse. I hope you will not send him over, for if the business of Franch Comte should be attempted, that matter will be left to the management of a major generall in the Emperor's service, and I am very confident he will not trust this man. So that I beg 6 [Sunderland] may dispose of him some otherway. You may remember he gott mony last summer, and he has no other thought but the doing the same for this yeare, it having been his constant practice the last warr. I am the more sensible of this, having dayly sollicitations of this kind.

By the time this coms to you, I hope Lieutenant General Earle will be ready to embarke. He is a brave man. However, you must incorage him.

Pray make my court to Lady Hariott, and assure her, though I do not write, I am very much hers.

1025. GODOLPHIN *to* MARLBOROUGH [*22 June 1708*]

Source: Blenheim MSS. A2-38.

June 22, 1708

I have the favour of yours of the 25th and 28th,[3] with the enclosed from Prince Eugene, in which I see a great deal of good will to joyn you as fast as he can. But the delays have been so great at Vienna, that 'tis impossible but the French must bee aware of your intentions, and consequently are not like

---

[1] 15/26 June, Blenheim MSS. B1-15. Pleas for Marlborough's protection. He sent another petition to Godolphin for the Queen as he received no answer from the last.
[2] 15/26 June, Blenheim MSS., B1-15, enclosing the above and recommending his case.
[3] Letters 1015, 1020.

to bee much surprised, though I hope they may not bee able to prevent the execution of your designs.

The same delays have (I doubt) been the occasion of retarding the Duke of Savoy's motions, which are more backward (as well as others) than were to bee wished. However, I can't but hope he will endeavour to doe somthing considerable, since (as Mr. Stanhope observes in his letter) the charge of those troops now with him, will never bee allowed another year, unless they appear to have been very usefull in this. And as I intend to press this argument to Comte Briancon, with all the earnestness I can, so (I think) it will have the more effect, if you please to doe the same to Comte Maffei.

I am sorry for the postscript in your last, that the Elector of Hannover has resolved not to pass the Rhyne till he hears that Prince Eugene is in motion, because when he does hear it, I doubt he will like that motion so little, as not to doe it at all; which may prove very inconvenient, in case the Duke of Savoy should enter Dauphinè, for then the Elector's being on that side of the Rhyne would be a very great distraction to the enemy.

I wish Lieutenant Generall Erle's expedition may oblige the French to make some detachment as you seem to think; but I rather believe they will depend upon their militia for the guard of their coasts.

I have pressed the Prince's counsell with all possible earnestness for the wintering of a squadron in the Mediterranean. They will putt their thoughts of it in writing which shall bee sent to Holland.[1] But the great question upon it is, how they shall then bee safe from the insults of the French att Thoulon, with a superior force. For my part, I cannot see any security for such a squadron (as you propose) in the ports of Italy, while the French have Tholoun; but if the King of Spain can gett Port Maon, a squadron may winter there in safety. I have written to Mr. Stanhope[2] to this effect, and the necessary stores shall bee providing here in view of it.

1026. GODOLPHIN *to* MARLBOROUGH   [*24 June 1708*]

Source: Blenheim MSS. A2-38.

June 24th 1708

My last was of the 22th,[3] in which I answered yours of the 25th and 28th; and there being very little appearance of hearing from you again before this

[1] In May Sunderland wrote Stanhope: 'As to what you have so often mentioned about the wintering of a squadron in the Mediterranean, everybody here is of the same mind with you as to the usefulness of it. . . . It has been referred to the Prince's Council ever since I received your first letter on that subject, but they have not yet made any report' (14 May, P.R.O., S.P. 104/208, pp. 211–12). On 23 June Sunderland received a report from the Admiralty which said wintering a fleet in the Mediterranean was practicable only if Port Mahon could be taken. Sunderland sent the news on to Marlborough on 25 June (Blenheim MSS. B1-1). Godolphin urged Stanhope to make the attempt in his letter (see below), Stanhope acted on his advice and was successful.
[2] 22 June, Chevening, Stanhope MSS. 66/7.   [3] Letter 1025.

post, I shall only trouble you with the enclosed packett from my Lord Gallway,[1] under a flying seal, as he sent it to mee. This will give you a very particular account of the position of affairs there; and you will see by it, that he insists still upon having the 8 battalions sent; which will goe out with Mr. Erle,[2] with orders to goe thither afterwards, in case ther bee no occasion more pressing for their service on this side.

Lieutenant General Erle takes Seymor for his major generall; Gorge and Wynn[3] will bee the brigadiers. Most of the collonells and (I doubt) of their soldiers too, are but raw, and I find Erle's greatest dependance is upon 600 marines, if they should have anything to doe; but in such a sort of expedition, there is not much appearance of that.

Upon 25th June

Talking with Mr. Erle since I had written this last paragraph I find Seymour goes as lieutenant generall, Gorge as major generall, and Wynn as a brigadier.

The winds have been so cross here, for our shipps to goe to Ireland that I doubt the 2 regiments[4] expected from thence will not come so soon as wee hoped.

The Queen seems resolved to goe to Windsor tomorrow. I don't trouble you with any home news, not having any that will please you, and I am sure you have too many things where you are, to make you uneasy without any addition from mee.

1027. GODOLPHIN *to* MARLBOROUGH   [*28 June 1708*]

Source: Blenheim MSS. A2-38.

St James's June 28, 1708

Tomorrow there will bee two posts due from you, and being in doubt whether wee shall have them before this packett goes, I begin to tell you today, that since my last wee have had fresh letters from Lisbon of the 15/26th. I need not trouble you with many particulars since I enclose a letter from my Lord Gallway to you,[5] unsealed, as he sent it to mee.

By the account he gives, it looks to mee as if the Portughese might have gained some advantage upon them, if they had not thought it necessary,

---

[1] Untraced.   [2] On the descent.

[3] Owen Wynne (died 1737), served in Royal Irish Dragoons (commanded by his brother, Brigadier-General James Wynne), under William III; continued under Ross who succeeded Wynne in 1695; lieutenant-colonel commanding at Blenheim; colonel, Regiment of Foot, 1705; brigadier-general 1706.

[4] Lepell's and Munden's.

[5] Untraced; reply, 19/30 July, Murray, iv. 136–7. Galway gave details for his plan to attack Cadiz in the autumn campaign and expressed concern that the Portuguese troops taken prisoner at Almanza were still not exchanged.

to draw their army into order of battell, which gave the enemy time to retire. My Lord Gallway is very pressing that the troops should bee hastned thither, and I think, he is in the right, if they intend to doe anything materiall in this autumn. But what I fear, is, that when they have the troops there, they will doe nothing, and wee shall lose the use which might have been made of them, on this side, in the meantime.

Our regiments expected from Ireland are not yett come,[1] and if that expedition bee delayed above 10 days or a fortnight, I doubt, wee shall bee too much streightned in time for the severall views wee have before us. I take it for granted, that whenever the Queen of Portugall comes to Portsmouth the troops must goe thither, under the same convoy with her Majesty, so that they cannot bee at liberty to act on this side, in any days after her arrivall.

Bergeyck had worked out a plan for retaking Bruges and Ghent by the French with the aid of French sympathizers among the inhabitants. Ghent was the key to the whole waterways system in Flanders, and Bruges controlled the canals to the Channel and Ostend so that the two towns were of great strategic importance.[2]

On the 22 June/3 July Vendôme sent a detachment towards Enghien, ostensibly to forage. The next day this force, under Grimaldi, made a dash for Ghent which it reached early on the morning of the 24th/5th. The town, guarded only by citizens, immediately surrendered to the first arrivals. As Grimaldi crossed the Dender at Aalst on 23 June/4 July a second advance party under Count de la Motte crossed the French lines at Comines and headed for Bruges, which also capitulated without giving opposition in the early hours of the 24th/5th.[3]

Vendôme ordered his main army to move at seven in the evening of 4 July. Crossing the Senne at Tubize on the morning of the 5th. Continuing with only a short rest the French crossed the Dender at Ninove and camped on the 6th at Lede.

On the 23rd/4th Marlborough received reports of the several French movements and put his own army in motion at two in the morning of the 24th/5th. At noon he ordered Bothmar to cross the Dender at Dendermonde to protect the Pays-de-Waes when he received notice of Grimaldi's crossing at Aalst. His main concern was Brussels, however, and he directed the main body of his army to a camp west of Anderlecht to await further evidence of French intentions. When Vendôme halted momentarily at Gooik, hard by Marlborough's right at St. Kwintens Lennik, Allied intelligence postulated an attack when in fact Vendôme was only protecting

---

[1] Lepell's and Munden's for the descent.   [2] See the map in Churchill, ii. 348.

[3] For a discussion of the charge of ill-treatment of the Flemish by the Dutch which encouraged them to give up their towns to the French, see A. J. Veenendaal, 'Opening Phase of Marlborough's Campaign of 1708', *E.H.R.*, 65. 34–48. But see also p. 1060, below.

his main force while they crossed the Dender. Too late, early on the morning of the 25th/6th, Marlborough discovered the French scheme, and he moved his own troops again to Asse for the better protection of Brussels.

1028. MARLBOROUGH *to* GODOLPHIN   [*28 June/9 July 1708*]

Source: Blenheim MSS. A2-39.
Printed: Coxe, ii. 466–7.

[Asse] Jully 9th 1708

I should answere two of your letters,[1] but the treachery of Gand, continual marching, and some letters I have received from England, has so vexed me, that I was yesterday in so great a feaver that the doctor would have persuaded me to have gone to Bruxelles, but I thank God I am now better, and by the next post I hope to answere your letters. 116 [the States] has used this country so ill, that I no ways doubt but all the towns in this country will play us the same trick as Gand have done, whenever thay have it in their power. I have been desired by the deputys to write that her Majesty would be pleased to lett the troupes now in the Ile of Wayt,[2] be sent for their relief to Ostend, so that it is likely you will be desired the same thing by Monsieur Vriberg; but I hope the Queen will continu in the resolution of imploying those troupes as she first designed, for I think that will be much more for hers and the nation's honour. But Vriberg must not know my opinion. I beg with my humble duty you will make my excuses to the Queen for my not acknowlidging the honour of hers[3] til the next post. I am so extreamly troubled at what has been write me concerning my brother George and Mr. Walpole, that I beg you will acquaint mee, with what you know of that matter.[4] Having made a halt of five hours, I am continuing my

1 Letters 1022, 1026.

2 The forces for the descent, assembled on the Isle of Wight.

3 18, 22 June, Brown, pp. 249–50. Sunderland had supported the Squadrone candidates for the representative peers to be chosen in Scotland, in opposition to those put up by the Court (p. 968, n. 1). Marlborough wrote the Queen that Sunderland had spread word that the Queen favoured the Squadrone candidates. This so angered Anne that she was ready to demand Sunderland's resignation. Marlborough did not answer these letters until 22 July/2 Aug. (in Coxe, ii. 505–6) when he implored her, successfully, to take no action until his return.

4 The affair concerned the disposal of Lillingston's Regiment of Foot to his lieutenant-colonel, James Jones, which was effective 2 June (see p. 996). Marlborough heard that Harley was responsible for the grant to Jones and wrote to George Churchill to this effect. Churchill in turn told the Queen and the Prince that Walpole had written to Marlborough that he (Walpole) and Harley had recommended Jones to the Prince, and that Walpole had publicly admitted it. The Queen was incensed and expressed her anger to Godolphin. Walpole responded that he had never heard the man's name and demanded an apology from George Churchill. Walpole to Marlborough, 22 June, W. Coxe, *Memoirs of the Life and Administration of Sir Robert Walpole, Earl of Orford* (London, 1798), ii. 9–11; Lewis to Harley, 26 June, H.M.C., *Portland MSS.*, iv. 494.

march, as I intend to do all the night, in hopes of getting to the camp of Lessings before the enemy, who made yesterday a detachement of 16 thousand men for the investing of Audenar. If I get the camp of Lessings before them, I hope to be able to hinder the siege, being resolved to ventur everything rather then lose that place.

Lessings the 10th

Mr. Cardonel telling me that by a mistake the letters were not gone, I have opened mine to lett you know that the head of the army is gott hether. I have received advice this morning from the governor of Audenar that he was invested on both sides of his town yesterday morning. I should think myself happy, since I am gott into this camp, if thay continu in their resolution of carrying on that siege.[1]

1029. MARLBOROUGH *to the* DUCHESS   [*28 June/9 July 1708*]

Source: Blenheim MSS. E4.
Printed: *Private Correspondence*, i. 146.
Addressed: For the Dutchesse of Marlborough.

[Asse] Jully the 9th 1708

Collonel Sutton being come, I have three of your letters to answere. But the treachery of Gand and the parpetual marching I have had, has made me so very uneasy, that I have sleep very litle these three last night, [so] that I am so hote, that I must beg of you not to answere yours til the next post. We are to continu our march al this night, in hopes of gaining a camp which may be of use to us, for I can't be att ease til I regain Gand, or make the enemy pay dear for itt. I am with all my heart and soull yours.

The army rested only briefly at Lessines for by 1 o'clock on the morning of 30 June/ 11 July Cadogan was off to Oudenaarde to bridge the Scheldt for the army which was to follow. The French meanwhile, on an unintentional converging path, planned a leisurely crossing at Gavere, sending out an advance party to forage under Biron. At three in the afternoon Cadogan attacked Biron's forward battalions. From that time on the battle waged ever fiercer as both sides poured in reinforcements as fast as they could be brought up. When darkness fell the miscalculations of Vendôme had resulted in his defeat and disgrace and he gave the order for the

[1] Marlborough wanted to bring the French to battle. When they laid siege to Oudenaarde, only 22 kilometres from Marlborough's camp at Lessines, and did not move further west (which they had contemplated) the French gave Marlborough an opportunity to bring them to battle in less than a day's march.

uncommitted troops to retire as best they could to Ghent. The fortunes of the Allies, shaken by the betrayal of Ghent and Bruges, were once again raised to new heights by the daring and luck of their commander.

1030. MARLBOROUGH *to* GODOLPHIN   [*1/12 July 1708*]

Source: Blenheim MSS. A2-39.
Printed: Coxe, ii. 480–1.
Addressed: To my Lord Treasurer, Whitehall.

[Oudenaarde] Jully 12th 1708

I have been so very uneasy, and in so great a hurry for some days, that I should not be able to write, were I not supported by the good sucess we had yesterday. The particulars you will have from Lord Stairs, who will give you this. You know his pretentions[1] and the friendshipe I have for him, and I will own to you, that I hope her Majesty may have by this messidge an excuse for others, if she is pleased to distinguish him at this time. I must ever acknowlidge the goodness of God in the success he was pleased to give us, for I beleive Lord Stairs will tel you that thay were in as strong a post as is possible to be found, but you know when I left England I was possitivly resolved to endeavour by all means a battel, thinking nothing else could make the Queen's busines go on well. This reason only made me ventur the battel yesterday, otherways I did give them to[o] much advantage; but the good of the Queen and my country shall always be preferred by me, before any personall concern, for I am very sensible if I had miscaried I should have been blamed. I hope I have given such a blow to their foot that thay will not be able to fight anymore this yeare. My head eakes so terribly that I must say no more.

1031. MARLBOROUGH *to the* DUCHESS   [*1/12 July 1708*]

Source: Blenheim MSS. E4.
Printed: Churchill, ii. 382.
Addressed: For the Dutchesse of Marlborough.

[Oudenaarde] Jully the 12th 1708

I have neither sperits nor tim to answere your three last letters, this being to bring the good news of a battaile wee had yesterday, in which it pleased God to give us at last the advantage. Our foot on both sides having been all ingaged has occasioned much blood, but I thank God the English have suffered less then any of the other troupes, none of our English horse having ingaged. I do, and you must give thankes to God for his goodness in

---

[1] For a British peerage. See pp. 1028 and 1200 for the reason he did not receive it.

protecting and making me the instrument of so much happyness to the Queen and nation, if she will please to make use of itt. Farwell my dear soull.

1032. GODOLPHIN *to* MARLBOROUGH   [*2 July 1708*]

Source: Blenheim MSS. A2-38.

July 2d 1708

Three posts are now due from Holland but the wind continues still so contrary that I don't hope to hear from you before this night's packett goes out.

The same cross winds will not suffer our shipps to gett to Ireland, and consequently the 2 regiments[1] are there still; which makes mee resolve to propose tomorrow, that the other 9 may bee embarked, and the expedition proceed without those 2. And as soon as the Queen of Portugall shall arrive at Spithead, it seems (at present) designed, to recall them from the coast of France, and to send 8 of the 9 regiments under the same convoy to Portugall with her Majesty.

Wee have had very hott alarms from Jersey and Guernsey, that the French squadron at Brest was come to St. Malo's with landmen on board, and that they had a design upon those islands. But there was nothing in it, (I think) more than a pannick fear, of which all our people seem to bee a good deal more susceptible ever since the late intended invasion than they were before.[2] And wee have often jealousy's and rumours spredd, that all the transports which Monsieur Fourbin carryed to Scotland with him, are still at Dunkirk, in view of renewing that attempt, when they see a proper opportunity. This I believe may bee true. But my hope is, they will never see that opportunity, and that wee shall not bee troubled with them again. For nothing is more certain than that generally the people of Scotland are dissatisfyed, and ready to embrace any new schemes that can bee offered to them.

1033. MARLBOROUGH *to* GODOLPHIN   [*5/16 July 1708*]

Source: Blenheim MSS. A2-39.
Printed: Coxe, ii. 484.

[Wervik] Jully 10 1708

My blood is so extreamly heated, that I must refer you to what Mr. Cardonell will write to the Secretary's office[3] of what has passed since my Lord Stairs

---

[1] Lepell's and Munden's, for the descent.
[2] On 29 June Boyle wrote to Marlborough (Blenheim MSS. B1-1): 'Lord Sunderland received this morning an express from Lieutenant Colonel Collier, deputy governor of Jersey', that they were in great apprehension of an invasion from France. He enclosed a copy of Collier's letter. On 2 July Boyle reported that by another express Collier wrote the cause of their alarm was only some French merchantman with privateers.   [3] In Murray, iv. 112-13.

left the army. If we had been six hours laitter, I am afraid we should not have been able to have forced these lins,[1] for Monsieur de La Mott was gott with his litle army to Ypres, and the Duke of Berwick was at the same time at Lille. We are now masters of marching where we please, but can make no siege til we are masters of Gand, from whence only we can have our canon.[2] The camp the French are now in behind the canal of Bridges, makes them intierly masters of Gand and Bridges. But at the same time thay leave all France open to us, which is what I flatter myself the King of France and his Councell will never suffer, so that I hope by Thursday[3] Monsieur de Vandome will receive orders from court not to continue in the camp wher he is, from whence we are not able to force him but by famin. I am taking measures for the attacking Gand as soon as he marches, and if the Duke of Vandomé's resolution of staying wher he is be approved of at court, I shall then endeavour to cutt off all provissions, as much as possible, from going to him. For if he stays and we can ruin that army, France is undone; but if thay can subsist longer then we can, thay will be able by that to hinder us from doing anything considerable for want of our canon. Upon the whole, the hazard to them is so very great that I can't think the King of France will ventur it. Four or five days will let us see their intentions. In the meantime, I shall take what rest I can in order to be the better able to serve, for att this minut my head is so very hott, that I am obliged to leave of[f] writting.

Prince Eugen's foot came last night to Bruxelles. My humble duty to the Queen.

1034. MARLBOROUGH *to the* DUCHESS   [5/16 *July 1708*]

Source: Blenheim MSS. E4.
Printed: Coxe, ii. 483-4.

[Wervik] Jully 16, 1708

I hope before this you have had the news by Lord Stairs of the good success we had on last Wensday.[4] I have been obliged ever since to be in perpetual motion, so that I am a good deal out of order. I was in good hopes that the dilligence I have made in getting into the French country, for I am now behind their lins, would have obliged them to have abandoned Gand, but as yet it has not had that effect. But on the contrary, Monsieur de Vandome says he will sacrifise a strong garison rather then abandon that town, which if he keeps his word, he will give me a great deal of trouble; for til we are masters of Gand we can have no canon. The governor of Audenar, to whom we sent our prisoners, assures me that the number is above seven thousand,

---

[1] Between Warneton and Ypres.
[2] By the waterways which Ghent controlled. See pp. 1034-5.
[3] 8/19 July.   [4] 30 June/11 July.

besides seven hundred and six officers. We have had a great many killed and wou[n]ded on both sides.[1] Thay were forced to leave the greatest part of theirs on the place where thay faught. We did take care to send all ours into Audnar, after which I ordered such of the French as were yett alive should be carryed into the town. I have had no account of what that number may be, but it being a weet night I beleive a great many of them suffered very much. If we had been so happy as to have had two hours more daylight, I beleive we should have made an end of this warr. The Duke of Barwick came to Lille the day before yesterday, but his troupes will not be here this three or four days. Those of Prince Eugene came last night to Bruxelles, so that both our armys will be abundantly recruted. However, I beleive the French will be carefull not to ventur anymore this yeare. But the greatest mischief thay can do is to ventur all for the preserving of Gand. I shall labor with pleasur the rest of this campagne in hopes it may be the last, so that I may be blessed with you and quietness.

1035. GODOLPHIN *to* MARLBOROUGH   [*6 July 1708*]

Source: Blenheim MSS. A2-38.
Printed: *Private Correspondence*, ii. 272-5.

Windsor 6 July 1708

It is not easy to express to you the joy wee had here yesterday upon my Lord Stair's arrivall. You must endeavour to conceive it, by your own satisfaction at Oudenard, which could not bee greater than ours upon this happy occasion. The Queen will order a publick thanksgiving as soon as possible, but it will require near 2 months to give the necessary notice over England and Scotland.

My Lord Stair's pretensions[2] are very just and reasonable, but the Queen is under such difficultys in that matter by the resolution openly declared already of contesting the Duke of Queensberry's admission in the House of Lords,[3] that till it bee seen what success that will have, I have endeavoured to satisfy my Lord Stairs that it would not bee advisable, neither for himself, nor for the Queen, to press it at this time, farther than the assurance of her Majesty's favorable intentions which she was very ready to give him.

You may doe mee the right to observe I never trouble you with storyes from hence being sensible I ought not to make you uneasy, upon whom all our hopes and safetys depend. But since you require an account of the noise about [1]82 [George Churchill] and Mr. Walpool,[4] I cannot but think he was very much to blame in that whole affair from the beginning to the end. But nobody is able to give you so exact an account of the particulars as [1]85

---

[1] The French had 3,000 killed and wounded. The Allies took 6,000 to 7,000 prisoners. Their own losses were not quite 3,000. Wijn, VIII. ii. 313.

[2] For a British peerage.   [3] See p. 992, n. 2.   [4] See p. 1023.

[James Craggs, Sr.], who was himself a witness to the most materiall part of it. I must need add upon this occasion that [1]82 [George Churchill] does certainly contribute very much to keep up both in 41 [Prince George] and in 42 [the Queen] the naturall, but very inconvenient averseness they have to 89 [the Whigs] in generall, and to Sir George Bing in particular, though Mr. Montgomery [Godolphin] took all imaginable pains to reconcile them, and to give promises and assurances to each other; and nothing is more certain than that the generall dislike of [1]82 [George Churchill] in that station is stronger than ever, and much harder to bee supported. But nothing less than your express command should have made mee say so much to you upon so disagreable a subject.

I make no doubt but you will judg best yourself how to prosecute the victory you have gained with most advantage. But if (as my Lord Stairs hinted to mee) you follow your first thoughts of going to *Lisle*, I hope you may bee able to make the siege of Dunkirk before the end of the year, even though it should bee late. The rains I should think would not doe much harm among those sand hills, and wee could help you by sea with all manner of provisions for the army. Forgive this hint from mee, since nothing can contribute so much to give us a quiett winter, as this would doe, the late attempt upon Scotland having very much unsettled our people's minds; and that part of the kingdome is still in all the ferment and discontent imaginable.

Wee reckon here, that it will not bee possible for the enemy to stay in the Pays de Waes, and consequently wee hope Gant and Bruges must fall to you again without your losing any time about them. If 50 [Elector of Hanover] and 58 [Duke of Savoy] would now think fitt to exert themselves upon the encouragement of this success, I don't see how it would bee possible for 43 [King of France] to weather even this present campagne. But perhaps they are not so desirous of a speedy end of this warr, as some of their neighbours. But I will not trouble you with more of my reflections till I know more certainly what measures you intend to take, for the rest of this campagne, and where the enemyes propose to make their next stand.

1036. GODOLPHIN *to* MARLBOROUGH [6 *July 1708*]

Source: Blenheim MSS. A2-38.
Printed: Coxe, ii. 500.
Addressed: To his Grace the Duke of Marlborough.

Windsor July 6, at night

I have troubled you this morning with so long a letter[1] that I shall only make use of this opportunity of enclosing a letter from the Queen,[2] to tell you,

---

[1] Letter 1035.
[2] 6 July, in Brown, p. 252, congratulating him on his victory and assuring him of her friendship and conviction that he would approve her conduct if he were properly informed.

that when you answer it, I wish, (in case you are of my opinion) you would take that occasion to lett her see, that when God has blessed her arms with so great success, it would bee a right time for her to show mercy and forgiveness to those who may have displeased her, and to putt an end to her resentment against Sir James Montague[1] which is a thing extreamly essentiall to her Service; and I have hitherto been but just able to keep her from coming to extremityes in it with all the industry, and skill imaginable.

1037. GODOLPHIN *to* MARLBOROUGH   [*8 July 1708*]

Source: Blenheim MSS. A2-38.

Windsor July 8, 1708

Since my last,[2] imediatly upon the arrivall of my Lord Stairs, the winds have continued so cross that wee have not been able to hear any news of you, though wee are in all the impatience imaginable to learn whether the enemy thinks of making any stand; and where it shall bee, if they doe; and what resolutions you have taken. What I wish most to hear is, that you are gon, with the body of the army to Lisle, and Prince Eugene with a detachment to Doüay. What other people's notions are of these matters, you will have some light into from the 2 letters enclosed.[3] The short one is civill and decent. The other is chiefly upon another subject, but I send it to you, that I may know your thoughts how farr this may bee a seasonable time to pursue such a design.[4] For I own myself very apprehensive that 116 [the States] may bee alarmed and jealous of this project, and possibly take a handle from it to run with more violence into any tempting offers relating to 81 [peace], which I think 43 [King of France] cannot fail of making to them.

Ever since the news of your victory I have looked upon this as our greatest danger, and therfore I was very glad to see a letter t'other day from 62 [Heinsius], in which he is very pressing that everything ought to bee done by the Allyes in all places towards making the best use of this great advantage; and particularly that the Queen would lose no time in sending her ships and troops upon the coast of France, to augment their consternation and hinder them from taking the militia of those countryes to recruit their foot.

[1] In the debates on the bill to abolish the Scottish Privy Council which took place in Parliament at the beginning of 1708 Montagu had supported the bill, a Whig measure, in opposition to the Court. Godolphin wanted to retain the Council, at least until after the spring elections, because of the influence it could bring to bear in helping to elect Court nominees. The Whigs were able to pass it and the Queen took a grudge against all who supported it, especially Sunderland and Montagu, who were both in the ministry. See Halifax to Marlborough, 10 June, Blenheim MSS. B1-7.

[2] Letter 1035 (and 1036).   [3] Untraced.

[4] The second letter referred to was from Coningsby (p. 995) and was mainly concerned about the need to reach an accommodation between the Court and the Whigs before Parliament met in the autumn (p. 1138). The Whigs threatened to set up Sir Peter King for Speaker in opposition to the Court candidate Richard Onslow if they did not receive a share of places in the government.

I have answered that he will bee very soon complyed with in this particular, but that to prevent our receiving any affront in that attempt, it would bee necessary for them to continue their squadron before Dunkirk, that so *Fourbin* might not bee able to come out and joyn the Brest squadron. This they promise to doe; but all this may bee altered, in case you have any more usefull employment for our little floating army.

I am very much of 62's [Heinsius] opinion that the Allys ought to bee pressed to exert themselves at this time in all places, and accordingly I have taken upon mee to write very fully to Mr. Palmes, to Mr. Stanhope, and to my Lord Gallway upon that subject.

Lieutenant Generall Erle went yesterday to Portsmouth and an express is sent to Sir George Bing who is crossing in the Channell to fetch him thither.

1038. MARLBOROUGH *to* GODOLPHIN　　　[8/19 July 1708]

Source: Blenheim MSS. A2-39.
Printed: Coxe, ii. 485-6.

[Wervik] Jully 19th 1708

I have this day had the favour of yours of the 28th and 2d of this month,[1] and am very sorry to see that England is capable of being so easily frigh[t]ned, for I dare say thay have not one thousand men on all their coast. This country lies all open to us, but for want of canon we are not able to do anything considerable. One of our partys have burnt the suburbes of Aras.[2] That and some other burnings have given a very great consternation, in so much that thay are already come to tell us that thay have sent to the King for leave to treat for the contribution. That which hinders us from acting with vigor is, that as long as the French are masters of Gand, we can't make use neither of the Schell nor the Lys. But we are using our utmost endeavours to gett some by land, which meets with infinet difficultys; but we must overcome them, or we shall have very litle fruit of our victorie. The Duke of Vandome is not contented with having the canal before him, but he is also retrenching, as if he intended to stay there the rest of this campagne. But when the King of France shall see that we have a probabillity of getting a battering train, I beleive he will not lett his own country be abandoned for the maintaing their treacherous conquest of Gand. We have this day returned our sollome thankes to God for the good success he has been pleased to give us, and in the evening the canon and both lins fired three tims.

You know my opinion as to La Braconier, but since he is come, I shall write to the Elector of Hanover by him; but he must not be trusted with the project we hope to put in execution. I wish I may be mistaken, but I fear he

---

[1] Letters 1027, 1032.
[2] Arras, an important French town 45 kilometres south-west of Lille.

has no other designe but that of getting [money]. However, I have promised him that Mr. Stanion[1] shall have 13 blank commissions which thay may fill on the place. You will be pleased to speak to Lord Sunderland to dispatch them; one must be for a collonel, and the other 12 for captain. These will cost her Majesty only the trouble of putting her name, and if thay should not be sent he will pretend all would have succeded if he had had these commissions.[2] Prince Eugene has desired me to write to you to hasten the 20 crowns a man for the 4,000 foot;[3] for til thay receive that mony, thay can't begine to raise those men, which will be prejudicial to the Service, so that I beg you will speak to the Comte de Gallas about it.

1039. MARLBOROUGH *to the* DUCHESS   [8/19 *July* 1708]

Source: Blenheim MSS. E4.
Printed: Coxe, ii. 500–2.

[Wervik] Jully 19th 1708

Since my last I have had none from you. But having had for some time two or three of your former letters to answere, I begine this morning very early, though the letters do not go till the evening, so that I may hear from you before this is sealed. You give me an account in one of yours of a conversation that 13 [Somerset] had with 7 [Wharton], and by 7 [Wharton's] answere it lookes as if he thought that 13 [Somerset] spoke the thoughts of 38 [Godolphin] and 39 [Marlborough].[4] You know that I have already assured you that I will be very farr from endeavouring to devide 89 [the Whigs], and I beg you will have so kind an opinion of me, as to beleive I can't be so indiscrit as to imploye 13 [Somerset] in anything that is of consequence. You seem to thinke that the designe of removing 6 [Sunderland] is over, but by the two inclosed letters[5] I think it is not. My not being well, the battel, and hurry I have bin in, has been my excuse hethertoo for my not having answered either of them. I beg that you will lett nobody know that I send them to you, only Mr. Mongomery [Godolphin], with whome I desire you will advise what answere I should give.[6] I am very sorry to see by yours that 42 [the Queen] is fonder of 256 [Mrs. Masham] then ever. I am sure as long as that

---

[1] Abraham Stanyan, British envoy at Zürich.
[2] Breconniere's project was to raise Huguenot troops in Switzerland and make a foray into Franche-Comté to foster a rebellion there by French Protestants against Louis XIV. See Marlborough to the Elector of Hanover, 10/21 July, Murray, iv. 122–3. There is a copy of Breconniere's project, sent to the Elector, in P.R.O., S.P. 87/3, fols. 148–9.
[3] The subsidy granted by the Queen to recruit replacements for the Palatine foot in Italy, who were taken into the pay of the Maritime Powers and sent to Spain. See p. 949, n. 3.
[4] The Duchess had her information from Maynwaring. See his letters to her on 15 and [*c.* 20] June, in *Private Correspondence*, i. 153–7, 252–4.
[5] The Queen's letters of 18, 22 June. See p. 1023, n. 3.
[6] He did not reply until 22 July/2 Aug. See p. 1049.

is, there can be no happyness; I mean quietness. By what you write me of 253 [Lady Tyrconnel], I beleive their discorse to you has been much the same as it was with mee, which was not to relye upon anybody, and persuading me to think the government of this country to be the greatest and happyest thing that could happen to mee.[1] I could also perceive that she thought 240 [Lady Marlborough] and 39 [Marlborough] were not so well with 42 [the Queen] as formerly. I do not wonder att that, for I beleive it is the opinion of everybody; but if I can end this warr well and you are kind, nothing can make be unhappy.

Having write thus far I have received your two letters of the 28th of the last month, and the 2d of this. The two inclosed you have sent me of Mrs. Morley's [the Queen][2] are as one would wish. God knows only what is in the heart, but I think in prudence you must not seem to have any doubts, and that may in length of time enable you to do good to the nation and 42 [the Queen]. I am very sensible of the very unreasonable opiniatrety of 239 [the Queen]. However, knowing the faults of those which were before them, what I fear will be in those that are to follow them, I do from my heart wish a long and prosperous reigne, so that you must take pains, for the happyness of 108 [England] depends upon their doing what is right and just. Besides my love to my country, I own to you I have a tenderness for 239 [the Queen], being persuaded that it is the faults of those whome she loves, and not her own when she dose what is wrong. God has been pleased to make me the instrument of doing her againe some service. I wish she may make a right use of itt. I send you back your two letters as you desire, with the two write to me, which I againe beg nobody may know but Mr. Montgomery [Godolphin].

1040. GODOLPHIN to MARLBOROUGH   [12 July 1708]

Source: Blenheim MSS. A2-38.

Windsor 12 July 1708

The winds continue still so cross, that since my Lord Stair's arrivall, they doe not allow us the least news from you, which is extreamly uneasy in many respects. But one ease you have by it; that you will not bee troubled with my reasonings upon anything you may design to doe next, for that will have taken its fate, long before I shall come to hear what your intentions are.

What the first notions and impressions were, among our people here, you will judge in some measure by the letters I enclosed to you in my last,[3] and will therfore give you no further trouble upon that subject.

---

[1] The offer made by Charles III in 1706 but refused because of the objections of the Dutch. It was renewed in August. See p. 1089.

[2] Untraced.   [3] Letter 1037.

The continuall westerly winds keep our transports still in the Downs, where they have stayd this long time, and there are not men of warr enough at Spithead to take in so many regiments, without making use of them, at least, of some of them. This is very unlucky, and putts us almost under the same inconveniences and of the same kind, as in my Lord Rivers's expedition. For by that time wee can gett our troops under sail, wee are told the Queen of Portugall will bee come; and then a part of our squadron, lying before Dunkirk, if not all, must bee withdrawn to bring her to Portsmouth; and then our ships with Sir George Bing, and the troops too, must bee recalled from the coast of France, to goe alltogether to Lisbon. 'Tis a great deal of trouble these Queens give us. However when these troops gett to Lisbon, I cannot but hope they may bee of very good use there. For after the siege of Tortosa, bee the event what it will, upon the arrivall of our succors, from Italy, the Duke of Orleans's army must needs want very considerable reinforcements; and from whence he can have them I doe not see, except from the Marquis de Bay, who will then bee forced to leave all the frontier of Spain, on that side, quite open, and exposed to the Portugheses, if they please to make use of that opportunity.

These are my notions upon the posture of affairs in Spain. For what is doing in Italy, on the Rhine, or the Moselle, you will both hear the news sooner, from every one of these places, and judg of it better, than I can.

The Queen has appointed the 19th of August for the thanksgiving all over the kingdome. The town is always very empty at that time of year, but she had no mind to deferr it so long, as till winter.

1041. MARLBOROUGH *to* GODOLPHIN [*12/23 July 1708*]

Source: Blenheim MSS. A2-39.
Printed: Coxe, ii. 489–90 (small omission).

[Wervik] Jully 23d 1708

I am extreamly obliged to you for your friendly and kind expressions in yours of the 6th,[1] as I would never wish the Queen should do anything that might hurt her Service. I am at the same time very glad to find by Lord Stair's letter[2] that she has been so good as to say that to him, which has made him happy.[3] Wee continu stil under the great difficulty of getting canon, for whielst the French continue att Gand we can make no use of the Schell and Lys, which are the only two rivers that can be off use to us in this country. We have ordered 20 battering peaces to be brought from Mastrick, and we have taken measures for 60 more to be brought from Holland. The calculation of the

---

[1] Letter 1035. [2] Untraced.
[3] The Queen had promised to make him a peer of Great Britain when conditions permitted, but the threat of the House of Lords to obstruct British creations of Scottish peers necessitated a delay (see p. 1028). Stair never did receive a British peerage.

number of draught horses to draw this artilliry amounts to sixteen thousand horses, by which you will see the difficultys we meet with, but we hope to overcome them. In the meantime, we send dayly partys into France which occasions great terror, so that I can't think the court of France will suffer the Duke of Vandome's army to continue where thay are, as soon as thay shall know we have a probabillity of getting canon. For by the intercepted letters, we find that both in France, as well as in the Duke of Vandome's army, thay think it impossible for us to gett a battering train, which makes them as yett bare the inroads of our troupes into their country. I have this morning sent 1,600 men to Armentier[e]s for the greater security of our partys. I am very glad you have sent Lieutenant General Earle to hasten the troupes on board, for though the number is not great, thay will alarme the coast. I hope you will not determin to send those troupes for Portugale, til we first see whether thay may not be of much more use on the coast of France. You know formerly you sent me a project for Ab[be]ville.[1] I have looked for it, but can't find itt. I should be glad you would send itt [to] me, for I think something of that kind might be practicable, and in that case those troupes as well as the fleet will be necessary. The Duke of Vandome's army is so frightned, I am very confident if we could gett them out of their retrench-ments, and from behind the canal of Gand and Brudges, we should beat them with half their numbers, expecialy their foot. This is one of their reasons for their staying where thay are. It lookes affected to be complaining in prosperity, but I have so many vexsations that I am quit tiered, and long extreamly for a litle ease and quiet. It has happened upon the Rhin as I formerly write you,[2] and the French talke of having another detachement from thence. This that the Duke of Barwick has brought consistes of 55 squadrons and 34 battalions. He has been obliged to put some of his troupes into Lille and Tournay, and is incamped with the rest att Douay.[3]

1042. MARLBOROUGH *to the* DUCHESS   [*12/23 July 1708*]

Source: Blenheim MSS. E5.
Printed: Coxe, ii. 512–13.

[Wervik]

Since my last[4] I have had time to read a second time your three letters of the 16, 18 and 22th of the last month, by which I see that I have not yet

[1] See pp. 433, 557, 1041, 1051.
[2] e.g. letter 1020. Marlborough wanted the Elector of Hanover to take the offensive on the Rhine, but he had not moved, confirming reports he would not until Prince Eugene's army, now in the Low Countries, would act in conjunction with him.
[3] Douai, an important fortress on the Scarpe, connected by canal to the Deule. A key fortress on the most direct invasion route to Paris.
[4] Letter 1039.

answered some things in your letters. In the first place, you may depend upon my joining with 89 [the Whigs] in oposition to 84 [the Tories] in all things. But as to the invitations[1] or what else that may be personall to 42 [the Queen], in regard to myself, as well as concern for them, I must never do anything that lookes like flying in her face. But as to everything else, I shall always be ready to join with 89 [the Whigs] in oposition to 84 [the Tories], for whome I shall have no reserve. I am intierly of your opinion as to 37 [Orkney] and 222 [Hamilton], that thay may be had by those that shall think it worth their while to bye them. The first has already told me that he will do whatever I shall think for the Service. But as I must be master of my own actions which may concern personally 42 [the Queen], so on the other hand I shall solicit nobody to be of my opinion, but be contented in giving my reasons and vote in the House.[2] You judge very right of 239 [the Queen] that nothing will go so near their heart as that of the invitation. I think the project very daingerous. I wish 89 [the Whigs] would think well of itt, but I am att to[o] great a distance to be advising. I find by yours the curiosity you have of knowing what I had done to gaine the kindness of 253 [Lady Tyrconnel]. I made them three vissets and had the patience to hear their pollatiques, which were of no great consequences. By the vissets I made her, she found all the people of quallity much civiller to her then thay had been in the winter, which I saw gave her great pleasure. Besides, I ordered it so that Mrs. Cadogane carryed her and her goods into Holland without any charge or trouble to her; which was another satisfaction, for she is very helpless, and has a great deal of lumber with her. I am very sorry that 11 [Devonshire] has had any objection to my letter[3] for I meant no reserve. For you know I have a great opinion of his honesty, but it is hard to write so freely at first. But upon all occasions yearafter I shall be carefull of doing what he may like, and if I can find a pretext of writting to him I shall do itt, so that I should be glad to know where he is. The businesse of Mr. Walpole has very much vexed me, for by what he write mee 182 [George Churchill] has been much to blame.[4] I wish with all my heart he would retier, for I have been long convinced it would be for his service, and everybody else. But as I am told 41 [the Prince] will not hear of itt, I shall never desist from being for itt. I would by no means endeavour to change any opinion that 6 [Sunderland] may have, but I think there is no necessity of his saying any thing to 42 [the Queen] that she will take ill, but one the

---

[1] An invitation for a member of the house of Hanover to come over and reside in England. This proposal, a perpetual irritant to the Queen and embarrassment to the ministry because of her strong aversion to it, had been aired by the Tories (p. 986) and Peterborough (p. 987) already this year. Now the report was spread that the Whigs planned one and Haversham carried this disturbing news to the Queen. The Queen to Marlborough, 22 July, Brown, pp. 253–4. There seems to have been no basis for it. But see p. 1217, n. 5.

[2] See p. 968, n. 1.   [3] Untraced. See p. 1012.

[4] See p. 1023, n. 4.

contrary that he would endeavour to please as much as is consistant with his opinion, for it will be very mortefying to me upon many accounts, if she should persist to have him removed; so that I beg of him upon my account, that he would do all that is in his power. Having write thus farr I have received your dear kind letter of the 6th, and as my happyness depends upon your kindness, be asured, as long as I have life, I shall do all I can to deserve your estime and love.

I inclose to you Mrs. Morley's [the Queen] letter[1] and a copie of my answere.[2] You will lett Mr. Montgomery [Godolphin] see them both, but nobody else must know that I send them. We continue under the great difficulty of getting canon. Til we have them, we must be contented with sending partys into France, which makes them very uneasy.

1043. GODOLPHIN *to* MARLBOROUGH   [15 July 1708]

Source: Blenheim MSS. A2-38.

July 15, 1708

While wee are expecting 3 posts from you with a good deal of impatience, give mee leave to enclose to you a letter from Mr. Robert Lowther[3] who was knight of the shire for Westmorland in the last Parliament, and will bee soe, I hope, in this, though the sheriff, my Lord Thanett's[4] deputy, would not return him.[5]

He is an honest and very modest young gentleman, and very well inclined. I have promised to make him a Comissioner of the Revenue in Ireland, when there shall bee a vacancy. In the meantime, he would bee glad, as you will see by his letter, of his cousin James Lowther's place in your office of the Ordnance, in case you have nobody else in your view to whom you would rather give this place. But if you have, you may freely lett mee know it, and I will tell him he is not to expect it. James Lowther has applyed to mee, to desire your leave to lay down.

Our expedition has (according to custom) stayd about a fortnight for some more transports, which have been detayned in the Downs by the contrary winds. But orders are now sent to them to embark the troops upon such

---

[1] See p. 1029, n. 2.

[2] 12/23 July, in Coxe, ii. 502-3, repeating his desire 'to serve you in the army, but not as a minister'. He made a plea for her to forget her resentment of the Whigs and employ them as the only way to carry on the war and preserve her crown.

[3] Robert Lowther, M.P., Westmoreland, 1705-8; appointed Keeper of the Stores in the Tower Sept. 1708; governor of Barbados 1710. See p. 1366.

[4] Thomas Tufton, sixth Earl of Thanet (1644-1729), Tory peer; Hereditary Sheriff, co. Westmorland, 1691; Privy Councillor 1703-7, 1711-14.

[5] A Whig, Daniel Wilson, and a Tory, James Graham, were returned and held their seats, uncontested, throughout the life of the Parliament.

transports as they have, and the remainder upon the men of warr, so I hope there will now bee no more delays in that matter.

I am now to acknowledg the favour of yours of the 16th and 19th,[1] not dated from any place, but I suppose you were then in the French lines. I find (as my Lord Stairs prepared us to expect) your difficulty will bee the want of your great cannon. I was in hopes they might have come to Vilvorden[2] or to Brussells by water. Afterwards I know they must bee carryd by land which will bee tedious. However, I am glad you seem inclined to turn your face rather towards France, than towards Ghendt, where I should hope, you might bee able to streighten the enemy by want of subsistance. I am sure you will doe what is really best, and I have hinted to you already, that nothing will please this country so much as Dunkirk.

My Lord Sunderland will take care to send Mr. Stanyan 13 commissions with blanks as la Breconniere, has desired. He is not trusted with particulars by anybody here.

I will speak to Mr. Secretary Boyle about the 20 crowns a man for the 4,000 men, but I have not yett heard a word of that from the Comte de Gallas.

I am much afraid those Italian succors will scarce come in time to relieve Tortosa.

1044. MARLBOROUGH *to* GODOLPHIN [15/26 July 1708]

Source: Blenheim MSS. A2-39.
Printed: Coxe, ii. 490–2 (small omission).

[Wervik] July 26, 1708

Since my last I have received the inclosed[3] from Monsieur Buys. You will by itt see the inclinations of the Burgemasters of 113 [Amsterdam]. Whenever their inclinations shall be known, you may depend upon itt that 116 [the States] will be of the same opinion; for lett our success by what it will, this campagne I find 110 [Holland] is determined for 81 [peace], which I am afraid 43 [King of France] knows. By our news from Paris, Tortose was taken the 11th, so that the troupes from Italie will come to late. You may see by the *Paris Gazett* the turn thay give to the battel of Audenar, taking no notice of the 706 officers, nor the 7,000 prisoners, we have also taken 95 coullors and standerds, besides 3 the Prusiens keep to send to their King. But that which is our greatest advantage is the teror that is in their army, so that it were to be wished that we could gett near them. What you aprehend in

---

[1] Letters 1033, 1038.
[2] Vilvoorde, a small town on the Senne, 10 kilometres north of Brussels, with water communication to Antwerp and the mouth of the Scheldt.
[3] 10/21 July, Blenheim MSS. B1-15, copy, B1-5. They expect Marlborough's victory will force the French to come to terms. Buys mentions the problem of obtaining contributions from Utrecht for troop subsidies. Cf. p. 1006.

yours of the 8¹ of the 116 [the States] is very just, for by what I have from 121 [The Hague] it is plain that thay think enough is done for 81 [peace], and I am afraid thay will not willingly give their consent for the marching their army into France, which certainly if itt succeded would put a happy end to the warr. I have acquainted 48 [Prince Eugene] with the earnest desire some have for our marching into France. He thinkes it impracticable til we have Lisle for a place *d'arme* and magazin, and then he thinkes we may make a very great inroad, but not be able to winter, though we might be helped by the fleet, unlesse we were masters of some fortefied town. If it depended upon 62 [Heinsius], he is so honest a man that he would not at this time think of 81 [peace], but he is in his nature so timorous, that he will never contridict whatever the inclinations of 116 [the States] may be. The letter I send you from Monsieur Buys was write before thay knew of the loss of Tortose,² by which you may be sure their inclinations for 81 [peace] will increase. I am assured that if this action had not happened, some proposal of peace was to have been made towardes the end of August.

Prince Eugene has desired me to send you the inclosed paper³ write in his own hand, so that he might have an answere to etch point, to send to the Emperor and King of Spain. I desire the answere may be in French, and in a paper apart, that he may have it.⁴ What he mentions of Mr. Stanhop and the 8,000 men is for the project Mr. Stanhope proposed by order of the King of Spain.⁵

You will very easily beleive me when I tell you that I am a good deal vexed and mortefied to see that finding fault is more naturall then helping to ease those that are forced to serve the publick. For I see by my letters from England, that if impossibillitys are not done after this success, your humble servant is to be blamed. I beg you to consider our situation. We are in a country where the Duke of Berwick, and Monsieur de Bernier⁶ the Intendant, in the King's name orders all the people to abandon their dwellings and retier to the strong towns. This joined with the difficulty of getting canon, makes me uneasy to the last degree. It is most certain that the success we had at Audenar has lessened their army att least twenty thousand men,⁷

¹ Letter 1037.   ² On 29 June/10 July.   ³ Untraced.

⁴ Untraced. The paper called for payment of the levy money to raise troops to replace the 4,000 Palatines sent from Italy to Spain. The money was a condition of their dispatch (p. 949). The second point was a request for 8,000 men to reinforce Charles III in Spain in 1709. For Godolphin's reply see p. 1057.

⁵ The King wanted to move from the defensive to the offensive, and 'get out of Catalonia, and enlarge our bounds'. The words of Stanhope quoted in Mahon, p. 248.

⁶ Charles Étienne Maignoet, Marquis of Bernières (1667–1717), Intendant of Hainaut 1698–1705, then in Maritime Flanders, 1705 until June 1708, where he was charged with supporting the army. Intendant of Flanders from July 1708 until 1715, he was sent by Villars to Louis XIV in 1709 to advise on measures for provisioning the army.

⁷ In addition to the loss of 6,000–7,000 prisoners and 3,000 killed and wounded the French sustained (p. 1028, n. 1), many thousands more were separated from the army in the retreat following the battle. It took several weeks for the army to collect all the stragglers and to reorganize.

but that which I think our greatest advantage consistes in, is the fear that is among their troupes, so that I shall seeke all occasions of attacking them. But their army is farr from being inconsiderable, for when the Duke of Burgundy's army shall join that of the Duke of Barwick, they will be at least one hundred thousand men. If it had pleased God that we had had one hour's daylight more at Audnar, we had in all likelywhode made an end of this warr. This is the treu state of our condition, which is proper for the Queen to know, and I beg you to asure her Majesty that I shall endeavour everything that I think may be for the publick good and her Service. In my last letter[1] you had my thoughts as to 201 [General Earle]. I long to hear thay are sailled.

1045. MARLBOROUGH *to the* DUCHESS   [*15/26 July 1708*]

Source: Blenheim MSS. E4.
Printed: Coxe, ii. 492–3.

[Wervik] July 26th 1708

Since my last I have the happyness of yours of the 8th. By that and some others from England, I find much more is expected from the success it has pleased God to give us, then I am afraid is possible. I am sure you and my friends are so just and kind as to beleive that I shall do my best. I have the advantage of having Prince Eugene and very good troupes, but our difficultys are much greater then can be imagined in England. I no ways doubt but 84 [the Tories] will endeavour all they can to vex me, but I hope 89 [the Whigs] will support me in this warr, and then I don't doubt but to bring France to such a peace as thay desire. But to effect it there must be one campagne more after this. This is not only my opinion but the opinion also of 48 [Prince Eugene], which I desire you will let 6 [Sunderland] know, and that I desire he would acquaint his friends with it, particularly 4 [Halifax], and 5 [Somers] and 7 [Wharton], if he be in town, after which I should be glad to hear from him on this subject; for 48 [Prince Eugene] and 39 [Marlborough] consult dayly, not only how to end this campagne, but also the warr, with advantage, so that it will be of great use for me to know the opinions of those Lords.

I should have been glad to have done what Sir Henry Furnesse desires, but the Duke of Vandome nor the Duke of Burgondy will not grant any passes for the sea, which Mr. Cardonel has acquainted Mr. Furnesse with.

You will see by the date of the inclosed letter[2] that I should have sent it

---

[1] Letter 1041.

[2] Halifax to Marlborough, 6 July, Blenheim MSS. B1-7; reply, 15/26 July, Murray, iv. 129. A congratulatory letter on Oudenaarde, pressing him to enter France, using Erle's force to seize Boulogne or some other French seaport to supply his army from England. Halifax added, 'after

you some time ago, but I have been in so continuall a hurry, that for this, and I am afraid other omissions, must be my excuse. I must end my letter with assuring you, that I am very sorry for what you mention in the begining of your letter, of the fondness of 239 [the Queen] for 256 [Mrs. Masham]. I do not mean it as a thing that may vex 240 [Lady Marlborough] or 39 [Marlborough], but as a thing that must at last have very ill consequences. I should have been glad on this occasion to have had a letter from 11 [Devonshire], so that I might have in some degree made amends for my last.[1] [Balance cut off by Duchess.]

1046. GODOLPHIN *to* MARLBOROUGH   [*18 July 1708*]

Source: Blenheim MSS. A2-38.

Windsor 18 July 1708

I have the favour of yours of the 23d,[2] and am desirous to begin to write my thoughts to you upon the chief part of it, though it bee 2 days before the going out of the post.

The news wee have from France, by these letters of the surrender of Tortosa, will make it harder upon us not to send the troops designed for Portugall as early as we can, to make a diversion on that side for the more ease of Catalonia. However, if you think they can bee of use in Picardie, that being a nearer service I am apt to think it will prevail. As for the project of Abbeville, I don't know that I have ever seen it, since you had it, but I very well remember the substance of it, which was to this effect, viz:

That our fleet should land 4 or 5,000 foot at St. Valery which is open, and march to Abbeville, not farr from it and likewise open, but so strong a post by the situation of it, that such a number might bee able to maintain themselves there against a much greater;

That a competent body of horse and dragoons should joyn them from Flanders;

That when joyned they would bee able immediatly to draw contributions from all Normandie, and even to the gates of Paris;

That being masters of the sea, their provisions and their retreat might bee always secure to them.

You will best judg how farr this is practicable [or] usefull. I think anybody may judg it would bee, for it might presently take the Duke of Berwick off of your hands, and oblige him to dislodg this little army, besides all other distraction and uneasyness that it would give to France.

all, we shall never get Spain, unless your Grace conquers it by the way of Flanders'. In the same letter Marlborough also acknowledged Halifax's of 25 June, on behalf of Captain Barton (see p. 869), perhaps the letter referred to here.

[1] See letters 1016, 1042.   [2] Letter 1041.

In case you incline that this should bee atempted, I think, for severall reasons, no time ought to bee lost in it; and I believe, your answer to this very letter ought to say, by what time you wish the fleet and the troops should bee there; and by what time you propose they should bee joyned by those you would send to meet them; and what stores and provisions they ought to bring with them, or ought (at least) to bee in a readyness here, to bee imediatly sent after them.

This is all I can at present think of to offer you upon this head. Your answer will determine it as you please, one way or other. You will be pleased to consider what officer you would send with your detachment, and whether it would not bee too great a mortification to Lieutenant Generall Erle not to comand the whole.

Windsor Sunday 18 10 at night

Since I had written the former part of this letter, upon having acquainted the Queen and Cabinet Counsell with the hint given in your letter, and my remembrance of this project for Abbeville, they all entered so readily both into the practicableness and importance of the thing, that they thought it not reasonable any time should bee lost to putt it in execution. This express is sent therfore to tell you that wind and weather permitting, the fleet and the troops about 6,000 men shall bee at St. Valery the last day of this month, old stile; with orders to make themselves masters of Abbeville as soon as they can; and to expect your detachment to joyn them there, with instructions from yourself to Lieutenant Generall Erle, for the better guidance of his future proceedings, as you shall judg most proper.

The reason why it has been thought advisable not to stay for your answer is, that it must needs bee a great advantage for you to know this intention, and the time of executing it, so long before the enemy can know it, which will not bee till the troops arrive at St. Valery; because you may bee able so to observe the Duke of Berwick's motions as to hinder him from sending a superior body of troops to ours; or to take what other measures you may judg more proper.

Our troops are all embarkd, but Erle and Bing are to bee here Tuesday[1] that they may bee more particularly made acquainted with this design.

1047. MARLBOROUGH *to* GODOLPHIN   [19/30 July 1708]

Source: Blenheim MSS. A2-39.
Printed: Coxe, ii. 493-4 (inc.).
Addressed: To my Lord Treasurer, Whitehall.

[Wervik] July 30th 1708

When we receive the English letters, the first thing Prince Eugene askes, is if the orders are given for the mony that is to enable them for the raising the

[1] 20 July.

4,000 foot sent to Catalionia, so that I beg you will let me know what orders you have given. I have write to Sir Philip Meadows that he should endeavour to inform himself from time to time what orders are given for the raising those men, so that the money may be imployed to no other use then that of raising the 4,000 men. I should think it might be fore the Service if her Majesty gave orders to the Secritary of State to write to the same effect.

Wee continue under very great difficultys of getting our canon. Lisle, Ypres, and Tournay which should have furnished 5,000 horses, have received possitive orders to furnish none, so that I am afraid we shall be obliged to bring from Bruxelles at twice, what we was in hopes to have done att once,[1] which must loss a great deall of time. We are assured that the Duke of Burgundy and Vandome have obtained the King of France's consent[2] to continu in their camp behind the canall of Brudges and Gand, thay having assured him that it will not be in our power to do anything considerable, but the setling some contribution, and the plundering the country, as long as thay continue masters by the situation of the town of Gand, [and] of the two Rivers of the Schel and Lys. Thay have another reason which thay do not give for their staying where thay are, which is thay dare not trust their men in any camp, where we might be able to come to them.

Monsieur de Bouflairs is come to his government of Lisle. I hope he will not have better success then he had att Namur,[3] if we were once so happy as to gett our canon. Monsieur de Chamilliard[4] was yesterday at Lisle, and it is sayde he is gone today to Valencien. The allarme in France is very great, so that we should bring them to reasonable terms, if Holande should lett us act as we aught to do.[5] But I hear this evening that the French have forced their passage into the Isle of Cassand,[6] which will give allarms to Zealand, and consequently make a great noyse at The Hague, and might occasion some unreasonable resolution, which might make us uncapable of acting in this country. My only hopes are that their eagerness for contribution, may incline them to suffer a litle, and lett us act with the troupes we have, we having already setled five hundred thousand crowns for the country of Artois, and

[1] That is, with only half the number of horse required to move the artillery, the horses that were available would be required to make two trips.

[2] For the King's consent see Louis XIV to Burgundy, 16/27 July, Vault, viii. 52–4.

[3] Boufflers was commander of the garrison at Namur in 1695 and surrendered it to William III, the first marshal of Franch to surrender a fortress.

[4] Michel de Chamillard (1651–1721), French Minister of War and member of the *conseil d'en haut* until his fall in 1709.

[5] Marlborough wanted to advance straight into the heart of France with Paris as his objective, while the disorganized French could not stop him. But the Dutch generals and Eugene were afraid of their supply lines and communications which might be cut by the French troops left behind and the fortresses, particularly Lille, still in French hands that lay in their path. Their caution prevailed and the siege of Lille was undertaken instead.

[6] Cadzand, a village and district north of Bruges, on the sea coast forming the south side of the mouth of the west branch of the Scheldt. Part of the province of Zeeland. For the French foray see Wijn, VIII. ii. 328–9.

we hope to gett them much more from Pickardy, this being a contribution that is likely to last as long as the warr. I did flatter myself it might have inclined them to continue the warr, til we might have had a good peace. We shall now see what use the party that is for peace will make of the French being in the Isle of Casand.

I am very sorry to find by yours of the 12th[1] that you think the Queen of Portugale as soon as she comes to Holand must be transported by the fleet, but I hope it will be thought more reasonable for her to continue on this side of the watter and let the fleet and landmen act for the publick good, or else be contented with two or three shipes which may carry her very safely. If my Lord Gallaway has not the command of the army in Portugale, as many troupes as you send thether this yeare, I take to be lost to the Service. On the other side, if thay make a noyse on the coast it will hearten the Dutch, and discorage the French, which is a much better service then they can do in Portugale. The loss of Tortose must, I am afraid, make us expect nothing good from Catalonia, this summer, and consequently that the Portuguess will be more cautious of venturing; so that in my opinion the hopes of having these troupes should be continued to them, but thay should not be suffered to goe till you see the end of this campagne; for I am very much afraid you will see 110 [Holland] do something very extravegant. I do not expect that my opinion should influence, but I beg you will advise with your friends what may be best for the publick and her Majesty's Service.

1048. GODOLPHIN *to* MARLBOROUGH   [*20 July 1708*]

Source: Blenheim MSS. A2-38.

Windsor 20 July 1708
morning

To my letter of the 18th[2] by *Nys*[3] the messenger I have only to add (at present) that Lieutenant Generall Erle and Sir George Bing are ordered to bee here some time today, the better to concert with them the manner of putting our project in execution. That is to say, whether the fleet shall first appear before St. Malo's to give them a jealousy for that place, and oblige them to draw what strength they have on the coast, that way; or whether they shall goe directly to the place designed [Abbeville], before they show themselves anywhere else upon the coast. Whatever is agreed upon with those 2 gentlemen, you shall know it before I close this letter.

I beleive our troops will amount to at [most] 6,000 men, which is all wee have now ready. But wee can soon have Munden and Lepell's regiments from Ireland, and one regiment may yett bee added more from hence, if, in case they shall take post in France, you shall think it necessary to send

---

[1] Letter 1040.   [2] Letter 1046.   [3] John Nijs.

them this reinforcement. I ought also to acquaint you, that by the end of this month (old stile) there will bee a convoy in Holland to bring over the Queen of Portugall. And in case you should have a mind to augment this little army yett farther, by any regiments that could be spared from any of the Dutch garrisons, this convoy might see them to the very place, in their passage from the Maez to Spithead. And therfore Rear Admirall Baker who is to command it, shall have orders to take under his convoy such transports as shall bee preparing to sail with him from Holland.

I have heard nothing yett from Comte de Gallas, about the 20 crowns a man,[1] but have had a long, and pretty obscure application from him about the orders which the Queen has given to Sir John Leak to demand reparations of the pope.[2] All that I could collect from his discourse, was that the court of Vienna was inclined to make up with the court of Rome, and had a mind to make use of the apprehensions which our fleet might occasion upon the coast of Italy to procure better terms for themselves, though those terms, are more like to bee a prejudice than an advantage to us and to the rest of the Allyes.

In the meantime, the loss of Tortosa makes us uneasy, and I should bee glad to hear Sir John Leak had brought the succours to Catalonia.

Since writing thus farr, Sir George Bing and Lieutenant Generall Erle have been here. They seem to approve very well of the undertaking, as it is projected and [they] will return this afternoon to Spithead, to putt it in execution. They will endeavour to bee at the place, as near as they can by the time appointed, rather a day sooner, than later. But they seem much to wish, that the detachment you send might have orders to come as near as is possible to the very place where they land, that they may bee assisting to them in their march and in taking the possession of the place; which if once done, it can not fail of having a very great effect, or (at least) of making a very great diversion from Flanders. You will best judg, what you can doe, in that side, to keep our little army from being oppressed, and lett us know, what you would have us doe further here, for the better support of it.

You will also bee pleased to consider that in case wee succeed in this attempt so as to keep our footing in France, it will bee impossible to send any troops to Portugall this autumn, but the thought of that matter must bee laid wholly aside, till next year.

---

[1] To recruit replacements for the Palatine troops sent to Italy. See p. 949.

[2] On 7 May Sunderland wrote to Leake to make a demonstration at one of the Papal ports and demand a compensation of 400,000 crowns from the Pope to assuage the insults he had given by encouraging the Pretender and recognizing Philip V as King of Spain. If the Pope did not comply Leake was to burn and destroy the Pope's ports and shipping. The instructions were dated 4 May (S. Martin-Leake, *Life of Sir John Leake* (Navy Records Society, 1920), ii. 227–9). He repeated his instructions on 22 June, ibid. 277–8.

1049. GODOLPHIN *to* MARLBOROUGH   [*20 July 1708*]

Source: Blenheim MSS. B1-2.

20 July Windsor 6 in the evening

Lieutenant Generall Erle left his letter[1] with mee to send you and left it open, which gives mee opportunity of blotting out *Montreuil*,[2] in his letter, and of inserting Abbeville. I find him very desirous that your detachment may joyn him at the sea side, and that you would doe all that is possible for sending more foot from Holland to strengthen this body, and enable them to maintain their ground, and keep onn the warr in Picardie and Normandie all the winter. But having troubled you so much upon that subject in my own letter of this day,[3] I shall add no more but that this expedition will take its life or death from you. If you determine it shall live, wee will give all possible nourishment from this side.

1050. GODOLPHIN *to* MARLBOROUGH   [*21 July 1708*]

Source: Blenheim MSS. A2-38.
Printed: Coxe, ii. 487 (inc.).

Windsor 21th July 1708

My 2 last letters of the 18th and 20th[4] have troubled you so much, about our project, that I would not mention some other things which I have often thought of offering to your thoughts. One of them, and the most materiall, is that finding the gazetts and newspapers take notice of Monsieur Plessen's[5] being to come very soon into England, and of his intentions to wait upon you in his way, in case he does so, I think it might not bee amiss for you to speak freely to him of the present condition and temper of 108 [England]; of the influence which his old friend and acquaintance Mr. Morley [Prince George] has with 42 [the Queen]; and consequently, of how much use and advantage it might bee to all who wish well, that right impressions should bee given to Mr. Morley [Prince George] of all that is necessary to bee done at this time for the strengthning of 42's [the Queen] only true interest. And that really the truth of the case is, that if this winter should slip without applying proper remedies to the uneasyness of 108 [England], it is but too probable wee should never see another opportunity for it. You know this man better than I. You can best tell whether you are like to see him, or what effect this

---

[1] Godolphin wrote this on the end of Erle's letter of this date, in which the general described his instructions, 'that we should land in Picardy near Saint-Valery and seize *Montreuil* on presumption of meeting a detachment of hors[e] and dragoons from your Grace in those parts'.

[2] Montreuil lay on the river Canche, some 40 kilometres north of Abbeville, located inland from Saint-Valery on the Somme.

[3] Letter 1048.   [4] Letters 1046, 1048.

[5] Danish minister and former envoy at The Hague and London. If he made the journey he did not do so in any official capacity.

proposall of mine is like to have, in case you should see him, so it must bee left entirely to you.

In the next place, 74 [Lord Raby] seems being near returning to his post. He talks somtimes of seeing you in his way, but in the same discourse takes notice of difficultys in it, and of the time it would lose. So I believe, upon the whole, you are not like to bee troubled with him. I really think 42 [the Queen] would have been willing to gratifie him in his request, if she had not seen that coppy of a letter written by him,[1] which has since been sent to you.

Lastly, I am sorry to tell you, that though I have often mentioned poor Sir Rowland Gwin to the Queen, and made use of your name in it, I never could find her easy that he should come over. She says she has forgiven him, and that she would not have him starve, but when one presses for leave that he may come over and have the honour to kiss her hand, she always says she thinks he is very well there. Pray tell mee therfore, when you have time to think of it, what you would have mee say to him, or doe farther in this matter.

July 23d

Since I had written thus farr, I have the favour of yours of the 26th[2] with the enclosed letter from 61 [Buys], and the paper from Prince Eugene's own hand.[3]

As to the former, you know so much of my apprehensions of the temper of 61 [Buys] and his neighbours, that you won't bee at all surprised when I tell you, I did not expect a letter less strong from 61 [Buys] upon that occasion taking it always for granted, that they will endeavour to make use equally, of good success, and of ill success towards their aim, which is 81 [peace]. And of the other side, wee must continue our endeavours as zealously to keep them onn as long as wee can in the expectation of farther advantages by doing so.

And I hope, you will not, upon second thoughts, bee so much disheartned by the idle notions and expectations of impossibilitys which you may hear of from hence. Somthing of this arises from malice and envy, and from a desire to raise expectations which they think can't bee made good. And when the Toryes talk at this rate, these are the true reasons of it. But you will consider, besides, that it is the temper of our nation, (confirmed by daily experience) that wee are at the top of the house in prosperity; and in misfortune, indeed, upon the least alarm ready to sink into the earth.

As to Prince Eugene's paper, I have given you, at very short warning, my own private thought upon it, in French (as you required) article by article in the paper enclosed.[4] But since his paper hints that the Imperiall and

---

[1] For the letter and Raby's request for an earldom see p. 980.　　　　[2] Letter 1044.
[3] On troops for Spain and levy money for replacements for those sent (p. 1039, n. 4).
[4] The paper is untraced, but see p. 1057 for what Godolphin told Gallas regarding the points raised.

Spanish ministers have orders to make application to the Queen upon the same heads, I suppose they will doe it next Sunday,[1] and you shall bee sure to have a coppy sent you, of the answer which the Queen shall bee advised to make them.

I can't conclude, (though I have troubled you too much) without observing that as you seem to think the French army under great terrour, and (as I think) with reason, yett all our Paris letters bragg of the contrary and would insinuate as if they had some great project ready to break out very soon. If there is anything in this, it must bee from some correspondence they have in some other of your great towns in Braband. But most likely ther's nothing in it at all more than idle talk.

Since mine of the 20th the winds have been so high, that (I believe) our expedition is not forwarder than it was at that time. But I hope wee shall have better weather before the end of the month and bee everyway in a condition to keep our appointment with you.

1051. MARLBOROUGH *to* GODOLPHIN

[*22 July/2 August 1708*]

Source: Blenheim MSS. A2-39.
Printed: Coxe, ii. 494 (inc.).

[Wervik] August 2, 1708

Since the arrivall of Lord Stairs, by whome I had no letter from you, I have received yours of the 15th[2] and have read Mr. Lowther's letter.[3] If his kindsman continues in the opinion of retiring, I have no objection against his having the place til you can provide better for him; but then it must be done at the same time the other quits, for I know of sollicitations that I shall be troubled with. That which governs me in this, is what I shall practice as long as I serve, to consent to whatever you think for her Majesty's Service. I thank you for Lord Coningsby's letter, and send it back, not knowing but you may think it proper to show to the Queen, if you have not already done it. I wish her so well, that I would be glad she might know what is in everybody's heart. The delay that has been occasioned by crose winds to the embarkation is a great *contretems*, but as I think most things are governed by destiny, having done all that is possible, one should submite with patience.

Wee have gott great part of our canon to Bruxelles, so that now our greatest aplication is to have it here. The allarme the French has given by getting into the Ile of Cassand, has weakned our army of 11 battalions.[4] As yet we

[1] 25 July.
[2] Letter 1043.
[3] Requesting a place in the Ordnance.
[4] Cadzand. See p. 1043. Seven battalions were sent to aid the Allied troops in the district according to Wijn, VIII. ii. 329.

do not know what effect it has had in Holand, but no doubt those that are for a peace will endeavour to make all the noyse thay can. We have an account that our partys have occasioned very great terror in Picardy, and that thay exclame very much against Monsieur de Vandome staying where he is; but by the measures he takes there can be no doubt of his intentions of staying there all this campagne. If we can succed in our undertakings, we must not think of winter quarters til we have obliged him to quitt that country. It must be by force, for it is not in our powers to hinder them from having subsistance, even for the whole winter, if thay should be permitted to stay. By a letter I have from Mr. Chetwood,[1] I find the 4,000 foot will fall short of 700 or 800 men, so that there must be care taken to pay the 20 crowns only for the efectives, and not to pay the rest til thay send the men. I should be glad in your next you would let me know where Lieutenant General Earle begins.

1052. MARLBOROUGH *to the* DUCHESS

[*22 July/2 August 1708*]

Source: Blenheim MSS. E4.
Printed: Coxe, ii. 504-5 (inc.).

[Wervik] August 2d 1708

The enclosed I send,[2] you will see is from Mrs. Morley [the Queen]. I have altered my answere[3] since I received yours of the 16. What I write is the truth of my heart. Nobody must see them but Mr. Mongomery [Godolphin]. You must keep all her letters and my answers for I keep no copies, and you must be carefull in the conversations you have not to lett them think that you have any account of their letters, for that would make them more shye when thay write. I am afraid what you say of Abigale is but to[o] trew, but 240 [Lady Marlborough] and 39 [Marlborough] must for their own reputations, have all the consideration imaginable for 42 [the Queen]. I beleive it is in the power of 256 [Mrs. Masham] to do very ill offices, but I do not think she could gett the blew ribon for anybody.[4] 74 [Raby] is in friendship with

---

[1] 21 June/2 July, Blenheim MSS. B1-3.

[2] 13 July, in Coxe, ii. 503-4 and Brown, pp. 254-5 (misdated as 24 July). In it she complained that the Duchess had shown her Marlborough's letter of 1/12 July (letter 1031) in which he suggested the Queen should make proper use of his victory. The Queen asked Marlborough: 'What is the use you would have me make of it?'

[3] Marlborough had received the letters of the Queen of 18 and 22 June on 28 June/9 July (see p. 1023). On 8/19 July (p. 1032) he sent them to the Duchess asking her to consult Godolphin about a reply. The Duchess returned him one on 16 July drawn up by Godolphin. Blenheim MSS. B2-32. For the final draft see Coxe, ii. 505-6. In it Marlborough pleads with the Queen not to dismiss Sunderland or discourage the Whigs in any other way, but to follow Godolphin's advice, 'for any other advisers do but lead you into a labyrinth, to play their own game at your expence'.

[4] For Kent (see p. 973) or Raby (see p. 1047).

199 [Harley] and all that cabal, so that I hope 38 [Godolphin] will give him as little countenance as possible. What you wish in yours of the 13th of my being able to make so good a campagne this yeare that I might never more stur out of England, I do with all my soull wish it, but I dare not flatter myself it will be so, for I fear there must be one yeare more to make a good peace. I am sorry that 182 [George Churchill] is gone to Oxford, fearing he may do what I shall not like.[1] I can't hinder being concerned for him, though I find he is not att all sensible of the trouble he is like to have this winter, so that I shall certainly have mortefications upon his account. I send you a letter I have received from Mr. St. Johns.[2] Nobody must see it but Mr. Mon[t]gomery [Godolphin], after which you may if you please burn itt.

Having ended my letter I received yours of the 16, so that I was obliged to make some alterations in my answere,[3] so that it might agree with what you sent me. I have corrected my copie, and have marked in yours what I have left out, beleiving that would rather do hurt then good, for I know thay would venture everything to effect the deviding of 89 [the Whigs], so that those expression would have no other effect but that of incoraging them to go on in the fatall way thay are now in. This is my opinion, but I submitt to better judgement. You may from me assure 6 [Sunderland] that I will always be in the intirest of 89 [the Whigs], [with] which assurance I desire he would acquaint 4 [Halifax], 5 [Somers] and 7 [Wharton]; and at the same time, for their sakes and that of the public, as well as my own reputation, I must be master of judgeing of my actions towardes 239 [the Queen], for sooner or latter we must have them out of the hands of 256 [Mrs. Masham], or everything will be labour in vain.

1053. MARLBOROUGH *to* GODOLPHIN

[*23 July/3 August 1708*]

Source: Blenheim MSS. A2-39.
Printed: Coxe, ii. 495 (inc.).

[Wervik] August the 3d 1708

I have this morning received yours of the 18th[4] by the express. I must refer you to Mr. Secretary's letter,[5] by which you will see Prince Eugene['s] and my opinion. I have speak of it to nobody but the Prince, for by severall

[1] He went to see Harley. See p. 1084.
[2] 6 July, in *Private Correspondence*, ii. 277, a congratulatory letter on Oudenaarde. See p. 840, n. 1.
[3] To the Queen, p. 1049, n. 3. above.   [4] Letter 1046.
[5] Marlborough to Boyle, 23 July/3 Aug., Murray, iv. 146–7. Eugene and the other generals prefer to besiege Lille before entering France, therefore the link-up that Marlborough had intended, between the forces for the descent and his own troops, is impracticable. Marlborough advises that Erle's destination be changed, and that Erle be sent instead to make a landing on the coast of Normandy to create a diversion and harass the French.

observations I have of late made of the deputys of our army, I am afraid 116 [the States] would not be for this expedition, nor anything else where ther is a venture; by which I am confident thay think themselves shure of 81 [peace], the thought of which may ruin themselves and 137 [the Allies]. For I veryly beleive the intentions of 43 [King of France] is to amuse them, in order to gaine time. After we have succeded at Lisle, and that we shall think it feasable to suport this project of Abville, I should agree with you that Lieutenant General Earle should have the chief command during this winter, so that he should endeavour to informe himself of the number of troups that will be necessary for the suporting him in that post. For as one of the difficultys will be his subsistance, he must not aske for more men then what is absolutly necessary.

It was Monsieur de Gatiny that gave you two years ago a schem for this project.[1] You should speak to him, and desire him to put in writting his thoughts on this matter, so that Earle and I might have copies. You should also speake to some knowing seamen, that the Queen might know how farr thay can assist, for most of the subsistance for the troupes must, during the winter, be sent from England. You will see by Mr. Secretary's [Boyle] letter, that we are taking the best measures we can for the security of our canon, which the enemy threatens, but I hope we are in no dainger, Prince Eugene having for their security 90 squadrons and 53 battalions. And if the Duke of Vandome should march with his whole army, I am ready to follow with the troups that remain with mee. I am in hast to send back this messinger, so that no time may be lost in sending Earle on the coast of Normandy.

1054. MARLBOROUGH *to the* DUCHESS

[*23 July/3 August 1708*]

Source: Blenheim MSS. E4.
Addressed: For the Dutchesse of Marlborough.

[Wervik] August 3d 1708

I write a long letter to you yesterday,[2] but having received yours of the 17 this morning by this messinger, I would not lett him return without telling you that I have keep him so few hours hear, that I have but just had time to write to Mr. Secretary [Boyle] and Lord Treasurer, to whose letter[3] I must refer you, and shall be sure to answere yours by the next post. You will see by my letter to Lord Treasurer the necessity of making such hast in sending back the messinger, otherways I should have keep him with pleasur to have answered yours, having no greater [pleasure] in this world then that of conversing with my dear soull.

---

[1] See pp. 433, 557.   [2] Letter 1052.   [3] Letter 1053.

1055. MARLBOROUGH *to* GODOLPHIN

[26 July/6 August 1708]

Source: Blenheim MSS. A2-39.
Printed: Coxe, ii. 496-7.

[Wervik] August the 6th 1708

Since my last I have received yours of the 20th,[1] as also the instructions of Lieutenant General Earle,[2] which makes me in pain, fearing he may be landed before he received contrary orders, which I hope were sent as soon as you received mine of the 3d,[3] it being impossible for us to send any detachement til our siege is over, I earnestly desire that though he should be landed, you will send orders for their reimbarking, and that thay loss no time in going to the coast of Normandy. I shall endeavour to send to Mr. Earle,[4] but it will be great odds it never comes to him, so that nothing is to be relyed on but one of the Queen's shipes. I am in hourly expectation of hearing that our cannon left Bruxelles this day. The French have severall detachements abroad in order to trouble the march, but I hope to no purpuse, for the Prince's army is now strenghned from hence by 47 squadrons and 30 battalions, so that I recon he has 50,000 men with him. By some letters I have from 108 [England], I find all maner of ways 39 [Marlborough] is to be found fault with; for when he is lucky, he is negligent and dose not make use of the ocasion; and if he should ever prove unfortunate, no doubt he would run the risque of being a fool or traytor. In my opinion it is hie time for him to think of retyring, by which he would be in nobody's power, but I know he will take no resolution but by the advice of 42 [the Queen] and 38 [Godolphin]. But as I wish him very well, I hope thay will allow him to do it this next winter, which may be a proper time, if what I hear from 121 [The Hague] be treu which is that thay are resolved to have 81 [peace]. I should have sent you before this, as you may see by the date of the inclosed letter. If it be not to[o] late, you will take notice to Aylmor[5] that I have sent it you.[6]

---

[1] Letter 1048.

[2] Two drafts by Sunderland of Erle's instructions are to be found in Blenheim MSS. VIII (23) and D2-1. Byng's orders are in *Byng Papers*, ii. 222-3.

[3] Letter 1053.

[4] Murray, iv. 152.

[5] Matthew Aylmer (died 1720), admiral; after serving in the navy since 1679, he retired from Service in 1702 upon George Churchill's being placed over him; returned to duty as commander-in-chief 1709-11, when Orford was made First Lord of the Admiralty.

[6] Aylmer to Marlborough, 25 May, Blenheim MSS. A2-39. Out of employment since 1702, Aylmer had asked to be governor of Greenwich Hospital or to 'be allowed some subsistence' the last winter. Marlborough had told him a governor would be appointed. Now Aylmer sees that Mr. Gifford has been granted the post he hopes for some relief.

1056. MARLBOROUGH *to the* DUCHESS

[*26 July/6 August 1708*]

Source: Blenheim MSS. E4.
Printed: Coxe, ii. 508–10.

[Wervik] August 6th 1708

I had not time by the messinger to answere yours of the 17 which he braught me. As to what you say of 182 [George Churchill], you will see by my former letters that I think him in as wrong measurs as is possible. It is a very great satisfaction the assurances you give me that there will be care taken to make the mortification as easy as such a thing can bare, but in this country it must have a very bad effect as to my reputation, since he is my brother. I know not from whome you may have heard what you write, but I am sure Mr. Walpole ought to be satisfied with 39 [Marlborough], for I did say enough to him[1] that he might see that I was farr from aproving, but on the contrary condemned the proceeding of 182 [George Churchill]. The account you give me of the commerce and kindness of 239 [the Queen] to 256 [Mrs. Masham] is that which will at last bring all things to ruin, for by all you write I see 42 [the Queen] is determined to support, and I beleive att last own 256 [Mrs. Masham]. I am of the opinion I ever was off, that 239 [the Queen] will not be made sensible or frighted out of this passion, but I can't but think some ways might be found to make 256 [Mrs. Masham] very much afraid.[2] The discovery you have made of 42 [the Queen] having the opinion that thay have friends which will support them, can be no other then 84 [the Tories]; and it is treu that thay would ruin 38 [Godolphin] and 39 [Marlborough]; and will be able to bring it about, if it can be thought ruin to be put in the condition of quietness, which of all things 39 [Marlborough] wishes for, but not to be forced to it which he will certainly bee, if 256 [Mrs. Masham] remains in that creditt you say, and I beleive thay have with 42 [the Queen]. I find you are in pain for my not being able to make use of the letter you sent mee. You will by the last post have seen how I have made use of itt, though I said nothing by way of excuse in my letter to Mrs. Morley [the Queen].[3] I did it by the same post to Mr. Mongomery [Godolphin] in his letter of the 23d,[4] which he acquainted Mrs. Morley [the Queen] without doubt, so that my letter may come very naturally, to her. By what I hear from 121 [The Hague], is that those people are resolved to have 81 [peace] on any conditions. This may prove fatal, but if thay are determined, we shall find it very difficult to hinder itt, so that you will have your thought how we may be most

---

[1] See p. 1023, n. 4.

[2] The anonymous letter, in Green, pp. 315–17, which the Duchess sent to the Queen, may have been inspired by this remark. Cf. Maynwaring to the Duchess, [4 Sept.], Blenheim MSS. E26, in which he encloses a letter she commissioned to 'vex or fright' Abigail. Ibid., p. 317 n.

[3] See p. 1049, n. 3.

[4] See p. 1037, n. 2, for the letter to the Queen, enclosed in letter 1041. See also p. 1055.

at ease. For when that happens I beleive nobody will be against my living quietly with you, and then the 91 [the Court] may govern as thay please, the consequence of which, I would flatter myself, will bee that we shall then, be more estimed by our friends as well as enimys, for the temper of 108 [England] is such that nobody in any great station can be liked; for if thay are luky thay do not make use enough of their advantage; if unfortunat thay run the risque of being called fools and traytors.

You will know from hence the publick news in the printed papers. By my letters yesterday from Cadogan I am in hopes the canon may begine their march from Bruxelles today or tomorrow.

Since I had finished this letter, I have received yours of the 20th, and have only time to assure you, that I am fully convinced that 84 [the Tories] would ruin me. You know my resolutions by my former letters, of being ferm to 89 [the Whigs], and if thay support 39 [Marlborough], thay will make him more capable of serving them and his country.

1057. GODOLPHIN *to* MARLBOROUGH   [*27 July 1708*]

Source: Blenheim MSS. A2-38.

Windsor 27 July 1708

I have none of yours to acknowledg since my last,[1] the contrary winds keeping back our letters from Holland to that degree, that it is not only uneasy, but prejudiciall to the Service.

The same westerly winds won't suffer the transport ships for our dragoons, nor those who carry the ordnance stores, now in the Downs to joyn the fleet at Spithead; for which reason the fleet is ordered to joyn them where they are, in the Downes (since the ordnance stores are indispensable); and I believe they will bee this night there altogether, and move from thence towards the coast of France, as soon as the winds will allow them. But I doubt, they must come a little more to the northward, before that can well bee done. In the meantime wee wait very impatiently for the return of the messenger with your thoughts and directions to us for what wee may bee capable of doing.

Power is given to Sir George Bing and to Mr. Erle, to send for Lepell and Munden's regiments from Ireland, when the wind serves for it, in case they take post in France and want a reinforcement of more foot. They have also power to send for 2 regiments from Scotland, Grant's and Strathnaver's, and Collonell Hill's regiment is ordered hither out of the North to send over to them if there bee occasion. This is all wee can bee able to gett together before winter, though the levy money bee ordered for the 4 regiments of Stuart, Portmore &c.

[1] Letter 1050.

The Comte de Gallas was not here Sunday last[1] (as I expected), nor has not yett delivered any memoriall upon the poynts mentioned in Prince Eugene's paper. As soon as any farther stepps are made in that matter you shall bee sure to have an account of them.

1058. MARLBOROUGH *to* GODOLPHIN

[*29 July/9 August 1708*]

Source: Blenheim MSS. A2-39.
Printed: Coxe, ii. 530–1 (inc.).

[Wervik] August 9th 1708

I had the favour of yours of the 23d[2] last night, and in it the honour of one from the Queen.[3] The enclosed answere,[4] with my humble duty, I beg you give her. As soon as Prince Eugene returns, I shall give him your answere to his six points. His difficulty will stil remain as to a squadron for the winter, for it is most certain that we aught not to expect any good from thence, if their can't be found means for the leaving a squadron their in the winter, so that I hope thay will apply themselves to be masters of *Port Mahon*.

I am very glad her Majesty dose forgive Sir Rowland Guyne, and that she would not have him starve. For his comming back, he never write to me anything about it, nor do I beleive he can come to England by reason of his debts. He has been ill used by the court of 141 [Hanover], so that if he could be of any use, I beleive he is to be trusted. But at the same time, I must own that I can't see any use that can be made of him, for it would not look well to give him any publick imployement. The behavior of 74 [Raby] in writting to Hanover[5] is not only foolish but also knavish. I am obliged to you for the good councell you give me, not to lay att heart the unreasonable behavior of some of my countrymen. I think what you say is reasonable, but as I act to the best of my understanding, with zeal for the Queen and my country, I can't hinder being vexed at such usidge. Our canon is come safe to Ath, so that we now think it out of dainger. The next thing we have to aprehend is the intelligences thay may have in our great towns, and particularly that of Bruxelles. For it is most certain the people are against us, so that wee have been obliged to leave eight battalions and six squadrons for the security of that town. I shall be in pain til I hear Earle is gone to the coast of Normandy.

---

[1] 25 July.   [2] Letter 1050.

[3] 22 July in Coxe, ii. 511–12 and Brown, pp. 253–4 (both abridged). The Queen said she would always regard him as both minister and general and 'never separate those characters'. As for his solicitations on behalf of the Whigs, she did not feel obliged to put herself 'entirely in the hands of any one party', especially as Haversham had told her the Whigs were to move an address in Parliament next session to invite over the Electoral Prince, and that the Prince would visit England after the campaign in Flanders was over. This she depended upon Marlborough to prevent.

[4] Untraced.

[5] To obtain the Elector's support for his request for an earldom. See p. 980, n. 1.

1059. MARLBOROUGH *to the* DUCHESS

[*29 July/9 August 1708*]

Source: Blenheim MSS. E4.
Printed: Coxe, ii. 510.

[Wervik] August 9th 1708

I have had the happyness of yours of the 23d. By the same post Mr. Mongomery [Godolphin] sent me one from Mrs. Morley [the Queen]. I have had a good deal of strugle with myself whether I should burn it or send it [to] you to show 38 [Godolphin]. As I would have you two know everything, that you might be the better able to act rightly, I have inclosed the letter I have received from the Queen, but I must conjure you that you will not in your discorse or any other way let anybody know of the contents of this letter, which has thorowly convinced me that there is no washing a blackamore white, and that we must expect this next winter all the disagreableness imaginable, for 84 [the Tories] have gott the heart and intier possession of 239 [the Queen], which thay will be able to maintain as long as 256 [Mrs. Masham] has creditt. I do earnestly beg, when Mr. Mongomery [Godolphin] has read Mrs. Morley's [the Queen] letter, and this of mine to you, that thay may both be torn to peeces, so that thay may never hurt Mrs. Morley [the Queen], who [I] can't but love and endeavour to serve her, as long as I have life; for I know this is not her fault, otherways then by being to[o] fond of 256 [Mrs. Masham], who imposes upon her.

1060. GODOLPHIN *to* MARLBOROUGH   [*30 July 1708*]

Source: Blenheim MSS. A2-38.
Printed: *Private Correspondence*, ii. 278–9 (slight omission).

Windsor 30th July 1708

Ever since my last,[1] thewinds continue so contrary and so strong, that wee cannot yett have the satisfaction of hearing from you; which is the more uneasy at this time, when wee hoped for the return of the messenger dispatched from hence the 18th at night,[2] with notice of the day upon which our fleet was designed to bee upon the coast of France (wind and weather permitting). But tomorrow is that day, and the wind and weather are now very bad, so God knows whether [we] shall bee able to perform our intentions, though the fleet arrived in the Downes the 28th in order to it. But unless you people are in a condition to assist them even at their landing, by the letters I have seen from Mr. Erle, which are not very sanguine, I don't expect any great advantage from what they will doe.

[1] Letter 1057.   [2] See p. 1042.

Mr. Secretary Boyle will have informed you of the misfortune hapned to the Moscovite Embassadour.[1] I am afraid it may have very ill consequences to our merchants and trade in those parts; besides that it is disagreable enough, that a government which makes so considerable a figure in the world should not bee able to preserve forreign embassadours from being insulted with barbarity.

I have nothing else to trouble you with by this post, but that my Lord Peterborow is come hither this morning with intentions to wait upon the Queen, for the first time since his return into England.[2] However I think this visitt not so extraordinary as one she had last week from my Lord Haversham.[3] I could not help observing to Mrs. Morley [the Queen] upon it, that it was not hard to make a judgment of what was like to happen next winter, when people of his behaviour could meet with encouragement to come to court.

My Lord and Lady Sunderland are gone to Althrope for 3 weeks.

1061. GODOLPHIN *to* MARLBOROUGH   [*2 August 1708*]

Source: Blenheim MSS. A2-38.

August 2d 1708

Nys the messenger is not yett returned[4] which makes us very uneasy and impatient; the more, for that [for] Sir George Bing and Mr. Erle there will bee very great difficultys in landing the troops at (or near) St. Valory. I don't trouble you with the particulars because you will have them more fully by this post from Mr. Secretary Boyle.

The Comte de Gallas spoke to mee yesterday of the severall poynts mentioned in Prince Eugene's paper,[5] but seemed to think they were all so much already adjusted, except two, that he did not think it proper to give in a memoriall upon them. The two poynts were: 1st, the 20 crowns a man for

---

[1] 23 July, Blenheim MSS. B1-1. Matvéev was arrested for debt by the action of several London merchants as he was on the point of leaving England. This action led to pioneer legislation safeguarding diplomatic immunity that set a pattern for the rest of Europe.

[2] Erasmus Lewis told Harley that Peterborough was introduced to the Queen by Godolphin (31 July, B.M., Portland Loan, 29/195, fols. 93–4). Luttrell reports ''tis beleived [Peterborough] will goe governor of Jamaica' (vi. 333). This seems incredible on the face of it, considering the disfavour into which Peterborough had fallen. However, the ministers may have felt that it was better to pacify him and get him out of the way rather than allow him to remain discontented and be in a position to cause trouble. He had been selected to go in 1702 but had refused because the enterprise planned was not on a sufficient scale to satisfy him (see p. 75, n. 6). If he was again offered the post at this time he may have refused it for the same reason, if a contemporary newsletter is correct: 'Peterborough some say cannot get such conditions and such powers in the West Indies as he thinks necessary. He is kindly and is angry very soon; now he has access to the Queen, he has quality, courage, and wit enough to speak his mind freely to the Queen, of which I will say no more.' 26 Aug., H.M.C., *Portland MSS.*, iv. 503.

[3] See p. 1036, n. 1.   [4] See letter 1048.   [5] See p. 1039.

the 4,000 men to bee payd at Franford, to the order of Prince Eugene. The other was, that measures might bee taken to provide 8,000 men more for the service of King Charles the 3d in the next year. To the 1st I told him he must bee pleased to give a memoriall because I must have orders upon it from the Queen for my justification in directing the money. And to the 2d I answered him much to the same purpose as I have already written to you.[1]

As to wintering a squadron in the Mediterranean upon Mr. Stanhope's earnest representations, directions are sent to Sir John Leak, now upon the place to give his opinion of that matter.[2]

Mr. Secretary Boyle will give you an account of the good fortune our ships have had to meet with the Galeons in the West Indies.[3] If your news from Lima[4] bee true, I believe this action may have (probably) been the occasion of it.

The consequences of this news cannot fail of being very good both in France, and in Spayn. In France it must quite compleat the ruine of their creditt. And in Spayn, it will enrage the people, and make them everywhere more inclinable to the settlement of King Charles the 3d.

I am going to Wiltshire tomorrow for 3 or 4 days, so I believe you will not bee troubled with any letter from mee by the next post.

I am very much obliged to you for what you have written to mee about Mr. Lowther.[5]

1062. GODOLPHIN *to* MARLBOROUGH [*2 August 1708*]

Source: Blenheim MSS. A2-38.

Windsor 2d of August 1708

Since my former letter[6] wee have letters from Mr. Erle, and Sir George Bing of yesterday off of Dover[7] with a coppy of yours of the 6th[8] by which you dismiss them from any farther intention (at present) of landing at St. Valery. So according to your desire, the Queen has just now directed them to pursue their first instructions for acting on the coast of Normandy and Brittany.[9]

---

[1] Letter 1050.
[2] Boyle to Leake, 4 Aug., P.R.O., S.P. 104/208, p. 242.
[3] A Spanish trade fleet, leaving America in June, had stopped at Portobello for bullion and was on its way to Cartagena for more when it was met by an English squadron under Admiral Wager. Wager destroyed two of the fourteen ships and captured a third. The remaining ships escaped to Cartagena and did not return to Spain until 1712. See H. Kamen, *The War of Succession in Spain 1700–15* (London, 1969), p. 185.
[4] Marlborough wrote to Boyle on 22 July/2 Aug. that Lima and much of Peru had recognized Charles III as King of Spain and that their viceroy had been murdered, according to Amsterdam newsletters (Murray, iv. 143).
[5] Letter 1051.
[6] Letter 1061.
[7] See the council of war, 2 Aug., in *Byng Papers*, ii. 228.
[8] In Murray, iv. 152.
[9] See the council of war, 4 Aug., *Byng Papers*, ii. 229–30.

Though till you can bee in circumstances to joyn them with a body of horse, I doe not think their appearing on those coasts is like to give the enemy any very considerable diversion. Nor doe I find them of an humour (as farr as I can perceive) where the success is like to bee doubtfull. I wish therfore, you would consider, as the occasion of it ripens a little more, where they may bee employd most usefully to you; and to give us the earlyest notice that is possible, whenever you can forsee you may bee able to give them a hand.

I goe away tomorrow, so unless it bee by great accident, you will not hear from mee by next post.

1063. MARLBOROUGH *to* GODOLPHIN   [2/13 August 1708]

Source: Blenheim MSS. A2-39.
Printed: Coxe, ii. 532 (inc.).

[Helchin] August 13th 1708

I read yesterday in the Dutch prints, that the embarkation was to land at St. Vallery. Fearing that her Majesty's orders might come to late, I sent an express by Ostend to Lieutenant General Earle and Admiral Bings, not to land but follow their first orders on the coast of Normandy, for fear of accedents. I hope the Queen has dispatched orders, and that she will be pleased to approve of what I have done, since it was ment for hers, and the publick Service.[1] You will know by this post that our cannon is arrived safely to Menin, and that I have reinforced Prince Eugene's army with 31 battalions and 34 squadrons. That with the detachements we have made for Flanders and Bruxelles, makes this army to consist only of 140 squadrons and 69 battalions, with which I am to obsarve the motions of the Duke of Burgondy's army; that of Prince Eugene is for the siege[2] and observation of the Duke of Berwick. Prince Eugen's army consist of 90 squadrons and 53 battalions by which you will see that when we join, which I believe we shall do, the whole will be 230 squadrons and 122 battalions. This day Lisle is invested; I pray God to blesse the undertaking. What I most fear is the want of powder and ball for so great an undertaking, for our inginiers feares we must take the town before we can attack the cittadel. I should have told you in my former letters, that I had given the Comte de Ruffe[3] a passe for 14 days. He has also letters from the Duke of Burgundy and Vandome, for the accomidating of the exchange of prisoners. He should return on the 16. If he be punctuall, I may be able to give you some account by the next post.

---

[1] See the preceding letter.   [2] Of Lille.
[3] Anne-Marie-Louis Dumas, Count, later Marquis of Raffey (died 1722), French officer, brigadier 1702; *maréchal de camp* 1704; taken prisoner by Byng on the *Salisbury* 1708. See Marlborough to Vendôme, 9/20 July, Raffey, 4/15 Sept., Chamillard, 9/20 July, 5/16 Sept., Murray, iv. 121–2, 224.

The greatest difficulty in that matter are the Portuguesse, who are more in number then the Dutch and English, which I would endeavour to exchange for the prisoners in Italie if the King of Spain will allow of it, for the greatest part of them are in Naples. I hear from Holand that Mr. Toland,[1] you know who suports him,[2] is so very free in all his discorses against 38 [Godolphin] and 39 [Marlborough], that some of the honest men in 110 [Holland] have a mind to send him out of their country. I think this a very unreasonable and ungentlemanlike proceeding of 199 [Harley]. I have this evening received yours of the 27th[3] with the letters of Bings and Earle, but as you know already my opinion of that matter, I shall not trouble you with any answer til the next post.

1064. MARLBOROUGH *to the* DUCHESS   [*2/13 August 1708*]

Source: Blenheim MSS. E3.
Printed: Churchill, ii. 427 (inc.).

[Helchin] August 13th 1708

I have had none of yours since my last,[4] so that I have no answere to any of yours, which will make my letter the shorter. Our canon being arrived in safety, we are devided in two armes. That of Prince Eugene is to invest Lisle this day. I am to observe as well as I can the motions of the Duke of Vandom's army. If his designe should be on Bruxelles he has it in his power of being there 2 days before me; but we having ten redgiments in it, if he has not intelligence in the place, I hope to come time enough for the relief of it. But the truth is that 116 [Holland] has been so very insolent, that we have generally the people against us, which att this time creates great difficultys. I could strugle with all this, knowing as I think the worst of itt, but that which gives me the greatest concern is the prospect we have in 108 [England], for by the enclosed letter I sent you by the last post,[5] it appeares plainly to me that 239 [the Queen] is determined to do everything that will hurt themselves, which will have the consequences of hurting everybody and everything. I have this evening yours of the 27th, and thank you for the verses, which I think very good. I should have been glad to have known the auther.[6]

---

[1] John Toland (1670–1722), writer, deist; edited works of Milton; visited Hanover 1701, 1705 Berlin, Holland, and other places on the Continent during Anne's reign. *D.N.B.*

[2] Harley sent him abroad by his own admission. Harley, autobiographical fragment, B.M. Loan 29/26/5.

[3] Letter 1057.   [4] Letter 1059.

[5] See p. 1055 n. 3.

[6] Probably 'Britain's Jubilee: A new Congratulatory Ballad on the Glorious Victories obtained by the Duke of Marlborough over the French; Writ by the Famous Comedian, Mr. Estcourt, and sung by him to most of our Nobility, with Great Applause.' In *Windsor Castle: a Poem* (London, 1708), pp. 15–16.

I have read in a newspaper that the Queen had given Mr. Harley, myself
and severall others our plate.[1] I supose it is not treu since you do not mention
itt. I am ever yours.

1065. GODOLPHIN *to* MARLBOROUGH   [4 August 1708]

Source: Blenheim MSS. A2-38.

Tillsett 4th of August 1708

I receive at this place the favour of yours by Nys the messenger.[2] Before I
left Windsor, I heard by yours of the 6th to Mr. Erle,[3] that you had putt off
the execution of the project, till a more convenient opportunity. I wish wee
may yett find one before the end of the campagne, for I think still the thing
might bee very usefull, and the necessary support from England of provisions
etc. very easy. In the meantime I will send for Gattigny, and give you an
account of what hee says.[4] In the meantime I wish you good success at
Lisle, for that place is of mighty consequence.

Duke of Marlborough.

1066. MARLBOROUGH *to* GODOLPHIN   [5/16 August 1708]

Source: Blenheim MSS. B2-9.
Printed: Coxe, ii. 568-9 (inc.).

Helchin

Yours of the 27th[5] came so late that I had not time by the last post[6] to give
you my thoughts, nor indeed have I as yett any time for other thoughts then
what is now acting in this country, on the success of which I think depends
the libertys of all Europe. The French are endeavouring to gett all the
troupes that is possible together, and by the intelligences we have from
Monsieur de Vandome's army, as well as the motions of the Duke of Berwick, it lookes as if their resolutions were to act in Braband. And though this
army is very much weakned by the siege, I am resolved to ventur everything
rather then lett them take Bruxelles, which I beleive is their designe,
beleiving me to[o] weake for the relief of itt. I beg you to assure the Queen
that I have that duty and love for her, that I shall have no reserve in venturing

---

[1] Sunderland had tried to make Harley return the customary issue of plate made to him on
his election as Speaker and again upon his appointment as Secretary, when he left office in February.
But Harley forestalled him by obtaining permission from the Queen to keep it at his last interview
with her before he retired (Harley to Godolphin, 23 Jan., 17 Mar., 1708, B.M. Loan 29/64/5
and 2). See Charlton to Harley, 16 Mar., recalling the plate; Lowndes to Harley, 11 May, informing him that the Queen has given him the plate (H.M.C., *Portland MSS.*, iv. 481-2, 488). The
grant was made to Marlborough and other recipients as well.

[2] Letter 1053.   [3] In Murray, iv. 152.

[4] Regarding his project for putting troops into Abbeville. See p. 1035.

[5] Letter 1057.   [6] Letter 1063.

everything that may be for her Service, hoping that God will protect her just cause. If it pleases God to give us one success more this campagne, I hope that may bring such a peace as may give her security abroad for the rest of her life. I do from my soull wish there were a better prospects att home, but by all the accounts I have, I see nothing but confusion, which is another argument for my ingaging the enemy if possible, for thay will otherways reap the advantage of our disunion. I find by my letters from the Brille that the messinger was by contrary winds detained there till Friday last,[1] so that I beleive Admerall Bings and Mr. Earle had my letters before her Majesty's orders could reach them. The Comte de Ruffeé is returned, and by what he has assured the deputys and myself, I beleive we shall agree upon the exchang of the prisoners.[2] In the meantime, the King of France has given leave to Arnott to vissett all the prisoners, so that you shall have an exact account of them.[3] By all that I can hear thay will not be 1,500 men, and the Dutch not above half so many; the Portuguese are much the greatest number. By our letters from Geneve we are assured the Duke of Savoye advances, and that Monsieur Villars desires more troupes, which I believe thay will send him from the Elector of Bavaria's army, if thay shall not think them more necessary in this country. For by the letters from the Rhin, we do not see that the Elector of Hanover makes any disposition for the passing of that river, by which the French will be able to make detachements from that army, if thay do not aprehend the a[n]greing the Elector of Bavaria.

1067. MARLBOROUGH *to the* DUCHESS   [*5/16 August 1708*]

Source: Blenheim MSS. E4.
Printed: Coxe, ii. 513–14.

Helchin August 16, 1708

Yours of the 27th came so late that I could not for want of time do any more then thank you for it by the last post. You say that 6 [Sunderland] has assured you that 39 [Marlborough] may depend upon the friendship of 89 [the Whigs], if 39 [Marlborough] will make it possible.[4] You and 6 [Sunderland] may be assured that 39 [Marlborough] has no intentions or thoughts but that of deserving from 108 [England], and consequently must and will depend on the friendship of 89 [the Whigs]; and if his good intentions are not seconded with success, he thinkes he shall have nothing justly to reproch

---

[1] 30 July/10 Aug.
[2] See p. 1051. The French agreed to exchange man for man, officer for officer. Marlborough to Heinsius, 5/16 Aug., 't Hoff, p. 396.
[3] See pp. 993–4.
[4] On 28 July Sunderland wrote a long letter to Marlborough on the deteriorating state of affairs in England. He sent it to the Duchess to review before forwarding it to the General. Blenheim MSS. E15.

himself withall, so that he may retire with quietness and honour. The siege of Lisle which was begune on Munday last[1] is of that consequence to France, that I no wais doubt of their drawing all the troupes that is in their power together, to give us what disturbance thay can. I pray God to bless this undertaking, and all others that may tend to the bringing of us to a safe and lasting peace, and then I am sure 39 [Marlborough] will not put the visset of Lord Haversham to Abigall much to heart.[2] But as that angry Lord has not for some yeares made any vissett to any belonging to the Court, I think his visset to Abigall will not be much for her service, nor that of 42 [the Queen], since it must apear to all the world, that she is the protectorise of those who would distroy the Queen's ministers, which must occasion very great prejudice to her Service. But I think we are now acting for the libertys of all Europe, so that til this matter is a litle more over, though I love the Queen with all my heart, I can't think of the business of England til this great affaire is decided, which I think must be by another battel; for I am resolved to risque rather than suffer Bruxelles to be taken, though the number of this army is very much deminished by the siege. But I rely on the justness of our cause, and that God will not forsake us, and that he will continue to keep our troupes in good heart, as thay are att present. I beg you to be so kind and just as to be assured that my kindness for you is such, that my greatest ambition is bounded in that of ending my days quietly with you my dear life.

1068. GODOLPHIN *to* MARLBOROUGH   [6 *August 1708*]

Source: Blenheim MSS. A2-38.

Windsor 6th of August 1708

I am just come hither time enough just to acknowledg the favour of yours of the 6 and 9th[3] but doe not say anything in answer to them not having eaten today, and being a little faint for want of it. However I have been above with the Queen to give her your letter of the 9th.[4] She said she was writing to you when I came into the room, so before she has done, I believe she will take notice also of the letter which I gave her of the 9th.[5]

[1] 2/13 Aug.
[2] On 21 July Haversham waited on Mrs. Masham after visiting the Queen. Mrs. Masham in turn reiterated Haversham's warning to the Queen that the Whigs would propose in Parliament an invitation for a member of the house of Hanover to come and reside in England. See p. 1036, n. 1. The Queen to Marlborough, 22 July, Brown, pp. 253-4; Duchess to the Queen, 26 July, in Green, pp. 318-21; Mrs. Masham to Harley, 21 July, in H.M.C., *Portland MSS.*, iv. 498.
[3] Letters 1055, 1058.   [4] Untraced.
[5] In Coxe, ii. 507-8 and Brown, pp. 255-6. The Queen insisted she advised with no one but Marlborough and Godolphin and that her refusal to admit more Whigs to office was consistent with her previous conduct and beliefs.

The wind has been so fair while I was in Wiltshire that I hope to hear from you tomorrow morning, that your cannon is come up and Lisle invested. By the next post I will endeavour to answer your 2 letters of the 6th and 9th, and add nothing more now. [The last two lines have been marked out, probably by Godolphin, and are illegible.]

1069. GODOLPHIN *to the* DUCHESS [*8 August 1708?*][1]

Source: Blenheim MSS. E20.
Printed: *Private Correspondence*, i. 315.
Addressed: To her Grace the Dutchess of Marlborough.

Sunday past 2

I have obeyd your commands in returning your letters as soon as ever I had time to reade them, immediatly, by good luck, as soon as I came home from chappell, before any company came to mee.

I think nothing can bee written stronger and more to the purpose at present than Lord Marlborough's letter,[2] and nothing can bee more just than your annotations and observations upon it;[3] but whether they will augment or allay the present fury, I am not able to judge. I wish only it were possible it could have as much effect, as I have readiness and inclination to obey and please you.

I will call at your lodgings before I goe upstairs. Possibly your company may be gone. If not, I will not troble you.

This letter was drafted by Godolphin to be sent to the Queen in reply to hers of 6 August (see p. 1063. n. 5). The Treasurer probably advised Marlborough at the end of his letter on 6 August (letter 1068) that he would prepare such a draft. (I presume this was the import of the lines scratched out.) The Queen would have given Godolphin her letter for Marlborough unsealed so that he had an opportunity to make a copy before forwarding it. After drafting the reply he gave it to the Duchess to revise. She returned it to him on Sunday, 8 August, with interlinear changes, and he acknowledged receipt of it in the foregoing. Godolphin then sent it to Marlborough on the 8th, which could explain the date added by the General, because he patently did not send it to the Queen on that date. It may even have been enclosed with the Queen's own letter. Marlborough wrote the Duchess on 23 August/3 September (letter 1084) that he had received the Queen's letter, having received mail of the 6, 7, 8, 12, 13, and 17 August (letters 1083, 1084). He decided

[1] The date of this can be conjectured by the reference to Marlborough's letter.
[2] The following letter.
[3] The annotations are indicated in the following letter. The observations made by the Duchess in her letter to Godolphin are not extant.

not to answer it until he could send a report of some success in the siege. It is reasonable to assume, therefore, that he sent it on 28 August/8 September, when he sent news of a lodgement on the counterscarp (letter 1087).

1069A. MARLBOROUGH *to the* QUEEN

[*28 August/8 September 1708*]

Source: Blenheim MSS., F1-31. In the hand of Godolphin, revised by the Duchess.
Endorsed by the Duchess of Marlborough: 'a copy of the Duke of Marl: ltr to the Queen' 'August the 8.'

[no heading]

I cannot delay returning my humble acknowledgments to your Majesty for your letter of the 6th[1] in which there are a great many obliging expressions to mee, whose heart and most earnest endeavours will always deserve it from your Majesty, both by doing and consenting[2] through all *discouragements* what I take to bee most necessary for your own service.

Your Majesty will have the goodness to forgive mee that word which is occasioned by your not taking notice of anything I had the honour to write to you[3] in answer to 2 of your letters[4] but only[5] of one expression of mine, which was to this effect, that I desired to *serve you as a generall but not as a minister*. This expression your Majesty is pleased to take notice of and with with dislike, in two letters together,[6] but you are not pleased to take any notice of the occasions I have for using itt,[7] which is that your Majesty is not inclined to follow[8] either my advice as a minister or to that of Lord Godolphin[9] in those particulars which are most effectuall to the carrying onn of your Service in the next Parliament, without which all the successes with which it has plased God to bless mee, and for which your Majesty is so truly thankfull, will bee of very little use.

Your Majesty is pleased to say you have the same opinion of Whigs that ever you had, but have you the same opinion of Torys that ever you had? Have you not had a thousand proofs[10] that they will take the crown from you whenever they can? And these proofs renewed no longer agoe than last winter? And have not you had a great many proofs of the zeal and inclinations of the

---

[1] See p. 1063, n. 5. [2] The first three letters are blotted out.
[3] See p. 1049, n. 3. [4] See p. 1023, n. 3.
[5] *only* has been added above the line by Marlborough.
[6] Marlborough's letter of 12/23 July, Coxe, ii. 502-3; the Queen's two letters of 22 July and 6 Aug., Brown, pp. 253-6.
[7] *itt* substituted for *this expression.*
[8] *is not inclined to follow* substituted for *will not hearken.*
[9] Added. Godolphin left a blank for his name.
[10] Added (by the Duchess?) above the line: 'You can't depend upon that party.'

others to support your Majesty in this warr, and to strengthen your government and many more you would have had from them I am really persuaded if they had mett with that encouragement which they had hoped their zeal might have deserved from your Majesty? But instead of that, at the same time they endeavour to show their zeal against your enemies, you show so much aversness to them, and so much countenance to their enemyes, that such a man as [Lord Haversham][1] can be encouraged to come to your Majesty and to speak to you as a faithfull Privy Counsellor after you yourself have heard him make the most disrespectfull and injurious proposalls that could be to your Majesty, and heard him utter all the scandalls imaginable upon those who had the honour to serve you and at that time to bee in your trust. And what have they done since that time to forfeit it, unless it bee[2] by endeavouring to serve your Majesty to preserve your government and authority at the hazard of their own reputation and life? Possibly your Majesty may think this is to[o] warm, but when you are pleased twice to take notice of my expression *that I can't serve you as a minister* I am obliged[3] to tell you, in the plainest and sincerest manner imaginable, and with the greatest duty and submission that a faithfull subject can pay you, the true reasons of it. Give mee leave Madame only to add, that while your Majesty by your own conduct and inclination is resolved to make it impossible for mee to serve you as a minister, I am very much afrayd that all the service I shall always endeavour to doe you as a generall, and all the success which these endeavours may have, will not bee sufficient to procure for your Majesty that lasting peace and quiett which I shall always wish you from the bottom of my soul.

1070. GODOLPHIN *to* MARLBOROUGH   [*8 August 1708*]

Source: Blenheim MSS. A2-38.

Windsor 8 August 1708

Since my last from this place which was very short,[4] I have the favour of yours of the 13th[5] with the account of your having invested Lisle. I pray God you may have success in it, for I look upon the event of this siege to bee of the greatest consequence. Next to the taking of Paris itself nothing will make a greater noyse in the world than this, nor really bee of greater importance. I conclude therfore that the French will not look on quietly while this is doing, but take the best measures they can to give you all the disturbance that is possible in the siege of that place. But you will probably know the

---

[1] Left blank by Godolphin. See p. 1063, n. 2.
[2] *Unless it bee* substituted for *but* by the Duchess.
[3] *I am obliged* substituted by Duchess for *it is time*.
[4] Letter 1068.   [5] Letter 1063.

certainty of this, from the motions of the enemyes before this letter comes to you, so, I will not trouble you any farther with my useless reflections upon this head.

You will see by the accounts which Mr. Secretary Boyle sends you[1] of the proceedings of the fleet, that Erle might have landed at St. Valery, and possessed himself both of that place, and of Abbeville too, without much difficulty. I hope therfore it may yett bee done at some other time when you shall bee in more proper circumstances to assist and sustain him. The supplying him from hence with all manner of provisions, will not bee a difficulty as long as wee are masters of the sea; but what number of troops it will require to maintain this post, I doubt he will not bee able to determine, till, he has possession of it.

As soon as I can see Gattigny, you shall have an account of what he says in this matter. The fleet in the meantime will sayl to the coast of Normandy and Brettany, to kill time, while you are at the siege of Lisle; though I see no other fruit of it than barely to harrass and alarm that part of the coast. For I cannot flatter myself, it will oblige the French to draw any of their regular troops from the places where they are now employed.

What you say of Toland's proceedings, I did not fail to read to 42 [the Queen] without offering to make the least observation upon it, having often found upon many other occasions, that it is always best to lett them make their own reflexions.

Monsieur de Guiscard seems very desirous to goe to the Duke of Savoy. His head is very roving, as you know. However, I have told him, in case he does goe, that he must call upon you at the army to see what comands you may have for him.

10 August

I was in hopes before I sent away this letter that wee might have had another post from Holland, but none being yett come, I shall only add, that our fleet is come back from Bologne Bay to Dover. [They] have taken the dragoons with them, and are gone to the coast of Normandie in pursuance of their first instructions.

Mr. Walpole tells mee that Carpenter[2] and Wills[3] are both come away from Spayn; the first (as I understand it) without any very good foundation; the

---

[1] The pilots had unanimously advised against a landing, but Byng was nevertheless prepared to try it when Marlborough's orders to halt the expedition arrived. Boyle to Marlborough, 4 Aug., Blenheim MSS. B1-1.

[2] George, first Baron Carpenter (died 1731); colonel, Regiment of Dragoons, 1703; brigadier-general 1705; major-general 15 Sept. 1708; created baron 1719; served at Almanza and Almenaca.

[3] Charles Wills (c. 1665–1741), lieutenant-colonel, Charlemont's Regiment of Foot, 1701; served at Cadiz and in West Indies 1702–3; adjutant-general to Peterborough in Spain 1705; colonel, Regiment of Marines, 1705; brigadier-general 1707; at Sardinia 1708; commander-in-chief of the forces with Baker, major-general 1709; at Almenara, Saragossa, after which he was imprisoned for some months.

latter, for want of timely notice that right had been done him in the matter of his rank. But bee their reasons for it good or bad, they are both good men and the service may suffer very much for want of them, in case of any misfortune to Stanhope. I find my Lord Shannon[1] is desirous to goe thither. But not being able to judge, if it be proper, or may not interfere with other pretensions, I have begged Mr. Walpole to write to you of it; and indeed of everything great and little, which relates to the army; being very sensible, that nothing will bee done right in those matters if you are not first acquainted with it. Though I know at the same time, you have so much to doe where you are, as to bee very willing not to bee troubled with our difficultys.[2]

Comte Gallas has now given a memoriall in form, for the 20 crowns a man to bee sent to Frankfurt payable to the order of Prince of Eugene [*sic*]. I shall give order for it next week, as farr as the men appear to have been effective.

1071. MARLBOROUGH *to* GODOLPHIN   [9/20 August 1708]

Source: Blenheim MSS. A2-39.
Printed: Coxe, ii. 532–3.

Helchin August 20th 1708

By the threatning of Monsieur de Vandome, I did not think we should have continued thus long in this camp, but as yett he is not marched from behind the canall. But the Duke of Berwick is drawing to his army all the troupes he can from their severall towns. Monsieur de Vandome declares in his army, that he has *cart blanch*;[3] and that he will attempt the relief of Lisle; that when the Duke of Berwick joins him, thay shall then have 135 battalions and 260 squadrons, which he flatters himself will be much stronger then we can be.[4] If we have a second action, and God blesses our just cause, this in all likelyhoode would then be the last campagne, for I think thay would not ventur a battal, but that thay are resolved to submit to any condition, if the sucess be on our side. And if thay should gett the better, thay will think themselves masters, so that if there be an action it is likely to be the last of this warr. If God continues on our side we have nothing to fear, our troupes being

---

[1] Richard Boyle, Viscount Shannon (1674–1740); colonel, Regiment of Marines, 1702; at Cadiz and Vigo; accompanied Peterborough to Spain as brigadier-general 1705; returned to England after taking of Barcelona; major-general 1707; lieutenant-general 1709. He did not return.

[2] On receipt of Walpole's letter of 10 Aug. (letterbook, Cholmondeley MSS. Ch(h)6, Cambridge University Library), Marlborough wrote to him suggesting that Carpenter be ordered to remain in Spain 'and a commission sent to him to command as major-general'. 20/31 Aug., Murray, iv. 200.

[3] This was not true. Vendôme and Burgundy, who took advice from Berwick, had disagreed on the strategy to be employed. Burgundy proposed a diversionary move to relieve Lille, and Vendôme was ordered by Louis XIV to support his plan. Vault, vi. 68–75.

[4] Vendôme had 107 battalions of infantry on 23/July/3 Aug. (Vault, viii. 412). Berwick brought 98 battalions of which 24 were cavalry and 16 dragoons. Ibid. 425.

good, though not so numberous as theirs. I dare say before half the troupes have fought the success will declare, I hope in God, on our side, and then I may have what I earnestly wish for, quiet, and [that] you [will] bee much more at ease then when you write yours of the 31. of the last month,[1] which I received yesterday. I find by Mr. Earle's letter[2] that mine was very welcome, since it gives them ease as to their not landing at St. Valery. I wish thay may be able to do anything on the coast of Normandy. I do think their resolutions at the councels of warr gives no great incoragement,[3] but thay can't avoyd giving great allarms. I wonder Count Gallas has not delivered those points I sent from Prince Eugene, who is very pressing for the 20 crowns a man for the raising the new redgiments.[4] It is certain the Service requiers thay should be now raising. I should think the Comte de Gallas should signe some short agreement for the 20 crowns a man which might appear to the Parliament, for all that was done by me was by letters to Prince Eugene, which letters can't apeare. Lord Haversham's visset makes a noyse.[5] I should be glad to know the occasion of 30 [Peterborough] [visit],[6] they being frends; no doubt it was concerted. If God puts it into the heart of 42 [the Queen] to do what is right, the projects of these gentlemen will signefie very litle.

62 [Heinsius] did acquaint me[7] with what Monsieur du Prye[8] had said to him concerning 81 [peace], which in effect was nothing more but to inform himself if his friends were willing to make any offers, and that accordingly he should receive instruction from 43 [King of France]. But I beleive nether he nor anybody else will have any orders till thay see the fate of Lisle, and consequently the issue of this campagne.[9] When I write you that I must

---

[1] Untraced

[2] 1 Aug., Blenheim MSS. B1-2, acknowledging Marlborough's of 25 July/6 Aug., Murray. iv. 152.

[3] See the *Byng Papers*, ii, *passim*. At a council of war on 29 July the pilots refused to take the ships in close to shore because of low water. The troops could not land west of the Somme because they had no means to cross it.

[4] See pp. 1039, 1047.　　　　[5] See p. 1063, n. 2.　　　　[6] See p. 1057.

[7] 31 July/11 Aug., 't Hoff, p. 395.　　　　[8] Louis Du-Puy Saint-Gervais.

[9] Du-Puy had spoken with Torcy while passing through Paris but had no commission. He advised that France could not give up Spain and the Indies (Stork-Penning, pp. 201-2; W. Reese, *Das Ringen um Frieden und Sicherheit in den Entscheidungsjahren des Spanischen Erbfolgekrieges 1708 bis 1709* (Munich, 1933), pp. 12, 17-18). He was quickly ignored as he was superseded the same month by Hermann Petkum, the Resident of the Duke of Holstein-Gottorp at The Hague. Petkum, who received money from Heinsius, Torcy, and Vienna as well, was invited by Torcy to come to Paris, which he did in July. He returned to the United Provinces in August, having delivered to him the Dutch stipulations for a peace, though without the cognizance of Heinsius. On his return Petkum advised Heinsius that France was willing to come to terms on all points but the cessation of Spain and the Indies ('t Hoff, pp. 397 ff.; Reese, pp. 5-39; H.M.C., *Round MSS.*, *passim*, for the correspondence between Torcy and Petkum). Heinsius asked Marlborough to keep it a secret, but Marlborough did pass on Heinsius's letter to Godolphin (below, p. 1076). At the same time Marlborough himself opened negotiations with his nephew Berwick, which were kept secret from both the Dutch and the English (A. Legrelle, *Une négociation inconnue entre Berwick et Marlborough 1708-1709* (Gand, 1893)). Churchill (ii. 496-7) errs in stating that Marlborough was not informed of Petkum's activities as a perusal of his correspondence with Heinsius and Godolphin clearly shows.

drive the French from Ghandt and Bruges,[1] I had no other thought then that it was absolutly necessary for the common cause. It certainly may occasion my coming ten days latter,[2] but if we are blessed with success in this part of the country, thay will have lesse heart for the defence of those towns, and then I may come home early.

1072. MARLBOROUGH *to the* DUCHESS [*9/20 August 1708*]

Source: Blenheim MSS. G1-7.
Printed: Coxe, ii. 515.

[Helchin] August 20th, 1708

I send you back yours to Mrs. Morley,[3] as also that of Mr. Montgomery, to her,[3] as you desired, having marked the lines which I desire her to reflect on.[4]
I am doing my best to serve 108 [England] and 42 [the Queen] and with all my heart and soul, pray for God's protection and blessing, but I am so tired of what I hear, and what I think must happen in England, that I am every-day confermed that I should be wanting to myself, and ingratefull to God Almighty, if I did not take the first occasion that can be practicable to retire from bussiness; and as I have for several yeares served my Queen and country with all my heart, so I should be glad to have some time, to recolect and be gratefull for the many mercys I have received from the hand of God. I would not live like a monk, but I can't with patience think of continuing much longer in business, having it not in my power to persuade that to be done, which I think is right. I forsee the difficultys of retiring during the warr, which is my greatest trouble at this time, but even that difficulty must be overcome, if I must be in some maner answerable for the actions of 42 [the Queen] who is noways governed by anything I can say, or do. God knows who it is that influences, but as I love her and my country, I dread the consequences. You say nothing of going to Bleinhiem, but the weather is so fine I could wish you there, by which the finishing with indoors I beleive would go on the faster. If it were possible I would flatter myself that I might be so happy as to see it the next sumer, especially if Monsieur de Vandome keeps his word in endeavoring the relief of Lisle, where the trenches are to be opened this night, and if thay let us be at rest for a fortnight longer, thay will very much oblige us.

[1] Page 1049.
[2] But see p. 967, where he reveals his real intentions.
[3] Untraced.
[4] When the Duchess forwarded the letter to the Queen (letter 1072A), she obliterated the italicized lines.

1072A. *The* DUCHESS *to the* QUEEN   [c. *16 August 1708*]

Source: Blenheim MSS. G1-7; a copy in the hand of the Duchess.

[no heading]

I beg leave to shew dear Mrs. Morley [the Queen] the inclosed leter from the Duke of Marlborough[1] and to asure her that what is struck out related only to our private concerns, which is a proof that hee had no design that I should shew it to anybody, for hee would not have mentioned his own buisness in a leter that hee intended should bee seen, and therefore you may be sure it contains nothing but his real thoughts. And though perhaps hee may be angry with me for it, I can't help leting you see them, because I must still think they ought to have some weight with you, and our conversations of late are so disagreeable, that this seems to bee the only way I have left of endeavouring to serve you. It is a melancholly thing to consider that whilest hee is venturing his life in your servise, hee should bee so tired out, as hee expresses it with what hee heares from England, as to wish for nothing so much as to bee got out of your businesse, and then hee complains what it is that thus tires him: that hee is not able to prevail to have anything don that is necessary for your own servise. And though hee forsees the difficulties of retiring during the war, he seems resolved to overcome them, reather then been answerable for what others doe, and that hee can no ways approve of or help, and that far I agree intirely with him, and in what hee says afterwards that hee dreads the consiquences, of what you are doing. But when hee comes to say that God knows who influences you, hee seems to make a doubt where there is non. For without being in the least uncertainty in that matter hee might safely have sworn who it is, for who else can it bee but one that I am ashamed to name,[2] and to which question I could never yet obtain an answer though I have taken the liberty to ask it so often. And here I can't help reflecting what a sad appearance it will make in the world when it shall come to bee known, that whilst a man is at the head of your affairs, and intrusted by most of your confederates hee has not so much credit with you as a dresser unknown to everybody but those that she has betrayed. And there is no doubt but it must bee thought a strange competition between one that has gaind you so many battles and one that is but just worthy to touch your limbs. And since you have seen it under his own hand, I hope you will no longer blame me for saying that hee has lost his credit with you, nor reproach me for not thinking you the same to me as I did when you told me all your thoughts; for if the Duke of Marlborough is as you say still in your favour 'tis plain that hee knows nothing of it himself. And therefore, without troubling you any more upon this subject at present I have but this request to make: that you would bee pleased to live with him as you used to do, when

---

[1] The foregoing letter.   [2] Mrs. Masham.

you harkened to his information and advise, that hee may write a leter quite contrary to his last; or else that you will give me leave to say that hee has quite lost his interest with you, and that you are resolved to make the best you can of the people recommended as friends to the person I have mentiond. And since it is certain that you must come very soon to one of these resolutions, if you really are determined as you seem to bee to declare youself in her favour, and to throw off your old and faithfull servants, I think the sooner 'tis don the better, for all disguises are mean, and below a great Queen.

1073. GODOLPHIN *to* MARLBOROUGH   [*12 August 1708*]

Source: Blenheim MSS. A2-38.

Windsor August 12th 1708

I am to acknowledg the favour of yours by the last post from Helchin, which I reckon was of the 16th, though you have not mentioned the day of the month.[1] I am not at all surprised that your thoughts should bee entirely taken up with the present business before you; since certainly there never yett was any business of greater consequence to all our world, than the event of the siege of Lisle, and the things which naturally depend upon it. For if the French should tamely look onn while that place is taken from them, there is an end, not only of their reall power, but of all their credit and reputation in Europe. For which reason, I have been a good while of opinion, that they would either turn their thoughts immediatly to 81 [peace] or hazard every thing to hinder you from being master of that place.

Now I believe they would have chosen the former of these, if they had miscarryed at Tortosa. But the taking of that place may perhaps have encouraged them to venture in Flanders once more, rather than submitt to give back all Spain, when they think themselves so near the entire possession of it. In case this should bee their resolution, I pray God to preserve you, and to give you that good sucess, which the well rounded confidence of all your officers and soldiers, does in great measure promise you.

I am sorry to see 50 [Elector of Hanover] makes so useless and insignificant a figure, in the whole business of this summer. I yett hope for better from 58 [Duke of Savoy], but one must always expect he should act for himself in the first place.

In my last[2] I acquainted that Monsieur de Guiscard had thoughts of going to the Duke of Savoy, and that he might bee of use in those parts towards exciting some diversion in Dauphinè or the Cevennes. Since which I have had letters from him upon that subject, and from Comte de Briancon recomending it. These letters I designe to enclose, by this post, to

<hr/>

[1] Letter 1066.   [2] Letter 1070.

Mr. Cardonell, that you may not bee troubled with them, till he sees a convenient time to read them to you. I will also send him in the same packett, a coppy of my Lord Gallway's last letter to my Lord Sunderland,[1] by which you will see how pressing he is for the sending our troops to Portugall, and even more troops than wee have, with his reasons for it. I am ready to own to you, my opinion is that wee ought to send some troops, but not soe many as he mentions, nor any at all till wee see how your campagne is like to end in Flanders. Because I think that must and ought to govern all the rest.

1074. MARLBOROUGH *to* GODOLPHIN   [*12/23 August 1708*]

Source: Blenheim MSS. A2-39.
Printed: Coxe, ii. 533-4.

Amougies[2] August 23d 1708

By yours of the 3d[3] I find you were going to be happy for some days in Wiltshire. If you have had the same weather we have had, you could not avoyd being abroad the whole day. The trenches being opened last night, and the Duke of Berwick having drawn all the troupes of this part of the country to his army at Mortagne,[4] I marched this morning to hinder his joining with the Duke of Burgundy between the Schel and the Dandre at Leissins, which I was assured was their designe, which now will be very heird for him to do. We expect the Duke of Burgundy will march tomorrow. His first march will let us see if he has any designe on any part of Braband, or if his intentions are what thay write from Paris, of releiving Lisle by a battel. As soon as I see what time the siege of Lisle is like to take us up, I shall then lett you know my thoughts as to the employing of the troupes with Lieutenant General Earle. In the meantime, thay will have a month or six weakes to do what mischief thay can on the coast of France. I thank you for your good news of the gallions. If it has the consequences you mention, it will help to make us easy. The first thing we shall see, will be the effect it will have on their creditt. I am afraid thay have found new methods of drawing mony from Holande.[5]

---

[1] 15/26 July, Blenheim MSS. C2-11.
[2] A village about 10 kilometres east of, and across the Scheldt from, Helchin.
[3] 2nd, letter 1061.
[4] At the Château-l'Abbaye, near Mortagne, a French village on the border 17 kilometres northwest of Valenciennes.
[5] The French did employ a new method after the siege of Lille. 'The method of creditt which the French did take to circulate after the siege of Lisle was by drawing on Lyons and Geneva and the bankes of the said places draw on Amsterdam and soe these draw againe for there reimbursement on Paris. Alsoe the bankers of Lyons and Geneva especially on[e] Salladyn and another Lullyn who have both houses or comptiors at Geneva and Lyons did remitt large summs in sham bills or bills made pro forma with the consent of one considerable banker here, he to whome they were payable upon his owne creditt as indorsed and upon the creditt of the acceptor a knowne rich man, did discount these bills here driveing up the price of discount by the greatness of the number and

1075. MARLBOROUGH *to the* DUCHESS   [*12/23 August 1708*]

Source: Blenheim MSS. E4.

[Amougies] August 23d 1708

[*first three lines rubbed out*]

You say Mrs. Morley [the Queen] has taken no notice of your letter.[1] I think that is a trew signe she is angry. There being three or four postes come from England since she has received Mr. Freeman [Marlborough] last letter,[2] I take it for granted the same methode will be taken of giving no answere. 39 [Marlborough] is no ways disatisfied at that maner of proceeding, for til 239 [the Queen] change their humour and resolutions, the less the conversations are, is for the better. What 185 [James Craggs, Sr.] has told you of the meettings and resolutions of 84 [the Tories],[3] and that thay think thay have good ground to stand on, is very naturall to people that have always flattered themselves. I both hope and think thay can succeed in nothing that can be of great consequence to the government, but thay will always have it in their power to vex those that are in business. For my own part, I shall be no ways surprised, when I see them act with all the mallice imaginable against mee. I shall aske no favour of them, being fully resolved of retiring as soon as possible, to such a sort of life, that it shall not be in their power to vex mee. I shall always endeavour to behave myself so, as that such of my friends as will be inclined to be kind to me shall have no reason to be ashamed of itt. I am very sorry that the inclinations of 182 [George Churchill] are so violent for 84 [the Tories] as that thay depend upon his intirest with 41 [Prince George]. But all that would quickly signifie very litle if it were not for the great power 256 [Mrs. Masham] has with 42 [the Queen]. I am so fully convinced of this, that I should never trouble 42 [the Queen] with any of my letters, but that I can't refuse 38 [Godolphin] and 240 [Lady Marlborough] when thay desire anything of mee. I am sure that the intirest of 256 [Mrs. Masham], is so setled with 42 [the Queen], that we only trouble ourselves to no purpose; and by endeavouring to hurt we do good offices to 256 [Mrs. Masham], so that in my opinion we aught to be carefull of our own actions, and not laye everything to heart but, submit to whatever may happen. I do not take 186 [Bromley] for a great negociater, but a less able man then himself will reconcil 31 [Rochester] and 199 [Harley] at this time. I beleive you may depend upon itt that thay will be all of one·mind, and

summs of the bills from 3-1/2 and 4 per cent to 5-1/2 and 6 per cent, and when such bills were discounted they remitted the value wherever the French intendants or paymaster of armyes required.' John Drummond to Brydges, 11–22 Feb. 1709, Stowe MSS. 58, III. 254–5, Huntington Library. Cf. above, p. 787, n. 2.

[1] Untraced. See p. 1070.   [2] 29 July/9 Aug. Untraced. See p. 1055.
[3] Perhaps of the plan to put up William Bromley for Speaker if the Court and the Whigs should split their vote between Onslow and King. They put this plan into execution in October, only to suspend action at the last moment when the Court and the Whigs were reconciled.

that thay think themselves assured of the hearts of 41 [Prince George] and 42 [the Queen], which is a very dismal prospect.

[August 24th]

If I had not made use of the leasure time I had yesterday, you had not been troubled with so long a letter, I having been on horseback all this day. The trenches were opened last night before Lisle, so that wee shall very quickly see what methode Monsieur de Vandome will take for the saving of that place.

1076. GODOLPHIN *to* MARLBOROUGH   [*13 August 1708*]

Source: Blenheim MSS. A2-38.

Windsor 13 August 1708

Since my letter of yesterday to you,[1] and my packett direct to Mr. Cardonell, I have the enclosed letter from Collonell Townhend[2] who is with his regiment on board the fleet. I think it proper to send it to you that you may consider how you will dispose of this regiment before the thing bee known, and consequently, before you can bee troubled with any importunitys for it.

I shall only putt you in mind that Collonell Honywood is here, who seems to expect and deserve your favour. But if I don't mistake you did design another regiment for him.[3]

1077. GODOLPHIN *to* MARLBOROUGH   [*16 August 1708*]

Source: Blenheim MSS. A2-38.

Windsor August 16th 1708

Your last of the 20th,[4] joyned with the other letters by that post from Brussells and The Hague, has given mee so much expectation of farther action, and consequently so much anxiety till I know the event, that though I am satt down to begin to write to you, I shall scarce bee able to write anything to the purpose. And really, if there should bee an action, 'tis certain the event of it must and will govern all future measures. But in case there should bee none, and that, after all their braggs, the French should endeavour to gett back to their own frontiers and suffer Lisle to bee taken,

---

[1] Letter 1073.

[2] Roger Townshend (died 1709), younger brother of Charles, second Viscount Townshend; M.P. 1701-2, 1705-9; colonel, newly raised Regiment of Foot, 1706; sent to Flanders in 1708. Townshend did not want to serve with the regiment for reasons of health. He died the following year. See p. 1079.

[3] The regiment was given to Honeywood on 29 May 1709 after Townshend's death on 22 May.

[4] Letter 1071.

I say in case this should happen, I have been thinking whether our body of foot now upon the coast of France with Mr. Erle, might not bee of use to you for the more speedy reducing of Bruges, and consequently of Ghendt also. For if Bruges were once regained, it follows that Ghent must be more streightned. And though you could bee able to recover these places without our assistance, yett if wee can contribute to the doing of it so much sooner as that it will give you opportunity of being sooner in England, give mee leave to repeat only to you that this is of greater consequence then it will perhaps appear to bee to anybody on the other side of the sea. And I shall not (at present) trouble you with any other answer to this part of your Letter of the 20th except just to observe to you, that 42 [the Queen] has not now in 2 days time, since I received it, taken the least notice to 38 [Godolphin] of any one word mentioned in that letter.

I need not trouble you with my reflexions upon our letters from Lisbon, since I send you enclosed 2 letters from my Lord Gallway to yourself,[1] which came in my packett under a flying seal.

You will see by them how pressing hee continues to bee for the immediat sending of the troops to Portugall, and how he seemes to take notice with satisfaction, that I was of the same opinion. I must agree I did wish always, wee might bee able to have sent them so as that they might have acted this autumn. But I acknowledg I doe not see any disposition in that court to concurr with us, as wee might have reason to expect. Besides that, while I am possessed with the thought I mentioned in the beginning of this letter, that they may bee of use to you for the more speedy recovering of Bruges and Ghendt. I can never bee of the opinion for sending them to Portugall till that view bee wholly at an end. However I should bee glad to bee guided by your thoughts upon this whole matter whenever you have time to give mee that satisfaction. In the meantime I shall give you no farther [trouble], till I have the pleasure to hear from you, for which I am very impatient.

Pray God send us good news from you, quickly.

1078. MARLBOROUGH *to* GODOLPHIN   [*16/27 August 1708*]

Source: Blenheim MSS. A2-39.
Printed: Coxe, ii. 534-6 (inc.).

[Amougies] August 27th 1708

The enclosed from the Pensioner[2] I send you, that you may make your observations on what was said on the subject of Spain by Monsieur de Torsy, to Monsieur Pethcum. You will see that the Pensioner is desirous it should be a secrit, which it shall be for me, since I shall say nothing of it to

[1] Untraced.   [2] 11/22 Aug., 't Hoff, pp. 398-9.

anybody but yourself. I am in expectation of hearing every minut that the army of Monsieur de Vandome and that of the Duke of Berwick are on their marches to join, so that I begine to write early this morning, fearing I may not have time in the afternoon. Our canon before Lisle begane this morning to fyer, so that whatever Monsieur de Vandome intends for the relief of that town, he must not lose much time, since our ingeniers promises that we shall have the town in ten days, after which we must attack the cittadel. But when we are once masters of the town, we shall have no occasion of so great a cercomvelation, by which the army will be much stronger, so that if the enemy will ventur it must be before we take the town. Our troupes are in good heart, and their foot in a bad condition. Thay are in horse stronger then wee, but upon the whole I can't think thay will ventur a battaille, though 'tis said thay have possitive orders to succor the place.[1] Thay write us from The Hague what I hope is not treu, that a French detachement is marching from the Rhin to this country, for my only hopes on that side was that 50 [Elector of Hanover] would act so as to hinder any detachement being sent heither, but it is so farr from that, that the same news says that thay have also sent another for Dophiny. Thay pretend these detachements should have begone their march on the 17th. Our next letters will informe us of the truth.

I have this minut advice that Monsieur de Vandome has begone his march, but as his army was very much seperated he will take his camp this night, his right half a league from Gavre, and his left towardes Ninove,[2] so that his army will not be above one league and a half from Gand, which has made me resolve not to march til tomorrow, that I know possitivly which way he takes for his second march. For as I am now posted it is impossible for him to gett between me and the siege and I have taken such measures with Prince Eugene for the strenghning etch other, that I no wais doubt of the preventing anything thay may flatter themselves with. And if thay will attempt the releif of Lisle, thay will be obliged to pass by Mons, which will cost them eight days, and I shall have it in my power to join Prince Eugene in less then three days with ease. I will keep the post til tomorrow, that I may give you an account of their further motions.

[28 August]

By the slow motions Monsieur de Vandome makes with his army, it lookes as if his intentions were to make the Duke of Barwick march round by Brabant to join him; for as I am posted he can do it no otherway. So that as to point of time, it is equall to us whether the Duke of Vandome marches by Mons, or obliges the Duke of Barwick to make the tour of Brabant. One day will informe us of his resolutions.

---

[1] See Louis XIV to Burgundy, 13/24 Aug. Vault, viii. 426.
[2] Ninove, a fortified town on the Dender, 22 kilometres west of Brussels.

1079. MARLBOROUGH *to the* DUCHESS   [*16/27 August 1708*]

Source: Blenheim MSS. E4.
Printed: Churchill, ii. 429–30.

[Amougies] August 27th 1708

I begine to write to my dear soull early this morning, beleiving I may be
obliged to march so that I should not have time in the afternoon; for if the
intelligence I received an hour ago that the Duke of Vandome's army as well
as that of the Duke of Berwick were on their march to join, I must march.
Our canon begone this morning to fyre at Lisle, so that in ten days we hope
to have the town, and after that we must attack the cittadel, which we think
will give us full as much trouble. My hopes are that God will bless us in this
undertaking, which will very much forward my being at quiet with you,
especially if we have another success against the Duke of Burgandy, who has
the King of France's possitive orders to ventur every thing rather then suffer
Lisle to be taken. We have for thes last ten days had extreame hott weather,
which I hope may give you good peaches att Woodstock, wher I should be
better pleased to eat even the worst that were ever tasted, then the good ons
we have here, for every day of my life, I grow more impatient for quiet.
Having write thus farr I have notice that Monsieur de Vandome has begone
his march, in order to camp this night at Gavre, which is not above one
league and a half from Gand, so that I shall not march till tomorrow,
when I shall be more certainly informed of his intentions. I intend to stop the
post til then, so that if there be anything new I may write itt.

[August 28th]

By the slow motions of Monsieur de Vandome, it lookes as if he resolved not
to march to join the Duke of Berwick, but to make that Duke march his
army to Gramont, where thay will then join.

1080. GODOLPHIN *to* MARLBOROUGH   [*17 August 1708*]

Source: Blenheim MSS. A2-23.

St James's 17th 9 at night

Though I have troubled you already with a great packett by this post,[1]
I cannot omitt acknowledging the favour of yours of the 23d[2] which I have
just now received, and am very glad to find by it, that you were posted so
well to your satisfaction for hindring the joyning of the two French armys.
For whatever their intention may bee after they are joyned (if they can
compass that), till they are joyned I dare say they will not fight, if they can
any way avoyd it. But if they were able to joyn, I think nobody could answer

---

[1] Letter 1077.   [2] Letter 1074.

how farr the consequence of losing such a place as Lisle, and a superior number of troops, might tempt them to venture. But upon the whole matter, since the arrivall of these letters, I am much less in pain than I was before, and I hope now every post will continue to make us easyer.

You will see by your letters of this post from the Secretary's office,[1] that our troops are not like to doe any great matter upon the coast of France, besides alarming the country; and I am much afrayd wee shall bee forced to bring them back again to Spithead, before you can bee able to give them better employment.

I sent you a letter from Collonell Townshend desiring to resign his regiment, in case it should bee ordered to Portugal.[2] But I find by his brother[3] who is now in town, that he would bee glad to continue in the service so [long as] he did not goe into that [aw]ful country, which would kill him; and he is so good a man, that I hope you may think of some way of turning that matter so as to keep him still in the service.

Our French letters by this post say the Duke of Savoy has had the worst of it in a small action at Sezane, though it has been in some measure recompenced by his having made himself master of [the Fort d']Exiles.[4] The same letters say that great detachments are going to Dauphinè from the Duke of Orleans's army in Catalonia, which, if true, must leave Count Starembergh pretty easy there.

1081. GODOLPHIN *to* MARLBOROUGH   [*20 August 1708*]

Source: Blenheim MSS. A2-38.

St James's August 20th 1708

In my last I acknowledged the favour of yours of the 23d,[5] since which time I have no letter from you. But wee continue in great impatience for the Holland letters, hearing by the way of Ostend that the armyes are in motion; but the accounts from thence (since the loss of Bruges and Ghandt) are very uncertain.

---

[1] Boyle to Marlborough, 17 Aug., Blenheim MSS. B1-1, enclosing the minutes of a council of war on 12 Aug. See the *Byng Papers*, ii. 235–63.

[2] Letter 1076.

[3] Charles, second Viscount Townshend (1674–1738), Privy Councillor 1707; ambassador at The Hague 1709–11; negotiated Barrier Treaty of 1709. Secretary of State 1714–17, 1721–30; married Walpole's sister 1713. *D.N.B.*

[4] The Duke of Savoy had sent a force under General Rehbinder from Saint-Jean-de-Maurienne by a back route to Mount Genèvre to take Cesana, thus cutting off the troops at Exilles and Fenestrelle from reinforcements. Cesana and Briançon were taken at the end of July and Exilles and Fenestrelle invested. On 31 July/11 Aug. the French retook Cesana, but Exilles capitulated to the Duke of Savoy on the 2/13th. Fenestrelle, the most important fortress on the frontier of Dauphiné, fell to the Allies on the 20/31st. This gave the Duke control of two passes into France from Turin.

[5] Letter 1074.

By the letters from the fleet which Mr. Secretary Boyle sends you by this night's post,[1] you will see they can doe nothing on the coast of Normandy and Brittany, more than continue to give alarms and putt the country to expence. You will also see, that (as the season of the year advances) they dare not venture to come so near St. Valery, as they did about a fortnight since. So that if you continue to think you shall bee able to find any detachment to joyn them, after the siege of Lisle is over, you must take your measures so as your detachment may assist them to land in Bulloin[2] Bay. For they can not with the fleet lie near enough to the shoar upon any other part of the coast of France. And therfore if you expect any thing more from them, the sooner you lett us know it, the better, that they may not bee detained from other services, upon an expectation which (at last) cannot bee complyed with.

Our late success upon the galeons in the West Indyes[3] gives great temptation and encouragement to send a farther strength thither, both of ships and landmen. But (I doubt) most of our land officers here, are either uncapable or unwilling to take the charge of such an expedition.

Mr. Secretary mentions also to you by this post, a proposall sent to him by Palmes about treating for more foot to serve in Catalonia.[4] I think wee ought by no means to discorage any proposall to that and though, if the last French letters are true, they have made a great detachment from the Duke of Orleans's army, in which case I should hope wee might bee superiour without any additionall strength.

Wee expect the Queen of Portugall here with the first wind; but till you can dismiss Sir George Bing, who is to attend her to Lisbon, she will bee obliged to stay at Spithead or in the Isle of Wight.

1082. GODOLPHIN *to* MARLBOROUGH [*23 August 1708*]

Source: Blenheim MSS. A2-38.

Windsor 23d August 1708

Wee are still without any letters from you since my last.[5] This day 2 posts are due, which is very disagreable at such a criticall time as this is.

I reckon Mr. Secretary Boyle sends you constantly such accounts, as come from the fleet. By the last, they were in the bay of La Hogue,[6] and seemed to bee very uneasy at finding every place so well guarded, and in so much

---

[1] Byng to Godolphin, 17 Aug., enclosed in Boyle to Marlborough, 20 Aug., in Blenheim MSS. B1-1.
[2] Boulogne. [3] See p. 1058, n. 3.
[4] Palmes to Boyle, 31 July/11 Aug., in Blenheim MSS. B1-1.
[5] Letter 1081.
[6] Saint-Vaast-La-Hougue, a port on the north-east coast of the Cotentin peninsular in the English Channel; off the coast Russell (Orford) won his famous victory over the French fleet in 1692.

readiness to receive them upon the coast, that they could not hope to make any significant impression; from which the conclusion seems very naturall that, unless you can support them in landing at Boloign Bay, or employ them more usefully by the way of Ostend, the sooner they were sent to Portugall, the better it would bee for the service.

By the letter from My Lord Gallway which I send you with this, under a flying seal as it came to mee,[1] I find hee seems too have great prospects and expectations, in case of the arrivall of our troops, as well as great demands, of which severall, I think, can not bee complyed with. But upon the whole matter, these troops which he expects just now, being a part of the establishment of Spain and Portugall for this year 1708, without apparent and more immediat advantage by employing them nearer home, it will bee pretty difficult to excuse the not sending them thither before the end of the year.

Though the wind bee so contrary that wee cannot have the satisfaction of hearing from you, yett the weather being very fair, I hope it helps you to carry onn your siege with better expedition and success.

I am going tomorrow to Quainton plate, from whence I hope to see Althrope before I return hither again. My Lord and Lady Sunderland are now there, and I have promised to wait upon them for a day or two this summer.

On 19/30 August Vendôme met Berwick with his troops at Lessines on the Dender, not far south of Geraadsbergen (Grammont) where Marlborough predicted they would meet (p. 1078). From there they moved to attempt the relief of Lille. On 21 August/1 September they were at Tournai. As soon as he ascertained Vendôme's plans Marlborough ordered ammunition and provisions brought out of Ath to prevent their seizure by the French. Soon 600 wagons crossed the path of the advancing French army and reached the Allied camp on the morning of the 19/30th. With these on hand the confederate army recrossed the Scheldt and came to Helchin the same day, to stay between the French and Lille, where they could join forces with Eugene and the siege forces to engage the enemy if necessary. Hearing of the French advance towards Tournai on the 20/31st Marlborough moved out at noon to Templeuve and continued the next day across the Marque to Peronne 'in the plains of Lille'. The French crossed the Scheldt on 22 August/2 September and camped that night between Blandain and Willemeau, their right resting on the road Marlborough had travelled the previous day. On the third Vendôme drew further south to Orchies 'and the source of the Marque, round which they must come if they design to attempt anything'.[2]

[1] Untraced.
[2] Marlborough to Boyle, 3 Sept., Murray, iv. 203–4.

1083. MARLBOROUGH *to* GODOLPHIN

[*23 August/3 September 1708*]

Source: Blenheim MSS. A2-39.
Printed: Coxe, ii. 536–7.

Paronne September 3d 1708

When I came to this camp on Saturday[1] I emediatly went to the siege, where I had the dissatisfaction of finding everything backwarder then was represented to me by letter. We have this morning seased a man that was endeavouring to gett into Lisle, who has confessed that he was to assur the Marishell de Boufflairs, from the Duke of Burgandy, that he would attempt the relief. Prince Eugene dyned with mee yesterday, and we have marked the camp where we are resolved to receive the enemy, if thay make good their boasting. The ground is so very much for our advantage, that with the blessing of God we shall certainly beat them, so that it were to be wished thay would ventur, but I really think thay will not. What I think thay may be most troublesome in, is in the hindring us from having provissions, which thay take all the measures thay can, having defended on pain of death to all the French subjects not to furnish any provissions.[2] I am afraid the town and cittadel will cost double the time which was first thought, by which the honestest people are like to loose their mony,[3] in Holland as well as in England. Since my last I have received yours of the 6, 8, 12, 13 and 17th.[4] I have so very litle time to myself that it will be impossible for me for some days to answere the perticulars in your letters. And as for my thoughts of the troupes with Mr. Earle, that will depend very much on the time we take Lisle. I see Lord Gallway presses very much for troupes. It is certain if the Court of Portugalle will not come into the Queen's measures, whatever troupes are sent will be useless to the common cause, for thay will do nothing but defend their own frontier. But I desire this opinion of mine may be known to nobody but the Queen and yourself. The enclosed from the Comte of Maffie[5]

---

[1] 21 Aug./1 Sept.

[2] The reason Marlborough had retrieved the stores from Ath. See the introduction to this letter.

[3] Wagering on the campaigns was a common and often profitable practice. It seems to have been particularly rife on the Toulon expedition and this siege. Maynwaring, for example, asked the Duchess for confidential information on the progress of the operation, and it is apparent from his letters the Duchess herself had placed bets on its outcome. 'Your Grace won't be angry if I say, I hope you will loose your bet with Mr. Cornwall, though, however that may happen, I doubt there are little hopes of mine for the 15th, upon the town and citadel both. They wager now upon the last of September and even of October with greater odds. And I believe I shall try to save myself that way; but then if the siege should be raised I must ruin my countrey' ([9 Sept.]. Blenheim MSS. E26). 'Pray Madam, if the Duke of Marlborough mentions in any letter the day that he thinks the castle and town of Lisle will be ours, be so charitable to let me know it, that I may try to save some of my ill bets' ([1 Oct.]. Blenheim MSS. E26). See also G. Davies, 'The Seamy Side of Marlborough's War', *H.L.Q.*, 15 (1951), 21–44.

[4] Letters 1068, 1069, 1073, 1076, 1080.

[5] 25 July/5 Aug. or 26 July/6 Aug., untraced; reply, 9/20 Aug., Murray, iv. 178. Maffei informed Marlborough that France had offered the Duke of Savoy peace on his own terms (see p. 1092).

should have been sent you some time since, but for mistake of Mr. Cardonel's. I should be glad to know if Comte Brianson has said anything of it. If not, you will be pleased to take no notice of the letter.

1084. MARLBOROUGH *to the* DUCHESS

[*23 August/3 September 1708*]

Source: Blenheim MSS. E4.
Printed: Churchill, ii. 430–1 (inc.).

Peronne September 3d 1708

I have received the pleasure of your three letters of the 6, 7, and 13th, with copies of those you write and received from Mrs. Morley [the Queen].[1] From my soul I wish the postur of affairs in England were better then I find thay are. I have writ[2] and shall speak very plainly to 182 [George Churchill] when I see him, but if he thinkes he can support himself, what I shall say will not have much weight. However, I shall have the satisfaction of having done what I think I aught to do. I shall not answere Mrs. Morley's [the Queen][3] til I see the success of this siege, which goes much slower then were to be wished. When I came into this campe last Saturday[4] I imediatly went to Prince Eugene, where I found the siege at least six days backwarder then I was made beleive by my letters, so that Mr. Crags' wagers in all likelywhode will be lost. Prince Eugene dined with me yesterday, and we have marked a camp where we are resolved to receive the French if thay will make their threats good. The post we have chose I think to be so very much for our advantage, that I am confident you may be at ease, that the French with the blessing of God will be beatten, which makes me think thay must be madd if thay ventur itt. I beleive their greatest application will be the endeavouring to starve us, thay having already in the King of France's name forbid on pain of death for any of his subjects to bring us any provissions. This is the greatest hurt I think thay can do us, but I hope we shall be able to strugle with itt. Yours of the 19th I had last night, by which I find your kindness makes you in pain for fear of a battaile. I hope this letter will make you easy, for I really think if thay do ventur a battaile on the disadvantages thay must have, it is the will of God thay should be beatten; for though thay have more redgments then wee, I think we have as many men. Whatever happens, do me the justice to believe, I am and ever will be tenderly yours.

This letter, prepared by Maynwaring at the request of the Duchess, was probably copied by Marlborough and sent to George Churchill on or about this date. It was

1 I have not been able to identify any of these.   2 Letter 1084A.
3 6 Aug., Brown, pp. 255–6.   4 21 Aug./1 Sept.

composed after Churchill's trip to Oxford in July (p. 1050). Marlborough must have requested the Duchess to send the draft in a letter which has not survived, perhaps on 19/30 July, for this is the only date between the middle of July and the beginning of September (old style) where there is obviously a letter to the Duchess wanting. His reference in the foregoing letter indicates he had sent off the letter recently if not on this date. He seems to make reference to it again on 30 August/ 10 September (p. 1090).

1084A. MARLBOROUGH *to* GEORGE CHURCHILL
[c. *23 August/3 September 1708*]

Source: Blenheim MSS. E28. A draft in the hand of Maynwaring.

[no heading]

I cannot help telling you that the more I am informd of the present posture of affairs in England, the more I am convinced of what I need not say I am sorry for, that it will be extream difficult, if not impossible for you to support yourself next winter in your present station. You know that even in the last session when the Tories were all for you, and the Whigs divided, and the power of the Court exerted to the utmost, you and the rest of the Prince's Council were not so well cleard as I could have wishd, though you avoided a direct censure. And the struggle then was so great, and the publick business so much obstructed by it, that I can by no means think of enduring the same uneasiness and trouble again, that I underwent last winter upon that single point. And you yourself must own that a good deal of the assistance you then had from the Whigs, was owing to the personal friends of Mr. Walpole, and to the defence he made in the House, from whom I fear you must expect no such service now,[1] but rather the contrary, after what passed between you this summer. And this Parliament is said to have near a third more Whigs than the last, who will most certainly be your enemies, if you continue where you are. For there is so little likelyhood of their being divided again in your favour, that even the D[uke] of Devon[shire] and some others that used to be the most moderate, are now entirely for sticking to their party, of which there is not one man, that I can hear of, who does not positvely declare for a change in the Admiralty, as a thing absolutely necessary to carry on the service. And your own foolish journey to Oxford, there to meet Mr. Harley,[2] and your declaring so frequently and publickly that you could and would support yourself, has made this load still more heavy upon you. Therefore upon the whole matter, that you may not be exposed to dayly affronts and questions in Parliament, and the misfortunes that generally

[1] See pp. 1023, 1028.   [2] See p. 1050.

attend them, I cannot but give you my sincere advice to think in time of quitting; which yet I would have done in the easiest way, and with the most honour and advantage to yourself that is possible. And I must be so plain to tell you, that as I think 'tis certain you cannot find friends enough of your own to prevent the storm that is coming upon you, so it will be impossible for Lord Treas[urer] and me to give you the assistance you might hope for, without ruining ourselves, and therefore you must not expect it. But if you will have so much regard to our interest, as well as your own, and indeed to the Queen's and Prince's, as to comply with my earnest desire in this matter, I promise you that as long as I have any credit or power, I will use it for your service, that you may not repent being governd by me in this affair, but may find your account in it, either in some office, or any other way that shall be most agreeable to you. And I have reason to believe that the like assurance will be given you at this time, by severall others that may be depended upon. But if you loose the opportunity, 'tis probable you will never have such another; and therefore I hope you will now seriously weigh this matter, and compare the advantage, ease, and security, which you may certainly enjoy one way, with the trouble, danger, or even ruin, which will probably fall upon you the other: and not upon you onely, but upon your nearest relations, and friends, the government itself, and the publick.

1085. GODOLPHIN *to* MARLBOROUGH [*25 August 1708*]

Source: Blenheim MSS. A2-38.
Addressed: To his Grace the Duke of Marlborough.

from Winchendon[1] August 25

I have received just now at this place yours of the 27th[2] with the enclosed from the Pensioner, and I would not delay to take notice, that as I shall bee carefull of the secrett he recomends in it, so I am inclined to believe the thing as he relates it is in great measure the truth of the case. And if it bee so, 'tis one argument more for sending our troops to Portugall, as soon as wee can.

I shall trouble you with no other reflexions, from this place, upon your letter, and the rather, for that, as the winds have been, I every moment expect fresher letters from you.

---

[1] Godolphin was visiting Lord Wharton, the Junto leader, at his country house. His visit was not a very agreeable one, at least to Wharton, who wanted to discuss the stalemate in efforts to bring himself and Somers into the Cabinet, to raise Montague to the Attorney-Generalship, and other political matters. 'He found Lord Treasurer had so little disposition to speake to him, that if he had not forced himself into his room at six a clock in the morning the day he was to go away he had not had a word's conversation with him: And what he said to him then was very dry and disagreeable.' Maynwaring to the Duchess [20 Oct. 1708?], in *Private Correspondence*, i. 254-5.

[2] Letter 1078.

This letter is incomplete. What survives is primarily a draft by Godolphin of a letter for Marlborough to write in reply to the Queen's of 27 August.[1] This may be ascertained by a comparison of its contents with those of the Queen's. Godolphin must have written in haste (see the close) on the 27th, the day he received the Queen's to forward to Marlborough. Marlborough received both on 9/20 September together with letters of the 31st. Having received two posts at once he confuses them and thus refers mistakenly to the Queen's as the 31st (see p. 1101). At the same time he wrote to Godolphin that he would not answer the Queen's until the next post (13/24 September). We can only presume he incorporated Godolphin's draft in his letter on that date.

1086. GODOLPHIN *to* MARLBOROUGH [*27 August 1708*]

Source: Blenheim MSS. F1-31.
Printed: Coxe, ii. 520-1.

[no heading]

As to the tyranny of the five Lords[2] which you seem so much to apprehend, and so much to desire that you might bee kept out of their hands, if your Majesty were disposed to hearken to the advices of those who have supported you for almost 7 years upon the throne, and much more before you came to it, you would bee in no danger of falling into any hands but ours whom you did not till very lately use to think dangerous, and certainly we are not altered. 'Tis a maxime I have often heard, that interest cannot lie. Wee can have no other interest but your Majesty's, and to make your throne powerful, and your government strong, but your Majesty will allow some people may have an interest to our prejudices. They may have an interest to create difficultys every day in your Majesty's mind against us, and by that means so to force us out of your service, and then indeed I am afrayd you may bee in very dangerous hands. But as to these 5 Lords, if your Majesty will bee inclined to doe such things only as in themselves, are not only just and reasonable, with regard to all that is past, but usefull and necessary for all that is to come, your Majesty needs not to apprehend falling into any hands but ours, who have done you very many faithful services and who (whatever return wee are like to have for them) will never fail to pray for your Majesty's long life and prosperity.

I have written this in a good deal of hast and disorder, and therfore I believe it wants no little correction; but you may omitt or alter any part of it just as you please.

[1] In Coxe, ii. 517-18 and Brown, pp. 256-8.
[2] The Whig Junto: Somers, Halifax, Sunderland, Wharton, and Orford.

On 24 August/4 September Marlborough moved his army to a position directly south of Lille and prepared for battle. His left was at Fretin, extending to the Marque, his right stretched beyond Noyelles to the river Deule. With both flanks anchored in marshes he left the French no choice but a frontal assault on a narrow front. The French came up to Mons-en-Pévèle on the 24th/4th but decided it was too late in the day to give battle. While their troops prepared positions opposite the Confederate lines, with their left on Phalempin, Vendôme and Berwick surveyed the situation for two days. The former wanted to attack. The latter, supported by Burgundy, believed it foolhardy to carry out the King's instructions. So instead of acting, all three wrote on the evening of the 25th/6th to Louis XIV, proferring their advice and asking for further instructions.

1087. MARLBOROUGH *to* GODOLPHIN

[*27 August/7 September 1708*]

Source: Blenheim MSS. A2-39.
Printed: Coxe, ii. 539-40 (inc.).

Fretin September 7th 1708

Since my last I have had yours of the 20th,[1] and am very sorry to see by the journall and letters from the fleet, that wee are not to expect much from that expedition, for it is certain if the sight of tents and mellitia can hinder them from landing, thay will in some degree find them all along the coast. Monsieur de Vandome having drawn all the troupes possible from the garrison, and having a great train of artillerie joined him from Doway, make his own army and ours beleive we should have had a battel on the 5th, which was the King of France's bearthday; so that Prince Eugene joined me that morning with 72 squadrons and 26 battalions. But thay not moving from their camp, which is in sight of ours, we sent back the foot the same night to the siege, resolving to intrench the front of our camp, which we begane to do yesterday. The intrenchment is so farr advanced, that I have this morning sent him back all his horse, as also a detachement of 2,000 foot, to assist him in the attacking of the counterscarp this night, and for the carrying on of the siege with more vigor then hethertoo; for it is certain our ingeniers finds much more work then thay expected. By the success of this night, we shall be able to guess when we may have the town, for should we be obliged to fyer much more powder and ball, we should be very much putt to, to find enough for the cittadel, this being the 12 day our battaries have fyered. Mr. Craggs[2] came to me yesterday from Bercelona, which place he left on the 5th of the last month. I shall dispatch him for England tomorrow, and by him send

---

[1] Letter 1081.
[2] James Craggs, the younger (1686–1721); Secretary 1708, Resident 1708–10, 1711 of English mission to Charles III. *D.N.B.*

copies of my letters from the King[1] and Duke of Molles,[2] which must be seen by nobody but her Majesty. By this post I send an abstract of part of the Duke of Molles' letter to Mr. Secritary Boyle,[3] by which you will see that the levy mony, and the charg of the transportation preposed by Comte Wratislaw, is not what the King of Spain expects the Queen should be att, he having proposed another methode to the Emperor; but Mr. Stanhop has promised the Queen should pay them when in Catalonia.[4] This abstract of the Duke of Molles must not be spoke of but at the Cabenet Councel, since it would do him an ill office at Vienna, if it should be known.

44 [King Charles] letter is to give assurances to 39 [Marlborough] that the *patent* he sent him two yeares ago, he intends to conferm for life. You will see the turn he gives to it by his letter which Mr. Craggs shall bring. This must be known by nobody but the Queen, for should it be known before 81 [peace], it would creat inconveniencys in 110 [Holland], and I beg you to assure the Queen that it is not compliment but real duty, that when 81 [peace] happens, that if she shall not think it for her honour and intirest that 39 [Marlborough] accepts of this great offer, I will be answerable that he shall decline it with all the submission imaginable. The Elector of Hanover has called a councell, and the opinions of the generals are given in writting, which are sent to Vienna, that the Emperor may give such orders as he thinkes proper. Mr. Bulau has promised me the whole in French. He says by their reasonings nothing can be done, so that the Elector, his master, is very uneasy, and that he is not sure, but that he may leave the army before the campagne is ended. 210 [Marlborough] has been informed that 50 [Elector of Hanover] is very much disatisfied at the success that 48 [Prince Eugene] and 39 [Marlborough] have had, and can't hinder showing it on all occasions.

September 8

I keep the post til this morning that I might lett you know, that we lodged on the counterscarp last night. I have not as yett the particulars of our lose.

1088. MARLBOROUGH *to the* DUCHESS
[*27 August/7 September 1708*]

Source: Blenheim MSS. E4.
Printed: *Private Correspondence*, i. 158–9 (inc.).

[Fretin] September 7th 1708

I had the pleasur of yours of the 20th yesterday when I was at the siege, which dose not go on so fast as were to be wished; but this night the counter-

---

[1] 25 July/5 Aug., part in Coxe, ii. 315, balance in Geikie, p. 92. In it the King revived the offer of the governorship of the Spanish Netherlands.

[2] 29 July/19 Aug., untraced; reply, 28 Aug./8 Sept., Murray, iv. 211. Don Francisco Moles, Duke of Paretti (died 1713), Imperial ambassador to Charles III 1706–11.

[3] P.R.O., S.P. 87/3, ff. 192–3.   [4] The 4,000 Palatines to be sent from Italy to Spain.

scarp is to be attacked, which we fear will cost a good many men. I have this morning sent 2,000 men to help them in their attack; and that I may be the better able to help them in the carrying on of the siege with vigor, we begane yesterday to intrench ourselves, which worke I hope will be finished tomorrow, after which I should think the French will have no mind to attack us, though thay will have double our numbers, now that I have sent all the troupes of Prince Eugene's army back to the siege, as also 2,000 of our men. The French army and we are about two English milles distance from each other. I do not think thay will come nearer, but endeavour all thay can to prevent provissions coming to us. I shall send by Mr. Craggs' son a letter I have received from 44 [King Charles] which must be a secritt. You will see by itt that he gives assurances to 39 [Marlborough] that he shall have for his life, what 253 [Lady Tyrconnel] was so desirous 210 [Marlborough] should have.[1] No doubt this is a great expression of 44 [King Charles], but if I know 39 [Marlborough], his happyness dose not depend so much on greatness as on your kindness and quietness. This must be known to nobody but 38 [Godolphin] and 42 [the Queen], without whoes consent I am sure 39 [Marlborough] would not accept of any offer, though of the greatest advantage. Besides, if this were known before 81 [peace] it would do hurt in 110 [Holland].

September 8th

The post was stopped til this morning, that I might lett you know that we are masters of the counterscarp. I have not the particulars, but what I hear, our killed and wounded may be about 1,600 men.

1089. MARLBOROUGH *to the* DUCHESS

[*30 August/10 September 1708*]

Source: Blenheim MSS. E4.
Printed: *Private Correspondence*, i. 159–60.

[*Fretin*] September 10th 1708

I begine to write this morning, beleiving that I shall not have any of yours this day. Since our last attack I am told that our ingeniers and those that governs the siege do not agree so well as thay did, which is no good sign for the siege. For if it should draw in lengh, I should much more fear the want of amunition, then what the French army could do, though we are in sight. Having write thus farr, contrary to my expectations, I this minut have the happyness of yours of the 24th, with the inclosed copies, by which I see Mrs. Morley [the Queen] is disatisfied with what Mrs. Freeman [Lady Marlborough] whispered at the church. I have torne all the enclosed papers

---

[1] The governorship of the Spanish Netherlands. For this new offer see above. For Lady Tyrconnel's comments see p. 1033.

as you desired.¹ I avoyd making answere to what you say concerning 182 [George Churchill], having fully answered itt in my former letters, that I had, and should assure him that it would not be in my power to protect him.² This being done, if it be expected that I must do some il-natured thing to convince that I do not approve of his actions, I must desire to be excused, for I shall content myself in letting him know, and see that he shall have no assistance from mee.

I am extreamly obliged to you for your kind assurances of your endeavours to make mee happy, when I shall retier. I find by your reasoning I did not explain myself enough on that subject, for my intentions is not to retier before a good and safe peace be made, unless I find myself made incapable by others' actions of doing good.

1090. MARLBOROUGH *to* GODOLPHIN

[*31 August/11 September 1708*]

Source: Blenheim MSS. A2-39.

[Fretin] September 11th 1708

I have had the favour of yours of the 24th,³ and very sorry to see the figure our embarkation makes, for from this time forward the French will have reason never to fear our landing, for thay certainly have this yeare no troupes on their coast but their melitia. You will see by a letter to me from the deputys, which I have sent to Mr. Secritary,⁴ the desire thay have of having the troupes of embarkation at Ostend. Thay do not pretend thay should stay above three weekes or one month att most. Thay, in my opinion, may be useful there, and though you should use all the dilligence imaginable, thay would not be of much use this campagne in Portugall; so that if thay be there by the begining of Febuarie, then I should think it might be better for the common cause. For besides the service thay might do towardes the

---

¹ At the thanksgiving service for Oudenaarde, held at St. Paul's, 19 Aug., the Duchess selected the Queen's jewels, over which there was a dispute, in her capacity as Mistress of the Robes, and accompanied the Queen in her coach. On arriving at the church the Duchess, fearful that the Queen might say something embarrassing about their disagreements, ordered the Queen to be silent, in a manner which aroused her wrath.

The Duchess had drafted a letter to the Queen to enclose Marlborough's of 9/20 Aug. (p. 1072), which she must have received 14 Aug. (see p. 1076). She apparently did not send this draft (in Blenheim MSS. G1-7), but waited, perhaps to see what she could accomplish in a personal interview as she attended the Queen on the thanksgiving. When the meeting ended so disastrously, she revised her letter (printed in *Conduct*, p. 219 (part)) and sent it off with Marlborough's. The Queen's reply, on 22 Aug., was short and cold (in Brown, p. 258). The Duchess wrote yet another chastising letter on 24 Aug. (in *Conduct*, pp. 220-2) and then their communications ceased until another interview on 9 Sept. (for which see Coxe, ii. 522-3).

² See letter 1084A.   ³ 23? Letter 1082.

⁴ 30 Aug./10 Sept., in S.P. 87/3, fols. 198-9, enclosed in his letter to Boyle, 30 Aug./10 Sept., Murray, iv. 216-18. Another copy in B.M., Add. MS. 5130, fol. 209.

reducing of Bridges and Gant, it might give time to Lord Galway to setle everything that is reasonable with the court of Portugall. And thay should be told plainly that no troupes should come if thay do not comply to what is reasonable; for thay can't make a peace or truce with France whielst wee are masters att sea.

Our siege dose by no means go so well as were to be wished. The French and we are very near, but I am so well posted and retrenched, that I do not aprehend their attacking; though thay are very much stronger then wee, by the necessity I lie under of sending almost every day very great detachements for the security of our convoyes. My Lord Albermarle is at this time with one of above 5,000 men at Audenar.

I should have been glad when you were in Wilshire you could have given 24 hours to Woodstock, for I fancy that would have incoraged the work. I fear it dose not lie in your way to Althrope.

When Mr. Secretary answers the paper I have had from the deputys, I desire it might be so answered, that I might send the letter[1] to the States, in which there will be an opertunity of the Queen's using some kind expression which will do good at this time.

1091. GODOLPHIN *to* MARLBOROUGH   [*31 August 1708*]

Source: Blenheim MSS. A2-38.

Windsor August 31th 1708

My last from Winchendon[2] acknowledged the favour of yours of the 27th[3] with the enclosed from the Pentioner relating to 81 [peace]. This morning I have also the favour of your letter of the 3d of September[4] with the enclosed from Comte Maffei. But I find no letter from you nor Lady Marlborough neither, by the post of the 30th, which I suppose may have been occasioned by your being on the march with the army, about that time; and I mention it only, because in yours of the 3d of September you doe not take notice of having missed writing by the former post; and that you might know (in case you did write by that post) those letters have never come to us. I have had time since my last to reflect a little upon the Pensioner's letter to you, and am more and more confirmed that what he says he had from Mr. Pettcum may bee the sincere and reall thoughts of 43 [King of France]; and I continue to think it will bee very naturall to inferr from thence, that more troops ought to bee sent to Portugall before the end of the year. But

---

1 Sunderland wrote on 6 and 7 Sept., telling Marlborough that all the troops on board the fleet except the Dragoons had been sent to Ostend. 'Nothing but their pressing insistence and the great desire the Queen has, of doing everything, they think may be of use to the common cause, or a security to Holland, could have induced her to comply in this matter.' Blenheim MSS. B1-1.

2 Letter 1085. Godolphin must also have written on the 27th. See p. 1086 and p. 1100.

3 Letter 1078.   4 Letter 1083.

'tis already too late to send them so as to bee of use in this autumn and I find Mr. Methuen, who is now arrived here, is entirely of that opinion.

Those troops are now returned with Mr. Erle to Spithead, in expectation of the event before Lisle, and of your thoughts after it, how they may bee best employed. In the meantime I am sorry to find by yours of the 3d of September that siege is not so forward as you had hoped. Wee have letters of the 8th from Ostend which speak of it more hopefully. At the same time, they pretend to tell us very positively the French will not venture a battell to relieve it. But all the letters from France, both publick and private, are quite in another style; so our impatience for farther news from you, is like to continue to a very great degree, till that matter bee absolutely decided.

I am not at all surprised at the letter you sent mee from Comte Maffei. It was very naturall to expect 58 [Duke of Savoy] should have *carte blanche* offered to him. I shall not take notice of it to Comte Briancon, not having heard of it from him. But I can't help wishing the thing itself were known to 116 [the States] and to 110 [Holland], for I don't at all doubt but the same offers will bee very soon made to them, and I should hope they would bee the more readily inclined to follow so good an example.

I shall not trouble you with anything now relating to our affairs at home. Everybody's mind and thoughts are in suspence upon the great event at Lisle, and the consequences of it. God send it may end to your own wish.

1092. GODOLPHIN *to* MARLBOROUGH   [*1 September 1708*]

Source: Blenheim MSS. A2-38.

Windsor September 1st 1708

I begin to acknowledg the favour of yours of the 7th of September with a postscript of the 8th[1] by which I am glad to see you were master of the contrescarp of Lisle. It seems now very plain, the French will have no more battells this year, and I doubt it is almost as plain you can make no more sieges, unless the taking of Lisle supplys the wants you seem to have of powder and ball.

Not knowing what your circumstances may bee upon taking that place, what I shall say (therfore) in this letter may bee much at random. But having had some discourse as I told you I intended with Monsieur Gattigny, I desired him to putt his thoughts into writing, and beg leave to send them to you in the enclosed paper[2] of which I have no coppy. What use you can make of it, or of our troops now at the Isle of Wight, I am not able to judg. But the sooner you can determine concerning the troops, it would bee the better, in many respects.

---

[1] Letter 1087.   [2] Untraced. See p. 1041.

The Queen of Portugall is not yett come but I expect this wind should bring us news of her, perhaps before I seal this letter. When she is come, wee shall bee much pressed to send the troops under the same convoy, and unless there bee some other immediat employment for them in view, I doubt it will not bee easy to resist those pressings, so as not to send, at least, some of the regiments now. Though at the same time, I must own that Mr. Methuen who was with mee this morning seems to think it impossible they can come time enough to bee of any use there in this autumn.

By the 2 last posts, we hear of Mr. Craggs his arrivall in Holland, but not yett of his being come hither. If the troops which you seem to think are embarking at Naples, arrive safely and speedily at Barcelona, they will not want any more reinforcement this year, nor more than recruits of the troops they have for the next. But I don't comprehend upon what those troops from Naples should embark, not having ever heard that Sir John Leak had sent a squadron thither for them, though he might safely have done it. And it would bee better a great deal for the Service, if he would separate his fleet more than he has yett thought fitt to doe; by which means severall services might bee performed at the same time, by 6 or 7 ships in a squadron, before the season were past.

By the Dutch prints he seems to have had success at Sardinia.[1] If so, that will prove a very necessary magazin for the army in Catalonia. And if wee could also gett Sicily before the fleet were obliged to return, Naples would than bee at liberty to furnish all the necessary recruits for that army. But this (I doubt) amounts to little more than a wish.

I am very well pleased to hear that 44 [King Charles] has renewed the patent to 39 [Marlborough] in the manner you speak of, and must also agree with what you seem to think that unless the secrett of it bee better kept than those things use to bee, it cannot fail of doing a great deal of mischief, not only with 110 [Holland] but in other places. So I think too much care can't bee taken to keep it quiett. I have never breathed it but to 42 [the Queen] who I hope will keep it. But if 42 [the Queen], tells it, t'will bee to those through whom it will pass in to the very worst hands that one can imagine.

Lady Marlborough is at Salisbury[2] and does not intend to return till Saturday.[3] Whether she will find any means of writing to you from thence, I doe not yett know, but if she does, I believe she will send mee her letter for you tomorrow, to this place.

My Lord Sunderland returns here next Sunday, and in a day or two after, Mr. Secretary Boyle goes into Wiltshire, for all this month of September.

I have been desired by Mr. Oglethorp,[4] he that is now the elder brother, to

---

[1] Cagliari, its capital, surrendered on 2/13 Aug.
[2] To visit the Bishop and Mrs. Burnet.   [3] 4 Sept.
[4] Theophilius Oglethorpe (1682–1720?), M.P., Haslemere, 1708–13; son of Sir Theophilius Oglethorpe (1650–1702); aide-de-camp to Ormonde; joined the Pretender after the accession of George I. His elder brother was Lewis Oglethorpe (1681–1704). *D.N.B.* under his father.

recommend him to your favour for some employment in the army. He is himself of the House of Commons, and tells mee he will bring in any one more whom I shall name to him. I remember he was always desirous to goe into the Service, butt his mother[1] was averse. Now he has either obtained her consent, or thinks he does not want it, which is much at one.

Though my letter is already very tedious, yett I shall add more tomorrow, in case the forreign letters come in, which as the winds have been here, wee may reasonably enough expect.

September 3d.

It is now Fryday noon and no letters come, and the wind now northwest, so I began to fear wee shall not have them before the [post] goes. The news of du Casse's[2] having brought the flota to Biscay,[3] and the thoughts people have that there may bee an opportunity this winter of attacking the galeons which have taken shelter at Carthagena,[4] makes a great ferment here at this time for sending some regiments to the West Indies upon that service. Those of Lepel and Munden are ready in Ireland,[5] but what more may bee necessary to make up 2,500 men, which is the number proposed, must bee taken from hence. I own, I think the thing is right, but wee want proper persons for the execution of almost anything.

1093. MARLBOROUGH *to* GODOLPHIN   [2/13 September 1708]

Source: Blenheim MSS. A2-39.
Printed: Coxe, ii. 541.
Addressed: To my Lord Treasurer, Whitehall.

[Fretin] September 13th 1708

Since my last[6] Monsieur de Vandome is come so near to us, that we did begine to beleive that his intentions was to attack us. But yesterday, and the day before, he did nothing but fyer a great quantity of canon; and this day we have been very quiet, he having drawn his canon from the batteries on our left, as we think with a designe to see what he can do on our right. We are camped so near that there is no possibillity of being at ease til Lisle is taken. I have been so disturbed these two last nights and days that I am as hotte as if I were in a feavor, so that you will excuse my saying no more by this post.

[1] Lady Eleanor Oglethorpe. See p. 1005.
[2] Jean-Baptiste Ducasse (1650–1715), French naval officer, governor of Saint-Domingue, 1691–1700; lieutenant-general of the navy 1707.
[3] The annual treasure fleet from America to Spain was brought under a French convoy to Los Pasajes on 16/27 Aug. by Ducasse because of the greater danger of interception from the Allied fleet if it was taken to Spain. Kamen, *War of Succession in Spain*, pp. 183–4.
[4] See p. 1058, n. 3.
[5] These regiments had been held in reserve to reinforce Erle, if required. See pp. 968, 973, 1054.
[6] Letter 1090.

1094. GODOLPHIN *to* MARLBOROUGH   [*3 September 1708*]

Source: Blenheim MSS. A2-38.

Windsor Fryday 3d of September
at 6 in the evening 1708

Since I had sealed my packett of this day[1] I have received the enclosed letters from my Lord Gallway,[2] which seem to bee of great consequence, and to putt the Queen under a good deal of difficulty every way.

On one side he says plainly, the court and the ministers will doe nothing for us unless they bee forced to it, by our sending a great body of troops to act there, and by furnishing greater subsidyes than wee have yett done. And on the other side, all this money, and all these men are to bee sent thither under very great uncertainty, at best, whether they are like to have any effect to our advantage, considering the great inclinations to a neutrality which he observes in that court.

It ought likewise to bee considered that provision was made in the last sessions of Parliament for 27 regiments to serve in Spain and Portugall, and not one has been sent to either, since the rising of the Parliament.

The reasonableness of sending some force to the West Indies, at this time, as I have touched in my former letter of this day, ought also to bee considered, before any decisive resolution bee taken upon the whole; towards which, it would bee a very great satisfaction to have your thoughts in answer to this letter, if the time will allow of our deferring to come to a resolution till then, since wee expect every hour to hear of the arrivall of the Queen of Portugall.

My own opinion at present is that 4 or 5 of the regiments on board the fleet[3] should bee sent imediatly to the West Indies, and the rest to Portugall with the Queen with an assurance at the same time of compleating them to the number promised, before the end of the winter. I think those wee take for the West Indies, might bee replaced by 2 from Ireland and 2 from Scotland. But I must own to you, I have no heart to take upon mee, in this or anything else any farther than barely to tell my opinion, which makes mee the more pressing in troubling you for your directions in these matters, in case you have liberty and inclinations to lett mee have them, without loss of time.

[1] Letter 1092.   [2] Untraced.
[3] With Erle and Byng.

1095. GODOLPHIN *to* MARLBOROUGH   [*6 September 1708*]

Source: Blenheim MSS. A2-38.

Windsor September the 6th 1708

I have the favour of yours of the 11th[1] and am very sorry to find that your loss has been greater and the advantage less than you expected, in the attack of the contrescarpe [of Lille], upon the 7th.

You will have seen by mine of the last post the severall service in view for the troops with Mr. Erle, and how pressing in their severall respects. However upon reading of your letter to Mr. Secretary Boyle with that from the deputyes to you, the Queen has dispatched her orders last night to Portsmouth that the fleet and troops should sail to Ostend without any loss of time. So that I veryly believe they are like to bee there before any orders are sent thither, either for receiving them, or how they shall bee made use of. I believe Lieutenant Generall Erle will both desire and expect to find 2 or 3 words from you upon his arrivall, how he is to guide himself.

Mr. Secretary Boyle going into the country tomorrow morning, my Lord Sunderland has the Queen's directions to make such an answer to your letter from the deputys, as may bee shown to the States, according to your desire.

My Lord Sunderland has likewise the Queen's orders for what he is to write to my Lord Gallway upon the troops not coming to Portugall with the Queen, as has been all along promised and expected. I will not trouble you with the particulars in this letter, because I intend to desire him to send you a coppy of what he writes upon this occasion.[2]

And as for getting the regiments wee want every moment to send to the West Indies, there remains no expedient but to take them from Ireland. But I must own I expect difficultyes in that matter from my Lord Lieutenant,[3] which in my own opinion are rather formall then effectuall difficultyes, and therfore I hope wee shall overcome them.

Mr. Craggs being not yett come thither, I doe not trouble you now upon any of the particulars which may have been the occasion of his coming. I have taken care with both the Secretarys of State that no mention shall bee made of the Duke of Moles's letter or so much as of his name. But I believe the

---

[1] Letter 1090.

[2] In his letter of 7 Sept., Sunderland enclosed a letter to Galway of the same date (Blenheim MSS. B1-1; copies in P.R.O., S.P. 104/208, pp. 244-6). He wrote: 'The season is so much advanced by the Queen of Portugall's long stay on the other side of the water, she having not yet left Holland, that it will be impossible for the troops that were designed for Portugall to arrive there time enough to be of any use this next campaign, besides that by the present posture of affairs on this side it will be absolutely necessary for them to be employed for a fortnight or three weeks to assist the Dutch in the reduction of Bruges and Gand . . . They shall be sent by the end of January or beginning of February, so as to be ready to act early in the spring, provided they do agree to your Lordship's proposalls about the payment of the troops.'

[3] Pembroke.

court of Vienna won't much like that 44 [King Charles] should take so much upon him in that matter.[1]

According to the leave you gave mee[2] I shall now speak to the Queen that Mr. James Lowther may resign his place in the ordnance to his cousin Mr. Robert Lowther, who is a very pretty, well tempered, young man. And I am sure you will like him much better than the other.

1096. MARLBOROUGH *to* GODOLPHIN   [6/17 *September 1708*]

Source: Blenheim MSS. A2-39.
Printed: Coxe, ii. 542.

Sanguin September 17th 1708

I came to this camp last night, the French having begone their march on the 15th towardes their right. I did not march till the next day, that I might be the better informed of their intentions, which seemes to be, for their taking a camp between us and Audnar, in order to hinder our convoye from Bruxelles, as also the provissions which comes from that side to the army.[3] Thay have carryed their battering trayne to Tournay, and thay say in their army, that thay will besiege and take Audenar before we shall gett Lisle. For these last five or six days the siege has advanced very litle, which makes everybody uneasy. No doubt there will be many letters, to the same effect, but I desire not to be named. If the enemy dose not oblige me to march, which I feare thay will, I shall go for two houres to the siege, so that I shall not seall this letter til my return, that if I have anything good from thence I may send it you.

I have this minut an account that the French army begine to pass the Schel by Tournay, which makes me resolve not to march til tomorrow.

I have been with Prince Eugene and the deputys at the siege and find everything in a bad way, which gives me the spleen.

1097. MARLBOROUGH *to* GODOLPHIN   [6/17 *September 1708*]

Source: Blenheim MSS. B2-9.
Addressed: To my Lord Treasurer, Whitehall.

[no heading]

Mr. Crags will give you an account of Monsieur de Vandome's movements. I cannot think he intendes to attack us, but to canonade, by which he thinkes

---

[1] See p. 1088.   [2] See pp. 1037, 1048.

[3] Marlborough had moved about 5 kilometres to the north-east, to Sainghin, with his right at Péronne and his left at Forest on the Marque, a line running north–south, parallel to the Scheldt. The French moved a greater distance to the east, some 25 kilometres to a camp east of the Scheldt on the north side of Tournai. Vendôme made his headquarters at Saulchoi. See Marlborough to Boyle, 6/17 Sept., Murray, iv. 226–7.

to make a noyse in the world. I should not have troubled you at this time but in feavor of Mr. Crags. For by what I find, I beleive Mr. Stanhope is of opinion, that if he had the carector of resident, it might enable him to do the Queen's business better, when Mr. Stanhope may be obliged to be at the army.[1] I shall give you no further trouble at this time, but what kindness you shoe this young gentleman, I shall take as a feavour done to your humble servant.

1098. MARLBOROUGH *to the* DUCHESS   [*6/17 September 1708*]

Source: Blenheim MSS. E2.
Printed: Coxe, ii. 541–2.

[Sainghin] September 17th 1708

Whenever I have a minutte to myself I make use of itt to write to my dear soull; for Monsieur de Vandome having geithered much more strengh to-geither then we could imagine, and being camped so near, that in one hour's time we might be ingaged, obliges us to be so very dilligent that we have very litle rest, by reason of the troupes we are obliged to have at the siege, which makes him have near twice as much foot as I have in this army. But I am so well intrenched that I no ways fear their forcing us. But the siege goes on so very slowly, that I am in perpetuall feares that it may continue so long, and consequently consume so much stores, that we may at last not have wherewithall to finish, which would be very crewell. These are my feares, but I desire you will lett nobody know them. I long extreamly to have this campagne well ended, for of all the campagnes I have made, this has been the most painfull. But I am in the gally, and must row on as long as this warr last. The Prince of Hanover has told me that as soon as the town is taken, he intends to return for Hanover. The French being marched by their right, I have been obliged to march by our left, so that we are now in our camp where I was before I came to that which I intrenched. I beleive the enemy will oblige us to march againe this night, thay having already sent a detachement towardes Audenard, which thay say in their camp thay will besiege. I am intierly yours.

Since I had finished this letter I have notice that the French are passing the Schell by Tournay, so that I shall not march til tomorrow morning.

[1] Craggs had gone as secretary to Stanhope. He was now given credentials as Resident bearing date of 29 Sept./10 Oct.

1099. GODOLPHIN *to* MARLBOROUGH   [*8 September 1708*]

Source: Blenheim MSS. A2-38.

Windsor 8th September 1708

I received yesterday the favour of yours of the 13th[1] and am sorry to hear you have been made so uneasy, and your rest so much disturbed by the French army. But by all the accounts that are come over, I hope those disturbances are now at an end. And by all the *working* of the French (to make use of a sea expression) I am very much perswaded that before you are in possession of the town of Lisle, they will take great care not to stay within your reach.

Monsieur de Gattigny has been with mee here this morning. I find him still very full of his notions in the paper which I sent you by the last post.[2] He says that if you can depend upon your having provisions for your army by sea, whenever you will march to possess yourself of Abbeville, and Amiens,[3] you necessaryly oblige the French army to putt themselves behind the river Oyse[4] to cover Paris and Versailles.

Wee have letters from Sir George Bing and Mr. Erle from Spithead that they would bee ready to sail as yeasterday, the 7th, with the troops to Ostend. But the weather has been stormy all this day, so I hope they did not sail. Besides that, I think our troops will always bee there too soon, if they doe not meet with particular orders from you how to govern themselves upon their arrivall.

Mr. Erle writes that he shall bee obliged to leave near 600 men sick, behind him. I am pressing therfore to have Maccartney and Hill's regiments ordered to follow him, as soon as possible. One of them is at Portsmouth, but not in a readyness to bee now embarked. The other is at Northampton.

9th of September at night

Since I began to write this letter I hear Sir George Bing sailed the 7th in the morning, and the wind having blown pretty hard ever since, I am persuaded he is now or will bee tomorrow at Ostend. I shall bee very glad to hear these troops may bee able to doe as much service as seems to bee expected from them. But when the campagne in Flanders is at an end, if they are to bee sent to Portugall at all, the sooner they are sent the more encoragement it must bee to those people, and the better effect it will have.

Another post will bee due from you tomorrow, but it has blown so hard that I doe not expect the letters, though everybody is very impatient to know the fate of Lisle, and how the armyes will part having been so near.

---

[1] Letter 1093. [2] Letter 1092.
[3] Amiens, capital of Picardy, an important provincial centre on the Somme, 40 kilometres up-stream from Abbeville.
[4] The Oise takes its rise in the north-east corner of Picardy at the border with the Spanish Netherlands and flows south-west to the Seine, which it joins just below its passage through Paris.

10th September

I have just now received notice that the stormy weather which continues still has forced Sir George Bing to come to an anchor in the Downs with the men of warr and transports.

The French had extended their lines from Tournai almost to Oudenaarde, 'which they have almost blocked up on that side'. On 6/17 September Marlborough wrote to Boyle:[1] 'It is likely we may march tomorrow towards Pont-Espierres, to observe their further motions.' Spiere lies about 15 kilometres north of Tournai on the Scheldt. The camp he chose to move to on the 7/18th was Templeuve, directly east of Forest where his left was fixed. From there he moved west again towards Lille on the 9/20th, stopping at Lannoy, a distance of some 10 kilometres, 'the better to observe the enemy and to cover the siege at the same time'.

1100. MARLBOROUGH *to* GODOLPHIN   [9/20 September 1708]

Source: Blenheim MSS. A2-39.
Printed: Coxe, ii. 543-4 (inc.).

[Lannoy] September 20th 1708

Since my last I have received your two letters of the 27th and 31.[2] By my letters I find Earle had leave to disembark the men. I could wish my letter had come time enough to have saved them that trouble, for if it be her Majesty's pleasure to lett them come for Ostend for some litle time, the sooner thay were there would be the better for the Service.

It is impossible for me to expresse the uneasyness I suffer for the ill-conduct of our ingeniers att the siege, where I think everything goes very wrong. It would be a crewell thing if after we have obliged the enemy to quit all thoughts of releiving the place by force, which thay have done by repassing the Schell, we should faile of taking it by the ignorance of our ingeniers, and the want of stores; for we have already fiered very near as much as was demanded for the taking the town and cittadell, and as yett we are not intier masters of the counterscarp; so that to you I may own my dispair of ending this campagne, so as in reason we might have expected. I beg you to assure the Queen that my greatest concern is on her account; for as to myself, I am so tierd of the world, that were she not concerned, my affliction could not be great. When the fate of Lisle is once known, we shall

---

[1] Murray, iv. 226-7.   [2] Letters 1086, 1091.

endeavour all we can to bring the enemy to a generall engagement. But as that is what we shall desire, I take it for granted it is what thay will avoid. Having drawn all the troupes thay can together, thay are stronger then wee; and our letters of yesterday from the Rhin assures us that the Elector of Bavier was to leave the army the next day, in order to drink the watters near Mettez; and that the troupes, Bavaroise and Spaniardes, had orders to march for this country; and that the Elector was to have his residence this winter att Mons. What you wish might be known in Holand as to the preposall made to 58 [Duke of Savoy] is impossible, for he desires it should be known to nobody but 42 [the Queen], 38 [Godolphin], and 39 [Marlborough].

I have this evening received a letter from Palms,[1] by which I find there is nothing more designed to be done this campagne. You must not take notice to Brianzon of anything Palms writes, but if he would have the four hundred thousand crowns, he should not end where it is only for his own conveniency. You will see by the enclosed copie of a letter,[2] write to me by the officer sent to Vienna by King Charles for these troupes that are now going to Catalonia, that it is not expected the Queen should give any leavy mony. I also enclose a letter and draft of what has passed at Lisle to this day, which I desire you will with my duty give to his Royal Highness,[3] and also lett the Queen know that I shall do myself the honour of answering hers of the 31,[4] which I received yesterday, by the next post; for my head eakes at this minut so extreamly, that I am not able to write any more at this time.

1101. MARLBOROUGH *to* GODOLPHIN

[*13/24 September 1708*]

Source: Blenheim MSS. A2–39.
Printed: Coxe, ii. 546–7.

[Lannoy][5] September 24th 1708

Since my last[6] Prince Eugene has received a wound in his head, which I thank God is no ways daingerous, and I hope tomorrow or next day he may be abroad. Ever since Friday[6] that he was wounded, I have been obliged to be every day att the siege, which with the vexation of it is going so ill, I am almost dead. We made a thord attack last night, and are not yett masters of the whole counterscarp. But that which is yett worse, those who have the charge of the stores have declared to the deputys, that the opiniatrety of the siege is such, that thay have not stores sufficient for the taking of the town,[7]

---

[1] 24 Aug./4 Sept., Blenheim MSS. B1–3.
[2] Marquis de Campos; 18/29 Aug., Blenheim MSS. B1–15.   [3] Prince George.
[4] 27 Aug., Brown, pp. 256–8; for date see introduction to letter 1086.
[5] The preceding letter.   [6] 10/21 Sept.
[7] Marlborough decided later that a considerable quantity of the stores had been embezzled. See pp. 1105, 1153.

upon which the Prince has desired to speak with me tomorrow morning. My next will acquaint you of what is resolved, but I fear you must expect nothing good. I have this afternoon a letter from Lieutenant General Earle from Ostend.[1] He is ill of the gout. The enemy has cutt in three severall places the canall of Newport, by which thay have putt that country under watter to hinder our comunication with Ostend. However, I shall find ways of letting him know what I desire. I am so vexed att the misbehavior of our ingeniers that I have no patience, and beg your excuse that I say no more til the next post.

1102. MARLBOROUGH *to the* DUCHESS [*13/24 September 1708*]

Source: Blenheim MSS. E4.
Printed: *Private Correspondence*, i. 160–1.

[Lannoy] September 24th 1708

I have received yours of the 6th this morning. Could you be thorowly sensible of the uneasyness I have had for these last six weekes, and stil lye under, you would not have used so hard an expression to Mr. Freeman [Marlborough], by saying that he was as cautious in his writting as if he write to a spy. I do assure you he would always, with pleasure, lett you know his heart and soull; and besides, that he has not time for anything but the present business. He has on severall occasions said so much on the obstenat perserverance of 42 [the Queen], that I would wish that Mrs. Freman [Lady Marlborough] would see what she so frequently obsarves, that 42 [the Queen] is not capable of being changed by reason, so that you should be quiet til the time comes in which she must chang. As to what you say concerning the offer of 44 [King Charles] to 39 [Marlborough],[2] my thought is the same with yours, that I had rather live a quiet life with your love and kindness, then the most ambitious employement that any prince can give. It is certain that this offer is at a distance, but be assured that if I were fond of it, as really it is otherwais, I would not accept it but by your good liking; for it is with you I must be happy, if I am to injoy any such days. As for 42 [the Queen] consenting, in order to be eased as to importunitys, I have deserved from them better, but thay need not be uneasy, for whenever I can dispose of my own time, it shall not be to importune them.

You will know by the publick nuse that last Friday Prince Eugene received a hurt in the head. I thank God it is not daingerous, and in two or three days I hope he will be abroad. Our affaires here goes every day worse, which I can't express my trouble.

---

[1] 11/22 Sept., Blenheim MSS. B1-2.   [2] See p. 1088.

1103. GODOLPHIN *to* MARLBOROUGH   [*14 September 1708*]

Source: Blenheim MSS. A2-38.

Windsor 14th of September 1708

I am sorry to see in yours of the 17th¹ that the position of your affairs on that side gives you the spleen. I have naturally so much of it myself, as to fear that word from you expresses more then a great many others together would have done. But I hope still wee shall soon hear you are masters of the town of Lisle; for till that bee taken, I see plainly, the French will bee at liberty to doe what they please elsewhere.

In the meantime what you may have found in both my last letters² is come to pass. Our troops arrived at Ostend the 10/21st without meeting there any orders from you, which I knew they would expect, and bee at a loss for want of them; though I am sensible that in point of time, it was utterly impossible for the notice of their being sent to reach you, so as that your orders could meet them there.

By the experience I have of their proceedings I believe they won't easily make any one stepp without your directions. However the very noise of their arrivall, may probably oblige the French to make a detachment from their army the better to observe them.

The Queen will grant the favour you have desired for Mr. Craggs,³ and send him back again (I believe) very soon. I much doubt whether the troops from Naples will embark by the time Sir John Leak's detachment will bee able to stay to convoy them. But if they should happen to have a lucky passage to Catalonia, 'tis certain our army there would then bee every way superior to that of the Duke of Orleans.

But though wee are so in Italy too, I very much doubt by what *Palmes* writes from Turin there is little more to bee expected from 58 [Duke of Savoy] in this campagne. 'Tis a very uneasy reflexion, that when wee so frankly and sincerely make all our efforts for the good of the whole Allyance, to find that every one of them, in particular, think only of what is best for themselves, without any consideration either of the whole Allyance or of us, by whom only they are enabled to act.

When I have said this, I reckon you will bee pressed by 58 [Duke of Savoy] for renewing the treaty with the King of Prussia,⁴ and I think it should bee done. But I submitt to you, whether, in case it bee done, some more particular agreement should not bee made for 58's [Duke of Savoy]

---

¹ Letter 1096.   ² Letters 1095, 1099.   ³ See p. 1098.

⁴ The treaty was negotiated by Raby at Berlin and signed 20/31 Mar. 1709 (P.R.O., Treaties, 408). The troops in Italy remained and an augmentation made of the Prussian troops in the Low Countries. See Schmettau's letter to Marlborough, enclosed in Marlborough to Sunderland, 20 Sept./1 Oct., Murray, iv. 244-5, for Marlborough's guidance in arriving at terms and Raby to Marlborough, 27 Nov./8 Dec., ibid. 385, for the King of Prussia's proposal regarding an augmentation.

operations in the next year. I doe but hint this to you. I am sensible you must bee able to judge better of it, than 'tis possible for mee to suggest.

Your letters of the 21th are not yett come to us here, but the wind has been so fair, that I expect them every hour.

1104. GODOLPHIN *to* MARLBOROUGH   [*16 September 1708*]

Source: Blenheim MSS. A2-38.

Windsor 16 September 1708

Since my last I have the favour of yours of the 20th[1] and have obeyed your commands in it to the Queen and to the Prince. I am very sorry to find your siege goes onn so slowly (by the want of good ingeniers), that if you take the place at last, it is like to cost too much time, as well as too much blood. And I must doe Monsieur de Gattigny that justice to say that from the very first he told mee, he was afrayd you wanted good ingeniers.

By letters wee had last night from Ostend wee have the satisfaction of hearing you had notice of the arrivall of our troops there and were sending an officer to them with orders. But the same letters say that country was all under water, and seem to doubt whether that officer would bee able to gett into the town, or the troops to march any way out of it.

They say farther that the horn work had been attacked and carryed the 21th, but with very great loss, and that Prince Eugene and my Lord Stairs were wounded. I hope the latter part of this news is not true, but till I hear again from you, I must own I am apt enough to apprehend the worst of any reports that come. Upon this head, I will trouble you with a letter I have received from Monsieur de Guiscard from Bruxelles.[2] You will bee able to judg if what he writes bee his own reflexions, or the thoughts and talk of the place where he is.

The terrible bad weather wee have here makes mee melancholly for fear it should bee the same with you; though it's plain, the winds have not been the same, for wee have expected to hear of the arrivall of the Queen of Portugall every day for a week together, and by the last Holland letters she had not yett left the Maez.

By letters from my Lord Gallway of the 7th of September[3] I find he is taking a great deal of pains towards this autumn campagne against the coming of those troops which have been so long hoped for by them. But that will bee all defeated now, by their not coming. However, I think they must still bee sent this winter, as soon as they can bee spared from their present engagements.

Till I can have the pleasure of hearing you are a little more at ease than by your last, I have very little heart myself to give you any farther trouble.

[1] Letter 1100.
[2] Untraced. See his letter to Marlborough, 3/14 Sept., Blenheim MSS. B1-7.
[3] To Sunderland, Blenheim MSS. C2-11.

1105. MARLBOROUGH *to* GODOLPHIN

[*16/27 September 1708*]

Source: Blenheim MSS. A2-39.
Printed: Coxe, ii. 554-5.

[Lannoy] September 27th 1708

You will have seen by my last letter[1] the unhappy circomstances we are in by the very ill conduct of our ingeniers and others. Upon the wounding of Prince Eugene, I thought it absolutely necessary to inform myself of everything of the siege, for before I did not medle in anything but the covering of itt. Upon examination I find thay did not deall well with the Prince, for when I told him that there did not remain powder and ball for above 4 days he was very much surprised. I own to you that I fear we have something more in our misfortunes then ignorance.[2] Our cercomstances being thus, and the impossibillity of getting a convoy from Bruxelles, obliged me to take measures for the getting some amunition from Ostend, which we could never have attempted but for the good luck of the English battalions being there. Having time I begine to write in the morning, but as the letters are not to go till the evening, I hope to send you some certainty of the convoy, I having sent yesterday Major General Cadogan with 26 squadrons and 12 battalions to meet them, so that thay might come withe the greater safety, with which we must do our best; for should this not come safe, I am afraid we must not flatter ourselves of hoping to gett any other, though you may be sure wee shall leave nothing unattempted. For it is impossible to express the trouble this matter has given mee; for I am sensible that not only her Majesty but all the common cause must suffer if we miscary in this undertaking, which we have but to[o] much reason to apprehend. Our letters from Garmany assures us that on the 15th of this month a great detachement was made for this country, and that the Elector of Bavaria is to come with them, which will give no litle allarm in 110 [Holland].

[Roncq] September 29th

I have keep this maile til now that you may be informed of the success we have had in bringing our convoye safe from Ostend.[3] I must refer you for the particulars sent to the Secretary's office,[4] my head having ecked extreamly for these last two days. I must own to you that I have not strengh to bare long the necessary trouble I undergo, but I now hope for some ease, since Prince Eugene will be abroad tomorrow. Last night the French attempted to send in succours and powder into Lisle. About 300 forced their way throw

---

[1] Letter 1101.   [2] See p. 1153.

[3] This was the action at Wijnendaal, in which Major-General John Richmond Webb held off the superior French forces under La Motte, sent to intercept the convoy, while it passed safely into Marlborough's lines.

[4] Murray, iv. 243-4.

a Pallatin Redgiment; severall were blowen up and killed, and about 40 men
and 4 officers taken prisoners, the rest returned to Doway. Our letters run
so much risque of being read by the enemy, which makes it not safe to write
some things I have a mind to say.

1106. MARLBOROUGH *to the* DUCHESS   [*16/27 September 1708*]

Source: Blenheim MSS. E4.
Printed: Coxe, ii. 524 (inc.), as 27 September.

[Lannoy] September 27th 1708

Since my last[1] there is very litle happened to putt me in better humour then
I was then in. The Duke of Berwick is with a body of troupes come to
Brudges for the endeavoring to hinder a convoy we have sent for from Ostend,
and which without accedent we may have tomorrow. This convoy is of that
consequence that I have sent Cadogen with the troupes that are to bring
them.

[Roncq] September 29th

I have not suffered the letters to go til this evening, that the account of the
convoye might go with them. I am in such a hurry that you will escuse me
that I refer you to the account that will be sent to the Secretary's office.
Having received yours of the 10th this afternoon, I would not omitt sending
back all the enclosed papers you have desired, and letting you know at the
same time that I have formerly write in other letters, that I am glad you have
taken the resolution of being quiet; for you are certainly in the right, that
whatever is said or writte by 240 [Lady Marlborough], 38 [Godolphin] and
39 [Marlborough] serves only for information to do hurt. The copie of the
letter you have sent[2] I think should be delivred, for if it dose no good, it can
do no hurt. For my own part, I am quit weary of all business, and if amongst
all these disagreable bussels I could be so happy as to have liberty of remaining quiet with you, I should be at the height of my wishes.

1107. GODOLPHIN *to* MARLBOROUGH   [*20 September 1708*]

Source: Blenheim MSS. A2-38.
Printed: Coxe, ii. 544–5 (inc.).

Windsor 20 September 1708

Yours of the 24th[3] which I received yesterday gave mee more trouble than
I can express to you, both upon the account of the publick, and more par-
ticularly from the part I take of so much disquiett and uneasyness which
I am sure you had upon you, when that letter was written.

[1] Letter 1102.   [2] Untraced.   [3] Letter 1101.

I beg of you, not to lett any misfortune which is occasioned by other people's faults prey upon your spiritts; for it will make you sick, and you must consider that all good people here, who wish well to the publick, look upon your life and health, as not only what has been, but what must and (I hope in God) will bee the support of us all. I beg you therfore once more not to neglect either of them. And I chuse to send this letter by the way of Ostend, hoping it may come some days sooner to you than by Holland, since by a letter from Mr. Erle of the 27th,[1] I find the comunication between that place and your army had been opened. And if wee may believe some extracts of letters which wee have seen from thence of the 30th, the attempts of the enemy to hinder it have been very much disappointed.

In case this should prove true, and that you find yourself able to preserve this comunication with Ostend, you will best judg whether any provisions or ordnance stores that wee could send from hence to Ostend, could either bee of use to you or arrive in time. There are 2 regiments at Portsmouth under orders to bee sent thither as soon as transports can bee any way had for them.[2]

I will give you no farther trouble now, because I intend to write again by the Holland post of tomorrow night, before which time I hope for the satisfaction and the ease of hearing from you.

1108. MARLBOROUGH *to* GODOLPHIN
[*20 September/1 October 1708*]

Source: Blenheim MSS. A2-39.
Printed: Coxe, ii. 555–6.

[Roncq] October 1, 1708

In my last[3] I had not time to give you any account of our last action,[4] but that of refering you to what was write to the Secretary's office. I have since had a particular account. Our loos of killed and wounded are very near 1,000. By what the enemy left dead on the place, thay must have lost at least three times as many as wee. Thay had above double our number, all our horse except 300, and 2,000 foot being sent on before for the security of the convoye, so that there was not above 8,000 men. And it is sayed by the officers which were left wounded on the field of battaile, that thay had 40 battalions and 46 squadrons, as also canon. Web and Cadogan have on this occasion, as thay will always do, behaved themselves extreamly well. The sucess of this vigorous action is in a great measure owing to them. If thay had not succeeded, and our convoye had been lost, the consequence must have been the raising of the siege the next day. All her Majesty's subject has

---

[1] Untraced.   [2] The regiments of Hill and Maccartney.
[3] Letter 1105.   [4] At Wijnendaal.

had the good fortune this campagne in all actions to distinguish themselves, so that I should not do them justice, if I did not beg of the Queen that when this campagne shall be ended, that she will be pleased to make a promotion amongest the generals of this army only, which will be a mark of her favour and their merit. For hetherto, though almost all the action has been in this army, yett every generall has advanced equally with them, though two parts of three of them has not so much as served this warr. If the Queen and Prince approves of what I desire in favour of this army, I should be glad it might not be known to anybody, til I have an opertunity of giving the names for their aprobation.[1]

Comte Cornell,[2] Monsieur Auverkirk's son, has on this occasion behaved himself extreamly well.

1109. MARLBOROUGH *to the* DUCHESS

[*20 September/1 October 1708*]

Source: Blenheim MSS. E4.
Printed: Coxe, ii. 524–5 (inc.).

[Roncq] October 1, 1708

By the French having taken all the postes along the Schell, makes it almost impossible for our letters to go that way without falling into their hands; and that by Ostend is very near as daingerous, so that we are obliged to be upon our garde of what we write, if we would not have them know itt, so that you must not expect perticulars as to news. But as for my personall estime and kindness for you, I should rather the world should know itt then otherwais; for if I am to be happy, it must be with you. I have read yours of the 10th three times, and am so intierly of your opinion as to 42 [the Queen], that I can't hinder repeating it againe in this letter. For the resolution you have taken of neither speaking nor writting is so certainly right, that I dare assure you that you will find a good effect of itt in one month. For I really am of opinion that when 42 [the Queen] shall be sensible, which thay will be in that time, that 240 [Lady Marlborough], 209 [Godolphin] and 210 [Marlborough] are in such dispaire, that thay offer nothing, but leave everything to the direction of those that have the present power with 42 [the Queen], it will so startle them, that thay will make them comply with what is necessary for the saving themselves, or nothing will do. I can't intierly agree with your opinion of 42 [the Queen]. I must own I have a tenderness for them, and I would willingly beleive that all which is amiss proceeds from the ambition and ill judgement of 256 [Mrs. Masham], and the knavery and artfulness of 199 [Harley].

---

[1] The promotion was made effective 1 Jan. 1709. See Dalton, vi. 17.
[2] Cornelis van Nassau, Baron of Woudenberg (1675–1712), brigadier-general in the Dutch army 1704; major-general 1709.

1110. GODOLPHIN *to the* DUCHESS   [*20 September 1708*]

Source: Blenheim MSS. E20.

Windsor near 3 Monday

I am farr from having any reproach to make you for your concern and kindness to your poor dead friend,[1] though it has hurryed you from hence before I could have the least possibility of seeing you, since I am very sensible this proceeds from the sincere goodness and tenderness of the best heart that ever was in any mortall. Yett some complaints I could desire to vent in behalf of one poor friend (who is yett living), if that were possible to bee done without being uneasy to you, which rather than I will bee (in cold blood), I will stifle them at any time, and myself with them. But I can remember when you would scarce have gon away upon any sudden occasion, without leaving behind you one line only of direction and comfort to poor mee, who can grieve myself to a shadow for every, the least mark of your indifference. Butt I have done, and should not I beleive have ventured to trouble you with this much, but that I had a mind to send you my letter to Lord Marlborough (which I design should goe this night by the post to Ostend), that you may enclose it in one of yours as you use to doe, if you care, or have lines to write tonight by that way; and if not, I would then beg the favour of you to seal my letter and send it to Mr. Tilson, with your directions to him to send it away tonight in the Ostend packett.

Now I am writing I have a mind to tell you Mr. Maynwaring was with mee this morning, to speak to mee upon the subject[2] you told mee he, or my Lord Sunderland himself, would speak to mee. It will not bee necessary for mee to troble you with the particulars of what passed, since you will have them from himself, possibly before this letter comes to your hands. I can only say, it did not seem to mee that there was much difference of opinion between us upon those subjects, no more than upon some others. I have ordered this bearer to return hither tomorrow whenever you order him. I must bee at London myself Thursday and Fryday[3] about the East India Company's affairs,[4] and should bee glad to goe sooner if I could hope to see you, with ease to yourself.

[1] Lady Fitzharding died 20 Sept.

[2] Sunderland came with proposals for accommodating the differences between the Court and the Whigs (see p. 1030), and arranged for a meeting between the Junto Lords and Godolphin at Newmarket in October where they could be discussed. (Sunderland to Wharton, 25 Sept., *Gentleman's Magazine*, 1803, i. 304.)

[3] 23–4 Sept.

[4] A merger of the old and new East India companies was in process, at the behest of and under the guidance of the Lord Treasurer, who had presided over the first steps towards a union in 1701–2.

1111. GODOLPHIN *to* MARLBOROUGH [*21 September 1708*]

Source: Blenheim MSS. A2-38.
Printed: Coxe, ii. 545 (inc.).

Windsor 21th September 1708

My last was of yesterday[1] by the way of Ostend, in hopes that comunication is kept open, and that you would have it, in case it bee so, both sooner and later than by the way of Holland.

I was indeed extreamly desirous to lett you know as soon as I any way could, that my greatest concern and uneasyness for the very ill posture of affairs at Lisle which appeared in yours of the 24th,[2] was least you should suffer your own mind to bee too much affected with it, and lett it prevail to the prejudice of your health, which must bee the support of all those who really love their country and the publick good. And when that comes to bee really the question, I make no question, for my part, but those will show themselves to bee the majority in England. Though in the meantime nothing appears so much as the ill will of those who care but little, either for one or t'other.

In the same letter by Ostend, I desired you to consider whether any stores or provisions to bee sent thither from hence could arrive in time to bee of any use to you. And I also told you, that wee should send over 2 regiments more with all possible expedition. There are also 2 regiments in Scotland, which have been for some time in a readyness to bee embarked, if you think it worthwhile to send transports and a convoy for them.

I have (without naming Mr. Palmes) spoken very coldly, and very fully to Count Briancon about the inaction of the Duke of Savoy, and the ill consequences of it to us. He seemed to bee a good deal out of countenance and uneasy at it, and as if he were impatient for the next letters in hopes they would contradict it.

I remember when you first thought of sending Mr. Palmes thither, it was, that being near the Duke of Savoy during the campagne, he might not only bee of use to him, but that by the accounts he sent you of his proceedings, you might bee the better able to judg what effect they were like to have. Now if his campagne bee at an end, I submitt to you whether Palmes might not bee of more use to you nearer home, or by returning through the same courts by which he went, being first instructed by you what he should say as he returns, at Vienna, at Berlin and at Hannover. Mr. Chetwynd might continue where he is all the next winter, or longer if there were occasion.

I find my Lord Lieutenant of Ireland has given comissions (for 4 regiments to bee replaced in that kingdome) to 4 collonells, whose names I never so

---

[1] Letter 1107.   [2] Letter 1101.

much as heard before.[1] If you are satisfyed of them, it is well. But otherwise, to putt 4 new Collonells at the head of regiments in time of warr to the discouragement of those who have served very well in that warr, in my humble opinion, this is not to bee supported if the case bee so. But I beg pardon for troubling you about it, since I really know no more of the fact than barely what I have told you in this letter.

1112. GODOLPHIN *to the* DUCHESS   [*21 September 1708*]

Source: Blenheim MSS. E20.

Windsor Tuesday morning past 9

The favour of your letter by the coach yesterday was extreamly welcome to mee, though I had not the satisfaction of having it till this morning. I have enquired into the reason of that delay, and was answered that when they came in late at night, they don't use to send about the letters till next day.

I would not lose the first opportunity of thanking you for it, though I desire to trouble you again before you sleep, by the messenger whom I shall send in the evening with my letter for Lord Marlborough to you.

I find I ghessed very right at the motives of your making so much hast to London,[2] and am glad you have the satisfaction in your own mind not to have neglected anything on your part that would have pleased her, but I am not less glad that in that poynt, you lost your labour, for as the sight of you must have been delightfull to her if she had been in her sences, so the sight of her in that condition must have been mortefying to you.

I have many reflextions upon occasion of this subject, but I think 'tis better not to trouble you with them, at least till I have the happyness to see you, which I hope will bee very soon, one way or other.

In case I find this very fine weather does not tempt you to make hast back to enjoy it at the Lodge, my present thought is, since I can't hope to dine with you at London, to dine with my Lord Halifax at Hampton Court tomorrow, and come to town at night, in hopes about tea time to see you. But this will be changed, in case I should hear today you design to bee here tomorrow, and I would bee sure to stay here till you come, though I must bee at London Thursday by noon, and all Fryday.

I cannot say anything to you about poor Lady Fitzeharding's lodgings, the Queen being gon a hunting this fine morning, though I should think there would not at this time bee any difficulty in it. In strictness, I know all the lodgings in that Tower have used to belong to the green cloth; but hers

---

[1] The colonels and the dates of their commissions: Christopher Fleming, later Lord Slane, 26 Aug. (a cousin of Sunderland's attainted 1691; pardoned 1704; outlawry reversed 1709); Kelner Brasier, 27 Aug.; Edward Jones, 28 Aug.; William Delaune, 30 Aug. See Dalton, vi. 250–7. The commissions were made without Marlborough's knowledge or approval (see p. 1123).

[2] The death of Lady Fitzharding. See p. 1109.

was the lodging of the Lord Steward himself, and hee is better provided for, over my head.

Your account of the letter, and of the porter is very diverting. I only wonder how my Lord Pembroke comes to bee marryed at all,[1] since it is plain his porter is against the match. I know he is a great favorite of his Lord (and you will think he deserves to bee soe), for he has the meritt of keeping out everybody living to a miracle.

You will think I need make no excuse for not troubling you any further, but I can't help telling you I have had many interuptions, and Mr. Hopkins[2] stays for my letter.

1113. MARLBOROUGH *to* GODOLPHIN

[*23 September/4 October 1708*]

Source: Blenheim MSS. A2-39.

[Roncq] October 4th 1708

I have had the favour of yours of the 14th.[3] You will have known by Mr. Earles second letter that he had directions from me[4] before all his troupes were landed, so that he was of use to us in the getting the convoye from Ostend. Our letters are so subject to be seen by the enemy, so that I shall give you no account of the 9 redgiments with Earle, nor of some things that passes here, but for the journall of what passes at the siege, [which] will be sent regularly to the Secretary's office.

What you mention in yours concerning 58 [Duke of Savoy] is but to[o] trew, and the methodes taken by 50 [Elector of Hanover] are, in my opinion, scandelous. By the accounts I have had from Vienna, the 4,000 men at Naples will have their orders and be in a readyness to embark att the arrivall of the men of warr. It is certaine 47 [King of Prussia] would be glad to have his goods [troops] from 119 [Italy], so that 74 [Raby] must be directed possitively upon their leaving them where thay are for this next season. If his orders are not very clear and possitive, he will be making his court to 47 [King of Prussia] by not pressing as her Majesty's Service requires he should do.[5] Besides, it will be absolutely necessary before 48 [Prince Eugene] and 39

---

[1] On 21 Sept. Pembroke, a widower, married Barbara (Slingsby), widow of John, Baron Arundel of Trerice.

[2] Thomas Hopkins, under-secretary to Sunderland and his most trusted assistant; M.P., Coventry, 1701; from an important family of merchants in Coventry; made a fortune in money-lending; had served in the secretariat under Trenchard and Vernon in William III's reign; a member of the Kit-Kat Club, he was a close friend of Maynwaring's, and through him a frequent attendant on the Duchess of Marlborough; worked closely with Maynwaring to maintain peace between the Whigs, especially Sunderland, and the Duumvirs 1708–10.

[3] Letter 1103.   [4] 10/21 Sept., Murray, iv. 231–2.

[5] See Marlborough to Sunderland, 20 Sept./1 Oct., with the enclosed letter from [Schmettau to the King of Prussia], Murray, iv. 244–5.

[Marlborough] separats, that thay may know what troupes thay have to dispose of for the next campagne, especially since the behaviour of 50 [Elector of Hanover] has been such this year that neither of them can take measures with him. By my letters from 119 [Italy], I find 58 [Duke of Savoy] would be glad of an interveu. But I confess I do not see that it can be off much use, so that unless the Queen and you are of another opinion, I should think it aught to be avoyded; for it would be impossible to have that interveu without the assistance of 50 [Elector of Hanover]. I should be desirous by your next, you would lett me have her Majesty's and the Lords of the Cabinett Councelle's directions, how farr I might proceed with King Augustus, for some part of his troupes for the next campagne. For as soon as the success of this siege is determined, he will be returning for his own country,[1] so that what can't be effected whielst he is here must not be exspected afterwardes.

1114. MARLBOROUGH *to the* DUCHESS

[*23 September/4 October 1708*]

Source: Blenheim MSS. E4.
Printed: Coxe, ii. 525 (inc.).

[Roncq] October 4th 1708

Since my last[2] I have had the pleasure of yours of the 14th. Notwithstanding the difficulty of the passage of the letters, I did in my last explain my thoughts so fully as to 42 [the Queen], that you must not think my opinion changed if I should not mention them any more this campagne. I do from my soull pity 38 [Godolphin], for his good sence must make him sensible how 39 [Marlborough] and he are exposed by the folly and opiniatrety of others. As to the secritt which you have recommended to Mr. Craggs,[3] I beleive it may be keep, for I cannot see any temptation 42 [the Queen] can have to acquaint 256 [Mrs. Masham] with itt. And as to what you have heard of the inclinations of 48 [Prince Eugene],[4] you may be assured, that as long as 39 [Marlborough] has any pretentions, 48 [Prince Eugene] will have no thoughts of that matter. But I say to[o] much of a thing that is at such a distance, and that nothing but ill usidge of 39 [Marlborough] from his own country can make him have a thought of liking itt, my heart and soull is intierly sett of being in quiet with you.

---

[1] He had served the campaign as a volunteer with Marlborough.
[2] Letter 1109.
[3] About the renewal by Charles III of the offer of the governorship of the Spanish Netherlands to Marlborough.
[4] For the governorship. It was granted to Eugene in 1716.

1115. GODOLPHIN *to* MARLBOROUGH   [*24 September 1708*]

Source: Blenheim MSS. A2-38.

St. James's 24th September 1708

I am very glad to hear by the favour of yours of the 27th,[1] with a postscript
of the 29th, that your convoy from Ostend has come safe to you, and with
so good sucess against the enemy in their attempts to hinder it. I hope this
will bee sufficient to keep you from future want of ordnance stores. But in
case it should not, wee are so much encouraged by this success, as to send
you 2 shiploads from the Tower to Ostend under the care of Mr. Craggs,[2]
who I hope will receive your directions not to unload them, in case you have
no occasion for them. Wee also send by the same convoy one month's provisions for 3,000 men, Mr. Erle having represented, that not only the troops
with him, but the garrison also of Ostend were in very great want of provisions.

I wish the 2 regiments[3] could have been ready to embark at the same time,
but I find they can't goe till next week. For I must own (considering how
necessary it is to keep your comunication with Ostend), my greatest fear is
that the enemies should force Mr. Erle from his post at Leffinghan.[4] For all
his letters describe those troops with him to bee very much diminished by
sickness, and those that are well very much fatigued. Since their numbers
are so much lessened, would it not bee right to send over some of their
officers now to bee raising recruits for them, without which they can never
bee in condition to goe to Portugall, when the time of the year requires their
being there?

I write this in the morning with intentions to send it by Ostend, that being
certainly the quicker and I should think the safer way, while your comunication with that place continues. But I hope to hear from you tonight and
then I will write again, by the way of Holland.

1116. GODOLPHIN *to* MARLBOROUGH   [*24 September 1708*]

Source: Blenheim MSS. A2-38.

[London] September 24th at night

I have written to you this day by the way of Ostend, and I have so little
doubt of that letters being with you before this, that I will not trouble you
with repeating anything that I said in it; except my fears least you should

---

[1] Letter 1105.   [2] The elder.   [3] Hill's and Maccartney's.
[4] Leffinge, a village 5 kilometres south of Ostend and 4 kilometres inland, on the canal connecting
Ostend to Nieuwpoort. Erle had taken possession of it because it protected the way between
Ostend and the confederate army, at the same time it obstructed French communications between
Nieuwpoort and Bruges.

lose your comunication with Ostend, by Mr. Erle's not being able to maintain his post at Leffingham, till wee send him 2 regiments more from hence, which is all wee can spare. And even those will not bee ready sooner than next week.

While you continue so uneasy under the difficultys created to [sic] you by the unreasonable delay of the siege, t'would bee too much to trouble your thoughts with matters so remote as Italy. But since I understand the Duke of Savoy is sending an officer on purpose to you,[1] to explain his thoughts more fully (I suppose) than he could doe by letter, I begg leave only to hint to you what I have already said to Comte Briancon. That unless wee can depend upon his making longer campagnes than barely 2 months in the year, our people here will not bee easily perswaded to continue such large subsidys to him as they have, and to maintain so great a number of forreign troops in his service only to secure his own territorys. And this is certainly the time to speak plain to him, or never. For the King of Prussia is making new difficultys and exactions every day upon us about renewing the treaty for his troops another year. And must wee submitt [to] whatsoever he thinks fitt to impose upon us in that matter before wee know what service wee have to expect from those troops which are to cost us so dear?

You may think perhaps I am too peevish upon this subject. But would not it vex anybody to bee disappointed 2 years together by those to whom wee have been so obliging, when they have certainly had it in their power to make us much better returns, if they had been pleased to have those reguards for us which wee have but too well deserved from them?

In the next place, I don't know what you will doe with 50 [Elector of Hanover]. By all I hear he is at least as much dissatisfyed with you as you may think you have reason to bee with him. And upon the whole, I think it would bee right to ease that matter before you come home, as farr at least as 'tis in your power.

1117. GODOLPHIN *to* MARLBOROUGH   [*27 September 1708*]

Source: Blenheim MSS. A2-38.
Printed: Coxe, ii. 556 (inc.).

Windsor 27th of September 1708

In hopes your comunication with Ostend continues still open, I design this letter to goe that way, being confirmed by the last letters from Mr. Cardonnell, that it is safer, as well as quicker, than to write by Holland. However I have not yett missed any of your letters by the Briell, and am now to acknowledg the favour of yours of the 1st of October,[2] which according to

---

[1] Palmes. See p. 1121.   [2] Letter 1108.

your commands I have communicated to the Queen and to the Prince. They both seemed very well pleased with the account of your sucess at Winnendal, and the satisfaction you express for the extraordinary good behaviour of your troops upon that occasion. They agreed very readily to the distinction you desire for the generall officers of your army at the next promotion, and the Prince added, it was his opinion that distinction ought to have been made much sooner.

My Lord Sunderland will give you an account (though perhaps not till tomorrow night by the Holland post) of the matter in which you desire my Lord Raby may bee instructed beforehand at Berlin, and follow your directions (I dare say) very exactly.[1] Upon this point I must begg leave to continue of the same opinion I was of in my last, which is, that if wee must take so much pains and continue soe great an expence for maintaining a strong army in that side another year, wee ought to bee very well secured that 58 [Duke of Savoy] will make another sort of use of them than he has been pleased to doe in this. And when he alledges (as an excuse) *that the victory at Oudenard was not so compleat as he at first believed it*, I am soe farr from allowing it to bee an excuse, that I look upon it as a very just aggravation of our complaint; since the less your success at *Oudenard* was taken to bee, the more occasion there was for his making a strong diversion. But I am weary of observing upon soe many occasions how wee are used by allmost all our Allyes except 116 [the States] who seem to have done very heartily all this year; though I am afraid it is little better than what wee call here *a brightning before death*. Upon the whole, I am as much in the spleen as you have been of late, and have no prospect from what side I can hope for any ease, unless it bee by hearing some good news from you, which will always bee a great satisfaction to mee. I goe to London tomorrow with the Queen. From thence, I believe I shall trouble you again tomorrow night.

On advice that Vendôme had left the safety provided by the canal of Bruges, to march to Oudenburg and cut Marlborough's communications with Ostend, Marlborough moved his army on 26 September/7 October from Roncq to Roeselare in hopes of bringing Vendôme to battle. The next day he continued towards Oudenburg but found that Vendôme had already retired, after cutting the dyke to

[1] See Sunderland's letter to Marlborough, 1 Oct., in which he enclosed copies of his letters to Raby, 28 Oct., Palmes, 1 Oct., and a paper listing the King of Prussia's reasons for withdrawing his troops from Italy and answers to his points by the English ministry: there are no winter quarters for them in the Low Countries or on the Rhine, where he wishes to send them; Augustus of Saxony can only offer horse to replace them, and they are overstocked with horse regiments in Italy; to withdraw the Prussian troops now would prevent the Duke from entering France the next campaign and would force him to make a separate treaty. See p. 1103, n. 4.

Nieuwpoort, which denied Marlborough the passage to Ostend. As a result the Confederate army camped that night at Torhout and returned to Roeselare on 28 September/9 October to study measures for reopening communication with Ostend.

1118. MARLBOROUGH *to* GODOLPHIN

[*27 September/8 October 1708*]

Source: Blenheim MSS. A2-39.
Printed: Coxe, ii. 559.

Tourout October 8th 1708

The uneasy march of this day can't hinder me from repeating againe the obligation the Queen and all the Allyes have to Major General Webb,[1] who will give you this letter, and I beg you will present him to the Queen. And were it not for measures I am obliged, for the Queen's Service, to keep with the States Generall, I should desire her Majesty would declare him a lieutenant generall, which he dose extreamly deserve. But as it must be done with management with them, I humbly desire the Queen will assure him, that when she makes a promotion this winter, he shall be one. And I will be answerable that not only now, but at all tims, he shall deserve itt from her.

1119. GODOLPHIN *to* MARLBOROUGH   [*28 September 1708*]

Source: Blenheim MSS. A2-38.

St. James's 38 September 1708

I writt you yesterday by the way of Ostend,[2] and was in hopes at my arrivall here this day to have found letters from you, but neither the Holland post nor that of Ostend is yett come. So I shall have very little to add to the trouble I gave you yesterday except to tell you that Mr. Craggs, *the father I mean*, being gon over to Ostend with ordnance stores, I have spoken very particularly to him about 82 [peace] and some other things of that nature, of which I am sure he will give you an account. And I mention it only to you, for fear you might otherwise have some distrust of the account he gives you, from knowing how little usuall it is for mee to speak very freely upon such kind of subjects.

My Lord Conningsby is come to town, I think chiefly at 38's [Godolphin] request, that he might have his assistance. I find him of the same opinion

---

[1] For his successful action at Wijnendaal.
[2] Letter 1117.

with most others I speak with that till Mr. Freeman [Marlborough] comes to town, there is no medling with 88 [Parliament] by any means in the world.

This is a matter for which I think one cannot prepare you too soon. And I hope you will not suffer anything but necessity to keep you from it.

1120. MARLBOROUGH *to* GODOLPHIN

[*28 September/9 October 1708*]

Source: Blenheim MSS. A2-39.
Printed: Coxe, ii. 558-9.

Roslar October 9th 1708

You will know by this post that we are in great want of another convoy, so that I marched on Sunday morning[1] with 110 squadrons and 60 battalions, and camped that night att Ruslar, and yesterday I was in hopes to have been in sight with the Duke of Vandome, who was enchamped at Oudenbourg[2] to hinder our having anything from Ostend. But as soon as he was informed of my being att Ruslar, he dechamped and marched to Brudges. But during the time he has been at Oudenberg he has cutt all the dikes, so that the whole country is under watter, which makes it impracticable for our carts to pass. But I have sent to Ostend to see if thay can put the powder into bags, which may be braught by horses, for we hope to find a passage by which thay may come. God knows how this siege will end. I have but litle faith and am quit weary, but resolved to persist as long as there is the least hopes. Major Generall Webb goes for England; I write to her Majesty by him.[3] I hope she will be pleased to tell him that she is very well satisfied with his services, and that when she makes a promotion this winter, he may be sure of being a lieutenant generall, which really this last action makes his due.

I am returned to this place, where I am conveniently camped for the assisting at the siege, as for the assisting and protecting what we may gett from Ostend. I dare not write some things I should be glad to say to you, which gives me a great deal of trouble, for I see everything is going to distraction, and that it is not in my power to help itt. The Electorall Prince of Hanover is this day gone for Ostend, in order to return to Hanover. The enemy has drowned all the country to that degree that he could take no part of his bagadge with him.

---

[1] 26 Sept./7 Oct.

[2] Seven kilometres inland from Ostend, on the Ostend–Nieuwpoort canal.

[3] Letter 1118.

1121. MARLBOROUGH *to the* DUCHESS

[*28 September/9 October 1708*]

Source: Blenheim MSS. E4.

Roslar October 9th 1708

I received at the same time yours by Mr. Harrison, with that of the 16 by the post, by which I see you had thoughts of going to Woodstock in this month of October. On many accounts I wish I had the happyness of being with you. You seem to be pleased with a conversation you have had with 6 [Sunderland]. I did some time ago write my mind very freely to him,[1] and shall always be ready to take measures with him, beleiveing him my friend as well as a man of honour, for whatever may be good for 108 [England], in which I shall have no reaserve. And as I do by no means approve of the measures I am persuaded 42 [the Queen] has resolved to persue this winter, I shall be governed by my friends, in not only of not helping, but by discountenancing; but must always have in my own power of doing whatever may be personally respectfull to 42 [the Queen], for that is what I shall never depart from, for my own sake as well as hers. I find by your expressions you are very fond of your new grant.[2] I do with all my heart wish you may live long to enjoye itt. As to the advice you are so kind as to say you will stay for, I would not have you lose any time, for I shall certainly be of your mind; but as the building can't well begine 'til the spring, you will have this winter to advise with whome you think fitt. But lett me now repeat what I think I have said formerly to you,[3] which is, make your bargains never so carefully, and that you have the good fortune of dealing with honest people, yett this building will cost you twice as much as thay shall at first propose. I do not say this to discorage you, but that you may be forwarned, so that you may take this juster measures. I did not say this to discorage you, but that you may be forwarned, so that you may be the more cautious. I did not say anything to you in my last letter of the march which I have now made, fearing it might have given you uneasiness, for I was in hopes by it to have had some action with the Duke of Vandome; but he dechamped in the night and marched to Brudges. The Electorall Prince of Hanover is gone this day to Ostend in his way homewardes.

1122. GODOLPHIN *to* MARLBOROUGH   [*29 September 1708*]

Source: Blenheim MSS. A2-38.
Printed: Coxe, ii. 596 (inc.).

September 29, 1708

I have just now received the favour of yours of the 4th of October[4] by which you are very cautious of what you write, for fear your letters should bee

---

[1] Untraced.   [2] Of land in St. James's Park for Marlborough House. See p. 1017, n. 4.
[3] Letter 1023.   [4] Letter 1113.

seen. [But] who indeed, [for] as they are now posted, [anyone] could, in my opinion, bee masters of them as often as they please. I mean of those sent by the way of Holland, but that [way] by Ostend, by which I design this, is (I hope) secure, since nothing appears to mee of greater consequence than your preserving of that comunication. And therfore I am glad to observe by this last letter of yours that you are sensible of the condition of those regiments with Mr. Erle, and will therfore I suppose think fitt to strengthen him till the other 2 regiments arrive which wee design him from hence.

To my apprehension the enemyes seem to sett all their stress upon keeping the Scheldt, and taking their winter quarters at Ghendt and Bruges, in which case, the preservation of Ostend is of the last consequence to the Allyes and from this time therfore in my [opinion] care ought to bee taking, for the victualling and garrisoning of that place for the whole winter. Not that I think they should bee suffered in the thought of keeping Ghendt and Bruges in quiett next winter, but I don't know how farr the season of the year will allow of endeavoring to dislodg them. And if that should fall out, so as to render that attempt next to impracticable, it will bee very necessary to think of some equivalent. And possibly there are few better to bee thought of, than that propose[d] in Monsieur de Gattigny's paper which I sent you some time since,[1] but you have never taken notice in any of yours that you had received it. However I hope it is not lost, and own myself ignorant enough not to bee sure, that use may not bee made of it.

There is to bee a Cabinet Counsell tomorrow after which I will write fully to you in answer to your comands relating to 74 [Raby], to 47 [King of Prussia] and also to King Augustus. In the meantime, I think I am sufficient of myself to answer you, as to the interview mentioned in yours which certainly is much better avoyded for the reason you give. But I must beg leave to add besides, that nothing of any kind in the world must bee admitted that can hinder 39 [Marlborough] and 108 [England] from seeing one another, as soon as is possible. And I can't possibly expect that any right measures will bee taken, either for next year, or even for this winter, till they two have mett. Since nothing is more plain to mee, that 42 [the Queen] has all the regard imaginable for Mr. Freeman [Marlborough] and very little for anybody else.

30 September

My Lord Sunderland tells mee he has written to you by the last post, in pursuance of your orders about 47 [King of Prussia] and 74 [Raby], and designs by this post, to send you coppys of the instructions he sends to 74 [Raby].[2]

As to 50 [Elector of Hanover] I agree that what you say of his conduct is certainly true. And yett I am of opinion that Mr. Freeman [Marlborough]

---

[1] Letter 1092. See p. 1127.   [2] See p. 1116, n. 1.

should endeavour to manage him, if possible as he can. For I can plainly see, by what 6 [Sunderland] throws out upon some occasions, and also by other ways, that 50's [Elector of Hanover] ill humour and uneasyness is fomented from hence, by some of both sides. And he is told that he has been very ill used by 39 [Marlborough] as well as by 48 [the Emperour], in not leaving him a *stock*[1] sufficient to carry on the trade in those parts to advantage. Now though nothing of this bee really true, yett one must allow a little for impressions, which people here are inclined to receive, whether they bee true or not true. My fear only is that people may take a handle from hence to doe ill offices to 39 [Marlborough] with 108 [England].

I am more tedious to you in this letter than I use to bee, because I am desirous to lett you know my thoughts now upon all particulars as fully as I can, being to goe to Newmarkett the beginning of next week. The Queen and the Prince talk of going thither, but her Majesty not being very well yesterday, I don't know till I have been at Kensington, whether that may not change her intentions.

The Queen and the Lords of the Counsell are of opinion you should lose no time in securing such troops from King Augustus as you think proper for the service, with this caution; that no money, by any agreement you make, is to bee paid to him for them till after the end of this year; that is to say out of the provision only which shall bee made by the Parliament for next year.[2]

I shall only add, that in pursuance of what Palmes writes, that in case of no meeting the Duke of Savoy inclines to send him to you, my Lord Sunderland sends him the Queen's orders by this post, to lose no time in comming to you.[3] This is done chiefly with this view, that when you are obliged to come over into England he may receive your orders to all the courts of Germany and Italy, and endeavour to execute your comands in those parts as Cadogan must doe in Holland and in Flanders.

1123. MARLBOROUGH *to the* DUCHESS
[*30 September/11 October 1708*]

Source: Blenheim MSS. E4.

Rousselaer October 11th 1708

Since my last[4] I have had none of yours, and wee are here in the same postur as when I write last. The season advancing our vollontiers begine to think of leaving us. The Prince of Hanover goes, I believe by sea from Ostend to Holland. His being a good husband is the excuse we make for his leaving us before the fate of the siege is known. Hethertoo we have great reason to give God thankes for the good weather we have had. By yours and other

---

[1] i.e. troops.
[2] This was accomplished by a treaty of 11/22 Feb. 1709., P.R.O., Treaties, 240.
[3] 1 Oct., P.R.O., S.P. 104/208, pp. 264–5.   [4] Letter 1121.

letters I find you have not had the same in England. The country between us and Ostend by the ill nature of the French will be like a sea in few days, so that thay will have ruined this country for many yeares in order to hinder us from having our stores from Ostend. However, I hope to be able before tomorrow night to gett above 500 barrelles of powder and other stores from thence, which will be of use to us at the siege. The French must have stoped the English post or we must have had your letters as the wind has been. I am impatient for them, my greatest pleasur being the hearing from you.

October 13th

For want of a postillion to carry our letters this has been stoped til evening, so that I have the pleasure of receiving two of yours. That of the 21 is so kind that it makes me happy beyonde expression. Whielst I live I shall endeavour to deserve from you. I hope in God poor Lady Bridgwatter will do well. Notwithstanding the sea comes in hourly upon us, we have gott 500 barels of powder from Ostend, and we continue in hopes of getting more, being resolved of doing everything that is in our powers for the reducing of Lisle.

1124. GODOLPHIN *to* MARLBOROUGH   [*1 October 1708*]

Source: Blenheim MSS. A2-38.

[London] October 1st 1708

I have written a very long letter to you yesterday[1] in answer to the favour of yours of the 4th,[2] and I send it this night by the way of Ostend, hoping still that comunication remains open to you. And if it does, that way is now become the safest as well as the quickest way of writing. I shall not therfore trouble you with repeating any part of it in this which I design to send by the way of Holland.

[I write] chiefly to acquaint you, that I have ordered Mr. Bridges to send by this night's post to Mr. Cardonell the necessary creditts at Francfort, payable to the order of Prince Eugene, for the 20 crowns a man for so many as were effective and did actually goe on board our ships to Catalonia; with an assurance at the same time, that whenever Mr. Chetwynd should certifie that so many more men were sent as should bee sufficient to compleat them to 4,000, the remainder of the levy money should bee paid. And this I hope is complying both with the agreement made in that case, and with your directions since in that matter.

Comte Briancon tells mee his master has sent very particular orders to his minister at Vienna to insist that all the Imperiall foot under his command may remain where they now are, desiring Sir Philip Medows may have the

---

[1] Letter 1122.   [2] Letter 1113.

same orders, which will bee sent him by this post. But I reckon nothing of this will bee so effectuall, as what you may please to say to Prince Eugene upon this subject.

I have been very much pressed this last post or two, to send provisions as well as ammunition to Ostend. The latter are sent, and I have encouraged merchants to send corn thither upon the presumption it will come to a good markett, which is as much as I have thought necessary to doe without particular comands from you in that matter.

The Queen does not find herself so well as to goe to Newmarkett, as she first intended. The time of my going is next Tuesday, but I will write to you upon Monday the 4th by the way of Ostend.[1]

[P.S. on cover] Since I had made up my letter I have heard, the ships and transports are ready to sail with the 2 regiments[2] for Ostend and 300 sick men now recovered, which were left behind by Mr. Erle. So you may count he is reinforced with at least 1,300 men by the time you have this.

1125. MARLBOROUGH *to* GODOLPHIN   [2/13 October 1708]

Source: Blenheim MSS. A2-39.

Rouslaer October 13th 1708

Our letters for England should have gone two days ago, but as the French makes the passage as uneasy as thay can, we had no postillion til our English letters of the 21 and 24th[3] come this evening. The watters which the enemy have lett into this country gives us a great deall of trouble: however, we have got 500 barrels of powder from Ostend, and are endeavoring to gett more. If I thought I had been anywais failling to 50 [Elector of Hanover], I should take pains to sett it right. But I take [the] matter of fact to be so much the contrary, that I am persuaded that 50 [Elector of Hanover] has done the litle that in him lay, that 48 [Prince Eugene] and 39 [Marlborough] might meet with difficultys. As to what you say of the colonels of the four redgements raised in Ireland, it is so farr from their having my approbation, that I do not so much as know who thay are. All the redgiments heretofore that were raised and sent into Ireland were always formed in England, and the lord lieutenant never gave commission but as the vacancys happened after their arrivall in Ireland. My being abroad is the occasion of many of these iregularitys, but that which is most uneasy is, that the officers here who are venturing their lives every day, have no share in the preferment of these four redgiments; and that besides this discoradgement, it is very likly her Majesty's Service will suffer by their having no good officers. I have sent to Lieutenant General Earle, that I beleive that 110 [Holland] have a sufficient quantity of

---

[1] Letter 1126.   [2] Hill's and Maccartney's.   [3] Letters 1111, 1115.

stores att Ostend, so that he should be carefull not to deliver any of her Majesty's til he sees an absolut necessity. In the meantime, I have desired him not to send them back for England til the end of the campagne, or that I shall give him directions for the doing itt. I do not doubt but he gives to Mr. Walpole the account of the redgiments, as he has done to mee. I have also derected him to send officers for the recrutting their redgiments emediatly for England, so that thay might raise theirs before our officers gett to England. What you said to 66 [Briancon] I think is extreame right, and I shall be sure to speake in the same maner to Major Generall Shulenbourg, when he comes to mee. No time should be lost in letting me receive her Majesty's commands concerning King Augustus' troupes, for as soon as the siege is finished he will be gone.[1] As Monsieur de Bouflarr has had but to[o] much time to have retrenchements behind the breach, we recon he will oblige us to storme the breach. God give us success, and thay may [pay] dearly for itt.

1126. GODOLPHIN *to* MARLBOROUGH   [*2 October 1708*]

Source: Blenheim MSS. A2-38.

St. James's October 3d 1708

Wee are still without letters from you, though the wind seems to bee fair, which makes us the more uneasy. However being to goe one day or 2 to Newmarkett, I have a mind to write once more to you by the way of Ostend, before I goe.

The regiments of Grant[2] and Strathnaver[3] are sent for from Scotland, partly to bee in more readiness here in case there should bee farther occasion to send troops to Ostend; and partly because it seems to bee agreed by all the Queen's servants in Scotland, that ther's no relying upon troops of that country in case of an invasion. Now in this latter view, it may bee worth your considering whether these two regiments I have named, and the 2 battalions of Scots Guards, which they say are very good men to look at, might not bee changed this winter, and sent to serve abroad, in the room of some of the weakest of those with Mr. Erle; and they sent into Scotland, to fill up there, or in the north of England. How farr this is practicable, you can judg better. But the notion seems to mee to bee right for the Service, both abroad and at home.

---

[1] See p. 1113.

[2] Alexander Grant of Grant (1679–1719), M.P. 1707–19, served under Marlborough in Flanders; taken prisoner 1710; brigadier-general 1711. His regiment was raised by Marlborough in 1702. Grant became colonel 6 Mar. 1706.

[3] William Gordon (1683–1720), heir to John, fifteenth Earl of Sutherland, whom he predeceased; styled Lord Strathmore from 1703; raised regiment 1702; resigned colonelcy 1710.

There are also a good regiments of dragoons in Scotland which might bee used in the same manner. But for Maitland's[1] regiment, who has the care of the highlands, the Duke of Queensbery sais, he can doe that business by his knowledg of those people much better than any stranger. You will bee pleased to think whether the whole or what part of this scheme ought to bee putt in practice, and when.

My Lord Dunmore who is coming hither has often desired mee very earnestly to recommend his eldest son[2] to your favour. He says he has served abroad in my Lord Orkney's regiment for some time, and with good reputation. When I have said this, I will trouble you no more at present about Scotland.

The Queen has this night ordered a proclamation to appoint the Parliament to meet upon the 16th of November, which is later than usuall, in the view that you may bee here some time before.

Wee have had an account from Portsmouth that the 2 regiments[3] sailed from thence upon Fryday, our first of October, so they must bee by this time at Ostend. I wish they may come time enough to assist in preserving the post at Leffinghen.

4th of October

Since I had written this an Ostend mail is come in with letters of the 7th which say that country is all under water, from whence I conclude they have at present no passage open to you. This makes mee resolve to send this letter by Holland.

The Prince has been very ill of a violent cold, and the Queen much alarmed at it. But he is much better, and she designs to goe Thursday[4] to Windsor for a week or 10 days more.

Sir Thomas Felton has the Comptroller's staff, and Mr. Dunch[5] has kissed the Queen's hand for his place.[6] He desires mee to give you his duty. Both their new elections are sure.

[P.S. on cover] I am afraid you will not have received my very long letter last week by Ostend.

---

[1] James Maitland (died 1716), served in Flanders under William III; succeeded Leven as colonel of the Cameronians 1694; commission renewed 1702; governor of Fort William, where his regiment served; lieutenant-general 1709; retired 1711.

[2] Lord Fincastle.   [3] Hill's and Maccartney's.

[4] 7 Oct.

[5] Edmund Dunch (1657–1719), Whig M.P. 1701–2, 1705–19; married 1702, Marlborough's niece, Elizabeth Godfrey; Master of the Household 1708–10; a nephew of Lord Wharton, the Junto peer.

[6] The Earl of Bradford died 2 Sept. The Earl of Cholmondeley succeeded him as Treasurer of the Household; Felton succeeded Cholmondeley as Comptroller; Dunch succeeded Felton as Master. The Duke of Richmond had tried to obtain Bradford's place through the Whigs, pleading 'it is not the sallary of a place makes one ambitious of one but being the only man of our party that yet has never been countenanced I think I have reason to desire my friends to shew themselves so' (Richmond to Sunderland, 15 Sept., Blenheim MSS. D1-32).

1127. MARLBOROUGH *to the* DUCHESS   [4/15 October 1708]

Source: Blenheim MSS. E4.
Addressed: For the Dutchesse of Marlborough.

[Roeselare] October 15th 1708

I have since my last received yours by the way of Ostend, as also that of the 24th by Mr. Craggs,¹ who will give you this. He will inform you of the discorse we have had, by which you will see that 39 [Marlborough] will be governed by 240 [Lady Marlborough] and 38 [Godolphin]. I am very free to write to 182 [George Churchill] whatever you and 38 [Godolphin] shall think proper to send mee. I should have write to him by this bearer, but he was desirous I would not do it til about a fortnight hence.² He will acquaint you with my thoughts as to our circomstances here. I beg you to beleive that I am with heart and soull yours.

I have this minut received yours of the 27th by Ostend, but am able to do no more, Mr. Crags being with me, then to thank you for that and three others I have received from you within these two days. For God sake never make excuses for the length or number of your letters, for thay are most acceptable to me, you being att this time dearer ten thousand times to me then my own life.

1128. GODOLPHIN *to* MARLBOROUGH   [7 October 1708]

Source: Blenheim MSS. A2-38.
Printed: Coxe, ii. 559-60.

Newmarkett October 7, 1708

Major General Webb brought mee your letter³ to this place. I had heard of his comming before I left London, so the Queen was prepared to use him very kindly, and with a great deal of distinction, as I find she has done, both by what he says himself, and by a letter which I have received from her by him. But I am very uneasy, and so I find he is, at his having made himself uncapable of serving with you for the rest of the campagne,⁴ when there may yett bee great occasion for men of service. Might it not bee an expedient, if the Queen should write to you, to give him the distinction of acting as a lieutenant generall now immediatly? Or (if this has its objections) might she not desire you now to acquaint the States that she intends a promotion?

---

¹ The elder. See p. 1117.

² Marlborough must have written 8/19 Oct. (See the letter in Coxe, ii. 600.) The Duchess sent him the draft for another in response to his remark here, but he did not send it owing to the death of Prince George. Churchill's office lapsed on this occasion. See p. 1150.

³ Letter 1118.

⁴ Apparently by refusing to return without his promotion. This was probably as much the cause of his dissatisfaction, which the Tories exploited, as the failure to mention his name in the first published accounts of the action at Wijnendaal. See p. 1176.

Pray lett mee have your answer, if either of these will doe, that I may speak to her Majesty to write accordingly, or what else you would have done in this matter.

Before I left London wee had sent you from thence all the stores and all the troops wee could. So I have nothing to trouble with from hence, but to wish you the same fine weather wee have, and to tell you that a great many of your friends and servants here drink every day to your good health and success. I shall direct this letter to bee sent by Ostend, in hopes of your answer so much the sooner.

1129. MARLBOROUGH *to* GODOLPHIN   [8/19 October 1708]

Source: Blenheim MSS. A2-39.
Printed: Coxe, ii. 560 (small omission).

[Roeselare] October 19th 1708

Having had no letters since Mr. Craggs went from hence, I have litle more to acquaint you from hence, than the watters are so grown upon us, that our communication with Ostend is at an end for some time. During the time we had the passage open, we have gott above 1,600 barrels of powder, and a great many other things which are of use. I aske your pardon for forgetting the thanking you for Gatteny's project, which came safe to me.[1] If the war continues for some time it may be attempted, but I fear this yeare is [too] far advanced.

Poor Monsieur Auverkerk dyed yesterday, by which her Majesty will save the pention I am told she gave to Lord Grantham. It would be an act of goodness and generossity if the Queen would be pleased to give some part of itt to Comte Corneil, who is as vertious and as brave a man as lives. His father has been able, I fear, to leave him nothing. If I were not sure that he did diserve and would be gratfull to the Queen, I would not say so much for him.[2] We hope in four or five days to give a generall storme, if thay will ventur it, which I fear thay will. I wish I may be mistaken since it will cost a great many lives. God continues to bless us with good weather.

1130. MARLBOROUGH *to the* DUCHESS   [8/19 October 1708]

Source: Blenheim MSS. E4.

[Roeselare] October 19th 1708

I have discorsed so very fully Mr. Craggs,[3] who has directions to acquaint you with all that has passed betwin us, that I have very litle to say, but to

[1] Letter 1122.
[2] Grantham was Ouwerkerk's elder son; Cornelis, Baron of Woudenberg, his younger.
[3] The elder. See p. 1117.

thank you with all my heart for your letters, which I have received by the way of Ostend, as well as that of Holland. And though I dare not write anything by the post but what I must expect may be seen by the French, so that I cannot give the account which otherways I should of what passes, yet you may, and I beg you will lett me have your thoughts of what passes in England, for by the cypher you have the French will not know what you write. Besides, thay are not so desirous of reading the letters that come to the Army, as those wee write. Since my last the watters are come in so fast upon us that I am afraid we shall not have any farther communication with Ostend.[1] However, we have made use of the time we had, having gott from thence above 1,600 barrels of powder and a great many other things which are of use to us. We hope in four or five days to be in a readiness of storming the town if thay will stand itt. You were very much to blame not to put off your journey when you found yourself not well, for though I was glad you were going to Woodstock, yett I would not willingly have you do anything that might hurt or make you uneasy, as I am sure such a journey must do when you had so great a cold, so that I shall be uneasy til I hear from you. Monsieur Auverkerk dyed yesterday, and as the Queen will by it save the thousand pounds a yeare she gave lately to the Earle of Grantham, it would be a good and generous thing to give some part of itt to Comte Corneil, who is a very honest and brave man, and his father has not been able to leave him anything. I shall write to Lord Treasurer,[2] and should be glad you could inclin him to serve Comte Corneil at this time. If the Queen will do anything for him, I should be desirous nobody might know it til I have first acquainted him with itt.

1131. GODOLPHIN *to* MARLBOROUGH   [*10 October 1708*]

Source: Blenheim MSS. A2-38.
Addressed: To his Grace the Duke of Marlborough.

Newmarkett 10th October 1708

This is only to acknowledg the favour of the 13th by the post,[3] and of the 15th[4] by Mr. Craggs;[5] who it seems has had a quick passage to England, and gives, as I hear, very good hopes that at last Lisle will bee in your hands. God send wee may hear it quickly.

I shall not now trouble you with any reflexions relating to that matter or any other, from this place, but beg I may reserve them till I come to London, which will bee about the end of this week. And after that, I shall not often bee soe mercyfull to you.

---

[1] 'The French have found means by flatt bottomed vessells armed with canon, to stop since the 8/19th all our correspondence and getting of ammunition from Ostend.' Hallungius to Brydges, 12/23 Oct., Stowe MSS. 58, III. 69, Huntington Library.
[2] Letter 1129.   [3] Letter 1125.   [4] Untraced.
[5] Craggs must have returned to the camp at once for he carried a letter from Marlborough to the Elector of Hanover bearing date of 14/25 Oct. In Macpherson, ii. 112–13.

1132. MARLBOROUGH *to* GODOLPHIN   [*13/24 October 1708*]

Source: Blenheim MSS. A2-39.
Addressed: To my Lord Treasurer.

[Roeselau] October 24th 1708

The two letters[1] you mention in yours of the 1st of the month,[2] which were
sent by Ostend, are not come to me, so that I desire you will always write
by the way of Holand. I send Sir Richard Temple to acquaint her Majesty
with the good news of our being at last masters of the town of Lisle. I have
acquainted him with the intentions of 48 [Prince Eugene] and 39 [Marl-
borough], so that you may from him know everything as to our intentions.
The risque our letters runs makes it impossible for me as yett to write freely
to you, so that I have instructed him the more fully. I am not uneasy at the
having trusted him for he is a discritt young man. Half of what you gave to
Lord Stairs will be enough for his present. As we are resolved to suport this
conquest, I hope it will give us such advantages for the next campagne that
we may hope by itt to procure a long and lasting peace, provided England
and Holland will do what I have desired by Sir Richard Temple.[3] The
French have been firing canon on the post of Leffin[4] yesterday and this day,
but as we can't sent to them we know not what thay have done. That post is
of so great consequence[5] that I am confident thay will do all thay can to
support it. I beg I may hear from you as soon as you have discorsed [with]
Sir Richard Temple, that I might the better take my measures.

1133. MARLBOROUGH *to* GODOLPHIN   [*13/24 October 1708*]

Source: Blenheim MSS. A2-39.
Addressed: To my Lord Treasurer, Whitehall.

[Roeselare] October 24th 1708

This bearer, Mr. Vain,[6] my Lord Westmoreland's brother, has been with
me this campagne. He has behaved himself very well, so that I am desirous
you would do him the honour of presenting him to the Queen. I like him
much better then his brother.

---

[1] Letters 1122, 1126.   [2] Letter 1124.

[3] Marlborough planned a large-scale invasion of France for 1709, supported by an amphibious
landing, and wanted an augmentation of his army, which he secured. See pp. 1132, 1142.

[4] Leffinge. It fell 15/26 Oct.

[5] 'Its certaine that there [the confederates] being able to keep it would have made us masters
of the canal of Bridges, which feeds the French army on the Scheld and att Bridges and Gent,
for all there provisions are sent now from Dunkirk to Newport and from thence by that canal to
Bridges and Gent, which we will now find difficult to reduce this winter.' Drummond to Brydges,
8/19 Nov., Stowe MSS., 58, III. 111-12, Huntington Library.

[6] John Fane, seventh Earl of Westmorland (1686-1762), fourth son of Vere, fourth Earl of Westmorland; M.P. 1708-11, 1715-34; captain, Cadogan's Regiment of Foot, 1709; succeeded to
the peerage in 1736.

1134. MARLBOROUGH *to the* DUCHESS   [*13/24 October 1708*]

Source: Blenheim MSS. E4.
Printed: *Private Correspondence*, i. 162 (inc.).
Addressed: For the Dutchesse of Marlborough.

[Roeselare] October 24th 1708

I have received yours of the 29th, but that which you mention to have write by Ostend is not come to me, so that I beg from henceforward you will always write by the way of Holland. I have sent Sir Richard Temple to the Queen with the good news of our being masters of the town of Lisle. The next step is the attacking the cittadell. I have fully acquainted Sir Richard with Prince Eugene and my intentions, which he is to tell Lord Treasurer, from whome you will know all, for I dare not put it in writting, fearing it might come into the enemy's hands. What you say of the vanity of 13 [Somerset] I know to be trew, for he dose not only think he has power with 7 [Wharton], but with many more. I am of your opinion that he dose do hurt with 42 [the Queen], but that must be suffered, for if he be a litle managed he will some-tims do good.[1]

1135. GODOLPHIN *to* MARLBOROUGH   [*14 October 1708*]

Source: Blenheim MSS. A2-38.
Addressed: To his Grace the Duke of Marlborough.

Newmarkett 14th October

I have received the favour of yours of the 19th[2] at this place. I am sorry for all the delays you meet with, and cross accidents. But I hope your comunication with Ostend will not bee long interrupted, since it seems to bee occasioned more by the Spring tides, than by the enemy.

I am concerned for the loss of poor Mr. d'Auverquerke. I doubt it may produce more uneasyness in Holland. As to his pension I can say nothing till I have seen the Queen, only that one of the arguments used to her to grant it, was, that it could not last.

I agree to your character of Comte Cornele. God send you may succeed in your storm at Lisle without too much loss.

1136. GODOLPHIN *to* MARLBOROUGH   [*17 October 1708*]

Source: Blenheim MSS. A2-38.

St James 17 October 1708

I received at Newmarkett the favour of yours of the 19th,[2] and have since my return acquainted the Queen with your request in favour of Comte

---

[1] See the letter from Maynwaring to the Duchess in *Private Correspondence*, i. 252-4 about Somerset's attempt to divide Wharton from his friends.
[2] Letter 1129.

Cornele. She is very sensible of his meritt, and willing to give him any mark of her favour that you shall think reasonable. But what she gave my Lord Grantham was not a pension out of the revenue in Ireland, but a bounty of 1,000 [pounds] only. He had indeed asked for 1,000 a year during his father's life, but the Queen chose rather to give him one £1,000 beleiving, as it has proved, that poor Monsieur d' Auverquerk, would not live to occasion a 2d payment. I have also putt her in mind of Major Generall Webb's service, and if you approve it, I should think the properest thing for him and the easyest for the Queen would bee to promise him the 1st government that should become vacant.

Last night an express from Mr. Erle brought us the welcome news that Lisle had capitulated, upon which the guns were fired, and bonfires all over the town. This received some allay by the loss of our post at Leffinghen. But wee are in hopes that as soon as you are at liberty to march with the army you will endeavour to gett your money for the army one way or other from Ostend, for at present I find 'tis all there.

I wish our men taken at Leffinghen might bee exchanged with the soonest, and that those officers which can bee spared from the regiments with Erle might bee sent over to recruit, or else they won't bee capable of serving anywhere next year.

You will see by my Lord Gallway's letter how great their disappoint-ment is like to bee in Portugall, at the want of our troops. However I am glad they did not goe. Nor doe I see how any measures can bee taken here for carrying onn the warr next year, before wee see the finall conclusion of your long campagne, which I hope will end at last to your full content and to our advantage.

The warr that seems ready to break out in Italy,[1] will bee very troublesome if the court of Vienna can't bee perswaded to putt an end to it either by a present accomodation, or by acting vigorously before the princes of Italy can bee in condition to oppose him. The Queen has caused letters to bee written to this purpose, and repeated to Sir Philip Medows and to Mr. Palmes, and to her other ministers in Italy.

I hope before I close this letter wee shall have an express from you with the capitulation of Lisle, and what motions you propose to make.

October 18

Sir Richard Temple arrived this day at noon and brought mee the favour of yours of the 24th.[2] It is a very great satisfaction that after so much agony and

---

[1] Between the Pope and the Duke of Modena, who had the support of the Emperor. See p. 1013.
[2] Letter 1132.

suspence, you are at last become master of this town, which I hope and believe is of so much reall consequence, as that the next year's campagne, if wee are to have another, will bee yett more glorious to you.

Sir Richard Temple has according to your commands very fully explained 48 [Prince Eugene] and 39's [Marlborough] intentions, and I think the plan is in their present circumstances, most reasonable. But there are very great precautions to bee used with regard to 110 [Holland] and 116 [the States] which I make no doubt, must bee in your thoughts, at least as much, as in any other body's whatsoever. You will also think it necessary to provide as much as possibly you can not only for the reall security, but even for the satisfaction of 108 [England] against any such attempt, as in the last spring. And I cannot forsee how that is to bee done so well as by having strong garrisons in Antwerp and Ostend, that so troops might bee drawn from those places upon any occasion. Mr. Craggs assures mee that latter place is miserably unprovided with all manner of necessaryes. Care ought to bee taken of this place in time.

I am very much pleased with the intentions of 39 [Marlborough] and 48 [Prince Eugene] that one of them shall bee all this winter upon the place. If one can ghess by the newsletters wee see from France, the enemys are taking the same kind of measures, whether of choyce or of necessity, you can best judg. But by all means 39 [Marlborough] must leave it to 48 [Prince Eugene] to stay there in the beginning of the winter, his presence being impatiently wanted with 108 [England] every hour in the day. And therfore I hope he will from this minute apply his thoughts to the taking of such methods as are likely to compass that meeting with the greatest expedition.

Your will have had from Mr. Stanhope the news of his being master of *Port Maon*, which is a very seasonable advantage to us at this time, because it must keep the princes of Italy in great fear of displeasing us. I wish the court of Vienna may make use of it, to gett better terms by a treaty, rather than take encouragement from it to prosecute a warr,[1] which cannot but bee prejudiciall to the Allyes, though it should succeed never so well.

As to the augmentation desired by 39 [Marlborough], the sooner Mr. Freeman [Marlborough] meets with 108 [England] the better that matter is like to bee digested.[2]

These are only my first thoughts upon hearing Sir Richard Temple, not having yett had time to see the Queen or any of the Lords. If what I hear from any of them tomorrow, should happen to differ from these notions, I will add yett to this tedious long letter before the post goes.

[1] The war in Italy between the Pope and the Emperor, concluded 4/15 Jan. 1709. See p. 1215, n. 4.

[2] For the augmentation of 1709 see the article by D. Coombs in *E.H.R.*, 72 (1957), 642–61.

1137. GODOLPHIN *to the* DUCHESS   [*17 October 1708*]

Source: Blenheim MSS. E20.

Sunday at 2

I came from last night in good time and good health, God bee thanked, without the least accident but that of finding no fire in my chamber, which hiendred mee from telling you last night by the post, there was a mail come in from Holland. This morning there is a 2d come, and finding I had no letters from Lord Marlborough by either of them, I sent for Mr. Tilson to know if he had any for you. He tells mee neither of these 2 posts have brought any letters from the army, and that by the Brussells' letters he finds the French keep so strict guard upon the passes over the Scheldt, that the letters stopp there. A 3d mail is expected tomorrow. Wee shall see if those can have any better luck; if not, this stop of the comunication may prove a reall inconvenience, as well as a great uneasyness.

I thought it was reasonable to trouble you with this account by a boy, for fear you should hear before tomorrow that the Holland post was come, and bee in pain about your own letters.

I have had this morning the conversation I had appointed with 7 [Wharton].[1] He continued to say a great many things that were very reasonable, but upon the whole, I think I could see that he begins to think the affairs he has undertaken has more nicety and difficulty in it than he was first aware of; but he concluded with saying he would see 5 [Somers] somewhere tomorrow, and then I should hear again from him.

6 [Sunderland] has been with mee this morning, very inquisitive to know if I have prevailled with you to come to town, not doubting as indeed he had no reason to doe, but that I endeavoured it as much as I could. I told him how little effect all I could say had upon that subject at which I thought he seemed to bee uneasy, but other company coming in, that discourse went off, at least (with him) at that time, but the thought of it, I own to you, remains a good deal with mee; for I see so many difficultys coming upon mee from all sides, that unless I would have recourse to you oftner, upon many occasions, than it is possible for mee to have at this distance when the ways grow bad, and the moon fails, that I am afraid they must needs bee too hard for mee; besides that, I would not willingly make any step, but what is first approved by you.

[1] About George Churchill. Godolphin proposed he retire. Wharton responded that the Prince would have to retire, and before Parliament met. Maynwaring to the Duchess, 18 Oct.; Blenheim MSS. E27.

1138. GODOLPHIN *to* MARLBOROUGH   [*19 October 1708*]

Source: Blenheim MSS. A2-38.
Printed: Churchill, ii. 457–8 (inc.).

[London] 19th October 1708

You will receive by this post a very great packett from mee, and yett I have not quite don troubling you, upon the subject of my talk with Sir Richard Temple.

By your letters to Mr. Erle, I see you always sett much weight upon keeping of Leffinghen.[1] You did not know it was lost, when Sir Richard Temple left you, yett he tells mee you expected it, which makes mee hope, you have had in your thoughts how it was to bee supplyed.

However I can't help being uneasy to think, wee are not to have any communication with you, but what is so very precarious as by the Holland post. How will you have your money from Antwerp or Brussells? How will you bee sure of provisions and subsistance for your army? Can you bee secure the French will not destroy all *Artois*, and even Picardie too, rather than they shall furnish subsistance to your army? I could ask a great many more of these which perhaps you will call idle questions, but I must own, I should bee glad to bee sure they were soe. And I think your business were more than half done, if you were once master of a port that could give your army a free comunication with us in England, from whence you might have your money, your provisions, and any other wants supplyed, not only with ease but with a great deal of satisfaction. I say no more at present upon this head, because I think this may not bee the right time to press it, though it could never bee more desirable, in my opinion, than at this time.

As to the augumentation which you desire of 108 [England] and 110 [Holland], in what method doe you propose to goe about it? Doe you think by yourself, or 39 [Marlborough] to sound 110 [Holland] about it first? Or would you have 42 [the Queen] desire it in form of 116 [the States]? And if this latter bee your thought, how and when would you have it done? I should bee very glad to know your mind in these things, with the soonest, though I don't forgett you have told mee you dare not write freely. But I don't find Sir Richard Temple is able to answer half the questions I could ask him, and that obliges mee to give you so much unreasonable trouble.

Sir Philip Medows writes as if the court of Vienna had thoughts of sending 48 [Prince Eugene] to head this new warr which I fear, is breaking out in Italy.[2] If that bee true, and he gives into it, nothing could bee more precarious.

[1] 23 Sept./4 Oct., Murray, iv. 251.
[2] Between the Emperor and the Pope. See p. 1013, n. 1.

1139. GODOLPHIN *to the* DUCHESS   [*20 October 1708*]

Source: Blenheim MSS. E20.

Wednesday night at 10

I received this afternoon the favour of yours with Mrs. Chantrell's[1] papers enclosed, and will bee sure to make good your promise of doing her what service I can upon my Lord Pembroke's coming to town.

I shall observe your directions in not writing so freely by the coaches as by the post, and hitherto I think I have hapned not to doe contrary to them, my letter last night by the post being written more freely than that of this day by the coach.

You will have seen by it that I had much the same thoughts of the visitts that passed this summer betwixt 4 [Halifax] and 188 [unidentified] that you seem to have in your letter today, and 'tis no small satisfaction to mee when I find our thoughts agree. I am very sure mine agree entirely in every word you did mee the favour to write to mee today, and I hope as long as I live they will never but agree in everything with you; but 'tis very hard when they doe soe, that I must not hope for the happyness of seeing you. I find my Lord Sunderland designs to dine with you tomorrow and stay all night. He drops my lady Sunderland at Hampton Court, and takes her up next day in his return. If he had not told mee of his intentions, I should have troubled you sooner, but now Lady Harryett and I, hand to fist, will pay our duty to you upon Saturday morning, and come back at night, if you will doe us the favour to lett you meet us by 10 in the morning att Belfond, a village between Stains and Hownslow.

I intend to send this letter to the generall post house, and not to trouble you tomorrow by the coach tomorrow, unless somthing extraordinary happens, being perswaded you will have but little spare time tomorrow. I waited upon 4 [Halifax] this evening to Mrs. Morley [the Queen] to make his complements,[2] of which he was pretty free, but our conversation in the coach had a great deal of what you described of yours in your letter, with this difference, that to my face he did not complain of mee, but much of 39 [Marlborough], which I liked full as little.

In one word, I should think myself very happy, and hope it would please you if I could find any way of satisfying 7 [Wharton] and 5 [Somers]; and for all the rest, I have no skill or they are not worth the pains one takes about them.

[1] Barbara, widow of Lieutenant-Colonel Francis Chantrell. On 5 Nov. Godolphin sent a warrant to the Lord-Lieutenant of Ireland to give her a pension of £100 a year in recognition of the services of her husband, 'an officer in the service of the crown for over 30 years . . . [whose] commission having been taken from him by the late Earl of Tyrconnell because he was a protestant' (*C.T.B.*, XXII. ii. 428).
[2] Upon the appointment of his brother James as Attorney-General. See Maynwaring to the Duchess, [21 Oct.], in *Private Correspondence*, i. 162–6.

1140. MARLBOROUGH *to* GODOLPHIN
[*21 October/1 November 1708*]

Source: Blenheim MSS. A2–39.
Printed: Coxe, ii. 564 (inc.).

[Roeselare] November 1, 1708

Since my last[1] I have had none from you; besides I have instructed Sir Richard Temple so fully with all my thoughts, that I should not for some time trouble you with long letters. We are carrying on our attack on the cittadell, and hope by the midle of this month to be masters of itt, for we do not think thay will stay the last extreamity. If thay do thay must expect no capitulations. We have been blessed with extraordinary good weather, so that we have very few sick in the army. Though we are now afraid the weather is changing, yett it will not be so troublesome to us as it must have been before we were masters of the town, for now the greatest part of the men that attack the cittadell are quartered in the town, which is a very great ease. I have had no particular account as yett from Mr. Earle of the maner of the loosing the post of Leffin, but the account we have from the French is not to the advantage of those that were there. I have write to Mr. Earle that he should endeavour to informe himself of the particulars, for the maintaining of that post would have made it impossible for the enemy to have continued at Brudges.[2] Upon the news of Port Mahon's being taken, the Dutch have resolved to leave shipes there this winter. I hope the same resolution is taken in England, for besides the necessity for the good of the Service on the account of the warr in Spain, it will also hinder any of the Italien princess joining with the Popp. I have assured 39 [Marlborough] that he may depend upon having leave of going for England, as soon as I shall be able to take measures for the winter quarter, which I beleive can't well be til we first see where the French are likely to take theirs. But I hope he will thank you by this post, since I have told him if it had not been to comply with your desire, he must have stayed here with me this winter, which the service dose requier, particularly that of his redgiment. But I must not refuse you anything that is in my power.

---

[1] Letter 1132.

[2] For the siege of Leffinge see *Compleat History for 1708*, pp. 334–5. An Allied relief force had made its way to Leffinge on 13/24 Oct. The troops celebrated in too joyous a fashion and were caught off guard; they were incapable of defending the town when the French made a surprise attack that night (Churchill, ii. 457). The garrison 'suffered themselves to be surprized by men that waded in the night breast high in water'. Even then 'they had another redoubt to retire too after they had beene beat from Leffengen'. See Cardonnel and Drummond to Brydges, 25 Oct./5 Nov., 29 Oct./9 Nov., Stowe MSS. 58, III. 111–12.

1141. MARLBOROUGH *to the* DUCHESS
[*21 October/1 November 1708*]

Source: Blenheim MSS. E4.

[Roeselane] November 1st 1708

Your two last letters from Blenheim, of the 3d and sixth of the last month, you may be sure were very agreable to me, since thay lett mee see you are in good health, and that you are very well pleased with the building. I do not doubt but the Duke of Shrewsbury's house[1] is very well contrived, and that is built much cheaper then our house; but if we live to see them both finished, you will find in the performance such a difference as you cannot now imagine, and which I shall certainly put you in mind off if I have then the happyness of being with you. I should have been glad to have known Monieur Vriberg's opinion as to the building and place, for he is a great crittick, [particularly] his thoughts as to the bridge, which you say nothing off, which makes me fear you do not like itt. I am of your opinion that it is far from 42 [the Queen] thoughts, the removing of 38 [Godolphin] and 39 [Marlborough], but I beleive thay have taken such resolutions as to some points, that will make it very difficult if not impossible for them to do much service to 42 [the Queen]. We are pressing on the attack of the cittadell, which as yett thay do not deffend with the vigor thay did the town.

1142. GODOLPHIN *to the* DUCHESS   [*21 October 1708*][2]

Source: Blenheim MSS. E20.
Addressed: To her Grace, the Duchesse of Marlborough at the lodg in Windsor Great Park.

Thursday 10 at night

I received the favour of a letter from you about one a clock, and immediatly sent your packett to Benjamin. I did not write by the coach, because nothing has hapned worth your trouble, and that I thought you would not have much time to spare. I thank you very much for the leave you have given mee to come, and I hope to make use of it Saturday, unless you forbid it. When I asked Lady Harryett if she would goe with mee, she told mee she liked it extreamly, with an air very naturall and sincere. But I doubt she won't like to come back in the night as I must doe, for Sunday I have a great many appointments.

I hope the wind is coming fair tonight for letters, so as that I may bring them to you upon Saturday; but I can't reckon so certainly as sometimes I have don, because of their uncertainty on the other side.

---

[1] At Heythrop, Oxfordshire, a house he built on property purchased after his return from Italy.
[2] The letter is postmarked $\frac{OC}{21}$.

I saw Mrs. Morley [the Queen] today. She seems much easyer to 38 [Godolphin] than she used to bee. How long it will hold, or which way it comes about, are equally unknown to mee. But I can see there are considerable mysterys stirring, though I cannot yett see through them. I had some talk this morning with 7 [Wharton],[1] who seemed much to wish that Mrs. Freeman [Lady Marlborough] would come to town. All my answer was, that I wished it at least as much.

1143. GODOLPHIN *to* MARLBOROUGH   [*22 October 1708*]

Source: Blenheim MSS. A2-38.
Printed: Coxe, ii. 601 (inc.).

St. James's 22 October 1708

Not having any letter from you since my last[2] and having troubled you then more then enough for one week, I think I should scarce have written by this post, but to cover the enclosed which I just now received from Lady Marlborough at the Lodg.

Mr. Stanhope's express is sent back by this packett with assurances of a squadron to winter at Port Mahon.

My Lord Gallway seems very much disappointed in his measures from the troops not coming with the Queen of Portugall. [He] is very pressing to know when they may bee certain of them, and to what number, both which questions are (I am afraid) too hard for us to answer.

I have a letter from Collonell Maine from Berwick giving an account that the Regiments of Grant and Strathnaver, making together about 1,000 effective men, passed by that place, in order to bee embarked at Newcastle for Ostend. Though as your affairs seem now to stand in that side I see no other use of troops at Ostend, unless it bee in order to keep a strong garrison in that place all this winter. But since they are there, I believe they will not bee drawn away by any orders from hence, but as you shall think proper.

42 [the Queen] is at last come to allow 38 [Godolphin] to make such condescentions,[3] which (if done in time) would have been sufficient to have eased most of our difficultyes, and would yett doe it in great measure, if 89

---

[1] See Maynwaring to the Duchess [21 Oct.], *Private Correspondence*, i. 162–6.

[2] Letter 1138.

[3] The Queen agreed to let Somers and Wharton come into the Cabinet, through the retirement of Pembroke from his two posts. One cannot ascertain if she intended to put Pembroke at the Admiralty in her husband's place, or if this only came about through his death on the 28th. The Whigs agreed to drop Sir Peter King as their candidate for Speaker. But all was not well, for Sunderland wrote on the 26th to Newcastle, Sutherland, and Montrose in terms that indicated a struggle in Parliament between the Whigs and the Court. Trevelyan, ii. 415–16; Montrose MSS., S.R.O.; Fraser, *Sutherland Book*, i. 328; Maynwaring to the Duchess [27 Oct.], Blenheim MSS. E29.

[the Whigs] will bee but tolerably reasonable. And I am really of opinion that if 39 [Marlborough] and 108 [England] were together at this moment but 48 houres all might yett goe well. I mean, as to the publick.

1144. GODOLPHIN *to the* DUCHESS   [*25 October 1708*]

Source: Blenheim MSS. E20.
Printed: *Private Correspondence*, i. 167–70.

Monday night at 6

I received this afternoon the favour of a letter from you by the boy, and I give you (as I ought to doe) a thousand thousand thanks for a great many things in it, which were very obliging. I beg leave to return you not by the post, but by the first safe hand, the letter you sent mee from 4 [Halifax][1] because it ought to bee kept, in the first place, as a curiosity, and next because whoever could write such a letter in his present circumstances, may hereafter give so much provocation, that one would not but have it in one's power to shew so much impertinence under his own hand. When I have said this, I must own I think the impertinence of it is greater to mee than to you, but I shall not take any notice of it to him, nor never make any court to him for his assistance, which I see by the letter he expects, but rather lett him have his full swing in joyning with 208 [Harley] and his friends (whom for 7 years together he has called enemies to the government) rather than not receive those who have done all that was possible for men to doe to oblige him.

Now as for what answer you should make, I am very much of the opinion which you yourself seem to have, that 'tis best to send him his venison, and not to write. The first preserves civility, and the second will shew his letter has not cured what he must needs know you complained of to 6 [Sunderland].

As to your thoughts relating to 6 [Sunderland] himself, I don't so entirely agree in them, but I can entirely submitt my thoughts in that matter, even though I could not doe it in others, but I doe assure you I can very freely doe it in all.

I think then, that what you write to *eyelashs*[2] [Lady Sunderland] upon this subject, will bring you in return a very kind tender letter, and perhaps bee the occasion of a visett to you from 6 [Sunderland], chiefly to complain, and say he is sure some ill offices must have been don him to you; and I think I knew him well enough to satisfie myself, he cannot doe this but in such a manner as will rather give you more reason to bee displeased then less; whereas if other things reconcile, he will probably think fitt to take up a little This is my opinion but I submitt it to you.

---

[1] 24 Oct., in *Private Correspondence*, i. 166–7.   [2] A cant name.

You seem to think I must have known what company was to bee with you yesterday, but your letter is the only knowledge I have of it to this moment, by which I find the Vice[1] was one, and Sir Richard Temple, another. As to what the Vice told you of his project, I have very little faith in any project, and not much in Sir John Germain. The African Company has been managed from a great many years by a pack of knaves (to speak in poor Mr. Guydott's stile), who have cheated all their adventurers. If a peace comes that trade is capable of being much improved, but not upon the present foundation, which is in my opinion a very rotten one; and I think this Parliament, nor any other, ought not to establish them without first dissolving the present company.[2]

I wonder very much that wee have not the forraign letters today. I make no doubt of them tomorrow.

The Prince seems to bee in no good way at all (in my opinion) as to his health, and I think the Queen herself seems now much more apprehensive of his condition, than I have formerly remembered upon the same occasion.

Monday night at 10

I had written thus much when David brought mee the favour of your letter. I have desired him to call here tomorrow morning, by which time I hope for some letters to send you from Lord Marlborough, and I send this to the generall post house, as I intended before hee came, and by him I will return your letter from 4 [Halifax]. I think I told you in my letter this morning that Lady Harryett was well, and had a very good stomach today. Wee have dined together these 2 days head to head, and Mr. Guy dozing by us. I scarce ever stir abroad, now you are not in town, but to the Treasury or to Kensington.

1145. GODOLPHIN *to* MARLBOROUGH   [*26 October 1708*]

Source: Blenheim MSS. A2-38.
Addressed: To his Grace the Duke of Marlborough.

St. Jame's 26 October 1708

I must begin my letter with repeating to you how disagreable it is to see 3 Holland mails come in successively without one letter from you, or from your camp, since the 24th by Sir Richard Temple,[3] But finding by the

[1] Peregrine Bertie.

[2] The Royal African Company of England, a chartered trading company, had ceased to make money because of mismanagement, interlopers, and the war, and was bankrupt by the end of 1708. After the failure of three schemes (proposed between 1709 and 1711) to accommodate the differences between the Company and its creditors, a fourth scheme proved acceptable in 1712 through the assistance of an Act of Parliament. The shareholders were also called 'adventurers' from the title of the Royal Adventurers into Africa, the predecessor of the Royal African Company. Germain was elected to the Court of Assistants (board of directors) in the years 1709, 1711–12. See K. G. Davies, *The Royal African Company* (London, 1957).

[3] Letter 1132.

Hague letters they hear there pretty regularly from Lisle, I wish for the future you would send your letters that way. 'Tis better to have them late than not at all.

The condition of the Prince's health has been languishing more than ordinary for above a month. But since Saturday last[1] he is much worse, and has such a generall weakness and decay of nature upon him, that very few people that see him have any hopes of his recovery. The Queen herself who did not use to bee in so much apprehension upon these occasions, as others who were not so much used to him, begins to think 'tis hardly possible for him to hold out long. I pray God her own health may not suffer by her perpetuall watching and attendance upon him.

This melancholly subject and the great uncertainty of my letters coming to you makes mee not care to give you any farther trouble at this time.

1146. MARLBOROUGH *to* GODOLPHIN

[*26 October/6 November 1708*]

Source: Blenheim MSS. A2–39.
Printed: Coxe, ii. 564–5 (inc.).

Rousselare November 6, 1708

Having a safe opertunity of sending this letter to Bruxelles, I shall write with more fredome then I have done for some time past. The greatest difficultys we now meet with is the want of corn, so that we are more aprehensive of wanting bread, then of anything the enemy can do. In order to see what corn we can gett from the country of Artoise, I sent yesterday Major Generall Cadogan to La Bassée,[2] where there are already two thousand horse and ten battalions of foot. He has taken with him ten squadrons more. He is to return the 10th, he being to meet the Comte de Ruffey the 12th att Turquin,[3] to see if it be possible to agree the exchang of prisoners. If it be treu what the enemy tels us of the beheavior of those that were taken att Leffin, thay deserve to be punished, having been a scandle to the nation. I have write to Lieutenant General Earle to inform himself of the truth, for some example must be made for the honour of the nation.[4] The French are expecting detachements both from the Rhin and Dophinée, being resolved to make their utmust effort in this country. I hope we may take the cittadell before thay come, though we go on very slowly, being very carefull of loosing as few men as possible, for we cannot yett guesse when this campagne may end. But

---

[1] 23 Oct.

[2] La Bassée, a fortified town in France 51 kilometres south-west of Roeselare, lying on a tributary of the Deule and connected by a canal to the Lys (Leie).

[3] Tuscoing, 25 kilometres south of Roeselare.

[4] Erle to Marlborough, 22 Oct./2 Nov., Blenheim MSS. B1–2; reply, 1/12 Nov., Murray, iv. 304.

as soon as wee have the cittadel we shall then be more att liberty to act against the enemy, and I do assure you that our intentions are, to do all that lyes in our powers to bring them to action. Thay give out that as soon as the troupes thay expect join them, thay will seek us. These resolutions seems more agreable to the begining of a campagne, then the month of November. If God blesses with further success before we go into winter quarters, ther is no doubt of having a good peace. But if everything remains as thay now are, the only way of having a speedy and good peace is to augement the troupes, so as that we may enter France the next campagne with a good superiority; and that the fleet may be assisting to us,[1] which, with the assistance of Almighty God, is what will in all likelywhoode bring this troublesome warr to a happy end, which is, I beleive, more wished for by your humble servant then by any other body living.

1147. MARLBOROUGH *to the* DUCHESS
[*26 October/6 November 1708*]

Source: Blenheim MSS. E5.
Addressed: For the Dutchesse of Marlborough.

[Roeselare] November 6, 1708

I have not had the satisfaction of any of yours these five or six days. I thank God we have now againe very fine weather, which is of great use to us. What you mentioned in on[e] of yours of mony being given to 254 [Mrs. Godfrey],[2] I do assure you upon my word that I cannot recolect that thay did ever recomend any officer to me. Having write thus farr I have notice that by mistake the officer that should have carryed this letter is gone, so that I can't write by the post with that freedome I intended.

November 8th

I have keep the post till this day, in hopes to have had something more to have write, but as our inginers think we have time enough and that thay would save the men as much as possible, our attack against the cittadel goes on slowly. I shall go to the siege tomorrow, so that my letters by Munday's post[3] may give you more perticulars. I am heart and soull yours.

[1] The plan he communicated to Godolphin by Sir Richard Temple. See p. 1129.
[2] Someone had apparently charged that Arabella Godfrey, Marlborough's sister, had taken money for using her influence with Marlborough to obtain a commission.
[3] 1/12 Nov.

1148. GODOLPHIN *to the* DUCHESS   [*26 October 1708*]

Source: Blenheim MSS. E20.
Endorsed by Duchess: upon good news Lord Treasurer.

Tuesday at 10

Though I have heard nothing since I wrott to you by the boy, I can't lett this keeper goe home without telling you, my heart was fuller of thanks than I had time or words to express last night in my letter by the post;[1] and that pleasure is still increased by the favour of yours of last night which I received but an hour agoe, and am entirely pleased that you take so kindly my diligence and concern for your service. I assure you my heart is always the same in everything you doe not see, as in this which you have the goodness to take kindly; and though you think it is my fault that I don't master the difficultys I meet with,[2] yett I feel the contrary every day. But I will not now trouble you with so disagreable a subject, having this minute received the enclosed letter[3] to the postmasters here, which contains so many particulars, which I hope will satisfy you, and with such circumstances, that I think it is impossible but thay must bee true.

I shall only add, that I beleive I can't have time to write again by the keeper that will call upon mee at 2, but by this night's post I will not fail. I hope in 2 or 3 days at most you will have the satisfaction of a letter from Lord Marlborough, the communication being now open, and the wind in my opinion coming faire.

1149. GODOLPHIN *to* MARLBOROUGH   [*29 October 1708*]

Source: Blenheim MSS. A2-38.
Printed: Coxe, ii. 601–2.
Addressed: To his Grace the Duke of Marlborough.

29 October 1708

My last[4] will have prepared you in some measure not to bee surprised with the news of the Prince's death, which hapned yesterday about two, in the afternoon. Nature was quite worn out in him and no art could support him long.

The Queen's affliction, and the difficulty of speaking with that freedom and plainness to her, which her service requires, while she has soe tender a concern upon her, is a new additionall inconvenience which our circumstances did not need, and will make it still more necessary than ever that 39 [Marlborough] and 108 [England] should not delay their meeting. For I really foresee that unless that can bee compassed, very very soon, it will bee next to impossible to prevent ruine.

---

[1] Letter 1144.   [2] From the Whigs.
[3] Untraced.   [4] Letter 1145.

I should [not] write so pressingly upon this head, if I were not entirely convinced of the necessity of it, and I won't mingle anything else in the same letter, because I think nothing else that I could say, is of half so much consequence.

1150. GODOLPHIN *to* MARLBOROUGH   [*1 November 1708*]

Source: Blenheim MSS. A2-38.

November 1st 1708

After having been 3 posts without hearing from you, I have had the satisfaction of 2 letters this morning from you, of the first and the 6th[1] by which I see you have had some accounts from the enemy of the scandalous behaviour of the troops at Leffinghen. However, wee are in so much want of the men, that I hope you won't lett that bee a reason why they should not bee exchanged, since the fault was probably in the commanding officer and not in the poor men.

And I seriously wish you would consider how weak and also how useless, in my opinion, all those regiments are now at Ostend, which went over with Mr. Erle, and send them back to recruit, that they may bee of service another year, either in Portugall or in Flanders, where I am in great hopes you will bee allowed the augmentation of troops which you desire next year. The grounds of these hopes you will have more particularly in the letter which enclosed this.

And if the augmentation you desire bee complyed with, I believe you will not think it very possible, at the same time, to comply with the proposalls you will find in the enclosed letters from my Lord Gallway. But it may bee the more necessary for the regiments with Erle to come over and recruit, that they may bee in condition to bee sent to Portugall; at least, as many of them as shall bee necessary towards a defensive warr in that side, and for preserving our allyance with those people; who are at present in very good humour by the quick passage of the Queen of Portugal to Lisbon, and the safe return of the greatest part of their Bresil fleet; though du Goè[2] has been in quest of them these 2 months. As soon as Sir George Bing has chased him from their coast, he has orders to proceed through the Streights and to winter at Port Maon, which I hope will bee a satisfaction to the Emperour, and to King Charles the 3d, as well as a bridle upon all the Italian princes.

However, I can't but bee in pain about this warr with the Pope, chiefly for fear 58 [Duke of Savoy] should play us some trick in that matter. All his discourses about it hitherto, of which I have had an account, seem very dark

[1] Letters 1140, 1146.
[2] René Du Guay-Trouin (1673–1736), commander of the Brest squadron. See *Vie du Monsieur Du Guay-Trouin écrite de sa main*, ed. by H. Malo (Paris, 1922).

and uncertain concerning it. But of this I believe you will soon bee more fully and particularly informed from Major Generall Palmes.

If I can give any ghess at the intentions of France by the accounts wee have from thence, all their bragging of seeking another battell will end in proposing 81 [peace] to 110 [Holland] as soon as they can. But 'tis not good to bee so sure of this, as not to take all the reasonablest precautions against a desparate attempt.

1151. GODOLPHIN *to* MARLBOROUGH   [*5 November 1708*]

Source: Blenheim MSS. A2-38.

November 5, 1708

I am to return you my thanks for the favour of yours of the 8th,[1] which came to mee by the way of Ostend. And 'tis a great satisfaction to mee that you can write by that way, since the way of Holland is of late so very uncertain, that for this last month wee have not received half the letters wee ought to have had. I shall send this therfore by the way of Ostend, and am very much in hope, by yours of the 8th, that your going to the siege will so hasten that affair, as that you may bee able (as you seem to intend) to send the news of it hither before the sitting down of the Parliament, which will bee a very good preliminary towards the Augmentation of troops that you have desired for the next year.

Upon Sir Richard Temple's arrivall I did write to know your thoughts, in what manner 116 [the States] should bee sounded about that augmentation. It would bee very convenient that I had your answer to that letter,[2] but I am afraid the uncertainty of the posts may have hindred you from having received it.

By the same Ostend mail, which brought mee yours of the 8th, wee had letters from Mr. Erle very full of complaints of the state of his troops, which moulder away every day, and I find he is averse to having the 2 Scots regiments[3] joyn him. So they will bee kept here, till wee can hear what you would have done with them, and with the troops at Ostend with Mr. Erle. For wee don't see here that their staying longer there can bee of much use, in case you continue your intentions of extending the quarters of your army towards France, and have no thoughts of disturbing the French in Ghendt and Bruges this winter.

I am afraid there will bee great difficulty here, of getting your recruits in time. The behaviour of the officers in some places last year upon that occasion, makes the Justices of Peace unwilling everywhere to take any pains in that matter. I intend therfore to try [and see] if I can [get] anything mentioned upon this subject in the speech at the opening of this Parliament,

---

[1] Untraced.   [2] Letter 1138.   [3] Grant's and Strathnaver's.

which will bee spoken by my Lord Chancellour, the Queen's present circumstances being too uneasy for her to appear so soon in publick.[1]

I doubt there will bee some little disadvantage in this circumstance. There will not bee quite so much care taken of the speech, as when it is spoken by the Queen herself, nor will what is said have so much weight.

This being the post night, by Holland as well as by Ostend, I shall write only 2 or 3 lines by that post,[2] only to tell you I have troubled you with a very long letter by Ostend.

[P.S. by the Duchess] I can't help adding two lines upon reading this leter before I seal it, that I wonder very much that hee should think there can bee any difference who speakes the speech, which is known by all the world to bee equally aproved and made by the Councell; and if it bee not reasonable and good for the nation, I think 'tis all alike who speakes it. God Almighty bless you and send you soon home.

1152. GODOLPHIN *to* MARLBOROUGH   [*5 November 1708*]

Source: Blenheim MSS. A2-38.
Addressed: For the Duke of Marlborough by Holland.

5th of November 1708

I trouble you but with 2 or 3 lines only by the way of Holland, to tell you I have troubled you this very day with a long letter by the way of Ostend,[3] that seeming, by our last letters from thence, to bee the lesse uncertain of the two. In that letter I have thanked you for the favour of yours of the 6th and 8th which are the 2 last I have had from you. Wee are in hopes of hearing again tomorrow.

1153. MARLBOROUGH *to* GODOLPHIN   [*5/16 November 1708*]

Source: Blenheim MSS. A2-39.
Printed: Coxe, ii, 565-6 (inc.).

[Roeselare] November 16, 1708

I know not whethere it proceed from the enemy, or that the letters are not come from England, but we have had none these last ten days. Beleiving this letter will go safe to Bruxelles, I shall ventur to write more freely then by the post. We have been extreame uneasy for want of corn, not having in our stores for longer then this day, which obliged me to send Cadogan to La Bassé, where wee gott some, but not sufficient to make us subsist the

---

[1] No remark was included, but a more effective recruiting act was passed, in which rewards were authorized to pay £3 per man to the parish in which he was raised 'for the better enabling them to maintain their poor especially the poor relations of able-bodied men so raised' (7 Anne, c. 2).
[2] Letter 1152.   [3] Letter 1151.

remaining part of this month; so that Thursday last[1] I detached the Earle of Staires with 10 squadrons of horse, and as many battalions of foot for Dixmude,[2] with orders to attack the fort the enemy has on the canal at that place. He succeded so well, that he made a lieutenant collonel and upwardes of 200 men prisoners of warr, by which we have secured a passage into that country, and I hope to draw subsistance sufficient for the army from thence.[3] Thay have already sent a thousand oxen and cowes, and great numbers of sheep to Lisle, where provission was much wanted. Notwithstanding the arbitrary government with which thay have been governed, thay are no ways inclined for us, but on the contrary give us litle assistance as is possible, suffering their bils to be protested, though thay have by them an advantage of 7 per cent.[4] But I hope when we have the cittadel everything will mend, which we think will be by the end of this month. It might be sooner, but that we have great management both of our men and amunitions. Besides, we imploye also this time in reparing the breeches of the town. As we have had the visible protection of God Almighty on severall occations this campagne, we both hope and pray that he will give us further success, which we shall endeavour to seeke when we are masters of the cittadell. Considering the looses we have had at this long siege, and the frequent actions with the enemy, yett we are in as good a condition as can be expected at this time of yeare, we having very few sick, and both men and officers full of resolution. I beg you to assure the Queen, that I act with all my heart and soull, that this campagne may end very much for her glory and safety. The scituation of the enemy, as well as ours, is such, that I think it impossible for either to take their winter quarters before we have action, which, if it can be braught to be a generall one, will decide the fate of this warr. I could wish it might come time enough for the opening of the Parliament, but I fear it must be the month of December before we shall be able to send you good news. Not knowing when I may have another oppertunity of writting freely, I must

---

[1] 28 Oct./8 Nov.

[2] Diksmuide (Dixmude), a fortified town in Spanish Flanders, on the Ijzer 23 kilometres north-west of Roeselare.

[3] Stair to Marlborough, 9, 10 Nov., Blenheim MSS. B1-9; Marlborough to Stair, 10 (2), 11 Nov., Murray, iv. 297-9, 301-2.

[4] Cardonnel made similar comments to Brydges, emphasizing the hostility of the citizens of this area which once formed part of the Spanish Netherlands, but was ceded to France in 1668. 27 Oct./8 Nov.: 'The gentry have entirely fallen into the French air and manners, the men of business much as in other places, and the commonal[t]y seem to be [in] as easy circumstances as [in] any part of the Netherlands. They were in general well pleased with the French government; the order and occonomy of the same was to the last nicety and everybody praises the affiable behaviour of Boufflers to the cittizens. We have always flattered ourselves that they onely wanted an opportunity to take of[f] the French yoake, but I assure you 'tis just the contrary, for they are under the least concerne for the change they are obliged to make, which they already foresee will be [the] ruin of there trade. And by all the information I could gett and the remarks I made while there [Lisle], I can't avoid being of there opinion.' 8/19 Nov.: 'I shall onely tell you that all the people of this towne [Lisle] are our mortal enemyes and o[w]ne us as such' (Stowe MSS. 58. III. 124, 128, Huntington Library).

againe presse you to what I take to be the only way of bring[ing] France to a speedy and good peace, [which] is, that you should not only resolve in England upon an augementation of troupes, but lose no time in prevailling with the States General to do the same, for their declaration would have a greater effect in France. I have and shal continue to presse them in Holand, which I hope may have its effect, their deputys here assuring me that thay are convinced there is no other way of bringing this warr to a happy end. Wee could wish here that the Elector of Hanover and the Duke of Savoye could have continued with their armys some time longer in the field, the French threatning us with the great numbers of troupes thay will bring into this country.

Whielst we continue in this scituation, you must not expect anything in my letters by the post, but what I must write with such caution as if the French were to read it, since thay have it in their powers. God knows when I shall be able to see you, but you may be sure when I leave the army, I shall stay very few days at The Hague.

1154. MARLBOROUGH *to the* DUCHESS   [5/16 *November 1708*]

Source: Blenheim MSS. E5.

[Roeselace] November 16, 1708

I am very uneasy at this time not having had any letters from you above these ten days. Our attack of the cittadel goes on very slowly, ther being great caution both for the saving our men an[d] amunition; but God that blesses us with faire weather, I hope will give us success in all we may undertake; so that we may send you good news about the end of this month. I have had the favour of a letter from Monsieur Vriberg, who seems to be very well pleased with his jorney to Bleinheim, as well as with the place. I wish the happy time were come that I might be there at quiet with you. Though I have a great many things that imployes my time here, I can't help having my apprehensions for the opening of this Parlaiment. For besides the uneasinessess any disagreement must give in England at this time, it would give so much advantage to France, that I really think it must ruin the whole, the consideration of which I hope will make all honest people agree in that principle of carrying on this warr with vigor. God knows when I may be att liberty to leave the army, but you may be sure as soon as I do I shall make hast for England, being resolved to stay very few days att The Hague.

1155. GODOLPHIN *to* MARLBOROUGH   [*9 November 1708*]

Source: Blenheim MSS. A2-38.

November 9th 1708

Wee had yesterday 2 posts from Holland, without any letters from you, or from the siege, which is very disagreeable and uneasy at all times. But at this time, 'tis more particularly inconvenient, the sitting of the Parliament being now so near, when it will bee very necessary to speak of the state of the warr abroad, with as much certainty as that matter can admitt. I believe therfore wee must goe on to take it for granted you are or will soon bee, masters of [the] cittadell of Lisle, and consequently masters of taking your winter quarters in that country, so as that nothing but an army betwixt you and France itself can hinder you from entring it in the next campagne.

This being (as I hope) a true state of the matter, I perswade myself, it will also bee, a very strong argument, to procure for you such an augmentation of troops as you desire, and seem to think, absolutely necessary. But upon this head, would it not bee as necessary to know the mind of 116 [the States] upon this matter, before it comes to bee provided for by the Parliament? And in what manner, or by whom 116 [the States] should bee applyed to, is another question with which I have often troubled you in my late letters. But now wee hear so seldom from you; and while wee remain so uncertain whether you receive our letters or not, you must have the goodness to forgive repetitions; for my letters can bee filled with nothing else, till I can have the ease and the pleasure of hearing more regularly from you.

1156. GODOLPHIN *to* MARLBOROUGH   [*12 November 1708*]

Source: Blenheim MSS. A2-38.
Printed: Coxe, ii. 567–8.

November 12th 1708

'Tis above a fortnight since wee have any letters from you by the post. I had the favour of yours of the 6th[1] by Brussells, of the 8th[2] by Ostend, and this day it was no small pleasure to mee to see the outside of yours of the 16th[3] by the way of Brussells. But the inside of it does not give mee so much satisfaction. I am sorry it will bee at least a week before you have the cittadell, and after that, to find you think of beginning a new campagne when you have been in the field a month longer already than ever was known. Can you hope the good weather will continue to the end of the year? I am sorry (besides) to find you think there must bee yett more action. If that must bee, I believe it will bee because you have a mind to disturb their winter quarters, for

---

¹ Letter 1146.   ² Untraced.   ³ Letter 1153.

I can't think they will pretend to hinder yours. Lastly, I am sorry to find that, bee the event of these things as one could wish, wee must not hope to see you here till Christmas, or very near it.

In the meantime till you doe come give mee leave to assure you no endeavour shall bee wanting, nor pains omitted on my part, to make every[thing] goe onn, as you could wish it might doe at the opening of the Parliament. I have gott it into the speech that an augmentation should bee desired for Flanders, and I hope it will bee granted.

I have been a good while of opinion that somebody should bee sent on purpose from 42 [the Queen] to 116 [the States] to press them very earnestly to declare themselves upon that matter. I have written to know your thoughts upon this for a month together, but not having any answer, I believe my letters have not come to your hands. Upon the whole, as things now stand, I beleive nobody will bee sent, till there bee a return from the Parliament to the speech, by the addresses of either house; and I hope they will bee such as may very much contribute to the success of him that carryes them over.

I have had the honour to read your letter to the Queen. She seemed to bee much concerned that wee were like to bee so long without seeing you.

I think you have but too much reason to repine at the coldness and in-difference of 50 [Elector of Hanover] and 58 [Duke of Savoy]. For my part, I cannot help thinking there is most cause to complain of the latter. He has had most done for him, and had most in his power to doe for us.

1157. MARLBOROUGH *to the* DUCHESS [*14/25 November 1708*]

Source: Blenheim MSS. E4.
Printed: Coxe, iii. 10 (inc.), as November 28.

[Roeselare] November 25th 1708

Since my last I have had the happyness of four of your letters. As the French very often stop our postillions, I received all four at the same time, so that the letter I should have write to 182 [George Churchill],[1] and your desire that I would not write, came time enough to hinder mee. I wish with all my heart that matter may be setled so as to give content, as I am of opinion that 108 [England] can't be safe but by a right understanding between 42 [the Queen] and 89 [the Whigs]. I am pleased at what you write that 38 [Godolphin] has reason to beleive that some of 89 [the Whigs] are making up with 256 [Mrs. Masham], for I hope you are of my mind, that when 108 [England] is safe, I had rather anybody should govern then 39 [Marlborough]. I have in a former letter[2] assured you that 254 [Mrs. Godfrey] never spoke to 39 [Marlborough] for any office. And as for Lieutenant Collonel Woods-worth,[3] I do not know that he pretends to the redgiment you mention, so

---

¹ See p. 1126.   ² Letter 1147.   ³ Unidentified.

that al that has been told you is certainly mallice, of which this world is so full that it is impossible for anybody to serve with pleasure.

What you say of 4 [Halifax] I have beleived for a long time. If he had no other fault but his unreasonable vanity, that alone would be capable of making him guilty of any fault. For God sake do not endeavour to hinder anybody making their intierest with 256 [Mrs. Masham], but agree with me in contemning anything that others may think vexes; for I sware to you sollumly, that your love and quiet I prefer to all the greatness of this world, and had rather live a privatt life than be the greatest man England ever had. I do not wonder nor shall be much troubled at anything 199 [Harley] shall say of me, for I shall desire nobody's friendshipe, but that my actions shall speak for mee, which shall be governed by the understanding God has given me to what I shall judge best for England.

[Oudenarde] November 28th

Having write thus far I resolved not to send my letter til I knew the success of what had been resolved by Prince Eugene and myself for the forcing the Skeel [Scheldt], which we executed yesterday with good success, which I from my heart praise the Almighty God for we having beaten good numbers of their troupes and lost but few of our own. The Prince is this morning returned for the siege of Lisle, and I am marching for the relief of that of Bruxelles, so that if it holes out til tomorrow night I hope to hinder the Elector's taking of itt.[1] The news I now write has given me a good deal of pleasure, knowing that it will be a great mortification to the Duke of Vandome and the French army. But yours of the 2d of this month old stile, which gives me an account of all things going well in England, gives me an intier content of mind. I am really to[o] tiered and so many orders to give that I can say no more, but beg you will make my excuse to Lord Sunderland that I do not thank him for his,[2] but hope to do it by the next post from Bruxelles.

Audenard November 28

1158. GODOLPHIN *to* MARLBOROUGH [*15 November 1708*]

Source: Blenheim MSS. A2-38.

November 15th 1708

In mine of the last post,[3] I acknowledged the favour of yours of the 16th[4] and gave you my thoughts of what was like to bee done here, in the affair

---

[1] On 11/22 Nov. the Elector of Bavaria had arrived before Brussels and demanded its surrender. Marlborough, after pretending to prepare for winter quarters, pierced the French lines on the Scheldt at three places, Eugene crossing at a fourth. By the 16/27th the French had retired to Ghent and Tournai, the Elector to Mons. The Lower Scheldt was once more in the hands of the confederates, Brussels relieved, and good communications reopened between Lille and Brussels.

[2] Untraced.   [3] Letter 1156.   [4] Letter 1153.

of the augmentation. Since that time, the States have written a letter to the Queen,¹ which I hope may contribute very much to make it succeed the better here. Though there are some expressions in the letter, that seem to insinuate as if they were not in a possibility of bearing their part of the expence, in proportion to what they have done upon other occasions.

Wee have letters of the 21th from Mr. Erle, by which he appears to bee uneasy enough at the condition of the troops with him, and the uncertainty how long he is to remain where he is. I have desired Mr. Walpole to lett him know that the latter depends wholly upon you, and that wee shall never order the return of those troops, till you lett us know they are of no more use on that side.

November 16th

This day the Parliament is assembled and Sir Richard Onslow² is chosen Speaker without any opposition, so there will bee one happy man this winter in England. But for many more I am sure I cannot answer.

1159. MARLBOROUGH *to* GODOLPHIN [*17/28 November 1708*]

Source: Blenheim MSS. A2-39.
Printed: Coxe, ii. 572-3.

Audenard November 28th 1708

The disagreableness of the French having it in their powers to see all our letters, has made me for some time not very regular in writting. But from henceforward I shall write very punctually, for yesterday morning we forced the Skeel [Scheldt], and beat the troupes that were posted about this town. Prince Eugene is gone back this morning for Lisle, and I am marching for the releif of Bruxelles, which if it be not taken by tomorrow's night, I do not doubt with the blessing of God the saving itt. After which, ther is an necessity of my getting more powder to Lisle, by which you may see that our campagne is not at an end, though my next letter must be dated in December, which is very unusuall in this country. My Lord Haversham may be angry, but Prince Eugene and myself shall have that inward satisfaction of knowing, that we have strugled with more difficultys, and have been blessed by God with more success then ever was known in one campagne. If at last it shall bring a safe and honorable peace to the Queen, I shall estime myself happy. When you see a proper time, you will assure her of my concern for the death of the Prince. I have four of your letters to thank you for, but I am in such a hurry with the many orders I am obliged to give for this march to Bruxelles,

¹ 9/20 Nov., B.M., Add. MS. 5130, fols. 228-9, summarized in D. Coombs, 'The Augmentation of 1709', *E.H.R.*, 62 (1957), 649.
² Richard Onslow, first Baron Onslow (1654-1717), M.P. 1679-87, 1689-1716; Speaker 1708-10; Lord of the Admiralty 1690-3; Privy Councillor 1710; Chancellor of the Exchequer 1714-15; created peer 1716; a leader of the Country Whigs or Whimsicals. *D.N.B.*

that I have not time. But I can't end this without telling you, that I very much approve of Mr. Webb's being gratified with a government, but I do not think if for her Majesty's service to give a promis before the vacancy happens, especially since he will be made a lieutenant general this winter. I have for some days been so tormented with a sore throat, that if the time could permit it, my chamber were the proprest place for mee.

1160. MARLBOROUGH *to* GODOLPHIN [*18/29 November 1708*]

Source: Blenheim MSS. A2-39.
Printed: Coxe, ii. 572–3 (inc.).

Bruxelles November 29th 1708

I have you an account in mine of yesterday[1] of our having forced the passage of the Sckeel [Scheldt]. At my arrivall last night at Allost, I had an account of the precipitated retreat of the Elector of Bavaria. He begane to draw off from the siege[2] two hours after he had knowlidge of my passage, fearing I might have fallen upon him, if he had stayed for the carrying off of his canon and wounded men, the leaving of which is most scandalous, and consequently must be a great mortefication to the Elector. Lord Harford having a mind to return for England,[3] I send these letters by him, so that there neds no present. But the opertunity being safe, I shall venture to tell you that the forcing of the Schell was not only necessary for the saving of Brabant, but also for the sending more amunition to Lisle, so that as soon as I have given the necessary orders in this town, I shall return this evening to the army, to take such measures as may secure the passage of one thousand barrelles of poweder from Ath to Lisle.

I cannot prove what I am going to say, but I really beleive we have been from the very begining of that siege been betrayed, for great part of our stores have been embasseld. The man I suspect is *Gilder Malsen*.[4] God is most certainly with us, or it would have been impossible to have overcome the many difficultys we have meet with. You are so pressing in your letters for my return, that I must tell you truth, and beg you will not think it vanity, that if I should leave the army, it would not be in anybody's power to keep them in the field, so that you see the necessity. The truth is that I am very ill in my health, so that if we should have very ill weather it may kille me, but I must venture everything rather then quit before we have perfected this campagne. My heart is in England and nobody living has a greater desire for

---

[1] Letter 1159.   [2] Of Brussels.
[3] Hertford had served this campaign as a volunteer.
[4] Geldermalsen was one of the Dutch field deputies; he was apparently in charge of the ammunition stores at Brussels, acting for the States ('t Hoff, p. 412). Wijn, VIII. ii. 360–2, in discussing the ammunition shortage, states that Goslinga and Geldermalsen favoured abandoning the siege, but he makes no mention of any embezzlement of stores.

the enjoying quietness then myself, but should I take ease at this time, I should hurt the Queen and my country more then my whole life could repare.

By yours of the 5th[1] which I have received this morning I find you have write me a long letter by Ostend,[2] which I may never receive. You will be pleased to write from henceforward to Holland, which will now come safe. I am in such hast that I can't read my letter, so that you must excuse mistakes.

1161. MARLBOROUGH *to the* DUCHESS   [*18/29 November 1708*]

Source: Blenheim MSS. E4.
Addressed: For the Dutchesse of Marlborough.

Bruxelles November 29th 1708

Since mine of yesterday[3] I have received yours of the 5th, by which I see you have write at large by Ostend. But that letter will find difficulty of getting to mee, so that henceforward yours should always come by Holland. I have not time to write you what passes. The publick papers will informe you. Do as I do, praise God, for certainly his hand is with us. I have not been well for some time but Lord Hartford will tell you that I am this day much better. I have not time to say more but that I am with heart and soull yours.

1162. GODOLPHIN *to* MARLBOROUGH   [*19 November 1708*]

Source: Blenheim MSS. A2-38.

November 19, 1708

Our letters goe and come so uncertainly of late, that one has little heart to write. However, I can't but take notice how much wee are alarmed, by the last post from Holland, for Brussells and Antwerp, by the motions of the Elector of Bavaria, as yett mere former friends by the consequences of those motions, which must have obliged your army to march. But I hope in God wee shall soon bee relieved by hearing some good news from you.

Wee have 2 Scots regiments here,[4] which wee would not send to Ostend, thinking them useless there. And hearing 5 or 6 regiments were gon from thence to Antwerp, we thought that whatever dangers threatned that place they must bee over, one way or other, before wee could land them there.

Here is another Scots regiment like to bee vacant, my Lord Polwort[5] being dead or dying. I believe you must have had many applications about

---

[1] Letter 1152.   [2] Letter 1151.
[3] Letter 1157.   [4] Grant's and Strathnaver's.
[5] Patrick Hume (died 1709), eldest son of Patrick, first Earl of Marchmont; served from 1689 in the army; brevet colonel 1704; colonel, Regiment of Dragoons (7th Hussars) 28 Apr. 1707; styled Lord Polworth after 1697; died Jan. 1709. See p. 1325.

it. Among others, I am earnestly desired to recommend my Lord Dunmore's son,[1] who is in your service now, as I am told. The Queen will not make any engagements to anybody before you come over.[2]

Nothing has yett passed in Parliament worth naming to you, but the address of the House of Lords, of which I send you a coppy. The Duke of Queensberry has been introduced there today, without one word sayd to his pattent.[3] The Commons have not done their swearing. There is a prospect of their being very hearty in the publick business, but I doubt wee shall have no money next year under 6 per cent, even upon the land tax.

1163. GODOLPHIN *to the* DUCHESS   [*21 November 1708*]

Source: Blenheim MSS. E20.
Addressed: To her Grace the Duchess of Marlborough att the Lodge.

Sunday night at 9 21th of November

I have just now received the favour of 2 letters from you, and the man that brought them having left word he must bee gon tomorrow morning before 8, I would not deferr troubling you with my thanks for your letters till then, for fear I should delay him. I am sorry you would not employ mee in distributing your letters, since I am sure nobody would have been more carefull of them, and I am more sorry you won't give mee leave to come to you tomorrow; but whatever satisfaction I proposed to myself in it, I shall not buy it at the rate of disobeying you.

I have never sayd more to the Duke of Somersett about Lord Brooke's affair,[4] than that the Queen did not seem in hast to take any resolution about it. 'Tis true he has often spoke of it to mee, and I believe as often to the Queen, by what she said to mee, and I am sure I will never meddle in it all but as you direct mee in it; for whatever is done in it, neither of them will bee pleased, and I have mett with so many mortifications, even since I saw you, that I can take no pleasure in any thought so much, as never speaking for anything.

As for Mr. Shute's[5] affair, since he will not accept of my proposall, I am engaged to bring him into the Customes if I can; but it is not in my power, for I proposed it to Mrs. Morley [the Queen] 2 yeares agoe, when I had another sort of credit with her than now, and she said no poor man,[6] I won't putt him out, hee's one of the oldest acquaintances I have. But I shall bee very

---

[1] Lord Fincastle.
[2] It was given to William Ker, brother of the first Duke of Roxburghe, on 10 Oct. 1709.
[3] See p. 996, n. 2.   [4] Not further identified.
[5] John Shute Barrington, first Viscount Barrington (1678–1734), Scottish lawyer; sent to Scotland by Somers to reconcile the Cameronians to the Union, for which he was promised a place; Commissioner of Customs Nov. 1708; advisor to Sunderland on the dissenters. *D.N.B.*
[6] Samuel Clark, Commissioner of the Customs 1701–8; died Nov. 1708.

desirous upon the first occasion to obey your commands relating to Mr. Congreve,[1] or indeed in any other thing great or little, as long as life and soul remains in mee. But for Mr. Vernon, as you seem indifferent about it, I think the thing itself is not to bee countenanced in any respect. Besides the place he has lost,[2] he is now a Clerk of the Counsell, which has been thought a very good provision heretofore for one of his age.

Nor is his case particular as to the Prince's family. There are 5 or 6 more who are of the House of Commons, and while they are so cannot receive pensions from the Queen, but must bee content with what consideration she will have of them hereafter upon that account.[3] I am afrayd I have troubled you too much upon these disagreable subjects, but there are no forreign letters and the winds are still directly contrary.

Mr Cardonell's letter was by Ostend. Lord Marlborough never cares to write that way because of the uncertainty of it, but now the other way is become as uncertain, I should think there were little choyce in the matter. But I have the letter itself in my pockett as it was enclosed to mee from the postmasters. I will look it out before I seal this and enclose it to you.

1164. MARLBOROUGH *to* GODOLPHIN

[*22 November/3 December 1708*]

Source: Blenheim MSS. A2-39.
Printed: Coxe, ii. 577–9 (inc.).

[Beerlegem]⁴ December 3d 1708

I have received the favour of yours of the 12th,[5] but those of the 16 going by the way of The Hague, thay will not be here for me to answere by this post. I beg from henceforward Mr. Secretary may derect the letters as formerly, and I shall take care for their coming quick and safe. I agree with you that this campagne is already much longer then has been usuall in this country, but you will remember that I have formerly told you that we must end this campagne with the retaking of Gant, if possible. The lengh of the siege of Lisle puts us under great difficultys, for from henceforward if we will continue the army together, we must subsist them with dry forage, which is very difficult and expencefull. This expence must be made by England and Holland; for even with that, we shall find it very difficult to persuade the forain troupes that it is reasonable att this time of the yeare to be from their

---

[1] William Congreve (1670–1729), dramatist: Commissioner of Hackney Coaches 1695–1707; of Wine Licences 1705–14; a friend of Maynwaring's; member of the Kit-Kat Club; devoted friend and reputed lover of the Marlboroughs' daughter, Henrietta. *D.N.B.*

[2] As Teller of the Exchequer.

[3] 30 Dec., the Queen 'signed a warrant for continuing the salaries to the Prince's servants during her life, provided they keep no publick houses'. Luttrell, vi. 390.

[4] Beerlegem, a village 15 kilometres south of Ghent.   [5] Letter 1156.

winter quarters. But I think the taking of Gant and Bridges, with the augementation which I hope will be made by England and Holande, will procure and honorable and safe peace. I have proposed this expence to Holand by the last letters, and if thay agree to it, I hope her Majesty will aprove of it. I acquainted you in a former letter that I had ordered Lieutenant General Erle to send five battalions to Antwerp, upon the first notice I had of the attempt on Bruxelles. I have now ordered him to leave at Ostend a bregadier with the six battalions, and himself and the rest of the generall officers to return for England. I have also directed him to take as many officers as is possible of those six redgiments with him for England, so as to recrut them, if possible, thay being extreame weake. The passage of the Scheel [Scheldt] and the raising the siege of Bruxelles has put the French so out of humor, that the exchang of prisoners is at a full stope. The enclosed is what I have under King Augustus' hand,[1] for I think it is of use it should not be known. I have not yett comunicated it to the Pensioner, but I shall do it by the first safe opertunity.[2] And for the troupes of augementation, if their be early care taken with the King of Prussia and others to lett them see that there must be no advance mony given, but that we shall be willing to pay such troupes as are not already in the Service, if there be not great care taken in this matter my Lord Raby, by his flatterie to the King of Prussia and that court, will spoile all. The 50 odd thousand crowns was last yeare promised so solomly, that thay must be payd as soon as he has signed the treaty for this yeare, but I think it should stay for that. You know also that the Queen is ingaged in honour to pay this winter the 200,000 crowns to the Langrave of Hesse. I know all these things must give you great trouble, but for God sake lett the Queen's promises be keep sacred, for that will forever eastablish her reputation, which is now very great.[3]

I can't end this letter without assuring you that I know the difficultys of Holland to be so great, that I hope every honest man in England will be contented with their furnishing only one thord in the augementation, for it is most certain that thay now subsist only by creditt, and that the ill affected in that country have no hopes left but that England will insist upon their giving one half.

I have been troubled some time with the Comte Guiscard, which has given me the opertunity of being sure that his head is turned to impracticable projects. He has desired me to send you the enclosed paper,[4] and at the same

[1] 13/24 Nov., Blenheim MSS. A2-36, copy, B2-15, concerning the hire of his troops; to be on the same basis as those of Prussia.

[2] He sent it the next day ('t Hoff, p. 412).

[3] Payment of the armies to the King of Prussia and the Landgrave of Hesse were both voted by the Commons on 12 Feb. *C.J.*, xvi. 107.

[4] In a memorial of 9/20 Dec. to Marlborough, Guiscard refers to his project for a descent in Roussillon and also plans to enter Dauphiné with a force of refugees with the assistance of the Duke of Savoy. Then he follows with a project to take Cavalier's regiment and to raise two

time tels me he has no mony. You must lett mee know what I am to say to him. If you can make any use of him, he is better anywhere then in England. I have this minut received a letter from Prince Eugene,[1] write last night, that he hopes by Thursday[2] to have all his batteries ready, and then he will summons the Mareshall,[3] and att the same time let him know that he may send an officer to see our canon and amunition. After which, if he obliges us to make the breach, he must expect no other capitulation but that of being prisoners of warr. The 1,000 barrelles of powder I send to Lisle, are this morning come out of Ath, and will be with the Prince on Wensday night, so that on Thursday or Friday, I hope the French will be obliged to see or hear them. I think the last will be the best, for though there are not above 4,000 men in the cittadel, but thay consist of 2 redgiments of horse, 2 of dragons, and 22 of foot, so that there will be a great number of officers, and consequently an impossibillity of raising the redgiments for the next campagne. If we can be so happy as to get everything necessary for the attack of Gant, I think to direct itt, and the Prince to cover the siege with the troupes that shall march with him from Lisle.

God has so blessed us for a long time with good weather that it would be ungratfull to complain, but this day we have rain with a southerly wind which makes us fear we must exspect much more. The letters you sent by Ostend I have not received.

1165. MARLBOROUGH *to the* DUCHESS
[*22 November/3 December 1708*]

Source: Blenheim MSS. E4.
Printed: Coxe, ii. 575 (inc.).

[Beerlegem] December 3d, 1708

As my greatest happyness is your kindness, and that I do flatter myself of your having a tender consarn for mee, I have endeavoured all I could not to lett the army know the ill condition of my health for these last three weekes, fearing some officers might write it to England, by which you might be made uneasy. But I think God I am now much better, and if I would have two or three days quiet, I do not doubt but it would sett me right, for my greatest uneasiness now is a constant drouth. By your last letter I find you apprehend that 256 [Mrs. Masham] has that intirest with 42 [the Queen],

---

additional regiments, one to be commanded by himself, another by de Rifier. He wants the fleet to take them next June to the coast of France near Béziers and Agde. The coast there is always bare of troops and there are many sympathizers and friends with whom he can join, moving into the mountains where he can be out of the reach of the French army. Blenheim MSS. B1-7.

[1] See reply, 21 Nov./2 Dec., Murray, iv. 331.
[2] 25 Nov./6 Dec.
[3] Boufflers.

that thay will always have it in their power of giving caracters and recomending such churchmen as may not be in the trew intirest of 42 [the Queen].
I beleive you judge very right, but pray consider that perfection is not to be
found on this side heaven, so that if 239 [the Queen] be governed by 97
[the Cabinet] in their affaires of consequence, I should hope everything
might mend, especially since you think that 38 [Godolphin] is as well with
42 [the Queen] as ever.[1] If that continues, 256 [Mrs. Masham] may vex, but
never do much mischief. I received yesterday yours of the 12th. Those of the
16 are all come to the army except yours, Lord Treasurer and the Secretary's
for me, which are sent by the way of The Hague, so that I shall not have them
to answere by this post. I beg henceforward that your letters may come as
formerly, and I shall take care to have them lose no time in coming to mee.
God Almighty has blessed us for a long time with good weather. If it had
been his pleasure to have continued it for one month longer, it would have
been of great use, for I beleive we shall be obliged to stay one month longer
in the field. This day we have a good deal of rain with a south wind, which
I fear will bring much more. If we end the campagne as I hope and think we
shall, it will make ample satisfaction for the trouble and lengh of itt, since it
may occasion my being for the remainder of my life with you.

1166. GODOLPHIN *to* MARLBOROUGH   [*23 November 1708*]

Source: Blenheim MSS. A2-38.
Addressed: To his Grace the Duke of Marlborough.

November 23d 1708

Never was there so great an impatience as to hear from you now, and to
know you are well. For by Ostend wee have reports of your having passed
the Scheldt, with so many particulars and circumstances of truth in them,
that I can't doubt of your success in generall. My only concern now is to hear
that you have no hurt.

Finding by Mr. Erle's letters that the regiments designed for Antwerp
were still at Ostend, orders will bee sent from hence to stop them. Since if
our accounts bee true, as I hope they are, those men are like to bee of more
use at Ostend.

Mr. Secretary will send you the address of the House of Commons,[2] which
is as full as you can desire, and cannot fail, I hope, of having a good effect.
The letter from Lady Marlborough which I enclose was brought mee this
morning from the Lodg.

I can't write anything more till I have the satisfaction of hearing from you.

---

[1] See p. 1138. Cf. p. 1155.
[2] The address of 23 Nov. in reply to the Queen's speech opening Parliament, *C.J.*, xvi. 8.

1167. MARLBOROUGH *to* GODOLPHIN

[*25 November/6 December 1708*]

Source: Blenheim MSS. A2-39.
Printed: Coxe, ii. 579–80.

[Beerlegem] December 6, 1708

Since my last I have received yours of the 19th,[1] by which I see the letters from Holand had given you feares for Bruxelles and Antwerp. There was but to[o] much reason for feares, for had not God favored our passage of the Schelde, thay must have been in dainger; for not only the towns, but all the people of this country hatte the Dutch. Our passage of the Schelde has so disordered Monsieur de Vandome's projects, that I hope in God we shall succeed in this undertaking of Gand, which is of the last consequence, not only for the finishing of this campagne, but also for the operations of the next. As it is impossible for me to stay for her Majestys orderes, without hurting the Service very much, I have taken upon me, hoping the Queen will approve of it, to send this day Major General Cadogan to Bruxelles, in conjunction with the deputys of the States, to contract for the dry forage that must be delivered to the army during the siege of Gand, the States having resolved to give it to those troupes thay pay. This extreordinary is absolutly necessary so that I must beg you to lay itt favourably before the Queen and the Lords of the Cabinet. For should I have stayed for orders, we might have lost the opertunity of making the siege, for both our horse and foot already suffer very much by the cold weather we now have. As we are assured by our letters from all parts, that the French draw all the troupes in their power into this country, we have resolved to keep as many of the Garmain troupes as we can persuade to stay; so that I could wish you had sent as I desired formerly the 2 Scoth redgiments of foot,[2] and if it be possible I could wish thay might yett be sent to Antwerp; for God knows when this campagne may end, and we have many of our redgiments very weake. Yet I think we must have Gand and Bridges, lett it cost what it will. Our men are very hearty and desirous of taking those two towns, so that I hope thay will suffer a great deal before thay grumble. This country is not used to see an army so late in the field, but thay all suffer patiently, believing it is what will forward the peace.

1168. MARLBOROUGH *to the* DUCHESS

[*25 November/6 December 1708*]

Source: Blenheim MSS. E4.
Printed: Coxe, ii. 575 (inc.).

[Beelegem] December 6, 1708

I have received your dear letter of the 19th, by which I see the kind concern you had at that time for mee, which I shall ever by my kindness endeavour to

[1] Letter 1162.   [2] Grant's and Strathnaver's.

deserve. You will have known by Lord Hartford by this time the success God has been pleased to bless us with. Considering the pains thay had taken by fortefying every place of the river where thay thought we could passe, I think it next to a mericle our surprising them as we did. Our passage has had all the happy effects we could propose to ourselves, which has encoraged mee to take measures for the siege of Gand, though the season is so advanced that I tremble every day for fear of ill weather. If we take Gand I think we have a certinty of a good peace, which is every day more and more wished for by mee. Yours, Lord Treasurer's and Mr. Secretary Boyle's letter of the 16 for me are not come, though the officers of the army have received theirs, so that I should be glad to know what was in them. As I am likely to continu for four or five days in this camp, I intend tomorrow to begine to take some fisick, which I hope will sett me right. Finding by the letters of the 19th no notice taken of Lord Pembrook and the other changes you mentioned to mee,[1] I should be glad to know the reason of the delay, for sure no time is more proper then that of opening the Parliament. I do with all my heart wish myself with you, but I see so many things that of necessity must be done by mee, that I am not able to guesse at the time. But what makes me suport it with patience is that I think this winter campagne will hasten the peace.

I have opened my letter to lett you know that I have just now received yours of the 16, but have not time to say more.

1169. GODOLPHIN *to* MARLBOROUGH   [26 November 1708]

Source: Blenheim MSS. A2-38.

November 26th 1708

Though wee had news here the 23d in the morning by Ostend of your having passed the Scheldt with great success, upon the 16/27th, which is now 10 days since, yett to this moment, wee continue under the very great uneasyness of being without any particulars by the way of Holland. And what makes it more wonderfull, is, that to our thinking here, the wind and weather for the last 3 or 4 days has not appeared to bee unfavorable. But surely the wind must have been otherwise in Holland, for I can't think the packetboat has been taken; or if it had, the rest are on that side and wee have three posts due this day. Imagine now, if you please, what heart one can have to write of anything else, while one [is] in soe great a suspence; and how wild and impertinent all our reasonings must bee upon events, which though wee had good grounds, in the main, to hope are true, yett not being certain of the

---

[1] Pembroke succeeded Prince George as Lord High Admiral on 25 Nov.; Somers succeeded him as Lord President, Wharton as Lord-Lieutenant of Ireland. A number of other office holders were changed to accommodate the Whigs.

particulars or the extent of them, 'tis impossible, as yett, to draw any reasonable consequences from what may have hapned.

26 at night

Since the former part of my letter my Lord Hartford is arrived, and I have the favour of yours of the 28th[1] from Oudenard, and of the 29th[2] from Brusselles. I am extreamly concerned that you have not been well, but my Lord Hartford gives mee hopes you are something better. Sore throats have been very common here and very troublesome. Therfore I hope you won't neglect to take care of yourself, expecially now, that it seems to mee, there is no possibility of any more action. Since it is plainer than ever by this last, that their troops won't stand you anywhere.

The news wee had from Ostend is a little dwindled by my Lord Hartford's arrivall. They had bragged of your having more prisoners, but I find by yours there was very little resistance. But the main advantages prove true; Brussells is relieved, and the communication restored, and ammunition enough (I hope) carryed to Lisle, to make you masters of it.

But as to your winter quarters, I don't see clear, yett, how they are to bee settled. I don't much wonder that the troops are unwilling to continue in the field, but rather, how they can endure it. This terrible cold weather, which wee have here to that degree, that if it holds (I doubt) they will bee frozen up in Holland.

I believe the troops designed for Antwerp from Mr. Erle did not goe, for want of convoy. If you have no more use of them on that side, should they not come home to recruit? I am told, there is at this time pretty good disposition in the House of Commons to provide the necessary recruits, if they could bee rightly informed what would bee wanting for the whole.[3] And therfore the sooner you can send Mr. Walpole an account of what will bee sufficient for your army, the better.

I was indeed very desirous of your [coming] into England before the Parliament, but that occasion being now over, and I hope pretty well over, and I doe not now look for you till about Christmas. My chief concern, at present, is for your health, and that you should gett some good warm clothes, which are to bee had at Brussells, or Lisle, as well as at Paris or London.

As to the person you suspect, since you doe but suspect, and have no certaintys against him, I think that matter ought to bee managed very tenderly, so as not to make a noyse. He can doe no more hurt in this year, and before another campagne, you may possibly bee able to give that a turn to 62 [Heinsius] and 116 [the States] so as to gett him changed, and sent to encourage 50 [Elector of Hanover].[4]

---

[1] Letter 1159.   [2] Letter 1160.   [3] See p. 1146, n. 1.

[4] Geldermalsen was apparently relieved of his duties at Brussels in 1709, for he was again assigned to attend Marlborough as a field deputy, representing the Council of State. He did not serve in that capacity thereafter.

1170. MARLBOROUGH *to* GODOLPHIN

[*29 November/10 December 1708*]

Source: Blenheim MSS. A2-39.
Printed: Coxe, ii. 581-2.

[Beerlegem] December 10th 1708

I am very glad to tell you that Prince Eugene sent Collonel Cromstron[1] to me yesterday, to lett me know that he was to have possession of one of the gattes of the cittadel that day. I have taken measures with him for their sending 20 battalions and 30 squadrons to join me with all expedition, so that I might give as litle time as possible to those in Gand to strenghen themselves, which thay now do by working day and night. You will see by the enclosed letter which we have intercepted[2] the number of troupes the enemy have for the defence of Gand and Brudges, which are so numerous that I am afraid thay will be able to give us more trouble then were to be wished at this season. But the consequences of taking thes places are so great, that we must ventur everything for the being masters of them. I never in my life felt colder weather then we have had for these last three days, so that our men and horses must suffer. I shall march tomorrow, so that my next march will be for the investing the town, which shall be as soon as I shall be able to have the canon att Dendermont. I hope my next will acquaint you of the day. If God blesse us with the taking of this place, and a good augementation be made, I think a good peace must follow before the midel of next summer.

1171. MARLBOROUGH *to the* DUCHESS

[*29 November/10 December 1708*]

Source: Blenheim MSS. E4.
Printed: Coxe, ii. 580 (inc.); *Private Correspondence*, i. 174-5 (abr.).

[Beerlegem] December 10th 1708

Yours of the 16 came so late that I could not by the last post say any more then that I had received itt. You may assure 6 [Sunderland] that the expression he had used to you gives mee great pleasure, since I see by it that his friends are satisified with my endeavours. I am now strongling with my own health and the season, that if it be possible to finish this campagne with the taking of Gand and Bridges, which if God blesses us with success, I think we may without vanity say that France will with teror remember this campagne for a long time, there never having been any in which there has been such variety of action. You know my greatest desire is ending my days

---

[1] Isaacq, Baron van Cronström, Dutch officer, colonel, Regiment Brandenburg, 1704; Lieutenant-General of Infantry 1709.

[2] The marquis of Grimaldi, governor of Bruges, to the duc de Popoli, 24 Nov./5 Dec., in Murray, iv. 346.

in quiet with you. As for wealth, I have as much as I desire, but if 6 [Sunder-land] and our friends can think of anything that will lett the people here abroad and the people in England, see how far thay approve of my actions, that would be a lasting obligation and satisfaction to mee, say and do in this matter what you think best.[1]

You have an expressions in yours concerning 272 [Godolphin] which you hope nobody else will ever know, that I should be glad you would explain to mee. As our letters will now come safe, you may venture to do itt. I am of your opinion that 28 [Shrewsbury] will not be very fond of the alterations, but I take his temper to be such that I beleive 89 [the Whigs] if thay think thay can make any use of him, thay may governe him as long as our affaires have success. I do not much approve of such a temper, but I take it to be his. Before the Queen disposes of the stables the Prince had att St. Jeamses, I should be glad a proper time might be taken to let her know that I have none, and that I hope she would be inclined to make me easy sooner then severall others that will be asking. But if her Majesty has occasion of them for herself, you will then say nothing.[2] Since my last we have had a very hard frost and as cold weather as ever I felt in my life, so that the poor men incamped grieves my heart to see them; but this is better then rain. The whole army is so convinced of the necessity we are in to have Gand, that thay will suffer everything to have itt, which makes me hope God will bless us with success, though we have reason to fear many accedents that might make us miscarry at this season. You will know by the letters of this post that we are in possesion of the cittadel of Lisle, so that great trouble is ended. I wish with all my soull that of Gand were also well over.

1172. GODOLPHIN *to* MARLBOROUGH   [*30 November 1708*]

Source: Blenheim MSS. A2-38.

November 30th 1708

I have the pleasure of yours of the 3d of December[3] which is so much longer than you use to write that I flatter myself you find your health begins to mend, and if you have the same clear frosty weather wee have here, I hope

---

[1] For discussion of a further memorial, see letter 1188A.

[2] The Duchess made the request to the Queen who replied: 'When dear Mrs. Freeman spoke to me about the stables I had soe little of anything of that kind in my thoughts that I realy did not know very well what answer to give you, but upon considering of it since I beleeve there are several of the dear Prince's servants have lodgings in the stables. I intend to order an account of the stables and what servants is in them, to be layd before me, and when the Duke of Marlborough com's home, he may see whether there is conveniences enough for him besides, and if there be, I shall be very glad to gratefye him in his desires. Munday [6 Dec.]' (Blenheim MSS. E19). The balance is printed in Green, p. 139. In an endorsement to this letter the Duchess attributed the Queen's refusal to Mrs. Masham, whose husband had been an Equerry to Prince George.

[3] Letter 1164.

this will find you perfectly well. But since Lady Marlborough says you complain to her of a draught upon you, give mee leave to tell you there is no better remedie in the world for that complaint than spâ waters; 2 or 3 little glasses in a days time, till you are well. But you must take them either in bed, or when you can bee by a fire, or walk yourself warm. In short, you must not lett them chill your blood for fear of an ague.

As to the augmentation the addresses of Parliament give so good hopes of that matter, that the Queen makes an answer by this night's post to the letter from the States to her Majesty upon that. I will speak to Mr. Secretary Boyle to send you a coppy of it.[1] Wee avoyd to enter into the particular proportions of that expence, since that would only create difficultys in it here, and if (at last) wee are to have any disputes about it, 'tis better still to deferr them as long as wee can.

Mr. Secretary has received the Queen's commands very distinctly for what he is to write too my Lord Raby, according to your desires, about the Prussians.[2] I think you ought to take them, in the 1st place preferably to King Augustus's troops, or else it will bee a mortall quarrell with the King of Prussia, who with all his humours is one of our best and most usefull allyes.

The 2 Scots regiments[3] will bee sent to Antwerp immediatly, but some few of their officers being of the House of Commons will bee allowed to stay behind, for the present.[4] Wee are taking the best and speediest measures wee can, in recommending the recruits to the House of Commons.

As to the expence for dry forage which you mention in yours of the 6th of December (which I must now acknowledg) I hope you need not bee so nice, for want of the Queen's orders in that matter, since there can bee no doubt but it will be approved. But you may please to direct *Cadogan* to send over authentick coppys of the particulars of the Queen's share of that expence, in order to its being laid (with the soonest) before the House of Commons.

I am very sorry to find you are going to begin a new campagne, though I agree, 'tis necessary to have Ghendt and Bruges; but sieges, in that country, must needs be very fatiguing at this time of year. God send you good success with them.

Before I end this letter I must yett mention 2 particulars to you, of a nature very different from those with which I generally trouble you. The first, is at the pressing instances of Sir Henry Furnese, to complain of one

---

[1] Printed in Lamberty, v. 154–5.

[2] Boyle's letter to Raby was enclosed with the Queen's letter to the States in his letter to Marlborough, 30 Nov., Blenheim MSS. B1-1.   [3] Grant's and Strathnaver's.

[4] 'Grant's regiment and [my son's] had orders to embarque att Shields the fourth . . . There being five members of the House of Commons in them it might have been as well that they who are members in the House had gone past to the electing of a Speaker and afterwards gone to their posts as her Majesty should think. I believe that it has been with a design in which our enemies shall be disappointed.' Sutherland to Sunderland, 9 Nov., Blenheim MSS. C1-20.

Andrew Peltz,[1] a merchant of Amsterdam who since the taking of Lisle gives excessive rates for the ready money of that town, which he sends to the French army. The two ill consequences of this are: 1st, that the enemyes find money to pay their troops by this means when they could not have it by any other; 2dly, that wee are forced by it to give much greater rates for the money wee want to pay our own troops. You can best judg of the proper remedy for this pernicious practice.[2]

The other particular is this: I am informed by 5 [Somers] that Toland, who is now at The Hague or Amsterdam, was upon the point of coming into England, but stopped by his correspondents here in order to his finishing and printing a book on that side against 39 [Marlborough].[3] In order to which, he has lately sent for the libell for which *Stephens* was punished here,[4] also for another book for which one Gilden stood in the pillory here some years since.[5] From these sort of materialls with which he is furnishing himself, wee ghess he must have some such design. You will bee able to judg whether you could not take some measures with 62 [Heinsius] for watching him, and for seizing his book, and papers, or finding out his printer, so as that you may bee master of what villany he is doing there.

Since I had written this I have received the enclosed letter from Sir Henry Furnese[6] which will more fully explain to you the former of my two last particulars, and may bee shown, if you see occasion for it, to anybody in Holland.

1173. MARLBOROUGH *to the* DUCHESS   [1/12 December 1708]

Source: Blenheim MSS. E2.
Addressed: For the Dutchesse of Marlborough.

[Melle][7] December 12th 1708

Though I beleive you will receive severall letters from me before this is delivered, yet I would not let Doctor Hare go without a letter. He will acquaint you that my health is much better, as also that we have the misfortune of having a very heard frost, so that we can't attack the town til it

---

[1] Andreas Pels, 'one of the greatest merchants in Europe', and a principal French agent in Amsterdam for remitting funds to the French armies. *New C.M.H.*, vi. 303.

[2] See p. 1073, n. 5.

[3] No work of this nature by Toland has been identified.

[4] See p. 544.

[5] Charles Gildon (1665–1724), writer to whom the Queen had once given money at the request of Lord Jersey upon Gildon's dedicating a play to her (Queen to Duchess, 7 June, Blenheim MSS. E18). This sentence came for his hand in *Sir Roland Gwynne's Letter to the Earl of Stamford* (see p. 800). He was also fined £100 and Maynwaring interceded for him for remission of the fine; H.M.C., *Portland MSS.*, viii. 349, 353. *D.N.B.*

[6] Untraced.

[7] Melle, a town on the Scheldt, 12 kilometres north-east of Beerlegem, and 8 kilometres south-east of Ghent.

pleases God to send a tha[w]. This place [Ghent] is so necessary that we must suffer everything in order to have it, if it be possible. God bless you, and make you happy, and be assured that I long to be with you, but the troupes can't be keep together but by my stay.

1174. GODOLPHIN *to* MARLBOROUGH   [*2 December 1708*]

Source: Blenheim MSS. A2-38.
Printed: Coxe, ii. 579 (inc.).

December 3d 1708

By the last post[1] I acknowledged the favour of yours of the 3d and 6th, and answered to all the particulars of both, except what related to Monsieur de Guiscard. I agree entirely in your character of him, and that he is better anywhere than here, as also that he wants money to carry him anywhere, though he had 500£ when he went from hence, to carry him first to you, and afterwards, by your approbation, to 58 [Duke of Savoy] and to concert with him, how he might bee of most use to his operations next year either by his intelligences in Dauphiné or in the Cevennes, to both which he pretends. I can propose nothing better for him than to follow this first intention, and if in order to it you will direct Mr. Cardonell to help him, by his credit at Amterdam or Brusselles with any sum not exceeding 4 or 500£ more, I will see it repaid; and he must give Mr. Cardonnell an account of his proceedings from time to time.

By the present posture of the affairs of France, I am very much of opinion they will bee forced to leave few or no troops either in Provence, or in Roussillon, at the beginning of next campagne. Hee might have your instructions, (if you think fitt) to observe and improve this hint, as he finds the occasion offers for it, either with 58 [Duke of Savoy] or 44 [King Charles].

All the necessary orders are given here for hastning the two Scots regiments[2] to Antwerp, which I reckon is all that will bee possible for us to contribute to your assistance, in this year. And for the next, if you can gett the augmentation you propose of forreign troops, I should think it would bee most for the service that the extraordinary regiments you have of ours should return to bee employed upon the fleet next year, as they were in the last.

You may depend the great jealousy of the French next year, will bee for Ypres and Dunkirk. Now if 39 [Marlborough] and 110 [Holland] have other views, it would not bee amiss to give out they have intentions upon those towns, that so they (the French) might make their preparations in the wrong place, for they won't bee in a condition to prepare in all places.

As the wind is at this time, I am in hopes to hear from you tomorrow and if the Dutch letters come before the post goes, I shall beg leave to trouble you again.

[1] Letter 1172.   [2] Grant's and Strathnaver's.

1175. MARLBOROUGH *to* GODOLPHIN   [*2/13 December 1708*]

Source: Blenheim MSS. A2-39.
Printed: Coxe, ii. 583, 596 (inc.).

[Melle] December 13th 1708

The wind having been for some time in the east, we have had no letters from England. Til this frost breakes, we can neither break ground for our batteries nor open our trenches, and which is yett worse, if this weather continues all the canals will be froze, so that we shall not be able to gett forage from Holand, which is the only place that can furnish us. But my reliance is that God who has protected and blessed us hethertoo, will enable us to finish it with the taking this town, which you will be sensible of the use it will be to us when you read the inclosed letter.[1] We begine to give dry forage tomorrow. We have contracted for as much as will serve us for three weekes, but after that time the towns of this country, as well as the army, will, I am afraid, find no forage but what must be brought from Holande, so that we should have a thaw.

The enclosed from Monsieur Guiscard[2] I received yesterday. I should be glad to know what answere I shall make, for I am quit weary of his corrispondance. Mr. Cardonell having shown me Mr. How's letter,[3] I would not omitt sending itt to you, but I think it should be comunicated only to 42 [the Queen]. For if Mr. How be not mistaken, their behavior is very extraordinary, and very wrong, I think, for their own intirest. But pation [passion] is very capable of making men blind.

Our last letters from England were of the 19th.

1176. MARLBOROUGH *to the* DUCHESS   [*2/13 December 1708*]

Source: Blenheim MSS. E4.
Printed: *Private Correspondence*, i. 175-6.

[Melle] December 13th, 1708

Since my last Doctor Hare is gone for England. As he is like not to make much hast I have write only to wordes by him to you. I could wish the time were come that I might be thinking of that jorny, but I can't guesse when that may be; for til this frost ends we can neither begine to make our batteries nor open the trenches, the ground being as hard as iron, which you may beleive gives me uneasiness. As the greatest part of our subsistance from

---

[1] An intercepted letter from the Elector of Bavaria's secretary, Baron of Maleknecht to the Count of Solar Monasterol at Danzig, 27 Nov./8 Dec. 1708, Blenheim MSS. B2-15.

[2] Untraced.

[3] 24 Nov./5 Dec., Blenheim MSS. B1-15. Howe congratulates him on relief of Brussels. News had arrived the day before that the French had taken it at which 'ther spirretts were raised here [Hanover]'.

henceforwards, particularly our forage must come from Holande if this frost should frieze the canals, we should be putt very hard for the carrying on our designe. But as God has blessed us on so many occations, I trust in his goodness that he will give us in due time such weather as may give us an opertunity of finishing this campagne so as that we may have quiet hearafter. I send Lord Treasurer a letter we have intercepted write by the Elector of Bavaria's secritary, that will let you see the necessity of having Gand, if possible, and that he is not very well pleased with the French. The comfort I have amongest the many troubles, is that you do not doubt of everything's going well in England. Your last letter was of the 18th.

1177. GODOLPHIN *to* MARLBOROUGH   [*3 December 1708*]

Source: Blenheim MSS. A2-38.

December 3d 3 in the afternoon

The forreign letters being not yett come, though the wind bee very fair, I shall only add for the present, that if 116 [the States] can bee made sensible of the mischief which Peltz and his correspondents doe to the publick service, the best and perhaps the only effectuall way of preventing it, will bee to stopp wholly the intercourse of letters with France. And if 116 [the States] could bee brought to doe this but for 6 weeks, wee are made to believe here, that it would hinder all the French preparations for next year. Now if this bee true in fact, the naturall consequence from it, is that they must come to a peace upon our terms, which is an argument that I should think likely to have a good deal of weight with 116 [the States]. And the tryall which is proposed being but for 6 weeks time, in case it had not the effect expected, nobody would give them the trouble of desiring a further prohibition of the letters.

The enclosed paper[1] was given mee by 50's [Elector of Hanover] minister [Schütz] here, with great recommendations to manage him in it. 'Tis the subject of a letter, betwixt France and Sweden, which has been intercepted by his court.

1178. GODOLPHIN *to* MARLBOROUGH   [*6 December 1708*]

Source: Blenheim MSS. A2-38.
Printed: Coxe, ii. 596.

[London] December 6, 1708

I have the favour of yours of the 13th.[2] In my last, you had all the answer I could make, as to Monsieur de Guiscard, who I find is so troublesome to

---

[1] Untraced.   [2] Letter 1175.

you, and I hope you will approve my answer, since it removes him so farr from you; and I am of opinion, the farther the better. For if he can bee usefull anywhere, it must bee by being near 58 [Duke of Savoy] or 44 [King Charles] by his intelligences in Dauphinè, and Languedoc.

As to the letter you send mee from Mr. How, I think it is so little fitt to bee shown to anybody, that I am not inclined to show it even to 42 [the Queen] who is but too apt, to take prejudices to that court, and I doubt, Mr. How is so too.

By your intercepted letter it looks as if they thought Monsieur de Véndosme might make some attempt to relieve Gandt, but I can't think there is any probability of that.

The frost has been gone here 3 or 4 days, and wee were sorry for it, believing that weather was good for you. But since by yours I find it otherwise, I hope you have the same open weather wee now have here, and that you will bee soon in a posture to close this long campagne, according to your own wish.

In order to this, you have (I hope by this time) our 2 Scots regiments,[1] as well as the 5 regiments from Ostend. But I hope you doe not look upon these, as to bee any part of your augmentation for next year, since they are upon our Spanish establishment. And besides, wee make account that all your augmentation is to consist of forreign troops, and chiefly of Prussians and Saxons. Though as to the former I find Monsieur Spanheim makes great difficultys of recovering the treaty for the troops in Italy without some better conditions. But if wee hold him, I believe they will not only comply in that, but also give a considerable number of troops for the augmentation.

Yesterday the House of Commons made one step towards a recruit bill, and I hope, that one way or other they will make it effectuall. But I doubt, they will scarce approve of fixing any certain proportion of men upon the severall countyes or parishes.[2]

I must always continue impatient for the end of your campagne.

1179. MARLBOROUGH *to* GODOLPHIN [6/17 December 1708]

Source: Blenheim MSS. A2-39.
Printed: Coxe, ii. 583-4 (inc.).

[Melle] December 17th 1708

I am to return you my thankes for yours of the 23d and 26th,[3] and I do with all my heart rejoice at what you write, that you beleive everything will go well in Parliament. I pray God we may succed in this necessary undertaking.

[1] Grant's and Strathnaver's.
[2] On 6 Dec. the Commons voted to consider recruiting in a committee on 13 Dec.
[3] Letters 1166, 1169.

The enemy knowing the consequence of our having Gand, have left 30 battalions and 19 squadrons for the defence of it, which in other countrys would be thought a good army. Their numerous garrison and the season of the yeare, have made them flatter themselves hethertoo, but now thay begine to see our amunition boates, so that I had this evening a deputation from the town, to desire that their houses might not be burnt. You will see my answere in the paper which goes to the Secretary's office, it being to[o] long to trouble you with in this letter.[1] Tomorrow the town will be invested on all sides, after which we must for some time have patience til we gett our canon. By the next post I intend to lett Mr. Walpole know what number of men we shall want for the twenty English battalions of this army. Those with Mr. Earle are in a much worse condition. He must let you know the numbers. Those in Spain and Portugalle should also be taken care off. The Pallatins are leaving us, and the deputys have write to the States for power to press Prince Eugene for the stay of the Imperial troupes in this country. Thay are willing to join with the Queen in the expence of giving them bread and forage, but I beleive the Prince will also insist on *agio*.[2] Whatever augmentation may be intended by England and Holande, I should think it would be for the Service to have it emediatly known, since the surest way of having a good peace is to be in a readyness for warr. Prince Eugene came here yesterday and goes tomorrow for Bruxelles. We shall have him here againe in two days.

1180. MARLBOROUGH *to the* DUCHESS   [*6/17 December 1708*]

Source: Blenheim MSS. E4.
Printed: Churchill, ii. 467 (inc.).

[Melle] December 17th 1708

Since my last[3] I have had the pleasure of receiving yours of the 22th from the Lodge, and that of the 26 by which I see you are returned to London, which I am glad of; for if you have had the same weather we have had, it has been so very cold that it must have done you hurt, for it has frozen so exsessive hard that the rivers have been al shut up, so that we could have nothing come to us, which if it had continued must have obliged us to have gone to our garissons. But I thank God we have now a gentle thaw, by which I hope the rivers will in a few days bring us our canon and amunition. The French knowing the consequence of this town have now in itt, 30 battalions and

---

[1] In S.P. 87/3, fols. 250–1. Sent 9/20 Dec.

[2] A percentage of charge for changing one currency into one more valuable, the value of one over another. *O.E.D.* In this instance the 'difference of the money current in the Empire and the rates the same money is current in the territories [the Spanish Netherlands] where the troops are employed.' *C.T.B.*, xxiii, part 1, xxiii.

[3] Letter 1176.

19 squadrons, so that I have desired the assistance of the foot of Prince Eugene's army, which will be with me tomorrow, and then I shall invest the place on all sides. The French hope by their numerous garrison to make such a defence, and by the advantage thay have of the season that we shall be forced to raise the siege; but my hopes are that God will enable us to deceive them, for to be in some quiet this winter, and to enable the making a good campagne the next yeare wee must be masters of this town. I have had this evening a deputation from the clergy, nobillity and citizens of the town in the nam of al the people desiring thay might not be bombarded. With all my hart I wish it could be taken without doing hurt, but in kindness to our own soldiers we must use all means for the reducing in the shortest time.

1181. MARLBOROUGH *to* GODOLPHIN [*9/20 December 1708*]

Source: Blenheim MSS. A2-39.
Printed: Coxe, ii. 584 (inc.).

[Melle] December 20th 1708

I have had the favour of yours of the 30th,[1] with the inclosed letter of Sir Stafford Fairborn.[2] I beleive what he writes is very trew, but I am afraid it is impossible to hinder itt; for though it be distruction, where mony is to be gott thay will have itt. However, I shall acquaint the Pensioner with itt.

I hope by this time the House of Commons are come to a resolution for an augementation, so that there may be time for the getting the men. Besides the advantage itt will be, that our friends as well as enimies may see that the warr next yeare is to be carryed on with vigor, I am earnest in this because I think it will make an end of the warr. The goodness of the Prussian troupes are such that I do asure you I estime them more then any other, so that whatever numbers the King will lett us have without leavy mony, we aught to entertain. What you write me of Mr. Toland dose no ways surprise me, for I know him to be a villain, and governed by a very mallicious man,[3] and is maintained by him in Holand as a spye. I have had an account of his behavior in the courts of Jarmany this last winter, where he spared nobody but his patron. I thank you for your kind care of my health, but as I must go abroad every day I dare not drink any quantity of the spa watters. But I have sent for some to Bruxelles, and shall drink two or three glasses every morning. I shall by the next post lett Mr. Walpole know what numbers we shall want for the recruting the 20 battalions I have had in the field. I guess it will be about 5,000 men, besides what we may lose at this siege. The 11 battalions

---

[1] Letter 1172.
[2] A mistake. The letter was from Sir Henry Furnese.
[3] Harley.

that came over with Earle, I beleive, will want near as many. The thaw continuing, the enemy now make use of the advantage of their sluces on the Scheld and Lys, by overflowing all thay can, so that we are forced to make new ways for the carrying of our canon, which I hope we shall begine to do in three days, all dilligence being used for the landing of them.

1182. MARLBOROUGH *to the* DUCHESS   [*9/20 December 1708*]

Source: Blenheim MSS. E4.

[Melle] December 20th 1708

I have had the pleasure of your obliging letter of the 30th, and if I had quiet and could stay within doors I should make use of some of your proscription. I have sent to Bruxelles for some spa watters, of which I intend to drink two or three glasses every morning when I dress, which I hope will do mee good for the heat I find when I wake in my mouth and throat. But I thank God it is less then it was, and dose not hinder me from going abroad every day. I am infinitly obliged to[o] for your kind offer of coming over, but I must not make so bad a return of letting you crose the seas at this time of the yeare. As I do expect, so it will be no surprise any mallice that shall come from 84 [the Tories]. And for 31 [Rochester], I dare say he would not only make his court to 256 [Mrs. Masham], but to the divell if he thought he could by itt hurt 240 [Lady Marlborough], 38 [Godolphin] and 39 [Marlborough]. I have write the two letters you sent me.[1] I think more might have been said to 5 [Somers]. I had a letter from 42 [the Queen] but lost it the same day out of my pocket, so that I do not know the date, but I beleive it was write the day Lord Harford arrived. We are using our utmust dilligence to gett our canon on shore, our next trouble will be to draw them to the severall places we would have them, for the ways are extreame deep. I long to have it over, and that of the happyness of being with you my dearest soull.

1183. GODOLPHIN *to* MARLBOROUGH   [*10 December 1708*]

Source: Blenheim MSS. A2-38.

[London] 10 December 1708

Having not the satisfaction of any letters from you, since my last, I shall trouble you at present only, with the result of a late conversation betwixt 5 [Somers] and 38 [Godolphin] upon the present condition of affairs abroad, in the view of your succeeding at Gand, and Bruges, as I hope you will.

[1] Untraced.

These 2 gentlemen seemed entirely to agree, that the chief motive at this time with 116 [the States] for pushing the warr, is because no other way appears of coming at 81 [peace] in such a manner as will bee pleasing in any degree to 108 [England]; but that in the bottom 116 [the States] has the same fondness for 81 [peace] and perhaps more than ever. And considering that 43 [King of France] in all probability may incline to leave that matter very much in the disposition of 116 [the States], that there may bee no room nor pretence for mistaking the opinion of 108 [England], 5 [Somers] and 38 [Godolphin] have resolved to digest some heads, relating to this business, and send them by the next post to 39 [Marlborough] for his approbation or objections as he shall think proper.

Wee are making all the strength wee can to have the augmentation and the recruit bill voted before Christmas and I hope wee shall have time enough for one or both. But the method which the House of Commons has taken of trying their [controverted] elections at the barr of the House, makes it impossible for them hitherto to proceed upon anything but elections one day, and supply the next.

The weather is now open, as you seemed to wish. But I doubt, this wind will scarce lett us have the satisfaction of hearing from you.

1184. MARLBOROUGH *to* GODOLPHIN   [*13/24 December 1708*]

Source: Blenheim MSS. A2-39.
Printed: Coxe, ii. 584–5 (inc.).

[Merelbeke] December 24th 1708

I have had the favour of yours of the 2d and 3d.[1] The inclosed letter of the 23d from Paris[2] the Pensioner had sent it me some time ago. I supose he had itt from Monsieur Bothemar. I shall be sure to follow your directions concerning Monsieur de Guiscard, and shall not lett him have any mony til I send him away from The Hague, which should not be til I have an opertunity of speaking with the Comte de Maffey. Cadogan came back yesterday from the conference at Leuse,[3] where the most material points are setled for the exchange of the prisoners. He has left Collonel Cromstron to finish what remains, so that we shall at last have both soldiers and officers which remain of the battel of Almanza. I do not beleive thay will amount to above 1,500. As soon as this expedition is over, if her Majesty approves of itt, I would send back those redgiments that are att Ostend. But for those att Antwerp, I should be glad to keep them so that thay might be used to the aire of the country, and consequently be in a condition of serving the next campagne. At this time the greatest part of them are sick.

---

[1] Letters 1174, 1177.   [2] See p. 1169.
[3] Leuze, near the head of the Dender, 16 kilometres east of Tournai, 39 kilometres east of Lille.

The inclosed is a copie of a letter write by Monsieur Chamilliard to the Comte de La Motte.[1] It should not be seen by many, for fear the French should hear of my having a copie. You will see by itt that he is not to manage his garrison, which, by a certain account we have from the town, consistes of 34 battalions and 19 squadrons. However, I have no doubt of God's blessing us with success, though it may last something longer then we first proposed to ourselves. At this time we have very faire weather, which we make use of by hutting and covering ourselves so, as that we may resist ill weather if we must have itt, for the soldiers as well as officers are convinced of the necessity of having this town. Prince Eugene is returned from Bruxelles and is desirous to be going for Vienna, where he says his pressence is necessary for the putting the troupes in a condition for the next campagne. But as he is also desirous of my going to The Hague with him for two or three days, he must stay til this siege is over, or not go to The Hague.

What you say as to the prohibition of letters is certainly very right, but 116 [the States] will never consent to itt. We shall open the trenches to the town this night, and that of the castel tomorrow.

1185. MARLBOROUGH *to the* DUCHESS [*13/24 December 1708*]

Source: Blenheim MSS. E4.

[Merelbeke] December 24th 1708

I have had the satisfaction of yours of the 2d, in which you are desirous to know what has occasioned my sickness. All the account I can give is that I have been for these last two months very much out of order. I thank God I am better, though the drouth continues, but dose no ways hinder me from going abroad every day, which is absolutly necessary at this time, so that I have been persuaded not to begine my spa watters til I can have a litle more quiet, fearing thay might go to my head.

I am extreamly of your mind that it is much the best for Lord Bridgwatter to have a sume of mony, but it [is] his temper that must make it easy or uneasy;[2] but I am very sure it will be a hardshipe to the Queen's masters of the horse[3] to take them from him without his consent, for naturally thay aught to be under his care. I think wee should do all we can to make our children easy, but it should be in things that are sollid and not in trifels that will only show partiallity.

The roades were so bad that we have been obliged to make new ones for

---

[1] Untraced.

[2] Bridgewater had been Gentleman of the Horse to Prince George, an office which had lapsed with his death on 28 Oct. It was a perquisite of the Master of the Horse to keep all of the horses in his charge upon the death of a sovereign and apparently of a consort also. See Luttrell, v. 154. The Queen must have offered to buy the Prince's horses from Bridgewater for her own stables.

[3] Somerset.

the carrying of our canon to their severall batteries. That joyned with the strengh of the garrison, which has obliged us to be very cautious, has occasioned our not being able hethertoo to open the trenches. But as it pleases God to give us moderat weather, and that our ways are all made, I hope everything will now go faster, and that in seven or eight days I may be able to lett you know the effect our canon and mortars may have had. This night we open the trenches against the town, and tomorrow against the cittadell.

1186. GODOLPHIN *to* MARLBOROUGH   [*14 December 1708*]

Source: Blenheim MSS. A2-38.

[London] December 14, 1708

In my last I acquainted you that I would send you my Lord President's thoughts, and my own, concerning 81 [peace]. You will see them most naturally and plainly in the 2 enclosed papers;[1] one written in my own hand, which contains the substance of what wee had discoursed together upon that subject; and the other a letter from him, by which he returns my papers, and putts the heads contained in it into a more proper method. The first part of his letter relates to the affair of the recruits, which is not yett soe well adjusted among us, as I could wish.

I am now to acknowledg the favour of yours of the 17th and 20th,[2] and am sorry to see by the latter that the deputation from Gand which you mentioned in the former has had no effect, for the shortning of your work, but that the enemys seem resolved to give you all the troble they can.

The augmentation is not yett voted, but it is resolved to propose it to the House tomorrow or next day. And there seems to bee a pretty good disposition towards it, except the Toryes, who take great pains to oppose that matter as well as the recruits. And at the same time that, as I have reason to think, they make all manner of professions in private to 42 [the Queen], they omitt no occasion of showing their malice to 39 [Marlborough] and to Mr. Montgomery [Godolphin].

Yesterday the House of Commons was surprised with a proposall of thanks to Mr. Webb, for the action at Winnendal;[3] which was brought on, not so much out of any reall kindness to him, but that one of their leaders might take that handle to show as much malice as he could to 39 [Marlborough]. But I take it for granted, that attempts of that nature always turn most to the prejudice of those who make them; and that in a very little time 39 [Marlborough] will have his entire satisfaction in that matter.

---

[1] Untraced. The heads included the restoration of the Spanish monarchy to Charles III; satisfaction to the other Allies for their just pretensions; a treaty of commerce with the Dutch and the settlement of a Barrier. Geikie, p. 101.

[2] Letters 1179, 1181.   [3] Voted 13 Dec., *C.J.*, xvi. 46.

1187. MARLBOROUGH *to* GODOLPHIN [*16/27 December 1708*]

Source: Blenheim MSS. A2-39.
Printed: Coxe, ii. 585.

[Merelbeke] December 27th 1708

I have received the favour of yours of the 7th.[1] Our frost left us about the same time yours did, and ever since we have had very fine weather, except yesterday and the day before, in which two days we had so great a fog, that we could not see ten yardes before us, so that we could not see til yesterday towardes the evening where to place our batteries. We are now working so dilligently that I hope our canon will fyer on Sunday morning[2] at farthest. In one of the sallyes the French made yesterday, thay carryed into the town Brigadier Evens[3] and Collonel Groves,[4] the latter daingerously wounded. Thay were so soon beaten back that we did not lose above 30 men, which were all of Lord North's redgiment. You will see by the letter I have received from the States,[5] which I have sent to Mr. Secretary Boyle, that thay are desirous I should stay here tile [the] begining of the winter, in hopes the Emperor will consent to send Prince Eugene in the begining of March. I have told the Prince, that provided the Queen allowes of itt, I will take care of the months of January and Febuarie, and that he must take care of March and Aprill, which he is willing to do. I am sure all the troupes can't be in their quarters til the be[ginn]ing of Febuarie, so that this will not keep me above three weekes longer abroad then naturally I must have been. But if the Queen will have it otherways I will not stay one day, which I desire you will assure her. This fogg, and my feet being weet every day in the trenches, has given me so great a cold and sore throat that it is uneasy to me to hold down my head, so that you will excuse my not answering your letter till the next post.

1188. MARLBOROUGH *to the* DUCHESS [*16/27 December 1708*]

Source: Blenheim MSS. E2.

[Merelbeke] December 27th 1708

I am now to thank you for yours of the 7th, and your kind concern for what might happen to mee. You may be sure that I shall not be lead by vanity, but I must not omitt anything that may presse on this undertaking, which I hope we may be able to accomplish by the midle of the next month.

[1] Letter 1178.

[2] 19/30 Dec.

[3] William Evans (died 1740), colonel, Regiment of Foot, 1703; brigadier-general 1707; major-general 1710.

[4] Henry Groves (1665–1736), brevet lieutenant-colonel, 1703; lieutenant-colonel 1704, North's Regiment of Foot; brigadier-general 1711; succeeded North as colonel 1715.

[5] 11/22 Dec., in Murray, iv. 375. For the genesis of this letter see Marlborough to Heinsius, 9/20 Dec., in 't Hoff, p. 416.

I agree intierly with you, and the author of the letter,[1] that precedency is what would give just reason for anger. The latter part of the letter is what would give 39 [Marlborough] imediat strengh in these countrys, so that whatever might be thought proper of that kind, he submits to the judgement of his friends. Nothing should be attempted that can meet with a strugle. Advise with 6 [Sunderland] and lett him govern, and lett him know that I had much rather have nothing done, then have a disagreable dispute.[2] You know that I never had a good opinion of 220 [Queensberry], so that I am sorry to hear of his being often with 42 [the Queen], expecially if 38 [Godolphin] be not acquainted with the subject of their conversations. He is a very daingerous false man.[3] By what you write me, I see there is difficultys about the stables.[4] I would not have them if it gives the least uneasiness, so that I desire there might be no more said of them. What you write concerning 43 [King of France] nephew was told me by Mr. Stanhope att The Hague this spring, but I thought it, as I do stil, so very extravegant, that I never mentioned it to anybody.[5] What you write of 33 [Ormonde] is very likely, but you will find his friends will not have creditt enough with him to keep him long from 108 [England].[6] My feet having been weet for two or three days has given me so great a cold, that it is uneasy to me to hold down my head, otherways I have time this day to have answered all your letters.

This letter was sent by the Duchess on 7 December to Marlborough and it is referred to in the foregoing (above). It could well have been the inspiration of Marlborough's request for his Captain-Generalcy for life, for which see Snyder, 'Captain-Generalcy', 67–83. (See p. 1189.)

---

[1] Letter 1188A.

[2] See p. 1164.

[3] He was appointed a Secretary of State, with responsibility for Scottish affairs, on 3 Feb. 1709. The Whigs wanted Montrose, the Duchess preferred Seafield. See pp. 788, 1197, 1208.

[4] See p. 1164, n. 2.

[5] Orléans was suspected of attempting to secure the throne of France for himself. He commanded the French army in Spain 1707–8. See p. 1200. He offered to help the Allies secure Spain if he were allowed to retain the northern portion with the title of King. Louis XIV, convinced the cause of his grandson was lost, appears to have acquiesced in the plan. For Orléans's schemes see A. Baudrillart, *Philippe V et la cour de France* (Paris, 1890), ii. 67–103.

[6] See p. 1186. The Duchess told Marlborough that Ormonde wanted to sell his employments, which consisted of the colonelcy of the 2nd Troop of Life Guards and a Regiment of Horse. He did not sell.

1188A. MAYNWARING *to the* DUCHESS   [*6 December 1708*]

Source: Blenheim MSS. E26.

Monday morning, December 6

Some addition of honour being onely intended, and not of wealth, I know at present but two ways of doing that; either by some new increase of his titles, or by some publick record of his actions. The first can onely be done by act of Parliament, giving him precedence of other dukes, or creating him a prince here as at Mindelheim. But I should apprehend that this would raise more envy and hatred in our ancient nobles than the thing would be worth. For none are so jealous of their dignities and preheminence as those that have nothing else to value themselves upon, and I am afraid the number of those is great. And the ill humour and resentment of those peers that would be disobliged by it would run through all their families and relations, so that if such a thing were attempted for the Duke of Marlborough I would not answer for it, that the Vice [Peregrine Bertie] himself would not impeach him. Besides, I think his reward should be as particular as his merit is, and since nobody can be said to have equaled his actions, the returns for them should be such as no other subject can pretend to. Now anyone that has power and favour enough may obtain the highest honours, especially in a weak reign, so that I do not think it quite impossible to see Mr. Masham a duke. But I shall never hear it said of him, nor of any other man alive, that he has gained four battels, and destroyed the French power.

Therefore I should think, if something were done in the second way I mentioned, it would be much more proper for the Duke of Marlborough and less lyable to the objections of others, if something like a Roman pillar or triumphal arch were set up in this great town, in memory of this prodigious war, that has saved Europe, with an inscription reciting all his actions in it; as it would be an act of gratitude that could be paid to nobody else, it woud surely be more valuable than any other. And such having been the rewards of great men, in better ages than this it would now, after so long a disuse, be revived with higher honour. And this would be a lasting security to him against his enemies of all kinds. For if ever anything should be said against him, it would be allways easy to answer it out of that inscription. But I think anything of this kind would be proposed with the best grace after a peace; though if it might be publickly discoursed of this winter, and especially if people might be employed in making some designs for it, it would have an imediate good effect, and a very great air abroad. And something like this, with the joint thanks of both Houses, carryed as high as is possible (as they may certainly be) would, in my poor opinion, be more expedient at this time, than an endeavour for more precedence. The rather because though this campaign has been a very extraordinary one, with respect both to the actions, and the consequences of it, yet it is not so shining nor so wonderfull as that of Blenheim. And as Woodstock was designed to perpetuate the memory of that campaign, I would have this pillar (or whatever else it is) to be an everlasting record of all the rest.

This is my first thought upon this subject, and if ever I have another, I will have the honour to send it to your Grace the same way.

1189. GODOLPHIN *to* MARLBOROUGH   [*17 December 1708*]

Source: Blenheim MSS. A2-38.

December 17, 1708

I have not yett any letter of yours to acknowledg since my last of the 14th.[1] But the wind has been so fair that wee may expect your letters tonight or tomorrow.

By the printed votes that goe over to Mr. Cardonell with this packett, you will see the sum voted for the augmentation.[2] It is above 40,000 more than was given last time, upon the same occasion, in view, that 3,000 of these[3] (at least) might bee horse or dragoons. I hear Mr. Foley[4] moved the following words or to that effect: *provided the same proportion bee furnished by the States.* But that was thrown off. However I believe it will bee the more expected of the Queen's minister should insist with the States to doe all that possibly they can upon this occasion, and to make even what they doe, appear rather more than less, than really it is.

I wish I were able to give you as good an account of the recruits but that matter meets with many of the same difficultys it did last year, and chiefly from the same persons. It was to have been considered this day, but our friends will rather chose to deferr it till Monday[5] if they can, hoping by that time to reconcile a little better the differing opinion about this thing.

The land tax will pass before Christmas, but I doubt money is not like to bee lent upon so quick as it use to bee, and you know of what consequence that is to our preparations for next year. The great reason of our present scarcity of money, is that in Holland they give such excessive rates for bills, as draws all our money thither. Now it is the account they find by it from France, which enables them to give such excessive rates. So that if that thing could bee obtained, which I mentioned to you about a fortnight since, I mean the stopping the intercours of letters with France, till the army was ready to take the field, the French would not find money to pay their troops at all, and wee should pay ours with much less difficulty than now wee must expect.

---

[1] Letter 1186.   [2] £220,000.
[3] Of a total of 10,000.
[4] Thomas Foley (died 1737), son of the former Speaker, Paul Foley, head of a family which had considerable influence in Herefordshire; a cousin of Robert Harley.
[5] 20 Dec.

Here are 2 very good officers, *Wills* and *Maccartney*, who long to bee employd in the West Indies, they say, rather than not at all. I perswade them all I can to bee patient, till you come over.[1]

Mr. Erle who has been here since Tuesday, tells mee it would bee very convenient the 6 regiments he left at Ostend should bee sent over with the soonest, that they may bee recruiting. But he says they are not at liberty to come away till the Dutch replace their garrison, which it seems they withdrew upon their arrivall, which is the reason of my troubling you upon this subject.

The House of Commons has agreed to putt of[f] the recruits till Monday.

1190. MARLBOROUGH *to* GODOLPHIN [*19/30 December 1708*]

Source: Blenheim MSS. A2-39.

[Merelbeke] December 30th 1708

I send to Mr. Secretary Boyle a copie of Monsieur de La Mott's letter to mee.[2] Thay are to give us possession of Gand on Wensday morning,[3] if not reliefed before. We have an account of the Merishall de Boufflairs being returned from court, and that he has given orders for the assembling the troupes, but I can't think he will attempt the relief of this place, so that I am taking measures for the reducing of Bridges, after which we shall be glad to go to our winter quarters.

Prince Eugene being desirous that I should goe with him to The Hague for two or three days, I should be glad to receive 38 [Godolphin] and 5 [Somers] thoughts concerning 81 [peace], for I am intierly of your opinions that it is absolutely necessary to speak plainly to 62 [Heinsius] on that subject. 240 [Lady Marlborough] has lett me know that 4 [Halifax] desires to be imployed in 81 [peace]. You all know what I have formerly said to 14 [Townshend] on that subject. As farr as I have anything to do in it, I am desirous of keeping my word to everybody, and obliging 4 [Halifax] as much as possible, so that you will be pleased to advise with 5 [Somers] and 6 [Sunderland] in this matter, and settel it to your own minds, and that will please your humble servant.[4]

As the scituation of this town will give us the conveniency of the Scheld and Lys, if we go on with our augmentations, and can recrute the army so as to be early in the field, I should hope with the blessing of God we might

---

[1] Wills was sent to Spain in 1709, Maccartney was chosen to lead an expedition to Newfoundland and to be governor of Jamaica. He lost both when he was charged with rape by his housekeeper.

[2] 18/29 Dec., P.R.O., S.P. 87/3, ff. 268-9.

[3] 22 Dec./2 Jan.

[4] See Snyder, 'British Diplomatic Service', pp. 62-3. Halifax finally withdrew his request.

have a good peace this next summer. I have been sollicited by Lord North and others to bring this good news, but I have excused it in order to save the Queen's mony.

1191. MARLBOROUGH *to the* DUCHESS   [*19/30 December 1708*]

Source: Blenheim MSS. E4.
Printed: *Private Correspondence*, i. 176.

[Merelbeke] December 30th 1708

You will by these letters know the good news that the garrison of Gand is to leave that place on Wensday morning,[1] if not reliefed before. I am now taking measures for the reducing of Bridges, with which we shall end this campagne. I have desired 38 [Godolphin] to advise with 5 [Somers] and 6 [Sunderland] concerning what you write me of 4 [Halifax].[2] In the meantime you may assure him that I shall be ready to do all that is in my power. When I write last I had so great a cold and sore throat, that it was very uneasy to me to write, otherways I should have acquainted you with a letter I had received from the States, which I sent to Mr. Secretary Boyle.[3] Their desire is absolutely necessary, so that I beleive the Queen must grant itt, which will deprive me of the satisfaction of being with you til the end of Febuary, Prince Eugene promising to return by the beginning of March. You may be sure I shall not stay one day longer then the Service obliges. My cold is not yett well, so that I shall say no more til tomorrow, but that I am heart and soull yours.

1192. MARLBOROUGH *to* GODOLPHIN   [*20/31 December 1708*]

Source: Blenheim MSS. A2-39.
Printed: *Private Correspondence*, ii. 279–80.

[Merelbeke] December 31 1708

I sent yesterday an expresse by Ostend, to acquaint her Majesty that the troupes of Gand were to march out on Wensday, if not reliefed before. This place will secure the conquest of Lisle, and give us great advantages for the next campagne. The Dutch thinking itt for the service, as really it is, to keep the Emperor's troupes in this country, have assured the Prince of Savoye that thay will be willing to give their part for the enabling them to subsist. I beg her Majesty will approve of my assuring, that whatever the Dutch allow that England may do the same. For should these troupes return for Garmany, we should not have them til the month of Jully at soonest. I have this morning sent a trompett with letters to the Governor and town of Bridges, offering them the same capitulations given to Gand; but if thay give

---

[1] 22 Dec./2 Jan.   [2] See the preceding letter.   [3] See p. 1177.

me the trouble of marching with the army, thay must not expect it. I am afraid I shall[not] have the returne of a civil answere, and the trouble of march-ing, which I shall give you an account of by my next. I have directed Major Generall Cadogen to take the best measures he can to send you exactly, so that you may lay itt before the Parliament, the forage and extraordinarys occasioned by this siege and the length of the campagne. But this can't be com-plyed with all, til the army is seperated. The Prince of Savoye bids me assure you that everything possible will be done to finish the dispute with the Pope. Yours of the 14th[1] I have this minut received, but it is so lait that I must answere it by the next post. I do not wonder att Mr. Brumley's barbarous ill natured proceeding,[2] since his anger proceeds from knowing that I will always serve my country to the best of my understanding, and that I shall never desire his friendshipe. But what mortefies me is, that gentlemen who do approve of my services could be silent.

1193. MARLBOROUGH *to the* DUCHESS   [*20/31 December 1708*]

Source: Blenheim MSS. E4.
Printed: *Private Correspondence*, i. 177–8.

[Merelbeke] December 31th 1708

I write yesterday by the expresse I sent by the way of Ostend to lett you know that the Comte de La Motte had capitulated to march out of Gand next Wensday, if not succored sooner. The Marishal Boufflairs is at Tournay, but we do not hear he has troupes enough to do that service. I have this morning write to the governor and town of Bridges to offer them the same capitual-tions I have given to this place. But I fear thay will only return a civill answere, and oblige me to march with part of the army thether, which if possible I would avoyd, especially now that it lookes like weat weather. The rain having begone yesterday, and God having hethertoo blessed us with extreme good weather, we may now reasonably exspect a great deal of rain. My next letter will lett you know what I shall be obliged to do, for if I do not go to Bridges I shall than go for two or three days to The Hague with Prince Eugene, and then return to this country, where I must continue til the end of Febuarie. The months of March and April will be under the care of the Prince of Savoye. By this you will see that I shall enjoye but a very litle time with my dear soull this winter in England. If we must have warr next summer, I do hope that the taking of these two towns will oblige the enemy to wish for a peace.

I have this minut received yours of the 14th, but have not time to say more by this post, then that Mr. Bromley's[2] and other gentlemen's good nature joined with the trouble I have here makes me quit weary of serving.

[1] Letter 1186.
[2] William Bromley, who moved the vote of thanks for General Webb.

1194. GODOLPHIN *to* MARLBOROUGH   [*21 December 1708*]

Source: Blenheim MSS. A2-38.

[London] December 21th 1708

Wee have no forreign letters since my last but are in hopes of them tonight or tomorrow the wind being fair, but the weather soe wett, that it makes one uneasy for fear you have the same.

The augmentation being fully settled the recruit bill is the only thing of any great consequence, relating to a vigorous prosecution of the warr, which remains yett unadjusted. But there is [e]very ground to hope that even before tomorrow night that will bee determined to your satisfaction, the proposall for the recruits from the severall parishes being so well considered, and made so much the interest of those parishes which shall furnish the men, that I don't see how either the House of Commons can decline accepting the proposall; or how, when accepted, it can fail of its effect. And if this should prove as I hope and think it will, you must give mee leave to mention once more to you, that I doubt it will not bee thought reasonable, when your army goes into quarters, to keep any of those regiments on that side, which went over with Lieutenant Generall Erle, and are part of the establishment of Spain and Portugall; especially if your desires are fully answered in those two poynts, of the recruits and the augmentation.

Mr. Secretary sends you the address of the House of Commons to the Queen upon that occasion.[1] It runs in generall to the Allyes, but 'tis particularly intended to 116 [the States]; and it will bee expected the Queen's ministers should use their endeavours with 110 [Holland] in that matter, how sensible soever they may bee that those instances will not have much effect.

The land tax will pass the 23d and the Parliament adjourn that day, I believe for a fortnight. I hope wee shall heare before that time, that you are well at The Hague.

1195. GODOLPHIN *to* MARLBOROUGH   [*23 December 1708*]

Source: Blenheim MSS. A2-38.

December 23d 1708

Upon receipt of yours of the 27th[2] the post was stopped last night, in order to send you this night, the Queen's resolution at the Cabinet Counsell, about your stay on that side of the water. And this day at one, wee were agreably surprised by the arrivall of the messenger with the good news of Gands having capitulated, which was very welcome for many reasons but chiefly

---

[1] 18 Dec. *C.J.*, xvi. 50 that the Queen would endeavour to engage the Allies to furnish their proportion for an augmentation in 1709.

[2] Letter 1187.

because, as it is near the very last day of the year, so I hope, it will bee the last of your fatigues. I doubt this will scarce alter the inclinations of the States, as to your staying abroad while Prince Eugene is at Vienna. But I must deal so plainly as to tell you when once he is there, I very much support his punctuality in returning.

You will have received, (I hope before this time) the thoughts of 5 [Somers] and 38 [Godolphin] concerning 81 [peace]. I wish they may have your approbation.[1] As to what you say 240 [the Duchess] has written about 4's [Halifax] inclinations to bee concerned in 81 [peace],[2] I can only say that I find 5 [Somers] is very intent and desirous that 4 [Halifax] should bee employd in that matter, but full as desirous of 14 [Townshend] too, and I can't see why they might not both bee pleased in it. And whatever may arise to create any struggle with 116 [the States] about that subject, 39 [Marlborough] will not have the uneasy part of it upon himself, but it will fall rather upon 14 [Townshend] and upon 4 [Halifax].

The House of Commons sitts today upon the recruits. I hope you will have a good account of it by this night's letters.

There will bee a generall thanksgiving day, for your successes in this whole year and prayers for blessings upon the next.

1196. MARLBOROUGH *to* GODOLPHIN

[*23 December 1708/3 January 1709*]

Source: Blenheim MSS. A2-39.
Printed: Coxe, ii. 587-8 (inc.).

Gand January 3d 1708

I was yesterday from ten in the morning til six at night seeing the garrison of Gand, and all that belonged to them, march by mee. It is astonishing to see so great numbers of good men to look on, suffer a place of this conse-quence to be taken at this season with so little a lose. As soon as thay knew I had possesion of the gates of this town, thay tooke the resolution of abandon-ing Bridges. This campagne is now ended to my own heart's desire, and as the hand of the Almighty is vissible in this whole matter, I hope her Majesty will think it due to him to return publick thankes, and at the same time to implore his blessing on the next campagne. I can't expresse enough to you the importance of these two towns, for without them we could neither be quiet in our winter quarters, nor have opened with advantage the next campagne. I shall tomorrow give the necessary orders for the seperating the army, so that in two days thay will be all on their March for their winter quarters. I must go with Prince Eugene for some few days to The Hague, after which I shall take a litle care of my health.

¹ Untraced. See p. 1176.   ² Letter 1186.

I am told that 33 [Ormonde] is desirous of parting with his imployements, but I hope att this time her Majesty will not allow of itt, since it must turn to her disarvice.[1] When I go to The Hague I shall follow your directions as to 81 [peace], but what I am afraid I shall be most pressed on, will be the Barier. I should be glad to have 38 [Godolphin] and 5 [Somers] thoughts how farr I might ingage on that subject.

I desire you will give my humble duty to her Majesty, and assure her that I do with all my hart pray that the Almighty God may blesse her armes the next campagne as vissibly as he has been pleased to do in this.

1197. MARLBOROUGH *to the* DUCHESS

[*23 December 1708/3 January 1709*]

Source: Blenheim MSS. E4.

Gand January 3d 1708

I send you open my letter to Mr. Crags,[2] so that I shall not repeat anything to you, how uneasy I am at that barbarous proceding of Mr. Bromley.[3] I no ways doubt but thay are incoraged by 256 [Mrs. Masham], and that thay are told by her and 208 [Harley] that 42 [the Queen] will not be displeased at this proceding. If 39 [Marlborough] can get happyly out of 80 [war], he is fully resolved to be quiet for the rest of his life.

I shall let 38 [Godolphin] know by this post, that if 42 [the Queen] suffers 33 [Ormonde] to sell his imployements, it is incoraging oposition. France is doing all that is possible for the strenghning of their army in this country, and if we should at the same time imploye ourselves in taring etch other to peaces, we may fear that the blessing of God will at last leave us; for it is his hand only that has preserved us and given success hethertoo, for the enemy have certainly a greater strengh of troupes then we. However, I may now assure you that this campagne has ended to my own heart's desire, for the French no sooner knew that I was master of this place, but thay emediatly took their measures for the abandoning of Bruges, which thay did yesterday morning, so that last night I had a deputation from the town, and this morning I have had their submissions, so that I am now imployed in sending the army to their severall garrisons. You will know by the publick papers, that this town has this day received me with all the publick markes of respect that can be given to a subject, so that my mortefycations must come from my own countrymen. My health is not yett as I could wish it, nor shall I have leasure to take care of itt til I have been att The Hague with Prince Eugene. As soon as he leaves that place I shall return to Bruxelles, and there shall have time to take care of myself.

[1] See p. 1178.   [2] Untraced.
[3] See p. 1183.